The Living Primates

The great apes are the chimpanzees, gorillas, and Asian orangutans, while the lesser, smaller apes are the gibbons and siamangs of South and Southeast Asia. Primates are the mammalian order that includes apes, monkeys, and humans. Prosimians, the most primitive of primates, are mainly small, solitary nocturnal creatures. Anthropoids, including apes, monkeys, and ourselves, have larger bodies, and are organized into social groups. All primates have a well-developed visual sense, forward-directed eyes, and larger brains for their body sizes than other mammals. Most live in the tropics, and move around in a variety of different ways.

Living Primates ▶

Apes
- Orangutan
- Chimpanzee
- Gorilla
- Gibbon

Other Anthropoids
- Platyrrhines
- Catarrhines

African Apes

African apes—bonobos, chimpanzees, and gorillas—live in the rain forests and woodlands of Central Africa, from the west coast to areas along the East African rift. Like their Asian relatives, they have long arms, no tails, and broad chests, features that enable them to climb and hang in trees.

Asian Apes

Gibbons and their relatives, the siamangs and orangutans, are confined to South and Southeast Asia. Gibbons are the smallest and most anatomically primitive of all apes, retaining many monkeylike traits. Orangutans are the largest arboreal mammals. Once widespread, they are now confined to forested regions of Borneo and Sumatra.

The Spread of Modern Humans

Fully modern humans evolved in Africa, probably between 200 000 and 100 000 years ago. By 30 000 years ago, they had colonized much of the globe. Rising temperatures at the end of the last Ice Age allowed plants and animals to become more abundant, and new areas were settled. By 8000 B.C., larger populations and

intense hunting had contributed to the near extinction of large mammals, such as mastodons and mammoths. In the Near East, groups of hunter gatherers were living in permanent settlements, harvesting wild cereals, and experimenting with the domestication of local animals. The transition to agriculture was under way.

The Spread of Agriculture

The appearance of farming transformed the face of the Earth. It was not merely a change in subsistence, it also transformed the way in which our ancestors lived. Agriculture, and the vastly greater crop yields it produced, enabled larger groups of people to live together, often in permanent villages. After agriculture emerged, craft, religious, and political specialization became more likely, and the first signs of social inequality appeared.

In 5000 B.C., only a limited number of regions were fully dependent on agriculture. In many parts of the globe, small-scale farming began to supplement hunting and gathering, the first steps in the gradual transition to the sedentary agricultural way of life.

The First Civilizations

The period between 5000 and 2500 B.C. saw the development of complex urban civilizations in the fertile river valleys of the Nile, Tigris, Euphrates, and Indus. Mesopotamian city states formed small kingdoms, which competed with one another. A literate elite ruled over each civilization, and their artisans experimented with new technologies such as bronze and copper metallurgy. Many village societies developed important ritual centres or buried their dead in communal sepulchres.

The Americas

- c.4750: First agriculture in Americas: maize grown in Central America's Tehuacan valley
- 4000: First pottery in the Americas from Amazon Basin
- 3500: Cotton cultivated in Central America; used to make fishing nets and textiles
- 3400: Farming villages established in Tehuacan Valley
- 2600: Large temple complexes built in villages along the Andean coast
- 2500: Evidence of long-distance trade throughout South America, mainly of valuables

Africa

- 3400: First walled towns appear in Egypt
- 3100: King Narmer unifies Upper and Lower Egypt, and becomes first pharaoh. City of Memphis is founded
- 3000: First evidence of hieroglyphic writing system
- 2650: The step pyramid of Djoser, the first Egyptian pyramid, is built at Saqqara
- 2530: Construction of Great Pyramid of Khufu, the largest of the Egyptian pyramids, at Giza

Europe

- **c.5000:** Metallurgy discovered in south-eastern Europe
- **4500:** Large cemeteries, for example on the western coast of the Black Sea, contain rich burials with elaborate gold jewellery
- **c.4500:** In western Europe, megalithic (large stone) chamber tombs, built as communal burial places
- **3800:** Ditched enclosures around settlements in central Europe create defended villages
- **3200:** Stone circles and rows of standing stones built throughout northern and western Europe
- **2900:** Earliest burials containing Corded Ware pottery in northern and central Europe

5000 BC – 4500 – 4000 – 3500 – 3000 – 2500 BC

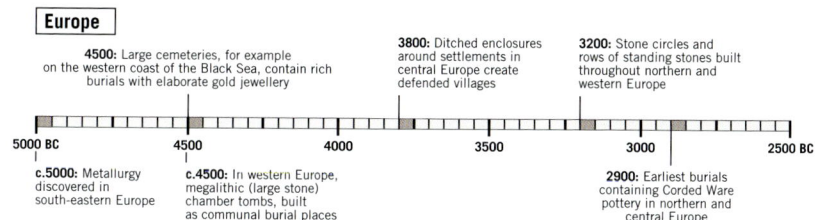

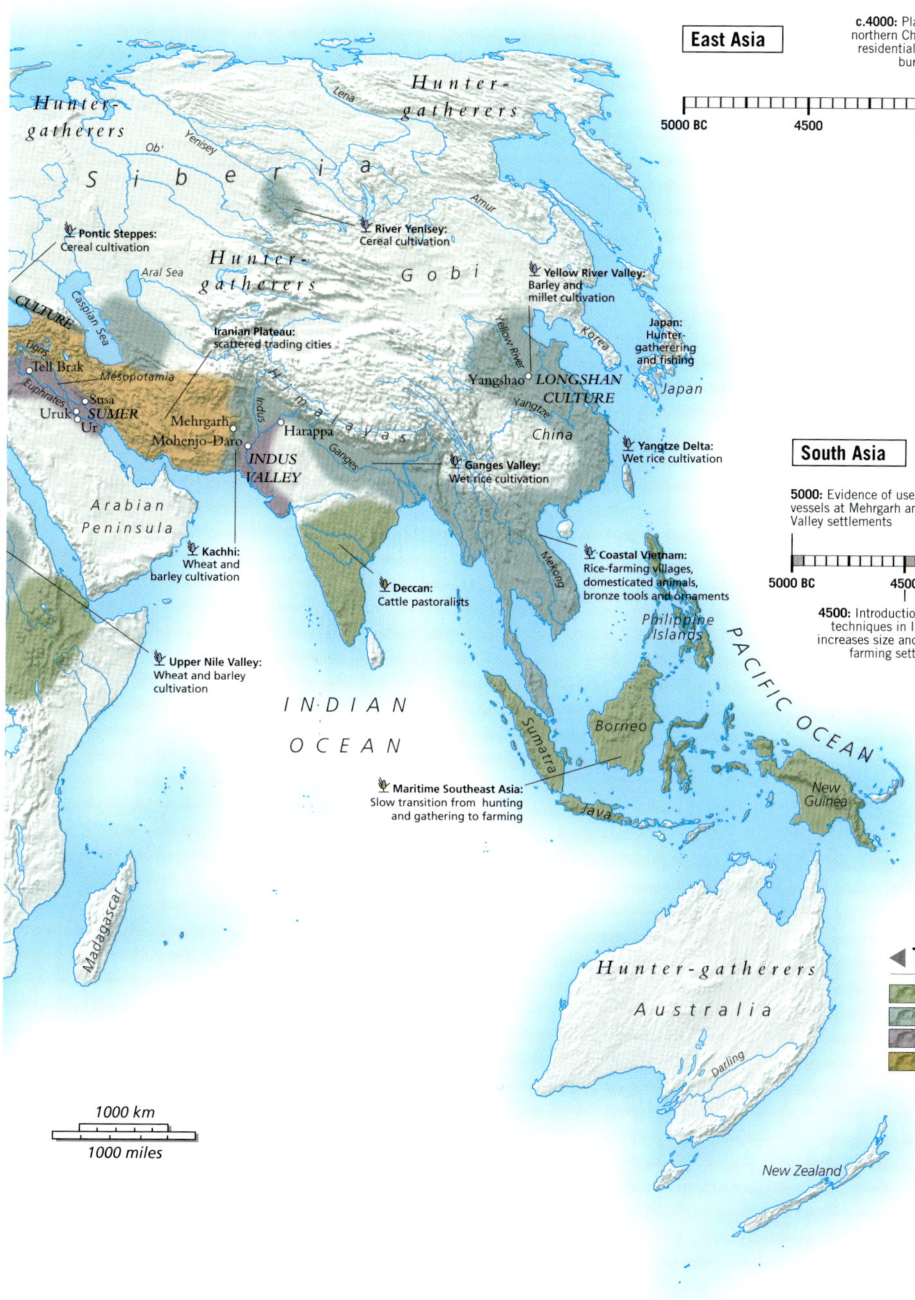

The world in 2500 BC

- transition from hunting and gathering to agriculture
- agricultural areas
- urban areas
- urban hinterland

East Asia

- **c.4000:** Planned villages in northern China, with distinct residential, workshop, and burial areas
- **3000:** First evidence of farming (millet cultivation) in Korea
- **c.3000:** Potter's wheel invented during formative phase of Longshan culture of eastern China
- **2750:** First Chinese bronze artefacts
- **2500:** Banshan culture of western China produces boldly painted burial urns

5000 BC – 4500 – 4000 – 3500 – 3000 – 2500 BC

South Asia

- **5000:** Evidence of use of pottery vessels at Mehrgarh and other Indus Valley settlements
- **4500:** Introduction of irrigation techniques in Indus Valley increases size and prosperity of farming settlements
- **3500:** Indus Valley lowlands settled by farmers; walled towns develop
- **2500:** True cities emerge in Indus Valley. Cultural uniformity throughout Indus plain. Evidence of trade links with Central Asia and Mesopotamia

5000 BC – 4500 – 4000 – 3500 – 3000 – 2500 BC

West Asia

- **3500:** Emergence of Uruk, the first city-state
- **c.3250:** Pictographic clay tablets from Tell Brak: earliest evidence of writing
- **2500:** City-states present throughout Mesopotamia and Levant
- **2500:** Rich array of grave goods at Royal Graves at Ur indicate extensive trade links

5000 BC – 4500 – 4000 – 3500 – 3000 – 2500 BC

Physical Anthropology and Archaeology

Carol R. Ember, Human Relations Area Files
Melvin Ember, Human Relations Area Files
Peter N. Peregrine, Lawrence University
Robert D. Hoppa, University of Manitoba
Kent D. Fowler, University of Manitoba

FOURTH CANADIAN EDITION

Editorial Director: Claudine O'Donnell
Acquisitions Editor: Loree Buchan
Marketing Manager: Christine Cozens
Program Manager: Madhu Ranadive
Project Manager: Colleen Wormald
Manager of Content Development:
  Suzanne Schaan
Developmental Editor: Joanne Sutherland
Production Services: iEnergizer Aptara®, Ltd.
Permissions Project Manager: Kathryn O'Handley
Photo and Text Permissions Research: iEnergizer Aptara®, Inc.
Interior and Cover Designer: Anthony Leung
Cover Image: Rolf Hicker/Getty Images
Vice-President, Cross Media and Publishing Services: Gary Bennett

Pearson Canada Inc., 26 Prince Andrew Place, Don Mills, Ontario M3C 2T8.

Copyright © 2018, 2009, 2006, 2002 Pearson Canada Inc. All rights reserved.

Printed in the United States of America. This publication is protected by copyright, and permission should be obtained from the publisher prior to any prohibited reproduction, storage in a retrieval system, or transmission in any form or by any means, electronic, mechanical, photocopying, recording, or otherwise. For information regarding permissions, request forms, and the appropriate contacts, please contact Pearson Canada's Rights and Permissions Department by visiting www.pearsoncanada.ca/contact-information/permissions-requests.

Authorized adaptation from Ember, Physical Anthropology and Archaeology 14e © 2015, Pearson Education, Inc. Used by permission. All rights reserved. This edition is authorized for sale only in Canada.

Attributions of third-party content appear on the appropriate page within the text.

PEARSON and ALWAYS LEARNING are exclusive trademarks owned by Pearson Education, Inc. or its affiliates in the U.S. and/or other countries.

Unless otherwise indicated herein, any third party trademarks that may appear in this work are the property of their respective owners and any references to third party trademarks, logos, or other trade dress are for demonstrative or descriptive purposes only. Such references are not intended to imply any sponsorship, endorsement, authorization, or promotion of Pearson Canada products by the owners of such marks, or any relationship between the owner and Pearson Canada or its affiliates, authors, licensees, or distributors.

If you purchased this book outside the United States or Canada, you should be aware that it has been imported without the approval of the publisher or the author.

ISBN: 978-0-13-335877-3

3 2019

Library and Archives Canada Cataloguing in Publication

Ember, Carol R., author
  Physical anthropology and archaeology/Carol R. Ember (Human Relations Area Files), Melvin Ember (Human Relations Area Files), Peter N. Peregrine (Lawrence University), Robert D. Hoppa (University of Manitoba), Kent D. Fowler (University of Manitoba).—Fourth Canadian edition.

Includes bibliographical references and index.
ISBN 978-0-13-335877-3 (softcover)

  1. Physical anthropology—Textbooks. 2. Archaeology—Textbooks. 3. Textbooks
I. Ember, Melvin, author II. Peregrine, Peter N. (Peter Neal), 1963-, author III. Hoppa, Robert D., 1967-, author IV. Fowler, Kent D., 1968-, author V. Title.

GN60.E42 2017   599.9   C2017-900801-3

Brief Contents

Part I   **Introduction to Anthropology**

     Chapter 1   What Is Anthropology?   1

Part II   **Introduction to Archaeological Methods and Theory**

     Chapter 2   Uncovering the Past: Tools and Techniques   26
     Chapter 3   Reconstructing the Past: Analysis and Interpretation   50

Part III   **Biological Evolution**

     Chapter 4   Historical Development of Evolutionary Theory   79
     Chapter 5   Modern Evolutionary Theory   95
     Chapter 6   Human Variation   115
     Chapter 7   The Living Primates   143
     Chapter 8   Primate Evolution: From Early Primates to Hominoids   175
     Chapter 9   Early Hominins   198
     Chapter 10   *Homo erectus* and Archaic *Homo sapiens*   231

Part IV   **Modern Humans**

     Chapter 11   Modern *Homo sapiens*   263
     Chapter 12   Origins of Food Production and Settled Life   291
     Chapter 13   Origins of Cities and States   325

Part V   **Applied Anthropology**

     Chapter 14   Applied Anthropology: Physical Anthropology and Archaeology   347

Contents

Boxes vi
Preface vii
About the Authors xii

Part I Introduction to Anthropology

Chapter 1   What Is Anthropology? 1

What Is Anthropology? 2
A Short History of Anthropology in Canada 2
The Scope of Anthropology 3
The Holistic Approach 4
The Anthropological Curiosity 4
The Fields of Anthropology 5
Explanations 13
Evidence: Testing Explanations 16
The Relevance of Anthropology 20
   Summary and Review 22
   Think On It 25

Part II Introduction to Archaeological Methods and Theory

Chapter 2   Uncovering the Past: Tools and Techniques 26

Site Formation Processes 27
Types of Sites 30
Evidence from the Past 30
Finding Archaeological Sites 34
Excavation 36
Dating Techniques 38
   Summary and Review 48
   Think On It 49

Chapter 3   Reconstructing the Past: Analysis and Interpretation 50

Analyzing Artifacts 51
Analyzing Human Remains 53
Reconstructing Past Diets 61
Reconstructing Past Environments 68
Reconstructing Settlement Patterns 69
Reconstructing Social Systems 72
Cultural Change 73
   Summary and Review 76
   Think On It 78

Part III Biological Evolution

Chapter 4   Historical Development of Evolutionary Theory 79

The Evolution of Evolution 81
The Principles of Natural Selection 88
The Origin of Species 89
   Summary and Review 92
   Think On It 94

Chapter 5   Modern Evolutionary Theory 95

Heredity 96
Sources of Variability 101
Natural Selection of Behavioural Traits 107
   Summary and Review 113
   Think On It 114

Chapter 6   Human Variation 115

Processes in Human Variation 116
Biological Diversity in Human Populations 118
"Race" and Racism 133
Cultural Diversity and Adaptation 138
The Future of Human Variation 139
   Summary and Review 140
   Think On It 142

Chapter 7   The Living Primates 143

Common Primate Traits 144
The Various Primates 151
Models for Hominin Behaviour 161
Primate Adaptations 164

Distinctive Human Traits 168
Summary and Review 172
Think On It 174

Chapter 8 Primate Evolution: From Early Primates to Hominoids 175

Interpreting the Fossil Record 176
The Emergence of Primates 179
The Emergence of Anthropoids 186
The Emergence of Hominoids 189
The Divergence of Hominins from the Other Hominoids 194
Summary and Review 196
Think On It 197

Chapter 9 Early Hominins 198

Trends in Hominin Evolution 200
The Transition to Hominins 209
One Model of Human Evolution 220
Early Species of *Homo* 220
Early Hominin Cultures 221
Summary and Review 228
Think On It 230

Chapter 10 *Homo erectus* and Archaic *Homo sapiens* 231

Homo erectus 232
Lower Palaeolithic Culture 240
Neandertals 247
Middle Palaeolithic Cultures 254
Summary and Review 261
Think On It 262

Part IV Modern Humans

Chapter 11 Modern *Homo sapiens* 263

The Emergence of Modern Humans 264
Upper Palaeolithic Cultures 270
The Earliest Humans in the New World 280
Summary and Review 289
Think On It 290

Chapter 12 Origins of Food Production and Settled Life 291

Food Collection and Production 293
Pre-agricultural Developments 296
The Domestication of Plants and Animals 304
Why Did Food Production Develop? 313
Consequences of the Rise of Food Production 315
Summary and Review 322
Think On It 324

Chapter 13 Origins of Cities and States 325

Archaeological Inferences about Civilization 326
Cities and States in Sumer 328
Cities and States in Mesoamerica 330
The First Cities and States in Other Areas 333
Theories about the Origin of the State 335
The Consequences of State Formation 337
The Decline and Collapse of States 338
Summary and Review 343
Think On It 346

Part V Applied Anthropology

Chapter 14 Applied Anthropology: Physical Anthropology and Archaeology 347

Applied and Practising Anthropology 348
Medical Anthropology 357
Environmental Anthropology 365
Forensic Anthropology 369
Nutritional Anthropology 371
Archaeology as Culture History 375
Landscape Archaeology 380
Making the World Better 380
Summary and Review 381
Think On It 383

Glossary 385
Literature Cited 394
Name Index 433
Subject Index 439

Boxes

CURRENT RESEARCH AND ISSUES

Archaeology Helps Brew Ancient Beer 64
You Are What You Eat: Chemical Analyses of Bones and Teeth 66
Selection Favours the Evolution of Drug-Resistant Diseases 92
Is Evolution Slow and Steady or Fast and Abrupt? 108
Hopping Across the Ponds 152
Why Are Primates So Smart? 167
A New Picture of *Dryopithecus* Emerging from Rudabánya Specimens 193
What Is Non-coding DNA? 195
Environmental Change and Evolutionary Consequences in Hominins 202
The First Migrants 233
Ancestors of the Hobbit 234
Inside the Zhoukoudian Cave 240
Neandertal Growth and Development 253
How Did Spoken Language Emerge? 278
Was Cahokia a State? 335

PERSPECTIVES ON GENDER

Getting Development Programs to Notice Women's Contributions to Agriculture 13
Women in the Shell Mound Archaic 54
Mother–Infant Communication and the Origin of Language 171
Effects of Imperialism on Women's Status 340
Eating Disorders, Biology, and the Cultural Construction of Beauty 364

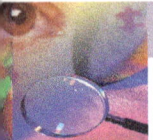

APPLIED ANTHROPOLOGY

Who Owns Your DNA? 100
Obesity, Hypertension, and Diabetes: Health Consequences of Modernization? 131
The Use of "Race" in Forensic Anthropology 134
Endangered Primates 162
Studying Biodiversity 183
Facial Reconstruction 248
Who Were the First North Americans? 282
The Archaeology of Environmental Collapse 316
The Effect of Food Production on the Environment 318
Predicting Societal Collapse 342
Exploring Why an Applied Project Didn't Work 355
Raised Field Agriculture 379

Preface

Physical anthropology explores the intriguing questions that surround the emergence and evolution of humans, what they were like in the past and how they lived, and why they vary biologically. New discoveries, from projects like the Human Genome Project on DNA, are providing evidence that the human past stretches back much further than scientists have predicted, and that humans share a genetic structure similar to other life forms. Archaeology deals with discovering and interpreting that past through remains of long-gone societies. Together, these two disciplines—physical anthropology and archaeology—attempt to reconstruct the past in a way that helps us to understand our roots and to have greater insight into ourselves and some of the problems that concern contemporary societies.

This fourth Canadian edition builds on a strong base. The original edition was designed to highlight the ideas, methods, and discoveries in physical anthropology and archaeology from a Canadian perspective within the framework of Carol R. Ember and Melvin Ember's successful first-year university textbook, *Anthropology*. The intent of this edition remains the same: to provide Canadian students with an introduction to physical anthropology and archaeology that highlights numerous examples of groundbreaking work that Canadian researchers are undertaking. In addition, this edition improves on previous ones by expanding the treatment of the history of anthropology in Canada; providing new sections on how social scientists answer "why" questions using the scientific method; updating the latest advances in archaeological methods and interpretation; and examining how new fossil and archaeological discoveries have changed our understanding of the human past. Many of the interest boxes help to illustrate the fields in which anthropologists toil, from the study of the earliest spoken languages, to how people adapt to and change environments, to the consequences of state formation and why states collapse. They also highlight work that shaped the questions anthropologists ask, new research that addresses them, and how old and new ideas, methods, and discoveries influence the emerging priorities in the discipline.

Foremost, this edition emphasizes to new students of anthropology that physical anthropology and archaeology are contiguous fields. The history of our biology and our cultures cannot be understood in isolation from each other if we are to comprehend our past, present, or future.

Highlights of the Chapters and What Is New in the Fourth Canadian Edition

Chapter 1: What Is Anthropology?

Chapter 1 introduces students to anthropology. We discuss what we think is special and distinctive about anthropology in general, and about each of its sub-fields in particular. We outline how each sub-field is related to other disciplines such as biology, psychology, and sociology. A Perspectives on Gender box highlights the work of a medical anthropologist.

Chapter 2: Uncovering the Past: Tools and Techniques

This chapter introduces the basic concepts behind locating, excavating, and recovering skeletal remains and material culture from the palaeontological and archaeological record. The processes that affect how fossils are formed and where they are found, as well as how archaeological sites form and change over time, are discussed. We also discuss the methods of dating fossils. Chapter 2 explains methods of site surveying and recording, and highlights the importance of provenience, or association, between objects. Finally, we review dating techniques for determining the relative or absolute age of a site and its artifacts.

Chapter 3: Reconstructing the Past: Analysis and Interpretation

Chapter 3 builds on the methods of recovery and analysis outlined in Chapter 2, and discusses a variety of aspects of interpreting archaeological data. The first section of the chapter examines how we reconstruct the past from artifacts, features, and the biological remains of once living peoples. Individual sections show how anthropologists and archaeologists reconstruct past diets, environments, settlement patterns, and social systems. The chapter ends with a discussion of cultural change. Interest boxes discuss interpreting women's roles from artifacts, reconstructing ancient brewing techniques as a means for reconstructing past lifeways, and studying ancient diets through chemical analysis of bones and teeth.

Chapter 4: Historical Development of Evolutionary Theory

This chapter discusses evolutionary theory as it applies to all forms of life, including humans. Following an extensive review of the historical development of the theory of evolution, this chapter ends with a discussion of natural selection and its importance to biological evolution, including how new species might develop. A Current Research and Issues box illustrates the concept of natural selection by examining the current increase in drug-resistant strains of diseases.

Chapter 5: Modern Evolutionary Theory

Chapter 5 introduces the modern theory of evolution, incorporating natural selection and genetics as the processes and basis on which change occurs over time. We also discuss how natural selection may operate on behavioural traits and how cultural evolution differs from biological evolution. We consider the ethical issues posed by the possibility of genetic engineering. A new Applied Anthropology box asks the question, "Who owns your DNA?" A Current Research and Issues box examines the evidence suggesting that evolution proceeds abruptly rather than slowly and steadily.

Chapter 6: Human Variation

Chapter 6, which is moved forward to follow on modern evolutionary theory, deals with biological variation in modern human populations and how biological anthropologists study such variation. In a section on race and racism, we discuss why anthropologists think that the concept of "race" as applied to humans is not scientifically useful. According to this view, human variation is more usefully studied in terms of clinal variation in particular traits. For example, we show how differences between populations—in physical features such as body build, skin colour, height, and susceptibility to disease—can be explained as adaptations to differences in the physical and cultural environment. We discuss the myths of racism and demonstrate that race is largely a social category in humans. We also discuss population variation in susceptibility to diseases and the co-evolution of diseases and humans. A new Applied Anthropology box discusses the use of "race" in forensic anthropology, while another Applied Anthropology box deals with obesity, hypertension, and diabetes in the context of long-term biocultural changes in populations.

Chapter 7: The Living Primates

This chapter describes the living non-human primates and their variable adaptations as background for understanding the evolution of primates in general and humans in particular. After describing the various species, we discuss some possible explanations of how the primates differ—in body and brain size, size of social group, and female sexuality. The chapter ends with a discussion of the distinctive features of humans in comparison with the other primates. A new Perspectives on Gender box explores mother–infant communication and the origin of language, while a new Current Research and Issues box discusses how lemurs and monkeys may have travelled to Madagascar and the New World, respectively, by island hopping.

Chapter 8: Primate Evolution: From Early Primates to Hominoids

Chapter 8 begins with the emergence of the early primates and ends with what we know or suspect about the Miocene apes and their relation to bipedal hominins. We describe the concept of the molecular clock for assessing timing of divergence between species, including hominins from other hominoids. A new Applied Anthropology box discusses the study of biodiversity, and a new Current Research and Issues box focuses on the topic of non-coding DNA. There is also a Current Research and Issues box that presents the work of a Canadian researcher who has studied the remains of a later Miocene ape.

Chapter 9: Early Hominins

Chapter 9 starts with the emergence of the first bipedal hominins. We first discuss trends in, and possible explanations of, the distinctive developments in the hominin line—bipedalism, the expansion of the brain, and the reduction of the face, teeth, and jaws. We then discuss the changing fossil evidence for understanding the evolution of early hominins. This chapter features a new Current Research and Issues box about environmental change and evolutionary consequences in hominins.

Chapter 10: *Homo erectus* and Archaic *Homo sapiens*

Chapter 10 discusses the transition between *Homo erectus* and *Homo sapiens* and the emergence of early modern humans. In keeping with our global orientation, we discuss fossil and archaeological evidence from many areas of the world, not just Europe and the Near East, including evidence indicating that people were hunting big game at least 400 000 years ago. We also explore how the earliest dating of *H. erectus* may affect ideas about when hominins first moved out of Africa. This chapter contains three new boxes: an Applied Anthropology box discussing facial reconstruction, a Current Research and Issues box about the ancestors of *Homo floresiensis*, and another Current Research and Issues box describing the Zhoukoudian cave site in China. A third Current Research and Issues box discusses the first hominins to leave Africa, while a fourth Current Research and Issues box examines growth and development in Neandertals as compared to anatomically modern humans.

Chapter 11: Modern *Homo sapiens*

Chapter 11 discusses the origins of anatomically modern human populations, contrasting the two major competing models—the "single-origin" and multiregional hypotheses. The chapter also covers key changes in cultural practices during the Upper Palaeolithic, including the flourishing of art and new forms of tools. We finish with a discussion of the peopling of the New World and briefly introduce the student to early Arctic cultures. A new Current Research and Issues box discusses the origins of spoken language, and a new Applied Anthropology box asks, "Who were the first North Americans?"

Chapter 12: Origins of Food Production and Settled Life

Chapter 12 deals with the emergence of broad-spectrum collecting and settled life, and the domestication of plants and animals in various parts of the world. Our discussion focuses mainly on the possible causes and consequences of these developments in Southeast Asia, Africa, the Andes, and eastern North America, as well as the Near East and Europe. We discuss puzzles such as why much of Indigenous North America switched to a dependence on corn, even though the earlier agricultural diet was apparently adequate. The chapter includes a new Applied Anthropology box about the archaeology of environmental collapse, and a second Applied Anthropology box discusses the impact of food-getting on the environment.

Chapter 13: Origins of Cities and States

Chapter 13 deals with the rise of civilizations in various areas of the world and the theories that have been offered to explain the development of state-type political systems. The chapter concludes with a discussion of the decline and collapse of states. Environmental degradation may be due to events in the natural world, but the behaviour of humans may sometimes be responsible. Civilizations may also decline because human behaviour has increased the incidence of disease. A new Applied Anthropology box discusses predicting societal collapse, and a new Current Research and Issues box discusses the question of whether Cahokia, a pre-Columbian city, was a state. A Perspectives on Gender box discusses the consequences for women's status of ancient imperialism in the Andes.

Chapter 14: Applied Anthropology: Physical Anthropology and Archaeology

The first part of Chapter 14 reviews the interaction between basic and applied research, a brief history of applied anthropology in Canada, the ethical issues involved in trying to improve people's lives, the difficulties in evaluating whether a program is beneficial, and ways of implementing planned changes. We point out how applied anthropologists are playing a role more as planners than as peripheral advisers to change programs already in place. The chapter examines several aspects of applied research in biomedical anthropology, environmental anthropology, forensic anthropology, nutritional anthropology, and archaeology as culture history. A new Applied Anthropology box describes raised field agriculture. Another Applied Anthropology box shows how anthropologists were able to explain why a health project in Guatemala did not work, and a Perspectives on Gender box explores the link between eating disorders, biology, and the cultural construction of beauty.

Features

Boxes in Each Chapter

Current Research and Issues. These boxes look at researchers at work or take an in-depth look at new research or a research controversy (for example, the chemical analyses of bones and teeth; interpretation of findings of *Dryopithecus*; Middle Palaeolithic hunting).

Applied Anthropology. These boxes deal with some of the ways anthropologists have studied or applied their knowledge to health and other practical problems (examples include primate conservation; modernization and obesity).

Perspectives on Gender. These boxes involve issues pertaining to sex and gender, both in anthropology and in everyday life (for example, depictions of women in art; changes in women's roles in prehistoric societies).

Readability

We get a lot of pleasure from describing research findings, especially complicated ones, in language that introductory students can understand. Thus, we try to minimize technical jargon, using only the terms students need to know to appreciate the achievements of anthropology and to encourage them to take advanced courses. Readability is important, not only because it enhances the reader's understanding of what we write but also because it makes learning about anthropology more enjoyable! When new terms are introduced, they are set off in boldface type and defined.

NEW! Learning Objectives

Learning objectives are new to this edition. Each chapter begins with learning objectives that indicate what students should know after reading the material. The learning objectives are reinforced with specific questions at the end of each chapter that unite the topics, help students gauge their comprehension, and signal what topics they might have to reread.

Key Terms and Glossary

Important terms and concepts appearing in boldface type within the text are defined at the bottom of each page on which the key term first appears. All key terms and their definitions are repeated in the Glossary at the end of the book.

Summaries

In addition to the learning objectives provided at the beginning of each chapter, each chapter has a detailed summary organized in terms of the learning objectives that will help students review the major concepts and findings discussed, along with review questions to reinforce and to complement the summary.

Think On It Questions

We also provide a series of questions at the end of each chapter to stimulate thinking about the implications of that chapter. The questions do not ask for repetition of what is in the text: we want students to imagine, to go beyond what we know or think we know.

Literature Cited at the End of the Book

The information and conclusions presented in this book are largely based on published research. These sources are cited in the text with full bibliographic references provided at the end of the book.

Supplements

The supplement package for this textbook has been carefully crafted to amplify and illuminate materials in the text itself. These instructor supplements are available for download from a password-protected section of Pearson Canada's online catalogue (www.pearsoncanada.ca/highered). Navigate to your book's catalogue page to view a list of those supplements that are available. Speak to your local Pearson sales representative for details and access.

Instructor's Resource Manual. For each chapter of the text, this manual provides the chapter outline, resources for discussion, discussion questions, paper topics and research projects, and a list of supplementary materials including films and readings.

Computerized Test Bank. Pearson's computerized test banks allow instructors to filter and select questions to create quizzes, tests, or homework. Instructors can revise questions or add their own, and may be able to choose print or online options. These questions are also available in Microsoft Word format.

PowerPoint Presentations. This instructor resource contains key points and figures to accompany each chapter in the text.

Learning Solutions Managers. Pearson's Learning Solutions Managers work with faculty and campus course designers to ensure that Pearson technology products, assessment tools, and online course materials are tailored to meet your specific needs. This highly qualified team is dedicated to helping schools take full advantage of a wide range of educational resources, by assisting in the integration of a variety of instructional materials and media formats. Your local Pearson Canada sales representative can provide you with more details on this service program.

Acknowledgments

We would like to thank a number of people for their contributions to this edition of the textbook. Erica Tennenhouse from the University of Toronto wrote several engaging new feature boxes for the text and provided some critical thinking questions. We also appreciate the input and assistance of the team at Pearson Canada, including Joanne Sutherland, Madhu Ranadive, Loree Buchan, Christine Cozens, Keriann McGoogan and Collen Wormald. Along with the production team and the Project Manager, Rakhshinda Chishty, at Aptara.

To colleagues and friends who provided material and comments, we thank Tina Moffat, Anne Keenleyside, the late Priscilla Renouf, Bob Park, Pascale Sicotte, Dongya Yang, Ariane Burke, Haskel Greenfield, the late Shelley Saunders, David Begun, Sarah Gaunt, Tracy Rogers, David Ebert, and Chris Meiklejohn. Finally, many students provided important feedback on the textbook.

—*Rob Hoppa and Kent Fowler*

About the Authors

Carol R. Ember started at Antioch College as a chemistry major. She began taking social science courses because some were required, but she soon found herself intrigued. There were lots of questions without answers, and she became excited about the possibility of a research career in social science. She spent a year in graduate school at Cornell studying sociology before continuing on to Harvard, where she studied anthropology primarily with John and Beatrice Whiting.

For her Ph.D. dissertation she worked among the Luo of Kenya. While there she noticed that many boys were assigned "girls' work," such as babysitting and household chores, because their mothers (who did most of the agriculture) did not have enough girls to help out. She decided to study the possible effects of task assignment on the social behaviour of boys. Using systematic behaviour observations, she compared girls, boys who did a great deal of girls' work, and boys who did little such work. She found that boys assigned girls' work were intermediate in many social behaviours, compared with the other boys and girls. Later, she did cross-cultural research on variation in marriage, family, descent groups, and war and peace, mainly in collaboration with Melvin Ember, whom she married in 1970. All of these cross-cultural studies tested theories on data for worldwide samples of societies.

From 1970 to 1996, she taught at Hunter College of the City University of New York. She has also served as president of the Society of Cross-Cultural Research and is one of the directors of the Summer Institutes in Comparative Anthropological Research, which are funded by the National Science Foundation. She recently served as president of the Society for Anthropological Sciences. Since 1996, she has been at the Human Relations Area Files, Inc., a nonprofit research agency at Yale University, first serving as executive director, then as acting president, and currently as president of that organization.

Melvin Ember majored in anthropology at Columbia College and went to Yale University for his Ph.D. His mentor at Yale was George Peter Murdock, an anthropologist who was instrumental in promoting cross-cultural research and building a full-text database on the cultures of the world to facilitate cross-cultural hypothesis testing. This database came to be known as the Human Relations Area Files (HRAF) because it was originally sponsored by the Institute of Human Relations at Yale. Growing in annual instalments and now distributed in electronic format, the HRAF database currently covers more than 385 cultures, past and present, all over the world.

Melvin Ember did fieldwork for his dissertation in American Samoa, where he conducted a comparison of three villages to study the effects of commercialization on political life. In addition, he did research on descent groups and how they changed with the increase of buying and selling. His cross-cultural studies focused originally on variation in marital residence and descent groups. He has also done cross-cultural research on the relationship between economic and political development, the origin and extension of the incest taboo, the causes of polygyny, and how archaeological correlates of social customs can help us draw inferences about the past.

After four years of research at the National Institute of Mental Health, he taught at Antioch College and then Hunter College of the City University of New York. He served as president of the Society for Cross-Cultural Research. From 1987 until his death in September 2009, he was president of the Human Relations Area Files, Inc.

Peter N. Peregrine came to anthropology after completing an undergraduate degree in English. He found anthropology's social scientific approach to understanding humans more appealing than the humanistic approach he had learned as an English major. He undertook an ethnohistorical study of the relationship between Jesuit missionaries and Native American peoples for his master's degree and realized that he needed to study archaeology to understand the cultural interactions experienced by Native Americans prior to contact with the Jesuits.

While working on his Ph.D. at Purdue University, Peter Peregrine did research on the prehistoric Mississippian cultures of the eastern United States. He found that interactions between groups were common and had been shaping Native American cultures for centuries. Native Americans approached contact with the Jesuits simply as another in a long string of intercultural exchanges. He also found that relatively little research had been done on Native American interactions and decided that comparative research was a good place to begin examining the topic. In 1990 he participated in the Summer Institute in Comparative Anthropological Research, where he met Carol R. Ember and Melvin Ember.

Peter Peregrine is professor of anthropology at Lawrence University in Appleton, Wisconsin, and external professor at the Santa Fe Institute in Santa Fe, New Mexico. He also serves as research associate for the Human Relations Area Files. He continues to do archaeological research, and to teach anthropology and archaeology to undergraduate students.

Rob Hoppa received a B.Sc. in physical anthropology from the University of Toronto in 1990. Subsequently he pursued graduate work and received a joint M.Sc. in osteology, palaeopathology, and funerary archaeology from the Universities of Bradford and Sheffield (UK) in 1991 and a Ph.D. in physical anthropology from the Department of Anthropology, McMaster University in 1996. His doctoral research focused on issues of sampling for skeletal biology, particularly the impact of bias on palaeodemographic estimates, under the supervision of Shelley Saunders. Following his doctoral research he undertook post-doctoral research in historical demography and epidemiology of a 19th-century subarctic Indigenous community during the decline of the fur trade. In 1998, he joined the Laboratory of Survival and Longevity at the Max Planck Institute for Demographic Research in Rostock, Germany. In July 1999, he joined the Department of Anthropology at the University of Manitoba.

Dr. Hoppa's research has broadly focused on issues of health and well-being in past populations. His research seeks to answer questions regarding the relationship between health and mortality, and changing social, economic, and cultural conditions. His training is strongly anchored in the biocultural tradition that recognizes the complex interaction of biological and social factors related to health and disease in populations.

Dr. Hoppa is currently professor in the Department of Anthropology at the University of Manitoba. His current program of research focuses on the biological anthropology of past populations. He held a Canada Research Chair in Skeletal Biology from 2002 to 2012, and two Canada Foundation for Innovation grants for the establishment of the Bioanthropology Digital Image Analysis Laboratory at the University of Manitoba. There, he and his students are exploring innovative approaches to examining and interpreting data from the past through advanced imaging techniques. Dr. Hoppa served as the president of the Canadian Association for Physical Anthropology from 2005 to 2011.

Kent Fowler received a B.A. and an M.A. in anthropology from the University of Manitoba, where he focused on funerary practices, pottery, and food remains in Early Bronze Age and Neolithic societies in Greece. His Ph.D. research at the University of Alberta shifted to South Africa, where he explored the socio-economic, political, and ritual uses of ceramic technology in early farming communities of the first millennium A.D. Dissatisfied with the kinds, quantity, and detail of ethnographic knowledge about pottery-making in southern Africa cultures, Dr. Fowler initiated the Nguni Ceramics and Society Project (NCSP) in 2002 while a post-doctoral fellow at the University of Calgary under the sponsorship of Dr. Nicholas David. The knowledge gained from this ethnoarchaeological research between 2002 and 2014 added southern Africa to a growing body of evidence concerning the social foundations of technical know-how.

Dr. Fowler's research has focused broadly on the long-term consequences of adopting food production in past societies. Work with colleagues has seen many kinds of data and approaches brought to bear on questions about the social consequences of food production during research in the eastern Mediterranean, the Near East, Africa, and Canada. His primary research aims to utilize ceramic technology as a means of understanding the organization of farming societies and, in particular, how the manufacture and use of ceramics are linked to routine and special activities people undertake during their lives. His training is deeply rooted in a multi-field approach to anthropology, one that sees a complicated but symbiotic interaction among socio-cultural anthropology, physical anthropology, and archaeology.

Dr. Fowler is currently associate professor in the Department of Anthropology at the University of Manitoba. He is passionate about teaching at both the undergraduate and graduate levels, and is the past recipient of the Faculty of Arts Teaching Excellence Award. For him, teaching and research are different sides of the same coin. His current research program combines ethnoarchaeology, archaeometry, and experimental archaeology to reconstructing ancient technology systems, and applies this research to understanding rural–urban relationships during the 19th-century Zulu kingdom. Research grants have provided the foundation for the Ceramic Technology Laboratory, where Dr. Fowler and his students work on exploring new approaches and methods to examining and interpreting ancient and modern societies through the lens of clay technologies.

Part I Introduction to Anthropology

What Is Anthropology?

Bruno Morandi/Robert Harding World Imagery

LEARNING OBJECTIVES

- **1.1** Define the purpose of anthropology.
- **1.2** Describe how anthropology started in Canada.
- **1.3** Describe the scope of anthropology.
- **1.4** Explain what the holistic approach means.
- **1.5** Explain anthropology's distinctive curiosity.
- **1.6** Describe the fields of anthropology.
- **1.7** Define *explanation* and discuss its role in anthropology.
- **1.8** Explain the process of operationalization, the importance of measurement, and the value of statistical evaluation in testing explanations.
- **1.9** Explain the relevance of anthropology.

What Is Anthropology?

Anthropology by definition is a discipline of infinite curiosity about human beings. The term comes from the Greek *anthropos* for "man, human" and *logos* for "study." Anthropologists seek answers to an enormous variety of questions about humans. They are interested in discovering when, where, and why humans appeared on the earth, how and why they have changed since then, and how and why modern human populations vary in certain physical features. Anthropologists are also interested in how and why societies in the past and present have varied in their customary ideas and practices. There is a practical side to anthropology too. Applied anthropologists solve practical problems using anthropological methods, information, and results.

Yet defining anthropology as the study of human beings is not complete, for such a definition would appear to incorporate a whole catalogue of disciplines: sociology, psychology, political science, economics, history, human biology, and perhaps even the humanistic disciplines of philosophy and literature. Needless to say, practitioners of the many other disciplines concerned with humans would not be happy if these disciplines were regarded as sub-branches of anthropology. After all, most of those disciplines have existed longer than anthropology, and each is somewhat distinctive. There must, then, be something unique about anthropology—a reason for its having developed as a separate discipline and having retained a separate identity over the past 100 years.

A Short History of Anthropology in Canada*

The founders of Canadian ethnology were the missionaries who lived in French Canada in the 1600s. These men, including Fathers LeClercq, Le Jeune and Sagard, were deeply interested in knowing the ways of life and beliefs of the Indigenous people they lived among, and they provided detailed descriptions that were later used by professional anthropologists. Other early Canadian anthropologists included explorer-traders such as Marc Lescarbot, and later teachers at early universities, such as Sir Daniel Wilson at Toronto or Sir John William Dawson at McGill (in the mid-1880s).

Government employees, in particular those with the Geological Survey of Canada, made important records of their travels, including details about Indigenous people they met and observed in the course of their work. The most important of these employees is George Mercer Dawson, who was employed by the Geological Survey from 1875 and rose to be its director in 1895. Dawson helped establish a professional basis for Canadian anthropology, though he died before it was given formal recognition.

In 1910 Prime Minister Wilfrid Laurier established a Division of Anthropology within the Geological Survey, marking the beginning of professional anthropology in Canada. Offices were in the Victoria Memorial Museum in Ottawa, and established anthropologists were recruited from England and the United States. Professor Franz Boas trained Edward Sapir, the first chief ethnologist at the Geological Survey of Canada. Charles Marius Barbeau, a pioneering anthropologist born in rural Québec, was an early contributor to the National Museum (now the Canadian Museum of History). Barbeau's collections of French Canadian material culture, songs, stories and tales provided the foundation for Les Archives de Folklore at Université Laval. Barbeau also recruited to the museum a fellow student from Oxford University, Diamond Jenness.

Like Dawson and Boas, Sapir and Barbeau both studied the Indigenous people of

---

*Courtesy of The Canadian Encyclopedia, Historica Canada. www.thecanadianencyclopedia.ca.

> **Anthropology:** the study of differences and similarities, both biological and cultural, in human populations. Anthropology is concerned with typical biological and cultural characteristics of human populations in all periods and in all parts of the world.

the Northwest Coast, while Jenness is best known for his research in the Arctic among the Inuinnait. William Wintemberg and Harlan Smith contributed to the collections of prehistoric artifacts.

These men, with a handful of others, had nearly sole responsibility for the development of the profession in Canada from 1910 until 1925, when Sapir left Canada and Thomas McIlwraith took the first academic position in anthropology at a Canadian university. Five years later, McIlwraith was still the sole member of his department at the University of Toronto. The next universities to hire anthropologists, the University of British Columbia and McGill, didn't do so until 1947.

Common trends dominated the development of anthropology in Canada despite differences in language and distances between the various universities and museums. Part of the reason for this uniformity was the widespread influence of the ideas of Franz Boas and his students. Moreover, anthropology in English Canada was built on an interest in Indigenous people living in small, isolated communities. This led to anthropological emphasis on the empirical field-study tradition, with participant observation and interviews with key informants, and resulted in reports that described the technology, economics, social organization, values and world view of each particular community. Research in other areas of Canada and the world gradually increased during the 1960s and 1970s.

In French Canada anthropology was built on rural and small-town studies of the Québec region and its people. The development of anthropology in Québec was based upon the classic studies of French Canadians by early sociologists. The most important figure was Léon Gérin, whose "L'Habitant de St-Justin" illustrated how, in rural Québec, the old European patriarchal system continued to organize the community's lifestyle. This interest in the study of non-Indigenous communities continued to grow throughout the 1960s and 1970s, particularly at the Université de Montréal and Université Laval. Research contributed to the cultural "mapping" of more isolated regions and helped draw attention to socioeconomic disparities. Canadian anthropologists also demonstrated a keen interest in the study of communities beyond Canada, namely in Africa (from the 1970s on), Mexico, Latin America, the Pacific and, later, Asia.

Anthropology first developed within museums and cultural institutions; today, however, it is firmly established at Canadian universities. Fifteen universities offer PhD-track programs in anthropology.

The Scope of Anthropology

Today, the field of anthropology is well established within Canada. Several professional organizations exist in support of the discipline including CASCA, CAA (see Wright 1985, and Mackie 1995 for a history of Canadian archaeology), and CAPA (for a recent history of bioarchaeology in Canada see Cybulski and Katzenberg 2014). Nevertheless, there remain misconceptions of what the discipline represents as it is not often taught in high schools, and is sensationalized in popular culture.

Anthropologists are generally thought of as individuals who travel to little-known corners of the world to study exotic peoples or who dig deep into the earth to uncover the fossil remains or the tools and habitations of people who lived long ago. These views, though clearly stereotyped, do indicate how anthropology differs from other disciplines concerned with humans. Anthropology is broader in scope, both geographically and historically. Anthropologists are concerned explicitly and directly with all people, in all places, and at all times. Beginning with the immediate ancestors of humans, who lived a few million years ago, anthropology traces the development of humans to the present. Every part of the world where a human population has lived is of interest to anthropologists.

Anthropologists have not always been as global and comprehensive in their concerns as they are today. Traditionally, they concentrated on non-Western cultures and left the study of Western civilization and similarly complex societies, with their recorded histories, to other disciplines. In recent years, however, this division of labour among the disciplines has begun to disappear. Now anthropologists work in a variety of societies, including their own.

What induces anthropologists to choose so broad a subject for study? In part, they are motivated by the belief that any generalization about human beings, any possible explanation of some characteristic of human culture or biology, should be shown to apply to many times and places of human existence. If a generalization or explanation does not prove to apply widely, we are entitled or even obliged to be skeptical about it. The skeptical attitude, in the absence of persuasive evidence, is our best protection against accepting invalid ideas about humans.

For example, when educators in the United States discovered in the 1960s that African-American schoolchildren rarely drank milk, they assumed that lack of money or education was the cause. Evidence from anthropology suggested a different explanation. Anthropologists had known for years that in many parts of the world where milking animals are kept, people do not drink fresh milk; rather, they sour it before they drink it, or they make it into cheese. Why they do so is now clear. Many people lack an enzyme, lactase, which is necessary for breaking down lactose, the sugar in milk. When such people drink regular milk, it actually interferes with digestion. Not only is the lactose in milk not digested, but other nutrients are less likely to be digested as well; in many cases, drinking milk will cause cramps, stomach gas, diarrhea, and nausea. Studies indicate that milk intolerance is found in many parts of the world (Harrison 1975; Durham 1991). The condition is common in adulthood among Asians, southern Europeans, Arabs and Jews, West Africans, Inuit, and North and South American Indigenous peoples, as well as African Americans. As many as 75 percent of all Native Americans are lactose intolerant. It is because anthropologists are acquainted with human life in an enormous variety of geographic and historical settings that they are often able to correct mistaken beliefs about different groups of people.

The Holistic Approach

Another distinguishing feature of anthropology is its **holistic**, or multifaceted, approach to the study of human beings. Anthropologists study not only all varieties of people but many aspects of human experience as well. For example, when describing a group of people, an anthropologist might discuss the history of the area in which the people live, the physical environment, the organization of family life, the general features of their language, the group's settlement patterns, political and economic systems, religion, and styles of art and dress.

In the past, individual anthropologists tried to be holistic and cover all aspects of a subject. Today, as in many other disciplines, so much information has been accumulated that anthropologists tend to specialize in one topic or area. Thus, one anthropologist may investigate the physical characteristics of some of our prehistoric ancestors. Another may study the biological effect of the environment on a human population over time. Still another will concentrate on the customs of a particular group of people. Despite this specialization, however, the discipline of anthropology retains its holistic orientation in that its many different specialties, taken together, describe many aspects of human existence, both past and present.

The Anthropological Curiosity

Thus far we have described anthropology as being broader in scope, both historically and geographically, and more holistic in approach than other disciplines concerned with human beings. This statement again implies that anthropology is the all-inclusive human science. How,

Holistic: refers to an approach that studies many aspects of a multifaceted system.

then, is anthropology really different from those other disciplines? We suggest that anthropology's distinctiveness lies principally in the kind of curiosity it arouses.

Anthropologists are concerned with many types of questions: Where, when, and why did people first begin living in cities? Why do some peoples have darker skin than others? Why do some languages contain more terms for colour than other languages? Why do women have more of a voice in politics in some societies than in others? Why do populations differ in their acceptance of birth control? Although these questions deal with very different aspects of human existence, they have at least one thing in common: they all deal with the *diversity* (both biological and cultural) within and between populations in both the past and present. Such diversity can represent variation in the colour of skin, a language with many colour terms, female participation in politics, or acceptance of birth control. This concern with variation, both biological and cultural, of populations is perhaps the most distinguishing feature of anthropology. For example, whereas economists take a monetary system for granted and study how it operates, anthropologists ask why only some societies during the last few thousand years developed and used money. In short, anthropologists are curious about the typical characteristics of human populations—how and why such populations and their characteristics have varied throughout the ages.

The Fields of Anthropology

Different anthropologists concentrate on different typical characteristics of societies. Some are concerned primarily with physical or biological characteristics of human populations; others are interested principally in what we call cultural characteristics. Thus these two interrelated branches of inquiry in anthropology can be divided into four major sub-fields:

- **Biological or physical anthropology**, which is concerned primarily with the biological diversity of humans, their ancestors, and closely related primates;
- **Archaeology**, which is the study of past human cultures, primarily through their material remains;
- **Socio-cultural anthropology**, which is concerned with the study of recent or contemporary cultures; and
- **Anthropological linguistics**, which is the anthropological study of languages.

Within each sub-field, a variety of research specialties exist, some of which overlap sub-disciplines (see Figure 1–1).

Physical Anthropology

Physical or biological anthropology seeks to answer a variety of questions about the human biological condition in both past and present populations. Some physical anthropologists are interested in the emergence of humans and their evolutionary relationship with other primates (this focus is called **human palaeontology** or **palaeoanthropology**). Others are interested in how and why contemporary human populations vary biologically, and in particular the interactions between biology, environment, and behaviour.

Biological (Physical) Anthropology: the study of humans as biological organisms, dealing with the emergence and evolution of humans and with contemporary biological variations among human populations. Also called *physical anthropology*.
Archaeology: the branch of anthropology that seeks to reconstruct the daily life and customs of peoples who lived in the past and to trace and explain cultural changes. Often lacking written records for study, archaeologists must try to reconstruct history from the material remains of human cultures.
Socio-cultural Anthropology: the study of cultural variation and universals.
Anthropological Linguistics: the anthropological study of languages.
Human Palaeontology: the study of the emergence of humans and their later physical evolution. Also called *palaeoanthropology*.

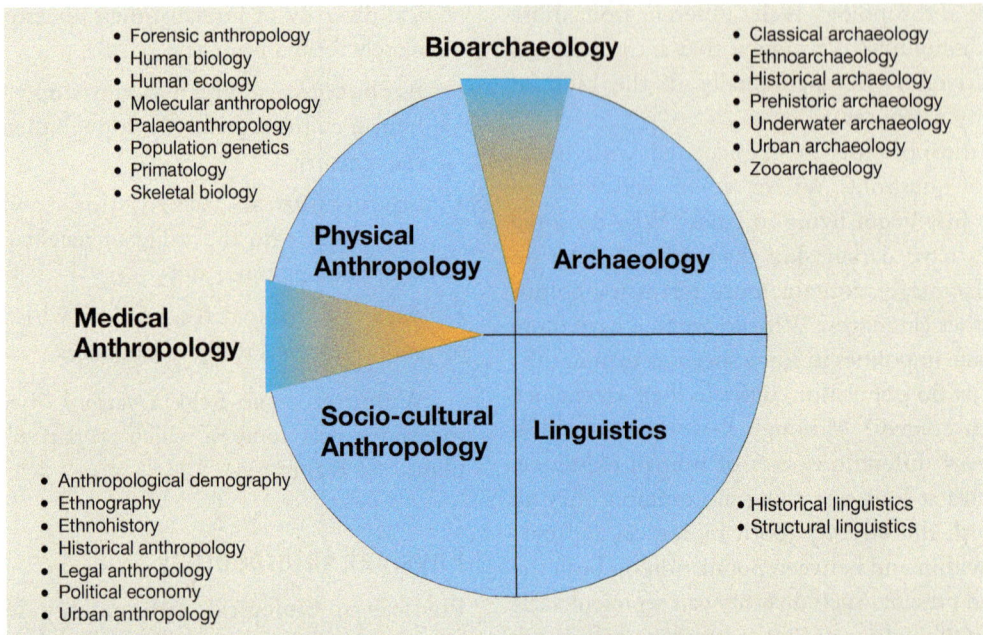

Figure 1–1 The Four Sub-fields of Anthropology

The four major sub-fields of anthropology, as promoted early on by Franz Boas. There are applications of anthropology in all four, and examples of specialties for each sub-field are shown in the lists. Bioarchaeology, drawing from both physical or biological anthropology and archaeology, and medical anthropology, drawing from both physical anthropology and socio-cultural anthropology, are two examples of areas that overlap sub-fields.

In order to reconstruct human evolution, palaeoanthropologists search for and study the buried, hardened remains or impressions, known as **fossils**, of humans, prehumans, and related animals. Palaeoanthropologists working in East Africa, for instance, have excavated the fossil remains of early human ancestors who lived more than 4 million years ago. These findings have suggested the approximate dates when our ancestors began to develop the facility to walk on two legs, very flexible hands, and a larger brain.

In attempting to clarify evolutionary relationships, palaeoanthropologists may use the fossil record and geological information about the succession of climates, environments, and plant and animal populations. Moreover, when reconstructing the past of humans, palaeoanthropologists are also interested in the behaviour and evolution of our closest relatives among the mammals—the prosimians, monkeys, and apes, which, like us, are members of the order of **Primates**. Anthropologists, psychologists, and biologists specializing in the study of primates are called **primatologists**. They observe the various species of primates in the wild and in the laboratory. One especially popular subject of study is the chimpanzee, which bears a close resemblance to humans in behaviour and physical appearance, has a similar blood chemistry, and is susceptible to many of the same diseases. It now appears that chimpanzees share over 95 percent of their genes with humans (Toder et al. 2001; Britten 2002).

Fossils: the hardened remains or impressions of plants and animals that lived in the past.

Primate: a member of the mammalian order Primates, divided into the two suborders of prosimians and anthropoids.
Primatologists: people who study primates.

Biruté Galdikas with two orangutans in Borneo.

From primate studies, physical anthropologists try to discover characteristics that are distinctly human as opposed to those that might be part of the primate heritage. Further, observed behaviours among modern living primates serve as a model for how human ancestors may have behaved under similar environmental conditions. With this information, these anthropologists may be able to infer what our distant ancestors were like. The inferences from primate studies are checked against the fossil record. The evidence from the earth, collected in bits and pieces, is correlated with scientific observations of our closest living relatives. In short, physical anthropologists piece together bits of information obtained from different sources. They construct theories that explain the changes observed in the fossil record and then attempt to evaluate their theories by checking one kind of evidence against another. Palaeoanthropology thus overlaps disciplines such as geology, general vertebrate (and particularly primate) palaeontology, comparative anatomy, and the study of comparative primate behaviour.

Another major focus of physical anthropology investigates how and why contemporary human populations differ in biological or physical characteristics. All living people belong to one species, *Homo sapiens*, for all can successfully interbreed. Yet there is much that varies among human populations. Investigators of **human variation** ask such questions as, Why are some peoples taller than others? How have human populations adapted physically to their environmental conditions? Are some peoples, such as Inuit, better equipped than other peoples to endure cold? Does darker skin pigmentation offer special protection against the tropical sun?

Physical anthropologists use the principles, concepts, and techniques of at least three other disciplines to further their understanding of human biological diversity: *human genetics* (the study of human traits that are inherited), *population biology* (the study of environmental effects on and

Homo sapiens: all living people belong to one biological species, *Homo sapiens*, which means that all human populations on earth can successfully interbreed. The first *Homo sapiens* may have emerged by 200 000 years ago.
Human Variation: the study of how and why contemporary human populations vary biologically.

interaction with population characteristics), and *epidemiology* (the study of how and why diseases affect different populations in different ways). Research on human variation, therefore, overlaps with research in other fields. Physical anthropologists, however, are concerned most with human populations and how they vary biologically.

Archaeology

The archaeologist seeks not only to reconstruct the daily life and customs of peoples who lived in the past but also to trace cultural changes and offer possible explanations for those changes. This goal is similar to that of the historian, but the archaeologist reaches much farther back in time. The historian deals only with societies that left written records and is therefore limited to the last 5000 years of human history. Human societies, however, have existed for more than a million years, and only a small proportion in the last 5000 years recorded their past in writing. For all those past societies lacking a written record, or where the written record is indecipherable or has disappeared, the archaeologist serves as historian. Lacking written records for study, archaeologists must try to reconstruct history from the remains of human cultures. Some of these remains are as grand as the Mayan temples at Chichén Itzá in Yucatán, Mexico. More often they are as ordinary as bits of broken pottery, stone tools, and garbage heaps.

Most archaeologists deal with the distant past—the time before written records. But there is a specialty within archaeology, called **historical archaeology**, that studies the remains of recent peoples who left written records. This specialty, as its name implies, employs the methods of both archaeologists and historians to study recent societies for which there is both archaeological and historical information.

In trying to understand how and why ways of life have changed through time in different parts of the world, archaeologists collect materials from sites of human occupation. Usually, these sites must be unearthed. On the basis of materials they excavate and otherwise collect, they then ask various questions such as these: Where, when, and why did the distinctive human characteristic of toolmaking first emerge? Where, when, and why did agriculture first develop? Where, when, and why did people first begin to live in cities?

To collect the data they need to find answers to these and other questions, archaeologists rely on techniques and findings borrowed from other disciplines as well as what they can infer from anthropological studies of recent and contemporary cultures. For example, to guess where to dig for evidence of early toolmaking, archaeologists rely on geology and physical geography to tell them where sites of early human occupation are likely to be found near the surface of the earth. To infer when agriculture first developed, archaeologists date relevant excavated materials by a process originally developed by chemists. To understand why cities first emerged, archaeologists may study information from historians, geographers, and others about how recent and contemporary cities are related economically and politically to their hinterlands. If we can discover what recent and contemporary cities have in common, we can speculate on why cities developed originally. Thus, archaeologists gather information from the present and recent past in trying to understand the distant past.

Socio-cultural Anthropology

Cultural anthropologists are interested in how populations or societies vary in their cultural features. But what is culture? To an anthropologist, the term **culture** refers to the customary ways of thinking and behaving of a particular population or society. The culture of a social group includes many things—its language, religious beliefs, food preferences, music, work habits, gender roles, how children are reared, how houses are constructed, and many other learned behaviours and ideas that have come to be widely shared or customary among the group.

Historical Archaeology: a specialty within archaeology that studies the material remains of recent peoples who left written records.

Culture: the set of learned behaviours, beliefs, attitudes, values, and ideals that are characteristic of a particular society or population.

Nadine Peacock, a biological anthropologist, studying reproduction and health among the Efe-Ituri Pygmies of the former Zaire.

Ethnologists seek to understand how and why peoples today and in the recent past differ in their customary ways of thinking and acting. **Ethnology**, then, is concerned with cultural patterns of behaviour, such as marriage customs, kinship organization, political and economic systems, religion, folk art, and music, and with the ways in which these patterns differ in contemporary societies. Ethnologists also study the dynamics of culture, that is, how various cultures develop and change. As well, they are interested in the relationship between beliefs and practices within a culture. Thus, the aim of ethnologists is largely the same as that of archaeologists.

Ethnologists, however, generally use data collected through observation and interviews with people. Archaeologists, on the other hand, must work with fragmentary remains of past cultures on the basis of which they can only make inferences about the customs of **prehistoric** peoples.

One type of ethnologist, the **ethnographer**, usually spends a year or so living with, talking to, and observing the people whose customs he or she is studying. This fieldwork provides the data for a detailed description (an **ethnography**) of many aspects of the cultural behaviours and customs of the group. The ethnographer not only tries to describe the general patterns of their life but also may suggest answers to such questions as these: How are economic and political behaviour related? How may a people adapt their customs to environmental conditions? Is there any relationship between beliefs about the supernatural and beliefs or practices about the natural world? In other words, the ethnographer depicts the way of life of a particular group of people and explains some of the customs observed.

Because so many cultures have undergone extensive change in the recent past, another type of ethnologist, the **ethnohistorian**, studies how

---

Ethnology: the study of how and why recent cultures differ and are similar.
Prehistoric: in the time before written records.
Ethnographer: a person who spends some time living with, interviewing, and observing a group of people so that he or she can describe their customs.

Ethnography: a detailed description of aspects of cultural behaviours and customs based on observation.
Ethnohistorian: an ethnologist who uses historical documents to study how a particular culture has changed over time.

the way of life of a particular group of people has changed over time. Unlike ethnographers, who rely mostly on their own observations, ethnohistorians rely on the reports of others. Ethnohistorians investigate historical documents, such as missionary accounts, reports by traders and explorers, and government records, to try to establish the cultural changes that have occurred. Often, they must attempt to piece together and make sense of widely scattered, and even apparently contradictory, information. Thus, the ethnohistorian's research is very much like that of the historian except that the ethnohistorian is usually concerned with the history of a people who did not themselves leave written records. The ethnohistorian tries to reconstruct the recent history of a people and may also suggest why certain changes in their way of life took place.

With the data collected and analyzed by the ethnographer and ethnohistorian, the work of a third type of ethnologist, the **cross-cultural researcher**, can be done. The cross-cultural researcher is interested in discovering why certain cultural characteristics may be found in some societies but not in others. Why, for example, do some societies have plural marriages (one spouse of one sex and two or more spouses of the other sex), circumcision of adolescent boys, or belief in a supreme being? To answer such questions and explain cultural variation, cross-cultural researchers rely on the data from samples of different cultures.

Because ethnologists may be interested in many aspects of cultural behaviour, from economic behaviour to political behaviour to styles of art, music, and religion, ethnology overlaps with disciplines that concentrate on some particular aspect of human existence, such as sociology, psychology, economics, political science, art, music, and comparative religion. The distinctive feature of **cultural anthropology** is its interest in how all these aspects of human existence vary from society to society in all historical periods and in all parts of the world.

Anthropological Linguistics

Linguistics, or the study of languages, is a somewhat older discipline than anthropology. The early linguists concentrated on the study of languages that had a written form for a long time—for example, the English language has had a written form for nearly a thousand years. Then anthropological linguists began to do fieldwork in places where the language did not have a written form. To learn the language, anthropologists had to first construct a dictionary and grammar. Then they could study the structure and history of the language.

Like physical anthropologists, linguists study changes that have taken place over time, as well as contemporary variation. Some anthropological linguists are concerned with the emergence of language and also with the divergence of languages over thousands of years. The study of how languages change over time and how they may be related is known as **historical linguistics**. Anthropological linguists are also interested in how contemporary languages differ, especially in their construction. This focus of linguistics is generally called **structural or descriptive linguistics**. The study of how language is used in social contexts is called **sociolinguistics**.

In contrast with the palaeoanthropologist and archaeologist, who work with physical remains to help them reconstruct change over time, the historical linguist deals only with languages, and usually languages do not have a written form. (Remember that writing is only about 5000 years old, and most languages were not written.) Because an unwritten language must be heard in order to

---

Cross-cultural Researcher: an ethnologist who uses ethnographic data about many societies to test possible explanations of cultural variation.
Cultural Anthropology: the study of cultural variation and universals.
Linguistics: the study of language.

Historical Linguistics: the study of how languages change over time.
Structural Linguistics: the study of how languages are constructed. Also called *descriptive linguistics*.
Sociolinguistics: the study of cultural and sub-cultural patterns of speaking in different social contexts.

be studied, it does not leave any traces once its speakers have died. Linguists interested in reconstructing the history of unwritten languages must begin in the present, with comparisons of contemporary languages. On the basis of these comparisons, they draw inferences about the kinds of change in language that may have occurred in the past and that may account for similarities and differences observed in the present. The historical linguist typically asks such questions as these: Did two or more contemporary languages diverge from a common ancestral language? If they are related, how far back in time did they begin to differ?

Unlike the historical linguist, the structural (or descriptive) linguist is typically concerned with discovering and recording the principles that determine how sounds and words are put together in speech. For example, a structural description of a particular language might tell us that the sounds *t* and *k* are interchangeable in a word without causing a difference in meaning. In American Samoa, one could say *Tutuila* or *Kukuila* as the name of the largest island, and everyone, except perhaps the newly arrived anthropologist, would understand that the same island was being mentioned.

The sociolinguist is interested in the social aspects of language, including what people speak about and how they interact conversationally, their attitudes toward speakers of other dialects or languages, and how people speak differently in different social contexts. In English, for example, we do not address everyone we meet in the same way. "Hi, Sandy" may be the customary way a person greets a friend, but we would probably feel uncomfortable addressing a doctor in this manner. Instead, we would probably say, "Good morning, Dr. Brown." Such variations in language use, which are determined by the social status of the persons being addressed, are significant for the sociolinguist.

Specialization

As disciplines grow, they tend to develop more and more specialties. This trend is probably inevitable because, as knowledge accumulates and methods become more advanced, there is a limit to the amount of information that any one person can reasonably keep track of. So, in addition to the general divisions we have outlined already, particular anthropologists tend to identify themselves with a variety of specializations. It is common for anthropologists to have a geographic specialty, which may be as broad as the Old World or the New World or as narrow as the West Coast of Canada. Those who study the past (archaeologists or palaeoanthropologists) may also specialize in different time periods. Socio-cultural anthropologists often specialize in more specific subject matters such as kinship, identity, symbolism, and complexity, often in addition to one or two cultural groups.

Some socio-cultural anthropologists identify themselves as *economic anthropologists*, *political anthropologists*, or *psychological anthropologists*.

Others may identify themselves by theoretical orientations, such as **cultural ecologists**, who are concerned with the relationship between culture and the physical and social environments. These specialties are not mutually exclusive, however. A cultural ecologist, for example, might be interested in the effects of the environment on economic behaviour, or political behaviour, or how people raise their children.

Does specialization isolate an anthropologist from other kinds of research? Not necessarily. Some specialties have to draw on information from several fields, inside and outside anthropology. For example, *medical anthropologists* study the cultural and biological contexts of human health and illness. Thus, they need to understand the economy, diet, and patterns of social interaction, as well as attitudes and beliefs regarding illness and health. They may need to draw on research in human genetics, public health, and medicine.

Increased specialization reinforces the division between the sub-disciplines of anthropology. Anthropologists are realizing, however, that many of the questions being asked cannot ignore the fundamental interactions between environment, behaviour, and biology for human populations.

Cultural Ecologist: a person concerned with the relationship between culture and the physical and social environments.

The Biocultural Model

In the 1990s, anthropology embraced the **biocultural model**—the idea that human biological diversity is interrelated to changes in environmental conditions, and that one of humankind's greatest adaptive strategies is the development of culture. Thus, the interactions of biology, behaviour, and environment are ultimately linked together, and changes in one can often be explained by changes in the others. Early incarnations of this concept are seen in the many arguments in the social and behavioural sciences that surround the debate of "nature versus nurture" or biology versus behaviour. However, anthropologists now recognize that both are interconnected, and to understand much of the evolutionary changes in the human species, we must understand the changing relationships between these associated factors.

The biocultural approach to reconstructing human evolution will become clearer in subsequent chapters that discuss the early **hominins**—early human ancestors—and the emergence of the genus *Homo*. For example, a current argument for the emergence of the first bipedal ape—that is, the earliest hominins—links changes in the environment in which these primates lived to changes in behaviour and biology related to new survival strategies to cope with these new conditions. Similarly, the genus *Homo* was originally classified and distinguished from other hominins by the presence of culture in the form of manufactured tools. This new adaptive strategy—the development of culture—represented the beginning of an integrated relationship between biology, behaviour, and culture. With a changing environment, important biological changes like increased brain size and complexity, and behavioural strategies, especially increased cultural complexity, improved survival, and eventually resulted in modern human populations. As the development of culture provided greater advantages for survival among early hominins, any genetic traits associated with these new behaviours were favoured in the population. Ultimately this relationship between biology and culture resulted in the rapid acceleration of human evolution.

Applied Anthropology

All knowledge is useful. In the physical and biological sciences it is well understood that technological breakthroughs like DNA splicing, a mission to Mars, and the development of minuscule computer chips could not have taken place without an enormous amount of basic research to uncover the laws of nature in the physical and biological worlds. If we did not understand these fundamental principles, the technological achievements we are so proud of would not have been possible. Researchers are often simply driven by curiosity, with no thought of where the research might lead, which is why such research is sometimes called *basic research*. The same is true of the social sciences. If a researcher finds out that societies with combative sports tend to have more wars, it may lead to other inquiries about the relationships between one kind of aggression and another. The knowledge acquired may ultimately lead to the discovery of ways to lessen social problems such as family violence and war.

Applied research is more explicit than basic research in its practical goals. Today many professional anthropologists are *applied anthropologists*. **Applied anthropology** is explicit in its concern with making anthropological knowledge immediately useful in public policy, for example (Chambers 1989). Applied anthropologists may be trained in any or all of the sub-fields of anthropology. In contrast to basic researchers, who are generally employed in colleges, universities, and museums, applied anthropologists are often

---

Biocultural Model: a holistic approach that recognizes the interaction between biology and culture in human populations.
Hominins: the group of hominoids consisting of humans and their direct ancestors. It contains at least two genera: *Homo* and *Australopithecus*.

Applied Anthropology: the branch of anthropology that concerns itself with applying anthropological knowledge to achieve practical goals, usually in the service of an agency outside the traditional academic setting. Also called *practising anthropology*.

PERSPECTIVES ON GENDER

Getting Development Programs to Notice Women's Contributions to Agriculture

When Anita Spring first worked in the field in Zambia in the 1970s, she was not particularly interested in agriculture. Rather, medical anthropology was her primary interest. Her work focused on customary healing practices, particularly involving women and children. She was surprised at the end of the year when a delegation of women came to tell her that she didn't understand what it meant to be a woman. "To be a woman is to be a farmer," they said. She admitted that it took her a while to pay attention to women as farmers, but then she began to participate in efforts to provide technical assistance to them. Like many others interested in women in development, Spring realized that all too often development agencies downplay women's contributions to agriculture.

How does one bring about change in male-centred attitudes and practices? One way is to document how much women actually contribute to agriculture. Beginning with the influential writing of Ester Boserup in *Woman's Role in Economic Development* (1970), scholars began to report that in Africa south of the Sahara, in the Caribbean, and in parts of Southeast Asia, women were the principal farmers or agricultural labourers. Moreover, as agriculture became more complex, it required more work in the fields, so the women's contribution to agriculture increased. In addition, men increasingly went away to work, so women had to do much of what used to be men's work on the farms.

In the 1980s, Spring designed and directed the Women in Agricultural Development Project in Malawi, funded by the Office of Women in the U.S. Agency for International Development. Rather than focusing just on women, the project aimed to collect data on both women and men agriculturalists and how they were treated by development agents. The project did more than collect information; mini-projects were set up and evaluated so that successful training techniques could be passed on to development agents in other regions. Spring pointed out that the success of the program was due not just to the design of the project but more so to the interest and willingness of Malawi itself to change. And it didn't hurt that the United Nations and other donor organizations increasingly focused attention on women. It takes the efforts of many to bring about change. Increasingly, applied anthropologists like Anita Spring are involved in these efforts from beginning to end, from the design stage to implementation and evaluation.

Source: Spring A. 1995. Agricultural development and gender issues in Malawi. Lanham, MD: University Press of America.

---

employed in settings outside of traditional academia, including government agencies, international development agencies, private consulting firms, businesses, public health organizations, medical schools, law offices, community development agencies, and charitable foundations.

Physical anthropologists may be called upon to give forensic evidence in court, work in public health, or design clothes and equipment to fit human anatomy. Archaeologists may be involved in preserving and exhibiting artifacts for museums and in finding and preserving cultural sites that might be damaged by construction or excavation. Linguists may work in bilingual educational training programs or may work on ways to improve communication. Ethnologists may work in a wide variety of applied projects ranging from community development, urban planning, health care, and agricultural improvement to personnel and organizational management, and assessment of the impact that changes in programs have on people's lives (Kushner 1991; Miracle 1998). We discuss applied anthropology more fully in Chapter 14.

Explanations

An **explanation** is an answer to a why question. There are many types of explanations, some more satisfying than others. For example, suppose we

> **Explanation:** an answer to a question. In science, there are two kinds of explanation that researchers try to achieve: associations and theories.

ask why a society has a long post-partum sex taboo. We could guess that the people in that society want to abstain from sex for a year or so after the birth of a baby. Is this an explanation? Yes, because it does suggest that people have a purpose in practising the custom; it therefore partly answers the why question. But such an explanation would not be very satisfying because it does not specify what the purpose of the custom might be. How about the idea that people have a long post-partum sex taboo because it is their tradition? That too is an explanation, but it is not satisfactory for a different reason. It is a tautology; that is, the thing to be explained (the taboo) is being explained by itself, by its prior existence. To explain something in terms of tradition is to say that people do it because they already do it, which is not informative. What kinds of explanations are more satisfactory, then? In science, investigators try to achieve two kinds of explanations: associations and theories.

Associations or Relations

One way of explaining something (an observation, an action, a custom) is to say how it conforms to a general principle or relationship. So to explain why the water left outside in the basin froze, we say that it was cold last night and that water freezes at 0°C. The statement that water solidifies (becomes ice) at 0°C is a statement of a relationship or association between two **variables**—things or quantities that vary. In this case, variation in the state of water (liquid vs. solid) is related to variation in the temperature of the air (above vs. below 0°C). The truth of the relationship is suggested by repeated observations. In the physical sciences, such relationships are called **laws** when almost all scientists accept them. We find such explanations satisfactory because they allow us to predict what will happen in the future or to understand something that has happened regularly in the past.

Variable: a thing or quantity that varies.
Law: associations or relationships that almost all scientists accept.

In the social sciences, associations are usually stated *probabilistically*; that is, we say that two or more variables tend to be related in a predictable way, which means that there are usually some exceptions. For example, to explain why a society has a long post-partum sex taboo, we can point to the association (or correlation) that John Whiting found in a worldwide sample of societies: societies with apparently low-protein diets tend to have long post-partum sex taboos (Whiting 1964). We call the relationship between low-protein diets and the sex taboo a **statistical association**, which means that the observed relationship is unlikely to be due to chance.

Theories

Even though laws and statistical associations explain by relating what is to be explained to other things, we want to know more: why those laws or associations exist. Why does water freeze at 0°C? Why do societies with low-protein diets tend to have long post-partum sex taboos? Therefore, scientists try to formulate theories that will explain the observed relationships (laws and statistical associations) (Nagel 1961:88–89).

Theories—explanations of laws and statistical associations—are more complicated than the observed relationships they are intended to explain. It is difficult to be precise about what a theory is. By way of example, let us return to the question of why some societies have long post-partum sex taboos. We have already seen that a known statistical association can be used to help explain it. If a society has a low-protein diet, it will generally have a long post-partum sex taboo. But most people would ask additional questions: Why does a low-protein diet explain the taboo? What is the mechanism by which a society with such a diet develops the custom of a long post-partum sex taboo? A theory is intended to answer such questions.

Statistical Association: a relationship or correlation between two or more variables that is unlikely to be due to chance alone.
Theory: a set of statements or principles intended to explain a group of facts or phenomena.

John Whiting theorized that a long post-partum sex taboo may be an adaptation to certain conditions. Particularly in tropical areas, where the major food staples are low in protein, babies are vulnerable to the protein deficiency disease called *kwashiorkor*. But if a baby could continue to nurse for a long time, it might have more of a chance to survive. The post-partum sex taboo might be adaptive, Whiting's theory suggests, because it increases the likelihood of a baby's survival. That is, if a mother puts off having another baby for a while, the first baby might have a better chance to survive because it can be fed mother's milk for a longer time. Whiting suggested that parents may be aware, whether unconsciously or consciously, that having another baby too soon might jeopardize the survival of the first baby, and so they might decide that abstaining from intercourse for more than a year after the birth of the first baby would be a good idea.

As this example of a theory illustrates, there are differences between a theory and an association. A theory is usually more complicated, containing a series of statements. An association usually states quite simply that there is a relationship between two or more measured variables. Another difference is that although a theory may mention some things that are observable, such as the presence of a long post-partum sex taboo, it contains other concepts or statements that could not be observed. For example, with regard to Whiting's theory, it would be difficult to find out if the people who adopted the custom of a long post-partum sex taboo had some awareness that babies would thereby have a better chance to survive. Then, too, the concept of adaptation—that some characteristic promotes greater reproductive success—is difficult to verify because of the challenge of finding out whether different individuals or groups have different rates of reproduction because they do or do not practise the supposedly adaptive custom. Thus, some concepts or implications in a theory are unobservable (at least at the present time), and only some aspects may be observable. In contrast, statistical associations or laws are based entirely on observations (Nagel 1961:83–90).

Why Theories Cannot Be Proved

Many people think that the theories they learned in physics or chemistry courses have been proved. Unfortunately, many students get that impression because their teachers present lessons in an authoritative manner. Scientists and philosophers of science now generally agree that no theory can be said to be proved or unquestionably true, although some theories may have considerable evidence supporting them. This is because many of the concepts and ideas in theories are not directly observable and therefore not directly verifiable. For example, scientists may try to explain how light behaves by postulating that it consists of particles called photons, but photons cannot be observed, even with the most powerful microscope. So, exactly what a photon looks like and exactly how it works remain in the realm of the unprovable. The photon is a theoretical construct, something that cannot be observed or verified directly. Because all theories contain such constructs, theories cannot be proved entirely or with absolute certainty (Nagel 1961:85; McCain and Segal 1988:75–79).

Why should we bother with theories, then, if we cannot prove that they are true? Perhaps the main advantage of a theory as a kind of explanation is that it may lead to new understanding or knowledge. A theory can suggest new relationships or imply new predictions that might be supported or confirmed by new research. For example, Whiting's theory about long post-partum sex taboos has implications that researchers could investigate. Because the theory discusses how a long post-partum sex taboo might be adaptive, we would expect that certain changes would result in the taboo's disappearance. For example, suppose people adopted either mechanical birth control devices or began to give supplementary high-protein foods to babies. With birth control, a family could space births without abstaining from sex, so we would expect the custom of post-partum abstinence to disappear. Additionally, we would expect it to disappear with protein supplements for babies because kwashiorkor would then be less likely to afflict the babies. Whiting's ideas might also prompt investigators to try to find out whether parents are consciously or unconsciously aware of the problem of close birth spacing in areas with low supplies of protein.

Although theories cannot be proved, they are rejectable. The method of falsification, which shows that a theory seems to be wrong, is the main way that theories are judged (McCain and Segal 1988:62–64). Scientists derive implications or predictions that should be true if the theory is correct. So, for example, Whiting predicted that societies with long post-partum sex taboos would be found more often in the tropics than in temperate regions and that they would be likely to have low-protein food supplies. Such predictions of what might be found are called **hypotheses**. If the predictions turn out not to be correct, the researcher is obliged to conclude that something may be wrong with the theory or something wrong with the test of the theory. Theories that are not falsified are accepted for the time being because the available evidence seems to be consistent with them. But remember that no matter how much the available evidence seems to support a theory, we can never be certain it is true. There is always the possibility that some implication of it, some hypothesis derivable from it, will not be confirmed in the future.

The Scientific Method

The Canadian Oxford Dictionary defines the **scientific method** as "a method of procedure that has characterized natural science since the 17th century, consisting of systematic observation, measurement, and experiment, and the formulation, testing, and modification of hypotheses."

So, using the scientific method, researchers can collect data through observation. These observations in turn result in generalizations about the way things work (the process of induction), which are called *hypotheses*. Hypotheses are then tested against predictions. When expected (predicted) results are observed, this supports (but does not prove) the stated hypothesis. If new observations contradict the predictions of an existing hypothesis, that hypothesis must be rejected and a new, more plausible explanation proposed. A hypothesis that is well supported by evidence and experimental testing is called a *theory*.

As anthropologist Philip Salzman explained,

> The scientific method, the heart of science, was invented because it was understood that human error, wish fulfillment, duplicity, dishonesty, and weakness would commonly distort research findings. The scientific requirements that the procedures of all studies must be specified in detail so that others could repeat them, and the actual replication of findings by other scientists in other venues, were established to minimize the distorting effects of human subjectivity and moral weakness in the quest for knowledge. (Salzman 2001:135)

Although one goal of anthropology is to understand what it means to be a human in a different cultural context, a goal for which science and its pursuit of explanations may not be appropriate, most anthropologists believe that objective knowledge about other cultures is possible through science.

Evidence: Testing Explanations

In any field of investigation, theories are generally the most plentiful commodity, apparently because of the human predisposition to try to make sense of the world. It is necessary, then, for us to have procedures that enable us to select from among the many available theories those that are more likely to be correct. As Peter Caws pointed out, "Just as mutations arise naturally but are not all beneficial, so hypotheses [theories] emerge naturally but are not all correct. If progress is to occur, therefore, we require a superfluity of hypotheses and also a mechanism of selection" (Caws 1969:1378). In other words, generating a theory or interpretation is not enough. We need some reliable method of testing whether or not that theory is likely to be correct. If a theory is not correct, it may detract from our efforts to achieve understanding by misleading us into thinking the problem is already solved.

> **Hypothesis:** a proposition intended to explain facts or phenomena.
> **Scientific Method:** a process that involves the formulation of a problem, the collection of data through observation and experiment, and the formulation and testing of hypotheses.

The strategy in all kinds of testing in science is to predict what one would expect to find if a particular theory were correct, and then to conduct an investigation to see if the prediction is generally consistent with the data. If the prediction is not supported, the investigator is obliged to accept the possibility that the theory is wrong. If, however, the prediction holds true, then the investigator is entitled to say that evidence supports the theory. Thus, conducting research designed to test expectations derived from theory allows researchers to eliminate some theories and to accept others, at least tentatively.

Hypotheses and Measurement

We test predictions derived from a theory, often in the form of hypotheses, to see if the theory may be correct—to see if it is consistent with observable events or conditions in the real world. A theory and the predictions derived from it are not useful if there is no way to measure the events or conditions mentioned in the predictions. If there is no way of relating the theory to observable events, it does not matter how good the theory sounds; it is still not a useful scientific theory (McCain and Segal 1988:114). To transform theoretical predictions into statements that might be verified, a researcher provides an operational definition of each of the concepts or variables mentioned in the prediction, in the form of a testable hypothesis using a specified method to measure the variables (McCain and Segal 1988:56–57, 131–132).

Whiting predicted that societies with a low-protein diet would have a long post-partum sex taboo. Amount of protein in the diet is a variable; some societies have more, others have less. Length of the post-partum sex taboo is a variable; a society may have a short taboo or a long taboo. Whiting operationally defined the first variable, *amount of protein*, in terms of staple foods (Whiting 1964:519). For example, if a society depended mostly on root and tree crops (such as cassava and bananas), Whiting rated the society as having low protein. If the society depended mostly on cereal crops (such as wheat, barley, corn, and oats), he rated it as having moderate protein because cereal crops have more protein by weight than root and tree crops. If the society depended mostly on hunting, fishing, or herding for food, he rated it as having high protein. The other variable in Whiting's prediction, *length of post-partum sex taboo*, was operationalized as follows: a society was rated as having a long taboo if couples customarily abstained from sex for more than a year after the birth of a baby; abstention for a year or less was considered a short taboo.

Specifying an operational definition for each variable is extremely important because it allows other investigators to check a researcher's results (McCain and Segal 1988:67–69). Science depends on *replication*, the repetition of results. Only when many researchers observe a particular association can we call that association or relationship a law. Providing operational definitions is also extremely important because it allows others to evaluate whether a measure is appropriate. Only when we are told exactly how something was measured can we judge whether the measure reflects what it is supposed to reflect. Specifying measures publicly is so important in science that we are obliged to be skeptical of any conclusions offered by a researcher who fails to say how variables were measured.

To **measure** something is to say how it compares with other things on some scale of variation. People often assume that a measuring device is always a physical instrument, such as a scale or a ruler, but physical devices are not the only way to measure something. *Classification* is also a form of measurement. When we classify people as male or female or employed versus unemployed, we are dividing them into *types*. Deciding which type they belong to is a kind of measurement because doing so allows us to compare them. We can also measure things by deciding which cases or examples have more or less of something (e.g., more or less protein in the diet). The measures employed in physical science are usually based on scales that allow us to assign numbers to each case; we measure height in metres and weight in grams, for example. However

> **Measure:** to describe how something compares with other things on some scale of variation.

we measure our variables, the fact that we can measure them means that we can test our hypotheses to see if the predicted relationships actually exist, at least most of the time.

Sampling

After deciding how to measure the variables in some predicted relationship, investigators must decide how to select which cases to study to see if the predicted relationship holds. If the prediction is about the behaviour of people, the sampling decision involves which people to observe. If the prediction is about an association between societal customs, the sampling decision involves which societies to study. Investigators must decide not only which cases to choose but also how many to choose. No researcher can investigate all the possible cases, and so choices must be made. Some choices are better than others. The best sample is almost always some kind of random sample. A **random sample** is one in which all cases selected have an equal chance of being included in the sample. Almost all statistical tests used to evaluate the results of research require random sampling because only results based on a random sample can be assumed to be probably true for some larger set or universe of cases.

Before researchers can sample randomly, they must specify the **sampling universe**, that is, the list of cases to be sampled from. For example, for archaeologists, the sampling universe might be an archaeological site where they are working. For physical anthropologists, it could be a skeletal collection from a specific location and time period.

Truly random sampling is not always possible in anthropology, and oftentimes there are specific criteria that need to be met in order for a case to be potentially selected (e.g., preservation, time period). As such, a nonrandom sample might still be fairly representative for the question being asked, as long as the strategy for selecting cases is independent of the anticipated outcome. We should be particularly suspicious of any sample that may reflect the investigator's own biases or interests. For example, if investigators pick only the artifacts that match their expectations, the sample is suspicious. A sampling procedure should be designed to get a fair, unbiased representation of the sampling universe. If we want to increase our chances of getting a representative sample, we have to use a random sampling procedure.

Statistical Evaluation

When researchers have measured the variables of interest for all the sample cases, they are ready to see if the predicted relationship actually exists in the data. Remember, the results may not turn out to be what the theory predicts. Sometimes researchers construct a contingency table, like that shown in Table 1–1, to see if the variables are associated as predicted. In Whiting's sample of 172 societies, each case is assigned to a box, or cell, in the table, depending on how the society is measured on the two variables of interest. For example, a society that has a long post-partum sex taboo and a low-protein diet is placed in the third row of the Long Duration column. (In Whiting's sample there are 27 such societies.) A society that has a short post-partum sex taboo and a low-protein diet is placed in the third row in the Short Duration column. (There are 20 such societies in the sample.) The statistical question is, Does the way the cases are distributed in the six central cells of the table generally support Whiting's prediction? If we looked just at the table, we might not know what to answer. Many cases appear to be in the expected places. For example, most of the high-protein cases (47 of 62) have short taboos, and most of the low-protein cases (27 of 47) have long taboos. But there are also many exceptions (e.g., 20 cases have low protein and a short taboo). So, although many cases appear to be in the expected places, there are also many exceptions. Do the exceptions invalidate the prediction? How many exceptions would compel us to reject the hypothesis? Here is where we resort to statistical tests of significance.

> **Random Sample:** a sample in which all cases selected have had an equal chance to be included.
> **Sampling Universe:** the list of cases to be sampled from.

Table 1–1 Association between Availability of Protein and Duration of Post-Partum Sex Taboo.

Availability of Protein	Duration of Post-Partum Sex Taboo		Total
	Short (0–1 Year)	Long (More Than One Year)	
High	47	15	62
Medium	38	25	63
Low	20	27	47
Total	105	67	172

Source: Based on Whiting JWM. 1964. Effects of climate on certain cultural practices. Goodenough W, editor. In: Explorations in cultural anthropology. New York: McGraw-Hill. p. 520.

Statisticians have devised various tests that tell us how "perfect" a result must be to convince us to believe that there is probably an association between the variables of interest, and that one variable generally predicts the other. Essentially, every statistical result is evaluated in the same objective way. We ask, What is the chance that this result is purely accidental, that there is no association at all between the two variables? Although some of the mathematical ways of answering this question are complicated, the answer always involves a **probability value** (or *p*-value)—the likelihood that the observed result or a stronger one could have occurred by chance. The statistical test used by Whiting gives a *p*-value of less than 0.01 ($p < 0.01$) for the observed result. In other words, there is less than 1 chance out of 100 that the relationship observed is purely accidental. A *p*-value of less than 0.01 is a fairly low probability; most social scientists conventionally agree to call any result with a *p*-value of 0.05 or less (5 or fewer chances out of 100) a **statistically significant** result. When we describe relationships or associations in the rest of this book, we are almost always referring to results that have been found to be statistically significant. However, we must be mindful that statistically significant relations are not always meaningful with respect to the questions being asked. For example, associations do not always equal causation. Point in case, the presence of fire trucks is almost always associated with the presence of fires; however, fire trucks are not the cause of the fire. But why should a probably true relationship have any exceptions? If a theory is really correct, shouldn't all the cases fit? There are many reasons why we can never expect a perfect result. Even if a theory is correct (e.g., if a low-protein diet really does favour the adoption of a long post-partum sex taboo), there may still be other causes that we have not investigated. Measurement inaccuracy is another source of exception.

Significant statistical associations that are predictable from a theory offer tentative support for the theory. But much more is needed before we can be fairly confident about the theory. Replication is needed to confirm whether other researchers can reproduce the predictions using other samples. Other predictions should be derived from the theory to see if they too are supported. The theory should be pitted against alternative explanations to see which theory works better. We may have to combine theories if the alternative explanations also predict the relationship in question. The research process in science thus requires time and patience. Perhaps most important, it requires that researchers be humble. No matter how wonderful one's own theory seems, it is important to acknowledge that it may be wrong. If we do not acknowledge that possibility, we cannot be motivated to test our theories. If we don't test our theories, we can never tell the difference between a

Probability Value (*p*-Value): the likelihood that the observed result could have occurred by chance.
Statistically Significant: refers to a result that would occur very rarely by chance. The result would occur fewer than 5 times out of 100.

better or worse theory, and we will be saddled forever with our present ignorance. In science, knowledge or understanding is explained variation. Thus, if we want to understand more, we have to keep testing our beliefs against sets of objective evidence that could contradict our beliefs.

The Relevance of Anthropology

Anthropology is a comparatively young discipline. It was only in the late 1800s that anthropologists began to live with people in faraway communities. Compared with our knowledge of the physical laws of nature, we know little about people, about how and why they behave as they do. The fact that anthropology and other sciences dealing with humans began to develop only relatively recently is not in itself a sufficient reason for this discrepancy. Why, in our quest for knowledge of all kinds, did we wait so long to study ourselves? Leslie White suggested that those phenomena most remote from us and least significant as determinants of human behaviour were the first to be studied. The reason, he surmised, is that humans like to think of themselves as citadels of free will, subject to no laws of nature. Hence, there is no need to see ourselves as objects to be explained (White 1968).

The idea that it is impossible to account for human behaviour scientifically, either because our actions and beliefs are too individualistic and complex or because human beings are understandable only in otherworldly terms, is a self-fulfilling notion. We cannot discover principles explaining human behaviour if we neither believe such principles exist nor bother to look for them. The result is assured from the beginning. People who do not believe in principles of human behaviour will have their disbelief reinforced by their finding none. If we are to increase our understanding of human beings, we first have to believe it is possible to do so.

If we aim to understand humans, it is essential that we study humans in all times and places. How else can we understand what is true of humans generally or how they are capable of varying? If we study just our own society, we may give explanations that are culture-bound (**ethnocentric**), that is, not general or applicable to most or all humans. Anthropology is useful, then, to the degree that it contributes to our understanding of human beings everywhere.

As well, anthropology is a relevant field of study because it helps us avoid misunderstandings between peoples. If we can understand why other groups are different from ourselves, we might have less reason to react to them in a negative way for behaviour that appears strange to us. We may then come to realize that many differences between peoples are products of physical and cultural adaptations to different environments. For example, someone who first finds out about the !Kung as they lived in the Kalahari Desert of southern Africa in the 1950s might think that the !Kung were "primitive." The !Kung wore little clothing, had few possessions, lived in meagre shelters, and enjoyed none of our technological benefits. But let us reflect on how a typical North American community might react if it woke to find itself in an environment similar to that in which the !Kung lived. People would find that the arid land made both agriculture and animal husbandry impossible, and they might have to think about adopting a nomadic existence. They might then discard many of their material possessions so that they could travel easily, in order to take advantage of changing water and food supplies. Because of the extreme heat and the lack of water for washing clothes, they might find it more practical to be almost naked. They would undoubtedly find it impossible to build elaborate homes. For social security, they might start to share the food brought into the group. Thus, if they survived at all, they might end up looking and behaving far more like the !Kung than like typical North Americans.

Physical differences, too, may be seen as results of adaptations to the environment. For example, in our society we admire people who are tall and

Ethnocentric: refers to judgment of other cultures solely in terms of one's own culture.

Tourism, shown here in Asmat county of western New Guinea, is one way to learn about other cultures. But anthropology is a better way. It not only tells us how cultures are different, but helps us to understand why.

slim. If these same individuals were forced to live above the Arctic Circle, however, they might wish they could trade their tall, slim bodies for short, compact ones, because stocky physiques conserve body heat more effectively and may therefore be more adaptive in cold climates.

Exposure to anthropology might help to alleviate some of the misunderstandings that arise between people of different cultural groups from subtle causes operating below the level of consciousness. For example, different cultures have different conceptions of the gestures and interpersonal distances that are appropriate under various circumstances. Arabs consider it proper to stand close enough to other people to smell them (Hall 1966). On the basis of the popularity of deodorants in our culture, we can deduce that North Americans prefer to keep the olfactory dimension out of interpersonal relations. We may feel that a person who comes too close is being too intimate. We should remember, however, that this person may only be acting according to a culturally conditioned conception of what is proper in a given situation. If our intolerance for others results in part from a lack of understanding of why peoples

Simplicity of technology should not be taken to imply backwardness. Inuit developed ingenious ways of dealing with their extremely difficult environment. Constructing an igloo out of specially shaped blocks of ice, as shown here in the Canadian Arctic, is not easy.

Even before the emergence of high-tech medical science, people all over the world had discovered how plants could provide effective medicine. Here are some medicinal plants used by Native Americans in Arizona.

vary, then the knowledge accumulated by anthropologists may help lessen that intolerance.

Knowledge of our past may also bring both a feeling of humility and a sense of accomplishment. If we are to attempt to deal with the problems of our world, we must be aware of our vulnerability so that we do not think that our problems will solve themselves. But we also have to think enough of our accomplishments to believe that we can find solutions to our problems. Knowing something about our evolutionary past may help us to understand and accept our place in the biological world. Just as for any other form of life, there is no guarantee that any particular human population, or even the entire human species, will perpetuate itself indefinitely. The earth changes, the environment changes, and humanity itself changes. What survives and flourishes in the present might not do so in the future.

Yet our vulnerability should not make us feel powerless. There are many reasons to feel confident about the future. Consider what humans have accomplished. By means of tools and weapons fashioned from sticks and stones, we were able to hunt animals larger and more powerful than ourselves. We discovered how to make fire, and we learned to use it to keep ourselves warm and to cook our food. As we domesticated plants and animals, we gained greater control over our food supply and were able to establish more permanent settlements. We mined and smelted ores to fashion more complex and durable tools. We built cities and irrigation systems, monuments, and ships. We made it possible to travel from one continent to another in a single day. Illnesses that once cut life short are being controlled, and human life prolonged.

In short, human beings and their cultures have changed considerably over the course of history. Human populations have often adapted to changing circumstances. Let us hope that we continue to adapt to the challenges of the present and future.

SUMMARY AND REVIEW

WHAT IS ANTHROPOLOGY?

1.1 Define the purpose of anthropology.

- Anthropology is the study of human beings.
- It seeks to understand both universals and differences in human populations in every part of the world and through time, from ancestral populations millions of years ago to the present.
- It seeks answers to biological and cultural questions about the past and the present for academic and practical purposes.
- Any generalization about human beings, any explanation of some characteristic of human biology or culture, must be applicable to many times and many peoples, not just a limited group.

 *Why are we unable to simply define anthropology as the study of human beings?*

A SHORT HISTORY OF ANTHROPOLOGY IN CANADA

1.2 Describe how anthropology started in Canada.

- While missionaries and explorer-traders provided detailed descriptions of Indigenous peoples in what is now Canada since the 1600s, professional anthropology was established by Prime Minister Wilfred Laurier in 1910 when he created the Division of Anthropology in the Geological Survey.
- Edward Sapir (a student of Franz Boas at Columbia) and Charles Marius Barbeau (a student of Edward Tyler and Robert Marett at Oxford) grew the Division of Anthropology over the next 15 years until Sapir joined the University of Chicago. That year, 1925, the first academic position in anthropology in Canada was offered to Thomas McIlwraith at the University of Toronto.
- Now, anthropology is taught at universities across Canada and many professional organizations represent anthropologists in the country. Unlike many universities in the United States, most anthropology departments in Canada retain the four-field approach to anthropology started by Franz Boas.

Who were the key players in the history of Canadian anthropology? What were their contributions to the development of the field?

THE SCOPE OF ANTHROPOLOGY

1.3 Describe the scope of anthropology.

- The field of anthropology has a broad scope, both geographically and historically.
- Anthropologists are interested in people of all periods, from millions of years ago to the present.
- The broad scope of anthropology is required to confirm that any suggested generalization about human beings, their biology or culture, is applicable to many times and places of human existence, not just a limited group.

How does anthropology differ from other disciplines concerned with humans?

THE HOLISTIC APPROACH

1.4 Explain what the holistic approach means.

- Anthropologists study the many aspects of human experience as an integrated whole.
- Anthropologists look for patterns of traits and attempt to explain them.
- Anthropologists tend to focus on *typical* characteristics of human populations as opposed to individual variation or the variation in small groups.
- The holistic approach leads anthropologists to find patterns of relationships between seemingly unrelated characteristics.

In what ways does anthropology take a holistic approach to the study of human beings?

THE ANTHROPOLOGICAL CURIOSITY

1.5 Explain anthropology's distinctive curiosity.

- Anthropology is distinct from other disciplines concerned with human beings in its scope, its holistic approach, and its distinctive curiosity.
- Because anthropologists view humans holistically, their curiosity may lead them to find patterns of relationships between seemingly unrelated characteristics.

Give some examples of the types of questions anthropologists would ask. What do they all have in common?

THE FIELDS OF ANTHROPOLOGY

1.6 Describe the fields of anthropology.

- The four traditional fields of anthropology (cultural anthropology, physical anthropology, archaeology, linguistic anthropology) can be divided into two branches depending upon the kinds of questions anthropologists ask.
- Biological anthropology poses questions about the emergence of humans and their later evolution (palaeontology) and about how and why human populations vary biologically (human variation).
- Cultural anthropology is the study of how and why cultures in the past and present vary or are similar in the ways that people in a society think and behave. This branch of anthropology includes cultural anthropology (or ethnology), linguistic anthropology, and archaeology.
- The biocultural model—the idea that human biological diversity is interrelated to changes in environmental conditions and that culture is humanity's greatest adaptive strategy—links the sub-fields together.
- A fifth field, applied anthropology, cuts across all four fields, and is concerned with the practical application of anthropological knowledge. Applied anthropologists may be trained in any or all of the fields of anthropology.
- Anthropologists specialize by focusing upon a geographic area; a period of time; a particular subject matter such as economics, politics, or psychology; or a particular theoretical orientation. Most anthropologists have more than one specialization.
- Applied anthropology makes its anthropological knowledge immediately useful in society, for public policy, for example.

What types of data are used in each of the four fields of anthropology?

EXPLANATIONS

1.7 Define *explanation* and discuss its role in anthropology.

- Scientists try to achieve two kinds of explanations: associations (observed relationships between two or more variables) and theories (explanations of associations).
- Associations are based only on observation, but theories are more complicated because there are concepts or implications in theories that are not observable. This is why theories can never be proved with certainty. There are always other possible implications, some hypotheses derived from a theory, which will not be confirmed by new research.
- Although one goal of anthropology is to understand what it means to be a human in a different cultural context, most anthropologists believe that objective knowledge about other cultures is possible through use of the scientific method.

What is the difference between an association and a theory? Why can't theories be proved?

EVIDENCE: TESTING EXPLANATIONS

1.8 Explain the process of operationalization, the importance of measurement, and the value of statistical evaluation in testing explanations.

- A theory needs to be tested to determine whether it is likely to be correct. A general strategy is to predict what one would expect to find if a particular theory were correct and then to conduct an investigation to see whether the prediction is generally consistent with the data.
- A satisfactory test specifies operationally how to measure the variables involved in the relationships that are expected to exist so other researchers can try to replicate, or repeat, the results.

- Tests of predictions should use samples that are unbiased and representative of the whole. The most objective way to obtain a representative sample is to select the sample cases randomly, but sometimes anthropologists must depend on a sample that is not random.
- We test predictions derived from a theory, often in the form of hypotheses, to see if they explain the facts or the phenomena we are interested in understanding.

 *What are the main steps in testing explanations?*

THE RELEVANCE OF ANTHROPOLOGY

1.9 Explain the relevance of anthropology.

- Anthropology contributes to our understanding of human beings everywhere because it considers both culture and biology of humans in all times and all places.
- Anthropology is relevant because it helps avoid misunderstandings between peoples. Anthropological studies can show us why other people are they way they are, both culturally and physically. Customs or actions that appear improper or offensive may be other people's adaptations to particular environmental or social conditions. Understanding and trying to respect cultural and physical differences is important in our increasingly interconnected world. If those in one culture understand why those in another are different from them, they might have less reason to condemn behaviour that appears strange.
- Anthropology helps improve our understanding of the past. Like any other form of life, we have no guarantee that any particular human population will perpetuate itself indefinitely. Yet knowledge of our achievements in the past may give us both humility and confidence in our ability to solve problems in the future.

 *How can anthropologists avoid being ethnocentric in their research?*

THINK ON IT

1. Why study anthropology?
2. What is unique about the anthropological approach?
3. What do you think about the suggestion that anthropology is the fundamental discipline concerned with humans?
4. Why are theories important?
5. On what grounds would you conclude that a theory is incorrect?
6. How does the biocultural approach inform anthropological questions?

Bruno Morandi/Robert Harding World Imagery

PART II Introduction to Archaeological Methods and Theory

2 Uncovering the Past: Tools and Techniques

Haskel Greenfield

LEARNING OBJECTIVES

2.1 Describe the processes that create sites.

2.2 Differentiate between fossil locales and archaeological sites.

2.3 Describe the different kinds of evidence that we can use to understand the past.

2.4 Describe the different ways that sites can be found.

2.5 Explain how sites are excavated.

2.6 Explain how sites are dated from different kinds of evidence.

Reconstructing the past using archaeological and palaeoanthropological evidence requires a firm understanding of the methods for acquiring data. This chapter deals specifically with the associated methods of site identification and recovery. The methods discussed are broadly applicable to both palaeoanthropological and archaeological research; in some instances issues are more relevant to one field than the other. The material covered in this chapter forms part of the foundation for subsequent chapters, which go on to introduce the biological and cultural evolution of human populations, through the archaeological and palaeontological record.

Understanding past life from the archaeological and palaeontological record requires expertise in a variety of areas. First, specialized methods, mostly borrowed from geological sciences and physics, have been developed to augment the traditional anthropological methods to locate *archaeological sites*—areas of human habitation or where fossil remains are found. Second, archaeological techniques are used for the excavation of remains—whether fossil remains of a hominin (a human, or the direct ancestor of a human), a prehistoric cemetery, or an entire settlement—so as to maximize and preserve the information that can be derived from the excavation of a site.

An important fact to remember is that archaeological remains are the most valuable source of data when the information about where they were buried in relation to all other remains is preserved—something called **provenience**. This is why it is so important that illegal or amateur excavation of sites is prevented. Archaeology, by its very nature, is destructive—once material has been removed, all information regarding its burial environment is lost. As a result, archaeologists have developed extremely rigorous methods for recording this information before and while remains are excavated from a site.

Reconstruction of the past is not an easy task. It requires careful analysis of the environment in which the materials are found in order to say something about the circumstances by which that material came to be there. **Material culture**—the objects that people have and make—is a direct reflection of human culture and behaviour. Archaeologists and their colleagues in related disciplines attempt to understand a complex process as it is reflected in the remains of the everyday belongings of past peoples. For example, if we want to understand how a community changed over the course of its history, we need to recognize that those changes would have been influenced by a variety of factors. These would include changes in the environment, the population numbers, religion, and culture, to name just a few. However, unravelling these factors is sometimes difficult, which is why the researcher has to pay careful attention to the context in which material culture is found. Further, while material culture is a direct reflection of past culture, the archaeological record is not always a direct reflection of material culture. A number of factors can affect where the remains of material culture are found and the patterns of deposition. Archaeologists must be able to recognize these influences.

Site Formation Processes

The archaeological record is not simply a sterile snapshot of society as it once was. Material culture is subjected to a host of **site formation processes**, including environmental and cultural, that affect how and where materials are deposited. Cultural factors can be as simple as past populations dumping waste in the same area for a long duration of time. This creates a garbage heap or **midden**, as it

---

Provenience: the location of an artifact or feature within a site. Also called *provenance*.

Material Culture: objects that people have and make.

Site Formation Process: environmental and cultural factors that affect how and where materials are deposited at an archaeological site or fossil locale.

Midden: a pile of refuse, often shells, in an archaeological site.

Modern landfill sites provide a cross-section of human material culture today.

is called in the archaeological record. The materials contained within a midden are waste products of the human population that produced them. However, examining the kinds of materials that were produced and how they were produced and contemplating their possible functions are fundamental aspects of archaeological reconstruction. Imagine what archaeologists 1000 years in the future might be able to say about life today by excavating a modern landfill site. Think about what a stranger could infer about your own life by what you throw out each week.

Similarly, how a community constructed its dwellings might have an impact on the formation of an archaeological site, such as whether its people were nomadic, moved around in an annual pattern, or lived a more sedentary life, building permanent or semipermanent dwellings. Locations where a community lived continuously over long periods tend to have layers of accumulated materials left by successive occupations, and these layers are superimposed on one another—people tend to build or rebuild on the rubble left from the dwellings of the previous occupants of a site. A community constantly on the move affects the quantity and distribution of the materials left in any one area. If a site is a product of seasonal habitation, the kind of material culture left behind will not be random, but will reflect the activities occurring at one time of the year but not another. Further, the composition and position of materials within the archaeological record can affect preservation of those remains. For example, in the contact period in Canada—when Europeans were first meeting with and interacting with Indigenous populations—burials that contain copper artifacts tend to show increased preservation of organic materials that are in direct association with the copper. Coffins provide a different burial environment for bodies than does burial directly in the soil.

People also reuse materials and trade materials over distances. Old timber may be used in the

Finding fossil hominins requires patience and endurance.

construction of a new house. Material from another region may be imported and valued for its rarity. For example, we see in the archaeological record the movement of native copper from northern Wisconsin and northwestern Canada into the interior regions of western Canada, where it was used by people who otherwise would not have had access to it.

Material culture can have functional, social, and aesthetic purposes. Consider the number of items in your own home that were once utilitarian but serve no functional purpose today. Pottery is a good example. Old glass and earthenware containers such as glass milk jugs or hand-thrown pottery that were used as everyday items in homes in the past might be used as decorative items within modern households. Fine ceramics may not be routinely used for food processing, storage, or service, but they do serve important social functions. These functions may be embedded in the meaning imparted to the vessels. Fine ceramics might be family heirlooms or expensive icons of social prestige. Such items might "function" to impart social messages about affluence and social position. So it can be difficult to untangle the many cultural processes that contribute to the formation of an archaeological site.

Natural physical processes can affect the survival of artifacts. Deposits from wind erosion and water can cover or submerge whole communities, depending on the environmental conditions at the time that they were occupied. Those same natural processes can cause erosion, exposure, and destruction of archaeological sites. Soil chemistry, temperature, water level, and bacterial action can all affect the rate of decay of organic and inorganic material. As a result, the archaeological record tends to favour the presence of inorganic materials, such as stone, metals, and baked clay, but under good preservation conditions organic materials such as bone, shell, hair, paper, and even soft muscle tissue can survive for extended time periods.

Taphonomy

The processes that affect an animal's remains following its death are important for understanding the context in which fossil remains are found. The study of the processes that affect the body of an animal following its death, known as **taphonomy**, is literally the science of burial. Taphonomic processes are certainly an important consideration in archaeological contexts, and palaeoanthropology requires an extensive understanding of them. For example, the distribution of bones observed in an area may reflect predation by a carnivore and subsequent disturbance by scavengers. This is relevant to the study of early hominins in particular, many of whom were often the prey for large carnivores rather than predators themselves. A carnivore may have brought a skull to a cave, for example, and it may be preserved because of the cave environment, yet the rest of the skeleton is missing from the cave. Of particular concern to palaeoanthropologists are any physical distortions to the fossil hominin remains. Skulls, for example, can be slowly crushed over the course of the fossilization process, leading to a distorted morphology, or form. Palaeoanthropologists need to try to determine the original morphology of the specimen in such instances.

Taphonomy: the study of changes that occur to organisms or objects after being buried or deposited.

Types of Sites

The first and most important aspect of archaeology is actually finding the remains of the past. Archaeologists have developed specialized techniques, some borrowed from other disciplines, to accurately identify, map, and excavate sites. However, identification of archaeological sites—that is, locations of human occupation—and fossil locales where fossilized remains of once-living organisms are found requires somewhat different prospection strategies.

Fossil Locales

Fossil locales are those places where the fossilized remains of animals are found. For the most part, a locale has no bearing on the life of the animal but is a product of a series of processes that affect the remains following death. Candidate locations for fossil sites are identified based on the environment that would have existed tens of thousands or even millions of years ago. Once the site is identified, the archaeologist undertakes a long and tedious process of field survey on foot, carefully looking for telltale signs in the hopes of finding that rare fossilized specimen. Oftentimes a whole field season can pass by without any new discoveries. Sometimes, though, the combination of skill and luck prevails, and the remains of a fossilized specimen are discovered.

Archaeological Sites

Archaeological sites are generally viewed as geographic areas that contain evidence of past human behaviour and activity. An archaeological site can range from a small campsite to a large city, a place for growing food or killing game, a place for mining or processing raw materials, or a place of worship or burial. All these activities can leave varying degrees of evidence in the archaeological record. Further, some sites may be clearly identifiable, such as the Great Pyramids of Egypt, while others may go relatively unnoticed for long periods.

Although many archaeological sites are discovered accidentally, the process of finding a site remains an important aspect of archaeology. Most development plans in Canada require an archaeological assessment to ensure that cultural heritage is not destroyed by modern development. By building archaeological research into the environmental assessment, the protection and investigation of these fragile non-renewable resources can be more carefully managed. Even with this level of planning, many archaeological sites are discovered by accident. Whether a site is discovered accidentally or as a consequence of a deliberate search, one of the first phases of archaeological investigation involves documenting the boundaries of a site. This enables the most efficient use of time and resources for site investigation. In most cases, only a portion of a site can be excavated, and proper survey techniques can help identify the areas of greatest interest to the archaeologist.

Evidence from the Past

Throughout a site, the remains of human culture are represented by fossils; **artifacts**, items manufactured by people; **ecofacts**, natural objects that have been used or affected by humans; and **features**, the non-portable portions of a site, some of which can include artifacts. Artifacts are tools like projectile points or bone tools, and items like clay pots or stone figurines. Ecofacts include bone from animals, seeds, and pollen. Features include things like hearths or fireplaces, burials, houses, fences, or middens. For the archaeologist, the most important aspect of an excavation is the proper mapping and recording of the provenience or location of all features and artifacts. This is critical as the **association** of artifacts or features with

---

Fossil Locales: places where fossilized remains of once-living organisms are found.
Archaeological Site: areas of past human habitation or where fossil remains are found.
Artifacts: items manufactured by people and found in archaeological contexts.
Ecofacts: natural objects that have been used or affected by humans.
Features: the non-portable portions of an archaeological site, some of which can include artifacts.
Association: the relationship between artifacts and features within archaeological sites.

one another is important for understanding past life at the site. Association is extremely important, for example, in the study of early hominins and the first appearance of manufactured stone tools. Unless the artifacts and fossils can be shown archaeologically to have been associated in the same *depositional context*, that is, from the same time period, one cannot assert that the tools were produced and used by that particular hominin species.

Fossils

What Are Fossils? A fossil may be an impression of an insect or leaf on a muddy or other surface that now is stone. Or it may consist of the actual hardened remains of an animal's skeletal structure. It is this second type of fossil—bone turned to stone—that has given palaeoanthropologists the most information about the evolution of primates.

Fossilization. When an animal dies, the organic matter in its body quickly begins to deteriorate. The teeth and skeletal structure are composed largely of inorganic mineral salts, and soon they are all that remains. Under most conditions, these parts eventually deteriorate too. But once in a great while conditions are favourable for preservation—for instance, when volcanic ash, limestone, or highly mineralized groundwater is present to form a high-mineral environment. If the remains are buried under such circumstances, the minerals in the ground may become bound into the structure of the teeth or bone and harden, thus making them less likely to deteriorate. This process of **fossilization** leaves a combination of inorganic bone and mineral, while retaining microscopic detail of the original material. Fossilization requires very specific environmental conditions—organisms need to be at the right place at the right time before there is even a chance of their remains becoming fossilized. Further, the process takes considerable time—more than 10 000 years,

> **Fossilization:** the process of becoming a fossil by the replacement of organic materials with an inorganic mineral matrix.

The fossil of a trilobite from the Cambrian period, 500 million years ago.

depending on soil chemistry and other factors. In fact, given the relative rarity of fossilization, palaeontologists have collected an exceptional amount of information about hundreds of past species from various periods.

Unfortunately, we have fossil remains of only some species and sometimes only fragments from one or a few individuals. So the fossil record is very incomplete (Bilsborough 1992). Robert Martin estimated that the earth has probably seen 6000 primate species, and remains of only 3 percent of those species have been found. While this number seems small, given the relative rarity of fossilization we should not expect to have as much information from the fossil record as we do. Nevertheless, primate palaeontologists continue to explore the evolutionary connections between early and later fossil forms. The task is particularly difficult with small mammals, such as the early primates, which are less likely to be preserved in the fossil record than are large animals.

Palaeoanthropologists have a more narrow interest in terms of the kinds of species they look at—primates at the broadest level, and more often hominins alone. Given these factors, it is amazing how much information we have actually accumulated regarding human evolution.

What Can We Learn from Fossils? Palaeontologists can tell a great deal about an extinct animal from its fossilized bones or teeth, but that knowledge is based on much more than just the fossil record itself. Palaeontologists rely on comparative anatomy to help reconstruct missing skeletal pieces as well as the soft tissues attached to bone. New techniques, such as electron microscopy, CT scans, and computer-assisted biomechanical modelling, provide much information about how the organism may have moved, the microstructure of bone and teeth, and how the organism developed. Chemical analysis of bone can suggest what the animal typically ate. Palaeontologists are also interested in the surroundings of the fossil finds. With methods developed in geology, chemistry, and physics, palaeontologists use the surrounding rocks to identify the period in which the organism died. In addition, the study of associated fauna and flora can suggest what the ancient climate and habitat were like (Klein 2009).

Since most of human evolution predates human material culture, palaeoanthropologists have only the biological remains of human ancestors from which to infer hominin behaviour. Because the environment in which these hominins lived and died was very different from that of today, palaeoanthropologists have turned to the expertise of geologists to interpret geological phenomena that reflect the environments that existed millions of years ago. Many fossils result from organic remains being deposited in lakes or rivers where they were quickly covered with sediment. Over time, lakes may have dried up, rivers may have changed course, and the land may have been uplifted. The old lake floors or riverbeds could now be represented by eroding sediments on hilltops. Consequently, the majority of fossil hominin remains found by palaeoanthropologists have been subject to long-term environmental processes before being found.

Artifacts

Anything made or modified by humans is an artifact. The book you are reading now, the chair you are sitting in, and the pen you are taking notes with are all artifacts. In fact, we are surrounded by artifacts, most of which we will lose or throw away. And that is exactly how things enter the archaeological record. Think about it: How much garbage do you produce in a day? What kinds of things do you throw away? Mostly paper, probably, but also wood (from the ice-cream bar you had at lunch), plastic (like the pen that ran out of ink last night), and even metal (the dull blade on your razor). Into the garbage they go and out to the dump or landfill. Under the right conditions many of those items will survive for future archaeologists to find. Most of the artifacts that make up the archaeological record are just this kind of mundane waste—the accumulated garbage of daily life that archaeologists may recover and examine to reconstruct daily life long ago.

By far the most common artifacts from the past are stone tools, which archaeologists call **lithics**. Indeed, lithics are the only artifact available for 99 percent of human history. Humans started using stone tools more than 2.5 million years ago, and some stone tools (grinding and polishing stones, for example) are still used today. Stone has been used for making almost any object you can think of, from cutting tools to oil lamps, but hunting, butchering, and hide-processing tools were commonly made from stone. Another common kind of artifact is **ceramics** (pots and other items made from baked clay). Humans started making ceramics about 10 000 years ago, and ceramic objects such as storage and cooking vessels quickly became widespread. Because they are both fragile and relatively easy to make, ceramics show up frequently in the garbage that makes up the archaeological record. Wood and bone artifacts are common too, and tools for hide working, cooking, hunting, and even butchering were made of these materials. Humans have used wood and bone tools at least as long as stone tools, but unlike stone tools, these tend not to survive well in the archaeological record. In some places metals and glass are common artifacts. These survive well in the archaeological record, and hence they are often found where they were used.

Lithics: the technical name for the tools made from stone.
Ceramics: objects shaped from clay and baked at high temperature (fired) to make them hard. Containers such as pots and jars are typical ceramics, though they can take on many forms and uses.

UNCOVERING THE PAST: TOOLS AND TECHNIQUES   33

A ceramic pot from China, dating to the period when agriculture first developed there—some 6000 years ago.

Ecofacts

Ecofacts are natural objects that have been consumed or affected by humans. A good example is the bones of animals that people have eaten. These bones are somewhat like artifacts, but they haven't been made or modified by humans, just used and discarded by them. Another example is pollen found at archaeological sites. Because humans bring plants back to their homes for a number of reasons, pollens from many plants are commonly found. These pollens may not have come from the same location. The only reason they are together is that they have been brought together by human use. Yet another example is the remains of insect and animal pests that associate with humans, such as cockroaches and mice. Their remains are found in sites because they associate with humans and survive by taking advantage of the conditions that humans create. Their presence is in part caused by the human presence, and thus they are considered ecofacts too.

Features

Features are a kind of artifact, but archaeologists distinguish them from other artifacts because they cannot be easily removed from an archaeological site. Hearths are a good example. When humans build a fire on bare ground, the soil becomes heated and is changed—all the water is driven out of it and its crystalline structure is broken down and re-formed. It becomes hard, redder, and even slightly magnetic (as we discuss later). When an archaeologist finds a hearth, what exactly is found? An area of hard, reddish soil, often surrounded by charcoal and ash. Here, then, is an artifact—an object of human manufacture. But it would be very hard, if not impossible, for the archaeologist to pick the hearth up and take it back to the lab for study like a lithic or ceramic. A hearth is really an intrinsic feature of a site—hence the name *feature*.

Hearths are common features, but by far the most common features are called *pits*. Pits are simply holes dug by humans that are later filled with garbage or eroded soil. They are usually fairly easy to distinguish because the garbage or soil they are filled with is often different in colour and texture from the soil the pit was dug into. *Living floors* are another common type of feature. These are the places where humans lived and worked. The soils in these locations are often compacted through human activity and are full of minute pieces of garbage—seeds, small stone flakes, beads, and the like—that became embedded in the floor. A large or very deep area of such debris is called a *midden*. Middens are often the remains of garbage dumps or areas repeatedly used over long periods of time, such as caves. Finally, *buildings* are a common feature on archaeological sites. These can range from the remains of stone rings that once held down the sides of tents to palaces built of stones that had been shaped and fitted together. Even the remains of wooden houses (or parts of them) have been preserved under some conditions. Features are a diverse array of things that can provide lots of information about the past.

Finding Archaeological Sites

Site Prospection

Detection of human modification of the landscape will depend on the scale of human activities. In the case of subtle landscape modifications, such as a single house or a burial, even a trained archaeologist may have difficulty recognizing the changes associated with these features. Often intuition, experience, and subsurface inspections will aid in the initial discovery of archaeological sites. The identification of a site is based on methods that can be broadly divided between *surface* and *subsurface surveying techniques* that can involve remote sensing or be intrusive, such as digging.

Surface Techniques.
Surface techniques include *field walking* and *field surveying*. Much like the palaeoanthropologist, an archaeologist will patiently walk and survey the surface of a location for signs of artifacts or surface irregularities that may indicate structures. Surface inspection is appropriate in situations where disturbances have exposed archaeological materials. These disturbances could be natural processes like erosion. Human activities like cultivation, construction, or clearing of forests are examples of modern practices that might reveal the presence of material culture from the past. Artifacts collected as part of field walking provide important clues about the potential distribution and boundaries of the disturbed archaeological materials, and can aid in identifying areas that remain undisturbed.

Field surveying can be as simple as the archaeologist walking through an area and carefully watching for sometimes subtle clues that indicate the presence of material culture, or as complex as the systematic survey of a region aided by local histories of land use and occupation by local residents. Once the archaeologist identifies an area of increased density of recovered surface artifacts or specific structures, he or she will use subsurface techniques to define where more comprehensive excavations will proceed.

Past changes to the landscape on a larger scale, such as irrigation systems for fields or whole cities, may still be sufficiently distinct to be identified through field inspection or the examination of air photographs or satellite images. *Aerial photography* and *satellite imaging* can even provide clues to the remains of structures buried under thick accumulations of sediment, particularly if the underlying cultural deposits alter the soil chemistry or soil moisture to the point that can change the pattern of vegetation. More recently, advanced imaging techniques using 3D laser scanners have been used to help identify sites (see Bryan 2015). For example, a team of researchers from the University of Calgary and Parks Canada used 3D laser scanning to document the site of a historic polar research camp on Ellesmere Island in the Canadian Arctic (Dawson et al. 2013). In another research collaboration, Robert Park of the University of Waterloo, Nunavut Director of Heritage Doug Stenton, and Brooke Milne of the University of Manitoba used laser-scanning technology to identify and document archaeological sites in the Arctic and monitor the impact of human activity, including tourism, on their preservation. Areas disturbed by past human occupation may produce differences in the kinds of vegetation that cover the area, and these may be detectable only from the air. Even when large-scale alterations to the landscape have been reduced through natural processes such as erosion or artificial processes such as plowing, they can leave distinct topographical patterns on the surface that are distinguishable from the air. Satellite imagery provides a similar tool, although the cost of using it and the observable level of precision make it currently impractical for archaeologists except for the documentation of large-scale disturbances such as roads, canals, irrigated fields, or large communities with monumental architecture.

Subsurface Techniques.
In most cases, surface surveying is not the most efficient means for locating archaeological sites. Those sites that have not yet been exposed, or whose distribution or pattern is not clearly recognizable on the surface, require other kinds of surveying techniques.

> **Surface Techniques:** archaeological survey techniques for finding and assessing archaeological sites from surface finds.

Archaeological test pits and trenching (shown here) help define the boundaries of a site.

Subsurface techniques can be mechanical or electronic. Mechanical techniques tend to be invasive and include *shovel shining*, *test pitting*, and *trenching*. Electronic techniques tend to be non-invasive and allow the archaeologist to survey or map below the surface without actually disturbing the site.

Shovel shining is a simple method where the edge of a shovel is used to scrape off thin layers of the immediate and usually disturbed surface layer to reveal undisturbed soil. This method is suitable for unearthing features like post moulds, hearths, house foundations, and refuse that can be identified through their different soil colour and composition. Shovel shining is also used to systematically explore a site that has been disturbed, perhaps through cultivation, for intact deposits that remain below the disturbed zone. The site is then further assessed by systematically removing layers of the surface from a small, contained area. This approach is most effective where the approximate extent and cultural identity of a disturbed site have been defined through a field-walking survey and surface collection.

Where a newly discovered site is relatively undisturbed, the excavation of test pits at intervals across the site might offer a better and less destructive understanding of the site's extent and its artifacts. Such test pits are usually excavated with a shovel, are generally quite small (about 50 cm in diameter), and are spaced at regular intervals across the site. The size, depth, and spacing of the test pits vary with the nature of the site deposits, the research objectives, and the resources available to the archaeologist. Each test pit should provide a sample of artifacts that can aid in dating the site's age and function. The density and position of what is recovered—that is, the recoveries—may aid in determining the size and shape of the site. As each test pit is associated with a specific location within the site, the archaeologist can use the shovel test pit data to examine the changing pattern and density of recoveries across the site. This serves as a useful preliminary assessment tool in planning a full-scale excavation.

In instances where material is suspected to be at great depths beneath the surface, boring and core samples can be taken to retrieve a column that reflects the overall layering of a small but deep area. This technique is being employed by archaeologist Aubrey Cannon of McMaster University in his analysis of middens from prehistoric Northwest Coast sites (Cannon 2000a, 2000b). The method has the advantage of providing a snapshot of all the layers within a site without the need for a complete excavation. The primary assumption of this method is that the distribution of artifacts within the core will be representative of the distribution within the immediate surrounding area. The same technique may be used to sample sediments that aid in reconstructing past environments. For example, how and when deposits were laid down may be inferred from sediment particle size, or pollen recovery can indicate past climatic conditions and vegetation cover.

Subsurface Techniques: archaeological survey techniques that map features beneath the surface.

A grid system is used at archaeological sites to accurately record the position of artifacts and features during excavation.

Non-invasive site inspection techniques have been borrowed from a variety of disciplines and applied to archaeological survey. These include *ground-penetrating radar* and methods based on *magnetic* or *electrical resistance* of subsurface features. Since archaeology is itself destructive, archaeologists would ideally like to obtain as much information as possible about the composition of a site without the need for excavation. Ground-penetrating radar involves radar waves that map subsurface sedimentary layers and buried archaeological features. Radar waves will "reflect" off subsurface features and produce pulses that can be detected on the surface. The speed at which the radar waves penetrate the surface varies due to soil composition, but when the velocity is known and the time between pulses recorded, the depth of features below the surface can be calculated. The radar can provide a subsurface map of the relative locations and depths of features over a large area.

Electrical resistivity meters measure differences in the ability of sediments and other materials beneath the surface to conduct electricity. For example, features like stone or brick walls are less conductive than the surrounding deposits. Alternatively, a concentration of metallic objects or a pit that has filled over time and has different soil moisture levels may be more conductive than the surrounding deposits. When soil resistivity is measured along controlled grids, patterns of variation in electrical conductivity can be detected and mapped to aid in site interpretation. Similarly, a *magnetometer* can measure the relative magnetism of items below the surface. Clay when fired acquires a small magnetic field that can be detected with this instrument. Rocks with trace amounts of iron in them and iron metal objects can also be detected. By examining the patterns in variation in sediment magnetism, the archaeologist can identify zones of particular interest that can be investigated through subsurface excavation.

Excavation

Once a site has been identified, excavation can begin. Before, during, and after excavation, the archaeologist follows a series of methods to maintain maximum control over the relationships between items in the three-dimensional space of the site. To begin with, *site evaluation* involves an assessment of the size of the site, depth of the deposits, site formation processes (including taphonomic processes that may bias site integrity, such as scavenger activity or water), and function.

While horizontal control is important, vertical control of the excavation process can be critical when there are dramatic differences in the time that various layers of sediment took to accumulate (see the discussion of stratigraphy for relative dating later in this chapter). A preliminary assessment of the information from the site evaluation is critical for planning an appropriate research design that includes budgeting for the costs of excavation and analysis, and implementing detailed excavation. Detailed excavation is generally conventional. However, because excavation is destructive, permanent (once an artifact is out of the ground, its context is lost), and expensive in terms of both time and money, archaeologists try to obtain a sample of deposits that they hope is representative of the whole site.

How a sample is chosen is based on a careful analysis of preliminary survey information regarding the distribution and function of the site. For example, determining the sampling strategy at a buffalo jump site like Head-Smashed-In Buffalo Jump in southern Alberta depends on the kinds of research questions that people have. If the researcher is interested in the antiquity, seasonality, and cultural association of a stratified sequence of bison kill events, then a deep excavation focused at the base of the jump would be appropriate. In contrast, if you are interested in the full sequence of events involved in the communal bison drive of past populations, then a broader perspective and more diverse sampling strategy would be warranted.

The first step of a controlled excavation is choosing a datum point. The **datum** represents a fixed, permanent reference point within or near the site.

This fixed reference point defines the location of all information and specimens collected from the site. As the datum is a permanent fixture, future investigations (perhaps using new, innovative techniques) can be spatially related to all previous work at the site. This enables an ongoing synthesis of information. Once a datum has been decided, a *grid system* is laid out, usually dividing the site into 1- or 2-metre squares. Under special circumstances, like cave archaeology or underwater archaeology (such as the discovery of the Franklin expedition's HMS *Erebus* in 2014 and HMS *Terror* in 2016 by Parks Canada), extra control over depth is necessary. Each square is defined by its location within the grid, and more detailed mapping and documentation of recoveries within the square are relative to the grid location of the control square. The careful recording of all information within the grid allows for all data to be incorporated into a single system at the end of the excavation, even though different people may have excavated certain grid squares at different times.

Depending on the scale of the excavation, archaeologists apply different techniques and equipment. For example, a backhoe or bulldozer might be used to remove disturbed or culturally sterile topsoil or sod from a location. Once this top disturbed layer has been removed, much finer excavation techniques using small hand tools are needed. In some circumstances, shovels are used to remove sediment. When beginning to excavate an area of interest, most archaeologists use small mason's trowels, whisk brooms and paintbrushes, root cutters, teaspoons, and dental picks to carefully remove the sediment and expose and recover the artifacts. This care is necessary to preserve and record the spatial context of recovery, prevent damage to the specimens, and enable discovery and documentation of features that might be represented by subtle shifts in sediment colour, texture, and degree of compaction.

Depending on the context and research objectives, sediment removed from the excavation unit is examined for minute objects that might have been missed during excavation. This involves removing the backdirt—or pile of soil left from excavating an area—in buckets, and sifting it through fine screens to identify small artifacts. The mesh size of the screen depends on the objectives of the researchers and the time and fiscal resources for the project. At most

> **Datum:** a fixed, permanent reference point within or near an archaeological site used to define the location of all information and specimens collected from the site. As the datum is a permanent fixture, future investigations can be spatially related to all previous work at the site.

modern excavation projects, sediment is screened through at least 5 mm (1/4-inch) hardware cloth, and a 2 to 3 mm (1/8-inch) screen size is routinely used at many projects. While the smaller screen size dramatically increases the rate of recovery of minute artifacts, there is a significant increase in associated time and costs of excavation and analysis. If the coarser 5 mm screen is used, then the archaeologist will often monitor artifact loss rates by regularly screening subsamples with the finer mesh.

Soil samples may also be bagged and labelled for future analysis. This might involve documenting sediment particle size, soil pH, charcoal and other organic materials, or the concentrations of chemicals such as phosphorus and nitrogen. The presence of *patterned variation*—systematic trends in the way in which material is distributed—of such materials may reflect the nature and intensity of past human activity, and is also very useful for reconstructing the past environmental context of the site. Such soil samples can also be useful for the recovery of minute organic materials. These could be charcoal and preserved wood fragments, carbonized seeds and other preserved plant parts, microscopic pollen, and **phytoliths** (microscopic granules of silicon dioxide that enter a plant's cells and take their shape), as well as land snails and other minute indicators of past climatic and vegetation conditions.

Dating Techniques

One must know the age of archaeological sites and fossils in order to reconstruct the evolutionary history of humans and their ancestors. For some time *relative dating methods*—that is, methods that could state that a fossil was older or younger than those from another area of the site—were the only methods available. These techniques generally addressed the sequence of layers by referring to the sedimentary context. The last 50 years have seen important advances in **absolute dating** or *chronometric dating*—methods that can estimate the age of a specimen or deposit in years—including techniques that allow the dating of the earliest phases of primate evolution (Bilsborough 1992). **Relative dating** allows the age of a specimen or deposit relative to another specimen or deposit to be determined.

Relative Dating Methods

The earliest and still the most common method of relative dating is based on **stratigraphy**, the study of how different layers of sediments and soils, artifacts, and fossils are laid down in successive deposits, or *strata*. The **law of superposition** states that older layers are generally deeper or lower than more recent layers (see Figure 2–1). On the basis of this law, researchers can make inferences about the relationship and relative date of cumulative layers of different strata.

Animals (*fauna*) and plants (*flora*) that spread widely over short periods, died out fairly rapidly, or evolved rapidly provide the most suitable indicator fossils for establishing a stratigraphic sequence for the relative dating of new finds. These life forms help in the relative dating of less well-known specimens found in association with them. Different animals and plants can serve as indicators of relative age in different areas of the world. In Africa, the fossils of elephants, pigs, and horses have been particularly important in establishing stratigraphic sequences. Once the stratigraphy of an area is

---

Phytolith: microscopic granules of silicon dioxide that enter a plant's cells and take their shape.
Absolute Dating: a method of dating fossils in which the actual age of a deposit or specimen is measured. Also known as *chronometric dating*.
Relative Dating: a method of dating fossils that determines the age of a specimen or deposit relative to a known specimen or deposit.
Stratigraphy: the study of how different rock formations and fossils are laid down in successive layers or strata. Older layers are generally deeper or lower than more recent layers.
Law of Superposition: a law that states that older layers at an archaeological site are generally deeper or lower than more recent layers. The law of superposition provides a framework with which to make inferences regarding the relationship and relative date of cumulative layers of different strata.

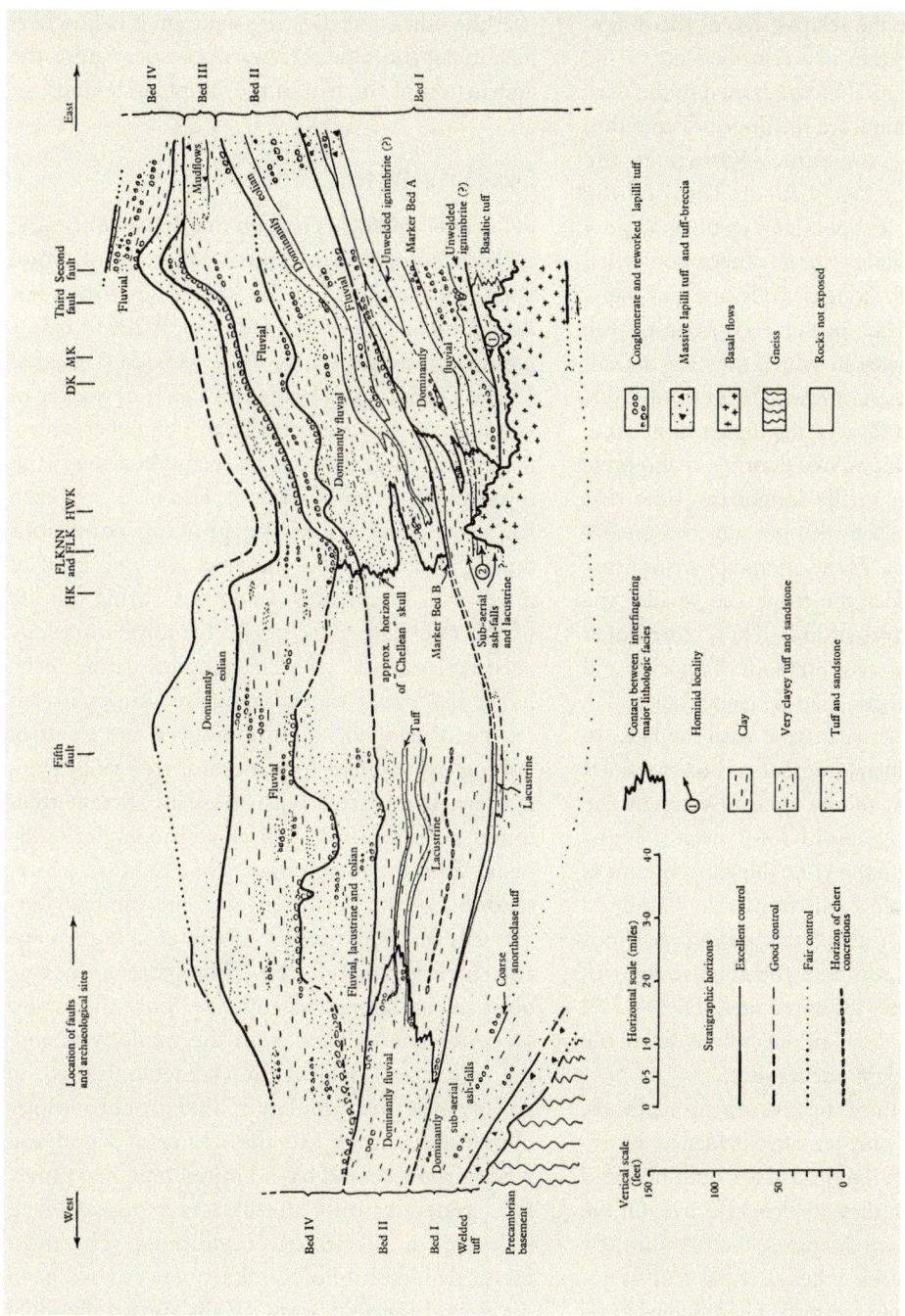

Figure 2-1 Stratigraphy of Beds I–IV along Olduvai Main Gorge

Notice how complex the four stratigraphic layers are—each has numerous layers of soil and rock within them. Index fossils, particularly those of pigs, along with a series of potassium-argon dates, allowed the researchers to identify the four major strata of the site, which correspond to four major periods of human occupation.

Source: Leakey LSB. 1965. Olduvai Gorge, 1951–1961, Vol. I: A preliminary report on the geology and fauna. Copyright © 1965. Cambridge University Press. Reprinted with the permission of Cambridge University Press.

established, the relative ages of two different fossils in the same or different sites are indicated by the associated flora and fauna (Klein 2009). Major transitions in flora and fauna define the epochs and larger units of geologic time. The dates of the boundaries between such units are estimated by absolute dating, described later in this chapter.

If a site has been disturbed, stratigraphy will not be a satisfactory way of determining relative age. A site may be disturbed in various ways: remains from different periods may be washed or blown together by water or wind, or a landslide may superimpose an earlier layer on top of a later layer. Still, it may be possible using chemical methods to estimate the relative age of the different fossils found together in a disturbed site.

Three of the chemical methods used in the relative dating of fossil bones are the fluorine, uranium, and nitrogen tests, sometimes known as the **F-U-N trio** (Oakley 1963). All are based on the same general principle: bones and teeth undergo a slow transformation in chemical composition when they remain buried for long periods, and this transformation reflects the mineral content of the groundwater in the area in which they are buried. Fluorine is one mineral present in groundwater; therefore, the older a fossil is, the higher its fluorine content will be. Uranium, like fluorine, is also present in groundwater, so the longer the time that bones or teeth remain in the ground, the greater their uranium content. The relationships are reversed for nitrogen: the older the fossil, the smaller the amount of nitrogen present in it. Thus, older bones have relatively higher concentrations of fluorine and uranium and less nitrogen than do recent bones.

However, a problem can arise with the F-U-N tests because the mineral content of bones reflects the mineral content of the groundwater in the area. A 30-million-year-old fossil from a high-mineral area may have the same fluorine content as a 50-million-year-old fossil from a low-mineral site. So these chemical relative dating methods cannot be used to compare the relative ages of specimens from widely separated sites. The F-U-N tests are restricted, then, to specimens from the same site or from neighbouring sites.

Each of the chemical relative dating methods, used alone, can give only tentative evidence. However, when the three methods are combined and confirm one another, they are very effective. Of the three methods we have discussed, the uranium test is by far the most reliable when used alone. It is not strictly a relative dating method. There seems to be some consistency in the increase in radioactivity with age, even in bones from different deposits. The uranium test has another distinct advantage over the other tests. Because uranium is radioactive, measuring the radioactivity does not require the destruction of any part of the sample in testing.

Absolute Dating Methods

Dendrochronology. Through **dendrochronology**, an archaeologist can estimate the age of wood samples by examining the annual growth rings. A.E. Douglass first used it in the 1920s to date a prehistoric settlement in New Mexico (Douglass 1929). During each year of its life, a new layer of wood grows in a tree's trunk and branches, creating annual rings that can be seen when the trunk is examined in cross-section. The nature of each ring is a function of the growing conditions during that year, and the rings act as a kind of fingerprint of climatic conditions during the life of the tree (Douglass 1947). Dendrochronology becomes useful as an archaeological dating technique if a *master chronology* of tree-ring patterns can be developed. A chronology is the result of linking overlapping sequences of tree rings from modern living trees with those in ancient trees found in palaeontological or archaeological contexts. With the establishment of a regional master chronology, analysts then examine the archaeologically recovered wood sample of unknown age and seek to match the ring pattern to one observed in the master sequence. Since the master sequence counts back from the modern period, the calendrical date of the archaeological wood sample can be calculated. Dendrochronology obviously is limited to the dating of wood and wood products, and has a limited temporal range. It is generally only useful at a regional level, reflecting local climatic conditions. The most useful dendrochronological sequences have been developed for arid areas. While most individual trees do not live for thousands of years, dendrochronological research has been considerably furthered by the study of very long-lived trees such

---

F-U-N Trio: fluorine (F), uranium (U), and nitrogen (N) tests for relative dating. All three minerals are present in groundwater. The older a fossil is, the higher its fluorine or uranium content will be, and the lower its nitrogen content.

Dendrochronology: an absolute dating technique based on counting annual tree rings in wood.

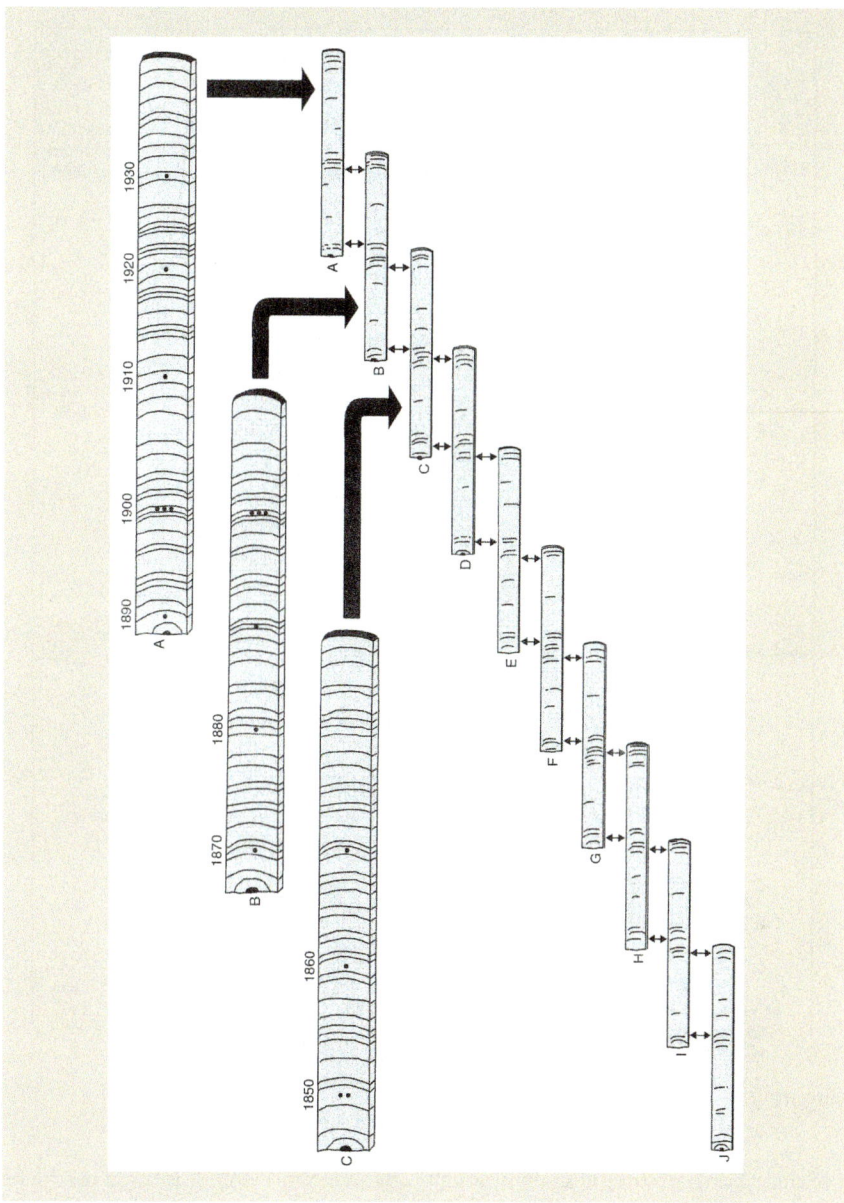

Figure 2–2 Dendrochronology

In order to establish a tree-ring chronology, core samples are removed from living trees, and the annual rings established. Wood specimens taken from other sources are matched up with specific years from the control cores in order to establish a date. In a similar manner, cores from trees of varying, overlapping ages can be compared in order to push back the dendrochronological record even further into the past.

Source: © Lindbriar Corporation

as the bristle cone pine (see Figure 2–2). In this way, dendrochronology is useful for measuring that age of wood that may be several thousand years old (i.e., before present or B.P.).

Many of the absolute dating methods are based on the decay rate of a radioactive isotope. The age of the specimen can be determined by measuring the remaining quantity of the isotope in the sample

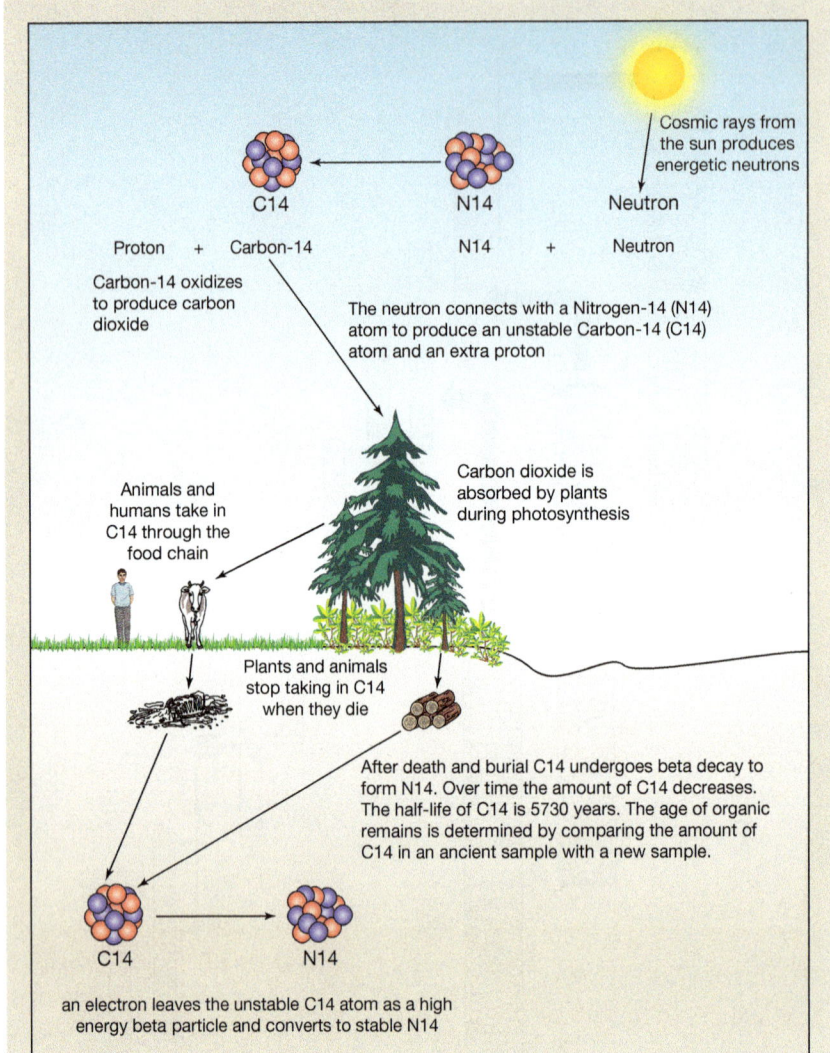

Figure 2–3 The Carbon-14 Cycle

since the rate of decay, or **half-life**, is known, and the original concentration of the isotope can be estimated, within a range of possible error. Radiocarbon, or carbon-14 (^{14}C), dating is perhaps the most popularly known method of determining the absolute age of an organic specimen.

Radiocarbon Dating. **Radiocarbon dating** is a reliable method for dating remains up to 50 000 years old (Brown 1992). It is based on the principle that all living matter possesses a certain amount of a radioactive form of carbon (^{14}C). Radioactive carbon is produced when atmospheric nitrogen-14 is bombarded by cosmic rays. This material is absorbed from the air by plants and then ingested by animals that eat the plants. After an organism dies, it no longer takes in any of the radioactive carbon (see Figure 2–3).

Half-Life: the time it takes for half of the atoms of a radioactive substance to decay into atoms of a different substance.

Radiocarbon Dating: a dating method that uses the decay of carbon-14 to date organic remains. It is reliable for dating once-living matter up to 50 000 years old.

Carbon-14 decays at a slow but steady pace and reverts to nitrogen-14. (By "decays," we mean that the ^{14}C releases a certain number of beta radiations per minute.) The rate at which the carbon decays is known: ^{14}C has a half-life of 5730 years. In other words, half of the original amount of ^{14}C in organic matter will have disintegrated 5730 years after the organism's death; half of the remaining ^{14}C will have disintegrated after another 5730 years; and so on.

To discover how long an organism has been dead—that is, to determine how much ^{14}C is left in the organism and therefore how old it is—we count the number of beta radiations given off per minute per gram of material. Modern ^{14}C emits about 15 beta radiations per minute per gram of material, but ^{14}C that is 5730 years old emits only half that amount (the half-life of ^{14}C) per minute per gram. So if a sample of some organism gives off 7.5 radiations a minute per gram, which is only half the amount given off by modern ^{14}C, the organism must be 5730 years old (Hole and Heizer 1973). This is why radiocarbon dating usually is not accurate for anything more than 50 000 years old—the amount of ^{14}C remaining in the organic matter is too small to permit reliable dating.

Is it really that simple, though? Unfortunately, the answer is no. One of the problems with radiocarbon dating is that it assumes the relative level of ^{14}C present in the atmosphere remains constant over all time. In fact we now know that this is not true, and that there are fluctuations because of variation in the intensity of solar radiation. The question is then, How do we compensate for these unknown fluctuations when estimating age using carbon-14 dating? The solution is to calibrate the expected values against observed values using dendrochronology. By taking samples of wood that can be dated accurately using dendrochronology and radiocarbon dating, we can assess any deviation between the two dates. By plotting the distribution of these two dates for many different samples that span the last several thousand years, we can create a *calibration curve* (see Figure 2–4). Then we can calculate the radiocarbon date of organic archaeological material, and the date can be calibrated against the curve. This method provides a calibration curve with a time range of about 9000 years ago for carbon-14 dating (Brown 1992).

Accelerated mass spectrometry (AMS) radiocarbon dating provides a number of advantages over traditional radiocarbon dating, and has revolutionized the dating of archaeological specimens.

First, this new method can date specimens that are up to 80 000 years old because it is more capable of accurately measuring minute quantities of ^{14}C (Brown 1992). It also has the advantage of requiring considerably less raw material to generate a useful date. Since the material to be dated is destroyed in the testing process, the smaller the sample required, the smaller the portion of the archaeological specimen that needs to be sacrificed. Taking only a very small sample is crucial when dating extremely rare items like a unique Northwest Coast atlatl (spear-throwing tool) (Fladmark et al. 1987). The reduced sample size also enables the dating of carbon that clearly derives from the organic component of bone (*collagen*). This greatly reduces the risk of sampling and dating carbon that may have percolated into the bone from groundwater.

Potassium-Argon Dating and Argon-Argon Dating. Potassium-40 (^{40}K), a radioactive form of potassium, decays at an established rate and forms argon-40 (^{40}Ar). The half-life of ^{40}K is a known quantity, so the age of a material containing potassium can be measured by the amount of ^{40}K it contains compared with the amount of ^{40}Ar (Gentner and Lippolt 1969) that it also contains.

Radioactive potassium's (^{40}K's) half-life is very long—1330 million years. This means that **potassium-argon (K-Ar) dating** may date samples from 5000 years old up to 3 billion years old.

> ^{40}**K (Potassium-40):** a radioactive form of potassium that decays at an established rate and forms argon-40 used in K-Ar dating.
> **Potassium-Argon (K-Ar) Dating:** a chronometric dating method that uses the rate of decay of a radioactive form of potassium (^{40}K) into argon (^{40}Ar) to date samples from 5000 to 3 billion years old. The K-Ar method dates the minerals and rocks in a deposit, not the fossils themselves.

(Variables: C13/C12 = −19.1:1ab.mult=1)

Laboratory number:	Beta-151217
Conventional radiocarbon age:	350 ± 40 BP
2 Sigma calibrated result: (95% probability)	Cal AD 1450 to 1650 (Cal BP 500 to 300)
	Intercept data
Intercepts of radiocarbon age with calibration curve:	Cal AD 1510 (Cal BP 440) and Cal AD 1600 (Cal BP 350) and Cal AD 1620 (Cal BP 330)
1 Sigma calibrated results: (68% probability)	Cal AD 1470 to 1530 (Cal BP 480 to 420) and Cal AD 1550 to 1630 (Cal BP 400 to 320)

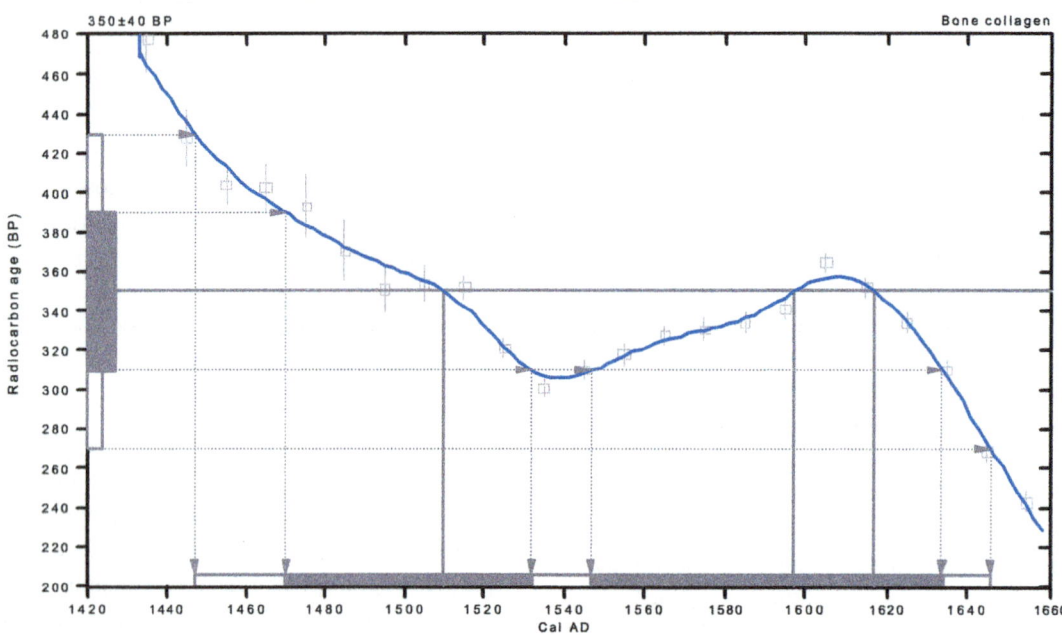

Figure 2–4 An Example of a Calibration Curve for a Carbon-14 Date

This example is based on AMS dating of collagen extracted from bone. Here a conventional radiocarbon age of 350 ± 40 years ago is obtained. In order to calibrate this age, the estimate and its outer limits (40 years on either side for a 66 percent probability and 80 years on either side for a 95 percent probability of being correct) are plotted against the C-14 dates taken on wood dated by dendrochronology. The resultant fluctuations reflect variations in atmospheric carbon during this time period. By examining the points at which the C-14 date limits cross the calibration curve, we come up with a calibrated estimate of the age of the specimen. In this case, the C-14 date of 350 years B.P. crosses the calibration curve at three different points—the years 1510, 1600, and 1620. As a result, the calibration makes the estimate less well defined with the specimen being between 300 and 500 years old or from between A.D. 1450 and A.D. 1650.

Source: Courtesy of Beta Analytic Inc., Miami, Florida.

The K-Ar method is applied to date potassium-rich minerals in rock, not the fossils that may be found in the rock. While it is an absolute dating technique, it is nevertheless indirect in that it is used to date geological deposits or layers that temporally surround the fossils or artifacts of interest. Very high temperatures, which, for example, occur during a volcanic event, drive off any original argon in the rock. Such volcanic events might involve the deposition of lava, or the accumulation of volcanic dust over top of the fossil-bearing strata. Therefore, the amount of argon that accumulates afterward from the decay of radioactive potassium is directly related to the amount of time since the volcanic event has passed. This type of dating has been extremely useful in East Africa, where volcanic events have occurred frequently since about 24 million years ago (Klein 2009). If the material to be dated is not rich in potassium, or the area did not experience any high-temperature events, other methods of absolute dating are required.

One problem with the K-Ar method is that the amounts of potassium and argon must be measured from different rock samples, so that researchers must assume that the potassium and argon are evenly distributed in all the rock samples from a particular stratum. Researchers got around this problem by developing the ^{40}**Ar-^{39}Ar dating** method. After measuring the amount of ^{40}Ar, a researcher, by using a nuclear reactor, converts another kind of argon, ^{39}Ar, to potassium so that the potassium/argon ratio can be measured from the same sample (Brown 1988; Bilsborough 1992).

Fission-Track Dating. The **fission-track dating** method is another way to determine the absolute age of fossil deposits (Fleischer et al. 1965). Like the K-Ar method, it dates minerals contemporaneous with the deposit in which fossils are found and it also requires the prior occurrence of a high-temperature event, such as a volcanic eruption. The kinds of samples it can date—such as crystal, glass, and many uranium-rich minerals—include a much wider variety than those that can be dated by the K-Ar method. The age range of fission-track dating, like that of K-Ar dating, is extensive—20 years to 5 billion years (Fleischer and Hart, Jr. 1972).

How does it work? This method is basically the simplest of all the methods discussed here. It entails counting the number of paths or tracks etched in the sample by the fission, or explosive division, of uranium atoms as they disintegrate. Scientists know that ^{238}U, the most common uranium isotope, decays at a slow, steady rate. This decay takes the form of spontaneous fission, and each separate fission leaves a scar or track on the sample, which can be seen through a microscope when chemically treated. To find the age of a sample, one counts the tracks, then measures their ratio to the uranium content of the sample.

The fission-track method was used to date Bed I at Olduvai Gorge in Tanzania, East Africa, where some early hominin remains were found (Fleischer et al. 1965). And the results corroborated earlier K-Ar estimates that the site dated back close to 2 million years. That the K-Ar and fission-track methods use different techniques and have different sources of error makes them effective as checks on each other. When the two methods support each other, they provide very reliable evidence.

Palaeomagnetic Dating. Most fossils of interest to anthropologists occur in sedimentary rocks, but the potassium-argon and argon-argon methods are suitable only for dating igneous rocks. When rock of any kind forms, it records the ancient magnetic field of the earth, which has reversed itself many times. **Palaeomagnetic dating** can identify the geomagnetic patterns in rocks and therefore date the fossils within those rocks. Strictly speaking, palaeomagnetic dating is not an absolute dating method, but geomagnetic time periods have been dated absolutely in conjunction with potassium-argon dating. Palaeomagnetic dating has been used

---

^{40}**Ar-^{39}Ar Dating Method:** used in conjunction with potassium-argon dating, this method gets around the problem of needing different rock samples to estimate potassium and argon. A nuclear reactor is used to convert the ^{39}Ar to ^{39}K, on the basis of which the amount of ^{40}K can be estimated. In this way, both argon and potassium can be estimated from the same rock sample.
Fission-Track Dating: a chronometric dating method used to date crystal, glass, and many uranium-rich materials contemporaneous with fossils or deposits that are from 20 to 5 billion years old. This dating method entails counting the tracks or paths of decaying uranium-isotope atoms in the sample and then comparing the number of tracks with the uranium content of the sample.
Palaeomagnetic Dating: a method used to identify the geomagnetic patterns in rocks, and to date the fossils within those rocks.

to date primate finds from the Eocene and Miocene epochs (Kappelman 1993).

Uranium-Series Dating. The decay rates of two kinds of uranium, ^{235}U and ^{238}U, into other isotopes (such as ^{230}Th, thorium) have also proved useful for dating *Homo sapiens* (modern human) sites, particularly in caves where there are stalagmites and other calcite formations. Because water that seeps into caves usually contains uranium but not thorium, the calcite formations trap uranium. The time that has elapsed since the formation of the materials can be estimated from the ratio of those isotopes—a process called **uranium-series dating**. The thorium–uranium ratio is useful for dating cave sites less than 300 000 years old where there are no volcanic rocks, which could be dated using the potassium-argon method. Early *Homo sapiens* from European cave sites in Germany, Hungary, and Wales were dated this way (Brown 1992; Schwarcz 1993).

Thermoluminescence Dating. Many minerals emit light when they are heated (*thermoluminescence*), even before they become red hot. This so-called cold light comes from the release under heat of "outside" electrons trapped in atoms within the crystal structure of the material. **Thermoluminescence dating** (Aitken 1985) is based on the principle that if an object is heated to a high temperature during its production or use, it will release all its trapped electrons. This is the process that clay undergoes when it is fired to produce a pot. Subsequent to heating, the object continues to trap electrons from radioactive elements (potassium, thorium, uranium) found in the sediments around it. The greater the time interval subsequent to its last firing, the greater the accumulation of electrons.

The amount of thermoluminescence emitted when the object is heated during testing allows researchers to calculate the age of the object. Of course, the analyst must have a sample of sediment that was associated with the object (for example, the surrounding soil in which a clay pot is found). This will determine the kind and amount of radiation that the object has been exposed to subsequent to its last heating event. Thermoluminescence dating is well suited to samples of ancient pottery, brick, tile, or terracotta that were originally heated to a high temperature when they were made. This method can also be applied to burnt flint tools, hearth stones, lava or lava-covered objects, meteorites, and meteor craters (Aitken 1985).

Electron Spin Resonance Dating. **Electron spin resonance dating** is a technique that, like thermoluminescence dating, measures trapped electrons from surrounding radioactive material. In this case, the method is different. The material to be dated is exposed to varying magnetic fields, and a spectrum of the microwaves absorbed by the tested material is obtained. Since no heating is required for this technique, electron spin resonance is especially useful for dating organic material such as bone and shell, which decompose if heated (Aitken 1985).

Amino Acid Racemization. **Amino acid racemization** is a non-radiometric technique that can be applied to organic material such as bone, mollusc shells, and eggshells. It is useful for dating materials

---

Uranium-Series Dating: a technique for dating *Homo sapiens* sites that uses the decay of two kinds of uranium (^{235}U and ^{238}U) into other isotopes (such as ^{230}Th—thorium). Particularly useful in cave sites. Different types of uranium-series dating use different isotope ratios.
Thermoluminescence Dating: a dating technique that is well suited to samples of ancient pottery, brick, tile, or terracotta, which (when they were made) were heated to a high temperature that released trapped electrons from radioactive elements around it; the electrons trapped after manufacture emit light when heated, so the age of the object can be estimated by measuring how much light is emitted when the object is heated.

Electron Spin Resonance Dating: like thermoluminescence dating, this technique measures trapped electrons from surrounding radioactive material. The material to be dated is exposed to varying magnetic fields in order to obtain a spectrum of the microwaves absorbed by the tested material. Because no heating is required for this technique, electron spin resonance is especially useful for dating organic materials, such as bone and shell, that decompose if heated.
Amino Acid Racemization: a non-radiometric technique for dating materials that can be applied to organic material such as bone, mollusc shells, and eggshells.

Table 2–1 Summary of Dating Techniques Available to Archaeologists

Name	Age Range	Materials Dated
Relative		
Stratigraphy		anything between two clearly defined sediment layers
F-U-N trio		bone and teeth
Absolute		
Amino Acid Racemization	2000 to 1 million years ago	bone, charcoal, other organic material
Dendrochronology	Up to 9000 years ago	Wood
Electron Spin Resonance	Up to 1 million years ago	bone and shell
Fission-Track	20 to 5 billion years ago	crystal, glass, and many uranium-rich minerals
Obsidian Hydration	Up to 800 000 years ago	volcanic glass
Palaeomagnetic	Up to 10 000 years ago	geological deposits
Potassium-Argon (K-Ar)	5000 to 3 billion years ago	volcanic rock
Radiocarbon (^{14}C)	Up to 50 000 years ago	bone, mollusc shells, eggshells
Thermoluminescence	Unlimited	baked clay, pottery, and burnt rocks
Uranium-Series	Less than 300 000 years ago	calcite formations

from a few centuries old to several hundred thousand years old. Most amino acids in protein occur in one of two forms termed *D-* and *L-isomers*. Both have the same molecular structure, but are mirror images of one another.

Only L-isomers are found in living organisms. When an organism dies, maintenance of the L-form ceases and there is a slow process toward equal distributions of the L- and D-isomers. This process of change in composition of the amino acids is called *racemization*, and can be applied to dating prehistoric shell and bone—the older a fossil shell or bone, the further along the process of racemization should be.

Obsidian Hydration. *Obsidian* is naturally formed volcanic glass, used by many prehistoric populations for the production of extremely sharp-edged tools. When a piece of obsidian is newly exposed to the atmosphere through natural forces or human activity, that surface begins to absorb water. This process is known as **obsidian hydration**. The layer that is being weathered is invisible, but its thickness can be measured. The thickness will depend on the time it has been exposed, as well as the amount of moisture available and what kind of sediment surrounded the artifact (Fagan 2000). Obsidian hydration can be used as both a relative and an absolute dating technique for tools fashioned from obsidian.

Each dating technique has its own benefits (see Table 2–1). Which ones are used will be determined by the material available and the expected age of the remains to be tested. Overall, anthropologists, whether examining archaeological sites or palaeoanthropological locales, use the techniques we have described to gather information about remains that they find. In the next chapter we will look at ways in which they interpret this information to reconstruct the past.

Obsidian Hydration: the absorption of water by a piece of obsidian when it is newly exposed to the atmosphere through natural forces or human activity. The layer that is being weathered is invisible, but its thickness can be measured and will depend on the time it has been exposed.

SUMMARY AND REVIEW

SITE FORMATION PROCESSES

2.1 Describe the processes that create sites.

- Site formation processes are environmental and cultural factors that affect how and where materials are deposited at an archaeological site or fossil locale.

- How sites form is important to understand because these processes affect the kinds and quantities of evidence for past lifeways. The study of taphonomy—post-depositional changes to remains—is crucial for reconstructing the past.

Why does the archaeological record tend to favour inorganic materials?

TYPES OF SITES

2.2 Differentiate fossil locales and archaeological sites.

- Archaeological sites are locations where evidence of the past has been buried and preserved. Archaeological sites are defined by assemblages of artifacts, ecofacts, and/or features. Fossil locales are places where fossils are recovered.

How are candidate fossil locales identified?

EVIDENCE FROM THE PAST

2.3 Describe the different kinds of evidence that we can use to understand the past.

- There are several categories of evidence about past lifeways, including fossils, artifacts, ecofacts, and features.

- Fossils are once-living organisms that have had their structure preserved in stone.

- Artifacts are materials manufactured by humans and found in the archaeological record.

- Ecofacts are natural objects that have been used or affected by humans.

- Archaeological context is the association of artifacts, ecofacts, and features with one another. The association of remains in three-dimensional space is called *provenience*. Archaeological data are of little value without controlled provenience.

What are some examples of features and ecofacts?

FINDING ARCHAEOLOGICAL SITES

2.4 Describe the different ways that sites can be found.

- Site prospection, or reconnaissance, is the primary way of finding sites and determining post-depositional effects on remains.

- Reconnaissance techniques can be divided into two groups: surface and subsurface. Surface techniques include surveying and field walking. Subsurface techniques include shovel testing, augering, test pitting, and trenching.

What are some non-invasive site inspection techniques, and how do they work?

EXCAVATION

2.5 Explain how sites are excavated.

- Excavation is the best, but most destructive, means of collecting information about the past.

- Careful and detailed recording of the relationships between and among artifacts, ecofacts, fossils, and features is key to excavation.

- Excavation requires control over spatial aspects of a site through the use of a grid system. Detailed mapping and documentation of recoveries are related to the grid system so that all data can be incorporated at the end of an excavation.

How might soil samples from an excavation site be analyzed?

DATING TECHNIQUES

2.6 Explain how sites are dated from different kinds of evidence.

- Techniques for dating archaeological material contribute to determining the context of finds. Both relative and absolute dating techniques can be used to assess the age of a site.

- Relative dating techniques determine the age of archaeological materials relative to material of known ages. Stratigraphy, for example, provides a basis for determining whether a feature or object is younger or older than other features or objects in adjacent layers.

- Absolute dating techniques determine the age of archaeological deposits or materials by providing the age in years. Each absolute dating technique has different sources of error, so it is important that different techniques be used as checks on each other. When the results of two or more dating techniques support each other, they provide more reliable evidence.

 *What is the main principle behind relative fossil dating using fluoride, uranium, or nitrogen?*

THINK ON IT

1. How does the formation of a site affect the kinds of evidence that are available?

2. Is one kind of archaeological evidence better than another? If so, why?

3. Why is careful mapping and recording of archaeological sites so crucial for interpreting the past?

4. What types of unexpected challenges do you imagine one might encounter when excavating an archaeological site? Think of ways in which researchers could deal with these challenges.

5. How do relative dating methods differ from absolute dating methods? Are there circumstances when one technique is more appropriate than another? Explain your answer.

3 Reconstructing the Past: Analysis and Interpretation

Adam Gault/Getty Images

LEARNING OBJECTIVES

3.1 Describe the different ways that we can analyze artifacts.

3.2 Describe the different ways that we can analyze human remains.

3.3 Describe the different approaches to reconstructing diet in the past.

3.4 Explain how archaeologists reconstruct past environments.

3.5 Explain how archaeologists reconstruct past settlement patterns.

3.6 Explain how archaeologists study social systems.

3.7 Explain the sources and processes of cultural change.

The relationship between humans and their environment has long been a focus of study, particularly among archaeologists and physical anthropologists. To reconstruct how past populations lived, researchers examine evidence from the archaeological record. They draw upon a variety of related disciplines to help reconstruct former ecological conditions, determine what people ate and how and where they obtained their food, and study the diseases of the past. Analysis of human remains is important for determining diet and disease, as well as revealing demographic information, such as lifespan and infant mortality. Settlement patterns are another focus of study, specifically, where people established permanent and seasonal dwellings, as well as the size of the settlements, how many people lived there, and how long the sites were occupied. The archaeological record can also give clues about the society itself—whether some people had a higher socio-economic status than others, for example, and what the patterns of resource distribution and allocation were. In this chapter, we explore some of the anthropological methods for reconstructing these aspects of lives of past populations.

Reconstructing the past is not an easy task. It is not enough to simply dig up material left behind by people who once lived in a place. Rather, it requires the careful analysis of the environment in which the materials are found in order to say something about the circumstances by which that material came to be there. Archaeologists and others attempt to understand a past society as it is reflected in the remains of the everyday belongings of past peoples. For example, if we want to understand how a community changed over the course of its history, we need to recognize that those changes would have been influenced by a variety of factors, including changes in the environment, in population numbers, and in culture, to name a few. However, unravelling these factors is sometimes difficult. The archaeologist has to pay careful attention to the context in which material culture is found. Further, while material culture is a direct reflection of past culture, the archaeological record is not always a direct reflection of material culture. A number of factors can affect where the remains of material culture are found in the archaeological record and the patterns of deposition. The archaeologist must also be able to recognize the influence of these factors.

Analyzing Artifacts

Conservation is the process of treating artifacts, ecofacts, and in some cases even features to stop decay and, if possible, even reverse the deterioration process. Some conservation is very simple, involving only cleaning and drying the item. Some conservation is highly complex, involving long-term chemical treatments and, in some cases, long-term storage under controlled conditions. The so-called Ice Man, for example, the frozen remains of a man who lived 5000 years ago found in 1993 in the Italian Alps, is kept in permanently glacial-like conditions after investigators found to their dismay that warming the remains for study induced the growth of mould. The archaeologists removed the mould but decided that his remains would have to be kept under the same conditions that preserved them in the first place, and so a complex storage facility had to be built to re-create the glacial environment in which he was originally found (Nash 2001; Makristathis et al. 2002; Dickson et al. 2003; Murphy, Jr. et al. 2003). Similarly, the remains of Kwäday Dän Ts'ìnchi, or "Long Ago Person Found" in the Tutchone language of the Champagne and Aishihik First Nations, discovered frozen in a glacier in British Columbia, required extensive conservation, including for the hat and cloak he was wearing (Beattie et al. 2000).

Reconstruction is like building a puzzle—but a three-dimensional puzzle where you're not sure which pieces belong and you know not all the pieces are there. First, materials have to be sorted into similar types. For example, to reconstruct ceramics from a site, all the ceramics have to be sorted into types with similar colour, decoration, and shapes. Then the similar pieces are compared to see if any seem to come from the same vessel. Once all the pieces thought to be from the same

Conservation: techniques used on archaeological materials to stop or reverse the process of decay.

A conservator applying preservative to a decaying Alaskan totem pole.

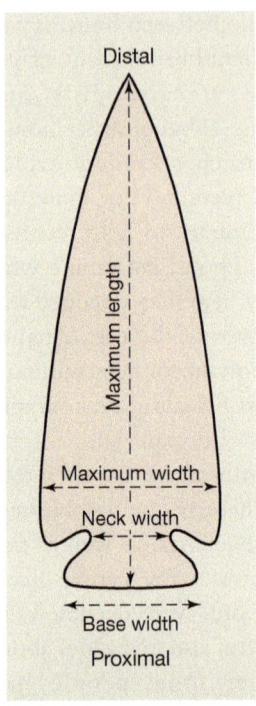

Figure 3–1 Standard Metrical Measurements of Chipped Stone Tools

vessel are located, they can be assembled. Reconstruction is clearly a long, difficult process—in some cases taking years.

What Can We Learn from Artifacts?

Once conservation and reconstruction are complete, the archaeologists or paleoanthropologists can begin to analyze the artifacts they've found. Archaeologists have developed specific and often unique ways to analyze the many different types of artifacts. Stone tools are examined in different ways from ceramics, and both are examined differently from bone. But there are some commonalities in the way artifacts are analyzed, regardless of what they are made of.

First, archaeologists typically examine the *form* of an artifact—how it is shaped. For most common artifacts, such as lithics and ceramics, forms are known well enough to be grouped into typologies. Placing artifacts into a **typology** is often the primary purpose of *formal analysis*, because typologies allow archaeologists to place a particular artifact into context with other artifacts found at the site or even at other sites. Typologies often provide a lot of information about an artifact, including its age, the species or culture with which it is affiliated, and in some cases even how it was made, used, or exchanged in the past. Second, archaeologists often measure artifacts, recording their size in various, often strictly defined, dimensions. Such analysis is used to group artifacts into a typology. Figure 3–1 shows the standard measurements taken from projectile points.

Third, archaeologists often attempt to understand how an artifact was made. By examining the material the artifact is made from and how that material was manipulated, archaeologists can learn about the technology, economy, and exchange systems of the people who made the artifact. For example, if the material is not locally available, that means the people traded for it. Archaeologists

Typology: a way of organizing artifacts in categories based on their particular characteristics.

can also study present-day peoples and how they make similar artifacts in order to understand how ancient artifacts were made.

Finally, archaeologists attempt to understand the function of an artifact. Knowing the function of an artifact allows the archaeologist a direct window into ancient life. Since this information is so important, a number of sophisticated techniques have been developed to determine how artifacts were used. For stone, bone, and wood tools, a technique called *use-wear analysis* has been developed, which can determine how a tool was used through the careful examination of the wear on its edges. For ceramic vessels, techniques have been developed to extract residues trapped in the clay and determine what the vessel held.

But what can archaeologists really learn by placing artifacts in typologies through formal and metric analysis, or by learning how an artifact was manufactured and used? Knowing how an artifact was made allows the archaeologist to understand the technology and technical abilities of peoples in the past. Artifacts and their context with other features can help inform us about the social organization of a past people and may also reveal religious beliefs. Even gender roles can be explored archaeologically (see Perspectives on Gender, "Women in the Shell Mound Archaic").

Analyzing Human Remains

Osteology, or skeletal biology, is the specialized sub-discipline of physical anthropology that deals with the biological remains of humans from past populations. Osteological reconstruction contributes a significant amount of information to our understanding of the past. The analysis of demographic structure (palaeodemography), health and disease (palaeopathology), diet and nutrition (palaeonutrition), and population affinity are just a few of the areas that skeletal biology can contribute to.

The first step in any analysis is identifying skeletal remains as being human. While this is relatively straightforward for well-preserved samples, it can be a difficult task for small fragmentary skeletal remains. For early hominins, the task of identification and classification becomes increasingly difficult. Estimation of the age and sex of individuals within a skeletal sample is the first step toward interpretation.

Estimation of Age

The age of an adult skeleton can be estimated using a variety of techniques. These methods are referred to as **skeletal age-indicator techniques**. These techniques depend on both *macroscopic*—visible by naked eye—observation and *microscopic* changes in the shape and structure of bone for estimating the age of an individual. Many macroscopic techniques focus on the pattern of age-related degeneration of bone. These include examination of the pubic symphysis and auricular surface on the hipbone, the closure of sutures between bones on the skull, and the ends of the fourth rib (see Figure 3–2). Other methods focus on **remodelling** to see how microscopic fractures may occur normally from everyday wear and tear. The physical anthropologist is trained to evaluate several criteria that indicate age, and then estimate an overall age range for the individuals within the sample.

The estimation of age from the skeletal remains of children is based on the development of dental and skeletal tissues—that is, the growing bones and developing teeth (see Figure 3–3, page 56). Age estimation for a child is much easier and more accurate than age estimation for an adult. While there are fewer specific techniques that can be used, these methods have a smaller range of error than do most adult aging techniques. Overall, estimation of age of a juvenile is accurate to within a range of about half a year.

Osteology: the study of the form and function of the skeleton.
Skeletal Age-Indicator Techniques: osteological techniques that are used to estimate the age-at-death of an individual from skeletal remains.

Remodelling: occurs after growth has ceased and replaces old tissue with new formed bone to maintain bone strength from microscopic fractures from normal biomechanical stress.

PERSPECTIVES ON GENDER

Women in the Shell Mound Archaic

One of the main issues addressed by archaeologists interested in gender is how we can learn about and understand gender roles in prehistoric cultures. Gender roles might seem impossible to study in archaeological contexts. How is gender preserved in the archaeological record? How can knowledge about gender roles be recovered? Information about gender roles can be recovered if one maintains an awareness of how material culture that is associated ethnographically with particular gender roles changes over time. Archaeologists argue that such an awareness leads not only to a better understanding of gender in prehistory, but also to a fuller understanding of prehistoric cultures overall.

An example is Cheryl Claassen's work on the Shell Mound Archaic culture of the Tennessee River valley. The Shell Mound Archaic represents the remains of people who lived in Tennessee and Kentucky between about 5500 and 3000 years ago. They were hunters and gatherers who lived in small villages, and probably moved seasonally between summer and winter communities. The most distinctive feature of the Shell Mound Archaic is the large mounds of mollusc shells they constructed for burying their dead. Tens of thousands of shells were piled together to create these mounds. Yet, around 3000 years ago, shellfishing and thus the creation of shell burial mounds stopped abruptly. Claassen wondered why.

Suggested explanations include climate change, overexploitation of shellfish themselves, and emigration of shellfishing peoples from the area. None has proven wholly satisfactory. In contemporary cultures shellfishing is typically done by women and children, and Claassen wondered whether an approach that considered gender roles might be more productive. She decided to approach the problem through the perspective of women's workloads, since women would have most likely have been the ones shellfishing. The end of shellfishing would have meant that women would have had a lot of free time—free time that could have been put to use in some other way. What might have changed to lead women to stop shellfishing? Would something else have perhaps become more important, so that women's labour was needed more for those other tasks?

Women's labour might have been redirected toward domesticated crops. There is archaeological evidence that about 3000 years ago several productive but highly labour-intensive crops became widely used. For example, *Chenopodium*, one of the more plentiful and nutritious of these new crops, has tiny seeds that require considerable labour to harvest, clean, and process. Women were likely the ones burdened with such work. They not only would have harvested these crops but also would have been the ones to process and prepare meals from them. Thus, the emergence of agricultural economies would have required women to undertake new labour in food production and processing that may well have forced them to stop other tasks, like shellfishing.

The development of agricultural activities might also have brought about changes in ritual and ceremonialism. The shell burial mounds were clearly central to Shell Mound Archaic death ceremonies. Considerable labour, mostly by women, would have been required to collect the shells and to build these mounds. Later societies in the region buried their dead in earthen mounds. Could this be a reflection of the new importance earth had in an emerging agricultural economy? If so, what role did women play in ceremonies of death and burial? If they were no longer the providers of the raw materials needed for burial, does that mean their status in society as a whole changed?

We may never know exactly why the Shell Mound Archaic disappeared, or how women's work and women's roles in society changed. But as Claassen pointed out, taking a gender perspective provides new avenues along which to pursue answers to these questions, and interesting new questions to pursue.

Source: Claassen C. 1991. Gender, shellfishing, and the shell mound archaic. In: Gero J, Conkey M, editors. Engendering archaeology: Women and prehistory. Oxford: Blackwell. pp. 276–300.

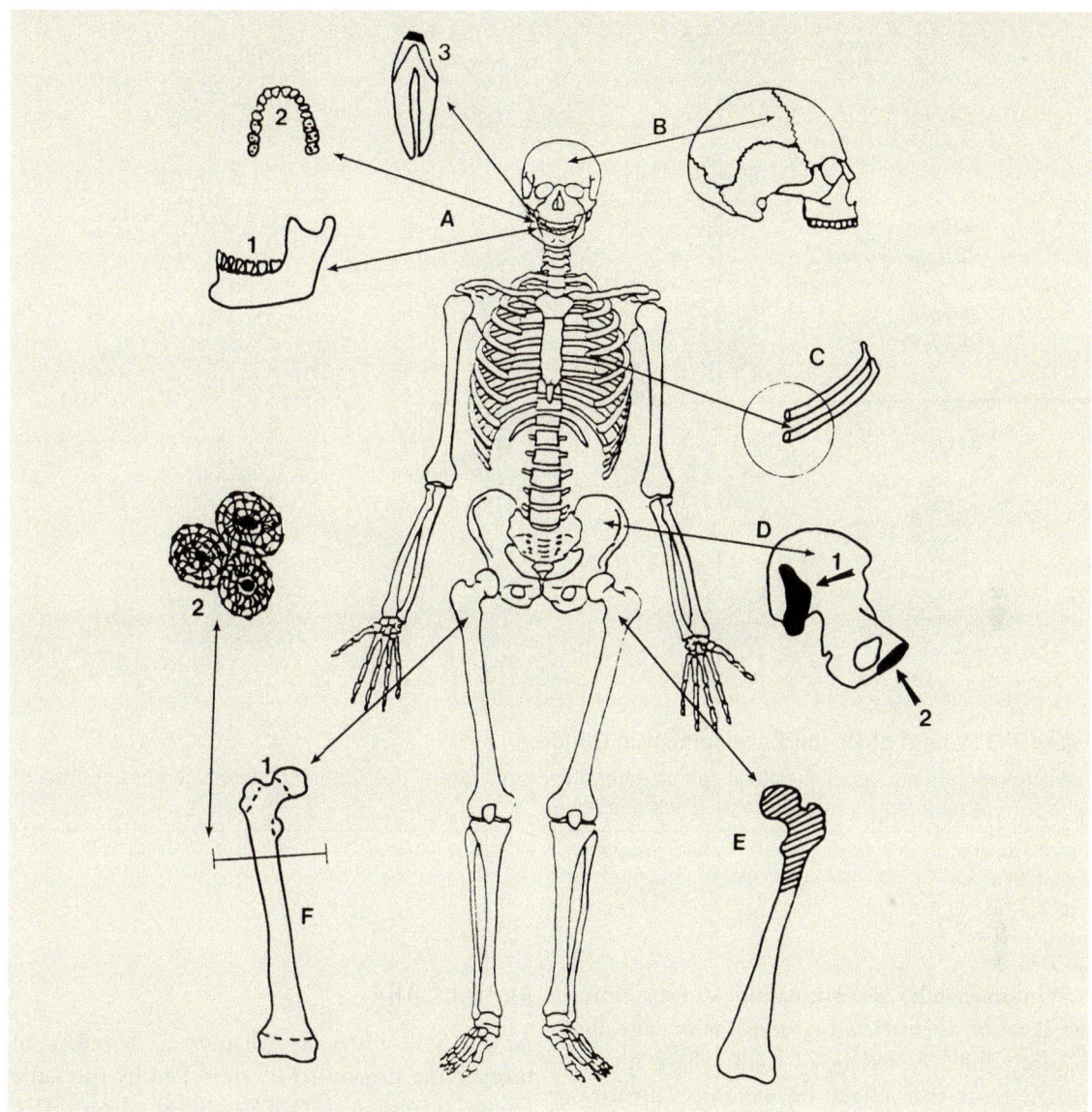

Figure 3–2 Commonly Used Skeletal Age-Indicator Techniques for Estimating the Age of Adult Remains

A: 1 dental development and eruption; 2 dental wear; 3 dental microstructure. **B**: cranial suture closure. **C**: sternal rib ends. **D**: 1 auricular surface; 2 pubic symphysis. **E**: radiographs of trabelucar bone from femur. **F**: 1 epiphyseal union; 2 cortical bone microstructure (osteon counting).

Source: Hunter J, Roberts C, Martin A. 1996. Studies in crime: An introduction to forensic archaeology. Chrysalis Books Ltd. Reprinted with permission.

Sex Determination

It is widely recognized by physical anthropologists that the pelvis or hipbone is the most reliable part of the skeleton for determination of sex. Both metric (based on measurements) and non-metric or morphological (based on size and shape) techniques are better than 95 percent accurate for correctly determining sex (see Figure 3–4, page 57). Accuracy rates based on other parts of the skeleton are usually lower than those using the hipbone.

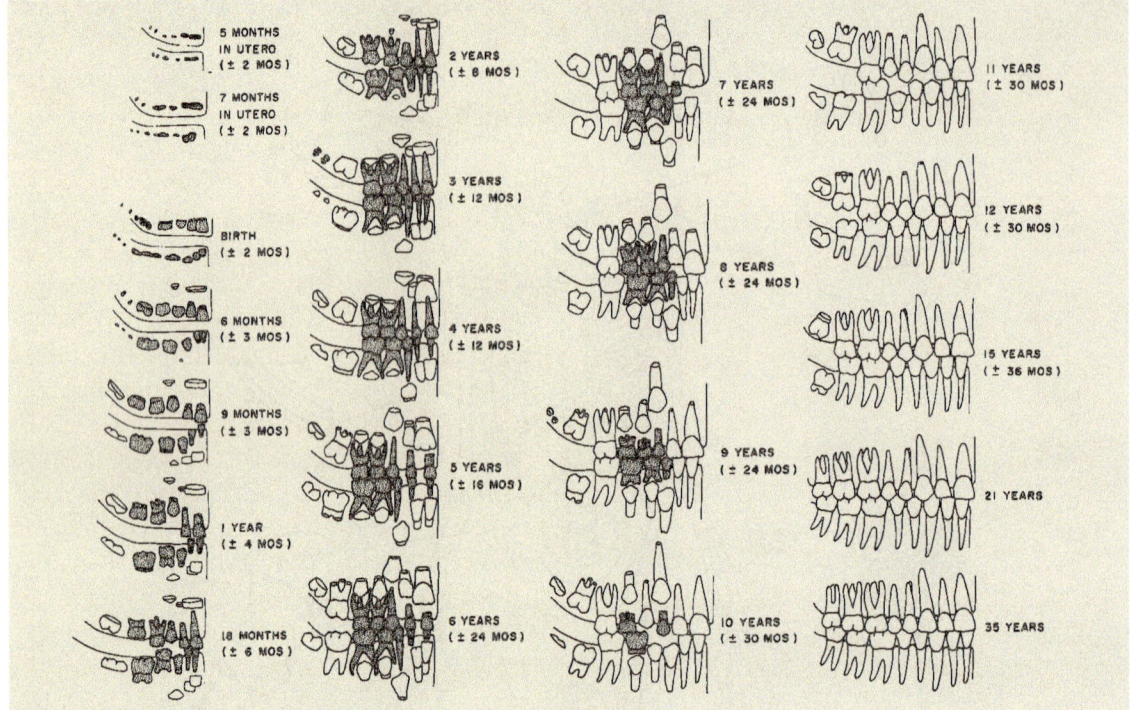

Figure 3–3 Pattern of Dental Development in Children
Age estimation in non-adult skeletons can be determined from dental development. Here a composite chart of development patterns is presented as a quick reference.

Source: Ubelaker D. 1989. Human skeletal remains: Excavations, analysis, and interpretation. Third edition. Washington: Taraxacum Press. Figure 71, p. 64. Reprinted with permission.

Unfortunately, determination of sex from the skeleton is restricted to remains of sexually mature adults. A variety of studies have investigated traits that might be **sexually dimorphic**—showing size and shape differences between males and females—in infants and juveniles, but only a few studies of such traits have demonstrated sufficient levels of accuracy to warrant applying these traits in osteological analyses. More promising, but still restricted by costs, are methods of sex determination that are based on *ancient DNA* extracted from the bones or teeth of individuals.

Ancient DNA

As we will learn in Chapter 5, heredity in most living organisms is controlled by the same chemical substance, **DNA—deoxyribonucleic acid**. The ability to extract DNA from prehistoric bone or other tissues led to the development of research in the field of **ancient DNA (aDNA)**. It was first proposed in the 1980s that DNA could be extracted from archaeo-

Sexually Dimorphic: refers to a species in which males differ markedly from females in size and appearance.

DNA (Deoxyribonucleic Acid): a long, two-stranded molecule in the genes; directs the making of an organism according to the instructions in its genetic code.
Ancient DNA (aDNA): DNA extracted from archaeologically recovered materials.

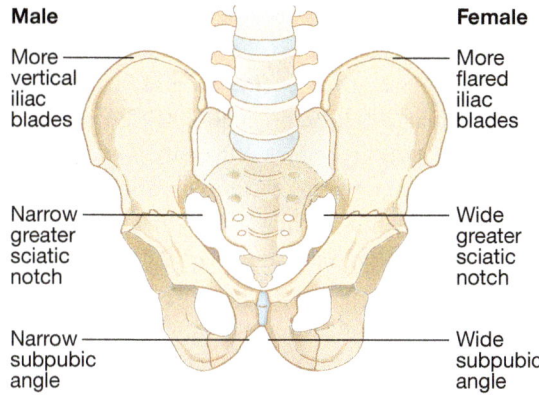

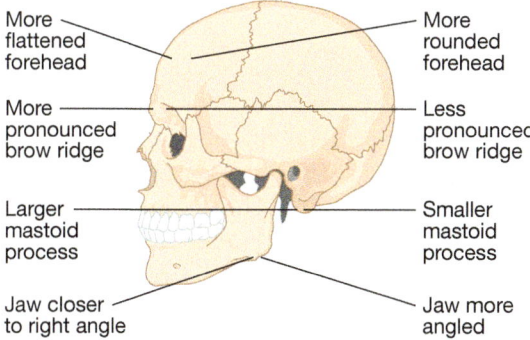

Figure 3–4 Common Traits of the Human Skeleton That Are Used to Assess Sex of Adults

Sex determination of the adult skeleton can be made from a variety of morphological techniques, as illustrated above. Determination of sex of children's skeletons cannot be done, as the growth process in children's skeletons is not yet complete.

logically recovered bone that was thousands of years old. Researchers around the world became excited by the possibilities of this new technology. However, like all new discoveries, several key methodological problems still had to be resolved. First, DNA is known to deteriorate over time. As a result, the actual quantity of DNA that might be present in a specimen could be very small and might represent comparatively fragmentary sections of the DNA sequence. Further, any DNA present might be damaged or degraded beyond the point of providing any useful information.

A significant advance in the field came with the discovery of the **polymerase chain reaction (PCR)** technique for the accurate recovery of ancient DNA. The major benefit of the PCR method is that it allows for the amplification of DNA sequences from trace amounts of the original genetic material. However, because the PCR method requires only a few molecules of DNA, it brought with it the heightened threat of sample contamination from both the burial environment and the laboratory environment. As a result, rigorous protocols have been developed to ensure the integrity of the original DNA sample and to minimize any possibilities of accidental contamination during the laboratory processing.

The ability to extract DNA from prehistoric remains has become an important aspect of anthropological research (Krause and Pääbo 2016). Determination of sex was one of the first areas of study for the application of DNA techniques to human skeletal samples. The ability to accurately identify sex from DNA is relatively straightforward now, although the time and cost associated with this methodology are still prohibitive for large samples. Another area of focus has been on population affinity or identification of maternal biological lineages through the analysis of mitochondrial DNA, from analysis of DNA extracted from skeletal samples. And most recently, researchers have begun trying to identify the DNA of agents associated with diseases that can be identified in the skeletal remains of individuals from the past. All these areas, and those that have yet to be explored, will greatly enrich our understanding of past populations and how they lived.

Polymerase Chain Reaction (PCR): technique for accurate recovery of ancient DNA. PCR requires only a few molecules for the amplification of DNA sequences from trace amounts of the original genetic material.

A variety of researchers in Canada have been working in the field of ancient DNA for over two decades now. In 1996, the Paleo-DNA Laboratory was established at Lakehead University. A number of projects have resulted from research and collaborations at this facility, including studies of the evolution of diseases (Spigelman et al. 2002; Donoghue et al. 2004, 2005; Larcombe, Nickerson et al. 2005), the bioarchaeology of ancient Egyptians (Graver et al. 2001), and the forensic archaeological analysis of soldiers from Vimy Ridge in 2007. The Institute for the Study of Ancient and Forensic DNA, established at McMaster University in 1999, is now the McMaster Ancient DNA Centre directed by Dr. Hendrik Poinar. A variety of research has been undertaken at the lab, including palaeopathological studies of humans and animals (Bathurst and Barta 2004; Yang et al. 2004) and forensic identification in historical archaeology (Dudar et al. 2003; Katzenberg et al. 2005). Dr. Poinar and his team continue to focus on a variety of areas, including the evolution of plague (Bos et al. 2012, 2016; Wagner et al. 2014), genetics of the woolly mammoth (Poinar et al. 2006; Schwarz et al. 2009; Palkopoulou et al. 2015), early Archaic hunter-gatherers (Poinar et al. 2001), and evolutionary genetic relationships (Nielsen et al. 2005; Poinar et al. 2006; Marciniak et al. 2015).

In particular, he is interested in the preservation and extraction of ancient DNA from archaeological and forensic sources (Poinar and Stankiewicz 1999; Poinar 2002; Pääbo et al. 2004; Poinar et al. 2006). At Simon Fraser University, Dr. Dongya Yang continues work on refining ancient DNA techniques begun at McMaster University (Yang et al. 1998, 2003; Yang and Watt 2005; Yang and Speller 2006), as well as the analysis of archaeologically recovered fish and animal remains from archaeological sites (Yang et al. 2004; Cannon and Yang 2006; Moss et al. 2006, 2015; Speller et al. 2006; Ames et al. 2015).

Palaeopathology

The study of **palaeopathology** seeks to answer questions concerning the origins, prevalence, and spread of diseases in past populations from human skeletal remains. The diagnosis and distribution of disease, within both individuals and the population, form the basis of interpretation for palaeopathological studies. Aided by macroscopic and microscopic examination, and some of the techniques already discussed, researchers attempt to identify and assess the prevalence of diseases within an archaeological sample. Then they may be able to draw conclusions about the prevalence of a disease within the population as a whole.

Like clinical medicine that deals with the whole person in his or her environment, palaeopathology must attempt to interpret the appearance, spread, and distribution of diseases in a biocultural context (Manchester 1987; Pinhasi and Mays 2008). Increasingly, palaeopathologists have become aware that human behaviour and its social and cultural determinants play a prominent role in the distribution and spread of infectious diseases. As a result, temporal and spatial differences in most disease patterns are largely the result of cultural differences in behavioural and not biological variation (Dunn and Janes 1986; Inhorn and Brown 1990; Sattenspiel 1990).

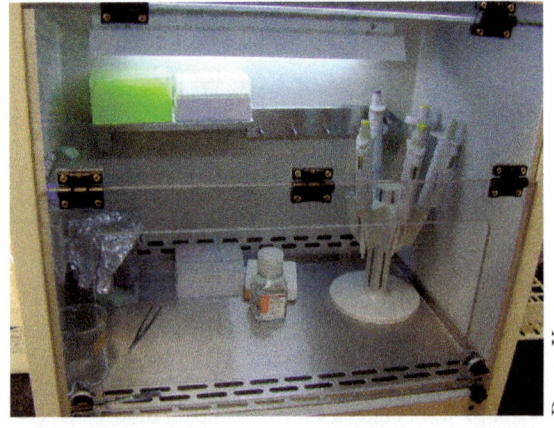

Processing ancient DNA requires meticulous control over the processing of samples. Seen here, an ultraviolet light is used to help prevent contamination.

Dongya Yang

Palaeopathology: the study of health and disease in the past from skeletal evidence.

A crucial aspect of palaeopathological studies has been to give precise descriptions and differential diagnoses from individual remains. **Differential diagnosis** is the process of listing each disease or condition that is consistent with the evidence observed, and then assessing which diagnosis is the most probable (Ortner 2012). The last few decades have seen a shift in emphasis to analysis of health and disease in populations. Interpretations of general population health from palaeopathological analyses have their limitations, however. First, only diseases that affect the hard tissues will generally be available for study, and of those, only a small percentage will actually result in changes to the skeleton. For example, pulmonary tuberculosis will affect the skeleton in only 3 to 7 percent of infected individuals (Steinbock 1976).

Skeletal evidence of health in the past is not limited to the effect of infectious diseases. Other conditions can leave distinct marks or lesions on bones and teeth, including but not limited to joint, autoimmune, and metabolic diseases, as well as other more specific maladies such as Paget's disease. The frequency of lesions caused by any of these conditions within archaeological samples is affected by factors such as differential preservation, incomplete or biased excavation, and the age and sex distributions within the sample. Anthropologists must attempt to deal with these issues before they can make interpretations of general population health from skeletal samples.

A primary question that palaeopathologists must ask themselves is, What does the presence of infectious lesions on the skeleton mean, for both the health of the individual and the population from which such an individual comes (Ortner 1991)? The basic assumption of palaeopathology is that there is a consistent relationship between the presence of skeletal lesions produced by a specific disease process in the individual (infectious or otherwise) and the risks of sickness and death associated with that disease within the population as a whole (Ortner 1991). Simply put, it is assumed that the more often you see evidence for a specific disease in the archaeological record, the greater the risk of illness or death from that disease for individuals in the living population who were exposed to it.

In the early 1990s, Jim Wood and colleagues cautioned palaeopathologists against drawing conclusions about past health based on this assumption (Wood et al. 1992). Palaeopathological interpretations of health assume that the individual immune response and environmental conditions do not influence the presence of skeletal lesions. Therefore, different levels of disease observed archaeologically must be related to cultural differences between populations (Cohen and Armelagos 1984a; Goodman et al. 1984b; Cohen 1989). Wood and co-workers, however, have strongly urged palaeopathologists to reconsider this supposition and critically examine the concepts of differential risk and susceptibility to disease and death within population samples. That is, each individual may or may not have the same chance of being exposed to a particular disease. Further, even when an individual is exposed, biological factors specific to the individual's immune response will result in some contracting the disease while others do not.

Many researchers have expressed concern over the fact that skeletal samples are intrinsically biased because they are the products of selective mortality (Cook and Buikstra 1979; Cook 1981; Saunders 1992; Wood et al. 1992; Saunders and Hoppa 1993). *Selective mortality* refers to the notion that skeletal samples represent not all the people who were susceptible (susceptibles) for a given age group, but only those individuals who died at that age. For example, 5-year-old individuals in a skeletal sample represent only those 5-year-olds who died and not all the 5-year-olds who were alive in the population at risk; other surviving susceptibles continued to live, in effect contributing to, or being members of, older mortality groups (Wood et al. 1992). The obvious problem, then, is whether the evidence of disease in a skeletal sample accurately represents the real prevalence of infectious agents in the living population during the past.

> **Differential Diagnosis:** the assessment of potential diseases that are consistent with the observable traits/criteria on bones within an individual.

A promising future direction is palaeopathological studies that seek to examine the epidemiology or the course taken by specific diseases (de Souza et al. 2003; Klaus 2014). For example, in order to better understand the true frequency of leprosy in medieval Denmark, Jesper Boldsen demonstrated that both sensitivity and specificity of skeletal lesions had to be assessed (Boldsen 2001). Using epidemiological concepts like this, researchers are better positioned to examine a variety of biocultural factors that might have influenced the population's response to the disease. This approach to past health has become an important focus of anthropological research. Another area that is beginning to immerge in palaeopathology is study of the developmental origins of disease and molecular study of epigenetic mechanisms (see Chapter 5) of risk (e.g., DeWitte and Stojanowski 2015; Gowland 2015).

Palaeodemography

Demography focuses on the age and sex structure of the population, and patterns of mortality, fertility, and population growth. **Palaeodemography** is the study of demographic structure in the past.

Palaeodemographic studies have focused primarily on the interpretation of human skeletal samples recovered archaeologically. The basic assumption is that mortality statistics derived from the skeletal sample are sufficient to make inferences about the past population. As well, archaeological evidence for settlement size and distribution of settlements has been used to estimate population growth or to address broader questions of population structure in the past.

Anthropological demography of contemporary or recent historic hunter-gatherer and foraging populations can also provide us with models for prehistoric populations. This is known as **ethnographic analogy**. However, ethnographic analogy based on patterns of subsistence or mobility is extremely problematic. More recently, evidence from genetic studies has begun to be used to make inferences about long-term evolutionary changes in demographic structure in modern human populations that have lived over the past 250 000 years or so. In particular, genetic studies that examine variation within living human populations provide information on human demography since patterns of gene differences contain information about the demographic history of a species (Harpending et al. 1998).

Traditionally, palaeodemographers place individuals into a series of age groups. They start by assuming that the past population numbers were **stationary**—in other words, that there was no in-migration or out-migration and the number of deaths equalled the number of births. They can then use the mean or average age at death in the skeletal sample to estimate life expectancy at birth. However, this assumption is not likely to apply in past populations, particularly over short periods and in small populations. In growing populations, age-at-death distributions are extremely sensitive to changes in birth rates but not to changes in death rates. Thus, if population numbers are not stationary—and changing populations never are—small variations in fertility have large effects on age-at-death distribution, while even quite large changes in mortality have virtually none (Wood et al. 1992). Recognizing this, many researchers have concluded that the age distribution of skeletal samples provides less information about mortality than it does about fertility. In fact, the same fertility and mortality patterns can produce different birth and death rates in populations with different age structures.

Two key factors that affect stationarity in populations are *growth* and *migration*. The immediate effects of migrations into or out of a population are obvious. People who move to a new location are not always representative of all age groups and

---

Palaeodemography: the study of demographic structure and processes in past populations from archaeological evidence.

Ethnographic Analogy: method of comparative cultural study that extrapolates to the past from recent or current societies.

Stationary: in demography, a population is considered to be stationary when there is no in-migration or out-migration and the number of deaths equals the number of births per year.

therefore can affect birth and death rates unequally at the new location. Similarly, potential changes in the gene pool or genetic background of migrants can change the overall susceptibility to different kinds of diseases. The impact of such changes depends on the source of migration and the cultural forces that are propelling the migration. War or invasion, persecution, plague, and social, political, or economic factors can alter the demographic structure of a population in both the short and the long term. Failure to recognize the possible effects of migration on the age structure of past populations can distort conclusions (Johansson and Horowitz 1986). If rates of population growth can be assessed independently of the skeletal evidence—that is, from other archaeological evidence—palaeodemographic analyses are less uncertain. However, such assessments are difficult to obtain (Moore et al. 1975; Milner et al. 1989).

Ultimately, physical anthropologists have tried to improve methods for estimating age from the skeleton in order to combine individual estimates to create a demographic profile of the age structure (e.g., Milner and Boldsen 2012), along with more sophisticated statistical approaches to estimate the age structure of a sample (see Konigsberg and Frankenberg 1994; Hoppa and Vaupel 2002; Müller et al. 2002; Bocquet-Appel 2008; Milner et al. 2008; Caussinus et al. 2010).

Reconstructing Past Diets

The only direct evidence for what people ate in the past is the preserved remains of the food itself. Such remains can be found in rare cases where mummified human remains may still have preserved stomach contents. Another form of direct evidence occurs in the form of *coprolites*—the fossilized remains of human feces. Other evidence for how people obtained their food and nutrition comes from a variety of sources. The study of the faunal or animal remains (*zooarchaeology*) and flora or plant remains (*palaeoethnobotany*) associated with settlement sites plays a major role in revealing the kinds of food people acquired and consumed. Evidence can also come from the analysis of human skeletons, that is, from biochemical analysis of bone.

Zooarchaeology

Zooarchaeology, or *archaeozoology*, is the study of animal remains from the archaeological record. The analysis of animal remains includes determining the number of different species represented, the minimum number of individuals of each species, and the age structure of those species. This information can provide clues about seasonal hunting strategies, specialized hunting practices, and the process of *domestication*—the modification of plants and animals for human use. However, it is critical to properly interpret the zooarchaeological data. For example, it is important to be able to distinguish between human-made butchering marks and marks from carnivore gnawing (e.g., Fisher 1995). Animals associated with human populations may reflect the kinds of foods that were consumed (including whether they were wild or domesticated, as we will see in Chapter 12). They may also reflect the strategies, such as big-game hunting techniques, used to acquire these food resources.

An example of the interpretation of animal remains is Aubrey Cannon's research on the Northwest Coast. Using zooarchaeological data from the site of Namu, downstream from Bella Coola on British Columbia's coast, Cannon argued that the increased focus on catching fish on the Northwest Coast was not the result of population pressure or lack of food from land-based sources. Rather, **sedentism**—living in one place for a prolonged period—and intensive salmon fishing seemed to be independent of increased salmon productivity and human population growth. He suggested that evidence of increased storage capacity associated with the development of wood-plank housing and social feasting could explain the apparent intensification of fishing economies on the Northwest Coast (Cannon 1998, 2002). By examining when and how this behaviour developed in a region, we can better understand its importance in a complex society where social and political power are based on resource control by the elite.

Zooarchaeology: the study of animals' remains from archaeological contexts.
Sedentism: settling in a single, permanent location.

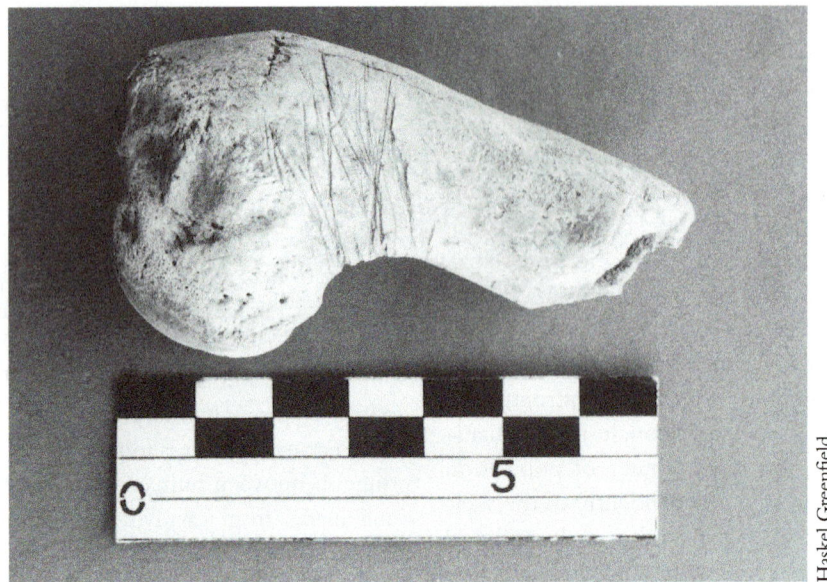

Interpreting butchering marks on animal bones helps us to reconstruct what people ate and how they procured and processed their food.

However, faunal remains are not associated only with food consumption. Jim Savelle of McGill University examined zooarchaeological assemblages of bowhead whalebone, which was a major component of house construction in Thule occupation sites throughout the Canadian Arctic around 1000 years ago. He suggested that the use of whalebone in house construction is the primary reason that we find whalebone at all Thule sites (Savelle 1997). This is of interest because most people would consider life in the Arctic, now as in the past, as involving small, widely dispersed populations of hunter-gatherers who are highly mobile and follow an intensive seasonal economy and settlement pattern. However, Thule people lived in winter villages in pit houses composed of whalebone rafters and covered with skins and turf. The question is, Why did these people invest in semipermanent housing given what we might expect regarding their seasonal subsistence and mobility patterns? Part of the answer is that there was an increase in whale hunting associated with warmer climatic conditions during this period. With the intensification of this kind of subsistence strategy, people became more sedentary because they did not have the technology, population size, or need to move all that material around.

Experimental Archaeology

Experimental archaeology explores a variety of historical questions, especially those related to diet and subsistence. The goal of experimental archaeology is to reproduce or replicate technological traits and patterns observed in the archaeological record. For example, many modern flint knappers attempt to reconstruct the process that would lead to the production of the kinds of chipped stone tools found in the archaeological record. Reconstruction may give the analyst insight into human behaviour and site formation processes. For example, animal carcasses were left to be scavenged to help palaeoanthropologists better understand the patterns in the distribution of bones found in sites associated with early hominins. The resultant tooth marks and distribution of bones were then analyzed and compared with those observed in the archaeological record (Hudson 1993; Schick and

Experimental Archaeology: a specialty within archaeology used to explore a variety of historical questions, especially those related to diet and subsistence, by reproducing or replicating technological traits and patterns observed in the archaeological record.

Toth 1994; see also Sala and Arsuaga 2016 for a recent review of such studies).

Similarly, Haskel Greenfield of the University of Manitoba is interested in food production and the origins of metallurgy. He conducted experiments in which meat was butchered using replicas of stone tools and early metal tools, fabricated in a manner consistent with early metallurgy, so as to better understand how the transition from stone tools to early metal tools could be observed in the archaeological record (Greenfield 1999, 2006). The results of this experiment provided information for better understanding this technological evolution associated with food production.

The analysis of polishes or wear patterns and organic residues left on the tools used in food-related tasks by past populations is another relatively new area of research. Because of experimental archaeology, scientists now know that butchering an animal carcass and processing vegetable matter with stone tools lead to different microscopic wear patterns or polishes on the edge of the tools. Archaeologists can now look at the stone tools used by prehistoric peoples and examine them microscopically for patterns that are consistent with ones produced by experiment.

Even more exciting is the potential of **molecular anthropology**, which examines anthropological questions using genetic evidence. Researchers in molecular anthropology analyze and identify microscopic traces of organic material left on prehistoric tools (Loy et al. 1990, 1992; Loy and Hardy 1992; Loy 1998). Stone tool edges can be examined for microscopic traces of blood from killed or butchered animals. Examples of success include blood retrieved from Australian stone tools, dated to 9000 years ago (Loy and Hardy 1992); mastodon blood on a tool found in Chile, dated to 13 000 years ago (Tuross and Dillehay 1995); and the identification of blood on a stone tool dated to 62 000 years ago (Lombard 2014). Blood residues of a variety of large mammal species, including mammoth, have also been detected on projectile points from Beringia, providing for the first time a direct association between the use of these tools and big-game hunting of Pleistocene mammals in Arctic and subarctic North America (Loy and Dixon 1998). Advanced spectroscopic techniques have also been used to examine protein residues (Prinsloo et al. 2014). Residue analysis on the interior of clay vessels has formed an important part of reconstructing aspects of ancient diet (see Current Research and Issues, "Archaeology Helps Brew Ancient Beer"). A variety of other organics have also been identified from residues, including wine, beeswax, and milk (see McGovern and Hall 2015 for an overview).

Palaeoethnobotany

Palaeoethnobotany, or archaeobotany, is the study of the relationships between plants and people in prehistory. Palaeoethnobotanists are especially trained in the identification of seeds found, often burnt or carbonized, in ancient garbage heaps (middens), cooking vessels, and hearths at archaeological sites. Soil removed from a site must be processed to recover the seeds from the archaeological record. The soil is placed in a flotation device in which the light seeds and charcoal float to the surface of the water, where they are skimmed off for analysis. The heavier sediments such as clay, rock, and pebbles sink. Phytoliths, which are microscopic particles of silica from plants, can also be collected from archaeological remains, including artifacts, teeth, and feces, to provide clues as to the kinds of plants that were being processed and consumed. Gary Crawford and David Smith of the University of Toronto are examining sites at the western end of Lake Ontario and in the lower Grand River Valley in south-central Ontario that were occupied during the period from about A.D. 500 to A.D. 1100. They hope to gain an understanding of the transition from earlier seed crops to maize (corn) agriculture in southern Ontario prehistory (Crawford and Smith 1996; Crawford et al. 1997). As we shall see in Chapter 12, the analysis of carbonized seeds from the archaeological record provides

Molecular Anthropology: the study of anthropological questions using genetic evidence.

Palaeoethnobotany: the study of plant remains from archaeological contexts.

CURRENT RESEARCH AND ISSUES

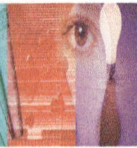

Archaeology Helps Brew Ancient Beer

Archaeological evidence from ancient civilizations in Mesopotamia, Egypt, and China has shown some of the earliest evidence for the brewing of beer. At Godin Tepe, a site in the Zagros Mountains in Iran, excavators from the Royal Ontario Museum found some of the earliest chemical evidence for beer. Clay pots were identified; these were used for the storage and fermentation of beer. Grooves on the interior of these vessels below the shoulder are consistent with early Sumerian examples for beer storage. Further, residue analysis from the grooves of some of these vessels found the chemical remnants of calcium oxalate—a primary component of barley beer that settles on the surface of storage tanks during fermentation. These findings represent some of the earliest evidence of beer production in the fourth century B.C.

For the second century B.C., evidence for beer production from the New Kingdom period in Egypt can also be observed from the archaeological record. During this period, which covers the reign of the Pharaoh Tutankhamen, evidence includes residue, from fermentation in vessels, and botanical remains. In 1990, the Egypt Exploration Society approached Scottish and Newcastle breweries in the United Kingdom to assist them in an investigation into beer making in ancient Egypt. Ancient Egyptian inscriptions and documents show that beer with bread was a daily food, giving nourishment to both the wealthy and poor. The established view of ancient Egyptian brewing, drawn from tomb scenes, was that beer loaves were made from a rich yeast dough, possibly with malt added. The dough was lightly baked and the resulting bread was then crumbled and strained through a sieve with water. Ingredients like dates or extra yeast might have been added at this stage. Fermentation occurred in large vats, and when complete, the liquid was poured into vessels and sealed for transportation.

Using a scanning electron microscope (SEM), researchers were able to examine residues on the interiors of fermentation pots, and they found evidence for yeast colonies and possibly lactic acid bacteria. In ancient Egypt, emmer and barley were the two major cereals for producing beer. Additional clues from SEM research on residues provide insight into the actual brewing process. For example, changes in the structure of starch granules, associated with starch being heated in water, can be observed in some residues. Comparisons between samples are difficult, though, given that contamination of the residues over the last 3000 years can obscure analyses. However, there now seems to be enough evidence from microscopic analysis of pot residues to suggest that the ancient Egyptians used a variety of techniques for brewing and that bread probably did not play a role in the production of beer in the ancient world.

Archaeologists recently reconstructed a beer recipe originating in China roughly 5000 years ago, during the Neolithic Yangshao period, using similar microbotanical analyses of residues found on vessels along with chemical analysis of calcium oxalate. Among the main ingredients recovered were millet and barley. The discovery of barley remains in these beer residues accounts for the earliest occurrence of this crop in China. It would be another three millennia before barley would become an important agricultural subsistence crop in the Central Plain region.

Sources: Armelagos G. 2000. Take Two Beers and Call Me in 1600 Years. Natural History. 109(4):50–53.

Samuel D. 1996. Archaeology of Ancient Egyptian Beer. Journal of the American Society of Brewing Chemists. 54:3–12.

Samuel D. 1996. Investigation of Ancient Egyptian Baking and Brewing Methods by Correlative Microscopy. Science. 273:488–490.

Samuel D, Bolt P. 1995. Rediscovering Ancient Egyptian Beer. Brewers' Guardian. 124(12):26–31.

Wang J, Liu L, Ball T, Yu L, Li Y, Xing F. 2016. Revealing a 5,000-Y-Old Beer Recipe in China. Proceedings of the National Academy of Sciences. 113(23):6444–6448.

---

us with clues as to the increasing dependence on seed crops at the beginning of the Neolithic era.

At Brandon University, Canada Research Chair in Archaeological Residue and Functional Analysis Mary Malainey is using **gas chromatography** to examine ancient fat (lipid) residues that remain from a variety of archaeological artifacts, including pottery, cooking rocks, and food-processing tools.

> **Gas Chromatography:** an analytical technique for determining the relative proportions of different substances within a sample.

From her analysis, she is trying to answer questions about the diet of and activities performed by the ancient inhabitants of sites (Malainey et al. 1999; Malainey 2011).

Coprolites

Coprolites, or fossilized feces, provide evidence for diet because humans do not digest all food that they consume. Some of what an individual consumed can be identified in coprolites. Of course, this kind of evidence represents a snapshot of dietary intake. Coprolites occur most frequently in cave sites, where the dry air naturally desiccates, or removes the moisture from, organic material. Only foods consumed by a specific individual within a very narrow time frame will be present in preserved coprolites. However, if cave sites are frequently used by certain groups of people, there may be a sufficient sample of coprolites to provide a broader cross-section of the kinds of foods being consumed by the group. Similarly, the analysis of coprolites was used by Lin and Connor (2001) to compare the diet of a 500-year-old Greenland Eskimo relative to a contemporary Inuit diet. More recently, coprolites at the Paisley Caves site in Oregon provided evidence for the oldest directly dated human remains (DNA) in the New World (Jenkins et al. 2012).

Stable Isotopes and Trace Elements

Researchers are often interested in changes in nutrition for past populations. These changes may provide a link to broad biocultural adaptations, such as changes in the environment or in how people obtained their food. Researchers make inferences regarding the general levels of nutrition from skeletal samples through biochemical techniques, including the analysis of **stable isotopes**—isotopes of the same elements with different atomic masses—and **trace elements**—elements found in extremely small amounts within the body (Klepinger 1984; Price 1984; Boutton et al. 1991; Katzenberg 1992, 2000; Sandford 1992, 1993; Schoeninger 1995) (see Current Research and Issues, "You Are What You Eat: Chemical Analyses of Bones and Teeth").

With respect to dietary reconstruction, the past consumption of two broadly different types of plants—tropical grasses and temperate climate plants—is commonly explored through stable isotope analysis. There are two types of photosynthetic pathways that plants can follow. The photosynthetic pathway for temperate climate plants is different than the pathway for the tropical plants. Maize, like other tropical grasses, is a C4 pathway plant. Temperate climate plants are called C3 plants. C3 plants tend to absorb proportionately more carbon-12 (^{12}C) because they discriminate more strongly against the carbon-13 (^{13}C) isotope. In contrast, C4 plants produce more complex sugar molecules, and tend to more readily accept the ^{13}C isotope. This means that organisms that regularly consume C4 plants will display a different ratio of ^{13}C to ^{12}C than animals that routinely consume C3 plants. As a result, stable carbon isotope analysis on skeletal remains can be used extensively to assess the importance of maize in North American populations. Stable isotope analyses have shown the absence of maize in the diet of prehistoric Ontario populations prior to about A.D. 700 (Schwarcz et al. 1985; Katzenberg 1993; Katzenberg et al. 1995). However, carbon isotope ratios increase after A.D. 1000 and peak around three to four centuries later, reflecting the adoption of maize agriculture in the region (Katzenberg et al. 1995). This is consistent with studies of other areas in eastern North America, although regional variations likely reflect a shorter growing season farther north.

Carbon isotopic analyses can also be used to study the diets of people who lived at coastal sites, particularly in determining the relative importance of marine versus terrestrial foods. Carbon absorbed by marine animals derives from dissolved carbonate, while terrestrial animals rely upon atmospheric carbon. As the relative abundance of

---

Coprolites: the fossilized remains of feces.
Stable Isotopes: isotopes of the same elements with different atomic masses.

Trace Elements: elements found in extremely small amounts within the body.

CURRENT RESEARCH AND ISSUES

You Are What You Eat: Chemical Analyses of Bones and Teeth

Physical anthropologists and archaeologists study ancient diets in several ways, which are mostly indirect. They can infer indirectly some of what ancient people ate from recovered food wastes. For example, if you find a lot of corncobs, chances are that the people ate a lot of corn. Physical anthropologists and archaeologists can also indirectly infer diet from the artifacts they find, particularly, of course, ones we can be pretty sure were used in obtaining or processing food. So, for example, if you find a stone with a flat or concave surface that looks similar to stones that some people use now in some places to grind corn, it is very likely that the ancient people also ground grain (or other hard things such as seeds) for food. However, plant remains or implements do not tell us *how much* people relied on particular sources of food.

There is a more direct way to study ancient diets. Anthropologists have discovered that in many ways "you are what you eat." In particular, chemical analyses of bones and teeth, the most common remains found in excavations, can reveal distinctive traces of the foods that metabolically went into the bones and teeth.

One kind of informative chemical analysis involves the ratio of strontium to calcium in bone. This analysis can indicate the relative amounts of plant and animal food in the diet. So, for example, we know from strontium analysis of bones that just before the beginnings of cereal agriculture in the Near East, people were eating a lot of plant food, probably wild cereals that were intensively collected. Then there was a temporary decline in such collecting, suggesting overexploitation of the wild resources, or at least their decreasing availability. This problem was presumably solved by the cultivation and domestication (modification) of cereals.

Carbon isotope ratios also can tell us what types of plants people were eating. Trees, shrubs, and temperate-zone grasses (for example, rice) have carbon isotope ratios that are different from those of tropical and subtropical grasses (such as millet and corn). People in China were relying heavily on cereals about 7000 to 8000 years ago, but the cereals were not the same in the north and south. Contrary to what we might expect, the carbon isotope ratios tell us that an originally temperate-zone cereal (rice) was the staple in subtropical southern China; in the more temperate north, an originally tropical or subtropical grass (millet) was most important. The dependence on millet in the north was enormous.

Non-chemical analyses of human bones and teeth were traditionally used by physical anthropologists and archaeologists to study similarities and differences between peoples in different geographic regions, between living humans and possible fossil ancestors, and between living humans and other surviving primates. In recent years, physical anthropologists and archaeologists have begun to study the "insides" of bones and teeth. The new kinds of chemical analysis mentioned here are part of that trend.

Sources: Larsen, CS. 2002. Bare Bones Anthropology: The Bioarchaeology of Human Remains. In: Peregrine PN, Ember CR, Ember M, editors. Archaeology: Original Readings in Method and Practice. Upper Saddle River, NJ: Prentice Hall/Simon & Schuster Custom Publishing.

van der Merwe NJ. 1992. Reconstructing Prehistoric Diet. In: Jones S, Martin R, Pilbeam D, editors. The Cambridge Encyclopedia of Human Evolution. New York: Cambridge University Press. pp. 369–372.

---

^{13}C is higher in marine environments than in the atmosphere, the entire marine food web reflects a high proportion of ^{13}C. This means the isotopic profile of human bones should show if past populations relied more heavily on marine foods than on terrestrial foods. For example, David Lubell and his colleagues have used this analysis to show an abrupt shift from marine to terrestrial food resources between Mesolithic and later Neolithic populations in Portugal (Lubell et al. 1994).

In the late 1980s researchers demonstrated that the ratio of stable isotopes of nitrogen could be used to detect the consumption of breast milk in an infant's diet (Fogel et al. 1989). The higher an organism is on the food chain, the more its tissues are enriched with the ^{15}N isotope. For example, carnivores that consume herbivores (plant-eating animals) have tissues enriched with ^{15}N. So we would expect that the tissues of breast-fed babies should be more enriched in ^{15}N than the tissues

In ancient Egypt, figures were made depicting household activities such as bread and beer preparation. Above is a Middle Kingdom model.

of their mothers. Many studies have explored whether high ^{15}N levels in infant skeletons, in contrast to decreased levels in older children, may reflect the weaning process (Katzenberg 1991; Tuross and Fogel 1994; White and Schwarcz 1994; Katzenberg and Pfeiffer 1995).

Annie Katzenberg, a physical anthropologist at the University of Calgary, and her colleagues have examined the issue of infant weaning, sickness, and mortality from a variety of skeletal samples. In a small protohistoric (around the time of contact with Europeans) sample from southern Ontario, Katzenberg and colleagues found that both carbon and nitrogen isotope ratios varied with age. This variation reflected a change in dietary intake associated with breast-feeding and weaning (Katzenberg et al. 1993). However, we must remember that infants and children in skeletal samples may reflect health and nutritional problems that prevented survival. As such, very young newborns might not have had the opportunity to nurse if very ill. Katzenberg analyzed skeletal samples of European descent from historic cemeteries. She found no difference in stable nitrogen ratios between newborns and adults, in contrast to very high levels among the infants and young children (Katzenberg 1991).

In their analysis of the skeletal remains of 64 individuals from a historic Methodist cemetery in Newmarket, Ontario, Katzenberg and Pfeiffer observed that nitrogen isotope ratios rose rapidly from birth to about one year of age, after which they declined to adult levels by about two years of age (Katzenberg and Pfeiffer 1995). In their study of infant mortality in a 19th-century pioneer cemetery in Belleville, Ontario, Ann Herring and colleagues suggested that the introduction of other food sources in relatively poor living conditions resulted in increased infant mortality by five months of age, even though breast milk remained a major component of infant nutrition until just over a year of age (Herring et al. 1998). It may be that the introduction of other foods in environments that were relatively unsanitary had an impact on infant mortality and morbidity patterns, not nutritional decline associated with the weaning process itself (Katzenberg et al. 1996; Schurr 1997; Herring et al. 1998).

Trace element analyses have also been used in reconstructing the diet of past populations. These studies have focused on identifying levels of calcium, strontium, and barium in bones. The pattern of absorption of strontium into the skeleton is opposite to the absorption pattern for nitrogen isotope ratios—instead of increasing from plant to herbivore to carnivore, it decreases. This means that amounts of calcium and strontium in skeletal remains can be analyzed for reconstructing prehistoric diets in animals and hominins (Katzenberg 1984). Herbivores have the highest levels of strontium in their skeletons, while carnivores have the lowest, and omnivores fall somewhere in between (Sandford and Weaver 2000). Calculating the ratio of strontium and calcium (Sr/Ca) in infant skeletons has also been a method for detecting the beginning of the weaning process. This approach was based on the assumption that supplemental foods in the early weaning stage in past populations were cereals that were enriched in strontium. Because the infant digestive system is less able to discriminate against strontium, infant bones absorb more than you would expect, and researchers need to take this into consideration. In addition, issues of **diagenesis**—the artificial uptake of trace elements from the burial environment—produce additional methodological problems to this approach. As a result, current studies now rely on the analysis of stable isotopes for understanding infant feeding practices.

Reconstructing Past Environments

Archaeological reconstructions of past environmental conditions are derived from the analysis of soils, sediments, and remains of former life forms. These life forms include pollen, plant macrofossil remains of all kinds, invertebrates (including parasitic nematodes, insects and other arthropods, and molluscs), and vertebrates (Reitz et al. 1996; Evans and O'Connor 1999; Dincauze 2000). For example, sediment from West Coast shell middens has provided clear evidence of human intestinal parasitism (Bathurst 2005). Researchers can make inferences about environmental conditions through time and in different locations based on changes in the relative abundance of these life forms. Once researchers reconstruct the past environmental conditions, they can then address whether there are observable changes in the human populations living in the region that might be a function of the shifting environmental conditions.

Environmental Archaeology

Environmental archaeology is distinct from *palaeoecology*. Palaeoecology identifies and explains past ecological phenomena like changes in forest growth or the numbers of types of organisms living in a given location. Environmental archaeology is interested specifically in ecological and climatic conditions of the past as a means for better understanding how various peoples lived—what conditions they lived in and how those conditions affected their lives. While the ultimate goals of these two disciplines are somewhat different, their research tools are similar.

Environmental archaeology employs a number of methods to assess both general and specific ecological conditions in the past. This evidence can be divided into two broad classes: *biotic evidence*, which represents the remains of biological organisms from the past, and *abiotic evidence*, or the remains of chemical components of sediments and their associated landforms. Biotic evidence includes the fossilized remains of bones, shells, seeds, and pollen. Abiotic evidence includes geological structures and the associated processes, soil sediments, and chemical makeup.

Another source of evidence is **palynology**—the study of pollen from different periods. Pollen

---

Diagenesis: chemical changes that occur in materials after deposition in the ground.
Environmental Archaeology: a field of study that is interested specifically in ecological and climatic conditions of the past as a means for better understanding how various peoples lived—what conditions they lived in and how those conditions affected their lives.
Palynology: the study of pollen from archaeological contexts.

can be preserved within sediments and in water-saturated conditions. The relative abundance of different plant species can be inferred from the relative abundance of pollen grains. This will give some indication of vegetative conditions within a given region. If the materials are recovered in a dated stratigraphic context, the analyst can document regional vegetation change over time. Since certain kinds of plants thrive under specific climatic conditions, palynology can offer indirect evidence of the general environmental conditions that existed in the past. Like pollen, phytoliths can also be collected from the soil, artifacts, and human teeth, and analyzed to identify plant species.

Another source of evidence for reconstructing past climatic conditions at a global scale is measuring the ratio of oxygen isotopes. Sea water naturally contains both ^{18}O and the lighter ^{16}O. The lighter ^{16}O evaporates first, and when this water vapour falls as snow, some remains "locked up" as glacial ice in northern latitudes. Thus, the relative abundance of ^{18}O goes up. During warmer periods, less precipitation falls as snow and glacial meltwater returns to the oceans, thereby reducing the relative abundance of ^{18}O. Past isotopic concentrations in sea water cannot be measured directly. Scientists use the fossilized remains of small marine organisms called *foraminifera* to measure these concentrations. Foraminifera absorb oxygen into their skeletal system, and their fossilized remains can be used as a proxy for broad changes in global temperatures.

At McMaster University, Henry Schwarcz engaged in research on beaver teeth to test seasonal changes in the ratio of ^{18}O to ^{16}O precipitation (Stuart-Williams and Schwarcz 1997). Fricke and co-workers traced changes over time in oxygen isotope ratios in the tooth enamel of Inuit and European populations in western Greenland and Denmark (Fricke et al. 1995). The results were consistent with an increasing cool trend in the North Atlantic region from A.D. 1400 to A.D. 1700. This may corroborate the theory that the abandonment of the Viking Greenland settlement was due to environmental stress (Scott et al. 1991; Buckland et al. 1996).

This same process of charting oxygen isotope values can also be used try to understand migration patterns in the past (see Lightfoot and O'Connell 2016). The idea is that people consume water that is local to the region in which they live. Therefore, if they move into a new area, they will have a different isotopic signature in their bones and teeth than those who grew up in the region. For example, Christine White and colleagues have similarly examined oxygen isotope data for understanding residency and geographic origins of peoples at ceremonial sites in ancient Peru (Webb et al. 2013; Toyne et al. 2014) and Mesoamerica (White et al. 2007, 2009). In one study, for example, they observed that there were more non-local individuals in a later sacrificial group, leading them to conclude that there was population mobility from the surrounding areas as the site was socio-politically important as a place of burial (Toyne et al. 2014). Dupras and Schwarcz (2001) used oxygen isotope values to suggest the presence of foreign individuals in the mortality sample excavated from the site in Dakhleh Oasis, Egypt. Similarly, Prowse and colleagues (2007) compared the ^{18}O ratio in teeth from the Imperial Roman site of Portus, and observed that about one-third of the children had signatures outside the range observed in a modern sample. This, they argued, could be explained by migration into the area at a young age by those individuals. For a broader review of isotopic analysis of migration in the Roman world, see Prowse (2016).

Reconstructing Settlement Patterns

Settlement archaeology is concerned with two aspects of human occupation: the distribution of sites across a landscape and the relationship of structures within a community.

We can learn a great deal about a past society from the distribution of archaeological sites, and the relationship of these sites to their surrounding physical environments. The size, organization, and location of buildings and other structures within a

Settlement Archaeology: the study of settlement patterns within the archaeological record.

community reflect the social and political structure of the community. Recognizing this, archaeologists undertake the analysis of settlement patterns to make inferences about past cultures.

Settlement data can tell us about such things as family organization and who performs certain tasks within a household. They can help us to understand the economy of a social group, what resources are important to them, and whether or not people moved during different seasons. They may also reveal clues regarding the different levels of social status, and perhaps even political or religious views within a community. By examining changes over time in the relationship between communities, and structures within communities, a researcher can gain considerable insight about the socio-cultural evolution of a society. For example, Brian Hayden analyzed a series of winter houses at Keatley Creek (about 20 kilometres north of Lillooet on terraces of the Fraser River) in British Columbia. The earliest occupation of the site was around 4800 B.P. (before present era). Hayden's analysis revealed that there was socio-economic variation in wealth between houses between 2400 and 1200 B.P. As well, he found possible evidence for long-term regional resource control by key families (Hayden 1997). In this instance there was one village that contained some huge pit houses that stand out in sharp contrast from other villages in the region. The question is, Why do we see these pit houses developing here at this particular time? Hayden argued that powerful families emerged because they were in a position to strategically control important resources. This in turn led to complex social alliances involving many families. As a result, the Keatley Creek sites provide a model for understanding the transition from small kin-based political systems based on family relationships—as we see in hunter-gatherer groups—to larger, more complex political units under the leadership of powerful chiefs.

Settlement archaeology is also interested in the distribution of sites and communities across the landscape as well as human changes to the landscape (for a discussion of landscape archaeology, see Chapter 14). Cultural ecology has become a central concept in settlement archaeology, and it is based on the notion that settlement distribution patterns are strongly related to local and regional changes in economic, environmental, social, subsistence, and technological factors (Fagan 2000). As an example, annual flooding of river systems might influence the distribution of dwellings or dwelling types within a community situated along a river shore.

A tool that has become established in archaeology over the past few decades is **geographic information system (GIS)** analysis (Allen et al. 1990; Wheatley and Gillings 2002). Andrew Stewart and colleagues (2000) combined archaeological evidence of seasonal site occupation and oral histories regarding caribou crossings, camps, and other places of cultural significance to interpret recent Inuit land use along the lower Kazan River, Nunavut. These researchers employed geographic positioning system (GPS) technology to record individual archaeological features (for example, tent rings, caches) at sites throughout the area. The resulting GIS database showed considerable variation in regional land use, including the types of sites observed and season of occupation (Stewart et al. 2000). GIS techniques can also help us to integrate complex data from a variety of sources. Using a GIS analysis of multiple surface and subsurface surveying techniques, Haskel Greenfield demonstrated distinct but complementary patterns of subsurface conditions at the stratigraphically complex Neolithic site of Blagotin in Serbia (Greenfield 2000).

Archaeological evidence can also shed light on issues of population size and composition (the number of men and women of different ages) in the distant past. Researchers can estimate population size and rates of growth—how fast a population is increasing in size—from settlement data. The size and area of the living site and how many dwellings are present can help the archaeologist to assess how many people were living in an area. As well, the distribution of artifacts and food remains can help the archaeologist to refine estimates. For example,

Geographic Information System (GIS): an integrated software package for the input, analysis, and display of spatial information.

Understanding the relationship within and between dwellings is a major component of settlement archaeology.

the archaeologist can tell the difference between a large dwelling of a single family versus a dwelling housing many families. Finally, ethnohistoric data of population size from recent populations living under similar conditions can serve as models for our estimates from the archaeological record.

However, even when data are available, estimates of population size must often be made through ethnographic analogy. This is a method where the relationship between population size and material remains seen in modern or historic groups is imposed on the archaeological site. One of the major questions that archaeologists have been interested in for many New World (North, South, and Central America) populations is demographic collapse—the drastic decline in population size. What factors led to the demise of entire populations? Can archaeology help us to understand the series of events associated with population collapse, such as that which affected the Maya?

Population collapse has been explored through analyses of *carrying capacity* and *site catchment area*. **Carrying capacity** is the estimated population number and density that a given area of land can support, given the technology used by the people at the time. However, because prehistoric resource patterns are difficult to determine, most studies have focused their efforts on the types and availability of raw resources, and the impact on population structure of changes in resources (Fagan 2000). **Site catchment analysis** is based on the simple assumption that the more dispersed

Carrying Capacity: the estimated population number and density that a given area of land can support, given the technology used by the people at the time.
Site Catchment Analysis: an analysis based on the assumption that the more dispersed resources are from habitation sites, the less likely they are to be exploited by a population.

resources are from habitation sites, the less likely they are to be exploited by a population (Bailey 1981). Of course, the technology, workforce size, and political organization of a population will have an impact on determining the relative "costs" associated with resource exploitation. For example, the benefits of acquiring labour-intensive resources for a large population may outweigh the costs, relative to a small population that would have to invest a greater proportion of their group's labour to acquire a smaller amount of material.

Alternative approaches to examining the relationship between resource availability and population structure have also been explored. Based on dietary trends from palaeopathological and stable isotope analysis, Lori Wright and Christine White argued that there is no evidence to link reduced food resources with the demographic collapse of the Maya civilization (Wright and White 1996). In addition, Katherine Emery and colleagues used stable isotopes to analyze the diet of deer, a common agricultural pest in ancient Mesoamerica, to suggest that ecological decline was not a factor associated with the collapse of the Mayan empire (Emery et al. 2000).

Reconstructing Social Systems

Reconstructing aspects of social systems from the archaeological record is possible by understanding the social context in which material culture accumulates. In addition, the items produced by past peoples can provide information about their social systems. For example, the manufacture of clay pots might include stylistic variations associated with the producer or the producer's family. Jewellery and other items of personal adornment can reflect aspects of self-identity and views of the world. The kinds of foods being consumed may also reflect broad class differences between groups within a society.

One of the major areas of archaeology concerning social status is burials. Human burials and burial practices are an important source of both biological and cultural information for the anthropologist. At the most extravagant, high-status burials like the tombs of pharaohs from ancient Egypt or a Chinese emperor buried with an army of life-sized ceramic soldiers capture the imagination of the public. Burials can reveal information about social status, as well as trade, religion, and economics. As well, burials and mortuary practices reflect the attitudes, values, symbolism, status, and other beliefs held by prehistoric peoples (Noble 1968). **Funerary archaeology**—the study of burials—can reveal information regarding social status, trade networks, population structure, and social organization within the society (Parker Pearson 1999; Gowland and Knüsel 2006). Lewis Binford proposed that increased social complexity resulted in increased variation in burial practices, and that social organization (not necessarily ritual practices or religion) was the primary cause of such variation (Binford 1972). Based on this notion, the more differences in the manner in which individuals were buried (including the type or number of any goods in the grave), the more socially complex and stratified a society was. By following the changing trends in mortuary customs, archaeologists may better understand the changing relationships between various peoples, as well as the changes associated with the influence of Indigenous and foreign cultures through time.

Using carbon isotope analyses of human skeletal remains, Christine White observed differences in the consumption of maize between high-status and low-status individuals. However, these differences are not always consistent. In Belize at the site of Pacbitun, the presence of maize in the diet was associated with high-status individuals, while at the site of Lamanai, maize was associated more with the diet of low-status individuals. White argued that this difference suggests that high-status individuals from Lamanai may have had better diets and greater access to protein than their counterparts at Pacbitun (White and Schwarcz 1989; White et al. 1993). At other Mayan sites like Copán in present-day Honduras, no differences in stable isotope ratios in bones have been detected between different classes (Reed 1994).

Funerary Archaeology: the study of burial customs from archaeological evidence.

Trading Patterns

Most prehistoric populations also engaged in some sort of long-distance trade. This can be inferred by the location of raw materials relative to the location of the produced artifact. Trade can also be inferred by observing the physical composition of the material and whether it was made locally or not. Interdisciplinary research at the University of Manitoba is combining geochemical approaches to the analysis of material sourcing for artifacts for this very purpose. For example, ten Bruggencate and colleagues (2014, 2015) compared lithic sources from chert and quartz quarries with archaeological artifacts to determine how far people travelled to acquire raw materials. Similarly, Hull (Hull and Fayek 2012; Hull et al. 2014) examined turquoise artifacts and their likely material source to make inferences about trade routes and the potential interactions between cultural groups over varying distances. Chia and colleagues (2014) undertook similar studies on obsidian from the Philippines, while Shaw and co-workers (2016) looked at the chemical composition of pottery in Papua New Guinea to posit trade routes in the past. Sometimes very precise chemical techniques are required to determine the specific composition of an item. Regardless, trade is an important part of *cultural diffusion*. Lowie believed that any given cultural trait is derived either from a *cultural antecedent* within the culture or through importing ideas from other foreign populations (Lowie 1988). The latter process, cultural diffusion, has been and continues to be a major area of investigation in the attempt to explain cultural change.

Cultural Change

The sources of all cultural change are discoveries and inventions, which may originate inside or outside a society. However, they do not necessarily lead to social change. If an invention or discovery is ignored, no change in culture results. It is only when society accepts an invention or discovery and uses it regularly that we can begin to speak of cultural change.

Discovery and Invention

The new thing discovered or invented, the *innovation*, may be an object—the wheel, the plow, the computer—or it may involve behaviour and ideas—buying and selling, democracy, monogamy.

One type of invention can be the consequence of a society's setting itself a specific goal, such as eliminating a disease or finding a way to preserve a food. Another type emerges less intentionally. This second process of invention is often referred to as *accidental juxtaposition* or *unconscious invention*. Ralph Linton suggested that some inventions, especially those of prehistoric days, were probably the consequences of literally dozens of tiny initiatives by "unconscious" inventors. These inventors made their small contributions, perhaps over many hundreds of years, without being aware of the part they were playing in bringing one invention, such as the wheel or a better form of hand axe, to completion (Linton 1936). Consider the example of children playing on a fallen log, which rolls as they walk and balance on it, coupled with the need at a given moment to move a slab of granite from a cave face. The children's play may have suggested the use of logs as rollers and thereby set in motion a series of developments that culminated in the wheel.

Some discoveries and inventions arise out of deliberate attempts to produce a new idea or object. It may seem that such innovations are obvious responses to perceived needs. Nevertheless, perceived needs and the economic rewards that may be given to the innovator do not explain why only some people innovate. We know relatively little about why some people are more innovative than others. The ability to innovate may depend in part on individual characteristics such as high intelligence and creativity. And creativity may be influenced by social conditions.

Types of Cultural Diffusion

The source of new cultural elements in a society may be another society. The process by which cultural elements are borrowed from another society and incorporated into the culture of the recipient group is called **diffusion**. Borrowing sometimes enables a group to bypass stages or mistakes in the development of a process or institution. There are three basic patterns of diffusion: *direct contact*, *intermediate contact*, and *stimulus* diffusion.

Direct contact occurs when elements of a society's culture are first taken up by neighbouring societies and then gradually spread farther and farther afield. The spread of the use of paper (a sheet of interlaced fibres) is a good example of extensive diffusion by direct contact. The invention of paper is attributed to Ts'ai Lun in China in A.D. 105. Within 50 years, paper was being made in many places in central China. While the art of papermaking was kept secret for about 500 years, paper was distributed as a commodity to much of the Arab world through the markets at Samarkand. But when Samarkand was attacked by the Chinese in A.D. 751, a Chinese prisoner was forced to set up a paper mill. Paper manufacture then spread to the rest of the Arab world; it was first manufactured in Baghdad in A.D. 793, Egypt about A.D. 900, and Morocco about A.D. 1100. Papermaking was introduced as a commodity in Europe by Arab trade through Italian ports in the 12th century. The Moors built the first European paper mill in Spain in about 1150. The technical knowledge then spread throughout Europe, with paper mills being built in Italy in 1276, France in 1348, Germany in 1390, and England in 1494 (Anonymous 1980; Anonymous 1998). In general, the pattern of accepting the borrowed invention was the same in all cases. Paper was first imported as a luxury, then in ever-expanding quantities as a staple product. Finally, and usually within one to three centuries, local manufacture was begun.

Diffusion by *intermediate contact* occurs through the agency of third parties. Frequently, traders carry a cultural trait from the society where it originated to another group. As an example of diffusion through intermediaries, Phoenician traders spread the idea of our alphabet, which may have been invented by another Semitic group, to Greece. At times, soldiers serve as intermediaries in spreading a cultural trait. European crusaders, such as the Knights Templar and the Knights of St. John, acted as intermediaries in two ways: they carried Christian culture to Muslim societies of North Africa and brought Arab culture back to Europe. In the 19th century, Western missionaries in all parts of the world encouraged peoples to wear Western clothing. The result is that in Africa, the Pacific Islands, and elsewhere, all peoples can be found wearing shorts, suit jackets, shirts, ties, and other typically Western articles of clothing.

In *stimulus diffusion*, knowledge of a trait belonging to another culture stimulates the invention or development of a local equivalent. A classic example of stimulus diffusion is the Cherokee syllabic writing system created by Sequoya, a Cherokee silversmith, so that his people could write down their language. Sequoya got the idea from his contact with Europeans. Yet he did not adopt the English writing system; indeed, he did not even learn to write English. What he did was use some English alphabetic symbols, alter others, and invent new ones. All the symbols he used represented Cherokee syllables and in no way echoed English alphabetic usage. In other words, Sequoya took English alphabetic ideas and gave them a new, Cherokee form. The stimulus originated with Europeans; the result was uniquely Cherokee.

The Selective Nature of Diffusion

Although there is a temptation to view the dynamics of diffusion as similar to a stone sending concentric ripples over still water, this view would be an oversimplification of the way diffusion actually occurs. Not all cultural traits are borrowed as readily as the ones we have mentioned, nor do they usually expand in neat, ever-widening circles. Rather, diffusion is a selective process.

We would expect societies to reject items from other societies that are repugnant to them and we would also expect them to reject ideas and technology that do not satisfy some psychological, social, or cultural need. Diffusion is also selective because

---

Diffusion: the borrowing by one society of a cultural trait belonging to another society as the result of contact between the two societies.

cultural traits differ in the extent to which they can be communicated. Elements of material culture, such as mechanical processes and techniques, and other traits, such as physical sports and the like, are not especially difficult to demonstrate. Consequently, they are accepted or rejected on their merits. But the moment we move out of the material context into the realm of ideas, we encounter real difficulties. For instance, how do you communicate the complex idea of democracy?

Finally, diffusion is selective because the overt form of a particular trait, rather than its function or meaning, frequently seems to determine how the trait will be received. For example, the enthusiasm for bobbed hair (short haircuts) that swept through much of North America in the 1920s never caught on among the Native American women of northwestern California. To many women of European ancestry, short hair was a symbolic statement of their freedom. To these Native American women, who traditionally cut their hair short when in mourning, it was a reminder of death (Foster 1962).

In the process of diffusion, then, we can identify a number of different patterns. Cultural borrowing is selective rather than automatic, and we can describe how a particular borrowed trait has been modified by the recipient culture. However, current knowledge does not allow us to specify when one or another of these outcomes will occur, under what conditions diffusion will occur, and why it occurs the way it does.

Acculturation

On the surface, the process of change called *acculturation* seems to include much of what we have discussed under the label of diffusion, since acculturation refers to the changes that occur when different cultural groups come into intensive contact. As in diffusion, the source of new cultural items is the other society. More often than not, though, the term **acculturation** describes a situation in which one of the societies in contact is much more powerful than the other. Thus, acculturation can be seen as a process of extensive cultural borrowing in the context of an unequal power relationship between societies (Bodley 1990).

External pressure for cultural change can take various forms. In its most direct form—conquest or colonization—the dominant group uses force or the threat of force to bring about cultural change in the other group. For example, in the Spanish conquest of Mexico, the conquerors forced many of the Indigenous groups to accept Roman Catholicism. Although such direct force is not always exerted in conquest situations, dominated peoples often have little choice but to change. Examples of such indirectly forced change abound in the history of Aboriginal peoples in Canada. A strong European missionary movement led to many Indigenous communities being forced to adopt non-religious aspects of Euro-Canadian culture. After Confederation, the federal government displaced many Indigenous populations from their lands, and obliged them to give up many aspects of their traditional ways of life, language, and cultures. Indigenous children were required to go to residential schools, which taught the dominant society's values. In order to survive, they had no choice but to adopt many of the dominant society's traits.

A subordinate society may acculturate to a dominant society even in the absence of direct or indirect force. The dominated people may elect to adopt cultural elements from the dominant society in order to survive in their changed world. Or, perceiving that members of the dominant society enjoy more secure living conditions, the dominated people may identify with the dominant culture in the hope that by doing so they will be able to share some of its benefits. For example, in some Arctic areas Inuit and Sami groups seemed eager to replace dogsleds with snowmobiles without any coercion (Pelto and Miller-Wille 1987).

In the following chapters, we will see how the interpretation and reconstruction techniques outlined in this chapter have been applied to tracing the evolution of humans.

Acculturation: the process of extensive borrowing of aspects of culture.

SUMMARY AND REVIEW

ANALYZING ARTIFACTS

3.1 Describe the different ways that we can analyze artifacts.

- Many artifacts will require conservation, in order to prevent them from further decaying, or reconstruction to put the pieces back together.
- The interpretation of past lifeways involves interpreting a wide range of data recovered from archaeological sites.
- Archaeologists will often study the form of an artifact, including through measurement, and try to understand how it was made.
- Archaeologists want to understand how an artifact functioned in the past in order to help understand issues of the human condition in the past.
- Many related disciplines provide data to help reconstruct past ecological conditions (environmental archaeology), diet (palaeonutrition), disease (palaeopathology), settlement patterns, socio-economic status, and resource distribution and allocation (political ecology).

What are typologies and what kinds of information can they provide about artifacts?

ANALYZING HUMAN REMAINS

3.2 Describe the different ways that we can analyze human remains.

- Osteology, or human skeletal biology, is a specialized sub-discipline of physical anthropology that deals with the biological remains of humans from past populations.
- Skeletal biologists use human remains to learn about the size, composition, and health of past populations. Palaeodemography is the study of the demographic structure and population processes of the past. Palaeopathology seeks to answer questions about the appearance, prevalence, and spread of diseases in past populations.

How can age be estimated from skeletal remains of children and adults?

RECONSTRUCTING PAST DIETS

3.3 Describe the different approaches to reconstructing diet in the past.

- The only direct evidence of what people ate in the past is preserved remains of food itself, such as food preserved in the stomach of a mummy, coprolites (fossilized feces), or extremely rare cases of preservation like the food at Pompeii.
- More often, past diet is studied through indirect evidence. What people ate in the past can explored from a variety of indirect sources: through animal remains (zooarchaeology), plant remains (palaeoethnobotany), stable isotopes, trace elements, and experimental archaeology.
- Unlike the study of animals and plants, stable isotope and trace element studies explore the biochemical evidence of diet using human and animal skeletal remains, and experimental archaeology examines how people used tools to process foods by matching wear patterns and organic residues on ancient tools with those on experimental ones.

How do the different photosynthetic pathways of plants aid in dietary reconstruction from skeletal samples?

RECONSTRUCTING PAST ENVIRONMENTS

3.4 Explain how archaeologists reconstruct past environments.

- Environmental archaeology reconstructs ecological climatic conditions of the past to better understand how people interacted with and were influenced by the environment.
- The study of past environments is concerned with both local and global environmental

conditions. Local conditions can be studied by reconstructing past vegetation through the study of pollen (palynology) and general conditions through the study of isotopic data, such as changes in temperature and rainfall conditions provided by the study of oxygen isotopes in ice cores.

- Geoarchaeology, a branch of environmental archaeology, is specifically concerned with the effects of changing climate on the terrain where archaeological sites are found.

How can oxygen isotopes be used to reconstruct past climatic conditions?

RECONSTRUCTING SETTLEMENT PATTERNS

3.5 Explain how archaeologists reconstruct past settlement patterns.

- Settlement archaeology is concerned with the distribution of sites across a landscape and the relationship structures in past communities.
- Settlement data can tell us about how many people lived at settlements, how families and larger social groups were organized, who performed different tasks in past communities, and the beliefs, values, and attitudes of people.
- Settlement archaeology is also concerned with how people lived on landscapes—the resources they used, and whether they moved often or lived a settled life.

What is population collapse? How is it studied in an archaeological context?

RECONSTRUCTING SOCIAL SYSTEMS

3.6 Explain how archaeologists study social systems.

- Reconstructing social systems also involves the study of burials because they can reveal much about social relations, beliefs, and how people interacted with other communities. Artifacts in settlements and burials provide evidence for exchange and trade among populations.

How can trade in prehistoric populations be inferred?

CULTURAL CHANGE

3.7 Explain the sources and processes of cultural change.

- Culture is always changing. Discoveries and inventions are the main sources of change.
- The process by which elements of culture are borrowed from one society and incorporated into another is called *diffusion*. This is a selective process, and it does not occur automatically. Often, people have a choice in what they borrow and what they do not.
- People do not always have a choice. When contact between two societies involves one being more powerful than the other, the dominant society can exert pressure on the subordinate society to adopt cultural changes. This is called *acculturation*.

What are the three basic patterns of cultural diffusion? How does each occur?

THINK ON IT

1. How do you think that cultural views of the past affect archaeological research in different societies?

2. Imagine you are an archaeologist in the future excavating your present-day apartment. What kinds of artifacts might you uncover? How would you analyze those artifacts and what would you be able to infer from them?

3. Anthropology is a holistic science, yet research is becoming increasingly specialized. How do you think this affects the way in which anthropologists are trained to do research?

4. For various levels of interpretation, different assumptions are made by anthropologists. What are these assumptions, and why do you think they are valid or not valid?

Part III Biological Evolution

Historical Development of Evolutionary Theory

4

Michael Willmer Forbes Tweedie/Science Source

LEARNING OBJECTIVES

4.1 Review the early thinkers who shaped the theory of evolution. Explain the contributions of both biological and geological views to the theory of evolution.

4.2 Explain the principles of natural selection.

4.3 Describe how new species emerge.

Astronomers estimate that the universe has been in existence for some 15 billion years, plus or minus a few billion. To make this awesome period of time more understandable, Carl Sagan devised a calendar that condenses this span into a single year (Sagan 1975). Sagan used as a scale 24 days for every 1 billion years and 1 second for every 475 years. This meant that if the "Big Bang," or beginning of the universe, occurred on January 1, for example, the Milky Way was formed on May 1.

Galaxies began to form as the universe cooled. By 4.5 billion years ago, our sun was formed, and the earth took shape shortly after that. Around 4 billion years ago, organic molecules existed on earth in the form of amino acids. Shortly thereafter, around 3.6 billion years ago, evidence for the first signs of life—bacteria-like organisms—is observable in the fossil record (Lopuchin 1975; Mojzsis et al. 1996; Schopf 2000). In Sagan's scheme, September 9 marks the beginning of our solar system, and September 25 the origin of life on earth.

It was originally assumed that life had evolved *in situ* on earth—the idea that life emerged from a primordial soup. However, the appearance of bacteria nearly 4 billion years ago creates a problem for this theory. It does not allow enough time between the formation of the earth and the first signs of life for the evolution of these first organisms. As a result, alternative theories have begun to emerge. One of these is that space provided the crucial chemical ingredients for life, and that bacteria from interstellar dust or even Mars was delivered to earth by way of asteroids and meteorites. This theory received heightened attention in 1996 with the announcement by NASA scientists that they had found possible evidence for fossil bacteria on Mars (see Figure 4–1).

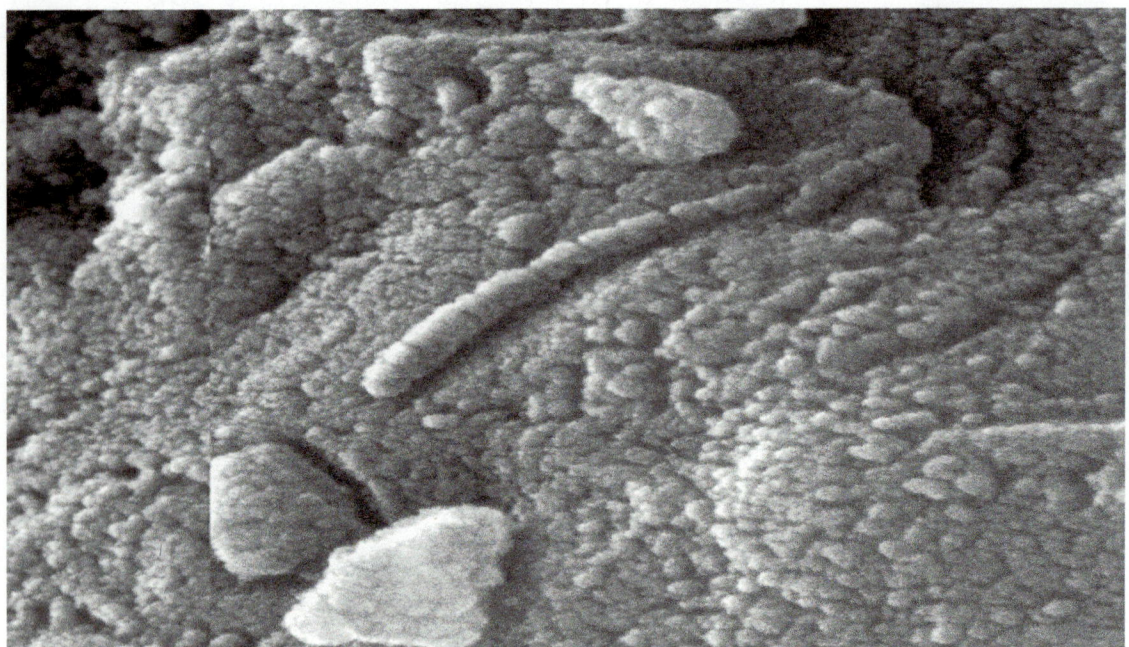

Figure 4–1 Life from Mars

This high-resolution scanning electron microscope image shows an unusual tube-like form that in size is less than 1/100th the width of a human hair. It was found in a 4.5-billion-year-old rock believed to have once been a part of Mars. This structure is suggested to be fossil evidence that primitive life may have existed on Mars more than 3.6 billion years ago. The rock is a portion of a meteorite that was dislodged from Mars by a huge impact about 16 million years ago and that fell to earth in Antarctica 13 000 years ago. The meteorite was found in Allan Hills icefield, Antarctica, by an annual expedition of the National Science Foundation's Antarctic Meteorite Program in 1984.

Source: SETI League photograph—used by permission, www.setileague.org.

Regardless of the origin of bacteria on earth, these early single-celled organisms photosynthesized; that is, they were able to make nutrients from water, sunlight, and carbon dioxide, a process from which oxygen is a by-product. As a result, by about 1.8 billion years ago an oxygen-rich atmosphere existed on earth, and soon afterward oxygen-using organisms evolved (Fortey 1999; Fry 2000). Around 1.7 billion years ago the first multicellular organisms appeared. At 1 billion years ago, organisms appeared that employed sexual reproduction strategies, that is, combining the genetic material from two parents. This is a key facet for the evolution of life, since for the first time natural selection had greater variation on which to act.

By 570 million years ago, at the beginning of the Cambrian period, a variety of complex organisms existed on the earth, starting with worms and jellyfish and later hard-shelled organisms. Sixty million years later the first organisms with internal skeletal structure evolved (*vertebrates*), and around 425 million years ago, plants and insects evolved on land and fish in the sea (Fortey 1999; Fry 2000). By 350 million years ago the first reptiles had emerged. By about 150 million years ago there was a proliferation of three major vertebrate groups: fish, amphibians, and reptiles. Reptiles showed evolutionary changes when compared with their amphibian ancestors, including the development of amniotic eggs for reproduction. This reflects a major **adaptation** (traits that increase the chances of surviving and leaving offspring that will survive) to terrestrial life (Fortey 1999; Fry 2000). Soon mammal-like reptiles appeared, and eventually we see the rise of mammals around 65 million years ago.

Mammals have a number of advantages over reptiles. They are warm-blooded, allowing them to live in a wider range of environments; have increased intelligence compared with reptiles; and have placental reproduction and an extended post-partum developmental period, both of which allow for increased brain development (Fortey 1999; Fry 2000). With the extinction of many reptiles around 65 million years ago, mammals had a variety of new evolutionary niches in which to adapt. The result was the rapid diversification, expansion, and proliferation of mammals into new and relatively unoccupied habitats.

Some 55 million to 65 million years ago, the first primates appeared. They were ancestral to all living primates, such as lemurs, monkeys, apes, and humans. The earliest primates may or may not have lived in trees, but they had flexible digits and could grasp things. Later, about 35 million years ago, the first monkeys and apes appeared. About 15 million years ago, some 20 million years after the appearance of monkeys and apes, the immediate ape-like ancestors of humans probably emerged. About 4 million years ago the first human-like beings appeared. Modern-looking humans evolved only about 100 000 years ago.

Using Sagan's scheme it was 10:30 in the evening of December 31 when the first human-like primates appear. Human-like beings have been around for only about 90 minutes out of Sagan's 12-month period! In this book we are concerned with what happened in those last few hours of that year.

How do we account for the biological and cultural evolution of humans? The details of the emergence of primates and the evolution of humans and their cultures are covered in subsequent chapters of this book. In this chapter we discuss the general evolution of life, and the historical development of ideas for understanding these changes, especially as relevant to humans. In Chapter 5 we will discuss more specifically the modern theory of evolution.

The Evolution of Evolution

Views from Biology

In the 19th century, Western ideas about forms of life on earth were very different from **Charles Darwin**'s *theory of evolution*, which suggested that

---

Adaptation: changes to biology or behaviour that increase the chances of surviving and leaving viable offspring in a new environment.

Darwin, Charles (1809–82): a British naturalist who proposed the theory of evolution by natural selection. Most people equate the theory of evolution with Darwin because of the historical controversy his theory created at the time.

different species developed one from another over long periods of time. In the fourth century B.C., the Greek philosophers Plato and Aristotle stated that animals and plants formed a single, graded continuum moving increasingly toward perfection. For Plato, who was a student and follower of Socrates, variation in animals had no meaning—only the essence of an organism mattered. Aristotle was trained first in medicine before he was sent to Athens in 367 B.C. to study philosophy with Plato. Aristotle's classification of animals grouped those with similar characters into *genera* and then distinguished subgroups of *species* within the genera. Humans, of course, were the species at the top of this scale.

Later Greek philosophers added the idea that the creator gave life or "radiance" first to humans, but at each subsequent creation some of that essence was lost (Lovejoy 1964). Macrobius, summarizing the thinking of Plotinus, used an image that was to persist for centuries, the image of what came to be called the "chain of being": "The attentive observer will discover a connection of parts, from the Supreme God down to the last dregs of things, mutually linked together and without a break. This is Homer's golden chain, which God, he says, bade hand down from heaven to earth" (Lovejoy 1964:63). Belief in the chain of being was accompanied by the conviction that an animal or plant species could not become extinct. In fact, all things were linked to each other in a chain, and all links were necessary. Moreover, the notion of extinction threatened people's trust in a supreme being; it was unthinkable that a whole group of these creations could simply disappear.

The idea of the chain of being persisted through the years, but it was not discussed extensively by philosophers, scientists, poets, and theologians until the 18th century (Lovejoy 1964). Those discussions prepared the way for *evolutionary theory*. It is ironic that, although the chain of being did not allow for evolution, its idea that there was an order of things in nature encouraged studies of natural history and comparative anatomical studies, which stimulated the development of the idea of evolution. People were also now motivated to look for previously unknown creatures. Moreover, humans were not shocked when naturalists suggested that humans were close to apes. This notion was perfectly consistent with the idea of a chain of being; apes were simply thought to have been created with less perfection.

Early in the 18th century, an influential scientist, **Carolus Linnaeus** (1707–78), looked at the similarities and differences among organisms and created a system that is still in use today for naming, ranking, and classifying organisms. This system defined the fundamentals of biology in terms of nomenclature and classification, from *kingdom* to *class*, *order*, **genus**, and *species*. Part of Linnaeus's innovation was the grouping of genera into higher groups, or *taxa*, that were also based on shared similarities. Thus, the kingdom Animalia contained the class Vertebrata, which in turn contained the order Primates. This order was further divided into genus and species, so that Primates contained the genus *Homo* with the species *sapiens*—or modern humans. The Linnaean classification scheme is hierarchical, and categories are based on inclusive traits—those at the top (kingdom) being the most inclusive, and those at the bottom (species) the least inclusive. Each category contains groups of related organisms that share common traits. Linnaeus's classification, or *systema naturae*, placed humans in the same order (Primates) as apes and monkeys. Linnaeus did not suggest an evolutionary relationship between humans and apes; he seems to have accepted the notion that all species were created by God and fixed in their form. Not surprisingly, then, Linnaeus is often viewed as an anti-evolutionist. However, Linnaeus's hierarchical classification scheme provided a framework for the idea that humans, apes, and monkeys had a common ancestor (Eiseley 1970; Mayr 1982). (See Figure 4–2.)

Linnaeus, Carolus (1707–78): a Swedish naturalist who looked at the similarities and differences among organisms and created a system for naming, ranking, and classifying organisms that is still in use today. This system defined the fundamentals of biology in terms of nomenclature and classification.

Genus: a group of related species; pl., *genera*.

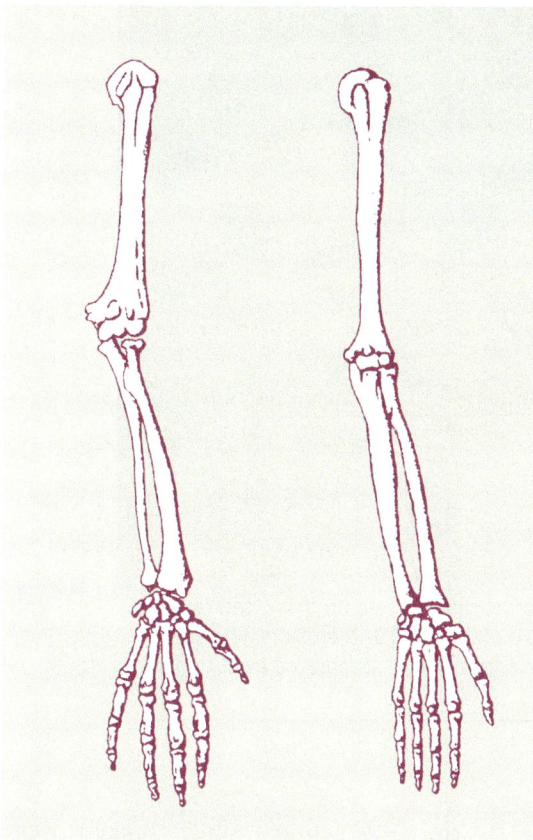

Figure 4–2 Chimpanzee and Human Upper Limbs

The idea that chimpanzees and humans descend from a common ancestor is suggested by anatomical similarities, such as in their forelimbs. Chimpanzee forelimb skeleton (left); human forelimb skeleton (right).

Others did not believe that species were fixed in their form. According to the French naturalist **Jean-Baptiste Lamarck** (1744–1829), acquired characteristics could be inherited, and therefore species could evolve; individuals who in their lifetime developed characteristics helpful to survival would pass those characteristics on to future generations, thereby changing the physical makeup of the species, a process that became known as the theory of **acquired inheritance**. Lamarck argued that the lower forms of life arise continually from inanimate matter by spontaneous creation, and progress inevitably toward greater complexity and perfection by "powers conferred by the supreme author of all things"—that is, by an inherent tendency toward complexity (Jordanova 1984; Bowler 1989). This evolutionary progress was guided by changing environments that altered the needs of organisms. For example, Lamarck explained that the long neck of the giraffe was the result of successive generations of giraffes stretching their necks to reach the high leaves of trees. The stretched muscles and bones of the necks were somehow transmitted to the offspring of the neck-stretching giraffes, and eventually all giraffes came to have long necks.

Lamarck was the first uncompromising advocate of a theory of evolution, and one of the first to try to provide a mechanism to explain this process. Lamarck also argued that evolution was progressive. One should note, however, that while the mechanism proposed by Lamarck is different from Charles Darwin's theory of evolution (discussed later in this chapter), the predictions are the same. But because Lamarck and later biologists failed to produce evidence to support the hypothesis that acquired characters can be inherited, this explanation of evolution was generally dismissed (Mayr 1982). Nevertheless, our current understanding of the impact of the environment on the modern genome, an area referred to as *epigenetics*, does suggest that "choice, behaviour, lifestyle and the external conditions could modify the genome and alter its activity by adding an additional biochemical dimension 'on top' of it, without changing the DNA sequence itself" (Gadjev 2015:245). So perhaps Lamarck wasn't as far off as history has suggested.

Lamarck, Jean-Baptiste (1744–1829): a French naturalist who proposed a theory of evolution through the inheritance of acquired characteristics.

Acquired Inheritance: a theory proposed in the late 18th century that acquired characteristics could be inherited and therefore species could evolve. Individuals who in their lifetime developed characteristics helpful to survival would pass those characteristics on to future generations, thereby changing the physical makeup of the species.

The history of the earth and the plant and animal forms that evolved on it is often revealed to us by rock formations that become visible because of uplifting and erosion. The emergence of geology—the study of the earth's structure and history—stimulated evolutionary thinking.

Views from Geology

One of the major components in the development of the whole idea of evolution was an understanding of how old the earth actually was. For most people in Western societies this understanding came from direct interpretation of the Bible, which made the earth relatively young. One of the earliest Western attempts at quantifying the earth's age was undertaken by Archbishop James Ussher, an Irish cleric who in 1650, referring to biblical events, calculated that the world was created in 4004 B.C. His result was based on simple mathematics and a thorough historical analysis of the events as detailed in the Bible.

The study of natural sciences emerged in the period of the 17th through to the 19th centuries. Most natural scientists then believed that natural catastrophes such as floods, volcanic eruptions, and earthquakes accounted for the variety of layers of rock that they observed. **Catastrophism**, as the theory became known, argued that the world changed over time by a series of divine catastrophic events like Noah's flood.

By the 19th century, some thinkers were beginning to accept the theory of evolution, while others sought to refute it (Mayr 1972). For example, Georges Cuvier (1769–1832) was a leading opponent of evolution. Cuvier, an anatomist who is considered one of the founders of the field of palaeontology, observed that different strata of sedimentary rock contained different kinds of fossils.

He supported the notion that changes in the animal world could be attributed to catastrophes that had destroyed whole populations of living things. Cuvier's theory of catastrophism proposed that a quick series of catastrophes accounted for changes in the earth and the fossil record. Cataclysms and upheavals such as Noah's flood had killed off previous sets of living creatures, which after each period of devastation were replaced by new creations.

Catastrophism: the theory that the earth was shaped by a serious of catastrophic events including volcanic eruptions, floods, hurricanes, etc. It preceded later theories to explain evolutionary changes.

Opponents to the catastrophist view slowly emerged, as geologists observed more slow-acting processes such as erosion by wind or water. They believed that these gradual processes, rather than natural catastrophes, accounted for changes over time. In the late 17th century, the Reverend Thomas Burnet believed the condition of the earth could be explained by the slow-acting processes of erosion by ice, wind, and water. Burnet still concluded that the earth was very young, arguing that if the earth were ancient, the process of erosion would have already worn away the greatest of mountains.

At the same time, a contemporary of Burnet, Robert Hooke, an English natural scientist, became interested in fossils. Up until this time, most natural scientists believed fossils were "tricks of nature." However, Hooke interpreted fossils as the remains of plants and animals that no longer existed, believing that these organisms became extinct as the earth changed. He thought that these changes included both catastrophes and slow-acting processes, but like Burnet, Hooke also thought the earth was very young because there was no historical record of fossilization in the ancient documents of China and Egypt. He did not realize, of course, how long the process of fossilization took.

In 1774, Georges Buffon (1707–88), a French natural scientist, published *A Natural History*, in which he proposed the notion of **uniformitarianism**. This was the idea that repeated uniform processes, such as rivers cutting channels, and wind and rain eroding mountains, operated throughout time. Shortly after, James Hutton (1726–97), a Scottish geologist, published *The History of the Earth*, in which he advanced the notion of studying the uniform, slow-acting processes of erosion to estimate the age of earth, and argued that using this measurement the earth was at least a few hundred thousand years old.

Uniformitarianism: the concept that processes in the past must have behaved in the same manner as they are observed to behave today, and will do so in the future. This is an assumption that is often applied to geological processes (e.g., erosion) or biological processes (e.g., interaction of mortality and fertility).

Major changes in geological thinking occurred in the 19th century. In contrast to Hutton's work, which was largely ignored, English geologist Sir Charles Lyell's (1797–1875) volumes of the *Principles of Geology*, published from 1830 to 1833, built on Hutton's earlier work and received immediate acclaim. The concept of uniformitarianism suggested that the earth is constantly being shaped and reshaped by natural forces that have operated over vast periods of time. By examining specific geological data, Lyell estimated the age of specific features of the earth, such as the Mississippi delta. Since the rate of silt deposition and the total size of the existing deposit at the delta could be measured or estimated, Lyell argued that the amount of time required for the delta to form could be calculated. Using this method of calculation, Lyell estimated the age of the delta to be 100 000 years (Lyell 1863). Ultimately, Lyell was proven incorrect, but his thinking represented the first step toward an understanding of the real antiquity of the earth. Lyell also discussed the formation of geological strata and palaeontology. He used fossilized fauna to define different geological epochs. Lyell's works were read avidly by Charles Darwin before Darwin's now-famous voyage on the *Beagle*. The two corresponded and subsequently became friends.

Many people in Western society were shocked by the implications of the works of Hutton and Lyell. However, when a 19th-century Scottish theologian and mathematician, Thomas Chalmers (1780–1847), the first Moderator of the Free Church of Scotland, accepted the principle of uniformitarianism, other scientists soon followed suit. After studying changes in plants, fossilized remains of animals, and varieties of domestic and wild pigeons, Charles Darwin (1809–82) rejected the notion that each species was created in a fixed form all at one time in the history of earth. The results of his investigations pointed clearly, he thought, to the evolution of species through the mechanism of *natural selection*. While Darwin was completing his book on the subject, Lyell sent him a manuscript by Alfred Russel Wallace (1823–1913), a naturalist who had independently reached conclusions about the evolution of species that matched Darwin's own (Wallace 1858). In 1858, the two men presented the astonishing theory of natural selection to their colleagues at a meeting of the Linnaean Society of London (Mayr 1982).

Both Darwin and Wallace observed that there was individual variation in appearance within a species. Lamarck's theory of acquired inheritance did not support such variation within a species since it predicted that eventually all organisms would adapt to the same form in the same environment. Expanding on Linnaeus's inference that similarities and differences among organisms represented biological relationships, they suggested that these relationships were the result of descent from previous similar organisms. Both Darwin and Wallace concluded that all species descended from other species.

In 1859, when Darwin published *The Origin of Species by Means of Natural Selection*, he wrote, "I am fully convinced that species are not immutable; but that those belonging to what are called the same genera are lineal descendants of some other and generally extinct species, in the same manner as the acknowledged varieties of any one species" (Darwin 1859:6). His conclusions outraged those who believed in the biblical account of creation, and the result was years of bitter controversy.

The major contributions of Darwin's work were that evolution has no direction and that selection acts on existing variation. Populations of species in different environments may have different selective pressures. Therefore, if such pressures select certain traits over very long periods, the populations may become so distinct as to become separate species. The idea of **natural selection** was that nature selects from existing variation those species best adapted to their environment and which will therefore have the greatest chance of surviving and reproducing successfully.

Natural Selection: the outcome of processes that affect the frequencies of traits in a particular environment. Traits that enhance survival and reproductive success increase in frequency over time.

In 1871 Darwin published *The Descent of Man and Selection in Relation to Sex*, in which he proposed that humanity was derived from an animal related to the progenitors of the orangutan, chimpanzee, and gorilla. In this work he also developed his important supplementary theory of sexual selection. Until then, Darwin avoided stating categorically that humans were descended from non-human forms, but the implications of his theory were clear. Controversy immediately ensued, with passionate advocates for each side. In June 1860, at the annual meeting of the British Association for the Advancement of Science, Bishop Wilberforce, representing the biblical view of creation, saw an opportunity to attack the Darwinists. Concluding his speech, he faced Thomas Huxley, one of the Darwinists' chief advocates, and inquired, "Was it through his grandfather or his grandmother that he claimed descent from a monkey?" Huxley responded,

> If . . . the question is put to me would I rather have a miserable ape for a grandfather than a man highly endowed by nature and possessing great means and influence and yet who employs those faculties and that influence for the mere purpose of introducing ridicule into a grave scientific discussion—I unhesitatingly affirm my preference for the ape.

At the same time as a theory of evolution began to develop, scientists began to explore cultural theories to explain the evolution of "civilization." During the mid-19th century, the discovery of stone tools prompted investigations into the origins of these items. In 1847, Jacques Boucher de Perthes published some of the earliest archaeological evidence for the association of human artifacts (chipped stone tools) and extinct animals that had been found together in a quarry (Bahn 1999). Forty years earlier, C.J. Thomsen (1788–1865), a Danish archaeologist and scholar, had published his idea that the development of civilization should be divided into three ages—the Stone Age, the Bronze Age, and the Iron Age (Bahn 1999). The validity of this model was later demonstrated in 1843. His colleague and successor at the Museum of Denmark, Jens Jacob Asmussen Worsaae (1821–85), whose

A 19th-century cartoon shows Charles Darwin with the body of a monkey while revealing the physical similarities between monkeys and humans.

structures and functions. Spencer believed that the level of evolution of a society was based on its structural differences from other societies (Bohannan and Glazer 1988).

One of the first cultural evolutionists, Edward Burnett Tylor (1832–1917), published *Primitive Culture* in 1871, in which he argued that the presence of what Western thinkers at the time considered "primitive societies" could be explained in one of two ways: either all cultures were created at an equal level and primitive societies represented degeneration, or modern societies developed over a very long period from an initial state of barbarism in which, for some reason, primitive societies remained. Tylor rejected the former explanation (Bohannan and Glazer 1988).

Lewis Henry Morgan (1818–81) was an American anthropologist who followed Tylor's explanation of cultural evolution. In 1877 he published *Ancient Society*, arguing that cultures passed through three stages from savagery to barbarism, and then to civilization. Morgan suggested that cultures could remain in certain stages if key inventions or innovations such as the bow and arrow, domestication, or iron smelting were not made (Bohannan and Glazer 1988). Both Tylor and Morgan, like their biological counterparts Linnaeus and Lamarck, believed that cultural evolution was unilinear—that all cultures passed through the same stages of technological innovation and cultural complexity.

By the early 19th century, a number of scholars began to challenge these notions of cultural evolution. Franz Boas (1858–1942) introduced the notion of **cultural relativism**—the idea that all societies are equal and comparable (Bohannan and Glazer 1988). There are no superior or inferior societies, and as a result, it is not possible to order cultures in an evolutionary scheme. Robert H. Lowie (1883–1957) also rejected Morgan's scheme for the evolution of society. He argued that diffusion or cultural contact was important

excavations uncovered stone tools in archaeological layers below bronze and iron tools, led to the widespread acceptance of Thomsen's system throughout Europe in the mid-19th century.

Herbert Spencer (1820–1903) borrowed the biological model of an organism for explaining changes in society. He believed that society was like a biological organism, being a system of

> **Cultural Relativism:** the attitude that a society's customs and ideas should be viewed within the context of that society's problems and opportunities.

for cultural development—borrowing ideas was always easier than originating ideas—and that both simple and complex societies participated in the exchange of ideas (Bohannan and Glazer 1988). Marshall D. Sahlins suggested that both biological and cultural evolution move in two directions at the same time, producing diversity and progress. He defined *diversity* as meaning adaptive changes that resulted in new forms from old forms, and *progress* as referring to the fact that evolution creates more complex forms (Bohannan and Glazer 1988).

The Principles of Natural Selection

Darwin was not the first person to view the creation of new species in evolutionary terms, but he was the first to provide a comprehensive, well-documented explanation—natural selection—for the way evolution had occurred. Natural selection is the main process that increases the frequency of **adaptive traits** through time. The operation of natural selection involves three conditions or principles (Brandon 1990). The first is **variation**: every species is composed of a great variety of individuals, some of which are better adapted to their environment than others. The existence of variety is important. Without it, natural selection has nothing on which to operate; without variation, one kind of characteristic could not be favoured over another. The second principle of natural selection is **heritability**: offspring inherit traits from their parents, at least to some degree and in some way. The third principle of natural selection is **differential reproductive success**: since better-adapted individuals generally produce more offspring over the generations than the less well adapted, the frequency of adaptive traits gradually increases in subsequent generations. A new species emerges when changes in traits or geographic barriers result in the reproductive isolation of the population.

When we say that certain traits are adaptive or advantageous, we mean that they result in greater reproductive success in a particular environment. The term *particular environment* is very important. Even though a species may become more adapted to a particular environment over time, we cannot say that one species adapted to its environment is "better" than another species adapted to a different environment. For example, we may like to think of ourselves as "better" than other animals, but humans are clearly less adapted than fish for living under water, bats for catching flying insects, or raccoons for living on suburban garbage. Because Darwinian evolution is not premeditated, the product of evolution is about being in the right place at the right time.

If certain kinds of variation are not selected for in one environment, then a species might follow a different evolutionary path than it would have if it had been in a different environment at that time. Similarly, if there is no adaptive variation within a species, it may have difficulty surviving a specific environment, and may run the risk of becoming extinct. To illustrate this point, consider that if there had not been a global catastrophic event in the form of a meteor impact that led to the extinction of the dinosaurs 65 million years ago, primates, including humans, might never have evolved. The presence of a group of dinosaurs that had some of the key morphological features we claim were important to human evolution—opposable digits, stereoscopic vision, and a large brain—led palaeontologist Dale Russell to propose in 1982 how dinosaurs may have evolved had they not become extinct (Russell and Séguin 1982). The earth would have been a very different place were it not for small mammals being in the right place at the right time.

Adaptive Trait: a trait that enhances survival and reproductive success in a particular environment. Usually applied to biological evolution, the term is also often used by cultural anthropologists to refer to cultural traits that enhance reproductive success.
Variation: differences in the genotype and phenotype of individual members of a species.
Heritability: the concept that traits are inherited from parent to offspring.
Differential Reproductive Success: differences in the chances of an organism surviving and leaving offspring that will also survive.

The giraffe's long neck is adaptive for eating tree leaves high off the ground. When food is scarce, longer-necked giraffes would get more food and reproduce more successfully than shorter-necked giraffes; in this environment, natural selection would favour giraffes with longer necks.

Although the theory of natural selection suggests that disadvantageous or maladaptive traits will generally decline in frequency or even disappear eventually, it does not necessarily follow that all such traits will do so. After all, species derive from prior forms that have certain structures. This means that not all changes are possible; it also means that some traits are linked to others that might have advantages that outweigh disadvantages. Choking may be very maladaptive for any animal, yet all vertebrates are capable of choking because their digestive and respiratory systems converge in the throat. This trait is a genetic legacy, probably from the time when the respiratory system developed from tissue in the digestive system of some ancestral organism. Apparently, the propensity to choke has not been evolutionarily correctable (Williams 1992).

Changes in a species can be expected to occur as the environment changes or as some members of the species move into a new environment. With environmental change, different traits become adaptive. The members of the species that possess the more adaptive traits will become more numerous, whereas those members whose characteristics make continued existence more difficult or impossible in the modified environment will eventually become extinct.

Consider how the theory of natural selection would explain why giraffes became long-necked. Originally, the necks of giraffes varied in length, as happens with virtually any physical characteristic in a population. During a period when food was scarce, those giraffes with longer necks that could reach higher tree leaves might be better able to survive and suckle their offspring, and thus they would leave more offspring than shorter-necked giraffes. Because of heredity, the offspring of long-necked giraffes are more likely to have long necks. Eventually, the shorter-necked giraffes would diminish in number and the longer-necked giraffes would increase. The resulting population of giraffes would still have variation in neck length but on the average would be longer-necked than earlier forms.

Natural selection does not account for all variation in the frequencies of traits. In particular, it does not account for variation in the frequencies of neutral traits—that is, those traits that do not seem to confer any advantages or disadvantages on their carriers. Changes in the frequencies of neutral traits may result rather from random processes that affect *gene frequencies* in isolated populations (*genetic drift*) or from matings between populations (*gene flow*). We discuss these other processes in Chapter 5.

The Origin of Species

One of the most controversial aspects of Darwin's theory was the suggestion that one species could, over time, evolve into another. A **species** is a

Species: a population that consists of organisms able to interbreed and produce fertile and viable offspring.

population that consists of organisms able to interbreed and produce fertile and viable offspring. In general, individuals from one species cannot successfully mate with members of a different species because of genetic and behavioural differences. If members of different species did mate, it is unlikely that eggs would be fertilized or, if they were, that the embryos would survive. If offspring were born, they would soon die or be infertile. So how could one species evolve into another? What is the explanation for the differentiation? How does one group of organisms become so unlike another group with the same ancestry that it forms a totally new species?

Speciation, or the development of a new species, may occur if one subgroup of a species finds itself in a radically different environment. In adapting to their separate environments, the two populations may undergo enough genetic changes to prevent them from interbreeding should they renew contact. Numerous factors can prevent the exchange of genes. Two species living in the same area may breed at different times of the year, or their behaviour during breeding—their courtship rituals—may be distinct. The difference in body structure of closely related forms may in itself bar interbreeding. Geographic barriers may be the most common barriers to interbreeding.

Once species differentiation does occur, the evolutionary process cannot be reversed; the new species can no longer mate with other species related to its parent population. Humans and gorillas, for example, have the same distant ancestors, but their evolutionary paths have diverged irreversibly.

Observed Examples of Evolution

Since the process of evolution may involve nearly imperceptible gradations over generations, it is usually difficult to observe directly. Nevertheless, because some life forms reproduce rapidly, some examples of natural selection have been observed over relatively short periods in changing environments. For example, scientists think they have observed natural selection in action in British moths. In 1850, a moth that was mostly black was spotted for the first time in Manchester. That was quite unusual, for most of that species of moth were speckled grey. A century later, 95 percent of the moths in industrial parts of Britain were black; only in the rural areas were the moths mostly grey. How is this to be explained? It seems that in the rural areas, the grey-speckled moth is hard to spot by bird predators against the lichen growing on the bark of trees. In industrial areas, though, lichen is killed by pollution. The grey-speckled moths, formerly well adapted to blend into their environment, became clearly visible against the darker background of the lichen-free trees and were easier prey for birds. In contrast, the black moths, which previously would have had a disadvantage against the lighter bark, were now better adapted for survival. Their dark colour was an advantage, and subsequently the darker moths became the predominant variety in industrial regions.

The changes that occurred in the moth population in different areas of England show natural selection in action. Before industrialization, tree trunks were lighter, and light-coloured moths predominated. With industrial pollution and the darkening of tree trunks, light-coloured moths became more visible to predators. Darker-coloured moths quickly increased in number in the new industrial environment. Rural areas today, with little or no industrial air pollution, show that natural selection in unpolluted areas still favours light-coloured moths.

Speciation: the development of a new species.

How can we be sure that natural selection was the mechanism accounting for the change? Consistent evidence comes from a series of experiments performed by H.B.D. Kettlewell. He deliberately released specially marked moths, black and grey, into two areas of England—one urban industrial and one rural—and then set light traps to recapture them. The proportions of the two kinds of moths recovered tell us about differential survival. Kettlewell found that proportionately more black moths compared with grey moths were recovered in the urban industrial area. The reverse happened in the rural area; proportionately more grey-speckled moths were recovered (Smith JM 1989). The same transformation—the switch to darker colour—occurred in 70 other species of moth, as well as in a beetle and a millipede. It did not occur only in Britain; it also happened in other highly polluted areas—the Ruhr area of Germany and the Pittsburgh area of the United States. Moreover, in the Pittsburgh area, anti-pollution measures in the last 30 years have apparently caused the black moth to dwindle in number once again (Devillers and Chaline 1993).

Another well-known example of observed natural selection is the acquired resistance of houseflies to the insecticide DDT. Beginning in the 1940s when DDT was first used to kill insects, several new DDT-resistant strains of housefly evolved. Many houseflies were killed but the few that survived were the ones that reproduced, and their resistant characteristics became common to the housefly populations. To the chagrin of medical practitioners, similar resistances develop in bacteria. A particular antibiotic may lose its effectiveness after it comes into wide use because new, resistant bacterial strains emerge.

A good example of the increased prevalence of highly virulent forms of old diseases that affect humans is *Streptococcus A*. Medical experts including Florence Nightingale recorded streptococcal toxic-shock syndrome (TSS) by names such as malignant ulcer, hospital gangrene, Fournier's gangrene, and phagedena. Streptococcal infections in the past, such as the scarlet fever epidemics that killed thousands of children during the 19th and early 20th centuries, also reached epidemic proportions.

In recent years, catastrophic *Streptococcus A*. infections have been observed in patients who are not normally affected by these diseases, that is, in young adults with no prior illnesses. Most disturbing, the progress of the disease in these new cases is much more rapid, earning some of the TSS effects the popular term "flesh-eating disease." Some high-profile cases, such as the 1990 death of Muppet creator Jim Henson, the media hype following a rash of TSS deaths in Britain in the mid-1990s, and the very public battle of former Quebec premier Lucien Bouchard with necrotizing fasciitis in 1993, spurred public awareness and fears over the last decade.

These new strains of common diseases will become more frequent than the original ones because of natural selection. In Canada now, an increasing number of disease strains are resistant to antibiotics currently on the market, a fact that worries medical practitioners (see Current Research and Issues, "Selection Favours the Evolution of Drug-Resistant Diseases"). One possible way to deal with the problem is to stop using certain antibiotics for a few years so that resistance to those antibiotics might not develop or will develop only slowly.

The theory of natural selection answered many questions but it also raised at least one whose answer eluded Darwin and others. The appearance of a beneficial trait may assist the survival of an organism, but what happens when the organism reproduces by mating with members that do not possess this new variation? Will not the new adaptive trait eventually disappear if subsequent generations mate with individuals that lack this trait? Darwin knew variations were transmitted through heredity, but he did not have a clear model of the mode of inheritance. As we will see in Chapter 5, Gregor Mendel's pioneering studies in the science of genetics provided the foundation for such a model, but his discoveries did not become widely known until 1900.

CURRENT RESEARCH AND ISSUES

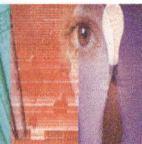

Selection Favours the Evolution of Drug-Resistant Diseases

Over the last decade or so, the threat of old diseases returning with renewed resistance to previously effective drug therapies has become a serious concern to public health officials. This unease has slowly gained the attention of the general public through media coverage of the breakout of virulent diseases in tropical "hot zones." An example of an old disease that is emerging as a renewed threat is tuberculosis (TB)—the "consumption" or "white plague" of the 19th and early 20th centuries.

Tuberculosis was once one of the most dreaded diseases in the world. In 1926, 1 in 13 North Americans died of the disease. Prior to the mid-1980s, the prevalence of tuberculosis cases was decreasing. Streptomycin and other antibiotics in use since the 1960s had been highly effective in steadily reducing new cases of tuberculosis. However, between 1985 and 1995, TB rates in industrialized countries stabilized, and in some cases increased slightly. This change in pattern was due in part to the rise of drug-resistant strains of *Mycobacterium tuberculosis*, the bacterium that causes the disease. The World Health Organization (WHO) estimates that approximately one-third of the world's population is now infected with latent TB. In 2014, an estimated 480 000 people developed multi-drug-resistant TB (MDR-TB) from a total of 9.6 million people who fell ill with TB and 1.5 million who died from the disease.

In Canada, tuberculosis rates have followed the pattern of most Western industrialized nations. The overall rate of tuberculosis in Canada has dropped from about 7.4 cases per 100 000 in 1992 to just under 5 cases per 100 000 in 2012. However, these figures do not tell the whole story. There is a substantial disparity in infection rates between Indigenous and non-Indigenous populations. In 2012, Indigenous peoples made up about 4 percent of the population of Canada but accounted for 23 percent of reported cases of active TB, with the rate for First Nations people 32 times higher and for Inuit almost 400 times higher than for Canadian-born non-Indigenous persons.

While "standard" TB is treatable with a 95 to 100 percent survival rate, multi-drug-resistant tuberculosis can have survival rates below 50 percent. In 2014, of 1376 TB cases tested in Canada, 107, or 7.8 percent, were resistant to one or more drugs and 1.3 percent were MDR-TB. As with many diseases, an important tool in the fight against MDR-TB is the sequencing of the *M. tuberculosis* genome. Researchers have begun to identify which mutations to the *M. tuberculosis* genome correspond to various drug resistances.

Sources: Health Canada and the Public Health Agency Canada. 2014. Tuberculosis Prevention and Control in Canada: A Federal Framework for Action. Publication 130511 (www.phac-aspc.gc.ca).

Public Health Agency of Canada. 2015. Tuberculosis: Drug Resistance in Canada 2014. Table 4: Overall Pattern of Reported Tuberculosis Drug Resistance in Canada, 2004 to 2014.

Stokstad E. 31 March 2000. Infectious Disease: Drug-Resistant TB on the Rise. Science. 287(5462):2391.

World Health Organization (WHO). March 2016. Fact sheet No. 104. Tuberculosis.

SUMMARY AND REVIEW

THE EVOLUTION OF EVOLUTION

 Review the early thinkers who shaped the theory of evolution. Explain the contributions of both biological and geological views to the theory of evolution.

- If we think of the history of the universe as represented by 12 months, the history of human-like primates would take up only about 90 minutes. The universe is some 15 billion years old; modern-looking humans have existed for about 100 000 years.

- It took a long time for ideas about evolution to be accepted into Western society because they contradicted the biblical view of events in which species were viewed as fixed in their form by the creator. But in the 18th and early 19th centuries, scientists increasingly interpreted evidence to suggest that evolution was a viable theory.

- In geology, the concept of uniformitarianism suggested the earth was constantly subjected to shaping and reshaping by natural forces working over vast amounts of time.
- A number of thinkers during this time began to discuss evolution and how it might occur.
- Carolus Linnaeus revolutionized the study of living things by classifying them according to similarities in form.
- Many pre-Darwin thinkers accepted evolution and put forward theories for the mechanism. Among these scholars were Georges Buffon and Georges Cuvier. Darwin was influenced by both of these natural historians.
- Lamarck proposed that the use of a trait—such as an elephant using its trunk to get food higher in a tree—could influence an offspring's phenotype in the next generation. Darwin instead showed that change could occur across generations based only on the selective retention of some traits and the filtering out of others.
- The 19th century also saw the emergence of cultural evolutionary theory by theorists like Herbert Spencer, Edward Burnett Tylor, and Lewis Henry Morgan.
- Anthropologist Franz Boas challenged many of these notions of cultural evolution and introduced the concept of cultural relativism.

What predictions derive from both Lamarck's and Darwin's theories of evolution?

THE PRINCIPLES OF NATURAL SELECTION

4.2 Explain the principles of natural selection.

- Charles Darwin and Alfred Russel Wallace proposed the mechanism of natural selection to account for the evolution of species.
- Charles Darwin spent much of his life thinking and writing about evolutionary change, and he developed the theory of evolution by natural selection to account for it.
- Alfred Russel Wallace was a contemporary of Darwin and co-discoverer of the theory of evolution by natural selection.
- There are three basic principles of the theory of natural selection: (1) every species is composed of a great variety of individuals, some of which are better adapted to their environment than others; (2) offspring inherit traits from their parents, at least to some degree and in some way; and (3) since better-adapted individuals generally produce more offspring over the generations than those that are more poorly adapted, the frequency of adaptive traits increases in subsequent generations. In this way, natural selection results in increasing proportions of individuals with advantageous traits.
- Natural selection depends upon variation within a population.

Why might a seemingly disadvantageous trait be retained in a given species?

THE ORIGIN OF SPECIES

4.3 Describe how new species emerge.

- How do new species emerge? Speciation, the development of a new species, may occur if one subgroup in a population becomes separated from other subgroups.
- In adapting to different environments, these two populations may undergo enough genetic changes over time to prevent them from interbreeding, even if they re-establish contact.
- Once species differentiation occurs, the evolutionary process cannot be reversed, and speciation has occurred.

What mechanisms prevent members of diverging populations from interbreeding?

THINK ON IT

1. Do you think the theory of natural selection is compatible with religious beliefs? Explain your reasoning.

2. Which is historically a more controversial concept—evolution or natural selection? Why?

3. How are humans influencing the evolution of other species? Of our own species?

4. How do you think human biology might be different 1000 years from now? Ten thousand years from now?

5. Under what conditions might a new species evolve?

Modern Evolutionary Theory

5

Nick Koudis/Getty Images

LEARNING OBJECTIVES

5.1 Explain the processes that lead to hereditary information being passed from generation to generation.

5.2 Describe the sources of biological variation.

5.3 Explain how natural selection can act on behavioural traits.

In the last chapter we learned that, according to Darwin's theory of evolution, natural selection is the process by which evolution occurred. Both Darwin and Wallace emphasized that natural selection operated on variation that already existed between individuals, but they did not know why or how that variation was created. Darwin thought that traits in offspring were somehow a blend of the parents' traits. At the same time that he was developing his theory of evolution by natural selection, an Augustinian monk from the Czech Republic was experimenting with how heredity worked. In this chapter we will discuss how the discovery of the gene influenced theories of evolution, and outline the modern theory of evolution. Biological evolution is not simply a process of change, but rather a process of changes in gene frequencies within a population.

In this chapter we begin by examining the roles of genes as the units of heredity—how they are inherited and how those genes are manifest in the individual. This section reviews the basis of cell biology and the structure and role of DNA in organisms. Next, we discuss sources of variation, that is, how similar genetic material is recombined in a variety of different expressions to produce variation, as well as how mutations occur within a species to also produce variation. These concepts form the fundamental basis for the modern theory of evolution. At the end of this chapter, we discuss the influence of genetics and environment on individual behaviour and the role of selection for behavioural traits.

Heredity

Mendel's Experiments

Gregor Mendel (1822–84), an amateur botanist, bred several varieties of pea plants and made detailed observations of their offspring. He chose as breeding partners plants that differed by only one observable trait. He crossed tall plants with short ones, and yellow ones with green, for example.

When Mendel transferred the pollen from a yellow pea plant to a green pea plant, he observed a curious phenomenon: all of the first-generation offspring bore yellow peas. It seemed that the green

Gregor Mendel.

trait had disappeared. But when he crossed seeds from this first generation, they produced both yellow and green pea plants in a ratio of three yellow pea plants to one green pea plant (see Figure 5–1). Apparently, Mendel reasoned, the green trait had not been lost or altered; the yellow trait was simply **dominant** and the green trait was **recessive**. Mendel observed similar results with other traits. Tallness dominated shortness, and the factor for smooth-skinned peas dominated the factor for wrinkled ones. In each cross, the 3-to-1 ratio appeared in the second generation. Self-fertilization, however, produced different results. Green pea plants always yielded green pea plants, and short plants always produced short plants.

From his numerical results, Mendel concluded that some yellow pea plants were pure for

> **Dominant:** the allele of a gene pair that is always phenotypically expressed in the heterozygous form.
> **Recessive:** an allele phenotypically suppressed in the heterozygous form and expressed only in the homozygous form.

MODERN EVOLUTIONARY THEORY

Genes: The Conveyors of Inherited Traits

Mendel's units of heredity were what we now call **genes**. He concluded that these units occurred in pairs for each trait and that offspring inherited one unit of the pair from each parent. Each member of a gene pair or group is called an **allele**. If the two genes, or alleles, for a trait are the same, the organism is **homozygous** for that trait; if the two genes for a characteristic differ, the organism is **heterozygous** for that trait. A pea plant that contains a pair of genes for yellow is homozygous for the trait. A yellow pea plant with a dominant gene for yellow and a recessive gene for green, although phenotypically yellow, has a heterozygous genotype. As Mendel demonstrated, the recessive green gene can reappear in subsequent generations. However, Mendel knew nothing of the composition of genes or the processes that transmit them from parent to offspring. Many years of scientific research have yielded much of the missing information.

The genes of higher organisms (not including bacteria and primitive plants such as green-blue algae) are located on ropelike bodies called **chromosomes** within the nucleus of every one of the organism's cells. Chromosomes, like genes, usually occur in pairs. Each allele for a given trait is carried in the identical position on corresponding chromosomes. The two genes that determined the colour of Mendel's peas, for example, were opposite each other on a pair of chromosomes.

Mitosis and Meiosis. Each body cell of every plant or animal carries a number of chromosome pairs, and this number is specific to each species. A human body cell has 23 pairs, or a total of 46 chromosomes, each chromosome carrying many times that number of genes. Each new body cell

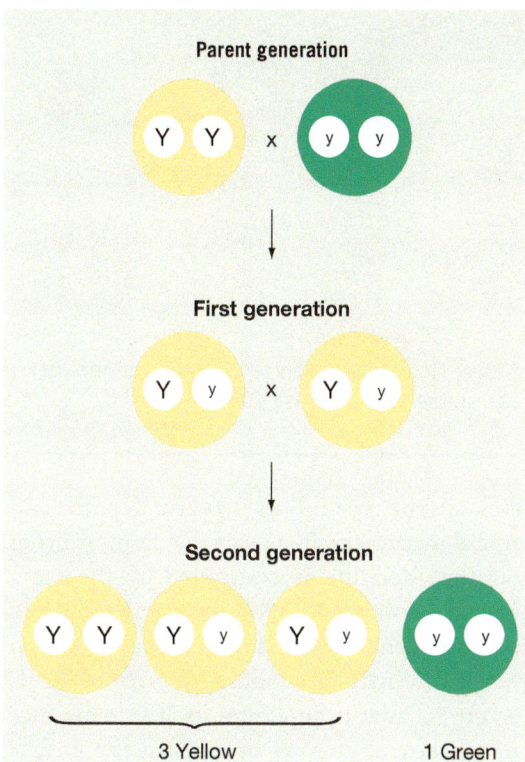

Figure 5–1 Green and Yellow Peas
When Mendel crossed a plant having two genes for yellow peas (YY) with a plant having two genes for green peas (yy), each offspring pea was yellow but carried one gene for yellow and one gene for green (Yy). The peas were yellow because the gene for yellow is dominant over the recessive gene for green. Crossing the first generation yielded three yellow pea plants for each green pea plant.

that trait, whereas others also possessed a green factor. That is, although two plants might both have yellow peas, one of them might produce green peas. In such cases, the genetic makeup, the **genotype**, differed from the observable appearance, or **phenotype**.

Genotype: the total complement of inherited traits or genes of an organism.
Phenotype: the observable physical appearance of an organism, which may or may not reflect its genotype or total genetic constitution.
Gene: chemical unit of heredity.
Allele: one member of a pair of genes.

Homozygous: possessing two identical genes or alleles in corresponding locations on a pair of chromosomes.
Heterozygous: possessing differing genes or alleles in corresponding locations on a pair of chromosomes.
Chromosomes: paired rod-shaped structures within a cell nucleus containing the genes that transmit traits from one generation to the next.

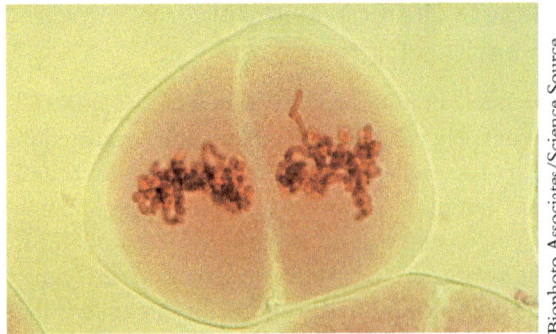 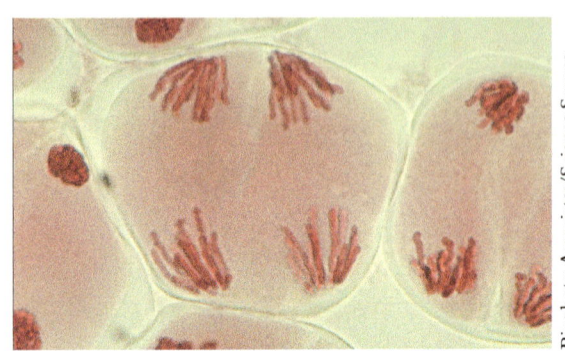

Meiosis in a plant cell. The left image shows the metaphase stage. Note how the chromosomes (stained dark red) lie against and even on top of one another. The right image shows the anaphase stage, when the chromosomes separate and the cell is ready to divide.

receives this number of chromosomes during cellular reproduction, or **mitosis**, as each pair of chromosomes duplicates itself.

What happens, though, when a sperm cell and an egg cell unite to form a new organism? What prevents the human baby from receiving twice the number of chromosomes characteristic of its species—23 pairs from the sperm and 23 pairs from the egg? The process by which the reproductive cells are formed, **meiosis**, ensures that this will not happen (see Figure 5–2). Each reproductive cell contains *half* the number of chromosomes appropriate for the species. Only one member of each chromosome pair is carried in every egg or sperm. At fertilization, the human embryo normally receives 23 *separate* chromosomes from its mother and the same number from its father, which add up to the 23 pairs.

DNA. As we have said, genes are located on chromosomes. Each gene carries a set of instructions encoded in its chemical structure. It is from this coded information carried in genes that a cell makes all the rest of its structural parts and chemical machinery. It appears that in most living organisms, heredity is controlled by the same chemical substance, DNA—deoxyribonucleic acid. An enormous amount of research has been directed toward understanding DNA—what its structure is, how it duplicates itself in reproduction, and how it conveys or instructs the formation of a complete organism.

One of the most important keys to understanding human development and genetics is the structure and function of DNA. In 1953, the American biologist James Watson, with the British molecular biologist Francis Crick, proposed that DNA is a long, two-stranded molecule shaped like a double helix (Alberts et al. 1983) (see Figure 5–3). Genetic information is stored in the linear sequences of the bases; different species have different sequences, and every individual is slightly different from every other individual. Notice that in the DNA molecule each base always has the same opposite base; adenine and thymine are paired, as are cytosine and guanine. The importance of this pattern is that the two strands carry the same information, so that when the double helix unwinds, each strand can form a template for a new strand of complementary bases (Alberts et al. 1983). Since DNA stores the information required to make up the cells of an organism, it has been called the language of life.

Once it was understood that genes are made of DNA, concerted efforts were begun to map DNA sequences and their locations on the chromosomes

> **Mitosis:** cellular reproduction or growth involving the duplication of chromosome pairs.
> **Meiosis:** the process by which reproductive cells are formed. In this process of division, the number of chromosomes in the newly formed cells is reduced by half, so that when fertilization occurs the resulting organism has the normal number of chromosomes appropriate to its species, rather than double that number.

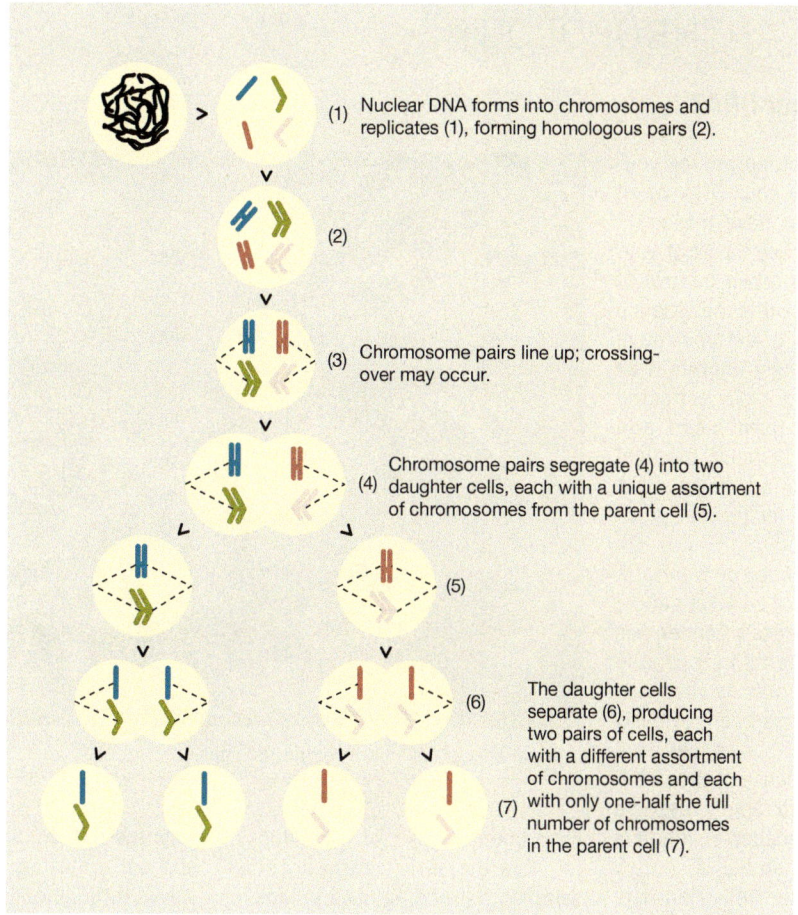

Figure 5-2 Meiosis (Sex Cells)

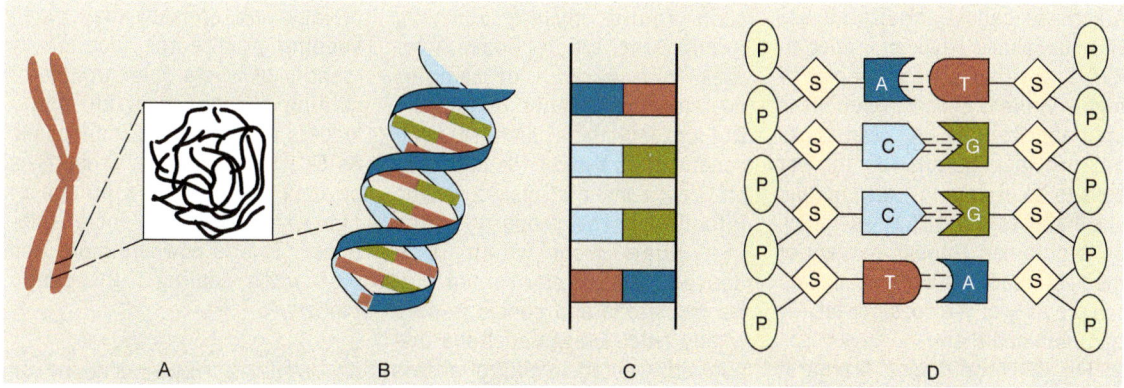

Figure 5-3 DNA

Chromosomes are built of DNA (A), which consists of two spiral sugar-phosphate strands (B) linked by the nitrogenous bases adenine, guanine, thymine, and cytosine (C). When the DNA molecule reproduces, the bases separate and the spiral strands unwind (D). Because adenine can bond only to thymine, and cytosine can bond only to guanine, each original strand serves as a mould along which a new complementary chain is formed.

APPLIED ANTHROPOLOGY

Who Owns Your DNA?

Your DNA is a blueprint for you. What happens to your DNA when you give blood or have a biopsy? Have you given away a part of you, or do you always retain control of your DNA because it is the essence of you? These questions have become increasingly important as DNA is now more easily extracted and sequenced from blood and body cells, and because medical research has found some DNA sources valuable for the design of new drugs.

Consider the case of Henrietta Lacks, who died of cervical cancer in 1951. Mrs. Lacks's cancer was particularly virulent; indeed, the cells grew more quickly than any human cells doctors had previously seen. Samples of her cancer were cultured and, because of their ability to reproduce so rapidly, became the targets of decades of medical research. More than half a century after her death, the cells Henrietta Lacks provided (referred to as HeLa cells) are still alive, growing in labs on every continent and interacting daily with thousands of scientists. Are these cells Henrietta Lacks? Has she gained a type of immortality? Or are they simply samples of highly virulent cancer tissue? It is important to note that Mrs. Lacks did not give permission for her cells to be used in this way, nor did she need to. In 1951, as today, cells obtained through surgery or medical treatment were considered the property of the doctor or facility that obtained them.

For anthropologist Margaret Everett, the question of who controls an individual's DNA came to the forefront of her research when her infant son Jack was diagnosed with, and later died from, a genetic disorder. Samples of Jack's DNA were taken as part of his autopsy. Dr. Everett later learned these samples were being used in labs in England and Italy and that several research papers had been published on them. As she related about one of these publications, "I soon found myself combing through the article, looking for Jack in a handful of samples described in a series of tables." But was Jack there? From research conducted to explore the impact of an Oregon law that makes genetic information the property of the individuals from which it is derived, Dr. Everett learned that her questions and concerns were widely held. Oregonians, she discovered, wanted to control access to their own DNA and felt that privacy and consent needed to be ensured when samples were taken.

In non-Western cultures, the situation may become even more complex. In the United States, we view the individual as autonomous and self-defining. We create ourselves through our work and contributions to our communities. But in many cultures, who you are may be mostly defined by others, not by you. In such situations, ensuring privacy and consent may mean keeping private the location or identity of whole communities or gaining consent from kin group leaders in addition to individuals. As Dr. Everett put it, "Property is never a thing—it is a bundle of rights, embedded in social relations." This is nowhere more true than when dealing with genetic property.

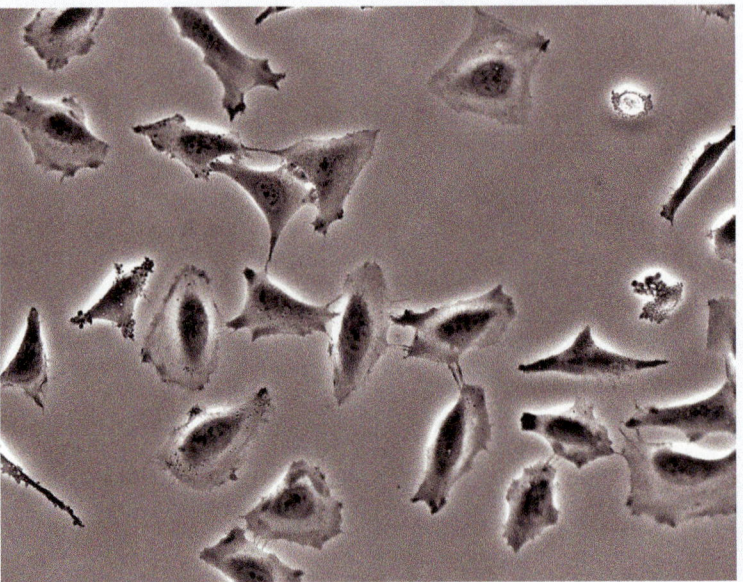
Cervical cancer cells from Henrietta Lacks.

Sources: Everett M. 2007. The "I" in Gene: Divided Property, Fragmented Personhood, and the Making of a Genetic Privacy Law. American Ethnologist. 34(2):375–386.

Landecker H. 2000. Immortality, In Vitro: A History of the HeLa Cell Line. In: Brodwin P, editor. Iotechnology and Culture: Bodies, Anxieties, Ethics. Bloomington: Indiana University Press. pp. 53–74.

of different organisms—that is, the **genome** of a species. A project known as the Human Genome Project (HGP) set out to assemble a complete genetic map for humans. Completed in 2003, this 13-year project to identify the 20 000 to 25 000 genes in human DNA was coordinated by the Department of Energy and the National Institutes of Health in the United States and involved collaborations with a number of international partners. This was a significant achievement and has already led to several breakthroughs in our understanding of how the genetic code functions (but see Applied Anthropology, "Who Owns Your DNA?") (Daiger 2005). For example, researchers recently reported finding two genes that appear to provide partial resistance to malaria. These newly found genes appear to have evolved recently, perhaps only a few thousand years ago. If researchers can discover how these genes help to defend their carriers against malaria, that may help medical science discover how to prevent or treat this devastating disease (Olsen 2002).

Messenger RNA. DNA stores the information to make cells, but it does not directly affect the formation of cells. One type of ribonucleic acid (RNA), **messenger RNA (mRNA)**, is copied from a portion of DNA and moves outside the cell nucleus to direct the formation of proteins (Alberts et al. 1983). Proteins have so many functions that they are considered to be responsible for most of the characteristics of an organism. They act as catalysts for synthesizing DNA and RNA and for the activities of cells; they also contribute many of the structural elements that determine the shape and movement of cells (Berg and Singer 1992). Messenger RNA is like DNA in that it has a linear sequence of bases attached to a sugar-phosphate backbone, but it is slightly different chemically. One difference is that messenger RNA has the base *uracil* instead of the base thymine. Messenger RNA also has a different sugar-phosphate backbone and is single- rather than double-stranded. Messenger RNA is formed when a double-stranded DNA molecule unwinds and forms a template for the mRNA. After a section of DNA is copied, the RNA releases from the DNA and leaves the nucleus, and the double helix of the DNA is re-formed (Alberts et al. 1983).

Protein Synthesis. Once the mRNA is released from the DNA, it travels out of the cell nucleus, through the cytoplasm, and into the body of the cell. There it attaches to a structure in the cell called a **ribosome**, which uses the information on the mRNA to make proteins. The ribosome essentially "reads" the chemical bases on the mRNA in commands that tell the ribosome the specific amino acids to join together to form a protein (see Figure 5–4). For example, the mRNA sequence adenine, adenine, guanine (AAG) tells the ribosome to place the amino acid lysine in that location, whereas the sequence adenine, adenine, cytosine (AAC) calls for the amino acid histidine. There are also mRNA commands that tell the ribosome when to begin and when to stop constructing a protein. Thus, the DNA code copied onto mRNA provides all the information necessary for ribosomes to build the proteins that make up the structures of organisms and drive the processes of life.

Sources of Variability

Natural selection proceeds only when individuals within a population vary. There are two genetic sources of variation: genetic recombination and mutation.

Genetic Recombination

The distribution of traits from parents to children varies from one offspring to another. Brothers and sisters, after all, do not look exactly alike, nor does

---

Genome: the complete genetic makeup of an organism.
Messenger RNA (mRNA): a type of ribonucleic acid that is used in the cell to copy the DNA code for use in protein synthesis.

Ribosome: a structure in the cell used in making proteins.

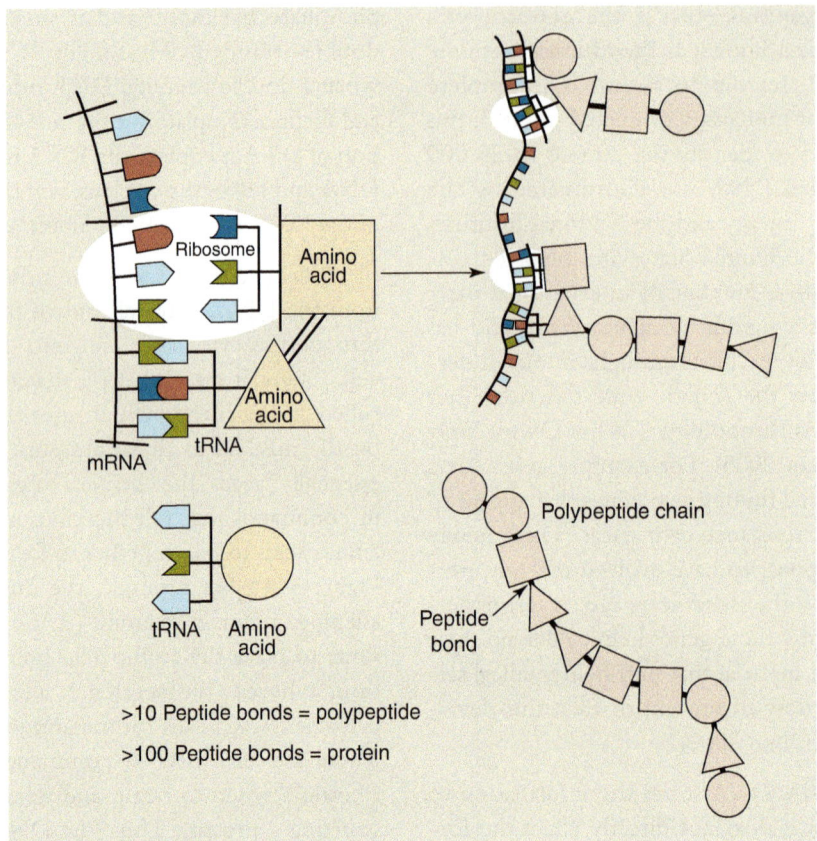

Figure 5–4 Translation and Protein Synthesis

The mRNA copy of the cellular DNA is "read" by a ribosome that attaches the amino acid with the corresponding transfer RNA (tRNA) to a growing chain of amino acids (called a *polypeptide chain* because the amino acids are linked together by peptide bonds). A chain more than 100 amino acids long is called a *protein*.

each child resemble 50 percent of the mother and 50 percent of the father. This variation occurs because when a sperm cell or an egg is formed from 23 chromosomes, each chromosome is randomly received. Each reproductive cell, then, carries a *random assortment* of chromosomes and their respective genes. At fertilization, the egg and sperm that unite are different from every other egg carried by the mother and every other sperm carried by the father. **Genetic recombination** then results in a *unique* offspring being produced through a random shuffling of the parents' genes. One cause of this shuffling is the random **segregation**, or sorting, of chromosomes in meiosis. Conceivably, an individual could get any of the possible assortments of the paternal and maternal chromosomes. Another cause of the shuffling of parental genes is **crossing-over**, the exchange

---

Genetic Recombination: a random shuffling of the parents' genes.
Segregation: the random sorting of chromosomes in meiosis.

Crossing-Over: exchanges of sections of chromosomes from one chromosome to another.

of sections of chromosomes between one chromosome and another (Alberts et al. 1983). Thus, after meiosis, the egg and sperm do not receive just a random mixture of complete paternal and maternal chromosomes; because of crossing-over they also receive chromosomes in which some of the sections may have been replaced (see Figure 5–5).

The traits displayed by each organism are not simply the result of combinations of dominant and recessive genes, as Mendel had hypothesized. In humans, most traits are influenced by the activity of many genes. Skin colour, for example, is the result of several inherited characteristics. A brownish shade results from the presence of a pigment known as *melanin*; the degree of darkness in the hue depends largely on the amount and distribution of melanin in the skin. Another factor contributing to the colour of all human skin is the blood that flows in blood vessels located in the outer layers of the skin. Humans carry at least five different genes for the manufacture of melanin, and many other genes for the other components of skin hue. In fact, almost all physical characteristics in humans are the result of the concerted action of many genes. Some traits are sex-linked. The X chromosome, which together with the presence or absence of a Y chromosome determines sex, may also carry the gene for hemophilia or the gene for colour blindness. The expression of these two characteristics depends on the sex of the organism.

Genetic recombination produces variety, which is essential for the operation of natural selection. Ultimately, however, the major source of new variation is mutation. This is because mutation replenishes the supply of variability, which is constantly being reduced by the selective elimination of less fit variants. Mutation also produces variety in organisms that reproduce asexually.

Mutation

A **mutation** is a change in the DNA sequence. Such a change produces an altered gene. The majority of mutations are thought to occur because of occasional errors in the chemical bases that make up DNA. Just as a typist will make errors in copying a manuscript, so will DNA, in duplicating itself, occasionally change its code (Beadle and Beadle 1966). A mutation will result from such an error. Some mutations have more drastic consequences than others. Suppose the error is in one base on a DNA strand. The effect depends on what that portion of the DNA controls. The effect may be minimal if the product hardly affects the organism. On the other hand, if the change occurs at a place where the DNA regulates the production of many proteins, the effect on the organism can be serious (Alberts et al. 1983). Mutations that are invisible to selection are neutral. Neutral mutations can, over time, replace regular alleles by simple chance (gamete sampling), although this occurs at a much slower rate

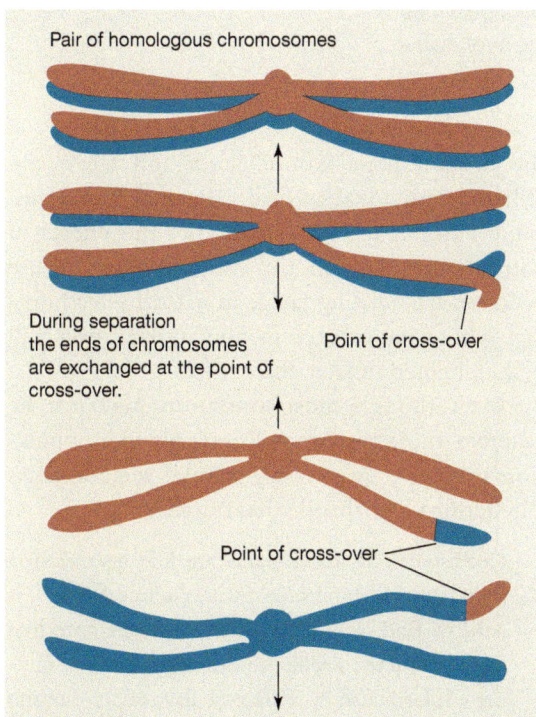

Figure 5–5 Crossing-Over

Source: Boaz NT, Almquist AJ. 1997. Biological anthropology. Upper Saddle River, NJ: Prentice Hall.

Mutation: a change in the DNA sequence, producing an altered gene.

A mutation in the fruitfly causes legs to grow where antennae should be. While most mutations are either neutral or harmful (like this one), some can be adaptive and spread rapidly through a population.

than if selection were influencing the replacement. The rate of neutral mutations being fixed within a population appears to be relatively constant—a fact that forms the basis of genetic comparisons between species (see "The Molecular Clock" in Chapter 8).

Although it is very difficult to estimate the proportions of mutations that are harmful, neutral, or beneficial, there is no doubt that some mutations have lethal consequences. We can discuss the relative merits or disadvantages of a mutant gene only in terms of the physical, cultural, and genetic environment of that gene (Dobzhansky 1962). Galactosemia, for example, is caused by a recessive mutant gene and usually results in mental retardation and blindness. However, it can be prevented by dietary restrictions begun at an early age. In this instance, the intervention of human culture through changes in diet can counteract the otherwise negative effects that the mutant gene would cause and allow the afflicted individual to lead a normal life. Thus, some cultural factors can modify the effects of natural selection. In this way, human culture becomes a mediating factor in natural selection, a fact whose importance in human evolution will be highlighted in later chapters.

Even though most mutations may not be adaptive, those that are will multiply in a population relatively quickly, by natural selection. As Theodosius Dobzhansky has suggested,

> Consistently useful mutants are like needles in a haystack of harmful ones. A needle in a haystack is hard to find, even though one may be sure it is there. But if the needle is valuable, the task of finding it is facilitated by setting the haystack on fire and looking for the needle among the ashes. The role of the fire in this parable is played in biological evolution by natural selection. (Dobzhansky 1962:139)

Darwin and Wallace proposed a mechanism for evolution—natural selection acting on existing variation. Mendel's work provided the foundation for genetics, which we now know are the source of existing variation and how it becomes established. As discussed earlier, new variation within a species can occur only through mutation—changes in the existing genetic structure of an organism. However, the distribution of individual variation within a species is based on two fundamental concepts—*genetic drift* and *gene flow*. In rare circumstances, the mating of two species can produce viable offspring and result in new variation in some populations.

Genetic Drift

The term **genetic drift** refers to various random processes that affect gene frequencies in small, relatively isolated populations. Genetic drift is the result of *population fission*—that is, the breaking apart of a previously large population into smaller, distinct groups. Thus, genetic drift may be the result of natural barriers (such as mountain ranges or oceans) or, in humans, cultural barriers (such as religious practices or marriage rules). In a small population, over time, genetic drift may result in a neutral or nearly neutral gene becoming more or less frequent simply by chance (Harrison et al. 1988).

One variety of genetic drift, called *founder effect*, occurs when a small group recently derived from a larger population migrates to a relatively isolated location (Harrison et al. 1988). If a particular gene is absent just by chance in the migrant group, the descendants are likely also to lack that gene, assuming that the group remains isolated. Similarly, if all members of the original migrant group carried a particular gene just by chance, their descendants would also be likely to share that gene. Isolation can occur for physical reasons, such as when a group moves to a previously uninhabited place and does not return. The populations that travelled over the Bering land bridge from Asia to North America could not readily return when the sea level rose. Or the isolation can occur for cultural reasons. For example, in 1918, there was a mass migration of Hutterites to Alberta and Manitoba by the descendants of the 100 Hutterite families who had settled in South Dakota by 1879. The fact that the families kept to themselves probably explains why some of their gene frequencies differ from what is found in both Germany and the broader population of both Canada and the United States.

Gene Flow

Gene flow is the process whereby genes pass from one population to another through mating and reproduction. Unlike the other processes of natural selection and genetic drift, which generally increase the differences between populations in different environments, gene flow tends to work in the opposite direction—it decreases differences between populations. Two populations at opposite ends of a region may have different frequencies of a particular gene, but the populations located between them have an intermediate gene frequency because of gene flow between them. The variation in gene frequency from one end of the region to the other is called a **cline**. In Europe, for example, there is a cline in the distribution of blood type B, which gradually diminishes in frequency from east to west (Harrison et al. 1988:198).

Most genetically determined characteristics in humans have gradually or clinally varying frequencies as one moves from one area to another. Neighbouring regions have more similar gene frequencies than regions widely separated. But these

---

Genetic Drift: the various random processes that affect gene frequencies in small, relatively isolated populations.
Gene Flow: the process by which genes pass from the gene pool of one population to that of another through mating and reproduction.

Cline: the gradually increasing (or decreasing) frequency of a gene from one end of a region to another.

A wolf–dog hybrid. Hybridization is sometimes a source of new variation.

clines do not always coincide, which makes the concept of "race" as applied to humans not very useful for understanding human biological variation (Brace 1996). We discuss this in more detail in Chapter 6 on human variation. Gene flow may occur between distant as well as close populations. Long-range movements of people, to trade or raid or settle, may result in gene flow. But they do not always do so.

Hybridization

A **species** is a population that consists of organisms able to interbreed and produce fertile and viable offspring. In general, individuals from one species do not successfully mate with members of a different species because of genetic and behavioural differences. If members of different species do mate, fertilization usually does not occur and, if it does, the embryo does not survive. In the cases where offspring are born, they are usually infertile. However, recent studies have suggested that **hybridization**, the creation of a viable offspring from two different species, may be more possible than once thought. Hybridization may be an important source of new variation in some populations.

The finches of the Galápagos Islands that Darwin used as evidence for natural selection and that we refer to in Current Research and Issues, "Is Evolution Slow and Steady or Fast and Abrupt?" also provide an example of hybridization in action. Many female cactus finches (*Geospiza scandens*) died during a period of severe drought, leaving an

Species: a population that consists of organisms able to interbreed and produce fertile and viable offspring.

Hybridization: the creation of a viable offspring from the mating of two different species.

abundance of males. High competition for mates led some female ground finches (*Geospiza fortis*) to mate with the abundant male cactus finches, something that would not normally occur. The result was hybrid offspring with unique characteristics. These hybrids, both male and female, went on to mate only with cactus finches, because they imprinted on the male cactus finch song as infants. The end result was a one-time influx of ground finch genes into the cactus finch population, adding new variations upon which natural selection could work (Grant and Grant 2002).

As we have already noted, populations adapt to the particular environmental niche that they live in. However, groups of species can over long periods of time adapt to differing environments, such that the allele frequencies in the populations are significantly different (genetic drift). With time, and if no gene flow exists, differences can become so substantive that the two populations can no longer breed. This process can be accelerated if an adaptive mutation occurs in a population. If particularly adaptive, the new traits can spread rapidly through the population.

So the question remains: Do new species diverge quickly or slowly from their ancestors? Palaeontologists disagree about the pace of speciation. The traditional view is that evolution occurs very slowly over time; new species emerge gradually. Others who espouse what is called "punctuated equilibrium" believe that species are very stable over long periods of time but that when divergence occurs it is quick (see the box titled "Is Evolution Slow and Steady or Fast and Abrupt?").

Epigenetics

As we saw in the last chapter, Lamarck proposed a mechanism for evolution, based on adaptations to the environment, which proved incorrect. With normal genetic replication, the environment does not alter the genome of an organism (save by environmentally induced mutation). However, we now know that biochemical signals in the body that are a result of environmental stresses may alter gene expressions in a way that may in fact be inheritable (Holliday 2006). This is known as **epigenetics**. Originally defined by British developmental biologist and palaeontologist Conrad Waddington, the term *epigenetics* referred to how a given genotype gives rise to a phenotype during the development of the organism (Bird 2007). Today, epigenetics is an exciting new field for understanding the mechanisms that may lead to differential expression of genes that may be inheritable. While most environmental influences that affect gene expression occur while the fetus is developing, current studies are examining the influence of environmental conditions on gene expression during life, and when such changes may be passed on to the next generation. The study of epigenetics is making important contributions to our understanding of gene/environment interactions, especially with respect to health and well-being, including diet-induced obesity and diabetes (Feinberg and Fallin 2015; Huypens et al. 2016), vitamin D deficiency and increased risk of cancer in black populations (Zhu et al. 2016), and tuberculosis in Aboriginal populations in Canada (Larcombe et al. 2012, 2015).

Natural Selection of Behavioural Traits

Until now we have discussed how natural selection might operate to change a population's physical traits, such as the colour of moths or the neck length of giraffes. But natural selection can also operate on the behavioural characteristics of populations. Although this idea is not new, it is now receiving more attention. The approaches called *sociobiology* (Barash 1977), **behavioural ecology** (Krebs and Davies 1984, 1987), *evolutionary psychology* (Badcock 2000), and *dual-inheritance*

> **Epigenetics:** changes in gene expression (without changes in the DNA itself) that are inheritable.
> **Behavioural Ecology:** the study of how all kinds of behaviour may be related to the environment. The theoretical orientation involves the application of biological evolutionary principles to the behaviour (including social behaviour) of animals, including humans. Also called *sociobiology*, particularly when applied to social organization and social behaviour.

CURRENT RESEARCH AND ISSUES

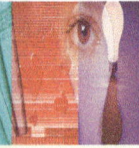

Is Evolution Slow and Steady or Fast and Abrupt?

Darwin's evolutionary theory suggested that new species emerge gradually over time. Through the process of natural selection, frequencies of traits would slowly change, and eventually a new species would appear. However, Darwin's theory did not allow for speciation (the development and divergence of different species). If trait frequencies change only gradually over time, wouldn't descendant populations retain their ability to interbreed and wouldn't they, therefore, continue to belong to the same species?

In the 1930s and 1940s, Theodosius Dobzhansky, Julian Huxley, Ernst Mayr, George Simpson, and others advanced what came to be called the "modern synthesis" in evolutionary theory, adding what was known from genetics about heredity. Mutation and the recombination of genes now provided for genetic variety. The driving force of change was still adaptation to environments through natural selection; gene frequencies of a population presumably changed slowly as adaptive traits (because of existing genes or mutations) increased in prevalence and maladaptive traits decreased. As for speciation, the modern synthesis postulated that it would occur when subpopulations became isolated by geographic barriers or when different subpopulations encountered different climatic conditions or moved into new ecological niches; those environmental isolating processes would eventually result in the development of reproductive isolation and therefore new species.

This gradualist view of evolution was challenged in 1972 by Niles Eldredge and Stephen Jay Gould. Their alternative model of evolution is referred to as *punctuated equilibrium*. They still assume that natural selection is the primary mechanism of evolutionary change, but they see the pace of evolution quite differently. In their view, new species evolve quickly; but once a successful species emerges, its characteristics are likely to change very little over long periods. Thus, in contrast to the modern synthesis, Eldredge and Gould do not think it is common for the world's species to change gradually into descendant species. Rather, individuals of a species are born more or less abruptly, they have lifetimes during which they do not change much, and they become extinct. As examples, Eldredge and Gould cited the history of North American trilobites and Bermudan land snails. In both groups of animals, the different species did not seem to change for a long time—millions of years for some species—but then certain species seem to have been quickly replaced by related species from nearby areas. In short, Eldredge and Gould believe that the succession of one species after another involves replacement more often than gradual change over time.

Another source of support for this theory is the Burgess Shale. A UNESCO World Heritage Site located in Yoho National Park in Canada, the Burgess Shale has been the source of over 170 plant and animal fossils finds that lend support to the theory of punctuated equilibrium. These fossils represent the remains of once tropical marine life from over 500 million years ago. In particular, these fossils reflect the so-called Cambrian explosion of life (including new phyla, not just new species) that seems to occur relatively quickly in geological terms after billions of years of only the simplest life forms existing on the planet.

Evolution may or may not occur according to the model of punctuated equilibrium, but most evolutionists today agree that change could occur relatively quickly. Recent research suggests that some relatively quick climate changes in the earth's history helped bring about massive extinctions of species and families of species and exponential increases in the subsequent number of new families. For example, there is

theory (Boyd and Richerson 2005) involve the application of evolutionary principles to the behaviour of animals. Behavioural ecology is interested in how all kinds of behaviour are related to the environment; sociobiology is particularly interested in social organization and social behaviour; evolutionary biology is interested in how evolution may have produced lasting variation in the way humans behave, interact, and perceive the world; and dual-inheritance theory looks at how cultural traits might be selected for and transmitted. The typical behaviours of a species are assumed to be

considerable evidence that a large meteorite collided with the earth at the end of the Cretaceous geological period, about 65 million years ago. Louis Alvarez and his colleagues proposed that so much dust was sent into the atmosphere by the collision that the earth was shrouded in darkness for months, if not longer. Some investigators now think that the impact of the meteorite may also have triggered a great deal of volcanic activity, even on the opposite side of the world, which would also have reduced solar radiation to the earth's surface. Not only the dinosaurs disappeared about 65 million years ago—so also did many sea animals and plants. Afterward, the earth saw the proliferation of many other kinds of animals, such as fish, lizards, birds, and mammals, as well as flowering trees. As we shall see in Chapter 8 on primate evolution, our own biological order, the Primates, is believed to have emerged around that time.

Peter Grant recently studied the same finches on the Galápagos Islands that partially inspired Darwin's theory. Unlike Darwin, though, Grant had the chance to see natural selection in action—and it was surprisingly quick. Central to Grant's study was the attachment of coloured bands to each individual bird, which allowed each bird to be identified at a distance. In the midst of the project, in 1977, when half the birds had been banded, there was a serious drought. Of the two main species of finch on one island, the cactus finch and the medium finch, only the cactus finches were able to breed, but they had no surviving offspring. During the next 18 months, 85 percent of the adult medium finches disappeared. Those finches that survived tended to be larger and to have larger beaks than the ones that died. Why larger beaks? Both species of finch eat seeds, but small seeds produced by grasses and herbs are scarce in a drought; bigger seeds are more available. So it seems that natural selection under conditions of drought favoured finches with bigger beaks, which are better at cracking the husks of large seeds.

If it were not for the fact that wet years, which favour smaller finches, occur between years of drought, we might see the rapid evolution of new finch species. It is estimated that 20 drought episodes would be sufficient to produce a new species of finch. Darwin's (and Grant's) finches do not really provide an example of punctuated equilibrium (no replacement from outside occurred), but they do suggest that evolutionary change could be a lot quicker than Darwin imagined.

Controversy continues over whether evolution is slow and steady or fast and abrupt. Many scholars, though, including Gould, point out that there is no need to pit one model against the other. Both may be correct in different instances. For example, recent research suggests that the pace of evolution has changed drastically over time. When life first arose billions of years ago, the earth was much hotter than it is at present; these high temperatures would have frequently triggered certain genetic mutations, providing greater genetic variation for natural selection to act on than is present today. In any case much more investigation of evolutionary sequences is needed to help us evaluate the competing theoretical models.

Sources: Devillers C, Chaline J. 1993. Evolution: An Evolving Theory. New York: Springer-Verlag.

Eldredge N, Gould SJ. 1972. Punctuated Equilibria: An Alternative to Phyletic Gradualism. In: Schopf TJM, editor. Models in Paleobiology. San Francisco: Freeman, Cooper and Co. pp. 82–115.

Gould SJ. 1989. Wonderful Life: The Burgess Shale and the Nature of History. New York: WW Norton & Company.

Grant PR. October 1991. Natural Selection and Darwin's Finches. Scientific American. 82–87.

Lewis CA, Crayle J, Zhou S, Swanstrom R, Wolfenden R. 2016. Cytosine Deamination and the Precipitous Decline of Spontaneous Mutation during Earth's History. Proceedings of the National Academy of Sciences. 113(29):8194–8199.

Tattersall I. 1998. Paleoanthropology and Evolutionary Theory. In: Ember CR, Ember M, Peregrine PN, editors. Research Frontiers in Anthropology. Upper Saddle River, NJ: Prentice Hall. Prentice Hall/Simon & Schuster Custom Publishing.

---

adaptive and to have evolved by natural selection. For example, why do related species exhibit different social behaviours even though they derive from a common ancestral species?

Consider the lion, as compared with other cats. Although members of the cat family are normally solitary creatures, lions live in social groups called *prides*. Why? George Schaller suggested that lion social groups may have evolved primarily because group hunting is a more successful way to catch large mammals in open terrain. He observed that not only are several lions more successful in catching prey than are solitary lions, but several lions are more likely to catch and kill large and dangerous prey such as giraffes. Then, too, cubs are generally safer from predators when in a social group than when alone with their mothers. Thus, the social behaviour of lions may have evolved primarily because it provided selective advantages in the lions' open-country environment (Schaller 1972).

It is important to remember that natural selection operates on expressed characteristics, or the phenotype, of an individual. Behaviour is also an expressed characteristic. If hunting in groups, which is a behavioural trait, gets the individuals in that group more food than if each individual were to hunt on his or her own, then individuals who hunt in groups will do better. We must also remember, though, that natural selection requires traits to be heritable. Can the concept of heritability be applied to learned behaviour, not just genetically transmitted behaviour? And, even more controversially, if the concept of heritability can include learning, can it also include cultural learning?

Early theorizing in sociobiology and behavioural ecology appeared to emphasize the genetic component of behaviour. However, Bobbi Low pointed out that although the term *biology* may have been interpreted to mean "genetic," most biologists understand that expressed or observable characteristics are the results of genes and environment and life history, all interacting (Low 1998). Behaviour is a product of all three. If we say that some behaviour is heritable, we mean that the child's behaviour is more likely to resemble the parents' behaviour than the behaviour of others (Wilson 1975, 1998). Learning from a parent could be an important part of why the offspring is like the parent. If the child is more like the parent than like others, then the likeness is heritable, even if it is entirely learned from the parent.

Nature or Nurture?

Many researchers have tried to discover if variation in child-rearing customs can account for observed psychological differences. Anthropologists and psychologists use the term **socialization** to describe the development in children of patterns of behaviour, attitudes, and values that conform to cultural expectations. Socialization occurs through the influence of parents, peer groups, and others. People often try to socialize children directly by rewarding certain behaviours and ignoring or punishing other behaviours. Socialization can be indirect or subtle as well as direct. By assigning tasks to children, parents can encourage the development of specific skills needed for adult life, and at the same time subtly communicate what kind of person they want their children to become. Whether children go to school may affect their psychological, particularly cognitive, development. Finally, parents may affect the psychological development of their children by the way they communicate how they generally feel about them.

Some researchers have suggested that genetic or physiological differences between populations predispose them to have different personality characteristics. Daniel Freedman found differences in "temperament" in newborn babies of different ethnic groups; because he observed newborns, the differences between them were presumed to be genetic. Freedman compared Chinese and European-American newborns in families that were matched in such factors as income, number of previous children, and so on. He found that European-American babies cried more easily, were harder to console, and fought experimental procedures more. Chinese babies, on the other hand, seemed calmer and more adaptable. Navajo babies were similar to the Chinese, showing even more calmness (Low 1998). Freedman also suggested that an infant's behaviour can influence how the parents respond. A calm baby may encourage a calm parental response; a more active baby may encourage a

> **Socialization:** a term used by anthropologists and psychologists to describe the development, through the direct and indirect influence of parents and others, of children's patterns of behaviour (and attitudes and values) that conform to cultural expectations.

One major difference in child rearing between Western societies and other places is the degree to which an infant is held by a caretaker during the day. In North America and other Western countries, an infant spends much of the day in a crib, playpen, or stroller. This Bai baby from Yunnan province in China (right) spends a good deal of time in physical contact with the mother.

more active response (Scarr and McCartney 1983; Low 1998). So, in Freedman's view, babies' genetically determined behaviour can lead to ethnic differences in adult personality and caretaking styles.

Nevertheless, we cannot rule out non-genetic explanations of babies' behaviour. For example, the mother's diet or her blood pressure could affect the baby's behaviour, and it may be that the baby can learn even in the womb. After all, babies in the womb apparently can hear and respond to sounds and to other stimuli. Therefore, it is possible that in societies in which pregnant women are calm, their babies may have learned calmness even before they were born. Last, we still do not know if the initial differences observed in newborn babies persist to become personality differences in adulthood.

Just as the diet of the mother, including the intake of alcohol and drugs, may affect the developing fetus, the diet of infants and children may also affect their intellectual development and their behaviour. Studies have shown that malnutrition is associated with lower levels of activity, less attentiveness, lack of initiative, and low tolerance of frustration. Behaviour of children can change with short-term nutrition supplements. For example, Guatemalan children who were given nutritional supplements were observed to have less anxiety, more curiosity, and greater involvement in games than children who were not given supplements (Barrett 1984; Dasen et al. 1988). The problem of malnutrition is not just a matter of nutrition, but also a matter of care and interaction with adults. For example, caretakers of malnourished children may interact with them less than do caretakers of healthy children. As a malnourished child shows reduced activity, caretakers tend to respond to the child with less frequency and enthusiasm. Then the malnourished child withdraws from interaction, creating a potentially serious vicious cycle (Dasen et al. 1988).

Physiological (not necessarily genetic) differences between populations may also be responsible for some personality differences in adulthood. Research by Ralph Bolton suggested that a physiological condition known as hypoglycemia may be responsible for the high levels of aggression recorded among the Qolla of Peru (Bolton 1973).

(People with hypoglycemia experience a big drop in their blood sugar level after they ingest food.) Bolton found that about 55 percent of the males he tested in a Qolla village had hypoglycemia. Moreover, those men with the most aggressive life histories tended to be hypoglycemic. Whether hypoglycemia is induced by genetic or environmental factors or both, the condition can be alleviated by a change in diet.

The sociobiological approach has aroused considerable controversy in cultural anthropology, probably because of its apparent emphasis on genes, rather than experience and learning, as determinants of human behaviour. Cultural ecologists have argued that the customs of a society may be more or less adaptive because cultural behaviours also have reproductive consequences. It is not just an individual's behaviour that may have reproductive consequences. So does natural selection also operate in the evolution of culture? Most biologists think not. They say there are substantial differences between biological and cultural evolution. How do cultural evolution and biological evolution compare? To answer this question, we must remember that the operation of natural selection requires three conditions, as we have already noted: *variation*, *heritability* or mechanisms that duplicate traits in offspring, and *differential reproductive success*. Do these three requirements apply to cultural behaviour?

In biological evolution, variability comes from genetic recombination and mutation. In cultural evolution, it comes from the recombination of learned behaviours and from invention (Campbell 1965). Cultures are not closed or reproductively isolated, as species are. A species cannot borrow genetic traits from another species, but a culture can borrow new things and behaviours from other cultures. The custom of growing corn, which has spread from the Americas to many other parts of the world, is an example of this phenomenon. As for the requirement of heritability, although learned traits obviously are not passed to offspring through purely genetic inheritance, parents who exhibit adaptive behavioural traits are more likely to "reproduce" those traits in their children, who may learn them by imitation or by parental instruction. Children and adults may also copy adaptive traits they see in people outside the family. Finally, as for the requirement of differential reproductive success, it does not matter whether the trait in question is genetic or learned or both. As Henry Nissen emphasized, "behavioral incompetence leads to extinction as surely as does morphological disproportion or deficiency in any vital organ. Behavior is subject to selection as much as bodily size or resistance to disease" (Nissen 1958).

Many theorists are comfortable with the idea of applying the theory of natural selection to cultural evolution, but others prefer to use other terminology when dealing with traits that do not depend on purely genetic transmission from one generation to the next. For example, Robert Boyd and Peter Richerson discussed human behaviour as involving "dual inheritance." They distinguished cultural transmission, by learning and imitation, from genetic transmission, but they emphasized the importance of understanding both and the interaction between them (Boyd and Richerson 1985, 2005). William Durham also dealt separately with cultural transmission, using the term *meme* (analogous to the term *gene*) for the unit of cultural transmission. He directed our attention to the interaction between genes and culture, calling that interaction "co-evolution," and provided examples of how genetic evolution and cultural evolution may lead to changes in each other, how they may enhance each other, and how they may even oppose each other (Durham 1991).

So biological and cultural evolution in humans may not be completely separate processes. As we will discuss, some of the most important biological features of humans—such as two-legged walking and relatively large brains—may have been favoured by natural selection because our ancestors made tools, a cultural trait. Conversely, the cultural trait of informal and formal education may have been favoured by natural selection because humans have a long period of immaturity, a biological trait.

As long as the human species continues to exist and the social and physical environments continue to change, there is reason to think that natural selection of biological and cultural traits will also continue. However, as humans learn more and more about genetic structure, they will become more and more capable of curing genetically caused disorders and even altering the way evolution proceeds. Today, genetic researchers are capable of diagnosing genetic defects in developing fetuses, and parents can and do decide often to terminate a pregnancy. Soon genetic engineering will probably allow humans to fix what society sees as defects and even try to "improve" the genetic code of a growing fetus. Whether and to what extent humans should alter genes will undoubtedly be the subject of continuing debate. Whatever the decisions we eventually make about genetic engineering, they will affect the course of human biological and cultural evolution.

SUMMARY AND REVIEW

HEREDITY

5.1 Explain the processes that lead to hereditary information being passed from generation to generation.

- Gregor Mendel's research on pea plants helped scientists to understand the biological mechanisms by which traits may be passed from one generation to the next.
- The basic units of heredity are genes. Genes occur in pairs, and each member of a pair is called an allele. Genes are inherited through sperm and egg cells, which are created through the process of meiosis.
- Genes, made up of deoxyribonucleic acid (DNA), provide instructions for cells to make proteins. Proteins are long chains of amino acids that make up the structures of organisms and drive life processes. Segments of DNA are transferred from the cell nucleus by mRNA. The mRNA is then "read" by a ribosome in the cell to construct proteins.
- Mitosis is the process of normal somatic cell division that occurs during the life of an organism. Meiosis is the process of cell division that ensures half the number of chromosomes appropriate for the species is carried in each sex cell.
- Although cells have very different functions they share the same basic anatomy: the nucleus sits within cytoplasm that houses genetic material, DNA.

- The major function of DNA is the make copies of itself, allowing hereditary information to pass from one generation to the next.
- The phenotype of an organism is the product of its genotype and the environment in which it developed and grew.

What is DNA, and why is it important to understanding evolution?

SOURCES OF VARIABILITY

5.2 Describe the sources of biological variation.

- There are two sources of biological variation: genetic recombination and mutation.
- Genetic recombination involves a random reshuffling of the parent genes as a consequence of segregation or crossing-over. Mutational changes in the DNA sequence can be detrimental to the fitness of an organism or they can beneficial, but many are neutral because they do not lead to any change in protein structure or function.

What are the basic mechanisms of evolution?

NATURAL SELECTION OF BEHAVIOURAL TRAITS

5.3 Explain how natural selection can act on behavioural traits.

- Natural selection can also operate on the behavioural characteristics of populations. Approaches such as sociobiology and behavioural ecology involve the application of evolutionary principles to the behaviour of animals.

- Much controversy surrounds the degree to which the theory of natural selection can be applied to human behaviour, particularly cultural behaviour. There is more agreement that biological and cultural evolution in humans may influence each other.

 *Can natural selection drive the evolution of culture? Why or why not?*

THINK ON IT

1. What are the moral and ethical implications of genetic engineering? How far should such processes be allowed to go?

2. How might the discovery of genetic cures and the use of genetic engineering affect evolution in the future?

3. What are the sources of genetic variability and how does each work?

4. There is a strong interrelationship between environmental and genetic influences on behaviour. How do these affect the way in which humans view and try to solve current social problems?

Nick Koudis/Getty Images

Human Variation

John Birdsall/The Image Works

LEARNING OBJECTIVES

6.1 Describe the processes that influence human physical and biological variation.

6.2 Describe the ways in which human populations can differ biologically, and how human biological adaptations are related to the physical and cultural environments.

6.3 Explain the contemporary views on race held by anthropologists.

6.4 Describe how cultural adaptations influence the evolution of a population.

6.5 Describe how advances in genetic engineering and gene therapy affect human biological variation.

In the preceding chapter we discussed concepts of modern evolutionary theory. Before moving on to discuss the progress of human evolution, we will review variation in modern *Homo sapiens sapiens*.

In any given human population, individuals vary in external features such as skin, hair, and eye colour or height, and in internal features such as blood type or susceptibility to a disease. If you measure the frequencies of such features in different populations, you will typically find differences on average from one population to another. So, for example, some populations are typically darker in skin colour than other populations.

Why do these physical differences exist? They may be largely the product of differences in genes. Or they may be largely due to growing up in a particular environment, physical and cultural. Or perhaps they are the result of an interaction between environmental factors and genes.

We turn first to the processes that may singly or jointly produce the varying frequencies of physical traits in different human populations. Then we discuss specific differences in external and internal characteristics and how they might be explained. Finally, we close with a critical examination of racial classification and whether it helps or hinders the study of human variation.

Processes in Human Variation

Natural Selection

Mutations, or changes in the structure of a gene, are the ultimate source of all genetic variation. Because different genes make for greater or lesser chances of survival and reproduction, natural selection results in genes associated with increased survival becoming more frequent in a population over time. How adaptive a gene or trait is depends on the environment; what is adaptive in one environment may not be adaptive in another. For example, in Chapter 4, we discussed the advantage that dark moths had over light moths when certain areas of England became industrialized. Predators could not easily see the darker moths against the newly darkened trees, and these moths soon outnumbered the lighter variety. Similarly, human populations live in a great variety of environments, so we would expect natural selection to favour different genes and traits in those different environments. As we shall see, variations in skin colour and body build are among the many features that can be at least partly explained by how natural selection works in different environments.

The type of natural selection in the moth example is called **directional selection** because a particular trait seems to be positively favoured and the average value shifts over time toward the adaptive trait. Figure 6–1 shows the effects of directional selection over time. But there can also be **normalizing selection**. In this type of selection the average value does not change, but natural selection removes the extremes (Harrison et al. 1988). An example is the birth weight of babies. Both very low birth weights and very high birth weights are disadvantageous and would be selected against. Directional selection and normalizing selection both assume that natural selection will either favour or disfavour genes, but there is a third possibility—balancing selection (Durham 1991:122). **Balancing selection** occurs when a heterozygous combination of alleles is positively favoured even though a homozygous combination is disfavoured. Later in this chapter we discuss a trait that apparently involves balancing selection—sickle-cell anemia—which is found in persons of West African ancestry, among other populations.

Natural selection does not account for variation in frequencies of neutral traits—that is, traits that do not seem to confer any advantages or disadvantages on their carriers. The sometimes different and sometimes similar frequencies of neutral traits in human populations may result, then, from genetic drift or gene flow.

Directional Selection: a type of natural selection that increases the frequency of a trait (the trait is said to be positively favoured, or *adaptive*).
Normalizing Selection: the type of natural selection that removes harmful genes that arose by mutation.
Balancing Selection: a type of selection that occurs when a heterozygous combination of alleles is positively favoured even though a homozygous combination is disfavoured.

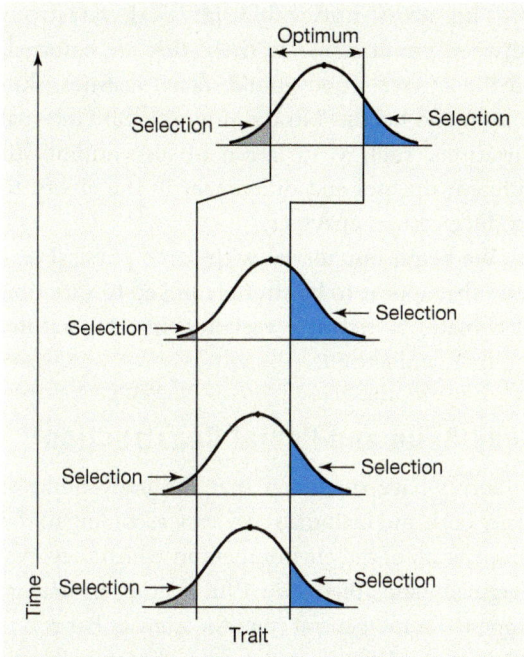

Figure 6–1 Directional Selection

Directional selection shifts the average value of a continuous trait (such as darkness of skin colour) in a population over time. The shaded grey area represents the individuals who are selected against in a particular environment; the blue represents the individuals who are selected for in that same environment. So, for example, in a very sunny environment, light skin colour would be selected against and dark skin colour would be selected for. Gradually, darker skin would become more common.

Influence of the Physical Environment

Natural selection may favour certain genes because of certain physical environmental conditions, as in the case of the moths in England. But the physical environment can sometimes produce variation even in the absence of genetic change. As we shall see, climate may influence the way the human body grows and develops, and therefore some kinds of human variation may be explainable largely as a function of environmental variation. Moreover, access to certain nutrients and exposure to certain diseases may vary from one physical environment to another, and this variation may also influence how one population differs physically from another. We call this process *acclimatization*. **Acclimatization** involves physiological adjustments in individuals to environmental conditions. Acclimatizations may have underlying genetic factors, but they are not themselves genetic. Individuals develop them during their lifetimes, rather than being born with them.

Many acclimatizations are simple physiological changes in the body that appear and disappear as the environment changes. For example, when we are chilled, our bodies attempt to create heat by making our muscles work, a physiological response to the environment that we experience as shivering. Longer exposure to cold weather leads our bodies to increase our metabolic rates so that we generate more internal heat. Both these physiological changes are acclimatizations, one short term (shivering), one longer term (increased metabolic rate).

As we discuss later in this chapter, some long-term acclimatizations are difficult to distinguish from adaptations because they become established as normal operating processes, and they may persist even after the individual moves into an environment that is different from the one that originally fostered the acclimatization. It also appears that some acclimatizations are closely related to genetic adaptations. For example, tanning, an acclimatization among light-skinned people when exposed to high levels of solar radiation, is related to the adaptation of light skin colour to environments with low solar radiation.

Influence of the Cultural Environment

Humans are not only influenced by their environments through adaptations and acclimatizations, but they can also dramatically affect their environments. Culture allows humans to modify their environments, and such modifications may lessen the likelihood of genetic adaptations and physiological acclimatizations. For example, the effects

Acclimatization: impermanent physiological changes that people make when they encounter a new environment.

of cold may be modified by the cultural traits of living in houses, harnessing energy to create heat, and clothing the body to insulate it. In these cultural ways, we alter our "microenvironments." Iron deficiency may be overcome by the cultural trait of cooking in iron pots. If a physical environment lacks certain nutrients, people may get them by the cultural trait of trading for them; for example, trading for salt has been common in world history. Culture can also influence the direction of natural selection. For example, the cultural practice of dairying seems to have increased the frequency of genes that allow adults to digest milk (Durham 1991; Laland et al. 2010).

In addition, individual cultures sometimes practise behaviours that lead to physical variations between their members and between members of one culture and another. For example, elites in many highland Andean societies (the Inca, for example) practised head binding. The heads of elite children were tightly bound with cloth. As the child grew, the binding forced the skull to take on an elongated, almost conical shape. This cultural practice, then, created physical variations among individuals that were intended to identify members of elite groups (Stewart 1950). Many cultures have practices that are intended to create physical variations that distinguish members of their culture from members of other cultures.

In the next section we discuss some aspects of human (biological) variation that involve one or more of the processes responsible for human variation.

Biological Diversity in Human Populations

While human adaptability to varying environmental conditions is a long-standing theme in anthropology, it is difficult to adequately define the term. In the broadest sense of the word, *adaptation* can refer to the basic biocultural flexibility of humans in responding to their environment. Ways in which humans adapt are through learned behaviours, species-wide physiological changes, and population-specific genetic characteristics (Harrison et al. 1988; Stinson 1992).

The most noticeable physical variations between populations are those that are external, on the surface—body build, facial features, skin colour, and height. No less important are internal variations, such as variation in susceptibility to different diseases and differences in the ability to produce certain enzymes.

We begin our survey with some physical features that appear to be strongly linked to variation in climate, particularly variation in temperature, sunlight, and altitude.

Body Build and Facial Construction

Scientists have suggested that the body build of many birds and mammals may vary according to the temperature of the environment in which they live. Bergmann and Allen, two 19th-century naturalists, suggested some general rules for animals, but it was not until the 1950s that researchers began to examine whether these rules applied to human populations (Harrison et al. 1988; Hanna et al. 1989; Leonard and Katzmarzyk 2010). **Bergmann's rule** describes what seems to be a general relationship between body size and temperature: the more slender populations of a species inhabit the warmer parts of its geographic range, and the more robust populations inhabit the cooler areas.

D.F. Roberts's studies of variation in mean body mass of human populations in regions with widely differing temperatures have provided support for Bergmann's rule (Roberts 1953, 1978; Leonard and Katzmarzyk 2010). Roberts discovered that the lowest body mass was found among residents of areas with the highest mean annual temperatures, and vice versa. Figure 6–2 shows the relationship between body mass of males and average annual temperature for four different geographic populations. Although the slope of the relationship is slightly different for each group, the trend is the same—with colder temperatures, mass is greater. Looking at the general trend across

Bergmann's Rule: the rule that smaller-sized subpopulations of a species inhabit the warmer parts of its geographical range and larger-sized subpopulations the cooler areas.

These East African young men live in a warm climate and have long limbs and torsos, which is thought to help dissipate body heat.

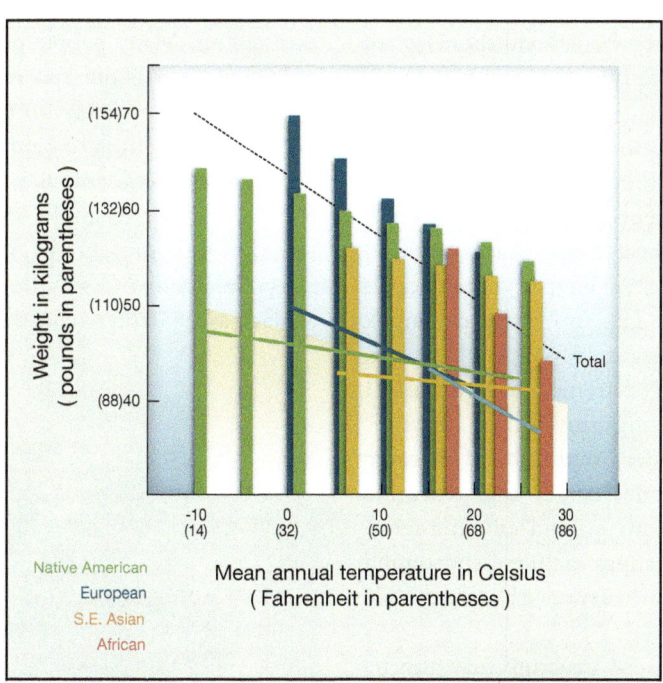

Figure 6–2 Relationship between Body Mass (Weight) of Males and Average Annual Temperature for Four Major Population Groups

Source: Roberts DF. 1953. American Journal of Physical Anthropology. Republished with permission of John Wiley & Sons, Inc.; permission conveyed through Copyright Clearance Center, Inc.

populations (see the "Total" line), we see that where the mean annual temperatures are about freezing (0°C; 32°F), the average body mass for males is about 65 kilograms; where the mean annual temperatures are about 25°C (77°F), male body mass is, on average, about 50 kilograms.

Allen's rule refers to another kind of variation in body build among birds and mammals: protruding body parts (for example, limbs) are relatively shorter in the cooler areas of a species' range than in the warmer areas. Research comparing human populations tends to support Allen's rule (Roberts 1953; Leonard and Katzmarzyk 2010).

The rationale behind these theories is that the long-limbed, lean body type often found in equatorial regions provides more surface area in relation to body mass and thus facilitates the dissipation of body heat. In contrast, the shorter-limbed body type found among residents of cold regions promotes retention of body heat because the surface area relative to body mass is less. The build of Inuit appears to exemplify Bergmann's and Allen's rules. The relatively large bodies and short legs of Inuit may be adapted to the cold temperatures in which they live.

It is not clear whether differences in body build between populations are due solely to natural selection of different genes under different conditions of cold or heat. Some of the variation may be induced during the lifespan of individuals (Harrison et al. 1988; Leonard and Katzmarzyk 2010). Alphonse Riesenfeld provided experimental evidence that extreme cold can affect body proportions during growth and development. Rats raised under conditions of extreme cold generally showed changes that resemble characteristics of humans in cold environments. These cold-related changes included shortening of the long bones, consistent with Allen's rule (Riesenfeld 1973).

Like body build, facial structure may also be affected by environment. Riesenfeld found that the facial width of rats increased in cold temperatures and their nasal openings grew smaller (Riesenfeld 1973). Because the rats raised in cold environments were genetically similar to those raised in warmer environments, we can confidently conclude that environment, not genes, brought about these changes in the rats. How much the environment directly affects variation in the human face is not clear. We do know that variation in climate is associated with facial variation. For example, people living in the humid tropics tend to have broad, short, flat noses, whereas people living in climates with low humidity (with cold or hot temperatures) tend to have long, thin noses. A narrow nose may be a more efficient humidifier of drier air than a broad nose (Weiner 1954; Steegman, Jr. 1975; Larsen 1998; Noback et al. 2011).

Skin Colour

Human populations obviously differ in average skin colour. Many people perceive skin colour as reflecting "racial" differences and sometimes treat others differently solely on this basis. But anthropologists, in addition to being critical of prejudice, also note that skin colour is not a good indicator of ancestry. For example, extremely dark skin is found most commonly in Africa. However, there are people native to southern India whose skin is as dark as or darker than that of many Africans.

This Inuit father and son illustrate Allen's rule. Both have relatively large bodies and short limbs, which help them maintain body heat in the cold climate they inhabit.

> **Allen's Rule:** the rule that protruding body parts (particularly arms and legs) are relatively shorter in the cooler areas of a species' range than in the warmer areas.

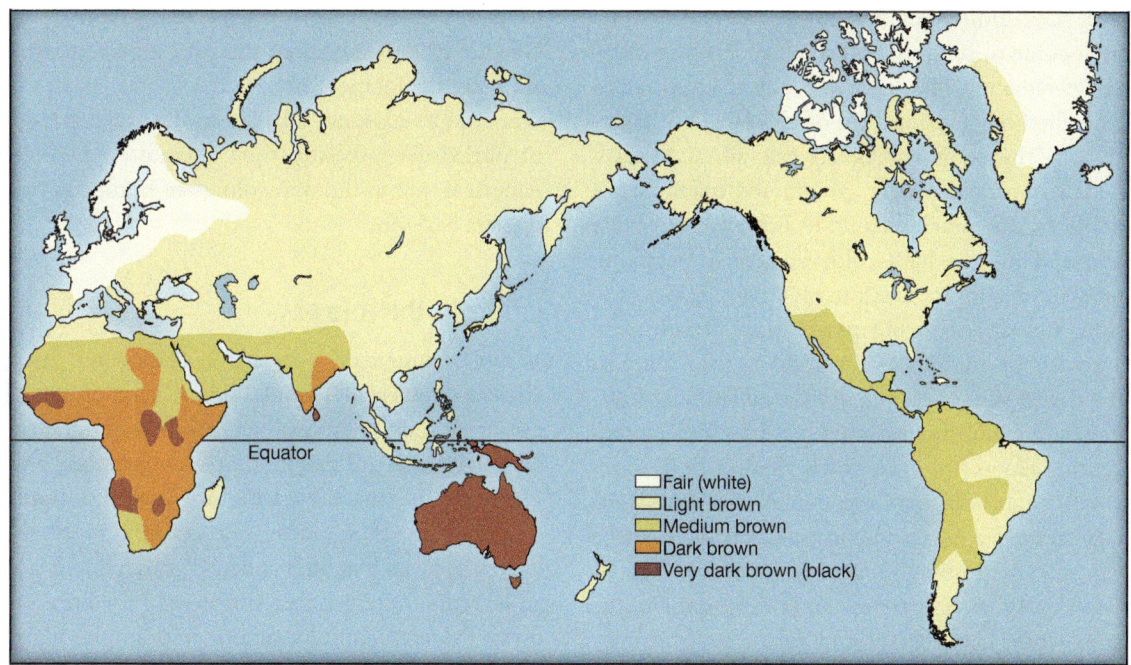

Figure 6–3 Variation in Skin Colour

Source: Robins, Ashley H. 1991. Biological perspectives on human pigmentation. New York: Cambridge University Press. Reprinted with the permission of Cambridge University Press.

Yet these people are not closely related to Africans, either genetically or historically.

How can we explain the wide range of skin colours among the peoples of the world? The colour of a person's skin depends on both the amount of dark pigment, or melanin, in the skin and the amount of blood in the small blood vessels of the skin (Jablonski 2010). Despite the fact that there is still much to understand about the genetics of skin colour, we do have some theories that may partly account for variation in skin colour.

The amount of melanin in the skin seems to be related to the climate in which a person lives. **Gloger's rule** states that populations of birds and mammals living in warmer climates have more melanin, and therefore darker skin, fur, or feathers, than do populations of the same species living

> **Gloger's Rule:** the rule that populations of birds and mammals living in warm, humid climates have more melanin (and therefore darker skin, fur, or feathers) than populations of the same species living in cooler, drier areas.

in cooler areas. On the whole, this association with climate holds true for people as well as for other mammals and birds.

The populations of darker-skinned humans do live mostly in warm climates, particularly sunny climates (Figure 6–3). Dark pigmentation seems to have at least one specific advantage in sunny climates. Melanin protects the sensitive inner layers of the skin from the sun's damaging ultraviolet rays. In fact, when someone gets a suntan, this is a product of the body's natural defence mechanism to produce more melanin to protect the skin from damage by solar radiation. Therefore, dark-skinned people living in sunny areas are safer from sunburn and skin cancers than are light-skinned people. Dark skin may also confer other important biological advantages in tropical environments, such as greater resistance to tropical diseases (Polednak 1974; Branda and Eaton 1978).

What, then, might be the advantages of light-coloured skin? Presumably, there must be some benefits in some environments; otherwise, human populations would all tend to have relatively dark skin. Although light-skinned people are more susceptible to sunburn and skin cancers, the ultraviolet radiation that light skin absorbs also facilitates the body's production of vitamin D. Vitamin D helps the body incorporate calcium and thus is necessary for the proper growth and maintenance of bones. Too much vitamin D, however, can cause illness. Thus, the light-coloured skin of people in temperate latitudes maximizes ultraviolet penetration, perhaps ensuring production of sufficient amounts of vitamin D for good health, whereas the darker skin of people in tropical latitudes minimizes ultraviolet penetration, perhaps thereby preventing illness from too much vitamin D (Loomis 1967). Light skin may also confer another advantage in colder environments: it is less likely to be damaged by frostbite (Post et al. 1975).

We now have direct evidence that confirms the connection between solar radiation and skin pigmentation. Anthropologists Nina Jablonski and George Chaplin used data from NASA satellites to determine the average amount of ultraviolet radiation people were exposed to in different parts of the world. They compared these average radiation amounts to data on skin reflectance (the lighter one's skin, the more light it reflects) and found that dark skin is more prevalent where ultraviolet radiation is more intense. Interestingly, there seems to be one notable exception—Native Americans tend to be lighter-skinned than expected. Jablonski and Chaplin (2000) suggested that this is because they are recent migrants to the New World, and their skin colours have not adapted to the varying levels of ultraviolet radiation they encountered in the Americas, just as the skin colours of European colonizers have not.

Lactase Deficiency

When American educators discovered that African-American schoolchildren very often did not drink milk, they assumed that lack of money or education was the reason. These assumptions provided the impetus for establishing the school milk programs prevalent around the country. However, it now appears that after infancy many people lack an enzyme, lactase I, that is necessary for breaking down the sugar in milk, lactose, into simpler sugars that can be absorbed into the bloodstream (Durham 1991). Thus, a person without lactase cannot digest milk properly, and drinking it may cause bloating, cramps, stomach gas, and diarrhea. A study conducted in Baltimore among 312 African-American and 221 European-American children in Grades 1 through 6 in two elementary schools indicated that 85 percent of the African-American children and 17 percent of the European-American children were milk-intolerant (Brodey 1971).

More recent studies indicate that lactose intolerance occurs frequently in adults in many parts of the world (Durham 1991). The condition is common in Southeast and East Asia, India, the Mediterranean and the Near East, sub-Saharan Africa, and among Indigenous North and South Americans. The widespread incidence of lactose intolerance should not be surprising. After infancy, mammals normally stop producing lactase (Relethford 1990; Stone and Lurquin 2007:102).

If lactose intolerance in adulthood in mammals is normal, we need to understand why only some human populations have the ability to make lactase I in adulthood and digest lactose. Why would selection favour this genetic ability in some populations but not in others? In the late 1960s, F.J. Simoons and Robert McCracken noted a relationship between lactose absorption

Human skin colour varies dramatically, and Gloger's rule explains this variation as an adaptation to climate. In humans, the intensity of sunlight is a key factor in skin colour variation.

Hans Neleman/Getty Images

and dairying (raising cows for milk). They suggested that with the advent of dairying, individuals with the genetic ability to produce lactase in adulthood would have greater reproductive success, and hence dairying populations would come to have a high proportion of individuals with the ability to break down lactose (McCracken 1971; Durham 1991).

But people in some dairying societies do not produce lactase in adulthood. Rather, they seem to have developed a cultural solution to the problem of lactase deficiency: they transform their milk into cheese, yogurt, sour cream, and other milk products that are low in lactose. To make these low-lactose products, people separate the lactose-rich whey from the curds or treat the milk with a bacterium (*Lactobacillus*) that breaks down the lactose, thus making the milk product digestible by a lactase-deficient person (McCracken 1971; Huang 2002).

So why in some dairying societies did natural selection favour a biological solution (the production in adulthood of the enzyme lactase) rather than the cultural solution? William Durham collected evidence that natural selection may favour the biological solution in dairying societies farther from the equator. The theory is that lactose behaves biochemically like vitamin D, facilitating the absorption of calcium—but only in people who produce lactase so that they can absorb the lactose. Because people in more temperate latitudes are not exposed to that much sunlight, particularly in the winter, and therefore make less vitamin D in their skin, natural selection may have favoured the lactase way of absorbing dietary calcium (Durham 1991). In other words, natural selection may favour lactase production in adulthood, as well as lighter skin, at higher latitudes (where there is less sunlight).

This is an example of how culture may influence the way natural selection favours some genes over others. Without dairying, natural selection may not have favoured the genetic propensity to produce lactase. This propensity is yet another example of the complex ways in which genes, environment, and culture interact to create human variation.

Adaptation to High Altitude

Oxygen constitutes 21 percent of the air we breathe at sea level. At high altitudes, the percentage of oxygen in the air is the same, but because the barometric pressure is lower, we take in less oxygen with each breath (Brutsaert 2010). We breathe more rapidly, our hearts beat faster, and all activity is more difficult. The net effects are discomfort and a condition known as **hypoxia**, or oxygen deficiency.

If high altitude presents such difficulties for many human beings, how is it that populations numbering in the millions can live out their lives, healthy and productive, at altitudes of 2000 metres, 3000 metres, or even 5000 metres? Populations in the Himalayas and the Andes have adapted to their environments and do not display the symptoms suffered by low-altitude dwellers if and when they are exposed to high altitudes. Moreover, high-altitude dwellers have also come to terms physiologically with extreme cold, deficient nutrition, strong winds, rough countryside, and intense solar radiation (Brutsaert 2010).

Early studies of Andean high-altitude dwellers found that they differed in certain physical ways from low-altitude dwellers. Compared with low-altitude dwellers, high-altitude Andeans had larger chests and greater lung capacity, as well as more surface area in the capillaries of the lungs (which was believed to facilitate the transfer of oxygen to the blood) (Greksa and Beall 1989). Early researchers thought that genetic changes had allowed the Andeans to maximize their ability to take in oxygen at the lower barometric pressure of their high-altitude environment. Recent research, however, has cast some doubt on this conclusion. It appears now that other populations living at high altitudes do not show the Andean pattern of

Hypoxia: a condition of oxygen deficiency that often occurs at high altitudes. The percentage of oxygen in the air is the same as at lower altitudes, but because the barometric pressure is lower, less oxygen is taken in with each breath. Often, breathing becomes more rapid, the heart beats faster, and activity is more difficult.

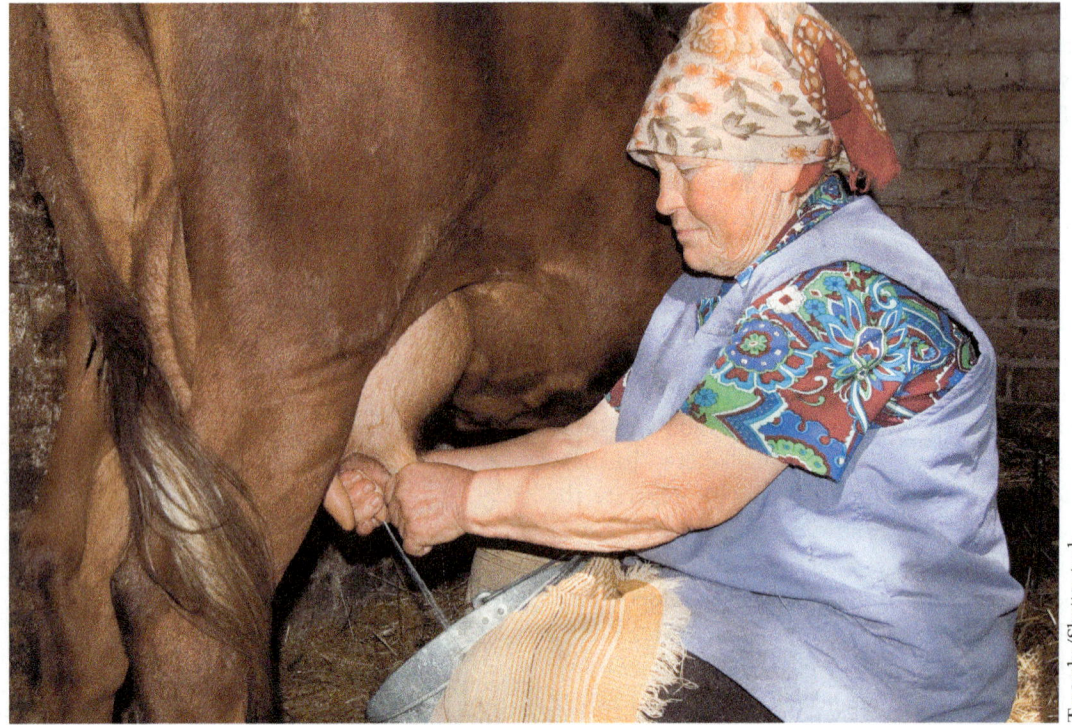
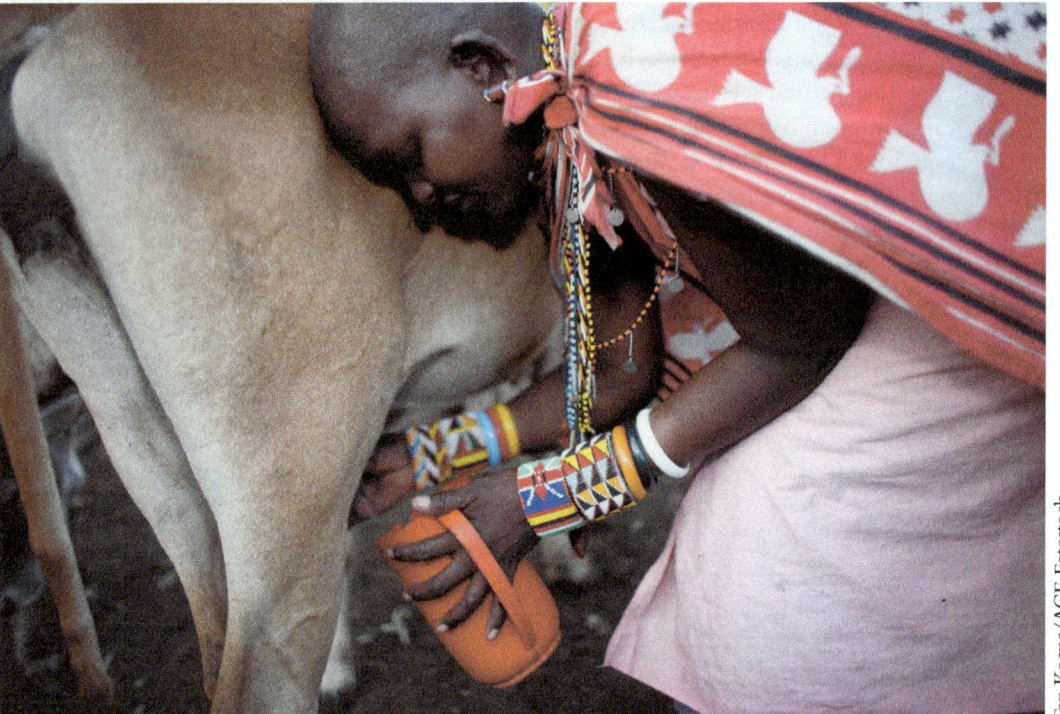

(Top) Milking a cow in Ukraine. Natural selection may favour production of the enzyme lactase, a genetic way of making milk digestible in dairying populations far from the equator. (Bottom) A Masai woman milking a cow in Kenya. Natural selection may favour the souring of milk, a cultural way of making it digestible in dairying populations close to the equator.

physical differences. In the Himalayas, for example, low-altitude dwellers and high-altitude dwellers do not differ in chest size or lung size, even though both groups show adequate lung functioning (Greksa and Beall 1989).

Thus, current research does not suggest that high-altitude living requires biological adaptations that are purely genetic. In fact, some evidence suggests that humans who grow up in a high-altitude environment may adapt to hypoxia during their lifetimes, as they mature. For example, Peruvians who were born at sea level but who grew up at high altitudes developed the same amount of lung capacity as people who spent their entire lives at high altitudes (Frisancho and Greksa 1989). Consistent with a presumed environmental effect, the children of high-altitude Peruvians who grow up in the lowlands do not develop larger chests. As with other traits that have been studied, it appears that life experiences can have profound effects on how the body grows.

Height

Studies of identical twins and comparisons of the height of parents and children suggest that heredity plays a considerable role in determining height (Eveleth and Tanner 1990), so genetic differences must at least partly explain average height differences between populations. For example, Hoppa and Garlie (1998) examined the pattern of height versus age for Toronto schoolchildren, from the late 19th century to the early and middle 20th century. The data clearly show a positive **secular trend**—change over time—toward increased attained height for age from the earliest to the most recent data, reflective of a global trend toward increased height and reduced age of sexual maturity over the last several centuries.

The considerable variation in average height among human populations may be partly explained by temperature differences. The Dutch of Europe are among the tallest populations in the world on average, and the Mbuti in central Africa are among the shortest (Bogin 1988). We already know that mass is related to mean annual temperature (Bergmann's rule). Body mass is also related to height (taller people are likely to be heavier). So, since the taller (heavier) Dutch live in a cooler climate, some of the population variation in height would appear to involve adaptation to heat and cold (Harrison et al. 1988). Other factors besides heat and cold must also be operating, however, because tall and short peoples can be found in most areas of the world.

Many researchers think that poor nutrition and disease lead to reduced height and body mass. In many parts of the world, children in higher social classes are taller on the average than children in lower social classes (Harrison et al. 1988), and this difference is more marked in economically poorer countries (Huss-Ashmore and Johnston 1985), where the wealth and health differences between the classes are particularly large. During times of war and poor nutrition, children's stature often decreases. For example, in Germany during World War II, the stature of children 7 to 17 years of age declined (as compared with similar data over previous periods), despite the fact that stature had generally increased over time (Harrison et al. 1988).

More persuasive evidence for the effects of poor nutrition and disease comes out of longitudinal studies of the same individuals over time. For example, Reynaldo Martorell found that children in Guatemala who had frequent bouts of diarrhea were on the average over 3 centimetres shorter at 7 years of age than children without frequent diarrhea (1980). Although malnourished or diseased children can catch up in their growth, follow-up research on Guatemalan children suggests that if stunting occurs before 3 years of age, stature at age 18 will still be reduced (Martorell et al. 1991).

As we noted earlier, in several areas of the world, people have been getting taller. What accounts for this recent trend toward greater height? Several factors may be involved. Researchers have generally agreed that improvements in health and nutrition in communities have likely contributed to the observed changes in patterns of growth (Tanner 1966, 1992;

Secular Trend: a change in growth and developmental measures over time.

In recent times there has been a dramatic increase in average height, which may be due to one or more environmental factors. Here we see a Chinese-American girl who is taller than her mother and almost as tall as her father.

Hauspie et al. 1996). Scientists agree that the positive secular trend in growth for many countries began in the 19th century, during the period of increased industrialization and subsequent improvements in socio-economic conditions (Tanner 1966; Cole 2003). However, others have noted that there are secular changes in height that predate the health and nutritional improvements of this time. Further, some studies have observed no secular shifts in the height of populations even where such improvements have occurred (Stulp and Barrett 2014). In short, both genetic and environmental factors seem to be responsible for differences in human size.

Susceptibility to Infectious Diseases

Certain populations seem to have developed inherited resistances to certain infectious diseases; that is, populations repeatedly decimated by certain diseases in the past now have a high frequency of genetic characteristics that ameliorate the effects of these diseases. As Arno Motulsky (1971) pointed out, if there are genes that protect people from dying when they are infected by one of the diseases prevalent in their area, these genes will tend to become more common in succeeding generations.

Infectious diseases seem to follow this pattern among human populations. When a disease enters a population that has not been previously exposed to it or has not had exposure for a considerably long time, this often results in what is called a **virgin soil epidemic**. In other words, because there is no previous immunity within a portion of the population, the disease tends to affect all members of the group equally, and can be extremely dangerous. The 1918 influenza *pandemic* that affected populations around the world is a good example. Other examples include new diseases brought by the explorers to the New World. We tend to think of measles as a childhood disease that kills virtually no one, and we now have a vaccine against it. But when first introduced into populations, the measles virus can kill large numbers of people. In 1949, the Tupari of Brazil numbered about 200 people. By 1955, two-thirds of the Tupari had died of measles introduced into the tribe by rubber gatherers in the area (Motulsky 1971). Large numbers of people died of measles in epidemics in the Faroe Islands in 1846, in Hawaii in 1848, in the Fiji Islands in 1874, and among Inuit in Canada very recently. It is possible that where mortality rates from measles are low, populations have acquired a genetic resistance to death from this disease (Motulsky 1971).

More recently diseases like the West Nile virus and SARS have had similar impacts on many populations. In North America, Toronto had the largest outbreak of SARS (severe acute respiratory syndrome) in the spring of 2003

Virgin Soil Epidemic: occurs when a disease enters a population that has not been previously exposed to it, or has not had exposure for a considerably long time. Because there is no previous immunity within a portion of the population, the disease tends to affect all members of the group equally.

(Naylor et al. 2004; Svoboda et al. 2004). In Toronto, 225 residents met the case definition of SARS, and all but three travel-related cases were linked to the original patient, who had returned to Toronto from a trip to Hong Kong (Svoboda et al. 2004). The disease spread to more than half of Toronto's acute care hospitals, and undiagnosed cases among patients caused a resurgence, or a second phase, of the outbreak. In total, Toronto Public Health investigated 2132 potential cases of SARS, identified 23 103 contacts of SARS patients as requiring quarantine, and logged 316 615 calls on its SARS hotline (Svoboda et al. 2004). Despite the relatively low and restricted spread among the Canadian population, the SARS outbreak had a significant psychological and economic impact (Blendon et al. 2004).

But why is a population susceptible to a disease in the first place? The epidemiologist Francis Black suggested that lack of genes for resistance is not the whole answer. A high degree of genetic homogeneity in the population may also increase susceptibility (Black 1992). A virus grown in one host is pre-adapted to a genetically similar new host and is therefore likely to be more virulent in the new host. For example, the measles virus adapts to a host individual; when it replicates, the forms that the host cannot kill are those most likely to survive and continue replicating. When the virus passes to a new host *with similar genes*, the pre-adapted virus is likely to kill the new host. If, on the other hand, the next host is very different genetically, the adaptation process starts all over; the virus is not so virulent at first because the host can kill it.

Populations that recently came to an area, and that had a small group of founders (as was probably true for the first Indigenous peoples in North America and the Polynesian seafarers who first settled many islands in the Pacific), tended to have a high degree of genetic homogeneity. Therefore, epidemic diseases introduced by Europeans (such as measles) would be likely to kill many of the Indigenous people within the first few years after contact. It is estimated that 56 million people died in the New World after contact with Europeans, mostly because of introduced diseases such as

Permanent settlements and high population densities allow diseases to spread rapidly and produce epidemics. Shown here is Banda Aceh's Peunayong Market in Indonesia. Close contact between chickens and humans in markets like this one provided the opportunity for the deadly H5N1 strain of bird flu to evolve.

smallpox and measles. Recent work by Linda Larcombe and colleagues at the University of Manitoba examined the genetics of the immune response of Indigenous populations in northern Canada. Analysis from both aDNA from archaeological remains and modern living populations in northern Manitoba suggested that these populations, in comparison to non-Indigenous groups, have an immune system that was adapted to a particular environment—more specifically, an environment in which helminthic, parasitic, and fungal infections predominated (Larcombe, Nickerson et al. 2005; Larcombe, Rempel et al. 2005; Larcombe et al. 2008).

Most researchers agree that non-genetic factors may also partly explain differential resistance to infectious disease. Increasingly, anthropologists have become aware that human behaviour plays an important role in the distribution and spread of infectious diseases. Differences in most disease patterns are, in fact, largely the result of cultural differences in behaviours and not biological variation (Dunn and Janes 1986; Inhorn and Brown 1990; Sattenspiel 1990). For example, Ann Herring and colleagues have been exploring the impact of socio-cultural behaviours associated with changing patterns of disease and mortality in central Canadian subarctic Cree populations during the 19th and early 20th centuries. Among the Western James Bay Cree at Moose Factory, a clearly seasonal pattern of epidemic diseases in this period can be observed. This reflects the seasonal socio-economic pattern of life that existed among these people. In the winter, the community dispersed in the small family units to trap furs, with population density reduced and contact between individuals minimized. However, during the summer, families congregated around the Hudson's Bay Company post, and increased population numbers and density, coupled with more inter-community travel, led to epidemic outbreaks of a variety of diseases like measles, whooping cough, and influenza (Hoppa 1998; Herring and Hoppa 1999). In fact, in modelling the patterns of travel—where people travelled to and when, how often, and how long they stayed—between communities during the 1918 influenza pandemic, Lisa Sattenspiel and Ann Herring observed that social organization and responses to the epidemic were more important than movement patterns between communities for explaining the differences in the impact of this virgin soil epidemic on the three study communities (Sattenspiel and Herring 1998). Epidemics of infectious disease may occur only if many people live near each other.

Early hunters and gatherers lived in small, mobile bands that seldom came into contact with other human groups. While they would have been susceptible to parasitic infections as well as non-specific infections, the high mobility of these groups would have made them relatively safe from diseases transmitted by humans. With little contact between the different groups, it would have been difficult for any human-transmitted disease to survive and spread. With the domestication of plants and animals, increase in sedentary life, and increased overall population size and density (discussed in Chapter 12), human beings became susceptible to a new range of diseases that they had been able to avoid in the past. Infectious diseases that required large populations to maintain themselves were now able to do so. As a consequence of humans and animals living in close proximity to each other and domesticated animals, easy transmission of diseases between both humans and animals alike was facilitated. Tuberculosis is an example of an infectious disease that, although very old, began to kill large numbers of people only after the emergence of sedentary, larger communities (Armelagos and Harper 2005).

Sickle-Cell Anemia

Another biological variation is an abnormality of the red blood cells known as **sickle-cell anemia**, or **sicklemia**. This is a condition in which normal,

> **Sickle-Cell Anemia (Sicklemia):** a condition in which red blood cells assume a crescent (sickle) shape when deprived of oxygen, instead of the normal (disk) shape. The sickle-shaped red blood cells do not move through the body as readily as normal cells, and thus cause damage to the heart, lungs, brain, and other vital organs.

disk-shaped red blood cells assume a crescent (sickle) shape when deprived of oxygen. The sickle-shaped red blood cells do not move through the body as readily as normal cells, and thus cause more oxygen deficiency and damage to the heart, lungs, brain, and other vital organs. In addition, the red blood cells tend to "die" more rapidly, and the anemia worsens still more (Stone and Lurquin 2007:96–98).

Sickle-cell anemia is caused by a variant form of the genetic instructions for hemoglobin, the protein that carries oxygen in the red blood cells (Durham 1991). Individuals who have sickle-cell anemia have inherited the same allele (Hb^S) from both parents and are therefore *homozygous* for that gene. Individuals who receive this allele from only one parent are *heterozygous*; they have one Hb^S allele and one allele for normal hemoglobin (Hb^A). Heterozygotes generally will not show the full-blown symptoms of sickle-cell disease, although in some cases a heterozygous individual may have a mild case of anemia. A heterozygous person has a 50 percent chance of passing on the sickle-cell allele to a child. And if the child later mates with another person who is also a carrier of the sickle-cell allele, the statistical probability is that 25 percent of their children will develop sickle-cell anemia. Without advanced medical care, most individuals with two Hb^S alleles are unlikely to live more than a few years (Stone and Lurquin 2007:104–105).

Why has the allele for sickle-cell persisted in various populations? If people with sickle-cell anemia do not usually live to reproduce, we would expect a reduction in the frequency of Hb^S to near zero through the process of *normalizing selection*. But the sickle-cell allele occurs fairly often in some parts of the world, particularly in the wet tropical belt of Africa, where frequencies may be between 20 and 30 percent, and in Greece, Sicily, and southern India (Harrison et al. 1988).

Because the sickle-cell gene occurs in these places much more often than expected, researchers in the 1940s and 1950s began to suspect that heterozygous individuals (who carry one Hb^S allele) might have a reproductive advantage in a malarial environment (Durham 1991). If the heterozygotes were more resistant to attacks of malaria than the homozygotes for normal hemoglobin (who get the Hb^A allele from both parents), the heterozygotes would be more likely to survive and reproduce, and therefore the recessive Hb^S allele would persist at a higher than expected frequency in the population. This kind of outcome is an example of *balancing selection* (Madigral 1989).

A number of pieces of evidence support the "malaria theory." First, geographic comparisons show that the sickle-cell allele tends to be found where the incidence of malaria is high (see Figure 6–4). Second, as land in the tropics is opened to yam and rice agriculture, the incidence of the sickle-cell allele also increases. In fact, recent studies suggest malaria may have evolved alongside agriculture in these regions (Pennisi 2001). The reason seems to be that malaria, carried principally by the *Anopheles gambiae* mosquito, becomes more prevalent as tropical forest gives way to more open land where mosquitoes can thrive in warm, sunlit ponds. Indeed, even among peoples of similar cultural backgrounds, the incidence of the sickle-cell allele increases with greater rainfall and surpluses of water. Third, children who are heterozygous for the sickle-cell trait tend to have fewer malarial parasites in their bodies than do homozygous normal individuals, and they are more likely to survive (Madigral 1989; Stone and Lurquin 2007). The sickling trait does not necessarily keep people from contracting malaria, but it greatly decreases the rate of mortality from malaria—and in evolutionary terms, the overall effect is the same (Motulsky 1971). Fourth, if there is no balancing selection because malaria is no longer present, we should find a rapid decline in the incidence of the sickle-cell allele. Indeed, we find such a decline in populations with African ancestry. Those who live in malaria-free zones of the New World have a much lower incidence of sickle-cell anemia than do those who live in malarial regions of the New World (Diamond 1993).

Hb^S is not the only abnormal hemoglobin to have a distribution related to malaria. It seems that

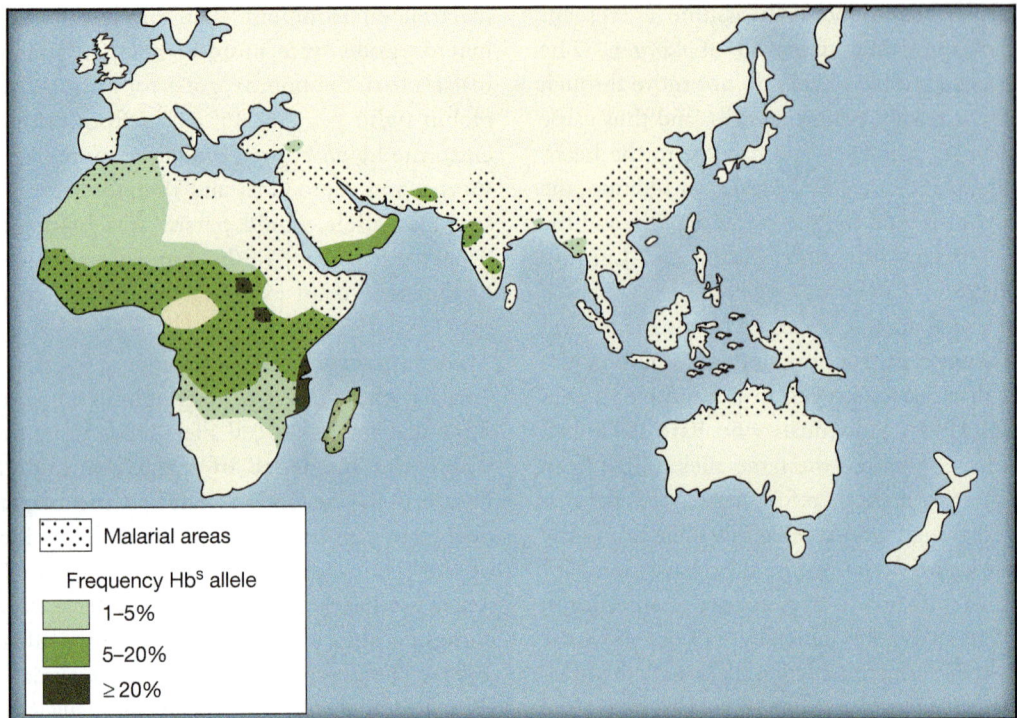

Figure 6–4 Geographic Distribution of Sicklemia and Its Relationship to the Distribution of Malaria

a number of abnormal hemoglobins may be much more widespread because of the advantage heterozygotes have against the disease. For example, another abnormal hemoglobin, Hb^E, occurs in populations from India through to Southeast Asia and New Guinea where malaria occurs, but Hb^S is not that common. Why should heterozygotes have resistance to malaria? One possibility is that malarial parasites are less able to survive in an individual's blood with some normal and some abnormal hemoglobin. Abnormal hemoglobin cells are more delicate and don't live as long, so they cannot readily support malarial parasites (Molnar 1998).

Type II Diabetes

Type II diabetes or *non-insulin-dependent diabetes mellitus (NIDDM)*, unlike insulin-dependent diabetes, tends to manifest itself in adult patients as a result of a sedentary lifestyle, chronic obesity, and excess sugar intake. The disease is particularly common in certain Indigenous populations, including First Nations people in Canada. In 1962 J.V. Neel suggested that a "thrifty gene" might exist in greater proportion in certain human populations (Neel 1962). This gene may have held survival value in periods of food shortage, but under a modern Westernized lifestyle characterized by food abundance, high carbohydrate intake, and sedentary living patterns, it would lead to increased obesity and diabetes incidence (see Applied Anthropology, "Obesity, Hypertension, and Diabetes: Health Consequences of Modernization?"). Critics have

Type II Diabetes: non-insulin-dependent diabetes mellitus (NIDDM), unlike insulin-dependent diabetes, that tends to manifest itself in adult patients as a result of a sedentary lifestyle, chronic obesity, and excess sugar intake.

APPLIED ANTHROPOLOGY

Obesity, Hypertension, and Diabetes: Health Consequences of Modernization?

Contact with the West first brought medical devastation to many populations previously unexposed to European illnesses. However, with the acceptance of modern medical care throughout much of the "developing world," infant mortality has declined and life expectancies have gone up. These achievements have largely come about because of the control of major epidemic diseases, such as smallpox (now eradicated), cholera, yellow fever, syphilis, and tuberculosis, as well as the inoculation of children against childhood diseases. Improvements in medical health are by no means uniform. The AIDS epidemic, which we discuss in Chapter 14, is spreading throughout much of the world. Overall deaths from infectious diseases may have declined, but other health problems have increased. As more people survive into older ages, problems of hypertension, heart disease, cancer, and diabetes increase. Some of the increase in these chronic diseases is due to the aging of populations, but much of it appears to be due to changes in lifestyle that accompany modernization.

A good deal of research has focused on the Samoans of the South Pacific, who traditionally depended on root and tree crop horticulture. As did many other people in the modern world, Samoans increasingly moved to urban areas, worked for wages, and started buying most of their food. Researchers reported substantial increases, within a relatively short time, in rates of hypertension, diabetes, and obesity across a wide range of age groups. For example, in 1990 about two-thirds of American Samoans were severely overweight, up substantially from the situation in the 1970s. And Samoans from more rural areas show less hypertension and physiological signs of stress. Among the lifestyle changes thought to be responsible are less physical activity and changes in diet to low-fibre, high-calorie foods. Stress may also increase as more individuals buy material things and status goods without having the economic resources to support them.

What about genetic factors? Could some genetic predisposition be interacting with modernization to create obesity in the Samoan population? One possibility is referred to as the "thrifty" gene. The geneticist James Neel suggested that individuals who have very efficient metabolisms and who can store calories in fatty tissue are most apt to survive and reproduce in environments with frequent famines or chronic food shortages. In time, populations in such environments would have a high prevalence of individuals with "thrifty" genes. What happens, though, when such individuals no longer need to exercise much or have access to high-calorie foods? Neel suggested that adult-onset diabetes might result, a scenario that is consistent with the increase in diabetes in Samoa and other parts of Polynesia. It is also consistent with the increase in obesity and hypertension.

The "thrifty" gene theory does not pertain just to the Samoans and other Polynesian populations. Several human populations likely had to cope with food uncertainty in the past. Neel originally proposed that famines during the Paleolithic selected for thrifty genes, but this idea has been since refuted. Based on molecular evidence, it is more likely that famines and food shortages occurring in sedentary agricultural societies over the past 10 000 to 12 000 years would have favoured thrifty genes via fertility selection.

If the food supply increases with modernization but it is accompanied by a reduction in physical activity and a switch to high-calorie diets, then increases in obesity, diabetes, and hypertension may frequently accompany modernization. Understanding both biological and cultural factors is essential in helping populations adapt to conditions of urban life.

Sources: Allen JS, Cheer SM. 1996. The Non-thrifty Genotype. Current Anthropology. 37:831–842.

When food is not plentiful, the "thrifty gene" helps people survive on less. But when the food supply becomes plentiful and reliable, people may become overweight, as in the Marquesas.

Bindon JR, Crews DE. 1993. Changes in Some Health Status Characteristics of American Samoan Men: Preliminary Observations from a 12-Year Follow-Up Study. American Journal of Human Biology. 5:31–37.

Bindon JR, Knight A, Dressler WW, Crews DE. 1997. Social Context and Psychosocial Influences on Blood Pressure among American Samoans. American Journal of Physical Anthropology. 103:7–18.

McGarvey ST. 1994. The Thrifty Gene Concept and Adiposity Studies in Biological Anthropology. Journal of the Polynesian Society. 103:29–42.

Pearson JD, James GD, Brown DE. 1993. Stress and Changing Lifestyles in the Pacific: Physiological Stress Responses of Samoans in Rural and Urban Settings. American Journal of Human Biology. 5:49–60.

Prentice AM, Hennig BJ, Fulford AJ. 2008. Evolutionary Origins of the Obesity Epidemic: Natural Selection of Thrifty Genes or Genetic Drift Following Predation Release? International Journal of Obesity. 23:1607–1610.

World Bank. World Development Report 1995. Workers in an Integrating World. Oxford: Oxford University Press.

---

noted that this theory assumes that carbohydrate intake exceeds daily energy requirements. The early occupants of North America subsisted in Arctic or subarctic environments, living on protein- and fat-based diets with few carbohydrates (Ritenbaugh and Goodby 1989; Szathmáry 1990, 1994). Alternative metabolic pathways to provide energy may have been favoured in them by natural selection (Young, Reading et al. 2000). Other explanations continue to be offered. Hegele observed the presence of a genetic mutation among Indigenous people in northern Ontario that is highly predictive of Type II diabetes (Hegele 2001). Alternatively, it has been suggested that Type II diabetes is the result of fetal malnutrition (Benyshek et al. 2001).

Of all the chronic conditions, Type II diabetes has been prominent in the epidemiological literature because of its high prevalence among many Indigenous populations in Canada and other parts of the world. According to a 2011 report from the Public Health Agency of Canada, the prevalence of diabetes among Indigenous groups in Canada is as follows: 15.3 percent of First Nations people on reserve, 8.7 percent of First Nations people off reserve, 5.8 percent of Métis people, and 4 percent of Inuit (Public Health Agency of Canada 2011). Of those with the disease, about two-thirds are women (Health Canada 1997). Compared with non-Indigenous rates in Canada, diabetes is between two and five times more prevalent among Indigenous people (Young et al. 1990; Waldram et al. 1995). Inuit are an exception to this pattern, with rates that are currently below the national average. However, there is some evidence that these rates may be on the rise, and that over time Inuit may be comparable to other Indigenous groups (Health Canada 1997). Between 2001 and 2006, the self-reported prevalence of diabetes among Inuit in Canada went from 2 percent to 4 percent (Tait 2008).

Up until the 1940s, diabetes was virtually unknown among Indigenous populations (Chase 1937; Szathmáry 1994; MacMillan et al. 1996). However, in 1983 a study in the Sioux Lookout Zone observed a prevalence rate of 2.8 percent for the disease. A decade later, it had risen to 3.8 percent, a pattern of increase that has been observed by a variety of studies (Young et al. 1985; Fox et al. 1994). For chronic illnesses of long duration, such as diabetes, the prevalence can be expected to increase over time as a function of survival of people with diabetes and aging of the population (Health Canada 1997).

Although Type II diabetes is classed as "adult-onset," concern has been raised by researchers who have observed increased incidence of the disease in recent years in Indigenous children as young as 5 to 8 years of age (Dean et al. 1992; Harris et al. 1996, 1997; Young, Dean et al. 2000; Kaler et al. 2006). According to Health Canada, the number of Indigenous children in Manitoba with a diagnosis of diabetes has been on the rise (Blanchard et al. 1996; Winnipeg Regional Health Authority 2004). A similar pattern was observed in the Sioux Lookout Zone, with diagnoses in children rising from 18 in 1994 to 52 in 1997 (Health Canada 1997). In both instances, girls outnumbered boys by more than five to one among the children with this condition (Health Canada 1997).

Diabetes, and in particular Type II diabetes (T2DM), has become perhaps one of the most important health concerns of First Nations people today. Understanding the impact (Daniel et al. 1999;

Rodrigues et al. 1999; Bruce 2000; Jacobs et al. 2000; Young, Reading et al. 2000) and addressing perception of health and disease among Indigenous communities (Daniel et al. 1999; Bruce 2000) are a critical facet of dealing with this disease. In addressing the health problems associated with diabetes, the First Nations have increased their leadership role in the First Nations and Inuit Health Branch (FNIHB). In 1994, the National Aboriginal Diabetes Association (NADA) was created, bringing together representatives of First Nations and Inuit national, regional, and tribal organizations. Successful models of such initiatives include the Sandy Lake Health and Diabetes Project (SLHDP) partnership, which formed in 1991 between Sandy Lake First Nation and researchers to address the high rates of T2DM in the community and undertake culturally appropriate interventions (Kakekagumick et al. 2013).

"Race" and Racism

For as long as any of us can remember, countless aggressive actions—from fistfights to large-scale riots and civil wars—have stemmed from tensions and misunderstandings between various groups commonly referred to by many as "races." *Race* has become such a common term that most of us take the concept for granted, not bothering to consider what it does, and does not, mean. We may talk about the "human race," which means that all humans belong to the same breeding population. Yet we are often asked to check a box to identify our particular "race." We discuss first how biologists sometimes use the term *race*; then we turn to why many biological anthropologists and others now conclude that the concept of race does not usefully apply to humans. We discuss how racial classifications are largely social constructions that have been used to justify the exploitation and even execution of certain categories of people.

The Biological Fallacy of Race

Biological variation is not uniformly distributed in any species. While all members of a species can potentially interbreed with others, most matings take place within smaller groups or breeding populations. Through the processes of natural selection and genetic drift, populations inhabiting different geographic regions will exhibit some differences in biological traits. When differences within a species become sufficiently noticeable, biologists may classify different populations into different *varieties*. Unfortunately, as applied to humans, racial classifications are the product of social and cultural beliefs that certain groups of people (often classed as different "races") are innately inferior to others. Historically, a number of populations have been subjected to discrimination on the basis of this concept, which unfortunately continues to be prevalent among many members of today's populations. However, biological anthropologists and others have argued that the concept cannot be applied to human biological differences. Nevertheless, racial profiling is often used in law enforcement, and within forensic anthropology it is associated with the determination of ancestry in order to help identify unknown skeletal remains (see Applied Anthropology, "The Use of 'Race' in Forensic Anthropology"). But as forensic anthropologist Norm Sauer noted, "the successful assignment of race to a skeletal specimen is not a vindication of the race concept, but rather a prediction that an individual, while alive was assigned to a particular socially constructed 'racial' category" (Sauer 1992:107; see also Ousley et al. 2009).

A second reason for not applying racial classification to humans is that humans have exhibited so much interbreeding that different populations are not clearly classifiable into discrete groups that can be defined in terms of the presence or absence of particular biological traits (Marks 1994; Shanklin 1994). Therefore, many argue that "race" is not scientifically useful for describing human biological variation. The difficulty in employing racial classification is evident by comparing the number of "races" that classifiers come up with. The number of "racial" categories in humans has varied from as few as 3 to more than 37 (Molnar 1998).

How can human groups be clearly divided into "races" if most adaptive biological traits show clines or gradual differences from one region to another (Brace et al. 1993)? Skin colour is a good

APPLIED ANTHROPOLOGY

The Use of "Race" in Forensic Anthropology

In this chapter, we have made the point that human "races" are not valid biological entities. There is more genetic variation within alleged "races" than between them, and the characteristics used to define "races" are primarily visual—skin colour, hair form, eye form, and the like. Most anthropologists (over 70 percent, according to a recent survey) disagree with the statement "There are biological races in the species *Homo sapiens*." Given this fact, it seems odd that many forensic anthropologists still employ "race" as one of the categories for identifying skeletal remains.

Diana Smay and George Armelagos suggested three reasons why forensic anthropologists still employ the concept of "race." First, some forensic anthropologists genuinely believe that "race" is a useful analytical tool. For these anthropologists, the fact that it is easy for anyone to categorize others into "races" must mean something is genuine about the concept. Indeed, some forensic anthropologists suggest that they can determine "race" with 80 percent accuracy from skeletal remains (although others argue that without clear information about the specific geographical location where the remains were found, accuracy drops to less than 20 percent). Second, in some circumstances the "race" concept seems to work. Within local areas, at least, a well-trained forensic anthropologist can determine whether a skeleton comes from one of the major "race" groups. But as forensic anthropologist Madeleine Hinkes explained, "sometimes it is only the anthropologist's experience that tells him there is an undefinable 'something' about the skeleton that suggests one race over another" (1993:51)—not a very convincing argument for the analytical utility of "race."

A third reason Smay and Armelagos gave for why many forensic anthropologists continue to employ the concept of "race" is that they are asked to do so. As Stanley Rhine pointed out, "The forensic anthropologist who can tell officials that an unknown skull is, for instance, Hispanic, provides datum useful in narrowing search parameters. By contrast, the forensic anthropologist who delivers a philosophical lecture to the sheriff on the non-existence of human races is unlikely to be consulted again" (1993:55). But is this a good reason to employ the concept of "race"? Might there be a better way to provide information to police and other officials to help them identify a set of human remains? Alice Brues thinks so. She argued that forensic anthropologists should focus on local, geographic variations among populations that we know do exist and avoid the large "race" categories that we

Forensic anthropologists are often asked to determine the race of a skeletal corpse.

know do not. In Alaska, for example, forensic anthropologists might be able to distinguish between Inuit and Aleut remains, or between Chinese, Japanese, and Polynesian in California. Brues argued that by lumping the real variation that is present in these local populations into predefined "racial" categories, forensic anthropologists limit their ability to use the full range of variation to identify unique, local variations that might be useful in identifying human remains.

Sources: Brues A. 1992. Forensic Diagnosis of Race—General Race versus Specific Populations. Social Science and Medicine. 34:125–128.

Hinkes M. 1993. Race, Ethnicity, and Forensic Anthropology. NAPA Bulletin. 13:51.

Lieberman L, Kirk R, Littlefield A. 2003. Perishing Paradigm: Race 1931–99. American Anthropologist. 105:110–113.

Rhine S. 1993. Skeletal Criteria for Racial Attribution. NAPA Bulletin. 13:54–67.

Smay D, Armelagos G. 2000. Galileo Wept: A Critical Assessment of the Use of Race in Forensic Anthropology. Transforming Anthropology. 9:19–29.

example of clinal variation. In the area around Egypt, there is a gradient of skin colour as one moves from north to south in the Nile Valley. Skin generally becomes darker closer to the equator (south) and lighter closer to the Mediterranean. But other adaptive traits may not have north–south clines, because the environmental predictors may be distributed differently. Nose shape varies with humidity, but clines in humidity do not particularly correspond to variation in latitude. So the gradient for skin colour would not be the same as the gradient for nose shape. Because adaptive traits tend to be clinally distributed, there is no line you could draw on a world map that would separate "white" from "black" people or "whites" from "Asians" (Brooks et al. 1993). Only traits that are neutral in terms of natural selection will tend (because of genetic drift) to cluster in regions (Brace et al. 1993; Dupré 2008:50).

Racial classification is extremely problematic because we know there is more physical, physiological, and genetic diversity *within* a single geographic group that might be called a race (for example, Africans) than there is *between* such supposed groups. For example, sub-Saharan Africans vary more among themselves than they do in comparison with people elsewhere (Brooks et al. 1993). Analyses of all human populations have demonstrated that 93 to 95 percent of genetic variation is due to individual differences within populations, while only 3 to 5 percent of genetic variation is due to differences among major human population groups (King and Motulsky 2002). "Race" when applied to humans is a social category, not a scientific one.

"Race" as a Social Construct

If race is not a useful device for classifying humans, why is it so widely used? Racial classifications should be recognized for what they are—social categories to which individuals are assigned, by themselves and others, on the basis of supposedly shared biological traits.

If racial categories are just social categories, we need to ask why they were invented. Part of the answer may be a desire to separate "my" group from others. People tend to be ethnocentric, to view their culture as better than other cultures. Therefore, racial classifications reflect the same tendency to divide "us" from "them." For example, German-speaking Hutterites who settled in parts of Canada in the early 20th century were viewed with suspicion when World War I broke out. Similarly, Japanese Canadians became "the enemy" in World War II, even though many of them were second-generation Canadians.

We do know that racial classifications have often been, and still are, used by certain groups to justify discrimination, exploitation, or genocide. Recent examples include the campaigns of "ethnic cleansing" in the Balkans. The most heinous 20th-century example, of course, was Hitler's vision of the blond-haired, blue-eyed, white-skinned "Aryan race" dominating the world, to which end he and others committed mass genocide. It is estimated that 6 million Jews, Slavs, and others were murdered in the Holocaust (Friedman 1980). But who are the Aryans? Technically, Aryans are any people, including the German-speaking Jews in Hitler's Germany, who speak one of the Indo-European languages. The Indo-European languages include such disparate modern tongues as Greek, Spanish, Hindi, Polish, French, Icelandic, German, Gaelic, and English. And many Aryans speaking these languages have neither blond hair nor blue eyes. Similarly, all kinds of people may be Jews, whether or not they descend from the ancient Near Eastern population that spoke the Hebrew language. There are light-skinned Danish Jews and darker Jewish Arabs. One of the most orthodox Jewish groups in the United States is based in New York City and is composed entirely of African Americans.

The arbitrary and social basis of most racial classifications becomes apparent when you compare how they differ from one place to another. Consider, for example, what used to be thought about the races in South Africa. Under apartheid, the system of racial segregation and discrimination, someone with mixed "white" and "black" ancestry was considered "coloured." However, when important people of African ancestry from other countries would visit South Africa, they were often considered "white." Chinese were considered "Asian," but the Japanese, who were important economically to South Africa, were considered "white" (Ross 1998). Biologically speaking, this makes no sense, but socially it was another story (Marks 1994).

The Myths of Racism

"Race" and Civilization.
Many people hold the racist viewpoint that the biological inferiority of certain groups, which they call "races," is reflected in the supposedly "primitive" quality of their cultures. They argue that the "developed" nations are "white" and the "developing" nations are not. (We put terms like "white," which are used as racial categories, in quotes to indicate the problematic nature of the categories.) But to make such an argument ignores much of history. As will be discussed in Chapter 13, many of today's "developing nations"—primarily in Asia, Africa, and South America—had developed complex and sophisticated civilizations long before European nations expanded and acquired considerable power. The advanced societies of the Shang dynasty in China, the Mayans in Mesoamerica, and the African empire of Ghana were all founded and developed by "non-whites."

Between 1523 and 1028 B.C., China had a complex form of government, armies, metal tools and weapons, and production and storage facilities for large quantities of grain. The early Chinese civilization also had writing and elaborate religious rituals (Ebrey 2010:22–37). From A.D. 300 to 900, the Mayans were a large population with a thriving economy. They built many large and beautiful cities in which were centred great pyramids and luxurious palaces (Coe 2011). According to legend, the West African civilization of Ghana was founded during the second century A.D. By A.D. 770, the time of the Soninke rulers, Ghana had developed two capital cities—one Muslim and the other non-Muslim—each with its own ruler and both supported largely by Ghana's lucrative gold market (Phillipson 2005:275–283).

Considering how recently northern Europeans developed cities and central governments, it seems odd that some "whites" should label others as backward in terms of historical achievement, or biologically inferior in terms of capacity for civilization. But racists, both "white" and "non-white," choose to ignore the fact that many populations have achieved remarkable advances in civilization. Most significantly, racists refuse to believe that they can acknowledge the achievements of another group without in any way downgrading the achievements of their own.

African metal workers created magnificent works of art like this golden head from Ghana long before Europeans arrived.

Werner Forman/Art Resource

"Race," Conquest, and the Role of Infectious Disease.
There are those who would argue that Europeans' superiority accounted for their ability to colonize much of the world during the last few hundred years. But it now appears that Europeans were able to dominate at least partly because many Indigenous peoples were susceptible to diseases brought by the Europeans (McNeill 1998; Crosby 2004). Earlier, we discussed how continued exposure to epidemics of infectious diseases, such as tuberculosis and measles, can cause succeeding

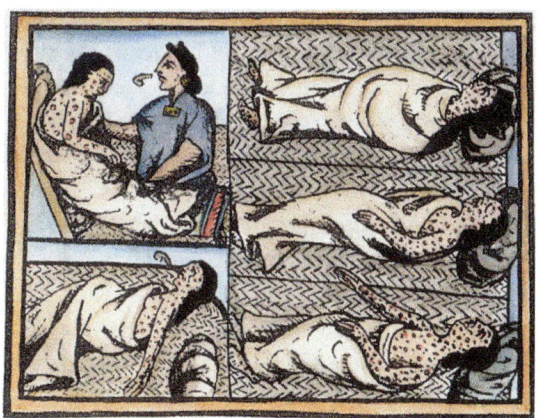

The conquest of the Aztecs was aided by smallpox contracted from the Spanish, which killed at least half the population.

generations to acquire a genetic resistance to death from such diseases. Smallpox had a long history in Europe and Africa; genetic resistance eventually made it mostly a survivable childhood disease. But in the New World it was quite another story. Cortés and the conquistadors were inadvertently aided by smallpox in their attempt to defeat the Aztecs of Mexico. In 1520, a member of Cortés's army unwittingly transmitted smallpox to the Aztecs. The disease spread rapidly, killing at least 50 percent of the population, and so the Aztecs were at a considerable disadvantage in their battle with the Spanish (Crosby 2004:195–216; Motulsky 1971). Germ theory alone may not completely explain these epidemics; Europeans may have deliberately encouraged the spread of smallpox by purposely distributing infected blankets to the Indigenous populations. Motulsky called the spread of smallpox "one of the first examples of biological warfare" (1971:232).

It is also known that there are associations between some infectious diseases and different blood types. For example, for the ABO blood system, certain disease organisms have ABO antigens on their cell walls, conferring some resistance on individuals who manufacture the appropriate antibodies, and increasing the susceptibility of people whose blood type matches the antigens. Examples include antigen A for syphilis and smallpox and antigen O for bubonic plague.

"Race" and Intelligence. In the 19th century, European white supremacists tried to find scientific justification for what they felt was the genetically inherited mental inferiority of "blacks." They did this by measuring skulls. It was believed that the larger the skull, the greater the cranial capacity and the bigger (hence, also better) the brain. However, we know that cranial capacity alone is not an appropriate measure of intellectual ability. For example, as discussed in Chapter 10, Neandertals had a cranial capacity that exceeded the modern range. Although the skull-measuring mania quickly disappeared and is no longer considered as a way to measure intelligence, other "facts" have been used to imply intellectual superiority of certain groups of people. Attempts to document differences in intelligence among the so-called races have a fairly long history. Two well-known attempts are the 1994 book *The Bell Curve*, by Americans Charles Murray and Richard Herrnstein (though see the response by Devlin et al. 1997), and the publications of the late Philippe Rushton, who had been a professor of psychology at the University of Western Ontario.

Rushton proposed a genetic evolutionary theory for what he claimed were consistent observations of East Asians and their descendants having larger brains, greater intelligence, more sexual restraint, slower rates of maturation, and a greater propensity to abide by the law and mores of social organization than Europeans and their descendants, who in turn had higher scores on those "traits" than Africans and their descendants (Rushton 1995, 1996). These observations were based on his synthesis of the international literature. One of the fundamental flaws in Rushton's arguments is, of course, his reliance on dividing the human species into three simple biological groups. As we have discussed earlier, these so-called races cannot be applied universally, and the biological and cultural diversity that is represented in each of these three groups makes any kind of comparison useless. Finally, while brain size and maturity can be readily quantified, the other traits are at best difficult to quantify, and would be highly ethnocentric in their construction.

To test Rushton's ideas, Peregrine, Ember, and Ember (2000) used information about the 186 cultures composing the Standard Cross-Cultural Sample (Peregrine et al. 2000). They examined 26 separate behaviours that Rushton predicted would differ among the "races." Contrary to Rushton's predictions, there were no differences between supposed "racial" groups for the most part. For only one behaviour were there the differences that Rushton predicted (frequency of homicide, which Rushton predicted would be higher among "Negroids" and lower among "Mongoloids," does indeed show this pattern), and the results for five behaviours (sexual restraint, acceptance of rape, degree of political integration, level of social stratification, and level of technological specialization) demonstrated a pattern that was the *opposite* of what Rushton predicted. So Rushton's gross division of humans into these "races" does not generally predict variation in human behaviour. His ideas appear plainly wrong and do not support the concept that it is scientifically useful to distinguish human "races" (Lieberman 1999). Rushton's work has been dismissed by the general anthropological and broader scientific community. Unfortunately, it continues to be exploited by groups interested in promoting racist socio-political agendas, and therefore needs to be continually addressed within the public arena.

Critics of genetic predisposition to intelligence within the "races" point to at least two problems. First, there is widespread recognition now that IQ tests are probably not accurate measures of "intelligence" because they are likely biased in favour of the subculture of those who construct the tests. That is, many of the questions on the test refer to things that middle-class children are familiar with, thus giving such children an advantage (Smith 1974). So far, no one has come up with a "culture-fair," or bias-free, test. There is more agreement that, although the IQ test may not measure "intelligence" well, it may predict scholastic success or how well a child will do in the primarily "middle-class"-oriented school system (Dobzhansky 1973).

A second major problem with a purely genetic interpretation of the IQ difference is that many studies also show that IQ scores can be influenced by the social environment. Economically deprived children, regardless of skin colour, will generally score lower than affluent middle-class children. And training of children with low IQ scores clearly improves their test scores (Dobzhansky 1973).

The geneticist Theodosius Dobzhansky reminded us that conclusions about the causes of different levels of achievement on IQ tests cannot be drawn until all people have equal opportunities to develop their potentials. He stressed the need for an open society operating under the democratic ideal, where all persons are given an equal opportunity to develop whatever gifts or aptitudes they possess and choose to develop (Dobzhansky 1962:243; Boyd and Richerson 1985). While some suggest that research on the genetics of intelligence can be undertaken from a "socially neutral" standpoint, others argue that this is not possible, and that such research simply reinforces social inequalities (Roberts 2015).

Cultural Diversity and Adaptation

Even though culture is learned and not genetically inherited like biological evolution, cultural practices can influence the evolution of a population. The frequency of certain genetic alternatives is likely to increase over time if those genetic traits increase their carriers' chances of survival and reproduction. Similarly, the frequency of a new learned behaviour will increase over time and become customary in a population if the people with that behaviour are most likely to survive and reproduce. Thus, if a culture is adapted to its environment, culture change should also be adaptive—not always, to be sure, but commonly.

One of the most important differences between cultural evolution and genetic evolution is that individuals often can decide whether or not to accept and follow the way their parents behave or think, whereas they cannot decide whether or not to inherit certain genes. When enough individuals change their behaviour and beliefs, we say that the culture has changed. Therefore, it is possible for culture change to occur much more rapidly than genetic change. It is particularly when circumstances change that individuals are likely to try new ideas or behaviours.

Whatever the motives for humans to change their behaviour, the theory of natural selection suggests that new behaviour is not likely to become cultural or remain cultural over generations if it has harmful reproductive consequences, just as a genetic mutation with harmful consequences is not likely to become frequent in a population (Campbell 1965; Boyd and Richerson 1985; Durham 1991). Still, we know of many examples of culture change that seem maladaptive—the switch to bottle-feeding rather than nursing infants, which may spread infection because contaminated water is used, or the adoption of alcoholic beverages, which may lead to alcoholism and early death. In the last few hundred years, the major stimulus to culture change, adaptive and maladaptive, has been the new social environment produced by the global spread of people from western European societies and the new globalization that is spreading American cultural values around the world.

Many of the cultural changes in the world from A.D. 1500 to the present have been caused, directly or indirectly, by the dominance and expansion of Western societies (McNeill 1967). Thus, much of the cultural change in the modern world has been externally induced, if not forced. This is not to say that cultures are changing now only because of external pressures, but externally induced changes have been the changes most frequently studied by anthropologists and other social scientists. Most of the external pressures have come from Western societies, but not all. Eastern societies, such as Japan and China, have also stimulated culture change. And the expansion of Islamic societies after the eighth century A.D. made for an enormous amount of culture change in the Near East, Africa, Europe, and Asia.

Measured in terms of travel time, the world today is much smaller than it has ever been. It is now possible to fly halfway around the globe in the time it took people less than a century ago to travel to the next province. In the realm of electronic communications, the world is even smaller. Although modern transportation and communications facilitate the rapid spread of some cultural characteristics to all parts of the globe, it is highly unlikely that all parts will end up the same. Cultures are bound to retain some of their original characteristics or develop some distinctive new adaptations. Even though television has diffused around the world, local people prefer to watch local programming when it is available. And even when people all over the world watch the same program, they may interpret it in very different ways. People are not just absorbing the messages they get; they may resist them or rework them (Kottak 1996).

Future research on contemporary culture change should increase our understanding of how and why various types of change are occurring. And if we can increase our understanding of culture change in the present, we should be better able to understand similar processes in the past. Another lead to understanding change in the past is the large number of cross-cultural correlations between a cultural variation and its presumed causes that have been discovered since the 1970s (Ember and Levinson 1991). All cultures have changed over time. Therefore, the variations we see are the products of change, and the "predictors" of those variations may suggest how and why the changes occurred.

The Future of Human Variation

Laboratory fertilization of an ovum, subsequent transplantation of the resulting embryo, and successful birth have been accomplished with humans and non-humans. *Cloning*—the exact reproduction of an individual from cellular tissue—has been achieved with frogs and sheep. And *genetic engineering*—the substitution of some genes for others—is increasingly practised on non-human organisms. Indeed, as we discussed in the last chapter on evolution, genetic engineering is now used on humans to eliminate certain disorders that are produced by defective genes. What are the implications of such practices for the genetic future of humans? Will it really be possible someday to control the genetic makeup of our species? If so, will the effects be positive or negative?

It is interesting to speculate on the development of a "perfect human." Aside from the serious ethical question of who would decide what the perfect human should be like, there is the serious biological question of whether such a development might in the long run be detrimental to the human species, for what is perfectly suited to one physical or social environment may be totally unsuited to another. The collection of physical, emotional, and intellectual attributes that might be "perfect" in the early 21st century might be inappropriate by the end of the century (Haldane 1963). Even defects such as the sickle-cell trait may confer advantages under certain conditions, as we have seen.

In the long run, the perpetuation of genetic variability is probably more advantageous than the creation of a "perfect" and invariable human being. In fact, biodiversity is crucial to the survival of all organisms. In the event of dramatic changes in the world environment, absolute uniformity in the human species might be an evolutionary dead end. Such uniformity might lead to the extinction of the human species if new conditions favoured genetic or cultural variations that were no longer present in the species. Perhaps our best hope for maximizing our chances of survival is to encourage the persistence of many aspects of human variation, both biological and cultural (Simpson 1971:297–308; Tattersall and DeSalle 2011:196–199).

SUMMARY AND REVIEW

PROCESSES IN HUMAN VARIATION

6.1 Describe the processes that influence human physical and biological variation.

- *Adaptation* and *acclimatization* are terms used to describe different physiological levels at which organisms make adjustments to cope with long- and short-term changes in their environments.

- Adaptation is genetic: it involves permanent genetic and physiological changes such as skin colour or body build that help people survive in an environment.

- Acclimatization involves temporary non-genetic physiological changes that help individuals survive in an environment, including physiological changes needed to live in extreme hot, cold, dry, and high-altitude environments.

- Culture may be the most important factor that allows people to survive in particular environments. Culture allows people to modify their environments and can lessen the likelihood of genetic adaptations and physiological acclimatizations.

How do the results of directional selection differ from those of normalizing selection?

BIOLOGICAL DIVERSITY IN HUMAN POPULATIONS

6.2 Describe the ways in which human populations can differ biologically, and how human biological adaptations are related to the physical and cultural environments.

- Physical variation in human populations includes differences in body build and weight (Bergmann's rule), the size of body parts (Allen's rule), skin colour (Gloger's rule), and facial features, such as nose shape, eye form, and hair form.

- These variations are thought to be adaptations to different climates, but research also suggests infant stress can produce some of these variations.

- Some physical variations, such as disease resistance or the ability to make lactase, might be adaptations to particular cultural environments. The ability to make lactase, for instance, is more prevalent in populations whose ancestors have long used domesticated animals for milk and milk products, like butter and cheese.

How is variation in skin pigmentation related to climate? What selective pressures might underlie this association?

"RACE" AND RACISM

6.3 Explain the contemporary views on race held by anthropologists.

- Species are composed of populations that can differ genetically and phenotypically. Subspecies or "races" are identified when populations are geographically separated and variation reaches a certain level. The "level" is ambiguous and has never been formally defined.
- "Racial" classifications are mostly social categories that are presumed to have a biological basis.
- Adaptive physical traits vary clinally; simply put, biological traits are more prevalent in certain geographically defined populations than others, such as skin colour—a trait of importance in classic and popular concepts of "race"—which is best explained as an adaptation resulting from population history (population interactions) and differences in sunlight exposure around the world.
- The study of clinal variation in biological traits demonstrates that there is more variation within geographically discrete human populations than between them. No human population unambiguously falls into a discrete group defined by particular biological traits. It is therefore meaningless to divide humans into separate "races" or "subspecies" because "race" as a category is not based upon biological facts.
- Racism is how people are treated based upon the perception that they belong to a "racial" group.

 *What role did infectious disease play in Europeans' colonization of various parts of the world over the last few hundred years?*

CULTURAL DIVERSITY AND ADAPTATION

6.4 Describe how cultural adaptations influence the evolution of a population.

- Whereas individuals within a population cannot choose their genetics, which are inherited, they may choose which cultural behaviours to follow.
- Regardless of motives, natural selection would suggest that behaviours that are harmful to reproductive success will not be maintained, although there are some examples of behaviours that seem maladaptive.

 *Why can cultural evolution occur more quickly than genetic evolution?*

THE FUTURE OF HUMAN VARIATION

6.5 Describe how advances in genetic engineering and gene therapy affect human biological variation.

- Advances in genetic engineering and gene therapy may certainly improve the lives of some people, but we must also think about the implications of these practices for the genetic future of humans.
- The notion of a "perfectly suited" human depends upon adaptation to a particular physical and cultural environment. If either or both of those environments change, the "perfect human" would not carry the genetic variability that could be more advantageous under those new conditions.

 *With the ability to develop cultural adaptations, how important is biological variation for modern humans?*

THINK ON IT

1. Why is skin colour used more often than hair or eye colour or body proportions in "racial" classifications?

2. If Europeans had been more susceptible to New World and Pacific diseases, how might the world be different today?

3. Can you think of examples of human behaviour that seem to be maladaptive? Explain why they have persisted.

4. Why might an increasing understanding of cultural variation also provide an increasing understanding of culture change in the past?

5. In what ways has culture influenced biological evolution in humans?

The Living Primates

7

R. Skilton/Shutterstock

LEARNING OBJECTIVES

7.1 Identify common primate traits.

7.2 Describe the major types of living primates and their geographical distribution.

7.3 Explain and contrast two models for understanding hominin behaviour in the past.

7.4 Describe the major ways in which living primates vary.

7.5 Describe the major traits that are distinctive to humans.

The goal of *primatology*, the study of primates, is to understand how different primates have adapted anatomically and behaviourally to their environments. The results of such studies may help us to understand the behaviour and evolution of the human primate.

But how can living primates such as chimpanzees tell us anything about humans or the primates that were our ancestors? After all, each living primate species has its own history of evolutionary divergence from the earliest primate forms. All living primates, including humans, evolved from earlier primates that are now extinct. Nonetheless, by observing how humans and other primates differ from and resemble each other, we may be able to infer how and why humans diverged from the other primates.

Together with fossil evidence, anatomical and behavioural comparisons of living primates may help us reconstruct what early primates were like. For example, if we know that modern primates that swing through the trees have a particular kind of shoulder bone structure, we can infer that similar fossil bones probably belonged to an animal that also swung through the trees. Differing adaptations of living primates may also suggest why certain divergences occurred in primate evolution. If we know what traits belong to humans, and to humans alone, this knowledge may suggest why the line of primates that led to humans branched away from the line leading to chimpanzees and gorillas.

In this chapter we first examine the common features of the living primates. Next we introduce the different animals that belong to the order Primates, focusing on the distinctive characteristics of each major type. Following this, we discuss briefly how we can apply what we know about behaviour in living primate groups as models for hominin behaviour. Then we discuss possible explanations for some of the adaptations exhibited by different primate species. We close with a look at the traits that make humans different from all other primates. The purpose of this chapter is to help us understand more about humans. Therefore, we emphasize the features of primate anatomy and behaviour that perhaps have the greatest bearing on human evolution.

Common Primate Traits

All primates belong to the class Mammalia, and they share all the common features of mammals. Except for humans, the bodies of primates are covered with dense hair or fur, which provides insulation. Even humans have hair in various places, though perhaps not always for insulation. Mammals are *warm-blooded*; that is, their body temperature is more or less constantly warm and usually higher than that of the air around them. Almost all mammals give birth to live young that, while still in the mother's womb, develop to a considerable size, and all are nourished once they are born by suckling from the mother's mammary glands. The young have a relatively long period of dependence on adults after birth. This period is also a time of learning, for a great deal of adult mammal behaviour is learned rather than instinctive. Play is a learning technique common to mammal young and is especially important to primates, as we shall see later in this chapter.

In addition to their mammalian features, the primates have a number of physical and social traits that set them apart from other mammals.

Physical Features

No single physical feature of the primates is unique to them; animals from other orders share one or more of the characteristics described below. However, the complex of all these physical traits is unique to primates (Napier and Napier 1967; Smuts et al. 1987).

Many skeletal features of the primates reflect an **arboreal** (tree-living) existence. All primate hind limbs are structured principally to provide support, but the feet in most primates can also grasp things. Some primates—orangutans, for instance—can suspend themselves from their hind limbs. The forelimbs are especially flexible, built to withstand both pushing and pulling forces. Each of the hind limbs and forelimbs has one bone in the upper portion and two bones in the lower portion (with the exception of the tarsier). This

Arboreal: adapted to living in trees.

feature has changed little since the time of the earliest primate ancestors. It has remained in modern primates (although many other mammals have lost it) because the double bones give great mobility for rotating arms and legs.

Another characteristic structure of primates is the clavicle, or collarbone. The clavicle also gives primates great freedom of movement, allowing them to move the arms at the shoulders both up and down and back and forth. Although humans obviously do not use this flexibility for arboreal activity, they do use it for other activities. Without a clavicle we could not throw a spear or a ball; no fine tools could be made and no doorknobs turned if we did not have rotatable forearms.

Primates generally are **omnivorous**; that is, they eat all kinds of food, including insects and small animals, tree gums, flowers, and nectar, as well as fruits, seeds, leaves, and roots. The teeth of primates reflect this omnivorous diet. The chewing teeth—the **molars** and **premolars**—are very unspecialized, particularly in comparison with those of other groups of animals, such as the grazers. The front teeth—the **incisors** and **canines**—are often very specialized, principally in the lower primates. For example, in many species of the suborder prosimians, the slender, tightly packed lower incisors and canines form a "dental comb" the animals use in grooming or for scraping hardened gum (which is a food for them) from tree trunks (Bearder 1987; Ankel-Simons 2007:224–227).

Primate hands are extremely flexible. As Figure 7–1 indicates, all primates have **prehensile**—grasping—hands, which they can wrap around an object. Primates have five digits on each hand and foot (in some cases, one digit may be reduced to a stub), and their nails, with few exceptions, are broad and flat, not clawlike. This structure allows them to grip objects; the hairless, sensitive pads on their fingers, toes, heels, and palms also help them to grip. Most primates have **opposable thumbs**, a feature that allows an even more precise and powerful grip.

Vision is extremely important to primate life. Compared with other mammals, a relatively larger portion of the primate brain is devoted to vision rather than smell. Primates are characterized by *stereoscopic vision*. Their eyes are directed forward rather than sideways, as in other animals—a trait that allows them to focus on an object (insects or other food or a distant branch) with both eyes at once. Most primates also have colour vision, perhaps to recognize when plant foods are ready to eat, although the extent of this vision varies by region and species. By and large, these characteristics are more developed in anthropoids (monkeys, apes, and humans) than in prosimians.

Another important primate feature is a large brain relative to body size. That is, primates generally have larger brains than do animals of similar size, perhaps because their survival depends on an enormous amount of learning, as we discuss later. In general, animals with relatively large brains seem to mature more slowly and to live longer than animals with relatively small brains (Richard 1985; Ankel-Simons 2007:199–206). The more slowly an animal grows up and the longer it lives, the more it can learn.

Finally, the primate reproductive system sets this order of animals apart from other mammals. Males of most primate species have a pendulous penis that is not attached to the abdomen by skin,

---

Omnivorous: eating both meat and vegetation.
Molars: the large teeth behind the premolars at the back of the jaw; used for chewing and grinding food.
Premolars: the teeth immediately behind the canines; used in chewing, grinding, and shearing food.
Incisors: the front teeth; used for holding or seizing food and preparing it for chewing by the other teeth.

Canines: the cone-shaped teeth immediately behind the incisors; used by most primates to seize food and in fighting and display.
Prehensile: adapted for grasping objects.
Opposable Thumb: a thumb that can touch the tips of all the other fingers.

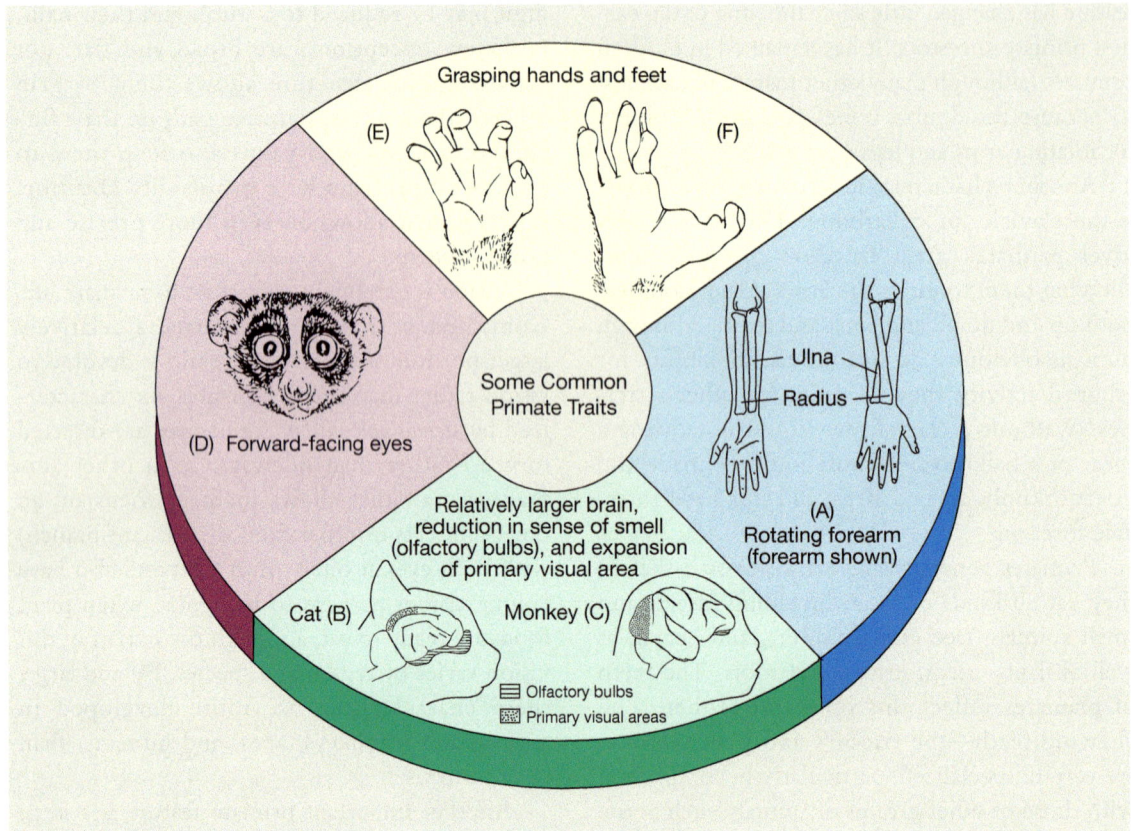

Figure 7–1 Some Common Primate Traits

Sources: (A) from Wolff 1991, 255. D.C. Heath; (B, C) from Deacon 1992, 110; (D) from Cartmill 1992b, 25; and (E, F) from Cartmill 1992b, 24.

a trait shared by a few other animals, including bats and bears. Females of most primate species have two nipples on the chest (a few prosimians have more than two nipples). The uterus is usually constructed to hold a single fetus (although some prosimians give birth to twins or triplets), not a litter, as with most other animals. This reproductive system can be seen as emphasizing quality over quantity—an adaptation possibly related to the dangers of life in the trees (Martin 1975). Primate infants tend to be relatively well developed at birth, although humans, apes, and some monkeys have helpless infants. Most infant primates, except for humans, can cling to their mothers from birth. Primates typically take a long time to mature. For example, the rhesus monkey is not sexually mature until about 3 years of age, the chimpanzee not until about age 9.

Social Features

For the most part, primates are social animals. Just as physical traits such as grasping hands and stereoscopic vision may have developed as adaptations to the environment, so may have many patterns of social behaviour. For most primates, particularly those that are **diurnal**—that is, active during the day—group life may be crucial to survival, as we will see later in this chapter.

Diurnal: active during the day.

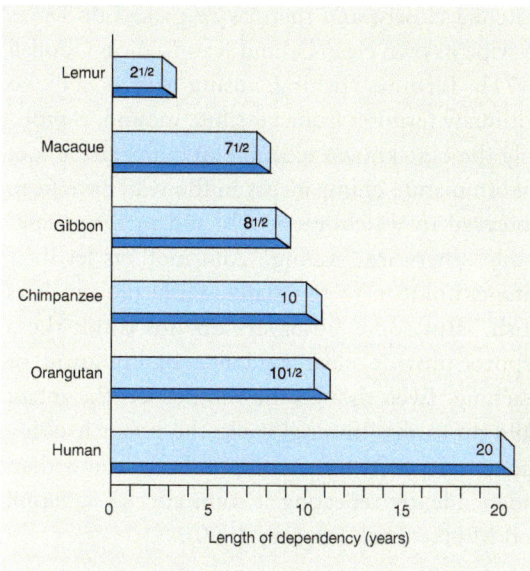

Figure 7–2 A Comparison of the Dependency Periods of Primate Offspring

Source: Data from Jolly A. 1985. The evolution of primate behavior. Second edition. New York: Macmillan. P. 292.

Dependency and Development in a Social Context. Social relationships begin with the mother and other adults during the fairly long dependency period of primates. (For the dependency period of primates, the infancy and juvenile phases, see Figure 7–2.) The prolonged dependency of infant monkeys and apes probably offers an evolutionary advantage in that it allows infants more time to observe and learn the complex behaviours essential to survival while enjoying the care and protection of mature adults.

Primates without a warm, social relationship with a mother or another individual do not appear to develop appropriate patterns of social interaction. In many primate groups the mother is not the only individual providing care to the dependent young. Among grey langur monkeys, the birth and subsequent rearing of a baby absorb the attention of most female members of the troop (Nicolson 1966). In some primate species, the father may expend as much time caring for infants as the mother (Gray 1985).

Primates at Play. We know, from early investigations of social learning in young primates, the importance of maternal care to baby rhesus monkeys. Play is another crucial ingredient of normal development during the dependency period. Just as monkeys raised without mothers showed abnormal behaviour as adults, so did monkeys raised with mothers but lacking peers to play with. In fact, when some of the monkeys raised without mothers were allowed a regular playtime with peers, many of them behaved more normally (Russon 1990).

Play is important for learning (Dohlinow and Bishop 1972; Fedigan 1982; Lewis 2000). It provides practice for the physical skills necessary or useful in adulthood. For example, young monkeys racing through the trees at top speed are gaining coordination that may save their lives if they are chased by predators later on. Play is also a way of learning social skills, particularly in interacting and communicating with other members of the group. In order to play, individuals must make adjustments to their behaviour to interact acceptably with other individuals. Thus there is a relationship between learning and socialization. Some dominance relationships seem to be established partly through the rough-and-tumble games that older juveniles play, where winning depends on such factors as size, strength, and agility. These qualities, or the lack of them, may influence the individual's status throughout adult life. Other factors also help determine an individual's status. For instance, the mother's status has been shown to be very important in some primates (Sade 1965; Hausfater et al. 1982).

Learning from Others. We know that primates, non-human and human alike, learn many things in social groups. Among humans, children often imitate others, and adults often deliberately teach the young. But do apes (and monkeys) imitate others, or do they just learn to do similar things whether or not a model is observed? There is controversy among researchers as to how much imitation versus independent learning occurs in non-human primates. Even more arguable is whether deliberate teaching occurs among non-human primates (Tomasello 1990; Visaberghi and Munkenbeck Fragaszy 1990). In a study of lowland gorilla infant–mother relationships, Maestripieri and colleagues (2002) observed that infants took a more active role in engaging mothers in active learning activities.

Some fieldworkers have suggested that chimpanzees may learn by imitation to use tools. For example, Jane Goodall cited an occasion when a female with diarrhea picked up a handful of leaves to wipe her bottom. Her 2-year-old infant watched closely, and then twice picked up leaves to wipe its own clean behind (van Lawick-Goodall 1971). Termite "fishing," using a grass stalk to withdraw termites from a termite mound, is probably the best-known example of chimpanzee tool use. Immature chimpanzees in the wild have been observed to watch attentively and pick up stalks while others are "fishing." And mothers let their infants hold on to the stalks while the mothers "fish." But some observers do not think these reports provide clear evidence of imitation or teaching. Even though the mother lets the infant hold on to the "fishing" stalk, the infant is doing the activity with her, not watching it and then independently repeating it soon after (Visaberghi and Munkenbeck Fragaszy 1990).

Primate Communication. Systems of communication are not unique to human beings. Other animal species communicate in a variety of ways, including sound, odour, and body movement. For example, chemical signatures (detectable by odour) may communicate information about identity, age, or sex of an individual (Zeller 1987). Facial expressions also are a means of communication in primates: Anne Zeller, a physical anthropologist at the University of Waterloo who specializes in primates, identified 33 different components of facial expressions in macaques. Primates can learn to interpret messages communicated through facial expressions. Infants are born able to communicate and understand only a few messages. The evidence is clear that social learning is the main source of this ability (Zeller 1992, 1994).

Although primates use all three methods of communication (sound, odour, and body movement), sound is the method that most concerns us because spoken language is human beings' major means of communication. Non-human primates also communicate vocally, but their range is limited in comparison with that of humans. Anne Zeller suggested that communication may have evolved to maintain social systems, although it also promotes survival and reproduction since it transmits ecological information as well (Zeller 1992).

Primates can learn from direct teaching, but they learn mostly by imitation and trial and error (Whiten et al. 2004).

Recent research suggests that some monkey and ape calls in the wild are also *referential* (vocalizations that seem to refer to an object or event). However, when we say that a communication (call, word, sentence) is *symbolic*, we mean at least two things. First, the communication has meaning even when its referent (whatever is referred to) is not present. Second, the meaning is arbitrary; the receiver of the message could not guess its meaning just from the sound(s) and does not know the meaning instinctively. In other words, symbols have to be learned. There is no compelling or "natural" reason that the word *dog* in English should refer to a smallish four-legged omnivore.

Vervet monkeys in Africa are not as closely related to humans as are African apes, but provide an example of symbolic communication. Scientists who have observed vervet monkeys in their natural environment consider at least three of their alarm calls to be symbolic because each of them *means* (refers to) a different kind of predator—eagles, pythons, or leopards—and monkeys react differently to each call. For example, they look up when they hear the "eagle" call. Experimentally, in the absence of the referent, investigators have been able to evoke the normal reaction to a call by playing it back electronically. Another indication that the vervet alarm calls are symbolic is that infant vervets appear to need some time to learn the referent for each. Very young infants apply a particular call to more animals than adult vervets do. So, for example, infant vervets will often make the eagle warning call when they see any flying bird. The infants learn the appropriate referent apparently through adult vervets' repetition of infants' "correct" calls; in any case, the infants gradually learn to restrict the call to eagles. This process is probably not too different from the way some North American infants in English-speaking families first apply the "word" *dada* to all adult males and gradually learn to restrict it to one person (Seyfarth and Cheney 1982).

All the non-human vocalizations we have described so far enable individual animals to convey messages. The sender gives a signal that is received and "decoded" by the receiver, who usually responds with a specific action or reply. How is human vocalization different? Since monkeys and apes appear to use symbols at least some of the time, it is not appropriate to emphasize symbolism as the distinctive feature of human language. However, there is a significant quantitative difference between human language and other primates' systems of vocal communication. All human languages employ a much larger set of symbols. Another and perhaps more important difference is that the other primates' vocal systems tend to be *closed*; different calls are not often combined to produce new, meaningful utterances. In contrast, human languages are *open* systems, governed by complex rules about how sounds and sequences of sounds can be combined to produce an infinite variety of new meanings (Hockett and Ascher 1964).

The idea that humans can transmit many more complex messages than any other animal does not begin to convey how different human language is from other communication systems. No chimpanzee could say the equivalent of "I'm going to the ball game next Wednesday with my friend Jim if it's not raining." Humans not only can talk (and think) with language about things completely out of context, but they also can be deliberately or unconsciously ambiguous in their messages. If a person asks you for help, you could say, "Sure, I'll do it when I have time," leaving the other person uncertain about whether your help is ever going to materialize.

Primates in the wild do not exhibit anything close to human language. However, recent successful attempts to teach apes to communicate with humans and with each other using human-created signs have led some scholars to question the traditional assumption that the gap between human and other animal communication is enormous. Chimpanzees Washoe and Nim and the gorilla Koko were taught hand signs based on American Sign Language (ASL, which is used by the hearing impaired in the United States and Canada). The chimpanzee Sarah was trained with plastic symbols, but Lana, Sherman, Austin, and a bonobo, Kanzi, were trained on symbol keyboards connected to computers.

Sherman and Austin began to communicate with each other about actions they were intending to do, such as the types of tools they needed to solve a problem, and they were able to classify items into categories, such as "food" and "tools." In contrast to other apes, Kanzi learned symbols just by seeing people point to them when they spoke to him. He did not need rewards or to have his hands put in the right position, and he understood a great deal of what was spoken to him. For example, when he was 5 years old, Kanzi heard someone talk about throwing a ball in the river, and he turned around and did so. Kanzi has come closest of all the "students" to having a primitive English grammar when he strings symbols together (Savage-Rumbaugh 1992). If chimpanzees and other primates have the capacity to *use* non-spoken language and even to understand spoken language, then the difference between humans and non-humans may not be as great as people used to think.

Are these apes really using language? There is a lot of agreement among investigators that non-human primates have the ability to "symbol"—to refer to something (or a class of things) with an arbitrary "label"—that is, a gesture or a sequence of sounds (Hill 1978). For example, the gorilla Koko (with a repertoire of about 375 signs) extended the sign for drinking straw to plastic tubing, hoses, cigarettes, and radio antennae. Washoe originally learned the sign *dirty* to refer to feces and other soil and then began to use it insultingly, as in "dirty Roger" when her trainer Roger Fouts refused to give her things she wanted. Even the mistakes made by the apes suggest that they are using signs symbolically, just as words are used in spoken language. For example, the sign *cat* may be used for "dog" if the animal learned *cat* first.

In spite of the new evidence, Jane Hill believes that the answer about whether apes use language is still controversial because language is not one unitary thing. Every human language has certain ways of combining sounds and ways of *not* combining those sounds. Although apes do not use sounds, the combination of symbols can be thought of as analogous to the combining of sound elements. Yet there does not appear to be anything comparable to linguistic rules that dictate how sound elements can be combined. Another major difference is that humans have many kinds of discourse. Humans may make lists and speeches, tell stories, argue, and recite poetry. Apes do none of those things, but as these experiments suggest, they do have some of the capacities for some of the elements of human language. Therefore, understanding their capacities may help us better understand the evolution of human language (Hill 1998).

Classification of Primates

Classification provides a useful way to refer to groups of species that are similar in biologically important ways. Sometimes classification schemes vary because the classifiers emphasize somewhat different aspects of similarity and difference. For instance, one type of classification stresses the evolutionary branching that led to the primates of today; another, the quantity of shared features. A third approach considers the evolutionary lines as well as similarity and difference of features, but not all features are equally weighted. More "advanced" and specialized features that develop in an evolutionary line are emphasized in this approach (Conroy 1990; Martin 1992). Figure 7–3 gives a classification scheme that follows this last approach, but this is not the only way to classify the primates.

Despite the different ways to classify, there is generally little disagreement about how the various primates should be classified. Most of the disagreement, as we shall see when we discuss the various primates, revolves around the classification of tarsiers and humans.

The order Primates is often divided into two suborders: the **prosimians** (literally, premonkeys) and the **anthropoids**. The prosimians include

> **Prosimians:** literally "premonkeys," one of the two suborders of primates; includes lemurs, lorises, and tarsiers.
> **Anthropoids:** one of the two suborders of primates; includes monkeys, apes, and humans.

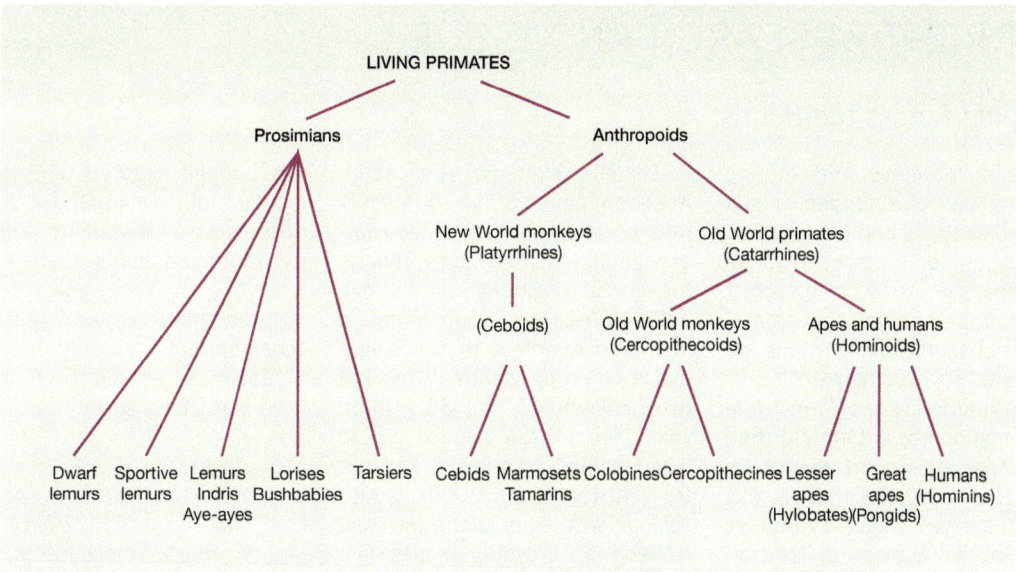

Figure 7–3 A Simplified Classification of the Living Primates

lemurs, lorises, and tarsiers. The anthropoid suborder includes New World monkeys, Old World monkeys, the lesser apes (gibbons, siamangs), the great apes (orangutans, gorillas, chimpanzees), and humans.

The Various Primates

Now that we have discussed their common features, let us focus on some of the ways in which the primates living in the world today vary.

Prosimians

The prosimians resemble other mammals more than the anthropoid primates do. For example, the prosimians depend much more on smell for information than do anthropoids. Compared with anthropoids, they typically have more mobile ears and whiskers, longer snouts, and little facial expression. The prosimians also exhibit many traits shared by all primates, including grasping hands, stereoscopic vision, and enlarged visual centres in the brain.

Lemur-like Forms. Lemurs and their relatives, the indri and the aye-aye, are found only on two island areas off the southeastern coast of Africa: Madagascar and the Comoro Islands. In fact, it is thought that these populations of lemurs were introduced to the Comoro Islands within the last 2000 years by humans since the time they first arrived on Madagascar (see Current Research and Issues, "Hopping Across the Ponds" for ideas about how primates got to Madagascar and the New World). These primates range in size from the mouse lemur to the 1.2-metre-long indri. Members of the lemur group usually produce single offspring, although twins and even triplets are common in some species. Many of the species in this group are **quadrupeds**—animals that move on all fours, in the trees as well as on the ground. Some species, such as the indri, use their hind limbs alone to push off from one vertical position to another in a mode of locomotion called **vertical clinging and leaping**. Lemurs are mostly vegetarians, eating fruit, leaves, bark, and flowers. Lemur species vary greatly in their group

Quadrupeds: animals that walk on all fours.
Vertical Clinging and Leaping: a locomotor pattern characteristic of several primates, including tarsiers and galagos. The animal normally rests by clinging to a branch in a vertical position and uses its hind limbs alone to push off from one vertical position to another.

CURRENT RESEARCH AND ISSUES

Hopping Across the Ponds

How did monkeys and lemurs seemingly all of a sudden appear in the New World and Madagascar, respectively (both places in which their ancestors were not present)? Island hopping and the closely related phenomenon of rafting are the prevailing hypotheses.

South America and Africa were once connected, but they drifted apart long before primates evolved. Researchers propose that roughly 36 million years ago, an intense storm ripped a piece of land off the African coast that just happened to be occupied by a few anthropoid primates. Currents would have pushed this raft of primates across the South Atlantic to their new home in South America, where they propagated and evolved into the New World monkeys of the present day.

There is an alternative scenario. At certain points in the earth's history, ocean levels have fallen low enough for land to emerge. Though the idea of a complete land bridge linking Africa and South America has been rejected, it is possible that a chain of islands linked the two between 40 and 50 million years ago. These islands would have enabled anthropoid monkeys from Africa to cross the South Atlantic with stops along the way, rather than crossing in a single long voyage.

Even earlier, but some time after 65 million years ago, ancestral lemurs began to populate the island of Madagascar. No geological evidence supports the presence of a land bridge linking Africa and Madagascar during that period, and it is unlikely that there was enough exposed land in the Mozambique Channel for island hopping to be a realistic possibility. That leaves natural rafts as the most likely vehicle, and research suggests that the prevailing flow of ocean currents between Africa and Madagascar at the time would have made for a speedy trip.

Sources: Ali JR, Huber M. 2010. Mammalian Biodiversity on Madagascar Controlled by Ocean Currents. Nature. 463:653–656.

Bond M, Tejedor M, Campbell K, Chornogubsky L, Novo N, Goin F. 2015. Eocene Primates of South America and the African Origins of New World Monkeys. Nature. 520:538–541.

De Oliveira FB, Molina EC, Marroig G. 2009. Paleogeography of the South Atlantic: A Route for Primates and Rodents into the New World? In: Garber PA, Estrada A, Bicca-Marques JC, Heymann EW, Strier KB, editors. South American Primates. New York: Springer. pp. 55–68.

---

size. Many lemur species, particularly those that are **nocturnal** (active during the night), are solitary during their active hours. Others are much more social, living in groups ranging in size from a small family to as many as 60 members (Doyle and Martin 1979; Tattersall 1982). An unusual feature of the lemur-like primates is that females often dominate males, particularly over access to food. In most primates, and in most other mammals, female dominance over males is rarely observed (Richard 1987).

Loris-like Forms. Representatives of the loris group, found in both Southeast Asia and sub-Saharan Africa, are all nocturnal and arboreal. They eat fruit, tree gum, and insects, and usually give birth to single infants (Bearder 1987). There are two major subfamilies, the lorises and the bushbabies (galagos), and they come from distinct geographic regions and show wide behavioural differences. Bushbabies, found only in sub-Saharan Africa, are quick, active animals that hop between branches and tree trunks in the vertical-clinging-and-leaping pattern. On the ground they often resort to a kangaroo-like hop. Lorises, which are found in sub-Saharan Africa as well as in southern India, Sri Lanka, and Southeast Asia, are much slower, walking sedately along branches, hand over hand in the quadrupedal fashion. Using searchlights and technical aids such as radio tracking, field researchers have learned a good deal about these nocturnal primates. For example, we now know that among bushbabies, females, particularly mothers and young adult daughters, stay together in small groups, whereas the males disperse. Newborns are born in nests or hollows of trees (which related females may share), and

Nocturnal: active during the night.

Prosimians such as these ring-tailed lemurs depend much more on smell than do anthropoids. Prosimians also have more mobile ears, whiskers, longer snouts, and relatively fixed facial expressions.

mothers return to nurse them regularly. A few days after birth, a mother may carry her infant in her mouth to nearby trees, "parking" it while she eats (Charles-Dominique 1977; Martin and Bearder 1979; Bearder 1987).

Tarsiers. The nocturnal, tree-living tarsiers, found now only on the islands of the Philippines and Indonesia, are the only primates that depend completely on animal foods. They are usually insect-eaters, but they sometimes capture and eat other small animals. They are well equipped for night vision, possessing enormous eyes, extraordinary eyesight, and enlarged visual centres in the brain. The tarsiers get their name from their elongated tarsal bones (the bones of the ankle), which give them tremendous leverage for their long jumps. Tarsiers are very skilled at vertical clinging and leaping. They live in family groups

Nocturnal tree-living tarsiers, like this one in the Philippines, are the only primates that depend completely on animal foods. Their enormous eyes equip them to find insects and other prey in the night. Their elongated ankle bones (tarsals) make them very good at vertical clinging and leaping.

composed of a mated pair and their offspring. Like some higher primates, male and female tarsiers sing together each evening, presumably to advertise their territories (MacKinnon and MacKinnon 1980).

The classification of tarsiers is somewhat controversial. Instead of placing them with the suborder prosimians, as we have done here, some classifiers group tarsiers with anthropoids. In this other classification scheme, the suborders of primates are labelled **strepsirhines** (which means *wet noses* and includes lemurs and lorises) and **haplorhines** (which means *single noses*, and includes tarsiers and anthropoids). Tarsiers have chromosomes similar to those of other prosimians; they also have claws on some of their toes that they use for grooming, more than two nipples, and a uterus shaped like the uterus of other prosimians (two-horned). Like bushbabies, tarsiers move about through vertical clinging and leaping. In other respects tarsiers are more like the anthropoids. They have a reduced dependence on smell; not only are their noses smaller, but they lack the wet, doglike snout of lemurs. In common with the anthropoids, their eyes are closer together and are protected by bony orbits (Fleagle 1999; Ankel-Simons 2007:31–32; Cartmill 2010).

Anthropoids

The anthropoid suborder includes humans, apes, and monkeys. Most anthropoids share several traits in varying degree. They have rounded braincases; reduced, non-mobile outer ears; and relatively small, flat faces instead of muzzles. They have highly efficient reproductive systems, including a placenta that is formed more fully than in any prosimian. They also have highly dextrous hands (Napier and Napier 1967). The anthropoid suborder is divided into two main groups: **platyrrhines**

This howler monkey, like all platyrrhines, has a broad, flat-bridged nose. Platyrrhines live in the wild only in Central and South America and are arboreal.

and **catarrhines**. These groups take their names from the nose shape of the different anthropoids, but as we shall see they differ in other features as well. Platyrrhines have broad, flat-bridged noses, with nostrils facing outward; these monkeys are found only in the New World, that is, in Central and South America. Catarrhines have narrow noses with nostrils facing downward, and include monkeys of the Old World (Africa, Asia, and Europe), as well as apes and humans.

New World Monkeys. Besides the shape of the nose and position of the nostrils, other anatomical features distinguish the New World monkeys (platyrrhines) from the catarrhine anthropoids. The New World species have three premolars, whereas the Old World species have two. Some New World monkeys have a prehensile (grasping) tail; no Old World monkeys do. All the New World monkeys are completely arboreal; they vary a lot in the size of their groups; and their food ranges from insects to nectar and sap to seeds, fruits, and leaves (Richard 1985).

Strepsirhines: lemurs and lorises.
Haplorhines: tarsiers and anthropoids.
Platyrrhines: the group of anthropoids that have broad, flat-bridged noses, with nostrils facing outward; these monkeys are currently found only in the New World (Central and South America).

Catarrhines: the group of anthropoids with narrow noses and nostrils that face downward. Catarrhines include monkeys of the Old World (Africa, Asia, and Europe), as well as apes and humans.

There are two main families of New World monkeys; one family contains marmosets and tamarins, the other cebid monkeys. The marmosets and tamarins are very small, have claws instead of fingernails, and give birth to twins who mature in about two years. Perhaps because twins are so common and the infants have to be carried, marmoset and tamarin mothers cannot take care of them alone. Fathers and older siblings have often been observed carrying infants. Indeed, males may do more carrying than females. Marmoset and tamarin groups may contain a mated pair (monogamy) or a female mated to more than one male (polyandry). The marmosets and tamarins eat fruit and tree sap, but like other very small primates, they obtain a large portion of their protein requirements from insects (Eisenberg 1977; Sussman and Kinzey 1984; Goldizen 1987; Cartmill 1992b).

Cebids are generally larger than marmosets, take about twice as long to mature, and tend to bear only one offspring at a time (Ankel-Simons 2007:526–527; Eisenberg 1977). The cebids vary widely in size, group composition, and diet. For example, squirrel monkeys weigh about 1 kilogram, whereas woolly spider monkeys weigh more than 7 kilograms, making them the largest New World monkey. Some cebids have small groups with one male–female pair; others have groups of up to 50 individuals. Some of the smallest cebids have a diet of leaves, insects, flowers, and fruits, whereas others are mostly fruit-eaters with lesser dependence on seeds, leaves, or insects (Crockett and Eisenberg 1987; Robinson et al. 1987; Robinson and Janson 1987).

Old World Monkeys. The Old World monkeys, or **cercopithecoids**, are related more closely to humans than to New World monkeys. They have the same dental formula as apes and humans. The Old World monkey species are not as diverse as their New World cousins, but they live in a greater variety of habitats. Some live both in trees and on the ground; others, such as the gelada baboon, are completely **terrestrial**, or ground-living. Macaques are found both in tropical jungles and on snow-covered mountains, and they range from the Rock of Gibraltar to Africa to northern India, Pakistan, and Japan. There are two major subfamilies of Old World monkeys.

Colobine Monkeys. The colobine group includes Asian langurs, the African colobus monkeys, and several other species from Asia. These monkeys live mostly in trees, and their diet consists principally of leaves and seeds. Their digestive tracts are equipped to obtain maximum nutrition from a high-cellulose diet: they have pouched stomachs, which provide a large surface area for breaking down plant food, and very large intestinal tracts.

One of the most noticeable features of colobines is the flamboyant colour typical of newborns in several species. For example, in one species dusky grey mothers give birth to brilliant orange babies (Blaffer Hrdy 1977). Observational studies suggest that the colobines are also unusual among the primates (except for humans) in that mothers let other group members handle their infants shortly after birth. However, males who are not members of the group are dangerous for infants; males trying to enter and take over a group have been observed to kill infants. Infanticide is not typical of colobines, and while documented first in colobines, it is found in several species outside of colobines. Although this description may

A troop of baboons spends most of its time on the ground.

Cercopithecoids: Old World monkeys.
Terrestrial: adapted to living on the ground.

suggest that a one-male group is the typical group structure, there does not appear to be a typical pattern for a given species. When more than one site of a species has been studied, both one-male and multiple-male groups have been found (Blaffer Hrdy 1977).

Cercopithecine Monkeys. The cercopithecine subfamily of monkeys is found primarily in Africa (in Asia the cercopithecines are represented only by the genus *Macaca*), and includes more terrestrial species than any other subfamily of Old World monkeys. Many of these species are characterized by a great deal of *sexual dimorphism* (the sexes look very different); the males are larger, have longer canines, and are more aggressive than the females. Cercopithecines depend more on fruit than do colobines. They are also more capable of surviving in arid and seasonal environments (Napier 1970). Pouches inside the cheeks allow cercopithecines to store food for later eating and digestion. An unusual physical feature of these monkeys is the *ischial callosities*, or calluses, on their bottoms—an adaptation that enables them to sit comfortably in trees or on the ground for long periods (Fedigan 1982; Ankel-Simons 2007).

Studies of baboons and macaques suggest that closely related females form the core of a local group, or *troop*. In large groups, which are common among rhesus monkeys, many social behaviours seem to be determined by degree of biological relatedness. For example, an individual is most likely to sit next to, groom, or help an individual who is closely related maternally (Fedigan 1982). Moreover, a closely related subgroup is likely to stay together when a large troop divides (Lee 1983).

The Hominoids: Apes and Humans. The **hominoid** group includes three separate families: the lesser apes, or **hylobates** (gibbons and siamangs); the great apes, or **pongids** (orangutans, gorillas, and chimpanzees); and humans. More recently, humans and their ancestors have been grouped together with the African great apes because of their evolutionary relatedness as *hominids*. Previously, the term *hominin* applied to only humans and their ancestors. While not all researchers utilize this classification, for our purposes we will refer to humans and their ancestors as hominins.

Several characteristics distinguish the hominoids from the other primates. Their brains are relatively large, especially the areas of the cerebral cortex associated with the ability to integrate data. The hominoids have several skeletal and muscular traits that point toward their common ancestry. All have fairly long arms, short, broad trunks, and no tails. The wrist, elbow, and shoulder joints of hominoids allow a greater range of movement than in other primates. Hominoid hands are longer and stronger than those of other primates. These skeletal features probably evolved along with the hominoids' unique abilities in suspensory locomotion. Unlike other anthropoids, who move quadrupedally along the ground or along tops of tree branches, hominoids often suspend themselves from below the branches and swing or climb hand over hand from branch to branch (Fleagle 1999). This suspensory posture also translates to locomotion on the ground (see a more detailed discussion of bipedalism in Chapter 9 on the first hominins).

The dentition of hominoids demonstrates some unique features as well (see Figure 7–4). Hominoid molars are flat and rounded compared with those of other anthropoids, and have what is called a **"Y-5" pattern** on the lower molars—that is, the lower molars have five cusps with a Y-shaped groove opening toward the cheek

---

Hominoids: the group of catarrhines that includes both apes and humans.
Hylobates: the family of hominoids that includes gibbons and siamangs; often referred to as the *lesser apes* (as compared with the *great apes*, such as gorillas and chimpanzees).

Pongids: hominoids whose members include both the living and extinct apes.
"Y-5" Pattern: refers to the pattern of cusps on human molars. When looked at from the top, the cusps of the molars form a Y opening toward the cheek.

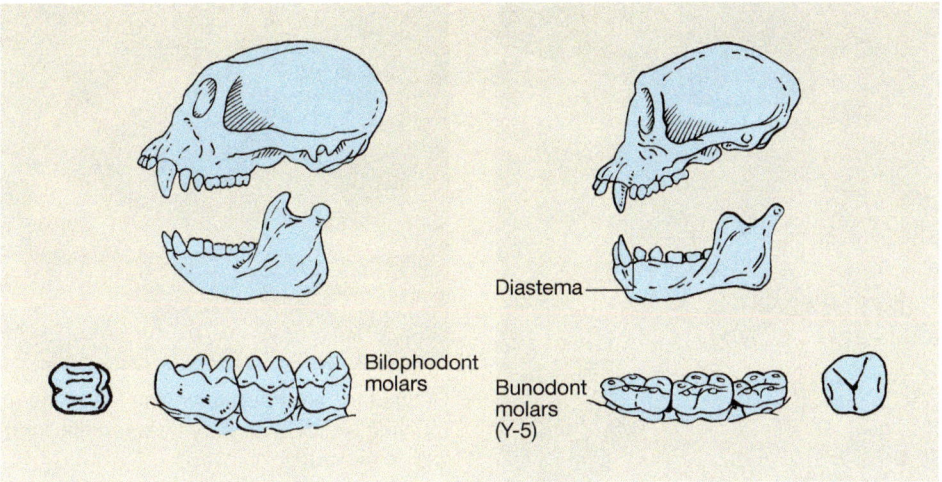

Figure 7–4 Dentition Differences

Difference in dentition between an Old World monkey (left) and an ape (right). In Old World monkeys, the cusps of the lower molars form two parallel ridges; in apes, the five cusps form a Y-shaped pattern. Apes also have a space between the lower canine and first premolar, called a *diastema*.

Source: Based on Boaz NT, Almquist AJ. 1999. Essentials of biological anthropology. Upper Saddle River, NJ: Prentice Hall. p. 164.

running between them. Other anthropoids have what is called a **bilophodont** pattern—their molars have two long ridges or "loafs" running parallel to the cheeks. All hominoids except for humans also have long canine teeth that project beyond the tops of the other teeth, and a corresponding space on the opposite jaw, called a **diastema**, where the canine sits when the jaws are closed. The contact of the upper canine and the lower third premolar creates a sharp cutting edge, in part due to the premolar being elongated to accommodate the canine (LeGros Clark 1964; Ankel-Simons 2007). These dental features are related to the hominoids' diets, which often include both fibrous plant materials, which can be efficiently cut with sharp canines against elongated premolars, and soft fruits, which can be efficiently chewed with wide, flat molars.

The skeletal and dental features shared by the hominoids point toward their common ancestry. Their proteins and DNA show many similarities, too. This genetic likeness is particularly strong among chimpanzees, gorillas, and humans (Pennisi 2007). For this reason, primatologists think chimpanzees and gorillas are evolutionarily closer to humans than are the lesser apes and orangutans, which probably branched off at some earlier point.

Gibbons and Siamangs. The acrobatic gibbons and their close relatives the siamangs are found in the jungles of Southeast Asia. The gibbons are small, weighing only about 5 to 7 kilograms. The siamangs are somewhat larger, no more than 11 kilograms. Both are mostly fruit-eaters, although they also eat leaves and insects. They are spectacular **brachiators**, with long arms and

Bilophodont: having four cusps on the molars that form two parallel ridges. This is the common molar pattern of Old World monkeys.
Diastema: a gap between the canine and first premolar found in apes.

Brachiators: animals that move through the trees by swinging hand over hand from branch to branch. They usually have long arms and fingers.

A white-handed gibbon demonstrates its ability as a brachiator.

Orangutans are unusual among the higher primates in living basically solitary lives, except for mothers with their young.

fingers that let them swing hand over hand through the trees (Preuschoft et al. 1984; Fleagle 1999). A gibbon can move more than 9 metres in a single forward swing.

Gibbons and siamangs live in small family groups, with each group consisting of an adult pair, who appear to mate for life, and one or two immature offspring. When the young reach adulthood, they are driven from home by the adults. There is little sexual dimorphism—males and females do not differ in size or appearance—nor is there any clear pattern of dominance by either sex (although some species have sex-specific colouring). These lesser apes are also highly territorial; an adult pair advertises its territory by singing and defends it by chasing others away (Carpenter 1940; Chivers 1974, 1980).

Orangutans. Orangutans survive only on the islands of Borneo and Sumatra. Unlike gibbons and siamangs, they are clearly recognizable as males or females. Males not only weigh almost twice as much as females (up to 90 kilograms), but they also have large cheek pads, throat pouches, beards, and long hair (Rijksen 1978; Ankel-Simons 2007). Like gibbons and siamangs, orangutans are primarily fruit-eaters and arboreal. They are the heaviest of the arboreal primates, and perhaps for this reason they move slowly and laboriously through the trees. Orangutans are unusual among the higher primates in living basically solitary lives, except for mothers and their young; however, a recent field study of orangutans on Sumatra found that groups of as many as 10 adults fed together in the same tree (Normile 1998).

Different ideas have been proposed about the solitary habit of the orangutans that live in the mountainous areas of Borneo. One is that there may be insufficient food in any one tree or home range to support more than a single adult orangutan, a pretty large animal, as animals go. Orangutans may therefore live alone rather than in groups to obtain sufficient food each day without having to travel over a huge area (Galdikas 1979). Another idea is that animals live in groups when they are subject to heavy predation; the large size of orangutans may make them immune to attacks from most animals, so living alone may be a viable option (Cheney and Wrangham 1987). In fact, the clouded leopard has been suggested as the primary predator of orangutans (Seidensticker 1985). A third idea, which on the face of it seems opposite to the second, is that living alone may be an adaptation to heavy predation by humans. The orangutan's best defence against humans with guns may be to hide alone in the trees (Rijksen 1978).

Gorillas. Gorillas are found in the lowland areas of western equatorial Africa and in the mountain areas of the Democratic Republic of Congo, Uganda, and Rwanda (Fossey 1983). Unlike the other apes, which are mostly fruit-eaters, gorillas mostly eat other parts of plants—stems, shoots (for example, bamboo), pith, leaves, roots, and flowers. The amount of fruit eaten by gorillas varies greatly. In many populations fruit eating is rare (for example, mountain gorillas); in some, such as the western gorillas and even some eastern populations, however, fruit is a common part of the diet (Tuttle 1986). Gorillas are by far the largest of the surviving apes. In their natural habitats, adult males weigh up to 205 kilograms and females up to 113 kilograms. To support the weight of massive chests, gorillas travel mostly on the ground on all fours in a form of locomotion known as **knuckle walking**: they walk on the thickly padded middle joints of their fingers. Gorillas' arms and legs, especially those of the young, are well suited for climbing. As adults, their heavier bodies make climbing more precarious (Schaller 1963, 1964; Ankel-Simons 2007:155–157), although Melissa Remis's work on lowland gorillas has shown that adult males stay close to the trunk while foraging for fruit in tree crowns, while the smaller and lighter females will venture into the crowns of trees by using major boughs as pathways (Remis 1995). They sleep on the ground or in tub-shaped nests they make from non-food plants each time they bed down (Fossey 1983).

Gorillas tend to live in groups, and each group consists of a dominant male, called a *silverback*, other adult males, adult females, and immature

> **Knuckle Walking:** a locomotor pattern of primates such as the chimpanzee and gorilla in which the weight of the upper part of the body is supported on the thickly padded knuckles of the hands.

Pascale Sicotte taking notes on a group of mountain gorillas.

offspring. Both males and females, when mature, seem to leave the groups into which they were born to join other groups. The dominant male is very much the centre of attention; he acts as the main protector of the group and the leader in deciding where the group will go next (Harcourt 1979; Ankel-Simons 2007:156). In her study of mountain gorillas in Rwanda, Pascale Sicotte, a biological anthropologist at the University of Calgary, observed that female and juvenile gorillas can and do take an active and intentional role in defusing conflicts between males in the same group. Availability of females for reproduction may partially explain the presence of multimale gorilla groups—more available females reduce the competition pressure on the dominant male, leading to the tolerance of young maturing silverbacks in the group. Some of these young males may end up staying in their natal group for many years past sexual maturity. Interestingly, once a group includes more than one adult male, the males can co-operate in trying to prevent their females from leaving during encounters with other groups. Indeed, Sicotte showed that herding of females during inter-group encounters occurred more often in groups that included more than one male (Sicotte 1993, 1995, 2002; Czekala and Sicotte 2000).

Chimpanzees. Perhaps because they form larger social communities and are easier to find, chimpanzees have been studied far more than gorillas. Chimpanzees live in the forested areas in

Africa, from Sierra Leone in the west to Tanzania in the east.

There are two distinct species of chimpanzee—the common chimpanzee (*Pan troglodytes*) and the bonobo, or pygmy, chimpanzee (*Pan paniscus*). While they share many features (indeed, they were not recognized as distinct species until 1929), bonobos tend to be more slender than common chimpanzees, with longer limbs and digits, smaller heads, darker faces, and a distinct part in their hair. Unlike common chimpanzees, bonobos show almost no sexual dimorphism in dentition or skeletal structure. More significant seem to be differences in social behaviour. Bonobos are more gregarious than common chimpanzees, and groups tend to be more stable. Groups also tend to be centred around females rather than males (Susman 1984; White 1996; Ankel-Simons 2007).

Although they are primarily fruit-eaters, chimpanzees show many similarities to their close relatives, the gorillas. Both are arboreal and terrestrial. Like gorillas, chimpanzees are good climbers, especially when young, and they spend many hours in the trees. Chimpanzees move best on the ground, though, and when they want to cover long distances, they come down from the trees and move by knuckle walking. Occasionally, they stand and walk upright, usually when they are travelling through tall grass or trying to see long distances. Chimpanzees sleep in tree nests that they carefully prepare anew, complete with a bunch of leaves as a pillow, each time they bed down (Goodall 1963; van Lawick-Goodall 1971).

Chimpanzees are only slightly sexually dimorphic. Males weigh a little more than 45 kilograms on the average, females somewhat less. Males do have longer canines, though. For some time it was thought that chimpanzees ate only plant food. Although most of their diet is vegetarian, a small proportion comes from meat (Stanford 1998). After three decades of studies at Gombe National Park in Tanzania and elsewhere, researchers found

Chimpanzees, though they spend much time in the trees, can also move very quickly on the ground.

that chimpanzees not only eat insects, small lizards, and birds, but they actively hunt and kill larger animals (Teleki 1973). They have been observed hunting and eating monkeys, young baboons, and bushbucks in addition to smaller prey. At Gombe, the red colobus monkey is by far the most often hunted animal. So it is not only humans who endanger other primates (see Applied Anthropology, "Endangered Primates"); the red colobus monkey population is quite small in areas of intense chimpanzee hunting. Hunting appears to be undertaken more often during the dry season when food is scarce—a time when the forest canopy is more open and the red colobus monkey is more visible (Stanford 1998). Prey is caught mostly by the males, which hunt either alone or, most successfully, in small groups. It is then shared with—or perhaps more accurately begged by—as many as 15 other chimpanzees in friendly social gatherings that may last up to nine hours (Stanford 1998).

Despite considerable observation, the organization of chimpanzee social groups is still not clear. Groups usually are multimale and multifemale, but the size may range considerably from a few to 100 or so members. In Gombe, males typically remain in their natal group throughout life, and females often move to a neighbouring group; but males in Guinea do not tend to stay in their natal groups (Normile 1998). It appears that chimpanzees come together and drift apart depending upon circumstances, such as the availability of food and the risk of predation (Tuttle 1986).

Hominins. According to the classification we use here, the hominoids we call hominins include only one living species—modern humans. Humans have many distinctive characteristics that set them apart from other anthropoids and other hominoids, which lead many to place humans in a category separate from the pongids. These traits will be discussed later in this chapter and also throughout much of the rest of the book. However, others believe that the differences are not so great as to justify a separate hominin category for humans. For example, humans, chimpanzees, and gorillas are very similar in their proteins and DNA, and it is widely agreed that the lines leading to humans, chimpanzees, and gorillas diverged from a common ancestor, perhaps 5 million to 6 million years ago (Goodman 1992). Whether we stress the similarities or differences between humans and apes does not matter that much; what does matter is that we try to understand the reasons for those similarities and differences.

Models for Hominin Behaviour

The idea that natural selection can operate on the behavioural or social characteristics of populations and not just on their physical traits is shared by cultural ecology and another, more recent, theoretical orientation called *behavioural ecology* (or, earlier, known as *sociobiology*). Developed mainly

Chimpanzees in the wild use tools—in this case, a stone to crack palm nuts. As far as we know, though, they don't use tools to make other tools, as humans do.

APPLIED ANTHROPOLOGY

Endangered Primates

In contrast to many human populations that are too numerous for their resources, many populations of non-human primates face extinction because they are not numerous enough. The two trends—human population growth and non-human primate extinctions—are related. Were it not for human expansion in many parts of the world, the non-human primates living in those habitats would not be endangered. Various lemur and other prosimian species of Madagascar; gorillas and red colubus monkeys of Africa; langurs, gibbons, and organutans of Asia; and the tamarin monkeys of Brazil are among the species most at risk.

Many factors are responsible for the difficulties faced by non-human primates, but most of them are directly or indirectly the result of human activity. Undoubtedly the biggest problem is the destruction of tropical rain forest, the habitat of most non-human primates, because of encroaching agriculture and cattle ranching and the felling of trees for wood products. The people who live in these areas are partly responsible for the threats to non-human primates—population pressure in the human populations increases the likelihood that more forest will be cleared and burned for agriculture, and in some areas non-human primates are an important source of hunted food. But world market forces are probably more important. The increasing need for "American" hamburger in fast-food restaurants has accelerated the search for places to raise beef inexpensively. There is also enormous demand for wood products from tropical forests; Japan imports half of all the timber from rain forests to use for plywood, cardboard, paper, and furniture.

Some would argue that it is important to preserve all species. Primatologists remind us that it is especially important to preserve primate diversity. One reason is scientific—we need these populations to study and understand how humans are similar and different and how they came to be that way. Another reason is the use of non-human primates in biomedical research on human diseases; we share many of our diseases, and most of our genes, with many of our primate relatives (chimpanzees share more than 98 percent of their genes with humans). Thus, understanding the way in which diseases affect our closest primate relatives may help us develop cures in human populations.

So how can non-human primates be protected from us? There are only two major ways the non-human primates can be protected from extinction. Either human population growth into primate habitats has to be curtailed, or we have to find a way to preserve substantial populations of non-human primates in their native habitats.

Anthropologists have joined the initiative toward conservation of primate populations. Dian Fossey's study site, Karisoke, became an international centre for gorilla research when she established the Karisoke Research Center in 1967. Her murder in 1985 is considered by many as retaliation for her efforts to stop the poaching of gorillas and other animals in Africa. As a result of her efforts, mountain gorillas are now protected by the government of Rwanda. Jane Goodall's years of experience studying the chimpanzees in the forests of Gombe National Park revolutionized our understanding of their behaviour. She has now turned that knowledge toward conservation with the establishment of the Jane Goodall Institute for Wildlife Research, Education and Conservation. Biruté Galdikas, another student of the famous Louis Leakey, and a colleague of Dian Fossey and Jane Goodall, has also focused on primate conservation. She is a professor of anthropology at Simon Fraser University in British Columbia, and is one of the world's foremost authorities on the life and behaviour of orangutans. In 1986, in order to assist her research and work in Borneo and to help support orangutans around the world, Biruté Galdikas co-founded the Orangutan Foundation International, which is based in Los Angeles and has chapters in Australia, Canada, Indonesia, Taiwan, and the United Kingdom.

Similar efforts have been aimed at ensuring that Madagascar's lemurs do not go extinct. In 2014 the International Union for Conservation of Nature (IUCN) Primate Specialist Group set out a plan to help drive eco-tourism and local conservation efforts in the region. Anthropologist Ian Colquhoun from the University of Western Ontario, who has studied lemurs for over three decades, is optimistic about these efforts. Colquhoun co-authored a "Policy Forum" commentary in *Science* titled "Averting Lemur Extinctions amid Madagascar's Political Crisis" (Schwitzer et al. 2014). The authors noted that Madagascar's lemurs are the most threatened primate species on earth, and while making up more than one-fifth of the world's primate species, are found only on the island. Madagascar is therefore considered a primate conservation hotspot.

The IUCN recently released its list of the world's 25 most endangered primates. Unsurprisingly, Madagascar topped the list of countries with endangered species, boasting five of those species. Indonesia and Vietnam are each home to three of the species; Brazil has two; and Cameroon, China, Colombia, Côte d'Ivoire, the Democratic Republic of Congo, Ecuador, Ghana, India, Kenya, Nigeria, Peru, the Philippines, Sri Lanka, Tanzania, and Venezuela each have one. Though the population sizes of many of these critically endangered species are unknown, among the lowest population estimates are the Hainan gibbon, with an estimated 25 individuals, the northern sportive lemur, with roughly 27 individuals, and the golden-headed langur, with an estimated 60 to 70 individuals remaining.

Sources: Mittermeier RA, Sterling EJ. Conservation of Primates. 1992. In: Jones S, Martin R, Pilbeam D, editors. The Cambridge Encyclopedia of Human Evolution. Cambridge: Cambridge University Press. pp. 33–36.

Nishida T. 1992. Introduction to the Conservation Symposium. In: Itoigawa N, Sugiyama Y, Sackett GP, Thompson RKR, editors. Topics in Primatology, volume 2. Tokyo: University of Tokyo Press. pp. 303–304.

Schwitzer C, Mittermeier R, Johnson S, Donati G, Irwin M, Peacock H, Ratsimbazafy J, Razafindramanana J, Louis EE, Chikhi L, Colquhoun IC, Tinsman J, Dolch R, LaFleur M, Nash S, Patel E, Randrianambinina B, Rasolofoharivelo T, Wright PC. 2014. Averting Lemur Extinctions amid Madagascar's Political Crisis. Science. 343(6173):842.

Schwitzer C, Mittermeier RA, Rylands AB, Chiozza F, Williamson EA, Wallis J, Cotton A., editors. 2015. Primates in Peril: The World's 25 Most Endangered Primates 2014–2016. Arlington, VA: IUCN SSC Primate Specialist Group (PSG), International Primatological Society (IPS), Conservation International (CI), and Bristol Zoological Society.

The Jane Goodall Institute (**www.janegoodall.org/**).

by biologists, particularly those who concentrated on the social insects (such as ants), the behavioural ecology or sociobiological orientation applies biological evolutionary principles to the social behaviour of animals, including humans. Some cultural anthropologists have employed behavioural ecology theory to explain some aspects of cultural variation (Irons 1979; Boyd and Richerson 1985).

How is behavioural ecology different from cultural ecology? Although both orientations assume the importance of natural selection in cultural evolution, they differ in important ways. Cultural ecology focuses mostly on what biologists would call **group selection**, or the natural selection of group characteristics. Cultural ecologists talk mostly about how a certain behavioural or social characteristic may be adaptive for a group or society in a given environment; a newly emergent behavioural or social trait that is adaptive is likely to be passed on to future generations by cultural transmission. In contrast, behavioural ecology focuses mostly on what biologists call **individual selection**—the natural selection of individual characteristics. Behavioural ecologists talk mostly about how a certain characteristic may be *adaptive* for an individual in a given environment (Irons 1979). By **adaptive** is meant the ability of an individual to transmit her or his genes to future generations. Does this viewpoint imply that behaviour is transmitted only through genes? No, say behavioural ecologists. What matters is that behaviour is *heritable*—transmitted in some way, by genes or learning, to persons (usually offspring) who share one's genes (Low 1998). If a certain behaviour is adaptive for individuals in a particular environment, it should become more widespread in future generations as the number of individuals with those traits increases.

The idea that behaviour is an adaptive mechanism to changing environmental pressures is the reason that anthropologists use living primates as models for understanding how early hominins may have behaved. Knowing something about

Group Selection: natural selection of group characteristics.

Individual Selection: natural selection of individual characteristics.

Adaptive: the concept that a trait or behaviour increases chances of survival under certain environmental conditions.

their changing biology from the fossil record and their changing environment from palaeoclimatic reconstructions, anthropologists can infer something about early hominin behaviour by observing modern primate behaviour under similar conditions. Culture, of course, is the ultimate extension of human behaviour and becomes an increasingly important aspect of evolutionary change, thus reinforcing the importance of the biocultural approach to anthropological research.

While studying a single primate species will not provide us with an ideal model for early hominins, understanding the variation in primate behaviour can help in understanding social organization in early hominins. There are two kinds of models for understanding the behaviour of human ancestors. The first is living non-human primates, which are primarily models for hominin behaviour. The second is contemporary and recent (because there are few societies today that are unaffected by Western culture) non-Westernized populations of small, foraging societies that may have behavioural patterns similar to prehistoric human populations existing under similar conditions for the last several tens of thousands of years. This second model is known as *ethnographic analogy*.

Non-human primate models are based on either *experimental* or *natural* observations, and either *referential* or *conceptual* perspectives. The advantage of experimental observation is that specific variables can be strictly controlled, so the results of changing only one variable can often be explained. Of course, the disadvantage of experimental observation is imposing an artificial environment on the animals to be studied. The effect of this on the behaviour of the animals cannot be completely known. Field observation of primates in their natural environment tends to provide a truer picture of animal behaviour. The disadvantage of field studies, however, is that they are very expensive and extremely time consuming. Stanford's (1998) research on chimpanzee hunting behaviour is a classic example of referential modelling (for example, the chimpanzee hunting behaviour serves as a model for the hunting behaviour of early hominins). The conceptual approach—known as ecological, or strategic, modelling—doesn't focus on one particular species. Rather, researchers look for behavioural patterns among species, and those patterns become a model of early hominin behaviour (Dunbar 1989).

Ethnographic analogy assumes that recent foraging or horticultural societies might have similar patterns of behaviour to prehistoric groups who lived under similar environmental conditions. However, two cautionary notes regarding ethnographic analogy are worth mentioning. First, modern or even recent historical groups are not completely isolated from the outside influences of the rest of the world, and therefore may exhibit behaviours that derive through cultural diffusion. Second, all such groups will have their own set of cultural qualities, which may not reflect any one universal behavioural pattern from prehistory. While there are no true completely foraging societies remaining, a number of cultures, including Inuit, several groups of Australian Aborigines, and !Kung San of the Kalahari, have served as classic models for anthropology over the last century.

Primate Adaptations

Thus far we have discussed the common features of primates and introduced the different primates that survive in the world today. Now let us examine possible explanations, suggested by research, of some of the ways in which the surviving primates vary physically.

Body Size

The living primates vary enormously in body size, ranging from the 50 grams or so of the average grey mouse lemur to the 160 kilograms of the average male gorilla. What accounts for this significant variation? Three factors seem to predict body size—the time of day the species is active, where it is active (in the trees or on the ground), and the kinds of food eaten (Clutton-Brock and Harvey 1977). All the nocturnal primates are small. Among the primates active during the day, the arboreal ones tend to be smaller than the terrestrial ones.

Finally, species that eat mostly leaves tend to be larger than species that eat mostly fruits and seeds.

Why do these factors predict size? One important consideration is the general relationship in mammals between body weight and energy needs. In general, larger animals require more absolute energy, but smaller animals require much more energy per unit of body weight. That being so, smaller animals (and small primates) need more energy-rich food. Insects, fruits, gum, and sap are full of calories and tend to be more important in the diet of small primates. Leaves are relatively low in energy, so leaf-eaters have to consume a lot of food to get enough energy. They also need large stomachs and intestines to extract the nutrients they need, and a bigger gut, in turn, requires a bigger skeleton and body (Jolly 1985; Aiello 1992). Small primates, which eat insects and other rich foods, probably would compete with birds for food. However, most very small primates are nocturnal, whereas most forest-living birds are diurnal. Energy requirements may also explain why arboreal primates are usually smaller. Moving about in trees usually requires both vertical and horizontal motion. The energy required to climb vertically is proportional to weight, so larger animals require more energy to climb. The energy for travelling horizontally, as on the ground, is not proportionate to weight, so larger animals use energy more efficiently on the ground than in the trees (Aiello 1992). An additional consideration is the amount of weight that can be supported by small tree branches, where foods such as fruits are mostly located. Small animals can go out to small branches more safely than large animals. Also, ground dwellers might be bigger because large size is a protection against predation (Jolly 1985).

Relative Brain Size

Larger primates usually have larger brains, but larger animals of all types generally have larger brains (see Figure 7–5). Primatologists are interested in *relative brain size*, that is, the ratio of brain size to body size.

Perhaps because human primates have relatively the largest brain size of any primate, we tend to think a larger brain is "better." However, a large brain does have "costs." From an energy perspective, the development of a large brain requires a great deal of metabolic energy; therefore, it should not be favoured by natural selection unless the benefits outweigh the costs (Parker 1990).

Fruit-eating primates tend to have relatively larger brains than do leaf-eating primates. This difference may be due to natural selection that favours more capacity for memory, and therefore relatively larger brains, in fruit-eaters. Leaf-eaters may not need as much memory, because they depend on food that is more readily available in time and space, and therefore they may not have to remember where food might be found. In contrast, fruit-eaters may need greater memory and brain capacity because their foods ripen at different times and in separate places that have to be remembered (Clutton-Brock and Harvey 1980; Milton 1981). The brain requires large supplies of oxygen and glucose. Because leaf-eating primates do not have as much glucose in their diets as fruit-eating primates, they may also not have the energy reserves to support relatively large brains (Milton 1988).

Group Size

Primate groups vary in size from solitary males and females with young (in orangutans) to a few individuals and young (as in gibbons) to the 100 or so individuals in some Old World monkey troops (Jolly 1985). What factors might account for such variation?

Nocturnal activity is an important indicator not only of small body size but also of small group size. Nocturnal primates feed either alone or in pairs (Clutton-Brock and Harvey 1977). John Terborgh noted that most nocturnal predators hunt by sound, so a nocturnal animal might best avoid attack by being silent (Terborgh 1983). Groups are noisy, and therefore nocturnal animals might be more likely to survive by living alone or in pairs. On the other hand, a large group might provide advantages in the daytime. The more eyes, ears, and noses a group has, the more quickly a would-be predator might be detected—and

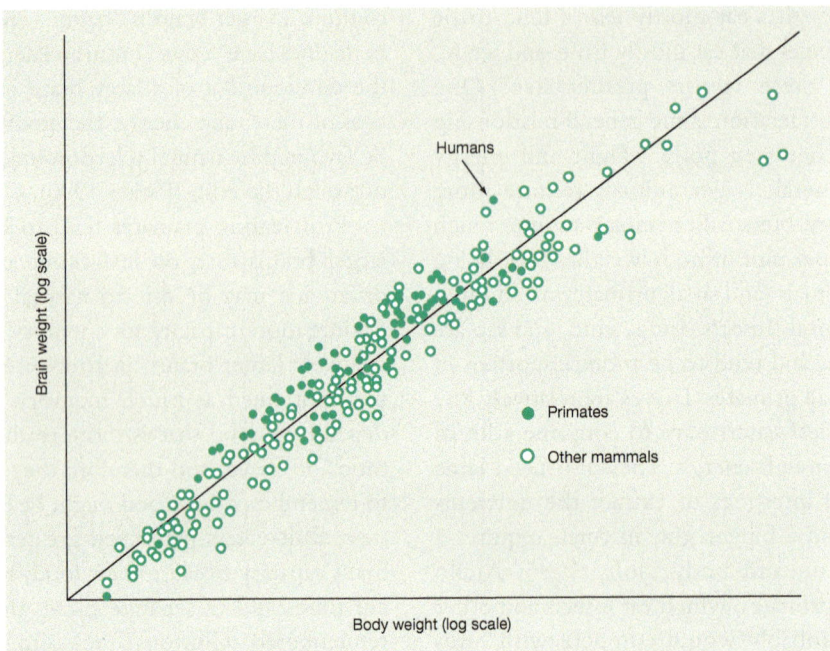

Figure 7–5 Brain Size

As this graph shows, larger animals generally have larger brains. Primates generally have even larger brains than we would expect from their body weight. Note that most of the primates (as indicated by the filled circles) fall above the line showing the relationship between brain weight and body weight. The brains in primates are about twice as heavy as the brains of non-primate mammals of the same body weight.

Source: Jones S, Martin RD, Pilbeam DR. 1992. The Cambridge encyclopedia of human evolution. ones. Reprinted with the permission of Cambridge University Press.

perhaps avoided—and a larger group would have more teeth and strength to frighten or mob a predator that actually attacked (Jolly 1985). Some groups, like the African savannah baboons, actually have co-operative defence strategies.

Other factors must also be taken into account, though. One seems to be the amount and density of food. If food occurs in small amounts and in separate places, only small groups can get enough to eat; if food occurs in large patches, there will be enough to support large groups (Jolly 1985). An additional factor may be competition over resources. One suggestion is that substantial but separated patches of resources are likely to be fought over, and therefore individuals living in larger groups might be more likely to obtain access to them (Wrangham 1980).

Group living provides a foundation for observational learning, including group traditions, innovative behaviours, and dealing with recurring problems (Perry and Manson 2003), for example, the washing of sweet potatoes by Japanese monkeys (Kawai 1965) or the dispensing of food pellets in zoos. (See Current Research and Issues, "Why Are Primates So Smart?")

Sexual Dimorphism

Males and females of many animal species cannot readily be distinguished even though they differ in chromosome makeup and in their external and internal organs of reproduction. In contrast, many primates including humans are sexually dimorphic—that is, the females and males of the species

CURRENT RESEARCH AND ISSUES

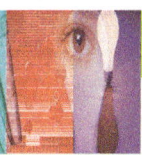

Why Are Primates So Smart?

The fact that you are capable of reading this sentence is one of the most unique aspects of who you are as a modern human. No other animal is capable of reading, much less of complex language. And researchers are not entirely sure that other animals are even capable of thinking in the self-reflexive way that allows you to consider how unique your ability to read is. We humans have unique intellectual abilities. One way of understanding which of our abilities are unique is to look at our closest relatives—the non-human primates—and compare their intellectual abilities with ours. Joan Silk and Robert Boyd do precisely this, and through their comparative look at primate intellectual abilities, attempt to answer the question "Why are primates so smart?"

Primates are unusual, if not unique, in the relatively large size of their brains and the complexity of their social behaviour. Monkeys and apes have larger brains in relation to their body size than members of any other taxonomic group, except the toothed whales and dolphins. Humans, of course, carry these evolutionary trends to even greater extremes.

One of the central questions of human evolution is, why has evolution made humans so smart? Understanding the nature and causes of the cognitive abilities of our closest living relatives, the non-human primates, will help us to answer this question. . . . There is now considerable debate about the primary factors that favoured the evolution of relatively large brains and enhanced cognitive capabilities among non-human primates. Ecological explanations, such as the "extractive foraging" and "cognitive mapping" hypotheses, posit that ecological factors associated with locating and processing inaccessible food items are principally responsible for the elaboration of cognitive skills and the increase in brain size within the primates. Alternatively, the "social brain" hypothesis holds that social demands associated with life in large and stable groups provided the primary selective force favouring cognitive complexity and intelligence among non-human primates.

Sources: Silk JB, Boyd R. 2002. Why Are Primates So Smart? In: Peregrine PN, Ember CR, Ember M, editors. Physical Anthropology: Original Readings in Method and Practice. Upper Saddle River, NJ: Prentice Hall. pp. 53–67. Also in: Ember CR, Ember M, editors. 2003. New Directions in Anthropology. Upper Saddle River, NJ: Prentice Hall. CD-ROM.

Dunbar RIM. 1998. The Social Brain Hypothesis. Evolutionary Anthropology. 6:178–190.

Dunbar RIM, Shultz S. 2007. Evolution in the Social Brain. Science. 317:1344–1347.

Milton K. 1988. Foraging Behaviour and the Evolution of Primate Intelligence. In: Byrne RW, Whiten A, editors. Machiavellian Intelligence: Social Expertise and the Evolution of Intellect in Monkeys, Apes and Humans. Oxford: Oxford University Press. pp. 271–284.

Parker ST, Gibson KR. 1977. Object Manipulation, Tool Use and Sensorimotor Intelligence as Feeding Adaptations in Cebus Monkeys and Great Apes. Journal of Human Evolution. 6:623–641.

---

are generally different in size and appearance. Gorillas are sexually dimorphic because there are significant differences in body size between males and females. Adult male gorillas also have much larger skulls, more dramatic musculature, and very large canine teeth relative to females.

In humans, females have proportionately wider pelvises. Males typically are taller and have heavier skeletons. A larger proportion of female body weight is fat; a larger proportion of male body weight is muscle. Males typically have greater grip strength, proportionately larger hearts and lungs, and greater aerobic capacity (greater intake of oxygen during strenuous activity). There is a tendency in our society to view "taller" and "more muscled" males as "better." Natural selection may have favoured these traits in males but different ones in females. For example, because females bear children, selection may have favoured earlier cessation of growth, and therefore less ultimate height in females so that the nutritional needs of a fetus would not compete with its mother's needs (Stini 1971). Similarly, there is some evidence that females are less affected than males by nutritional shortages, presumably because they tend to be shorter and have proportionately more fat (Frayer and Wolpoff 1985). Natural selection may have favoured those traits in females because they resulted in greater reproductive success.

Macaques staying warm in the hot springs.

Distinctive Human Traits

We turn now to some of the features that distinguish humans from the other primates. Although we like to think of ourselves as unique, many of the traits we discuss here are at the extreme of a continuum that can be traced from the prosimians through the apes.

Physical Traits

Of all the primates, only humans consistently walk erect on two feet, which is known as **bipedalism**. Gibbons, chimpanzees, and gorillas (and even some monkeys and lemurs too) may stand or walk on two feet some of the time, but only for very short periods. All other primates require thick, heavy musculature to hold their heads erect; this structure is missing in humans, for our heads are more or less balanced on top of our spinal columns with the foramen magnum centred in the bottom of the skull. A dish-shaped pelvis (peculiar to humans), straight lower limbs, and arched, non-prehensile feet are all related to human bipedalism. Since we are fully bipedal, we can carry objects without impairing our locomotor efficiency. In Chapter 9 we will discuss the origins of human bipedalism in more detail and consider its effects on a diverse set of traits, including tool-making, prolonged infant dependency, and the division of labour by gender. Although many primates have opposable thumbs that enable them to grasp and examine objects, the greater length and flexibility of the human thumb allow us to handle objects with more firmness and precision.

The human brain is large and complex, particularly the **cerebral cortex**, which is the centre of speech and other higher mental activities. The brain of the average adult human measures more than 1300 cc, compared with 525 cc for the gorilla, the primate with the next largest brain. The frontal areas of the human brain are also larger than those of other primates, so that humans have more prominent foreheads than monkeys or gorillas. Human teeth reflect our completely omnivorous diet and are not very specialized, which may reflect the fact that we use tools and cooking to prepare our food. Many other primates have long lower canines, which are accommodated by a space in the upper jaw; in humans, the canines both look and act very much like incisors, and there are no spaces between the teeth. The human jaw is shaped like a parabolic arch, rather than a U shape, as in the apes, and is composed of relatively thin bones and light muscles. Humans are relatively hairless compared with other primates.

One other distinctive human trait is the sexuality of human females, who may engage in intercourse at any time throughout the year; most other primate females engage in sex only periodically, just around the time they can conceive (Thompson-Handler et al. 1984; White 1996). Humans are also unusual among the primates in having female–male bonding. By this we mean that at least one of the sexes typically has sex with

---

Bipedalism: locomotion in which an animal walks on its two hind legs.

Cerebral Cortex: the "grey matter" of the brain; the centre of speech and other higher mental activities.

just one opposite-sex partner throughout at least one estrus or menstrual cycle. The bonding may not be monogamous—an individual may be bonded to more than one individual of the opposite sex (Ember and Ember 1979). The importance of this trait in the evolution of modern human beings is an area of great interest to many anthropologists, and there are several theories for its development. It used to be thought that more or less continuous female sexuality may be related to female–male bonding, but comparative research on mammals and birds contradicts this idea. Those mammals and birds that have more frequent sex are not more likely to have male–female bonding (Ember and Ember 1979, 1984).

Why, then, does human female sexuality differ from that of most other primates? One suggestion is that more or less continuous female sexuality became selectively advantageous in humans after female–male bonding developed through the growth of local groups consisting of at least several adult males and adult females (Ember and Ember 1984). More specifically, the combination of group living and male–female bonding—a combination unique to humans among the primates—may have favoured a switch from the common higher-primate pattern of periodic female sexuality to the pattern of more or less continuous female sexuality. Such a switch may have been favoured in humans because periodic rather than continuous female sexuality would undermine female–male bonding in multimale–multifemale groups.

Field research on non-human primates strongly suggests that males usually attempt to mate with any females ready to mate. If the female (or females) a male was bonded to was not interested in sex at certain times but other females in the group were, it seems likely that the male would try to mate with those other females. Frequent sexual relationships might jeopardize the male–female bond and thereby presumably reduce the reproductive success of both males and females. Hence, natural selection may have favoured more or less continuous sexuality in human females if humans were living in groups. If bonded adults lived alone, as do gibbons, non-continuous female sexuality would not threaten bonding, because sex with another individual would not be likely to occur. Similarly, seasonal breeding would also pose little threat to male–female bonds because all females would be sexually active at more or less the same time (Ember and Ember 1984). So the combination of group living and male–female bonding in humans may explain why continuous female sexuality developed in humans. The bonobo, or pygmy chimpanzee, female engages in intercourse throughout the year, but bonobos do not have male–female bonding and the females are not interested in sex as often as human females (de Waal and Lanting 1997). The difference here, though, is that much of bonobo sexual behaviour is not related to reproduction, but rather sex is used as a social tool to alleviate social stress and antagonism.

Behavioural Abilities

In comparison with other primates, a much greater proportion of human behaviour is learned and influenced by culture. As with many physical traits, we can trace a continuum in the learning abilities of all primates. The great apes, including orangutans, gorillas, and chimpanzees, are probably about equal in learning ability (Rumbaugh 1970). Old and New World monkeys do much less well in learning tests, and, surprisingly, gibbons perform more poorly than most monkeys.

Toolmaking. The same kind of continuum is evident in inventiveness and toolmaking. With few exceptions, there is no evidence that any non-human primates except great apes use tools, although several species of monkeys use "weapons"—tree-dwelling monkeys have been observed dropping branches, stones, or fruit onto predators as the predators pass below them on the ground. Chimpanzees both fashion and use tools in the wild. As we have noted, they strip leaves from sticks and then use the sticks to "fish" termites from mound-shaped nests. They use leaves to mop up termites, to sponge up water, or to wipe themselves clean (Boesch and Boesch 1990; Whiten et al. 1999). In fact, some researchers have observed Taï chimpanzees modifying tools before use, or using two tools at the same time to acquire a food source (Boesch and Boesch 1990).

One example of chimpanzee tool use suggests planning. In Guinea, West Africa, observers watched a number of chimpanzees crack oil-palm nuts with two stones. The "platform" stone had a hollow depression; the other stone was used for pounding. The observers assumed that the stones had been brought by the chimpanzees to the palm trees, because no stones like them were nearby and the chimpanzees were observed to leave the pounding stone on top of or near the platform stone when they were finished (Jolly 1985). Observers in other areas of West Africa have also reported that chimpanzees use stones to crack nuts. In one location in Liberia an innovative female appeared to have started the practice; it seems to have been imitated within a few months by others who previously showed no interest in the practice (Hannah and McGrew 1987). Julio Mercader, a Canada Research Chair in Tropical Forest Archaeology at the University of Calgary, is opening up a new research niche he has termed "chimpanzee archaeology." His research builds upon the observation of some chimpanzees using tools to open nuts. One reason that makes this kind of research so important is that many of these instruments are similar to, though cruder than, the rough utensils that palaeoanthropologists have associated with early hominins. Mercader and his co-workers have excavated a Taï forest site called Panda 100. The site, formerly the location of so-called Panda nut trees, revealed tree roots with pounding marks made by stones. Excavation around the roots revealed fragments of nutshells and nearly 500 stone artifacts, often including the remains of hammering stones, flakes, and pieces of shattered rock (Mercader et al. 2002).

In captivity, chimpanzees have also been observed to be inventive toolmakers. One mother chimpanzee was seen examining and cleaning her son's teeth, using tools she had fashioned from twigs. She even extracted a baby tooth he was about to lose (Anonymous 1973).

Humans have usually been considered the only toolmaking animal, but observations such as these call for modification of the definition of toolmaking. If we define toolmaking as adapting a natural object for a specific purpose, then at least some of the great apes are toolmakers too. As far as we know, though, humans are unique in their ability to use one tool to make another.

Language. Only humans have spoken or symbolic language, but, as with toolmaking abilities, the line between human language and the communications of other primates is not as sharp as we once thought. Vocalizations in non-human primates can carry information about the sex of the animal vocalizing, group membership, social status, and even an individual's identity. Many species of primates are now known to have vocalizations specific to certain kinds of threats, including different kinds of predators. There is an enormous selective advantage to those individuals that can distinguish predators by unique signalling. This advantage may have provided an evolutionary first step for the development of spoken language in humans. (See Perspectives on Gender, "Mother–Infant Communication and the Origin of Language.")

How long humans have had spoken language is not known. Some think that the earliest *Homo sapiens*, perhaps 100 000 years ago, may have had the beginnings of language. Others believe that language developed more recently. One set of theoreticians of grammar suggest that there may be a language-acquisition device in the brain, as innate to humans as call systems are to other animals (Chomsky 1975). As the forebrain evolved, this device may have become part of our biological inheritance. Whether the device in fact exists is not clear, but we do know that the actual development of individual language is not completely biologically determined. If it were, all human beings would speak the same brain-generated language. Instead, about 4000 to 5000 different and distinct languages have been identified. More than 2000 of them were still spoken as of recently, most by peoples who did not traditionally have a system of writing. Indeed, the earliest writing systems are not that old; they appeared only about 5000 years ago (Senner 1989).

PERSPECTIVES ON GENDER

Mother–Infant Communication and the Origin of Language

Most models for the origin of human language identify tool use and hunting as major factors driving the development of language skills in early humans. Problems with these models of language origin are well recognized. Flint knappers have suggested that observation and imitation are more important than vocal communication in learning to make stone tools. As well, most contemporary hunters communicate with hand signals rather than speech during hunts.

But despite these problems, the view that tool use and hunting promoted language is still widely accepted. Feminist scholars have raised another objection: gender bias. They have suggested that toolmaking and hunting are typically male roles, so these models of language origin see males as the producers of human language. Several have suggested alternative models that give women a primary role in language origins.

Catherine Borchert and Adrienne Zihlman argued that language may have developed through mother–infant communication. They suggested that the problems faced by hominin mothers and infants may also have played a key role in the origin of language. The extreme dependency of human infants on their mothers may have been one important factor. Infants would have had to convey both distress and desire to their mothers. Anyone who has ever been around infants knows that they are able to let you know when they are content, when they are in distress, and when they want something, even though they cannot talk. Borchert and Zihlman argued that many uniquely human traits like crying, smiling, laughing, and cooing may have evolved as ways for mothers and infants to communicate, and such communication may well have provided the beginnings of human language.

Borchert and Zihlman also pointed out that child rearing in human groups is a social process with many caretakers, not just the mother, looking after children. Communication would have been essential in these interactions as well, both for the mother and the child. The mother would have needed to be able to convey known needs and preferences to caretakers of her child, and more significantly, the child would have had to be able to communicate with caretakers who were not the mother. Sharing child care would have required a shared communication system that all members of the group, both adults and infants, could understand. Borchert and Zihlman suggested it may have been these social interactions among mothers, infants, and caretakers that formed the foundation for human language, not toolmaking and hunting. If so, language may have begun to develop before toolmaking and hunting.

Sources: Borchert CM, Zihlman AL. 1990. The Ontogeny and Phylogeny of Symbolizing. In: Foster ML, Botscharow LJ, editors. The Life of Symbols. Boulder, CO: Westview Press. pp. 15–44.

Knight C, Power C. 2006. Words Are Not Costly Displays: Shortcomings of a Testosterone-Fuelled Model of Language Evolution. Behavioral and Brain Sciences. 29:290–291.

Zihlman A. 1997. The Paleolithic Glass Ceiling. In: Hager LD, editor. Women in Human Evolution. London: Routledge. pp. 91–113.

Nevertheless, the ability for language is determined partly by biology. For example, chimpanzees are physically incapable of "speaking" because of the structure of their upper respiratory system. To answer the question of when human language originated, we need to look for clues in the fossil record that show the appearance of changes in anatomical structures related to language capability. The positioning of the *larynx* is an important anatomical factor in the ability to "speak." In most mammals, the larynx is high in the throat to prevent choking—allowing animals to breathe and swallow food at the same time. The same is true of human infants (and is related to breast-feeding), but in adults the larynx drops to a position, unlike in any other animal, that allows us to speak. Since soft tissues are not preserved in the hominin record, we must look to associated skeletal evidence for these structures. This evidence includes the increased flexion of the **basicranium**—the base of the skull (Laitman et al. 1978; Laitman and Heimbuch 1982; Lieberman et al. 1982; Lieberman 1992). Further clues come from the

Basicranium: the base of the skull.

structure of the brain, which can sometimes be preserved as an **endocast**—a preserved, fossilized impression of the interior braincase of a skull.

Efforts at reconstructing the skeletal anatomy associated with language in hominins suggest that australopithecines—an earlier form of hominin—had ape-like anatomy and brains that resemble living apes in both size and external form; thus, there is no apparent evidence for spoken language. However, as early as 2 million years ago, evidence from endocasts from Kenya of *Homo habilis*—the oldest species in the genus *Homo*—appear to show a more developed frontal lobe and **Broca's area**—the area that is responsible for the production of human speech (Tobias 1987). Thus, there is some tantalizing evidence that the changes associated with speech are observed in the fossil records as early as 2 million years ago. This is not to say that spoken language existed—simply that evolutionary changes occurred in these early hominins that would allow for the development of spoken language. Further details of the evidence of language capabilities in each hominin group will be discussed in subsequent chapters.

Other Human Traits. Only humans hunt very large animals, unlike other primates. Also, humans are one of the few primates that are completely terrestrial. We do not even sleep in trees, as many other ground-living primates do. Perhaps our ancestors lost their perches when the forests receded, or cultural advances such as weapons or fire may have eliminated the need to seek nightly shelter in the trees. As well, we have the longest dependency period of any of the primates, requiring extensive parental care for well into the second decade of life.

Finally, humans are unlike almost all other primates in having a division of labour by sex in food-getting and food-sharing in adulthood. Among non-human primates, both females and males forage for themselves after infancy. Humans have more gender-role specialization, perhaps because males, unencumbered by infants and small children, were freer to hunt and chase large animals.

Having examined our distinctive traits and the traits we share with other primates, we need to ask what selective forces may have favoured the emergence of primates, and then what forces may have favoured the line of divergence leading to humans. These questions are the subjects of the next two chapters.

Endocast: a preserved, fossilized relief of a hominin brain, created by the skull filling with minerals and taking on the morphology and structure of the brain. Endocasts are an important source of evidence for understanding the evolution of the brain and questions related to the origins of language, etc.

Broca's Area: the area of the brain related to language acquisition. It is important for understanding the origins of language in early hominins.

SUMMARY AND REVIEW

COMMON PRIMATE TRAITS

7.1 Identify common primate traits.

- No one trait is unique to primates. However, primates do share a distinct complex of features that include skeletal, dietary, sensory, brain, and developmental elements.
- Specific shared features include two bones in the lower part of the leg and in the forearm, a collarbone, omnivorous eating patterns, flexible prehensile hands, forward-facing eyes and stereoscopic vision, a large brain relative to body size, long maturation of the young, and a high degree of dependence on social life and learning.

 *Which primate skeletal traits reflect an arboreal existence?*

THE VARIOUS PRIMATES

7.2 Describe the major types of living primates and their geographical distribution.

- The order Primates is divided into two suborders: the prosimians and the anthropoids. Prosimians include lemur forms (found on Madagascar and the Comoro Islands, off the southeastern coast of Africa), loris forms (in Southeast Asia and sub-Saharan Africa), and tarsiers (on the islands of the Philippines and Indonesia). Anthropoids include monkeys, apes, and humans.

- Prosimians resemble other mammals more than anthropoids do and typically have mobile ears, whiskers, longer snouts, relatively fixed facial expressions, and more dependence on smell for information than other primates do. But they share with anthropoids grasping hands, stereoscopic vision, and enlarged visual centres in the brain.

- Anthropoids have rounded braincases; reduced, non-mobile outer ears; and relatively small, flat faces instead of muzzles. They also have highly efficient reproductive systems and highly dexterous hands.

- The anthropoid suborder is divided into two main groups: platyrrhines and catarrhines. Platyrrhines have broad, flat-bridged noses, with nostrils facing outward. The catarrhines are subdivided into cercopithecoids and hominoids.

- Hominoids have distinct locomotor patterns, including brachiation, knuckle walking, and bipedalism; high conceptual abilities; and relatively large brains.

- The hominoids include three groups: (1) the hylobates, or lesser apes; (2) the pongids, or great apes, which include orangutans, gorillas, and chimpanzees; and (3) the hominins (humans).

 *Why is the classification of tarsiers controversial?*

MODELS FOR HOMININ BEHAVIOUR

7.3 Explain and contrast two models for understanding hominin behaviour in the past.

- There are two models for understanding the behavior of our human ancestors: living non-human primates and ethnographic analogy.

- Non-human primate models are based on either experimental or natural observations of behaviours in living non-human primate groups.

- Ethnographic analogy relies on what we know from small, non-Westernized foraging or hunting-and-gathering societies that may be similar to such prehistoric populations.

 *What are some advantages and disadvantages of conducting natural observations of non-human primates?*

PRIMATE ADAPTATIONS

7.4 Describe the major ways in which living primates vary.

- No one trait is unique to primates, but they share the following features.

- Anatomical traits include two bones in the lower parts of the leg and the forearm; a collarbone; flexible prehensile (grasping) hands; and stereoscopic vision.

- Life history traits include a relatively large brain–body size ratio; having only one (or sometimes two) offspring at a time; and a long maturation of the young.

- Behavioural traits include daytime activity and a high degree of dependence on social life and learning (sociality).

 *What factors predict variation in primate body size? What are the reasons behind these associations?*

DISTINCTIVE HUMAN TRAITS

7.5 Describe the major traits that are distinctive to humans.

- Hominins differ from other anthropoids in ways that show us what makes humans unique as a species.
- Hominins are bipedal; they do not need arms for locomotion.
- Hominins have the largest and most complex brain of all the anthropoids, especially the cerebral cortex.
- Hominins move their jaws both vertically and horizontally when chewing.
- Hominin females are not limited to when they can engage in intercourse.
- Offspring have a much longer dependency stage, and more hominin behaviour is learned and culturally patterned.
- Hominins usually have a division of labour in food-getting and food-sharing in adulthood.
- The use of tools to make other tools and spoken, symbolic language is unique to modern humans.

 *Why might human female sexuality differ from that of most other primates?*

THINK ON IT

1. How could you infer that a fossil primate lived in the trees?
2. Why are primates so intelligent?
3. Under what conditions would the ability to communicate be adaptive?
4. Explain the differences between hominins and anthropoids and how those differences may have influenced hominins' ability to thrive.
5. How can studying living primates help us understand the lives of our extinct ancestors?

R. Skilton/Shutterstock

Primate Evolution: From Early Primates to Hominoids

8

The Trustees of the Natural History Museum, London

LEARNING OBJECTIVES

8.1 Describe the evidence that can be used to interpret the fossil record.

8.2 Discuss the emergence of primates in relation to environment and adaptation.

8.3 Describe the emergence of anthropoids.

8.4 Differentiate between early anthropoids and hominoids.

8.5 Discuss the challenges to identifying any clear emergence of hominins.

Primate palaeontologists and palaeoanthropologists focus on various questions about primate evolution. How far back in time did the primates emerge? What did they look like? What conditions, environmental and otherwise, favoured them? How did the early primates diverge after that point? What kinds of niches did the different primates occupy? Although our concern as anthropologists is largely with the emergence of humans and with the primates that are in the ancestral line leading to humans, we must remember that evolution does not proceed with a purpose or to give rise to any particular species; rather, organisms adapt, or fail to adapt, to the environments in which they find themselves. Thus, the primate fossil record is full of diversity; it is also full of apparent extinctions. Most of the primate lineages of the past probably never left any currently living descendants at all (Ciochon and Etler 1994).

The reconstruction of primate evolution depends upon the finding of fossil remains. Although many fossils have been discovered and continue to be discovered, the fossil record is still very incomplete. If geological strata are not uplifted, exposed by erosion, or otherwise accessible in the areas where ancient primates lived, palaeoanthropologists cannot recover their fossils. The fossils that are found are usually fragmented or damaged, and judgments about what the organism looked like may be based on one or just a few pieces. As we shall see, piecing together the evolutionary history of the primates requires much more than recovering fossil remains. The knowledge gained from anatomical studies of living species can allow us to make inferences about physical and behavioural traits that are likely to have been associated with the fossil features. Researchers use dating techniques developed in geology, chemistry, and physics to estimate the age of fossil remains (see Figure 8–1). Further, studies of ancient plants and animals, geography, and climate help us reconstruct the environments of ancient primates.

While there are many questions that continue to be asked about primate evolution, there are also a great many that we can answer at this point. We know that as of the early Eocene epoch, which began about 55 million years ago, primates with some of the features of modern prosimians had already emerged (see Figure 8–2). Primates with monkey- and ape-like features appeared in the Oligocene epoch, beginning about 34 million years ago. During the Miocene epoch, beginning about 24 million years ago, Old World monkeys and many different kinds of apes appeared. The ancient primates we know from fossils had some of the features of today's primates, but none of the ancient primates looked exactly like the primates of today.

In this and the following chapters we describe the main features of current theory and evidence about primate evolution, from the origin of primates to the origin of modern humans. In this chapter we deal with that part of the story before the emergence of definite bipedal hominins. Our overview covers the period from about 65 million years ago to the end of the Miocene, a little over 5 million years ago.

Interpreting the Fossil Record

How can palaeoanthropologists know about what may have happened millions of years ago? There is no

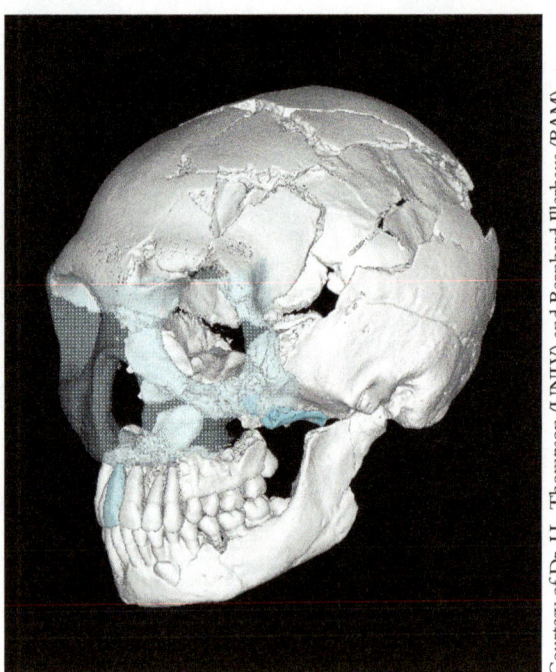

Juvenile Neanderthal Le Moustier 1. Virtual reconstruction by Jennifer L. Thompson (University of Nevada, Las Vegas) and Bernhard Illerhaus (Federal Institute for Materials Research and Testing).

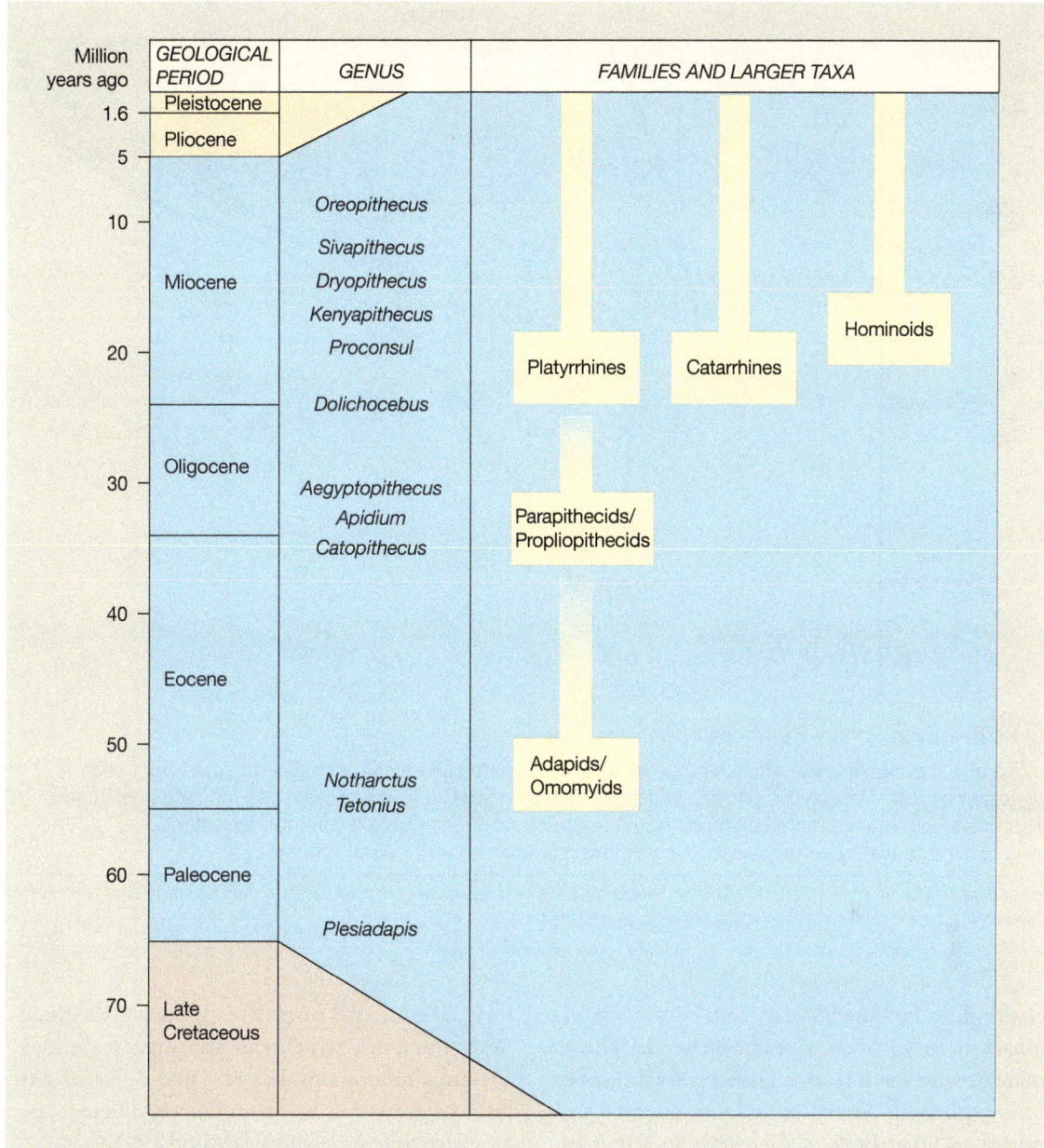

Figure 8–1 The Evolution of the Primates

written record from that period from which to draw inferences. However, we do have the fossil record, and as you have seen, we have ways of "reading" the record left by fossils and of telling how old fossils are.

Much of the evidence for primate evolution comes from teeth, which along with jaws are the most common animal parts to be preserved as fossils. Animals vary in **dentition**—the number and kinds of teeth they have, their size, and their arrangement in the mouth (see Figure 8–3). Dentition provides clues to evolutionary

Dentition: the type, number, and arrangement of teeth.

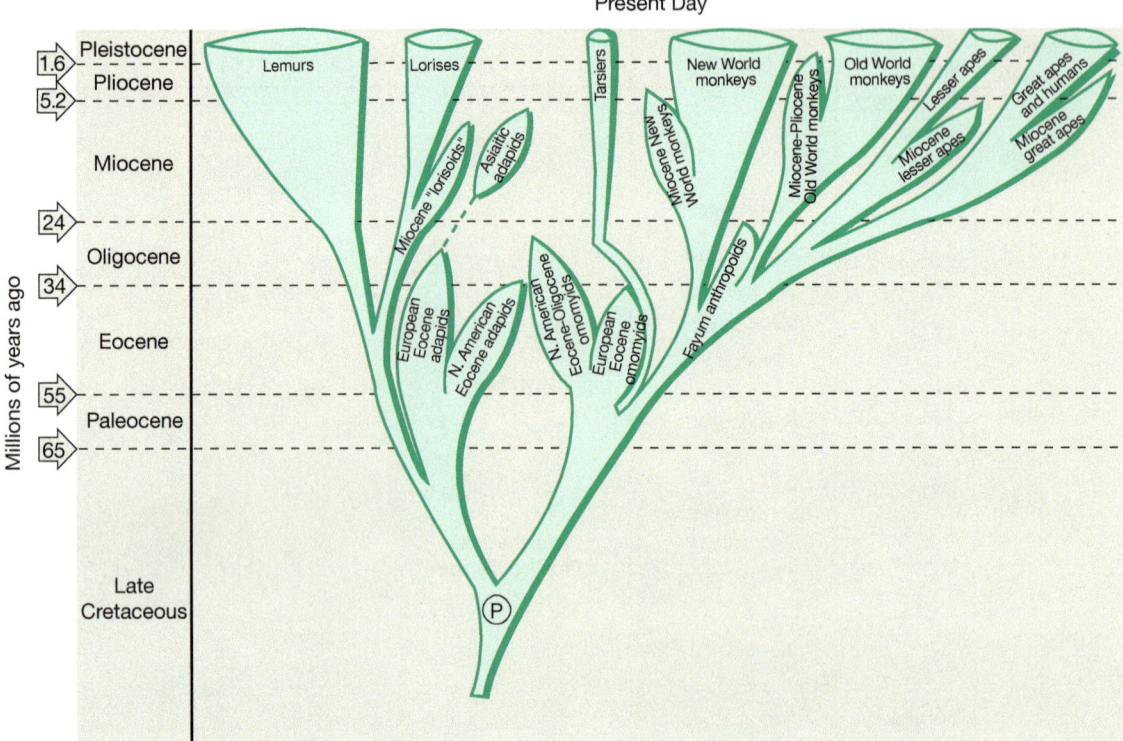

Figure 8–2 Evolutionary Relationships

A view of the evolutionary relationships between early primates and living primates, adapted from one suggested by R.D. Martin. The primate lineages that do not extend to the present day indicate presumed extinctions. Branching from a common "stalk" suggests divergence from a common ancestor. The circled P in the figure represents the unknown common ancestor of all primates.

Sources: Martin RD, Martin AE. 1990. Primate origins and evolution: A phylogenetic reconstruction. Republished with permission of Princeton University Press; permission conveyed through Copyright Clearance Center, Inc.

relationships because animals with similar evolutionary histories often have similar teeth. This is partly because teeth tend to change very little over time, both from an evolutionary standpoint and relative to other biological changes in a species. For example, no primate, living or extinct, has more than two incisors in each quarter of the jaw. That feature, along with others, distinguishes the primates from earlier mammals, which had three incisors in each quarter. Dentition also suggests the relative size of an animal and often offers clues about its diet. For example, comparisons of living primates suggest that fruit-eaters have flattened, rounded tooth cusps, unlike leaf- and insect-eaters, which have more pointed cusps (Kay 1988b). CT scan methodology has helped palaeontologists image the internal parts of teeth, such as the thickness of enamel, which can also suggest the diet. Electron microscopy has revealed different patterns of growth in bones and teeth; different species have different patterns (Wood 1994).

Palaeontologists can tell much about an animal's posture and locomotion from fragments of its skeleton. As you can see in Figure 8–4, *arboreal quadrupeds* have front and back limbs of about the same length; because their limbs tend to be short, their centre of gravity is close to the branches on which they move. They also tend to have long grasping fingers and toes. *Terrestrial quadrupeds* are more adapted for speed, so they have longer limbs and shorter fingers and toes. Disproportionate limbs are more characteristic of vertical clingers

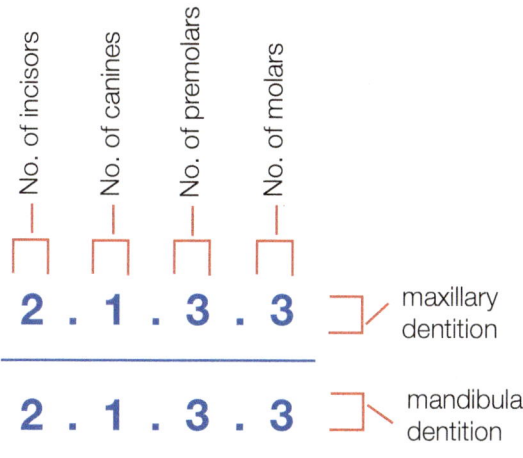

Figure 8–3 Dental Formula

Each row indicates the number of tooth types in the upper and lower jaws. From left to right the tooth types are incisors, canines, premolars, and molars.

and leapers, and brachiators. *Vertical clingers and leapers* have longer, more powerful hind limbs; *brachiators* have longer forelimbs (Conroy 1990). Even though soft tissues are not preserved, much can be inferred from the fossils themselves. For example, the form and size of muscles can be estimated by marks found on the bones to which the muscles were attached. The underside of the cranium may also provide information about the proportions of the brain devoted to vision, smell, or memory. The skull also reveals information about characteristics of smell and vision. For example, animals that rely more on smell than on vision tend to have longer snouts; nocturnal animals tend to have larger eye sockets.

The Emergence of Primates

When did the primates first emerge? This question turns out to be hard to answer from the current fossil record. Some palaeoanthropologists have suggested that fossil finds from the **Paleocene** epoch, which began about 65 million years ago, represent archaic primates, or *plesiadapiforms*. They have been found in both Europe and North America, which in the Paleocene were one land mass (see Figure 8–5).

A reconstruction of *smilodectes*, a primate found in western North America from 50 million years ago.

The most well known of the plesiadapiforms is ***Plesiadapis***. This squirrel-like animal had a large snout and large incisors. It also had a large nasal cavity and eye orbits located on the sides of the skull, suggesting a well-developed sense of smell and little or no stereoscopic vision (depth perception). The fingers of *Plesiadapis* had claws, and its hands and feet did not appear to allow for grasping. These features suggest that *Plesiadapis* was not a primate. However, the elbow and ankle joints suggest great mobility, and despite the large incisors the teeth suggest a primate-like omnivorous diet. The structure of their inner ears also resembled that of modern primates. Because it had these primate-like features, some scholars believe that the plesiadapiforms were archaic primates (Szalay 1972; Szalay et al. 1975; Gingerich 1986).

Other palaeoanthropologists find so few similarities between them and later obvious primates that they do not include the plesiadapiforms in the order of primates (Ciochon and Etler 1994; Fleagle 1994; Cartmill 2010). There is no dispute, however,

Paleocene: the geological epoch 65 million to 55 million years ago.

Plesiadapis: The most well known of the plesiadapiforms, possibly an archaic primate.

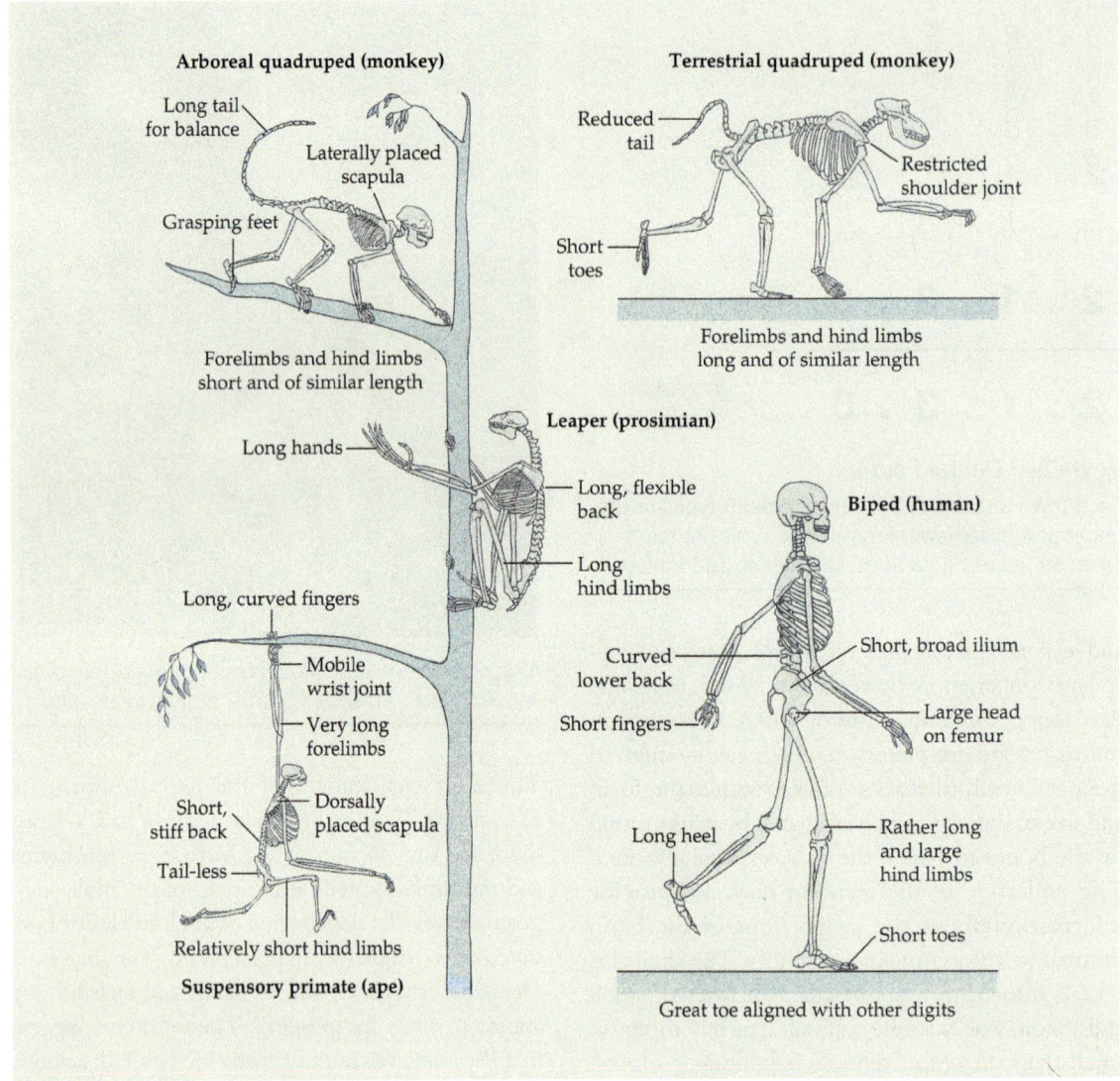

Figure 8–4 Primate Locomotion

The four major modes of primate locomotion include vertical clinging and leaping (prosimians), quadrupedalism (monkeys), brachiation (apes), and bipedalism (hominins).

Source: Fleagle JG. 1988. Primate skeletons. Primate adaptation and evolution. Second edition. San Diego: Academic Press. pp. 245–251. Reprinted with permission of Elsevier.

about fossils dating from the early **Eocene**, about 55 million years ago. These oldest definite primates appear in two major groups of prosimians—*adapids* and *omomyids*. The adapids led to modern lemurs and lorises (*strepsirhines*) and the omomyids led to tarsiers and anthropoids (*haplorhines*). Omomyids exhibit many characteristics that seem to be more anthropoid-like, including a larger brain, the beginnings of postorbital closure around the eyes, and a relatively short face.

Since these two kinds of primates are different from each other in major ways, and because they both appeared rather abruptly at the border of the Paleocene and Eocene, there presumably was an

> **Eocene:** a geological epoch 55 million to 34 million years ago during which the first definite primates appeared.

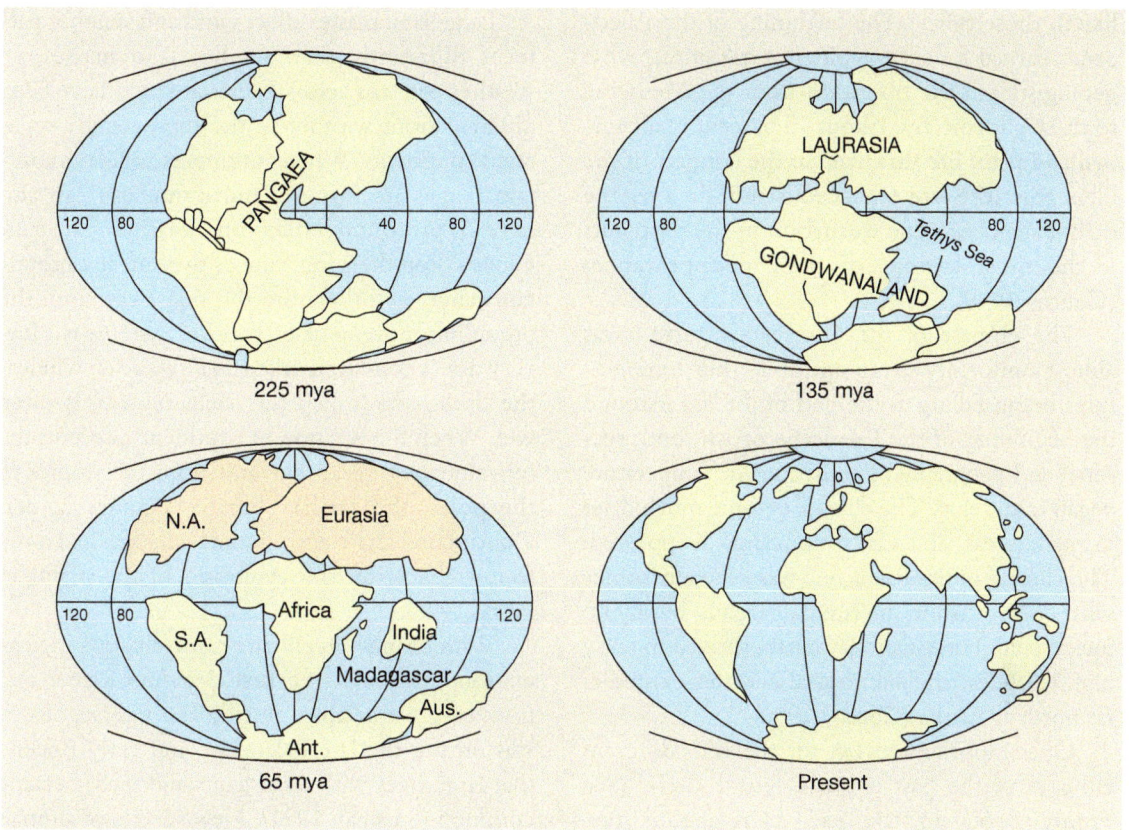

Figure 8–5 Continental Drift
The supercontinent Pangaea split into Laurasia and Gondwanaland 135 million years ago (mya). These further divided into the continents as we know them today.

earlier common primate ancestor. One strong candidate for the common primate ancestor is *Carpolestes simpsoni*, a mouse-sized arboreal creature from Wyoming dating to about 56 million years ago. *Carpolestes* has an interesting mix of primate and non-primate characteristics. While it lacks stereoscopic vision, *Carpolestes* has nails instead of claws on its big toes, and it has grasping hands and feet (Block and Boyer 2002). Not all scholars are convinced that *Caropolestes* is the common ancestor of all primates. In Figure 8–2 (page 178), the circled P represents the unknown common ancestor, which Robert D. Martin suggested lived in the late Cretaceous. Others think the common ancestor emerged in the Paleocene.

Now we turn to the environmental conditions in which we see the emergence of the primates.

The Environment

It is generally agreed that the earliest primate may have emerged by the Paleocene, 65 million years to 55 million years ago, and perhaps earlier, in the late **Cretaceous**. What was the environment

Carpolestes: A mouse-sized arboreal creature living about 56 million years ago; a strong candidate for the common primate ancestor.

Cretaceous: geological epoch 135 million to 65 million years ago, during which dinosaurs and other reptiles ceased to be the dominant land vertebrates and mammals and birds began to become important.

like in those times? The beginning of the Paleocene marked a major geological transition, what geologists call the transition from the Mesozoic to the Cenozoic era. About 75 percent of all animal and plant life that lived in the last part of the Cenozoic (the late Cretaceous) vanished by the early Paleocene. The extinction of the dinosaurs is the most famous of these disappearances (Conroy 1990).

The climate of the Cretaceous period was almost uniformly damp and mild, but temperatures began falling at the end of the era. Around the beginning of the Paleocene epoch, both seasonal and geographic fluctuations in temperature began to develop. The climate became much drier in many areas, and vast swamplands disappeared. The climate of the Paleocene was generally somewhat cooler than in the late Cretaceous, but by no means cold. Forests and savannahs thrived in fairly high latitudes, and subtropical climates existed as far north as Alaska (Conroy 1990).

One important reason for the very different climates of the past is **continental drift**. (See Figure 8–5.) In the early Cretaceous (ca. 135 million years ago), the continents were actually clumped into two large land masses or "supercontinents"—*Laurasia*, which included North America and Eurasia, and *Gondwanaland*, which included Africa, South America, India, Australia, and Antarctica. By the beginning of the Paleocene (ca. 65 million years ago) Gondwanaland had broken apart, with South America drifting west away from Africa, India drifting east, and Australia and Antarctica drifting south. As the continents changed position, they moved into locations with different climatic conditions. More importantly, however, the very movement of the continents affected the climate, sometimes on a global scale (Habicht 1979).

Large land masses affect wind and weather patterns differently than smaller land masses, so weather patterns across Laurasia would have been different from weather in the subsequently separated continents. When continents collide, mountain ranges are formed, and mountains can also have a profound effect on weather patterns. Clouds drop their moisture as they meet a mountain range, and therefore the side away from the prevailing movement of weather systems is often very dry (a condition called a *rain shadow*), whereas the other side (called the *windward side*) is often wet. When the location of continents prevents the movement of ocean currents from the tropics to the poles, the earth's climate becomes colder. Continental drift and climate change had profound effects on the evolution of the primates (Vrba 1995).

With changes in climate came changes in vegetation. Although the first deciduous trees and flowering plants arose during the Cretaceous, it was during the late Paleocene and early Eocene that large trees with large fruits and seeds became common (Sussman 1991). New species of animals evolved as the climate and environment changed. Although some mammals date from the Cretaceous, the Paleocene saw the evolution and diversification of many different types of mammals, and the expansion and diversification of deciduous trees and flowering plants probably played a large role in mammalian expansion and diversification (see Applied Anthropology, "Studying Biodiversity"). Indeed, primate palaeontologists think primates evolved from one of these mammalian *radiations*, or extensive diversifications, probably from the **insectivore** order of mammals, including modern shrews and moles, that is adapted to eating insects—insects that would have lived off the new deciduous trees and flowering plants.

Continental Drift: the movement of the continents over the past 135 million years. In the early Cretaceous (about 135 million years ago) there were two "supercontinents": *Laurasia*, which included North America and Eurasia, and *Gondwanaland*, which included Africa, South America, India, Australia, and Antarctica. By the beginning of the Paleocene (about 65 million years ago), Gondwanaland had broken apart, with South America drifting west away from Africa, India drifting east, and Australia and Antarctica drifting south.

Insectivore: the order or major grouping of mammals, including modern shrews and moles, that is adapted to feeding on insects.

To put it simply, the new kinds of plant life opened up sources of food and protection for new animal forms. Of most interest to us is that the new plant life provided an abundant food supply for insects. The result was that insects proliferated in both number and variety, and in turn there was an increase in *insectivores*—the mammals that ate the insects. The insectivores were very adaptable and were able to take advantage of many different habitats—under the ground, in water, on the ground, and above the ground, including the woody habitat of bushes, shrubs, vines, and trees. It was the last kind of adaptation, above the ground, that may have been the most important

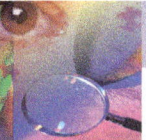

APPLIED ANTHROPOLOGY

Studying Biodiversity

The late Miocene is known as the age of the apes. Literally dozens of ape species were in the forests of Europe and Asia. What happened to all the diversity of apes, and why is there such a relative paucity of ape species today? We might ask the same question about humans. Two million years ago, there were at least four hominin species in Africa, and perhaps more, but today, there is only one. What leads to a great diversity of species, and what causes that diversity to diminish? These are central questions for applied anthropologists who study biodiversity.

Biodiversity refers to the richness of genes, species, and ecosystems within a given region. Regions with greater biodiversity are generally considered healthier and more stable than those with less biodiversity. However, there are also broad geographic differences in biodiversity, with tropical areas generally having greater biodiversity and polar areas having lower biodiversity. Biodiversity has also changed over time, with periods of mass extinction dramatically lowering global biodiversity. Although it is clear from the primate fossil record (and the fossil record of many other species) that biodiversity changes over time through natural processes, many scholars now believe that humans are having an impact on biodiversity in far more dramatic and rapid ways than ever before. And most scholars think this is a significant problem that needs to be addressed.

Biodiversity benefits humans in at least three ways. First, the maintenance of genetic variation in plant and animal species provides for innovations in agriculture such as increased yield and resistance to disease. Second, the maintenance of species diversity provides sources for new resources or technologies in things such as building materials and medicines. Finally, and perhaps most importantly, biodiversity appears to be a measure of environmental health and stability, and working to maintain biodiversity may, therefore, also serve to maintain a stable and healthy environment. Applied anthropologists who conduct research on biodiversity tend to focus on two related aspects of biodiversity. First, they document local knowledge of biodiversity. Second, they document local practices that help maintain biodiversity. For example, Terence Hays has spent much of his career documenting knowledge of plants among the Ndumba people of Papua New Guinea. Hays's research and that of other anthropologists has helped scholars to more fully understand the biodiversity of the New Guinea highlands. Similarly, Terence Turner documented the political struggles of the Kayapo peoples of Brazil, who have fought logging companies and miners to protect the rain forest environment in which they live. Turner hoped that the Kayapo example can be a model for other Indigenous groups struggling to protect the biodiversity of their homelands.

Even though the study of our ancient primate roots may appear to have little impact on the world today, applied anthropologists have recognized that an understanding of evolutionary patterns of biodiversity is essential to identifying trends in the modern world that point to human-imposed damage to the earth's living systems.

Sources: Abel T, Stepp JR. 2003. A New Ecosystems Ecology for Anthropology. Conservation Ecology. 7(3):12.

Hays TE. 2009. From Ethnographer to Comparativist and Back Again. In Ember CR, Ember M, Peregrine P, editors. MyAnthroLibrary. MyAnthroLibrary.com. Pearson.

Orlove B, Brush S. 1996. Anthropology and the Conservation of Biodiversity. Annual Review of Anthropology. 25:329–352.

Turner T. 1993. The Role of Indigenous Peoples in the Environmental Crisis: The Example of the Kayapo of the Brazilian Amazon. Perspectives in Biology and Medicine. 36(3):526–545.

Turner T. 1995. An Indigenous People's Struggle for Socially Equitable and Ecologically Sustainable Production: The Kayapo Revolt against Extractivism. Journal of Latin American Anthropology. 1:98–121.

for primate evolution. The woody habitat had been exploited only partially in earlier periods. But then several different kinds, or taxa, of small animals, one of which may have been the archaic primate, began to take advantage of the woody habitat.

What in Particular May Have Favoured the Emergence of Primates?

The traditional explanation of primate origins is called the *arboreal theory*. According to this view, the primates evolved from insectivores that took to the trees. Different palaeoanthropologists emphasized different possible adaptations to life in the trees (Sussman 1991). In 1912, G. Elliot Smith suggested that taking to the trees favoured vision over smell. Searching for food by sniffing and feeling with the snout might suit terrestrial insectivores, but vision would be more useful in an animal that searched for food in the maze of tree branches. With shorter snouts and the declining importance of the sense of smell, the eyes of the early primates would have come to face forward. In 1916, Frederic Wood Jones emphasized changes in the hand and foot. He thought that tree climbing would favour grasping hands and feet, with the hind limbs becoming more specialized for support and propulsion. In 1921, Treacher Collins suggested that the eyes of the early primates came to face forward not just because the snout got smaller. Rather, he thought that three-dimensional binocular vision would be favoured because an animal jumping from branch to branch would be more likely to survive if it could accurately judge distances across open space (Cartmill 1974; Richard 1985). In 1968, Frederick Szalay suggested that a shift in diet—from insects to seeds, fruits, and leaves—might have been important in the differentiation of primates from insectivores (Szalay 1968).

In 1974, Matt Cartmill highlighted some crucial weaknesses in the arboreal theory (Cartmill 1974, 1992a, 1998). He argued that tree living is not a good explanation for many of the primate features because there are living mammals that dwell in trees but seem to do very well without primate-like characteristics. One of the best examples, according to Cartmill, is the tree squirrel. Its eyes are not front-facing, its sense of smell is not reduced in comparison with other rodents, it has claws rather than nails, and it lacks an opposable thumb. Yet these squirrels live very successfully in trees. Furthermore, other animals have some primate traits but do not live in trees or do not move around in trees as primates do. For example, carnivores, such as cats, hawks, and owls, have forward-facing eyes, and the chameleon and some Australian marsupial mammals that prey on insects in bushes and shrubs have grasping hands and feet.

Cartmill proposed that the early primates may have been insect-eaters, and that three-dimensional vision, grasping hands and feet, and reduced claws may have been advantageous for hunting insects on the slender vines and branches that filled the undergrowth of tropical forests. Three-dimensional vision would allow the insect hunter to gauge the prey's distance accurately. Grasping feet would allow the predator to move quietly up narrow supports to reach the prey, which could then be grabbed with the hands. Claws, Cartmill argued, would make it difficult to grasp very slender branches. The sense of smell would have become reduced, not so much because it was no longer useful, but because the location of the eyes at the front of the face would leave less room for a snout.

One criticism of this idea by J. Allman was that if visual predation is such an important predictor of forward-facing eyes, why don't all visual predators have such eyes? Cats and owls have forward-facing eyes, but mongooses and robins do not. A second criticism, by Paul Garber, is that if claws were disadvantageous for moving on slender branches, why does at least one small primate—the Panamanian tamarin—feed on insects among small twigs and vines but have claws on four of its five digits of each paw? And Robert Sussman pointed out that most small nocturnal prosimians eat more fruit than insects. Sussman suggested that the need for precise finger manipulation to grasp small fruits and flowers at the ends of small branches, while hanging on by the hind feet, might favour both clawless digits and grasping extremities.

Robert Sussman's theory built on Cartmill's *visual predation theory* and on Szalay's idea about a dietary shift (Sussman and Raven 1978). Sussman accepted Cartmill's point that the early primates were likely to eat and move about mostly on small branches, not on large trunks and branches (as do squirrels). If they did, grasping hands and feet, and nails rather than claws (as squirrels have), would have been advantageous. Sussman also accepted Szalay's point that the early primates probably ate the new types of plant food (flowers, seeds, and fruits) that were becoming abundant at the time, as flowering trees and plants spread throughout the world. Sussman, however, asked an important question: If the early primates ate mostly plant foods rather than quick-moving insects, why did they become more reliant on vision than on smell? Sussman suggested it was because the early primates were probably nocturnal (as many prosimians still are): if they were to locate and manipulate small food items at the ends of slender branches in dim light, they would need improved vision. Thus, increased exploitation of flowering plants (*angiosperms*) promoted modern primate characteristics like sharp vision and the ability to distinguish colours.

Cartmill now believes that the earliest primates were probably nocturnal and they also probably ate fruit as well as insects, as Sussman suggested, just as many contemporary nocturnal prosimians do. If they ate fruit and insects at the ends of small branches and twigs, claws may have been disadvantageous. Cartmill thinks that his modified theory explains the changes in primate vision better than Sussman's theory does. For example, how can we explain stereoscopic, forward-facing eyes in the early primates? Sussman said that the early primates were fruit-eaters, but Cartmill pointed out that, although stereoscopic, forward-facing eyes are not necessary for getting fruit, they might be essential for helping to catch insects.

We still have very little fossil evidence of the earliest primates, although the emergence of flowering plants in the Paleocene roughly coincides with the emergence of the earliest primate ancestors. When additional fossils become available, we

Squirrels are arboreal, but lack many of the features that characterize primates. Matt Cartmill argued that primate features are adapted to the slender terminal branches of trees, while squirrel features are adapted to the trunks and main branches.

may be better able to evaluate the various explanations that have been suggested for the emergence of primates.

The Early Primates: What They Looked Like

The earliest definite (undisputed) primates, dating back to the Eocene epoch, appeared abruptly in North America, Europe, and Asia about 55 million years ago. At that time many land masses that are now separate were connected by land bridges. North America and Europe were connected by Iceland, Greenland, and the Faeroe Islands. Europe and North America became separated later in the Eocene. The beginning of the Eocene was warmer and less seasonal than the Paleocene, and vast tropical forests abounded (Conroy 1990).

The anatomy of the diverse Eocene primates suggests that they already had many of the features of modern primates—for example, nails rather than claws, a grasping, opposable first toe, and a bony bar around the side of the eye socket (Conroy 1990). Vertical clinging and leaping was probably a common method of locomotion. Eocene prosimians not only moved around the way modern prosimians do, but some were similar skeletally to living prosimians.

Early Eocene Primates: Omomyids and Adapids

Two groups of prosimians appear in the early Eocene. One group, the **omomyids**, has many tarsier-like features; the other group, **adapids**, has many lemur-like features. The omomyids were very small, no bigger than squirrels; the adapids were kitten- and cat-sized.

Omomyids are considered tarsier-like because of their large eyes, long tarsal bones, and very small size. The large eyes suggest that they were active at night; the smaller-sized omomyids may have been insect-eaters and the larger ones may have relied more on fruit (Fleagle 1994). Most of the omomyids have dental formulas characteristic of modern prosimians: two incisors and three premolars on each side of the lower jaw rather than the three incisors and four premolars of early mammals (Conroy 1990). The importance of vision is apparent in a fossilized skull of the Eocene omomyid *Tetonius*. Imprints in the skull show that the brain had large occipital and temporal lobes—the regions associated with perception and the integration of visual memory (Radinsky 1967).

The lemur-like adapids were more active during the day and relied more on leaf and fruit vegetation. In contrast to the omomyids, adapid remains show considerable sexual dimorphism in the canines and they retain the four premolars characteristic of earlier mammals (although there are fewer incisors) (Radinsky 1967; Fleagle 1994). One adapid known from its abundant fossil finds is *Notharctus*. It has a small, broad face with full stereoscopic vision and a reduced muzzle. It appears to have lived in the forest and had long and powerful hind legs for leaping from tree to tree (Conroy 1990; Alexander 1992).

There was a great deal of diversity among all mammals during the Eocene epoch, and the primates were no exception. Both the omomyids and adapids have a few features that suggest links between them and the anthropoids that appear later, in the Oligocene, but there is no agreement that either group gave rise to the anthropoids. Although the omomyids had some similarities to modern tarsiers and the adapids bear some resemblance to lemurs and lorises, palaeoanthropologists are not sure that either group is ancestral to modern prosimians. However, it is generally thought that the populations ancestral to lemurs and lorises as well as tarsiers did emerge in the Eocene or even earlier, in the late Paleocene (Conroy 1990; Martin and Martin 1990).

The Emergence of Anthropoids

Unfortunately, the fossil record documenting the emergence of the anthropoids is extremely spotty. The living anthropoids—monkeys, apes, and humans—have been very successful, and are represented by well over 150 species today. Who were their ancestors? There are several questions concerning the evolution of New World monkeys (platyrrhines). The first New World primates appear in the late Oligocene when South America was no closer to either Africa or North America than it is today. So the question remains, Where did New World monkeys come from? The earliest fossil evidence comes from Bolivia and dates to about 35 million years ago. It is represented by a variety of genera including *Branisella*, *Tremacebus*, *Dolichocebus*, *Homunculus*, and *Soriacebus*.

There is no clear fossil record of the Old World forms (the catarrhines) in the two areas where they are most abundant today—the rain forests of sub-Saharan Africa and Southeast Asia (Fleagle and Kay 1985). Some palaeoanthropologists think that recent Eocene primate finds from China, Southeast Asia, and Algeria have anthropoid affinities, but there is no clear agreement on their evolutionary status (Fleagle 1994). Undisputed remains of early anthropoids date from a somewhat later period, the early Oligocene, about 34 million years ago, in the Fayum area, southwest of Cairo, Egypt. One of the earliest fossil primates at

---

Omomyid: a type of prosimian with many tarsier-like features; appeared in the early Eocene.
Adapid: a type of prosimian with many lemur-like features; appeared in the early Eocene.

PRIMATE EVOLUTION: FROM EARLY PRIMATES TO HOMINOIDS

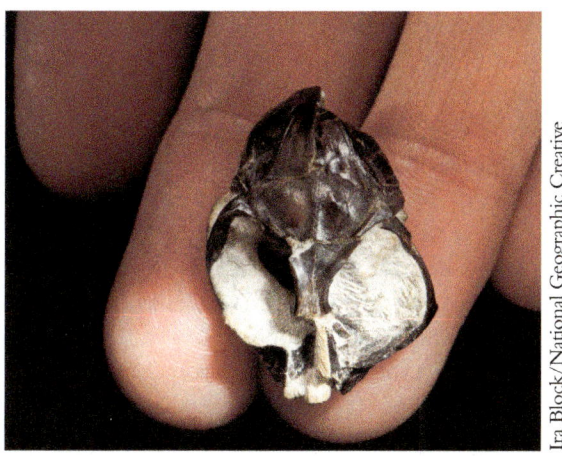

Although the Fayum depression is a desert today, it was a tropical forest in the Oligocene. The area is littered with the fossilized remains of tropical plants and the animals that fed on them, including primates.

A reconstruction of what two Oligocene primates might have looked like. In the foreground is a group of *Aegyptopithecus*; in the background are two individuals of *Apidium*. Some of the fauna that shared the Fayum region with these early primates are also shown.

Fayum is *Catopithecus*, dating to around 35 million years ago. Several recent finds have made it one of the best-known late Eocene primates. *Catopithecus* was about the size of a modern marmoset or squirrel monkey. Its dentition suggests a mixed diet of fruit and insects. Its eyes were small, suggesting it was active during the day (diurnal). The few skeletal remains of *Catopithecus* suggest it was an agile arboreal quadruped. It may be the best candidate for the earliest anthropoid, though how it was related to other primates is still debated (Simons 1995).

The Fayum Oligocene Anthropoids

The Fayum is an uninviting area of desert badlands, but during the **Oligocene** epoch, 34 million to 24 million years ago, it was a tropical rain forest very close to the shores of the Mediterranean Sea. The area had a warm climate, and it contained many rivers and lakes. The Fayum, in fact, was far more inviting than the northern continents then, for the climates of both North America and Eurasia were beginning to cool during the Oligocene. The general cooling seems to have resulted in the virtual disappearance of primates from the northern areas, at least for a time.

As well as a prosimian family related to tarsiers, the Fayum yielded two main types of anthropoid: the monkey-like *parapithecids* and the ape-like *propliopithecids*. Dating from 35 million to 31 million years ago (Fleagle 1994), the parapithecids and the propliopithecids had enough features to be classified as anthropoids.

Parapithecids. The monkey-like **parapithecids** had three premolars (in each quarter), as do most prosimians and the New World monkeys. They were similar to modern anthropoids in the presence of a bony partition behind the eye socket,

---

Oligocene: the geological epoch 34 million to 24 million years ago during which definite anthropoids emerged.

Parapithecids: small monkey-like Oligocene primates found in the Fayum area of Egypt.

broad incisors, projecting canines, and low, rounded cusps on their molars. But they had prosimian-like premolars and relatively small brains. The parapithecids were small, generally weighing under 1.3 kilograms; they resembled the squirrel monkeys living now in South and Central America (Kay 1988a). Their relatively small eye sockets suggest that they were not nocturnal, and their teeth suggest that they ate mostly fruits and seeds. From the remains of one of the parapithecids, *Apidium*, an arboreal quadruped, Kay (1988a) and Conroy (1990) inferred that this anthropoid did a considerable amount of leaping. Palaeoanthropologists still disagree as to whether the parapithecids preceded or followed the split between the New World monkeys (platyrrhines) and the Old World monkeys and apes (catarrhines). In any case, the parapithecids are the most primitive known anthropoids (Fleagle 1999).

That parapithecids may be ancestral to New World monkeys (platyrrhines) raises an interesting puzzle in primate evolution: the origin of the New World monkeys. Anthropoidal primates such as *Dolichocebus*, a small fruit-eating monkey similar to the modern squirrel monkey (Rosenberger 1979), appear suddenly and without any apparent ancestors in South America around 25 million years ago. Since the parapithecids predate the appearance of anthropoids in South America and resemble them in many ways, it seems reasonable to view them as part of the population ancestral to the New World monkeys (Fleagle and Kay 1987; Aiello 1993; Hartwig 1994).

But how did anthropoidal primates get from Africa to South America? Although the continents were closer together in the late Oligocene, when primates are thought to have first appeared in South America, the distance between South America and Africa was at least 3000 kilometres. An extended continental shelf and islands created by lower sea levels in the late Oligocene may have made it possible to "island hop" from Africa to South America over ocean stretches as short as 200 kilometres, but that is still a long distance for an arboreal primate to travel.

Going from Africa to Europe and North America, which were still joined in the late Oligocene, was not likely either. North America and South America were not joined until some 5 million years ago, so even if the ancestors of the New World monkeys made it to North America, they would still have needed to cross the Atlantic Ocean to reach South America. One suggestion is that the ancestors of the New World monkeys "rafted" across the Atlantic on large mats of vegetation. Even today, such "rafts," of matted plants, roots, and soil, break away from the mouths of major rivers, and they can be quite large. It seems an unlikely scenario, but many scholars believe such drifting vegetation must have been the means of bringing anthropoids to South America (Aiello 1993; Hartwig 1994; Andrews 2000).

Propliopithecids. The other type of anthropoid found in the Fayum, the **propliopithecids**, had the dental formula of modern catarrhines. This trait clearly places the propliopithecids with the catarrhines (Andrews 2000). In contrast with the parapithecids, which had three premolars, the propliopithecids had only two premolars, as do modern apes, humans, and Old World monkeys. Propliopithecids shared with the parapithecids the anthropoid dental characteristics of broad lower incisors, projecting canines, and lower molars with low, rounded cusps. Like parapithecids, propliopithecids also had a bony partition behind the eye socket.

Aegyptopithecus, the best-known propliopithecid, probably moved around quadrupedally in the trees, weighed about 6 kilograms, and ate mostly fruit. It had a long muzzle and a relatively small brain and showed considerable sexual dimorphism. Although its teeth and jaws are ape-like, *Aegyptopithecus*'s skeleton is monkey-like (Fleagle and Kay 1985; Conroy 1990; Rasmussen 2002).

Because the propliopithecids lack the specialized characteristics of living Old World monkeys and apes but share the dental formula of the catarrhines, some palaeoanthropologists think that the propliopithecids included the ancestor of both the Old World monkeys and the hominoids—apes

Propliopithecids: ape-like anthropoids dating from the early Oligocene, found in the Fayum area of Egypt.

The fossil skull of an *Aegyptopithecus* from the Fayum. Its dentition, its small, bony eye sockets, and its relatively large brain make it an unambiguous ancestor of Old World monkeys and apes.

and humans (Fleagle and Kay 1983; Fleagle 1999; Rasmussen 2002).

The Emergence of Hominoids

During the **Miocene** epoch, 24 million to 5.2 million years ago, monkeys and apes clearly diverged in appearance, and numerous kinds of apes appeared in Europe, Asia, and Africa (Begun 2010). In the early Miocene, the temperatures were considerably warmer than the temperatures in the Oligocene. From early to late Miocene, conditions became drier, particularly in East Africa (Fleagle 1999). The reasons for this relate again to continental drift. By about 18 million years ago, Africa came into contact with Eurasia, ending the moderating effect that the Tethys Sea, which separated Africa from Eurasia, had on the climates of both continents. The contact of Africa and, more significantly, India with the Eurasian continent also initiated mountain building, changing established weather patterns. The overall effect was that southern Eurasia and eastern Africa became considerably drier than they had been. Once again, these changes appear to have significantly influenced primate evolution.

Miocene: the geological epoch from 24 million to 5.2 million years ago.

We can infer that late in the Miocene, between about 8 million and 5 million years ago, the direct ancestor of humans—the first hominin—may have emerged in Africa. The inference about *where* hominins emerged is based on the fact that undisputed hominins lived in East Africa after about 5 million years ago. The inference about *when* hominins emerged is based not on fossil evidence but on comparative molecular and biochemical analyses of modern apes and humans. As we will see in the next chapter, the effect of a drier climate and the creation of more open grassland environments may have directly influenced the evolution of the hominins.

One of the Miocene apes (known or unknown) was ancestral to hominins, so our discussion here deals mostly with the early hominoids or *proto-apes*, or primates that possess some but not all of the key traits shared by apes, of the early Miocene, and the *definite* apes of the middle and late Miocene. Before we get to the apes, though, we should say something about monkeys and prosimians in the Miocene. Unfortunately, monkey fossils from the early Miocene are rare. In the New World, the whole Miocene fossil record is quite sparse. There have been only a few primate fossils found in Colombia and Argentina; they show close affinities with present-day South American monkeys. In the Old World, early Miocene monkey fossils have been found only in northern Africa. The situation is different for the middle and late Miocene: Old World monkey fossils are much more abundant than ape fossils (Conroy 1990). As for prosimians, fossils from the Miocene are scarce, but we know that at least some adapids survived into the middle Miocene in India and the late Miocene in China (Conroy 1990). Some loris-like prosimians appeared in East Africa, Pakistan, and India during the Miocene (Martin and Martin 1990).

Early Miocene Proto-Apes

Most of the fossils from the early Miocene are described as proto-apes. They have been found mostly in Africa. The best-known genus is

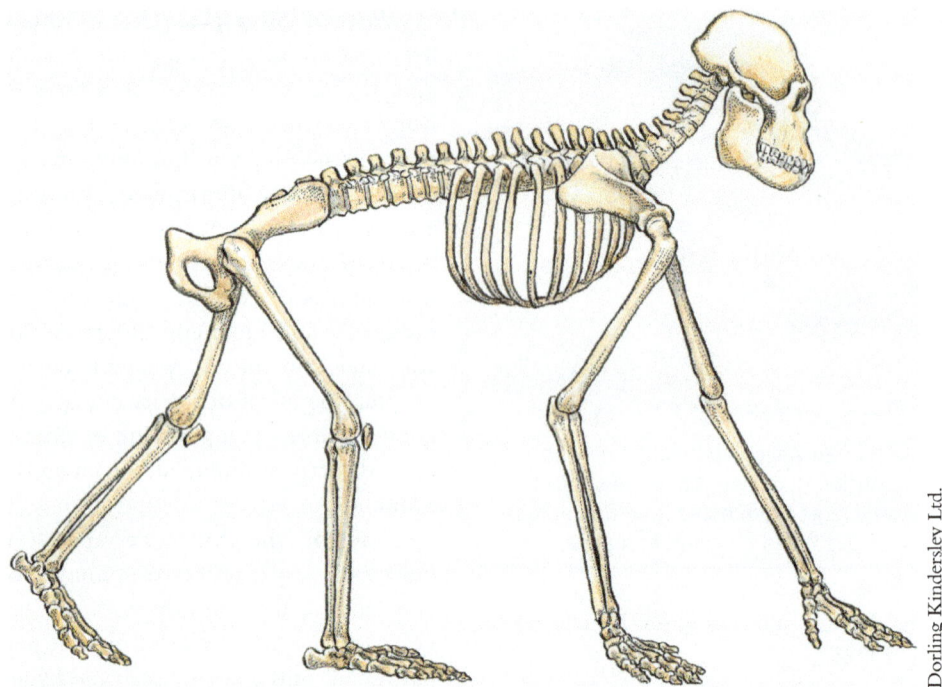

Figure 8–6 *Proconsul africanus*

The forelimbs and hind limbs of *Proconsul africanus* (dating from about 20 million years ago) are about the same length, suggesting that it moved on all fours on the tops of branches. *Proconsul africanus* was the smallest of the *Proconsul* species, weighing about 10 to 12 kilograms.

Proconsul, its fossils found in sites that are about 20 million years old in Kenya and Uganda (Begun 1998). (See also Figure 8–6.)

All of the various *Proconsul* species that have been found were much bigger than any of the anthropoids of the Oligocene, ranging from about the size of a gibbon to that of a female gorilla (Conroy 1990; Harrison 2002). *Proconsul* lacked a tail, which is one of the most definitive features of hominoids. Most palaeoanthropologists now agree that *Proconsul* was definitely hominoid, but quite unlike any ape living today. Modern hominoids have many anatomical features of the shoulder, elbow, wrists, and fingers that are adapted for locomotion by suspension (brachiation). However, suspension was apparently not *Proconsul*'s method of getting around because its elbows, wrists, and fingers may have permitted brachiation (Begun 1998, 2010; Harrison 2002). Like the Oligocene anthropoids, *Proconsul* was primarily an arboreal quadruped (see Figure 8–4, page 180), although some of the larger forms may have sometimes moved on the ground. Based on dental morphology, most *Proconsul* species appear to have been fruit-eaters, but larger species may have also consumed leaves (Andrews 2000; Harrison 2002).

Some recent finds from East Africa suggest that other types of early hominoids were also on the scene from the early Miocene, but these are quite fragmentary and not clearly classifiable. *Proconsul* may or may not have been ancestral to

Proconsul: the best-known genus of proto-apes from the early Miocene; found mostly in Africa.

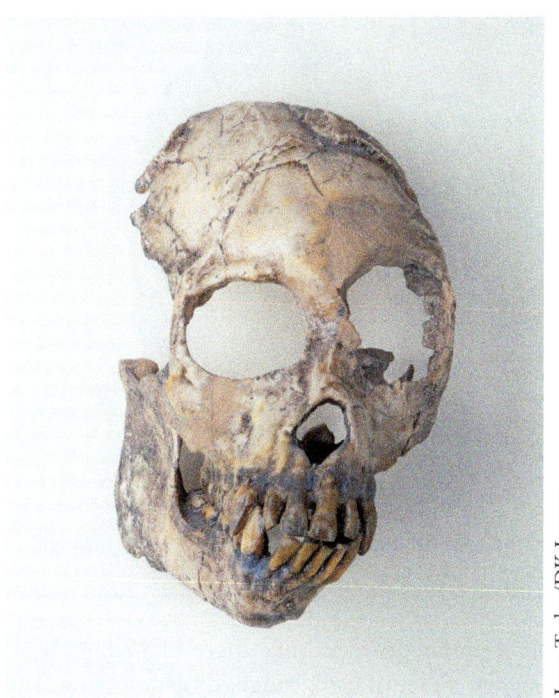

The skull of a *Proconsul* specimen from Kenya.

later apes and humans, but given its combination of monkey-like and ape-like features, it may have looked a lot like the common ancestor of apes and humans (Begun 1998, 2010).

Middle Miocene Apes

By about 17 million years ago, during the warmer Miocene epoch, a large number of distinct hominoid species emerged. These forms were distributed throughout Africa, Europe, and Asia, and included *Dryopithecus*, *Kenyapithecus*, *Oreopithecus*, *Ouranopithecus*, and *Sivapithecus*. While some of these species have been closely associated with modern forms, none of them appears to have any clear link with the earliest hominins. The oldest, dating to about 13 million years ago, is *Pierolapithecus*, and was recently found near Barcelona, Spain (Begun 2010). Another hominoid, *Kenyapithecus*, was found on Maboko Island and nearby locations in Kenya (Ward et al. 1999; Zimmer 1999).

Both *Pierolapithecus* and *Kenyapithecus* had many of *Proconsul*'s features, but their teeth and faces resembled those of more modern hominoids. And, in contrast to *Proconsul*, *Kenyapithecus* was probably more terrestrial. It also had very thickly enamelled teeth and robust jaws, suggesting a diet of hard, tough foods, or possibly a great deal of grit in the food because *Kenyapithecus* lived mostly on the ground. Whether *Kenyapithecus* is ancestral to the later apes and humans is something of a puzzle because its limbs do not show the capacity for brachiation that is characteristic of all the later apes (Kelley 1992; Begun 2010). *Pierolapithecus*, however, had wrists and vertebrae that would have made it capable of brachiation, but it also had relatively short fingers like modern monkeys. *Pierolapithecus* probably spent most of its time in trees, walking along larger branches as monkeys do, and also brachiating among smaller branches, as apes do (Moyà-Solà et al. 2004; Begun and Ward 2005). Thus, *Pierolapithecus* is a good candidate for the ancestor of later forest-dwelling apes.

According to Sue Savage-Rumbaugh, knuckle walking may have evolved as a mode of terrestrial locomotion only in later apes. Because they are knuckle walkers, living apes cannot make a snapping motion with the hand (which is called "abducting the wrist"), as humans uniquely can (Savage-Rumbaugh 1994). This last ability, along with other things hands can do if they are not involved in locomotion, may have been crucial in making complete bipedalism adaptive in the earliest humans, as we will discuss in the next chapter.

Late Miocene Apes

From the end of the middle Miocene into the late Miocene, the apes diversified and moved into many areas. Fossils are abundant in Europe and

Pierolapithecus: a middle Miocene ape that had wrists and vertebrae that would have made it capable of brachiation, but also relatively short fingers like modern monkeys.

Kenyapithecus: an ape-like primate from the middle Miocene found in East Africa. It had very thickly enamelled teeth and robust jaws, suggesting a diet of hard, tough foods. Probably somewhat terrestrial.

Asia, less so in Africa. This does not mean that apes were more numerous than monkeys. In fact, the fossil record suggests that monkeys in the Old World became more and more numerous than apes toward the end of the Miocene, and this trend continues to the present day. There are many more monkey than ape species now. The climate throughout the Miocene was turning cooler and drier, which probably favoured more drought-resistant plants with thicker cell walls. Modern monkeys tend to be more adapted than apes for eating leaves, so monkeys may have had an advantage in the changing environment toward the end of the Miocene, and since (Conroy 1990).

One well-known late Miocene ape from Europe is *Oreopithecus*, which dates from about 8 million years ago. It is particularly interesting because, despite being well represented by fossils, including nearly complete ones preserved in beds of hard coal, its classification is enigmatic. *Oreopithecus* was clearly adapted to life in thickly forested marshlands. It had extremely long arms and hands and mobile joints, and was likely an agile brachiator. Its dentition suggests it had a diet that consisted mostly of leaves. However, the dentition and skull of *Oreopithecus* also had a number of unique features that suggest affinity to some Old World monkeys. In short, *Oreopithecus* had an ape-like body and a monkey-like head. Because of its suspensory locomotion and other ape-like features, most scholars today consider it an early, albeit specialized, ape (Fleagle 1999).

Most palaeoanthropologists divide the later Miocene apes into at least two main groups: *Sivapithecines*, found primarily in western and southern Asia, and *Dryopithecines*, found primarily in Europe (Fleagle 1999; Begun and Ward 2005).

Sivapithecus, known for its thickly enamelled teeth, was remarkably similar in facial features to the modern orangutan, and is now thought to be

The reconstructed skull of a *Dryopithecus* strongly resembles that of modern African apes.

its ancestor. Its teeth, like those of *Kenyapithecus*, suggest a diet of hard, tough, or gritty items. The closely related *Gigantopithecus* has similar dentition, but, as its name suggests, it was huge, perhaps over 3 metres if it stood erect (Begun 1998). Some palaeoanthropologists have suggested that *Gigantopithecus* weighed over 270 kilograms and became even larger over the nearly 10 million years of its existence, eventually weighing perhaps as much as 545 kilograms (Ciochon et al. 1990).

Dryopithecus had thin tooth enamel, lighter jaws, and pointed molar cusps. In the palate, jaw, and midface, *Dryopithecines* looked like the African apes. In contrast to later hominoids, however, *Dryopithecines* had a very short face and a relatively small brow ridge (Begun 1998).

The fingers and elbows of *Dryopithecines* and *Sivapithecines* suggest that they were quite a bit more capable of suspending themselves than were earlier hominoids, but they did not have as much of that capacity as modern hominoids. *Sivapithecines* may have moved about more on the ground than

---

Sivapithecus: a genus of ape from the later Miocene known for its thickly enamelled teeth, suggesting a diet of hard, tough, or gritty items. Found primarily in western and southern Asia and now thought to be ancestral to orangutans.

Dryopithecus: genus of ape from the later Miocene found primarily in Europe. It had thin tooth enamel and pointed molar cusps quite similar to those of the fruit-eating chimpanzees of today.

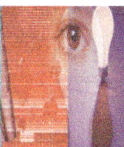

CURRENT RESEARCH AND ISSUES

A New Picture of *Dryopithecus* Emerging from Rudabánya Specimens

Evidence from newer and more complete specimens of *Dryopithecus* from Hungary are beginning to paint a better picture of the relation between these late Miocene apes and the evolution of hominoids. Dr. David Begun, a physical anthropologist at the University of Toronto, conducts palaeoanthropological research on Miocene primates in Europe. His research has focused on the excavation and analysis of fossil hominoids from Rudabánya, Hungary.

Rudabánya is a late Miocene hominoid site, dating to about 10 million years ago. All the hominoid specimens recovered from the site have been attributed to *Dryopithecus*. Living apes and humans share many skeletal features retained from a common hominoid ancestor. One key to unravelling the question of where *Dryopithecus* fits into later hominoid evolution is to compare morphological features of fossil remains with those of living hominoids. Begun's claim that *Dryopithecus* is more closely related to African apes and humans than it is to *Sivapithecus*

and orangutans has been further supported with the reanalysis of two preserved crania of *Dryopithecus*: RUD 77 and RUD 197-200, the latter being the most complete cranium of the taxon ever recorded. The fossil evidence has shed light on the question of the evolutionary relations among living hominoids, and supports the view that humans have an evolutionary relationship closest to chimpanzees, when compared with all the other apes.

The *Dryopithecus* specimens have offered not only insight into the connection between this fossil great ape and African apes and humans, but also indications that *Dryopithecus* had a great ape-sized brain relative to body size. This suggests that great ape brain size has remained about the same since the origin of hominids, with the sole exception of the human lineage.

If *Dryopithecus* did in fact establish the lineage of modern African great apes, this would indicate that the lineage first evolved in Europe. It would have been later in the Miocene, when climate change rendered Europe uninhabitable,

that they began their migration to Africa. In addition to his research in Hungary, Begun is involved in the survey, excavation, and analysis of Miocene hominoids from Turkey.

Sources: Begun DR, Kordos L. 1993. Revision of *Dryopithecus brancoi* Schlosser 1901 Based on the Fossil Hominoid Material from Rudabánya. Journal of Human Evolution. 25:271–286.

Begun DR. 1995. Late Miocene European Orangs, Gorillas, Humans or None of the Above? Journal of Human Evolution. 29:169–180.

Begun DR. 1995. Miocene Apes. In: Ember CR, Ember M, editors. Research Frontiers in Anthropology—Advances in Archaeology and Physical Anthropology. Englewood Cliffs, NJ: Prentice Hall.

Begun DR. 1996. Events in European Hominoid Evolution. Europa. 23:13–22.

Begun DR, Nargolwalla MC, Kordos L. 2012. European Miocene Hominids and the Origin of the African Ape and Human Clade. Evolutionary Anthropology: Issues, News, and Reviews. 21:10–23.

Kordos L, Begun DR. 1997. The Cranium of *Dryopithecus* from Rudabánya, Hungary: A New Reconstruction and Its Phylogenetic Implications. American Journal of Physical Anthropology. 103:277–294.

Kordos L, Begun DR. 2001. A New Cranium of *Dryopithecus* from Rudabánya, Hungary. Journal of Human Evolution. 41:689–700.

Dryopithecines, but both were probably mostly arboreal (Begun 1998).

As the climate became drier in the late Miocene, the majority of hominoid forms became extinct, leaving behind a few modern-day forms (*Pan*, *Gorilla*, and *Pongo*). It is still very difficult to identify the evolutionary lines leading from the Miocene apes to modern apes and humans (see Current Research and Issues, "A New Picture of *Dryopithecus* Emerging from Rudabánya Specimens"). Only the orangutans have been linked to a late Miocene ape genus, *Sivapithecus*, so presumably that lineage continued into modern times (Fleagle 1999). *Dryopithecines* disappear from the fossil record after about 10 million years ago,

A *Dryopithecus* cranium.

leaving no known descendants, perhaps because less rainfall and more seasonality reduced the forests where they lived (Bilsborough 1992).

The Divergence of Hominins from the Other Hominoids

The later Miocene apes are best known from fossils discovered in Europe and Asia. There has been an almost complete gap in the African fossil record between 13.5 million and 5 million years ago (Simons 1992); however, recently, two species, *Orrorin tugenensis*, from Kenya and dated to about 6 million years ago, and *Sahelanthropus tchadensis*, from Chad and dated to perhaps 7 million years ago, have provided a glimpse of hominoid evolution during this period. Still, this scarcity of fossils from this period is unfortunate for our understanding of human evolution because the earliest known bipedal primates (hominins) appear in Africa near the beginning of the Pliocene, after 5 million years ago. To understand the evolutionary links between the apes of the Miocene and the hominins of Africa, we need more fossil evidence from late Miocene times in both Europe and Africa (Begun 2010).

However, we do have some idea about the transition to hominins. The molecular biology of the various modern primates suggests when the most recent common ancestor of humans and our closest primate relatives, the chimpanzees, probably lived.

The Molecular Clock

In 1966, on the basis of biochemical comparisons of blood proteins in the different surviving primates, Vincent Sarich and Allan Wilson estimated that gibbons diverged from the other hominoids about 12 million years ago, orangutans 10 million years ago, and the other apes (gorillas and chimpanzees) from hominins only 4.5 million years ago. These estimates depended on the assumption that the more similar in chemistry the blood proteins of different primates are, the closer those primates are in evolutionary time. In other words, the more similar the blood proteins of related species, the more recently they diverged (Sarich and Wilson 1966; Sarich 1968; Lewin 1983).

This relationship between molecular closeness and evolutionary time is also based on another assumption: that molecular changes occur at a constant rate. After all, a reliable "molecular clock" should not slow down or speed up from one period of time to another. Because natural selection can speed up the rate of molecular change in the case of a characteristic that is very advantageous or very disadvantageous, researchers examine molecular characteristics that are probably neutral in terms of adaptation in order to calculate when related species might have diverged (see Current Research and Issues, "What Is Non-coding DNA?" for a discussion of research related to neutral and functional genome regions and the potential implications for the study of species divergence). The rate of change in a neutral characteristic is calculated from the time of some divergence that is absolutely dated. For example, if we know that two lineages split 20 million years ago, and we know the degree of molecular difference between a contemporary representative of each, we can estimate the rate of change that produced that degree of difference. Given such an estimated rate of change (in a particular characteristic), we can estimate the amount of time that has elapsed since other pairs of related species diverged from each other (Martin and Martin 1990; Jones et al. 1992). Today, it is possible to directly measure the mutation rate in modern humans, and it has been shown recently that the mutation rate is considerably less than that estimated from phylogenetic studies (Scally and Durbin 2012:751).

Subsequent comparative studies of the living primates have employed a variety of techniques, including comparisons of amino acid sequences and chromosomal structures, and the degree of matching of DNA strands from different species (Clark et al. 2003). These studies have confirmed the probable recent divergence of hominins from chimpanzees and gorillas. Although the different techniques yield slightly different estimates, the results are not that dissimilar. Most of the recent comparisons place the split somewhat earlier than the Sarich and Wilson estimates, but not by much. The common ancestor of chimpanzees and hominins is estimated to have lived 5 million to 6 million years ago, the common ancestor of gorillas and hominins a little farther back in time (Jones et al. 1992).

So what does the fossil evidence tell us about where and when hominins first emerged? Unfortunately, there is no answer to this question yet. We still do not have any definite hominin fossils in Africa from the end of the Miocene (8 million to 5 million years ago) and we have not found definite hominin fossils dating from the late Miocene anywhere else, nor do we know the place and time where and when hominins emerged. All we know for sure at present is that primates with indisputably hominin characteristics lived about 4 million years ago in East Africa. We turn to these hominins in the next chapter.

CURRENT RESEARCH AND ISSUES

What Is Non-coding DNA?

It was once believed that only a small fraction of the genome was made up of "functional" DNA. The remaining non-coding sequence, for which no known function could be resolved, came to be known as "junk DNA" back in the 1960s. In 1972, Tim Hunt, a British biochemist, used the term "junk DNA" to refer to "the large amount of nucleic acid that never finds its way out of the nucleus, which does not fit in with the old categories of genes and messages." Debate quickly ensued over how much of our DNA was truly non-functional. A mistake on the part of scientists was their failure to clearly define the term "functional." So how much of our DNA is really "junk"?

In 2012, the National Human Genome Research Institute published an extensive set of results of their unprecedented study of the genome. Among their findings was that, while only around 3 percent of the genome directly codes for proteins, an astonishing 80.4 percent of sequences serve some regularity function by controlling how protein-coding genes get turned on, turned off, expressed, and modified. Not only did this research show that a larger portion of the genome is functional than was previously believed, but it also highlighted the potential for future research to uncover additional functional regions.

Regardless of precisely how much of the genome is composed of coding and non-coding DNA, both of these types of sequences are imminently useful for researchers studying evolution at the genetic level. Mutation rates are known to vary among regions of the genome, even within a single species. Coding DNA sequences tend to be highly similar, or conserved, among organisms, reflecting key functions that are maintained through natural selection. By contrast, the portion of non-coding DNA that is presumably non-functional, or neutral, at the organism level is subject to higher rates of mutation. As a result, these non-coding stretches of DNA diverge more rapidly between species.

Although the rates of mutation differ between coding and non-coding DNA, these rates are often constant (clock-like), meaning that they can be used as "molecular clocks" to deduce how far back in the past two organisms shared a common ancestor. Specifically, coding genome regions, which mutate slowly, can provide estimates of changes that have accumulated between species over long time periods. By contrast, for species that are just recently diverged, non-coding DNA provides a better estimate of fine-scale changes that have occurred over a short time period.

If non-coding genome regions actually contain substantial amounts of functional sequence, presumably they will mutate more slowly than a true neutral clock. This can cause practical problems, such as overestimation of divergence times between species. Continued efforts to uncover hidden functions in non-coding DNA will therefore have implications for the study of species divergence using molecular clocks.

Sources: Ecker JR, Bickmore WA, Barroso I, Pritchard JK, Gilad Y, Segal E. 2012. Genomics: ENCODE Explained. Nature. 489(7414):52–55.

Gregory TR. 2005. The Evolution of the Genome. Amsterdam: Elsevier Academic Press.

Yi SV. 2007. Understanding Neutral Genomic Molecular Clocks. Evolutionary Biology. 34(3–4):144–151.

SUMMARY AND REVIEW

INTERPRETING THE FOSSIL RECORD

8.1 Describe the evidence that can be used to interpret the fossil record.

- Much of the evidence for primate evolution comes from the fossil remains of teeth and jaws.
- Dentition can provide clues about the size of the primate as well as its diet.
- Fragments of the skeleton can give palaeoanthropologists clues about locomotion.
- Evidence from the cranium can provide insight into vision, smell, and memory in early primates.

What types of fossil evidence can be used to differentiate among arboreal quadrupeds, terrestrial quadrupeds, vertical clingers and leapers, and brachiators?

THE EMERGENCE OF PRIMATES

8.2 Discuss the emergence of primates in relation to environment and adaptation.

- Plesiadapiforms are questionable primates that lack certain primate features; they have claws rather than nails but have specialized teeth.
- The visual predation hypothesis suggests primates originated as arboreal quadrupeds that preyed on insects in the smallest branches of trees. This niche would have selected for distinctive teeth, a reliance on vision over smell, binocular vision, and grasping hands and feet.
- The earliest definite primates (adapids and omomyids) date from the early Eocene, about 55 million years ago. Both possess more forward facing eyes, nails and not claws, and an opposable toe.
- Adapids (with lemur-like features) occur in the New and Old World but are more abundant in the Old World. They probably gave rise to strepsirhines (lemurs and lorises).
- Omomyids (with tarsier-like features) are also found throughout the world but are more common in the New World. They probably gave rise to haplorhines.

What are the major theories explaining primate origins?

THE EMERGENCE OF ANTHROPOIDS

8.3 Describe the emergence of anthropoids.

- The earliest undisputed anthropoids have been found in Egypt dating from the early Oligocene, about 34 million years ago.
- Early anthropoids include monkey-like parapithecids and the ape-like propliopithecids. Propliopithecids are the earliest definite anthropoid group and may be the ancestors of New World monkeys.
- The origins of anthropoids may be related to a tougher climate. Changing patterns of monkey and ape diversity in the Miocene reflect a drying climate and loss of forested areas.
- Platyrrhines appeared 25 to 30 million years ago when South America was an island. Their origin is uncertain: they may have originated from either African or Asian anthropoids, or from North American primates of the Eocene.
- *Aegyptopithecus* may be ancestral to all Old World monkeys and apes.
- There are few monkeys during the early Miocene, but they are abundant by the late Miocene.

How might anthropoidal primates have travelled from Africa to South America?

THE EMERGENCE OF HOMINOIDS

8.4 Differentiate between early anthropoids and hominoids.

- During the Miocene (24 million to 5.2 million years ago), monkeys and apes diverged in appearance and various kinds of apes appeared in Europe, Asia, and Africa.
- From the middle to the end of the Miocene, apes diversified and spread rapidly; they were bigger than earlier anthropoids and lacked a tail.
- Early apes, like *Proconsul*, had the Y-5 dental pattern of apes, but their postcranial skeleton was much like that of monkeys. True apes also have wide, not deep, chests and a shoulder reflecting a brachiating ancestor.
- The later Miocene apes are often divided into two groups: *Dryopithecines*, found primarily in Europe, and *Sivapithecines*, found mainly in western and southern Asia.
- Apes are abundant during the early Miocene, but there are very few by the late Miocene.

*In what ways did **Proconsul** differ from modern apes?*

THE DIVERGENCE OF HOMININS FROM THE OTHER HOMINOIDS

8.5 Discuss the challenges to identifying any clear emergence of hominins.

- Hominins probably diverged from the hominoids between 8 and 6 million years ago.
- The split is difficult to determine because there are few fossils dating to between 13.5 and 5 million years ago.

What is a molecular clock?

THINK ON IT

1. An animal's skeletal anatomy suggests what it eats and how it gets its food. Discuss possible examples in the evolution of the primates.
2. What environmental factors may have led to the emergence of primates?
3. We like to think of the human lineage as biologically unique, which of course it is (like all evolutionary lineages). But some palaeoanthropologists say that humans, chimpanzees, and gorillas are so similar that all three should be grouped as hominins. Think of arguments for and against this grouping.
4. What regions would likely be the best sources of evidence of hominin emergence, and why?

9 Early Hominins

LEARNING OBJECTIVES

9.1 Identify the main trends in hominin evolution.

9.2 Describe the fossils that chronicle the transition from hominoids to hominins.

9.3 Explain one model of the evolutionary relationships among hominins.

9.4 Describe the evidence for the early species of the genus *Homo*.

9.5 Describe the tools, lifestyle, and language abilities of early hominins.

Undisputed bipedal hominins lived in East Africa about 4 million years ago (see Figure 9–1). These hominins—meaning the bipedal ancestors of the human species—and some others who lived later in East and South Africa are generally classified in the genus *Australopithecus*. Some East African hominins who lived nearly 2.5 million years ago are classified in our own genus, *Homo*. In this chapter we discuss what we know or suspect about the emergence and relationship of the australopithecines and early *Homo*.

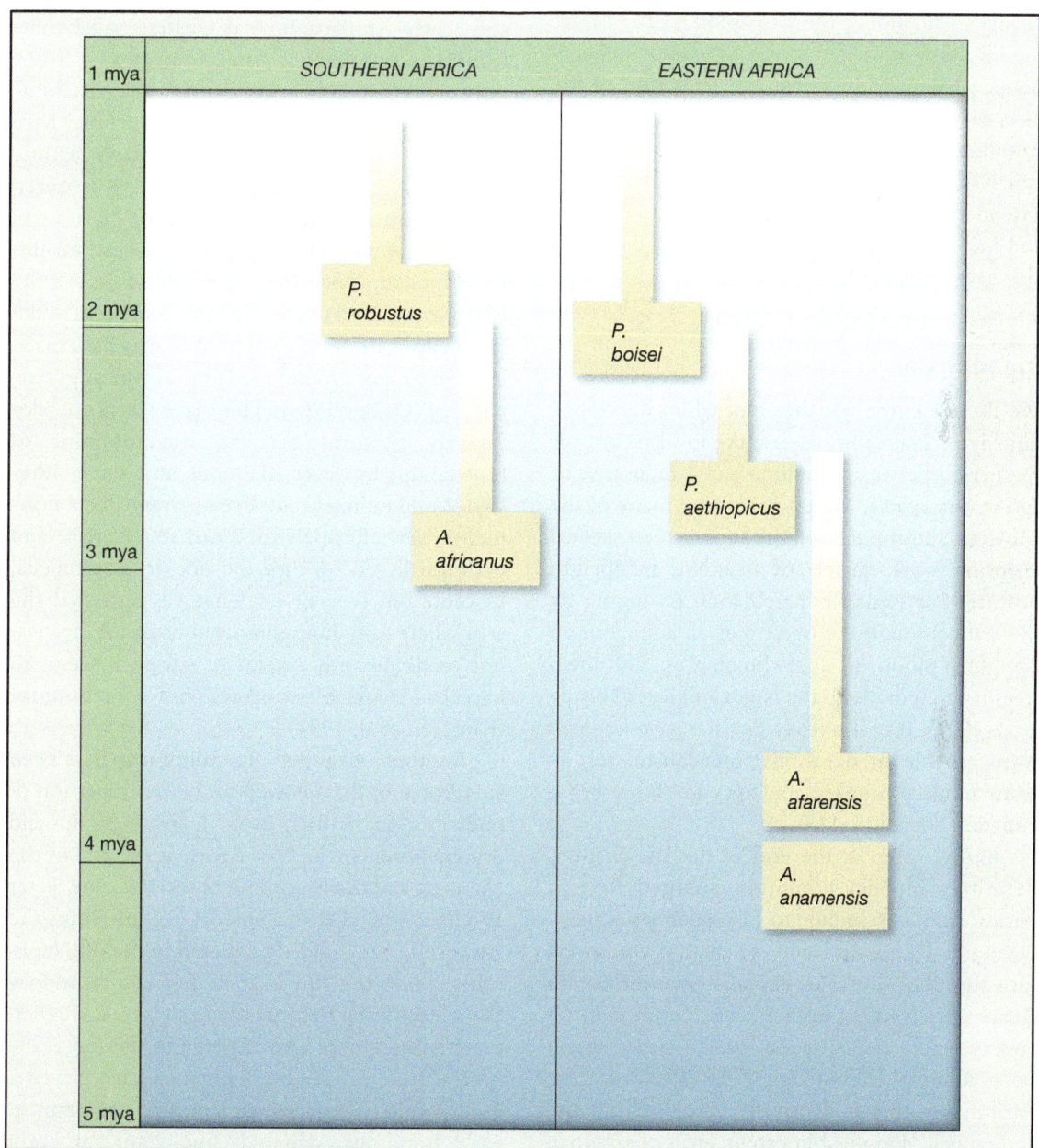

Figure 9–1 The Evolution of Australopithecines and Paranthropoids

Australopithecus: genus of Pliocene and Pleistocene hominins.

Homo: genus to which modern humans and their ancestors belong.

Trends in Hominin Evolution

Perhaps the most crucial change—and the defining characteristic of hominin evolution—was the development of bipedal locomotion, or walking on two legs (see Figure 9–2). We know from the fossil record that other important physical changes—including the expansion of the brain, modification of the female pelvis to allow bigger-brained babies to be born, and reduction of the face, teeth, and jaws—did not occur until about 2 million years after the emergence of bipedalism. Other human characteristics, including an extended period of infant and child dependency and increased reliance on meat in their diet, may also have developed after that time.

Bipedalism

We do not know whether bipedalism developed quickly or gradually, because the fossil record for the period between 8 million and 4 million years ago is very sparse. We do know that many of the Miocene anthropoids, on the basis of their skeletal anatomy, were capable of assuming an upright posture. For example, brachiation (swinging by the arms through the trees) puts an animal in an upright position; so does climbing up and down trees by grasping with the hands and feet (Thorpe et al. 2007). It is also likely that the *proto-hominins* were capable of occasional bipedalism, just as many modern monkeys and apes are (Rose 1984; Langdon 2005:116–117).

As we noted at the end of the last chapter, definitely bipedal hominins emerged first in Africa. About 16 million to 11 million years ago, a drying and cooling trend set in that continued into the Pliocene. The physical environment in Africa was changing from extensive tropical forest cover to more discontinuous patches of forest and open country (Bilsborough 1992). Gradually, the African rain forests, deprived of intense humidity and rainfall, dwindled in extent; areas of savannah and scattered deciduous woodlands became more common. The tree-dwelling primates did not completely lose their customary habitats because some tropical forests remained in wetter regions, and natural selection continued to favour the better-adapted tree dwellers in those forested areas. However, the more open country probably favoured characteristics adapted to ground living in some primates as well as other animals. In the evolutionary line leading to humans, these adaptations included bipedalism (see Current Research and Issues, "Environmental Change and Evolutionary Consequences in Hominins"). Since humans are the only living primate that is habitually bipedal, the question of what factors may have led to this adaptation is of evolutionary significance. So what in particular may have favoured the emergence of bipedal hominins?

There are several possible explanations for this development. One idea is that bipedalism was the adaptive response to life amid the tall grasses of the savannahs because an erect posture may have made it easier to spot ground predators as well as potential prey (Oakley 1964). This theory does not adequately account for the development of bipedalism, however. Baboons and some other Old World monkeys also live in savannah environments, yet, although they can stand erect, and occasionally do so, they did not develop bipedal locomotion. Recent evidence suggests that the area where early hominins lived in East Africa was not predominantly savannah; rather, it seems to have had a mix of woodland and open country (Kingston et al. 1994).

Another idea is that bipedalism may have been an adaptation that allowed for better dispersion of body heat, particularly in the increasingly hot and dry environments of East Africa at the end of the Miocene and the beginning of the Pliocene. Peter Wheeler argued that a bipedal posture limits the area of the body directly exposed to the sun, especially when the sun is at its hottest, at midday (Wheeler 1991). Because the head is raised higher, there is less surface area exposed to the sun at the hottest time of the day. This may have played a crucial role in thermoregulation of the brain in early hominins, which is important for brain development (Wheeler 1991; Chaplin et al. 1994). Bipedal posture would also facilitate convective heat loss by allowing heat to rise up and away from the body rather than being trapped underneath it.

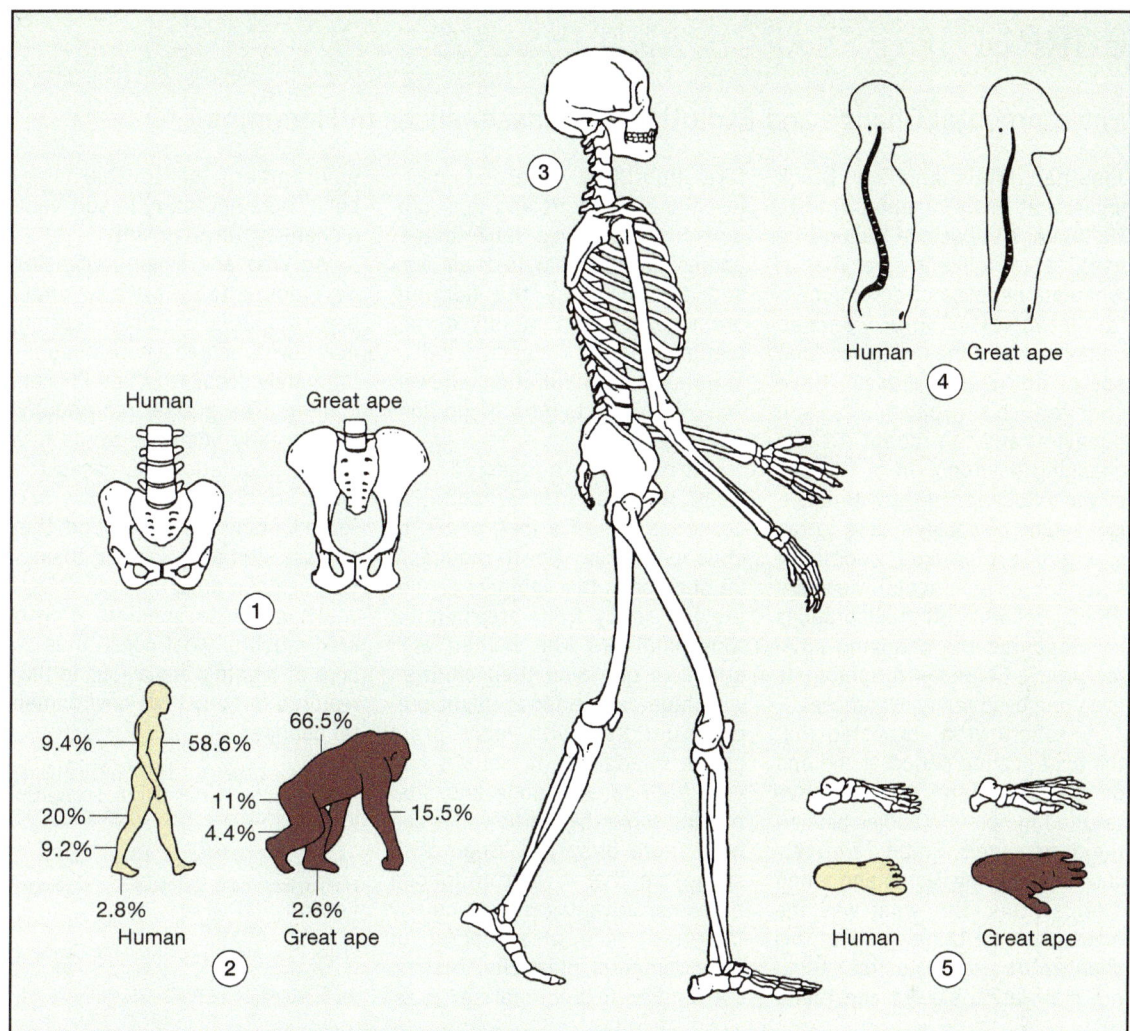

Figure 9–2 Skeletal Evidence of Bipedalism

The human skeleton differs from the skeleton of the great ape because humans move about on their legs only. The human head is more or less balanced on the backbone (see the feature marked 3 in the figure), so there is no need for powerful muscles at the back of the neck, as in the great ape. The human vertebral column (see 4 in the figure) has a forward curvature in the neck and lower back regions. These two extra curves, along with the curvature in the middle back region, allow the backbone to act more like a spring, which is advantageous given that the legs have to bear all the weight and given the need to balance on one leg with each stride. Bipedal locomotion has favoured a human pelvis (see 1 in the figure) that is lower and broader than the ape pelvis. In contrast to the apes, human legs are longer than human arms and represent a larger proportion of the body weight (see 2 in the figure); this lowers the body's centre of gravity and is advantageous for bipedalism. The most obvious adaptation to bipedalism is the human foot (see 5 in the figure). The big toe is not opposed to the other toes, as in the other primates, and the foot can no longer grasp. When we walk, the big toe is the last point of contact with the ground before the leg swings forward, which explains why the big toe has become aligned with the other toes.

Source: Jones S, Martin R, Pilbeam D, editors. 1992. The Cambridge encyclopedia of human evolution. New York: Cambridge University Press. p. 78.

CURRENT RESEARCH AND ISSUES

Environmental Change and Evolutionary Consequences in Hominins

Jonathan Wells and Jay Stock argue that environmental change led humans to become "colonizing apes," able to live in diverse environments because of developmental plasticity and learned behaviours. It makes sense that early hominins would have changed, both physically and behaviourally, to adapt to the changing environment at the end of the Pliocene. Indeed, bipedalism seems obviously linked to the emergence of mixed woodland-savannah environments in eastern Africa. But what other adaptations accompanied the changing environment? Palaeoanthropologists have proposed many hypotheses.

Elisabeth Vrba suggested that the long cooling period at the end of the Pliocene would have resulted in hominin bodies becoming larger and limbs relatively shorter following Bergmann's and Allen's rules. But what was the mechanism for bringing about this change? Vrba suggested that hominin maturation slowed and therefore hominins retained more juvenile body forms and limb proportions (juveniles have bigger bodies proportional to their legs and arms). Since the hominin brain grows most rapidly during maturation, the longer period of childhood or maturation allowed hominin brains to grow proportionally larger.

Barry Bogin suggested that there were additional adaptive consequences of a long period of childhood. Brain growth requires a lot of calories that mothers cannot provide solely from breast milk; those mothers who worked with others to provision their children with high-calorie foods might produce children with more brain power. In addition, if mothers provide high-calorie foods and stop nursing somewhat earlier, they can have more offspring. Bogin also suggested that a long childhood has other advantages. Particularly important is a great degree of developmental plasticity, that is, the ability to acclimatize to an environment or to learn new behaviours necessary to survival in a changing environment.

As Vrba and Bogin suggested, developmental plasticity and a brain capable of social learning may have emerged among hominins ultimately because of late Pliocene cooling. The greater reproductive rate in early hominins would have led to population increases that Wells and Stock argued may have forced hominins to expand their ranges, ultimately leading them to colonize new areas.

Thus, these scholars considered much of what constitutes the core of hominin behaviour to have resulted directly from environmental change.

Sources: Bogin B. 1997. Evolutionary Hypotheses for Human Childhood. Yearbook of Physical Anthropology. 40:63–89.

Vrba ES. 1996. Climate, Heterochrony, and Human Evolution. Journal of Anthropological Research. 52(1):1–28.

Wells JCK, Stock JT. 2007. The Biology of the Colonizing Ape. Yearbook of Physical Anthropology. 50:191–222.

(We radiate a lot of body heat through the head.) Cooling through the evaporation of sweat would also be facilitated by a bipedal posture, as more skin area would be exposed to cooling winds. Thus, natural selection may have favoured bipedalism because it reduced heat stress in the warming environments of East Africa.

Other theories stress the importance of allowing the hands to be free while the legs are moving. If some hand activity is critical while an animal is moving, selection may favour bipedalism because it frees the hands to perform other activities at the same time as the animal is moving. What hand activities might have been so critical? Gordon Hewes suggested that carrying food in the hands was the critical activity. If it were necessary to carry food from one locale to another, bipedal locomotion would have provided an adaptive advantage (Hewes 1961). Hewes emphasized the importance of being able to carry hunted or scavenged meat, but many palaeoanthropologists still question whether early hominins hunted or even scavenged (Shipman 1986; Trinkaus 1987). Regardless, the ability to carry any food to a place safe from predators may have been one of the more important advantages of bipedalism. C. Owen Lovejoy suggested that food-carrying might have been important for another reason. If males provided for females and their babies by carrying food back to a home base, the females would have been able to conserve energy by not travelling and therefore might have been able to produce and care for more babies (Lovejoy 1981). Thus, whatever the advantages of carrying food, the more bipedal a proto-hominin was, the more it might reproduce.

But carrying food or provisioning families might not have been the only benefit of freeing the hands; feeding itself may have been more efficient. Clifford Jolly argued that bipedalism would have allowed early hominins to efficiently harvest small seeds and nuts because both hands could be used to pick up food and move it directly to the mouth (Jolly 1970). Natural selection would have favoured bipedalism not just for locomotion, but also for more efficient foraging. In the changing environments of East Africa, where forests were giving way to more open woodlands and savannahs, an advantage in foraging for small seeds and nuts might well have proven important for survival, and thus have been favoured by natural selection. For example, Videan and McGrew (2002) also observed that food piles or raised foraging platforms introduced to wild chimpanzees increased the frequency of bipedal locomotion in the group. Similarly, Stanford's (2006) observation of bipedal activity in wild chimpanzees suggested that bipedal posture in hominins may have emerged in relation to foraging in fruit trees.

Bipedalism might also have been favoured by natural selection because the freeing of the hands would allow proto-hominins to use, and perhaps even make, tools that they could carry with them as they moved about. Consider how advantageous such tool use might have been. Sherwood Washburn noted that some contemporary ground-living primates dig for roots to eat, "and if they could use a stone or a stick they might easily double their food supply" (Washburn 1960:163). David Pilbeam also suggested why the use of tools by the more open-country primates may have appreciably increased the number and amount of plant foods they could eat: in order to be eaten, many of the plant foods in the grassy areas probably had to be chopped, crushed, or otherwise prepared with the aid of tools (Pilbeam 1972). Tools may also have been used to kill and butcher animals for food.

Many non-human primates walk upright occasionally, but the only primates that habitually walked or walk upright were our hominin ancestors and modern humans.

Without tools, primates in general are not well equipped physically for regular hunting. Their teeth and jaws are not sharp and strong enough, and their speed afoot is not fast enough. So the use of tools to kill and butcher game might have increased even further their ability to exploit the available food supply.

Finally, tools may have been used as weapons against predators, which would have been a great threat to the relatively defenceless ground-dwelling proto-hominins. In Milford Wolpoff's opinion, it was the advantage of carrying weapons *continuously* that was responsible for transforming occasional bipedalism to a completely bipedal locomotion (Wolpoff 1971). Sue Savage-Rumbaugh suggested that the ability to abduct the wrist in particular would have permitted early humans "to perfect both throwing and rock-striking skills [for toolmaking] and consequently to develop throwing as a much more effective predator defence system than apes could ever manage" (Savage-Rumbaugh 1994).

But some anthropologists question the idea that tool use and toolmaking favoured bipedalism. They point out that our first evidence of stone tools appears perhaps a million years *after* the emergence of bipedalism. So how could toolmaking be responsible for bipedalism? Wolpoff suggested an answer. Even though bipedalism appears to be at least a million years older than stone tools, it is not unlikely that proto-hominins used tools made of wood and bone, neither of which would be as likely as stone to survive in the archaeological record. Moreover, unmodified stone tools discovered in the archaeological record might not be recognizable as tools (Wolpoff 1983). This is still not a compelling argument, however. Chimpanzees use unmodified wood and stones for certain tasks, and yet they did not become bipedal. The key issue for humans and their ancestors is the use of tools to modify other tools, and the earliest evidence of modified tools in the hominin record is unequivocally associated with fully bipedal hominins.

Sylvester (2006) suggested that bipedalism emerged as an adaptation that maintains a highly mobile shoulder joint (important for continued arboreal activity) while retaining a high degree of locomotor stability. Some researchers have taken a closer look at the mechanics of bipedal locomotion to see if it might be a more efficient form of locomotion in the savannah-woodland environment, where resources are likely to be scattered. Compared with the quadrupedal locomotion of primates such as chimpanzees, bipedalism appears to be more efficient for long-distance travel (Zimmer 2004) (see Figure 9–2, page 201). But why travel long distances? Pat Shipman suggested that bipedalism was an appropriate adaptation for hominins to scavenge food (Shipman 1984, 1986). While bipeds are slower and less efficient than quadrupeds when running, they are much more efficient when walking. Thus, a biped could cover large areas, although very slowly. In addition, having the head elevated would allow one to see farther distances. Sinclair added to the scavenging hypothesis by suggesting that long-distance migration may have also been important—those who were able to walk long distances, for example, to follow migrating herds, would be able to rapidly increase their numbers (Sinclair et al. 1986). Sinclair argued that tool use developed in hominins as a response to the need to quickly butcher scavenged remains. However, Preuschoft (2004) suggested that load carrying was the critical adaptive advantage of bipedalism, after which other typical human morphology can be explained as reflective of energy savings over long distances.

It is of course not clear which theories regarding the origins of bipedalism are correct. It is difficult to collect direct evidence of the factors that may have led to bipedalism. Any or all of these factors—the abilities to see farther, to carry food back to a home base, to carry tools that included weapons, or to travel long distances more efficiently—may explain the transformation of an occasionally bipedal proto-hominin to a completely bipedal hominin.

The "Costs" of Bipedalism. We must remember that there are also "costs" to bipedal walking. Bipedalism makes it harder to overcome gravity to supply the brain with sufficient blood (Falk 1988), and the weight of the body above the pelvis and lower limbs puts greater stress on the hips, lower back, knees, and feet. As Adrienne Zihlman pointed out, the stresses on the lower body are even greater for females. Females have to support extra weight during pregnancy, and as mothers they usually are responsible for carrying nursing infants. Thus, human bipedalism is an evolutionary compromise—a biological trade-off that was maintained through natural selection. So whatever the advantages of bipedalism, they must be greater than the disadvantages or our ancestors never would have become bipedal (Zihlman 1992).

We must also remember that the evolution of bipedalism required some dramatic changes in the ancestral ape skeleton. While apes today can and do walk bipedally, they cannot do so efficiently or for long periods of time. To be habitually bipedal, the ancestral ape skeleton had to be modified, and the major changes that allowed the early hominins to become fully bipedal occurred primarily in the skull, pelvis, knees, and feet (Lovejoy 1988; Langdon 2005:116–121). Let's take a look at each of these changes.

In both ancient and modern apes, the spinal column enters the skull toward the back, which makes sense because apes generally walk on all fours, with the spine roughly parallel to the ground. In bipedal hominins, the spinal column enters the skull at the bottom, through a hole called the **foramen magnum**. Thus, when hominins became bipedal, the skull ended up on top of the spinal column.

Ancient and modern ape pelvises are considerably different in shape from that of a bipedal hominin. The ape pelvis is long and flat, forming a bony plate in the lower back to which the leg muscles attach. In bipedal hominins the pelvis is bowl-shaped, which supports the internal organs and also lowers the body's centre of gravity, allowing better balance on the legs. The hominin pelvis also provides a different set of muscle attachments and shifts the orientation of the femurs (the upper leg bones) from the side of the pelvis to the front. These changes allow hominins to move their legs forward in a bipedal stride (and do things like kick a soccer ball). Apes, in comparison, move their legs forward (when they walk bipedally) by shifting their pelvis from side to side, not by kicking each leg forward alternately as we do (Aiello and Dean 1990).

Another change associated with the hominin ability to kick the leg forward is our "knock-kneed" posture. Ape legs hang straight down from the pelvis. Bipedal hominin legs, on the other hand, angle inward toward one another. This configuration not only helps us move our legs forward but also helps us maintain a centre of gravity in the midline of our bodies, so that our centre of gravity does not shift from side to side when we walk or run; the lateral gluteus medius muscles are also crucial for this motion—for example, the right gluteus medius contracts when the right leg swings forward, thus preventing the upper body from pitching to the right side.

Finally, the feet of bipedal hominins and apes are different in two major ways. First, hominin feet have an enlarged group of ankle bones forming a robust heel that can withstand the substantial forces placed on them as a result of habitual bipedalism. Second, hominin feet have an arch, which also aids in absorbing the forces endured by the feet during bipedal locomotion. We know this arch is vital to our ability to be habitually bipedal because "flat-footed" people who lack it have chronic problems in their feet, ankles, knees, and back (Aiello and Dean 1990).

When did these changes take place? We don't know for sure, but fossils from East Africa—Ethiopia, Tanzania, and Kenya—clearly show that bipedal hominins lived there between 4 million and 5 million years ago, perhaps even earlier.

Expansion of the Brain

In the early 20th century, the question of brain size and bipedalism in human evolution was a bit like the chicken-and-egg question—it was unclear which came first. Early palaeoanthropologists assumed that the key to human evolution was a big brain, and therefore expected that the first hominins would be large-brained apes. The evolution of upright walking followed. However, as discussed below, the discovery of the Taung fossil fuelled that debate, since it provided the evidence for the implication that early hominins were in fact bipedal "apes," with increased brain development following later in evolution. Today, it is clear that bipedalism evolved first and that increased brain development followed later.

The australopithecines had relatively small cranial capacities, ranging from about 380 cc to 530 cc—not much larger than that of chimpanzees. Around 2 million years ago, almost half a million years after stone tools appeared, some hominins showed evidence of enlarged cranial capacity. These hominins, classified as early members of our genus, *Homo* (*Homo habilis*), had

---

Foramen Magnum: the hole in the base of the skull through which the spinal cord passes en route to the brain.

Homo habilis: early species belonging to our genus, *Homo*, with cranial capacities averaging about 630–640 cc, about 50 percent of the brain capacity of modern humans. Dating from about 2 million years ago.

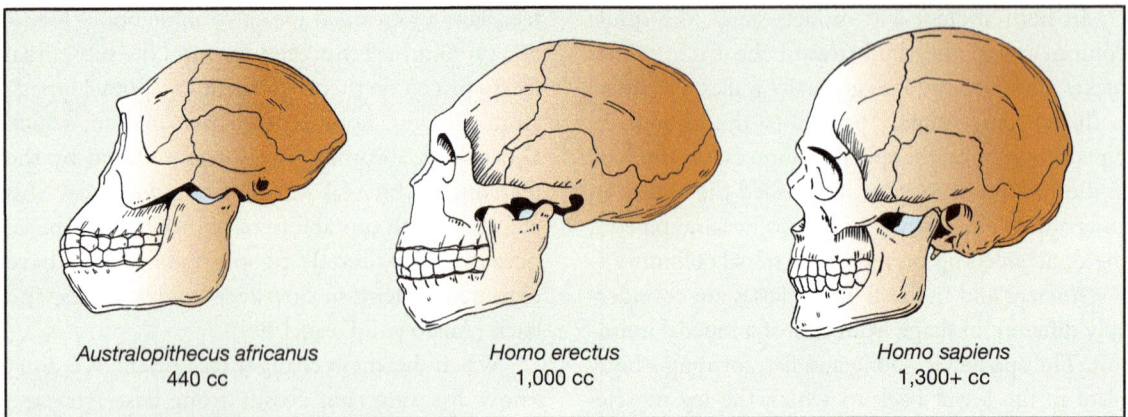

Figure 9–3 Estimated Cranial Capacities

Comparison of the estimated cranial capacities of *Australopithecus africanus*, *Homo erectus*, and *Homo sapiens*, demonstrating the expansion of the brain in hominin evolution.

Source: Tattersall I, Delson E, Van Couvering J, editors. 1998. Estimated cranial capacities. In: Encyclopedia of human evolution and prehistory. New York: Garland. pp. 80, 263, 268.

cranial capacities averaging about 630 cc to 640 cc, which is about 50 percent of the brain capacity of modern humans (the average is slightly more than 1300 cc—see Figure 9–3). A later member of our genus, **Homo erectus**, which may have first appeared about 1.8 million years ago, had a cranial capacity ranging from about 895 cc to 1040 cc, or about 70 percent of the brain capacity of modern humans (Tobias 1994; McHenry 1998b). *Homo erectus* is discussed in the next chapter.

The australopithecines were small, and the earliest *Homo* remains indicate that they were not much bigger, suggesting that much of the increase in brain size over time might have been a result of increasing body size in *H. erectus* and *H. sapiens*. When we correct for body size, however, it turns out that brain size increased not only absolutely but also relatively after 2 million years ago. Between about 4 million and 2 million years ago, relative brain size remained just about the same. Only in the last 2 million years has the hominin brain doubled in relative size, and tripled in absolute size (McHenry 1982; Langdon 2005).

What may have favoured the increase in brain size? Many anthropologists think that the increase is linked to the emergence of stone toolmaking about 2.5 million years ago. The reasoning is that stone toolmaking was important for the survival of our ancestors, and therefore natural selection would have favoured bigger-brained individuals because they had motor and conceptual skills that enabled them to be better toolmakers. According to this view, the expansion of the brain and more sophisticated toolmaking would have developed together. Other anthropologists think that the expansion of the brain may have been favoured by other factors, such as hunting, increased lifespan, and language (McHenry 1982; Langdon 2005). One intriguing theory is that life in complex social groups requires increased intelligence and memory, and that the creation of home bases and family groups may have fostered the expansion of the hominin brain (Dunbar and Schultz 2007; Herrmann et al. 2007; Silk 2007; Fuentes et al. 2010). Whatever the factors favouring bigger brains, they also provided hominins with an increased capacity for culture. Thus, along with bipedalism, the expansion of the brain marks a watershed in human evolution.

> ***Homo erectus***: the first hominin species to be widely distributed in the Old World. The earliest finds are possibly 1.8 million years old. The brain (averaging 895–1040 cc) was larger than that found in any of the australopithecines or *H. habilis* but smaller than the average brain of a modern human.

As the hominin brain expanded, natural selection also favoured an increased breadth of the female pelvis to allow larger-brained babies to be born (Simpson et al. 2008). But there was probably a limit to how large the pelvic outlet could be and still be adapted to bipedalism. Something had to give, and that something was the degree of physical development of the human infant at birth—for instance, the human infant is born with cranial bones so plastic that they can overlap. Because birth takes place before the cranial bones have hardened, the human infant with its relatively large brain can pass through the opening in the mother's pelvis.

Reduction of the Face, Teeth, and Jaws

As in the case of the brain, substantial changes in the face, teeth, and jaws do not appear in hominin evolution until after about 2 million years ago. We know that the australopithecines all had cheek teeth that were very large relative to their estimated body weight. The diet of the australopithecines may have been especially high in plant foods (Pilbeam and Gould 1974; Klein 2009), including small, tough objects such as seeds, roots, and tubers. We also know that the australopithecines had thick jawbones, probably also related to their chewing needs. The australopithecines have relatively large faces that project forward below the eyes. But when we get to the *Homo* forms, we see reduction in the size of the face, cheek teeth, and jaws (see Figure 9–4). It would seem that natural selection in favour of a bigger and stronger chewing apparatus was relaxed. One reason might be that members of the *Homo* genus started to eat foods that were easier to chew. Such foods might have included roots, fruits, and meat. As we discuss later, it may have been the development of habitual tool use and the control of fire that allowed members of the *Homo* genus to change their diet to include easier-to-chew foods, including meat. If food was cooked and easy to chew, individual humans with smaller jaws and teeth would not be disadvantaged, and therefore the face, cheek teeth, and jaw would get smaller on average over time (Leonard 2002; Wrangham 2009).

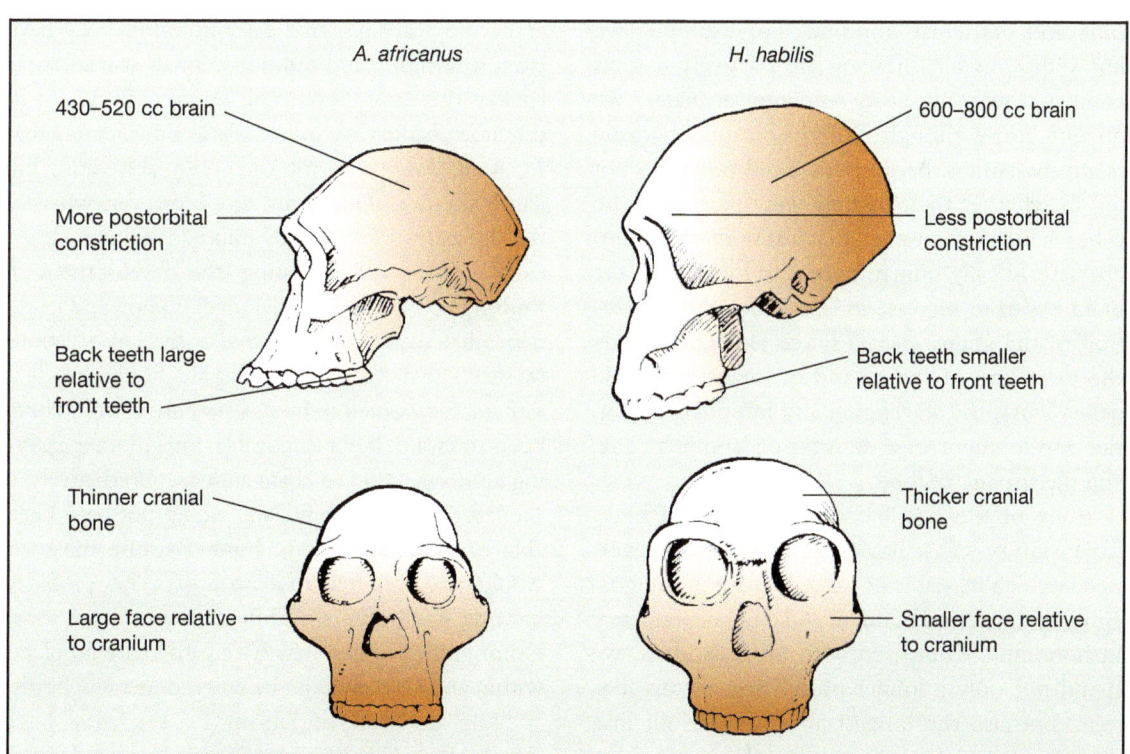

Figure 9–4 Comparison of *A. africanus* and *H. habilis*

The expansion of the brain and reduction of the face occurred at about the same time and were probably related. A recent discovery in human genetics appears to provide direct evidence of a connection. Researchers studying muscle diseases in modern humans discovered that humans have a unique form of a myosin gene called MYH16 (myosin is a protein in muscle tissue) that is present only in jaw muscles. Comparing MYH16 to related genes in primates, the researchers determined that the mutant form of MYH16 evolved about 2.4 million years ago—around the time the brain began to enlarge and the face and jaw began to shrink. So, the expansion of the brain may have been aided by a mutation in myosin that caused jaw muscles to shrink (Stedman et al. 2004).

Other Evolved Traits

The fossil evidence, which we will discuss shortly, suggests when, and in which hominins, changes occurred in brain size and in the face, teeth, and jaws. Other changes in the evolution of hominins cannot yet be confidently dated with regard to time and particular hominin. For example, we know that modern humans are relatively hairless compared with the other surviving primates. We do not know, though, when hominins became relatively hairless, because fossilized bones do not tell us whether their owners were hairy. On the other hand, we suspect that most of the other characteristically human traits developed after the brain began to increase in size, during the evolution of the genus *Homo*. These changes include the extension of the period of infant and child dependency, the scavenging and hunting of meat, the development of a division of labour by sex, and the sharing of food.

One of the possible consequences of brain expansion was that babies were born less developed, which may at least partly explain the lengthening of the period of infant and child dependency in hominins. Compared with other animals, we spend not only a longer proportion of our lifespan, but also the longest absolute period, in a dependent state. Prolonged infant dependency has probably been of great significance in human cultural evolution. According to Theodosius Dobzhansky,

> it is this helplessness and prolonged dependence on the ministrations of the parents and other persons that favours . . . the socialization and learning process on which the transmission of culture wholly depends. This may have been an overwhelming advantage of the human growth pattern in the process of evolution. (Dobzhansky 1962:196)

It used to be thought that the australopithecines had a long period of infant dependency, just as modern humans do, but the way their teeth apparently developed suggests that the early australopithecines followed an ape-like pattern of development. Thus, prolonged maturation may be relatively recent, but just how recent is not yet known (Bromage and Dean 1985; Smith 1986).

Although some use of tools for digging, defence, scavenging, or hunting may have influenced the development of bipedalism, full bipedalism may have made possible more efficient toolmaking and consequently more efficient scavenging and hunting. As we shall see, there are archaeological signs that early hominins may have been scavenging and hunting animals at least as far back as the early Pleistocene. As we will discuss in the next chapter, we have fairly good evidence that *H. erectus* was butchering and presumably eating big game after a million years ago. However, whether the big game were actually hunted is not yet clear.

Regardless of its timing, the development of hunting, combined with longer infant and child dependency, may have fostered a division of labour by sex. The demands of nursing might have made it difficult for women to hunt. Certainly, it would have been awkward, if not impossible, for a mother carrying a nursing child to chase animals. Alternatively, if she left the child behind, she would not have been able to travel very far to hunt. Because the men would have been freer to roam farther, they probably became the hunters. While the men were away hunting, the women may have gathered wild plants within an area that could be covered in a few hours.

The division of labour by sex may have increased the likelihood of food-sharing. If men primarily hunted and women primarily gathered plant foods, the only way each sex could obtain a complete diet would have been to share the results of their respective labours.

What is the evidence that the physical and cultural changes we have been discussing occurred during the evolution of the hominins? We shall now trace the sequence of known hominin fossils and how they are associated with the development of bipedalism, brain expansion, and reduction of the face, jaws, and teeth. We shall also trace the sequence of cultural changes in toolmaking, scavenging, and hunting, and other aspects of cultural development.

The Transition to Hominins

The windswept deserts of western Chad don't seem a likely place to find fossil apes or hominins, but palaeoanthropologist Michel Brunet thought it might be (Gibbons 2002). Western Chad was once covered by an ancient lake, and for several million years forest-dwelling mammals, including primates, congregated there. Around 7 million years ago a primate called *Sahelanthropus tchadensis* lived on the shores of the lake, where its bones were fossilized and recovered by Brunet and his colleagues in 2001. *Sahelanthropus*, represented by an almost complete skull, has a unique mix of hominin and hominoid traits. While the skull itself is hominoid, with a small brain, large brow ridges, and wide face, the teeth seem more hominin-like, especially the canines, which do not project below the tooth row (Brunet et al. 2002; Wong 2003). Unfortunately, it is unclear whether *Sahelanthropus* was bipedal. It has been tentatively suggested that the foramen magnum of *Sahelanthropus* is located relatively forward on the cranial base, suggestive of a more bipedal locomotion (Brunet et al. 2002).

There is, however, tantalizing evidence that another possible early hominin, *Orrorin tugenensis*, was bipedal. Discovered in western Kenya by Brigitte Senut and colleagues in 1998, *O. tugenensis* consists of 19 specimens of jaw, teeth, finger, arm, and leg bones, including the top of a femur (Aiello and Collard 2001; Pickford et al. 2002; Wong 2003). The femur in *Orrorin*, according to Senut (2006), shows adaptations to bipedalism, including a long, angled "head" with the presence of an obturator externus groove on the femoral neck, providing increased stability during upright locomotion (Galik et al. 2004). *Orrorin* dates to between 5.8 and 6 million years ago, and researchers now agree that it is one of the earliest bipedal hominids (Richmond and Jungers 2008; Almécija et al. 2013).

Recently, Ethiopia has yielded a fossil find dated 4.4 million years ago that has palaeoanthropologists intrigued (Fischman 1994). Is it a link between a Miocene ape and the australopithecines that lived about 4 million years ago? This specimen was initially classified as an early australopithecine, but has since been renamed *Ardipithecus ramidus* (White et al. 1994, 1995). Leakey and co-workers (Leakey et al. 1995, 1998) suggest that *A. ramidus* is a sister species to *Australopithecus anamensis* and all later hominins (see the following section). What makes *A. ramidus* unique is the combination of ape-like dentition with possible evidence of bipedal locomotion and an overall hominin-like skeleton. However, it is difficult to tell from the few available bones whether *A. ramidus* was mostly or only intermittently bipedal. Like apes, *Ardipithecus* has relatively small cheek teeth with thin enamel and relatively large canines. However, its arm bones seem hominin-like, and because of the position of the foramen magnum, this species appears to have been bipedal. The central location of the foramen magnum indicates that the head was carried directly over the spine. The feet of *Ardipithecus* also seem to be adapted to bipedalism (Haile-Selassie 2001; White et al. 2009). However, contrary to expectation for the ancestral hominin, *A. ramidus* appears to have lived in the forest, not in the savannah,

---

Sahelanthropus tchadensis: a hominoid found in Chad dating to about 7 million years ago.

Orrorin tugenensis: an apparently bipedal primate dating to between 5.8 million and 6 million years ago, making it possibly the earliest known hominin.

Ardipithecus ramidus: an intermittently bipedal species dated to 4 million years ago. It is a possible candidate for the hominin common ancestor.

as popular theories for the emergence of bipedalism would anticipate. However, the remains of this specimen continue to be analyzed, so we will have to wait to see how old bipedalism really is.

The First Definite Hominins

Fossil finds from East Africa—Ethiopia, Tanzania, and Kenya—clearly show that bipedal hominins lived there between 4 million and 3 million years ago, perhaps even earlier. Since the 1960s, important discoveries have come mostly from the Great Rift Valley of East Africa, an area where the underlying plates of the earth are pulling away from each other. In many places the Rift Valley drops precipitously from the rim, exposing layers and layers of older rock. Although some doubt remains about the status of *Ardipithecus* as a hominin genus, there is no doubt that the australopithecines (members of the genus *Australopithecus*) and paranthropoids (members of the genus *Paranthropus*) were hominins (Figure 9–5 shows some sites where australopithecines and

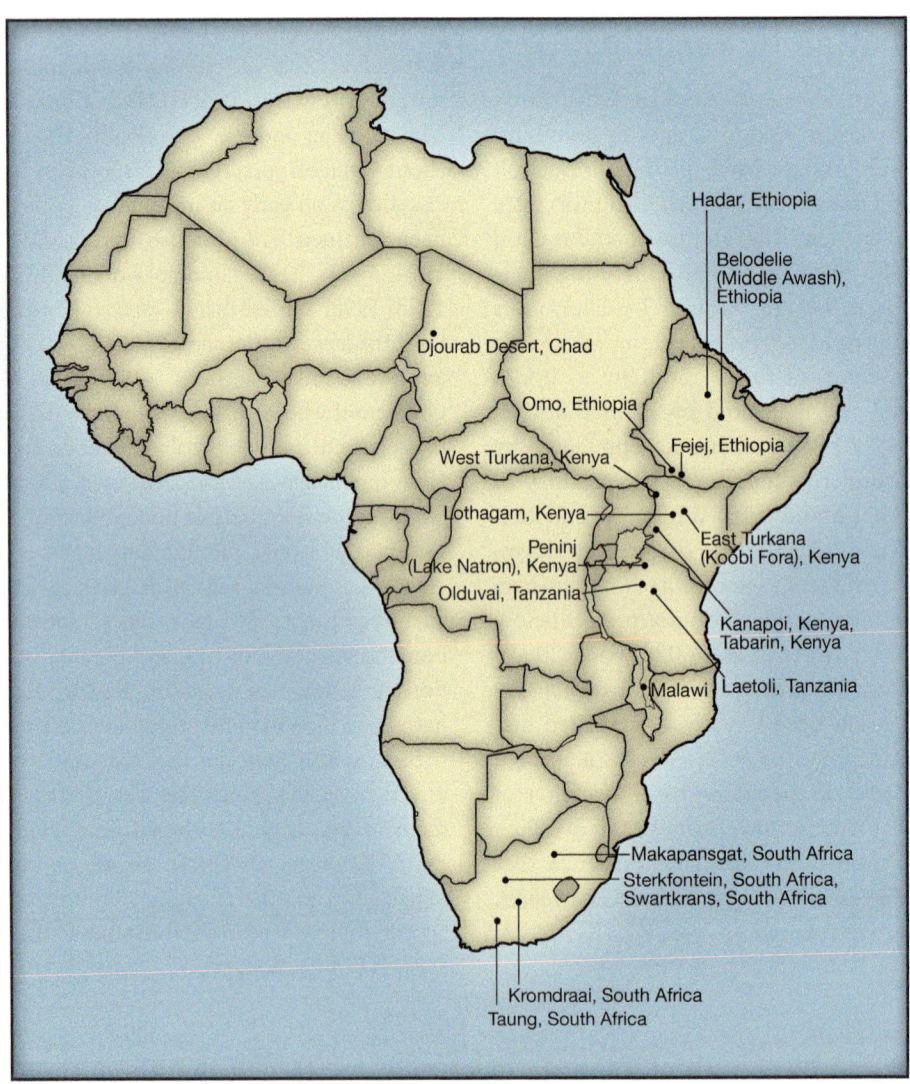

Figure 9–5 Australopithecine and Paranthropoid Sites

Source: Ciochon RL, Fleagle JG, editors. 1993. The human evolution source book. Englewood Cliffs, NJ: Prentice Hall. p. ix.

paranthropoids have been found). Their teeth share the basic hominin characteristics of small canines, flat and thickly enamelled molars, and a parabolic dental arch, and there is unambiguous evidence that even the earliest australopithecines were fully bipedal. Not only do their skeletons reflect bipedal locomotion, but at Laetoli, Tanzania, more than 50 hardened human-like footprints that are estimated to be about 3.6 million years old give striking confirmation that the hominins there were fully bipedal. Nevertheless, their bipedalism does not mean that these earliest definite hominins were completely terrestrial. All the australopithecines, including the later ones, seem to have been capable of climbing and moving in trees, judging by arm versus leg lengths and other skeletal features (Rose 1984; Susman et al. 1985). The South African specimen nicknamed "Little Foot" is the clearest indication yet of this—the hallux (or "big toe" of the foot, the importance of which has long been recognized in the proper function of the foot during gait) appears to have been slightly divergent, allowing good mobility of the big toe, and some prehension of the foot (Clarke and Tobias 1995).

The australopithecines of Africa show considerable variability, and palaeoanthropologists divide the genus *Australopithecus* into at least six species (Conroy 1990; Culotta 1995; Wilford 1995). Some argue that there may have been several more species. Recent finds are considered by some scholars to represent two new australopithecine species, *A. bahrelghazali* and *A. garhi*, as well as a related hominin, *Kenyanthropus platyops*, that some scholars believe is yet another australopithecine species. The **australopithecines** include *A. anamensis*, *A. afarensis*, and *A. africanus*. All of them have smaller dentition and lighter facial and dental musculature than the paranthropoids.

Australopithecus anamensis (found south of Lake Turkana in Kenya) may be 4.2 million years old (Leakey et al. 1998) and is suggested to be ancestral to *A. afarensis* (Kimbel et al. 2006). Other hominins found in East Africa that lived about 4 million to 3 million years ago are classified by most palaeoanthropologists as belonging to the species *Australopithecus afarensis*. A few palaeoanthropologists do not think that these hominins should be placed in a separate species because they resemble the later hominin species *Australopithecus africanus*, which lived between about 3 million and 2 million years ago.

In 1999, the remains of *Australopithecus garhi* were discovered in the Afar region of Ethiopia, dating to about 2.5 million years ago. *Australopithecus garhi* had a projecting ape-like face and small braincase, similar to *A. afarensis* but with much larger teeth, suggesting to some that it is descended from *A. afarensis* and is a candidate ancestor for early *Homo* (Asfaw et al. 1999). It may represent one end of the range of variation in *afarensis*, or it may represent an adaptation to eating tough foods, similar to that made by the paranthropoids, which we will discuss shortly.

It is interesting, however, that the remains of butchered animals were found in the same rock layer as the *A. garhi* remains. Several bones found near the *A. garhi* fossils show unambiguous cut marks and signs of having been broken with a stone tool. Unfortunately, no stone tools have been found, but the evidence for butchery suggests they must have been used. And since no other species of hominin have been found in the area, it is reasonable to think that *A. garhi* was the toolmaker and butcher. The fossil's discoverer, Berhane Asfaw, suggests that *A. garhi* is in the right place, at the right time, and has the right physical and behavioural traits to be the direct ancestor of early *Homo* (Brunet et al. 1995).

Australopithecines: a bipedal genus of hominin distinguished from the later genus *Paranthropus* by their lighter dentition and smaller faces.
Australopithecus anamensis: a species of *Australopithecus* that lived perhaps 4.2 million years ago.
Australopithecus afarensis: a species of *Australopithecus* that lived 4 million to 3 million years ago in East Africa and was definitely bipedal.
Australopithecus africanus: a species of *Australopithecus* that lived between about 3 million and 2 million years ago.
Australopithecus garhi: a species discovered in 1999 in the Afar region of Ethiopia, dating to about 2.5 million years ago. *A. garhi* had a projecting ape-like face and small braincase, similar to *A. afarensis* but with much larger teeth.

Equally intriguing is *Australopithecus sediba*. Found by Lee Berger in Malapa Cave in South Africa, the two skeletons representing *A. sediba* and dated to around 2 million years ago present a strange mix of australopithecine and early *Homo* features. While the legs and feet of *A. sediba* seem australopithecine-like, the pelvis is more like early *Homo*, as are the hands (Berger et al. 2010). The brain is smaller than that of other australopithecines but appears to have some features found in early *Homo*, and the teeth seem more *Homo*-like as well (Carlson et al. 2011; Pickering et al. 2011). Indeed, some have suggested that *A. sediba* may be better categorized as *Homo*, though this idea is controversial and certainly will not be resolved until more specimens are found.

Finally, **Australopithecus bahrelghazali** is interesting not so much because of its physical features but because it was found farther west than any other australopithecine, in what is now central Chad. Reported in 1995 by French researchers, *A. bahrelghazali* is the first early hominin to be found outside of the Rift Valley (a long valley in East Africa where the earth is pulling apart, exposing fossils from millions of years ago), and until *A. bahrelghazali* surfaced, few thought early hominins were present anywhere else. *A. bahrelghazali* dates to about 3 million years ago and is very similar to contemporary *A. afarensis* fossils from the Rift Valley. It differs from *A. afarensis* in some distinct ways (its premolars, for example, have thinner enamel and more well defined roots), but the important difference is where *A. bahrelghazali* lived. Most scholars assume the early hominins represent a specific adaptation to the Rift Valley. The discovery of an early australopithecine some 2500 kilometres west of the Rift Valley calls this assumption into question (Brunet et al. 1995).

A related hominin genus, **Kenyanthropus platyops**, is thought by some scholars to be yet another australopithecine (and hence should not be regarded as a separate genus). The nearly complete 3.5-million-year-old skull of *Kenyanthropus platyops* from western Kenya shows traits that Meave Leakey and her colleagues suggested separate it from the australopithecines that lived at the same time. Its face is smaller and flatter, and its molars are smaller than those of the australopithecines. Leakey believes *Kenyanthropus* may be a direct link to *Homo*, but others are not so sure. The skull is distorted, and scholars are not convinced that its features lie outside the range of the australopithecines (Leakey et al. 2001). The debate over the relation of *Kenyanthropus* to *Australopithecus* will continue until more fossils are found.

The **paranthropoids** have larger dentition than the gracile species australopithecines, and massive faces and jaws. Some robust individuals had a ridge of bone called a **sagittal crest** on the top of their heads; the ridge anchored the heavy musculature for their large teeth and jaws. The earliest species is *Paranthropus aethiopicus*, which lived in eastern Africa between 2.7 and 2.3 million years ago. Most palaeoanthropologists think that the later paranthropoids, who lived between 2.3 and 1 million years ago, consist of two species: the East African species *Paranthropus boisei* and the South African species *Paranthropus robustus*.

Australopithecus bahrelghazali: a species of *Australopithecus* discovered by French researchers in Chad in north-central Africa and reported in 1995. *A. bahrelghazali* is dated between 3.5 million and 3 million years ago and is thought to be a second hominin species contemporary with *A. afarensis*.

Kenyanthropus platyops: a nearly complete 3.5-million-year-old skull found in western Kenya. It is thought by some scholars to be a species of australopithecine (and hence should not be regarded as a separate genus).

Paranthropoids: a later group of hominin usually differentiated from the australopithecines by their heavier dentition and larger faces.

Sagittal Crest: a ridge of bone along the midline of the top of the skull for muscle attachment.

Paranthropus aethiopicus: the earliest paranthropoid.

Paranthropus boisei: an East African robust australopithecine species dating from 2.3 million to 1 million years ago with somewhat larger cranial capacity than *A. africanus*. No longer thought to be larger than other australopithecines, it is robust primarily in the skull and jaw, most strikingly in the teeth. Compared with *P. robustus*, *P. boisei* has even more features that reflect a huge chewing apparatus.

Paranthropus robustus: a South African species found in South African caves dating from about 2.3 million to 1 million years ago.

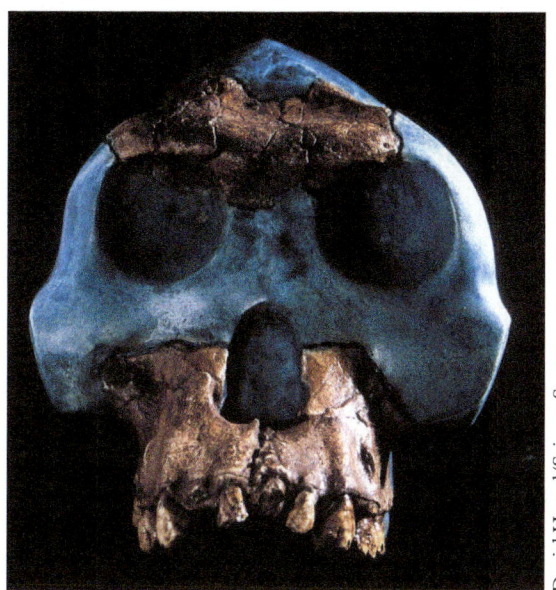

Reconstructed skull of *Australopithecus garhi*. Note the large molars but relatively small face.

Daniel Herard/Science Source

process itself (White 2003). Whatever the cause, diversity seems to be the key word when thinking about the australopithecines. Let's take a closer look at the diverse species of *Australopithecus*, and then the more robust *Paranthropus* species.

Australopithecines

Australopithecus anamensis. The earliest australopithecine species is *A. anamensis*, which has been found in several locations in northern Kenya and is dated between 3.9 and 4.2 million years ago (Culotta 1995). While there is controversy about some of the specimens included in *A. anamensis*, the general picture is that it was a small bipedal hominin with teeth similar to those of the later *A. afarensis* (Leakey et al. 1995). The more controversial specimens have long bones, suggesting well-developed bipedalism, but their elbow and knee joints look more like those of the later *Homo* genus than like those of any other species of *Australopithecus*. It has been said that *A. anamensis* is "*afarensis*-like from the neck up and *Homo*-like from the neck down" (Tattersall and Schwartz 2000:93).

Australopithecus afarensis. It appears that other bipedal australopithecines lived earlier in East Africa, before 3 million years ago. The fossils showing the clearest evidence of bipedalism come from Laetoli, Tanzania, and Hadar, Ethiopia. These finds, dated between 4 million and 3 million years ago, represent an earlier species of *Australopithecus*. The Hadar and Laetoli hominins, as well as those from some other East African sites, are classed as *A. afarensis*.

Remains from at least two dozen hominins were unearthed at Laetoli, Tanzania (Simpson 1998). Although the remains there consisted largely of teeth and jaws, there is no question that the Laetoli hominins were bipedal, because it was at the Laetoli site that the now famous trail of footprints was found. Two hominins walking erect and side by side left their tracks in the ground 3.6 million years ago. The remains of at least 35 individuals have been found at another site, Hadar, in Ethiopia. The Hadar finds are remarkable for their completeness. Whereas palaeoanthropologists often find just parts of the cranium and jaws, many parts of the skeleton were also

The picture that emerges from this brief overview of the australopithecines is one of diversity. There seem to have been many different species of australopithecine, and even within species there seems to be a relatively high level of variation (Fleagle 1999). All shared similar environments in eastern and southern Africa, but those environments were diverse and changing. Forests were giving way to open woodlands and grasslands. Large lakes were formed and then broken apart through uplifting and volcanic activity in the rift valley of eastern Africa. And the climate continued to warm until the end of the **Pliocene**, some 1.6 million years ago. The apparent diversity of the australopithecines may reflect an *adaptive radiation* (a dispersal and divergence) of bipedal hominins to these dynamic environmental conditions (deMenocal 2011). On the other hand, Tim White suggested that we really do not know enough about the australopithecines to judge how many species there are. He also suggested some variations may be the result of differences in the fossilization

Pliocene: the geological epoch 5.2 million to 1.6 million years ago during which the earliest definite hominins appeared.

Mary Leakey's expedition discovered a trail about 64 metres long of 3.8-million-year-old fossilized footprints at Laetoli, Tanzania. Shown here is one part of the trail left by two adults who were clearly upright walkers. The footprints show a well-developed arch and forward-facing big toe.

found at Hadar. For example, palaeoanthropologists found 40 percent of the skeleton of a female hominin they named Lucy, after the Beatles' song "Lucy in the Sky with Diamonds" (Johanson and Edey 1981). At the time, Lucy was the most complete australopithecine specimen found. An analysis of Lucy's pelvis indicates clearly that she was a bipedal walker (Lovejoy 1988). However, she probably spent some time in the trees, if we judge by her leg bones and joints; they are not as large proportionately as those of modern humans (Jungers 1988). More recently, Sellers and colleagues (2005) used evolutionary robotics to predict the most energy-efficient upright walking gait for the fossil remains of Lucy and matched their predictions to the Laetoli footprints. Their results suggested that Lucy was a fully adapted biped. Similarly Berge et al. (2006) examined the Laetoli footprints using shape analysis of the outlines, compared to modern humans and chimpanzees. They also suggested the Laetoli prints were produced by a modern human-like, bipedal gait.

Dating of the hominin remains at Laetoli suggests that the hominins there lived between 3.8 million and 3.6 million years ago (Johanson and White 1979). Although Lucy and the other hominins at Hadar were once thought to be about as old as those at Laetoli, recent dating suggests that they are somewhat younger—less than 3.2 million years old. Lucy probably lived 3.2 million years ago (Walter 1994). The environment when Lucy lived there was semi-arid, upland savannah with rainy and dry seasons (Conroy 1990; Simpson 1998).

Those palaeoanthropologists, such as Donald Johanson and Tim White, who believe the Laetoli and Hadar hominins should be given the separate species name *A. afarensis* base their decision primarily on some features of the skull, teeth, and jaws that they feel are more ape-like than those of the later hominins classified as *A. africanus*. For example, the incisors and canines of the Laetoli and Hadar hominins are rather large, their tooth rows converge slightly at the back of the jaw, and the palate (roof of the mouth) is flat and narrow. Many *A. afarensis* specimens also display a sagittal crest, and some have a *temporo-nuchal crest*—a compound crest that forms at the back of the skull (Johanson and White 1979; White et al. 1981).

In some other respects, the Laetoli and Hadar fossils resemble *A. africanus*. Like *A. africanus*, individuals were very small. Lucy, for example, was about 105 centimetres tall, and the largest individuals at these sites, presumably males, were about 150 centimetres tall (Campbell 2001:202). The brains of the Laetoli and Hadar hominins also tend to be small; cranial capacity is estimated at 415 cc, just slightly less than that of *A. africanus* (McHenry 1982).

In 2006, the remains of a fairly complete juvenile skeleton of *A. afarensis* were finally uncovered

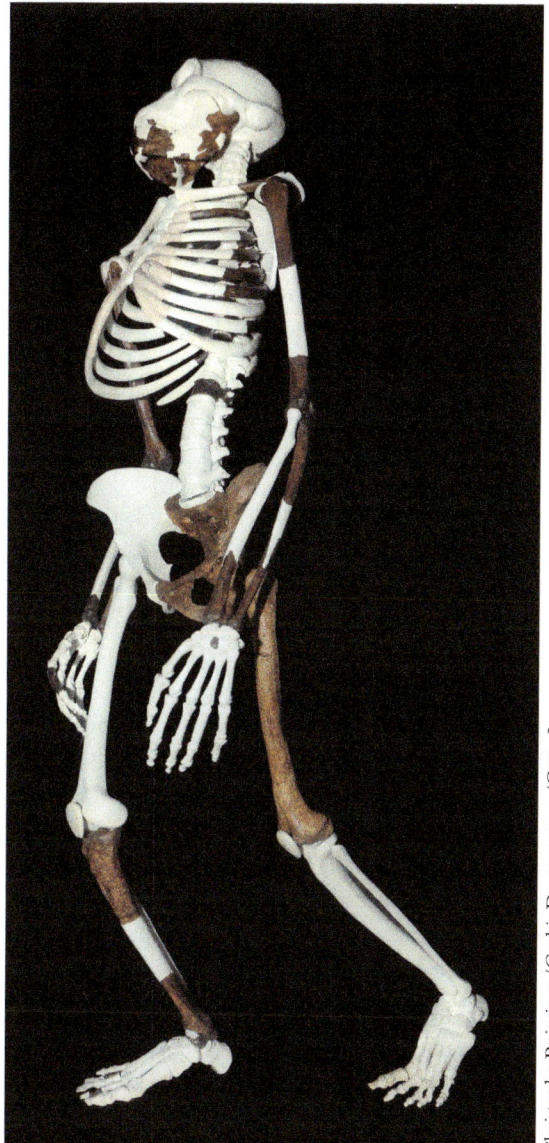

A reconstruction of a female *Australopithecus afarensis* skeleton. Note how long the arms are relative to the legs, and the long fingers. Both suggest *A. afarensis* was at least partially arboreal.

from a block of sandstone first discovered in 2000 not far from where Lucy was found, in Dikika, Ethiopia; it is referred to as DIK-1-1. The fossil specimen includes the skull, torso, and segments of the upper and lower limbs. CT scans showed that the jaw still had unerupted teeth, suggesting that the child was about 3 years old (Alemseged et al. 2006). In their preliminary description of the remains, Alemseged and co-authors (2006) suggested the morphology of the face of the 3.3-million-year-old child resembles *A. afarensis* and differs from *A. africanus*, including the Taung skull, which is discussed below. The DIK-1-1 skeleton is an important find because of its completeness, but also because of the light it sheds on juvenile australopithecine skeletal biology (Alemseged et al. 2006; Wood 2006). Further, the DIK-1-1 lower limbs, including the foot, provide clear evidence for bipedal locomotion, but other aspects of the skeleton, including the scapula and phalanges, raise questions about the importance of arboreal behaviour in *A. afarensis* (Alemseged et al. 2006).

Australopithecus africanus. Although the oldest australopithecine fossils come from East Africa, they were not the first australopithecine discoveries. The first finds identified as *Australopithecus* were discovered in caves in South Africa in the 1920s.

In 1925, Raymond Dart, professor of anatomy at the University of Witwatersrand in Johannesburg, South Africa, presented the first evidence that an erect bipedal hominin existed in the Pliocene epoch. As he separated bones from a matrix of material originally found in the Taung cave on the edge of the Kalahari Desert, Dart realized he was looking at more than the remains of an ape. He described the experience:

> On December 23, [1924,] the rock parted. I could view the face from the front, although the right side was still embedded. The creature that had contained this massive brain was no giant anthropoid such as a gorilla. What emerged was a baby's face, an infant with a full set of milk teeth and its permanent molars just in the process of erupting. (Dart 1925)

From the teeth Dart identified the fossil as the remains of a 5- to 7-year-old child, although more recent analysis by electron microscope suggests that the child was no more than 3.5 years old (Bromage and Dean 1985; Smith 1986). He named the specimen *Australopithecus africanus*, which means "southern ape of Africa." Dart was certain the skull was that of a bipedal animal. He based his conclusion on the fact that the foramen magnum was centrally located. (In monkeys and apes, this passageway is near the back of the skull, in a position more appropriate for quadrupedal locomotion.) Furthermore, the Taung child's incisors and canine teeth were short, and therefore definitely more human than ape-like.

Dart's conclusion met with widespread skepticism and opposition. Not the least of his problems was that scientists at the time believed hominins had originated in Asia. There were other reasons. Dart had found only one fossil; it was an infant rather than an adult; and no other hominin fossils had yet been found in Africa. Other australopithecines were not discovered until the 1930s, when Robert Broom recovered some fossils from the Sterkfontein cave near Johannesburg. Dart's and Broom's conclusions did not begin to be accepted until after 1945, when Wilfrid Le Gros Clark, a professor of anatomy at Oxford, supported the hominin status of their finds (Eldredge and Tattersall 1982).

Since the Taung child's discovery more than 75 years ago, the remains of hundreds of other similar australopithecines have been unearthed from the caves at Sterkfontein and Makapansgat in South Africa. From this abundant evidence a fairly complete picture of *A. africanus* can be drawn: "The brain case is rounded with a relatively well-developed forehead and moderate brow ridges surmount a rather projecting face" (Pilbeam 1972:107). The estimated cranial capacity for the various finds from Taung and Sterkfontein is between 428 cc and 485 cc. In contrast, modern humans have a normal cranial capacity of between 1350 cc and 1450 cc (Holloway 1974). Like *A. afarensis*, *A. africanus* was very small; the adults were only about 105 to 135 centimetres tall and weighed about 20 to 40 kilograms (Szalay and Delson 1979:504).

Australopithecus africanus retained the large, chinless jaw of the Miocene apes, but some of the dental features of *A. africanus* were similar to those of modern humans—broad incisors and non-projecting canines. Although the premolars and molars were larger than in modern humans, their form was very similar. Presumably, function and use were also similar.

The broad, bowl-shaped pelvis, which is very similar to the human pelvis in form and in areas for muscle attachments, provides corroborating evidence for bipedalism. The australopithecine spine also suggests they walked erect. The bottom part of the vertebral column forms a curve, causing the spinal column to be S-shaped (seen from the side). This **lumbar curve** and an S-shaped spinal column are found only in hominins (see Figure 9–2, page 201). Analysis of the hip-joint and femoral bone fossils also indicates that the australopithecines walked fully upright and that at least the later ones walked with the same direct, striding gait observed in modern humans (Lovejoy et al. 1973).

Dating of the australopithecine finds from the South African limestone caves is somewhat difficult because none of the absolute dating techniques can be applied. Relative dating is possible, though. Comparisons of the fauna found in the strata with fauna found elsewhere suggest that the South African *A. africanus* lived between 3 million and 2 million years ago. The climate was probably semi-arid, not too different from the climate of today (Conroy 1990; Klein 2009).

Paranthropoids

There is little disagreement that the so-called robust species of paranthropoids lived in East Africa and in South Africa from about 2.7 million to 1 million years ago. Paranthropoids were found first in South African caves, in Kromdraai and in Swartkrans, and later in East Africa, in the Omo Basin in Ethiopia, on the east and west sides of Lake Turkana in Kenya, and in the Olduvai Gorge in Tanzania (Conroy 1990; Klein 2009). Most palaeoanthropologists classify the South African paranthropoids from about 1.8 million to 1 million years ago as *P. robustus*, and the East African robust forms from 2.3 million to 1.3 million years ago as *P. boisei* (McHenry 1998b). The third species, *P. aethiopicus*, is even earlier, dating back more than 2.5 million years ago, and may have been ancestral to *P. boisei*.

In contrast to australopithecines, the paranthropoids generally had thicker jaws, with larger molars and premolars but smaller incisors, more massive muscle attachments for chewing, and

Lumbar Curve: found only in hominins; the bottom part of the vertebral column forms a curve, causing the spinal column to be S-shaped (as seen from the side).

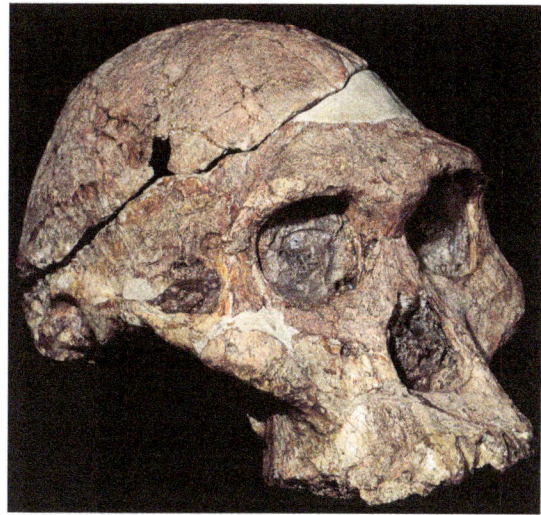

Fossil skull of an *Australopithecus africanus* (STS 5) nicknamed "Mrs. Ples," found by Robert Broom at Sterkfontein cave in 1947.

well-developed sagittal crests to support heavy chewing (Szalay and Delson 1979; Wood 1992; Klein 2009), although this has been suggested to be a sexually dimorphic trait among males. In addition, *P. robustus* and *P. boisei* have somewhat larger cranial capacities (about 490 cc to 530 cc). Compared with *P. robustus*, *P. boisei* has even more extreme features that reflect a huge chewing capability—enormous molar teeth and expanded premolars that look like molars, a massive thick and deep jaw, thick cheekbones, and a more pronounced sagittal crest (McHenry 1998b).

It used to be thought that the paranthropoids were substantially bigger than the australopithecines. But recent calculations suggest that they were not substantially different in body weight or height. The robustness is primarily in the skull and jaw, most strikingly in the teeth. If the paranthropoids were larger in body size, their slightly bigger brain capacity would not be surprising, since larger animals generally have larger brains. However, the body of the paranthropoids is similar to that of *A. africanus*, so the brain of the robust australopithecines was relatively larger than the brain of *A. africanus* (Jungers 1998; McHenry 1998a).

Paranthropus aethiopicus. *P. aethiopicus* is the earliest and also the least known of the paranthropoids.

A reconstruction of an *Australopithecus africanus* mother and child picking berries in a tree. Like *A. afarensis*, *A. africanus* probably spent time in trees both feeding and avoiding predators.

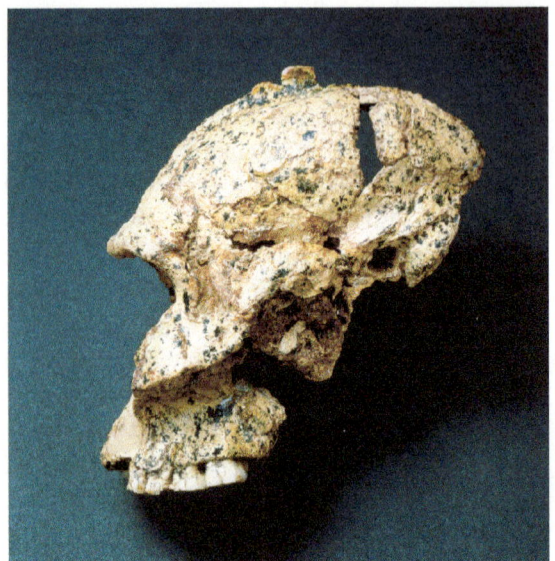

Fossil skull of *Australopithecus robustus* (SK46) found by Robert Broom at Swartkrans cave in 1949. Note its sagittal crest, massive cheekbones, and huge molars.

A reconstruction of what *Paranthropus boisei* may have looked like.

P. aethiopicus is represented by a small group of fossils found in northern Kenya and southern Ethiopia dating between 2.3 million and 2.7 million years ago, including one spectacular find—a nearly complete skull (known as the "Black Skull" because of its dark colour) found in 1985 (Fleagle 1999; Klein 2009). Even though we have only a few fossils, it seems clear that *P. aethiopicus* was quite different from other australopithecines. They differ from *P. afarensis* specimens from roughly the same region and perhaps even the same time period by having much larger dentition, particularly molars, huge cheekbones, projecting and dish-shaped (round and flat) faces, and large sagittal crests. But they are similar to *A. afarensis* in most other ways. Overall, *P. aethiopicus* resembles *A. afarensis* with a massively "scaled-up" dental apparatus (Walker and Leakey 1988; Grine 1993).

Paranthropus robustus.

In 1936, Robert Broom, then curator of vertebrate palaeontology at the Transvaal Museum in South Africa, began visiting quarries seeking fossils for the museum, particularly hominins that might support Raymond Dart's earlier discovery of the Taung child. In 1938, a quarry manager gave Broom a hominin jaw that had been found in a nearby cave called Kromdraai. Broom immediately began excavating in the cave, and within days was able to piece together the skull of what would prove to be a new australopithecine species—*Paranthropus robustus* (Broom 1950).

While Broom had expected another example of *Australopithecus africanus* (he had found an *A. africanus* skull in 1936), this one was different. It had larger teeth, a massive jaw, and a flatter face than *A. africanus* (Fleagle 1999; Klein 2009). Indeed, after further study, Broom decided that the fossil represented an entirely new hominin genus: *Paranthropus*. Broom's genus designation was not widely accepted at the time (scholars thought the specimen represented a species of *Australopithecus*), but as we noted earlier, many scholars today believe the robust australopithecines are unique enough to warrant classification in a separate *Paranthropus* genus.

During the 1940s Broom added many new fossils of *P. robustus* and *A. africanus* to the collections of the Transvaal Museum. But his discoveries also raised a problem. How did two strikingly different hominin species evolve in the same environment? In 1954, John T. Robinson proposed that *A. africanus* and *P. robustus* had different dietary adaptations—*A. africanus* being an omnivore (van der Merwe et al. 2003) and *P. robustus* a vegetarian, with a need for heavy chewing. Robinson's view was hotly debated, but recent evidence from electron microscopy and the analysis of carbon isotopes in the teeth suggests that *P. robustus* and *A. africanus* did not have very different diets, probably a mix of grasses and fruits (Ungar and Sponheimer 2011). Analyses also suggest that *A. africanus* practised fairly heavy chewing (McHenry 2002).

The idea that *P. robustus* was only vegetarian is also questioned by a chemical technique that analyzes strontium–calcium ratios in teeth and bones to estimate the proportions of plant versus animal food in the diet. This new kind of analysis suggests that *P. robustus* was an omnivore (McHenry 1998b). Thus, *P. robustus* may have needed large teeth and jaws to chew seeds, nuts, and tubers, but that does not mean that it didn't eat other foods.

Was *P. robustus* adapted then to a drier, more open environment than *A. africanus*? This is a possibility, but the evidence is somewhat controversial. At any rate, most palaeoanthropologists think that *P. robustus* died out shortly after 1 million years ago (Grine 1998) and therefore could not be ancestral to our own genus, *Homo* (Stringer 1985; Klein 2009).

Paranthrpus boisei.

Legendary palaeoanthropologist Louis Leakey began his search for a human ancestor in 1931 at Olduvai Gorge in western Tanzania. It was not until 1959 that his efforts paid off with the discovery of *Paranthropus boisei* (named after a benefactor, Charles Boise). The nearly 30 years that Leakey, his wife, Mary Leakey, and their children (including palaeoanthropologist Richard Leakey) worked at Olduvai before finding *P. boisei* were not wasted. The Leakeys assembled a rich collection of non-hominin fossils and established a detailed understanding of the ancient environment of the region (Leakey 1971, 1979). As we discuss later in the chapter, they also amassed a remarkable collection of ancient stone tools. So, on a hot July morning, when Mary Leakey rushed to tell Louis, who was sick in bed, that she had discovered the hominin they had long been searching for, the Leakeys were able immediately to place their find into a rich environmental and perhaps cultural context.

The discovery of *P. boisei* was particularly important because it demonstrated that early hominins were present in East Africa. Until the Leakeys found *P. boisei*, it was thought that South Africa was the homeland of the hominins. Indeed, Leakey initially assigned *P. boisei* to a new genus—*Zinjanthropus*—to highlight its location (*Zinj* means "East Africa" in Arabic). Today we know that the most ancient fossil hominins are all found in East Africa, but in 1959 simply finding a fossil hominin in East Africa was remarkable.

What did *P. boisei* look like? Compared with *P. robustus*, *P. boisei* had even more extreme features that reflected a huge chewing apparatus—enormous molar teeth and expanded premolars that look like molars; a massive, thick, and deep jaw; thick cheekbones; and a more pronounced sagittal crest (McHenry 2002). Indeed, *P. boisei* has been called a "hyper-robust" australopithecine—a name that definitely captures the species.

P. boisei lived between about 2.3 and 1.3 million years ago. Like *P. robustus*, it seems to have lived in a dry, open environment and ate a lot of coarse seeds, nuts, and roots. Most palaeoanthropologists think that, like *P. robustus*, *P. boisei* is not ancestral to our genus, *Homo* (Fleagle 1999; Klein 2009). We don't know for sure whether *P. boisei* was the maker of the stone tools the Leakeys found at Olduvai for, as we will learn in the next chapter, it lived alongside at least two other hominin species—*Homo habilis* and *Homo erectus*—who are perhaps the more likely toolmakers. Susman's studies of the thumb and musculature required to make tools suggest that all the australopithecines and paranthropoids after about 2.5 million years ago were capable of making tools with their hands (Susman 1994). However, this doesn't mean that they made tools, only that they could have.

One Model of Human Evolution

Figure 9–6 shows one model of how the known fossils may be related. The main disagreement among palaeoanthropologists concerns which species of *Australopithecus* were ancestral to the line leading to modern humans. For example, the model shown in Figure 9–6 suggests that *A. africanus* is not ancestral to *Homo*, only to one line of *Paranthropus*, *P. robustus*. *Australopithecus afarensis* is viewed as ancestral to both paranthropoids and to the line leading to modern humans. Those who think that *A. afarensis* was the last common ancestor of all the hominin lines shown in Figure 9–6 also think the split to *Homo* occurred over 3 million years ago (Wood 1992; Klein 2009). Despite the uncertainty and disagreements about what species was ancestral to the *Homo* line, there is widespread agreement among palaeoanthropologists

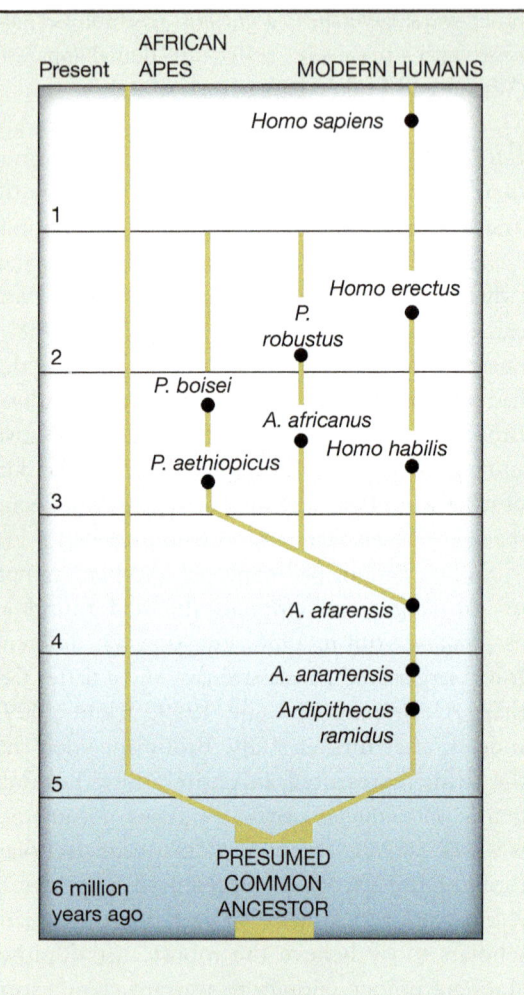

Figure 9–6 Phylogenetic Timelines

Source: Leakey M, Tattersall I. 5 September 1995. The fossil trail. New York Times C9. Dates changed slightly to reflect recent redating. Copyright © 1995 by the New York Times Company.

about other aspects of early hominin evolution: (1) there were at least two separate hominin lines between 3 million and 1 million years ago; (2) the paranthropoids were not ancestral to modern humans but became extinct by 1 million years ago; and (3) *Homo habilis* (and successive *Homo* species) were in the direct ancestral line to modern humans.

Early Species of *Homo*

Hominins with a brain absolutely and relatively larger than that of the australopithecines appeared about 2.5 million years ago. These hominins, classified in our own genus, *Homo*, are generally divided into two species: *Homo habilis* and **Homo rudolfensis**. Fossils of both were primarily found in the western parts of Kenya and Tanzania, but remains have been found elsewhere in eastern and southern Africa, including the Omo Basin of Ethiopia and Sterkfontein cave in South Africa (Conroy 1990). Both lived in the same place and time as *Paranthropus boisei*, and may have lived at the same time as *Homo erectus* (Simpson 1998).

Homo habilis appears to be the earlier of these two species, appearing around 2.3 million years ago. Compared with the australopithecines, *H. habilis* had a significantly larger brain, averaging 630–640 cc (Tobias 1994; McHenry 1998b), and reduced molars and premolars (Simpson 1998). The rest of the skeleton is similar to the australopithecine skeleton, including the presence of powerful hands and relatively long arms, suggesting that *H. habilis* was at least partially arboreal. *H. habilis* might also have been sexually dimorphic like the australopithecines, as individuals seem to have greatly differed in size.

Homo rudolfensis is roughly contemporary with *H. habilis*, and shares many of its features. In fact, many palaeoanthropologists make no distinction between the two species, putting them both together as *H. habilis*. Those who do not see them as distinct species point to the larger and more thickly enamelled cheek teeth of *H. rudolfensis*, its flatter and broader face, and its more modern-like limb proportions. Even with its large teeth and broad face, the dentition of *H. rudolfensis* is considerably reduced compared with that of the australopithecines and, like *H. habilis*, its brain is at least a third larger.

We have few postcranial skeletal remains for either of these early species of *Homo*, so it is impossible to tell whether the female pelvis had changed. But, with the brains averaging a third larger than the australopithecines', it seems likely that some modifications must have developed to

Homo rudolfensis: early species belonging to our genus, *Homo*. Similar enough to *Homo habilis* that some palaeoanthropologists make no distinction between the two.

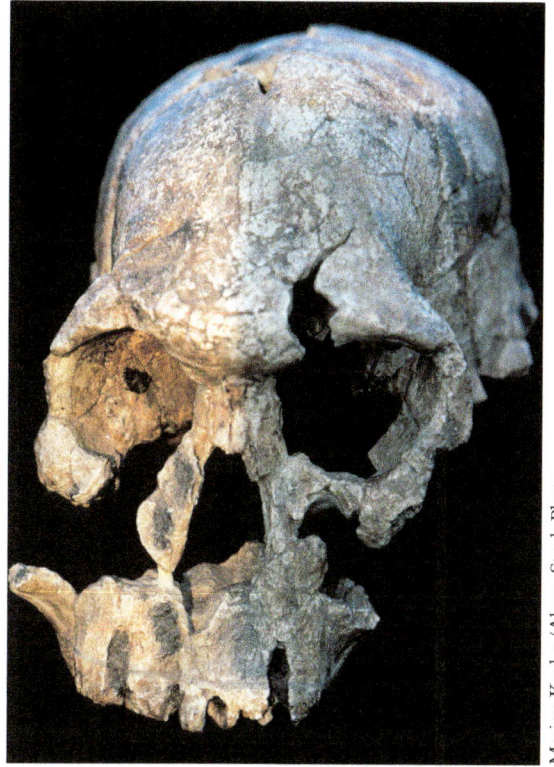

The skull of a *Homo habilis/rudolfensis* (ER-1470) found by Richard Leakey in 1972. Note its high forehead and large braincase.

allow for larger-brained offspring to be born. We do know, though, that changes in the female pelvis to accommodate larger-brained babies can be seen in *Homo erectus*, discussed in the next chapter.

Early Hominin Cultures

Tool Traditions

Because stone tools found at various sites in East Africa date to about the time of *H. habilis*, some anthropologists surmise that *H. habilis*, rather than the australopithecines, made those tools (see Figure 9–7). After all, *H. habilis* had the greater brain capacity. But the fact is that none of the earliest stone tools are clearly associated with *H. habilis*, so it is impossible as yet to know who made them. All the hominins that lived from at least 2.5 million years ago had a thumb capable of toolmaking, so all of them may have been toolmakers (Susman 1994). We turn now to those tools and what archaeologists

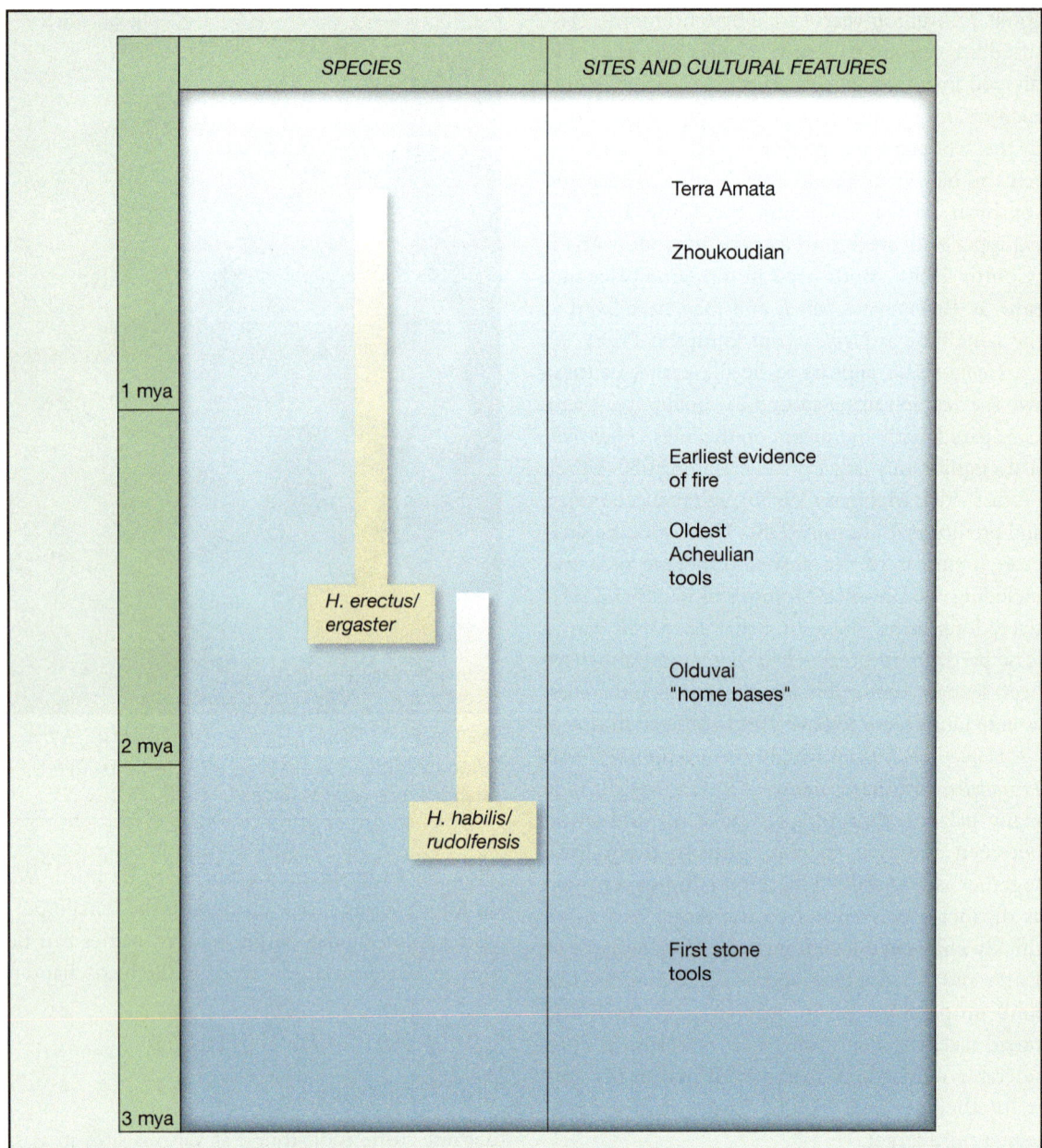

Figure 9–7 Early Evolution of the Genus *Homo*

infer about the lifestyles of their makers, the hominins (whoever they were) who lived between about 2.5 million and 1.5 million years ago.

The earliest identifiable stone tools found so far come from various sites in East Africa and date from about 2.5 million years ago (Susman 1994; Klein 2009), and maybe earlier. The oldest tools, some 3000 in number, were discovered recently at Gona, Ethiopia. The tools range from very small flakes (thumb-size) to cobble or core tools that were fist-size (Anonymous 1997c). These early tools were apparently made by striking a stone with another stone, a technique called **percussion flaking**. Both the sharp-edged flakes and the

Percussion Flaking: a toolmaking technique in which one stone is struck with another to remove a flake.

sharp-edged cores (the pieces of stone left after flakes are removed) were probably used as tools.

What were those earliest stone tools used for? What do they tell us about early hominin culture? Unfortunately, little can be inferred about lifestyles from the earliest tool sites because little else was found with the tools. In contrast, finds of later tool assemblages at Olduvai Gorge in Tanzania have yielded a rich harvest of cultural information. The Olduvai site was uncovered accidentally in 1911, when a German entomologist followed a butterfly into the gorge and found fossil remains. Beginning in the 1930s, Louis and Mary Leakey searched the gorge for clues to the evolution of early humans. Of the Olduvai site, Louis Leakey wrote,

> [It] is a fossil hunter's dream, for it shears 300 feet [91.4 metres] through stratum after stratum of earth's history as through a gigantic layer cake. Here, within reach, lie countless fossils and artifacts that but for the faulting and erosion would have remained sealed under thick layers of consolidated rock. (Leakey 1960)

The oldest cultural materials from Olduvai (Bed I) date from early in the Pleistocene. The stone artifacts include core tools and sharp-edged flakes, but flake tools predominate. Among the core tools, so-called *choppers* are common. A chopper is a core tool that has been partially flaked and has a side that might have been used for chopping. Other core tools, with flaking along one side and a flat edge, are called *scrapers*.

Whenever a stone has facets removed from only one side of the cutting edge, we call it a **unifacial tool**. If the stone has facets removed from both sides, we call it a **bifacial tool**. Although there are some bifacial tools in the early stone tool assemblages, they are neither as plentiful nor as elaborated as in later tool traditions. The kind of tool assemblage found in Bed I and to some extent in later (higher) layers is referred to as **Oldowan** (see Figure 9–8) (Clark 1970; Schick and Toth 1994).

Olduvai Gorge, Tanzania. Bed I, where evidence of early human culture was found, is at the very bottom of the gorge.

Lifestyles

Archaeologists have long speculated about the lifestyles of early hominins from Olduvai and other sites. Some of these speculations come from analysis of what can be done with the tools, microscopic analysis of wear on the tools, and examination of the marks the tools make on bones; other speculations are based on what is found in association with the tools.

Archaeologists have experimented with what can be done with Oldowan tools. The flakes appear to be very versatile; they can be used for slitting the hides of animals, dismembering animals, and whittling wood into sharp-pointed sticks (wooden spears or digging sticks). The larger stone tools (choppers and scrapers) can be used to hack off branches or cut and chop tough animal joints (Schick and Toth 1994). Those who have made and tried to use the stone flake tools for various purposes are so impressed by the sharpness and versatility of flakes that they wonder whether the core tools were really routinely used as tools. The cores could mainly be what remained after flakes were struck off (Schick and Toth 1994:129; Klein 2009:257–258). Archaeologists surmise that many early tools were also

Unifacial Tool: a tool worked or flaked on one side only.
Bifacial Tool: a tool worked or flaked on two sides.
Oldowan: the earliest stone toolmaking tradition, named after the tools found in Bed I at Olduvai Gorge,

Tanzania, from about 2.5 million years ago. The stone artifacts include core tools and sharp-edged flakes made by striking one stone against another. Flake tools predominate. Among the core tools, so-called choppers are common.

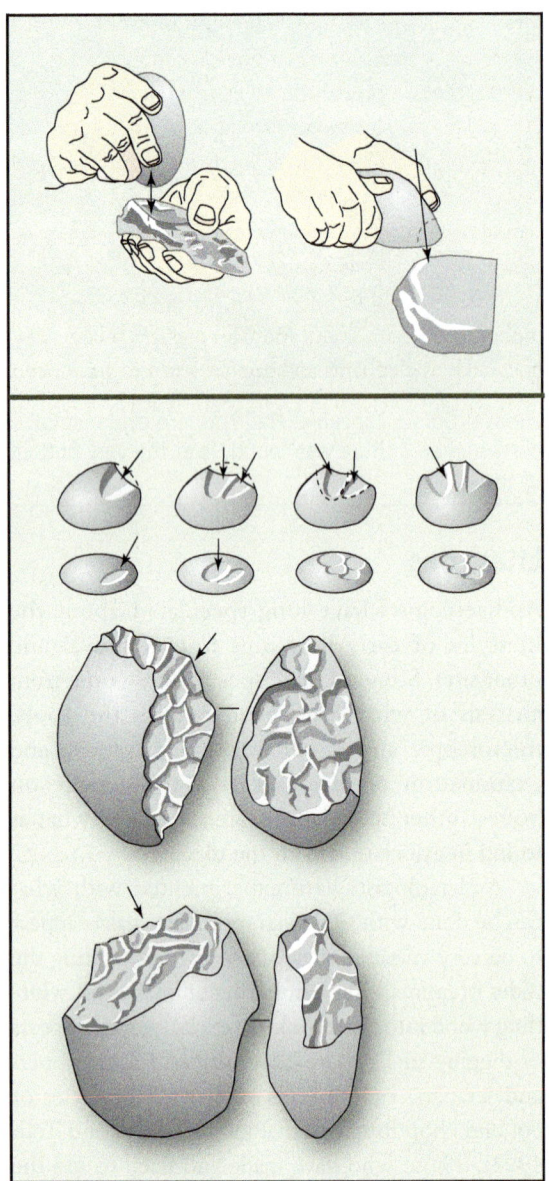

Figure 9–8 The Production of a Simple Oldowan Chopper Core and the Resultant Flakes

made of wood and bone, but these do not survive in the archaeological record. For example, present-day populations use sharp-pointed digging sticks for extracting roots and tubers from the ground; stone flakes are very effective for sharpening wood to a fine point (Schick and Toth 1994).

None of the early flaked stone tools can plausibly be thought of as weapons. So if the toolmaking hominins were hunting or defending themselves with weapons, they had to have used wooden spears, clubs, or unmodified stones as missiles. Later Oldowan tool assemblages also include stones that were flaked and battered into a rounded shape. The unmodified stones and the shaped stones might have been lethal projectiles (Isaac 1984).

Experiments may tell us what can be done with tools, but they cannot tell us what was actually done with them. Other techniques, such as microscopic analysis of the wear on tools, are more informative. Early studies focused on the microscopic scratches formed when a tool was used in different ways. Scratches parallel to the edge of a tool often occur when a tool is used in a sawing motion; perpendicular scratches suggest whittling or scraping (Whittaker 1994). Lawrence Keeley used high-powered microscopes in his experimental investigations of tools and found that different kinds of "polish" develop on tools when they are used on different materials. The polish on tools used for cutting meat is different from the polish on tools used for woodworking. On the basis of microscopic investigation of the 1.5-million-year-old tools from the eastern side of Lake Turkana, Keeley and his colleagues concluded that at least some of the early tools were probably used for cutting meat, others for cutting or whittling wood, and others for cutting plant stems (Schick and Toth 1994).

In the 1950s and 1960s, Olduvai Gorge revealed the presence of both Oldowan tools and the remains of broken bones and teeth from many different animal species. For many years it seemed plausible to assume that hominins were the hunters and the animals their prey. However, archaeologists had to re-examine this assumption with the emergence of the field of *taphonomy*, which is the study of the processes that can alter and distort a sample of bones. So, for example, flowing water can bring bones and artifacts together, which may have happened at Olduvai Gorge about 1.8 million years ago. (The area of what is now the gorge bordered the shores of a shallow lake at that time.) Also, other animals such as hyenas could have brought carcasses to some of the same places that hominins frequented. Taphonomy requires archaeologists to consider all the possible reasons that might explain why things may be found together (Speth 1998).

Regardless, there is little doubt that hominins shortly after 2 million years ago were cutting up animal carcasses for meat. Microscopic analyses show that cut marks on animal bones were unambiguously created by stone flake tools, and microscopic analyses of polish on stone tools show the polish to be consistent with butchering. We still do not know for sure whether the hominins around Olduvai Gorge were just scavenging meat (taking meat from the kills of other animals) or hunting the animals. On the basis of her analysis of cut marks on bone from Bed I in Olduvai Gorge, Pat Shipman suggested that scavenging, not hunting, was the major meat-getting activity of the hominins living there between 2 million and 1.7 million years ago. For example, the fact that cut marks made by stone tools usually (but not always) overlie teeth marks made by carnivores suggests that the hominins were often scavenging the meat of animals killed and partially eaten by non-hominin predators. The fact that the cut marks were sometimes made first, however, suggested to Shipman that the hominins were also sometimes the hunters (Szalay 1975; Shipman 1986). On the other hand, prior cut marks may indicate only that the hominins scavenged before carnivores had a chance to.

The artifact and animal remains from Bed I and the lower part of Bed II at Olduvai suggest a few other things about the lifestyles of the hominins there. First, it seems that the hominins moved around during the year; most of the sites in what is now the Olduvai Gorge appear to have been used only in the dry season, as indicated by an analysis of the kinds of animal bones found there (Speth and Davis 1976). Second, whether the early Olduvai hominins were hunters or scavengers, they apparently exploited a wide range of animals. Although most of the bones are from medium-sized antelopes and wild pigs, even large animals such as elephants and giraffes seem to have been eaten (Isaac 1971). It is clear, then, that the Olduvai hominins scavenged or hunted for meat, but we cannot tell yet how important meat was in their diet.

There is also no consensus yet about how to characterize the Olduvai sites. In the 1970s, there was a tendency to think of these sites (which contain tools and animal bones) as home bases to which hominins (presumably male) brought meat to share with others (presumably nursing mothers and young children). Indeed, Mary Leakey identified two locations where she thought early hominins had built simple structures (see Figure 9–9). One was a stone circle that she suggested formed the base of a small brush windbreak.

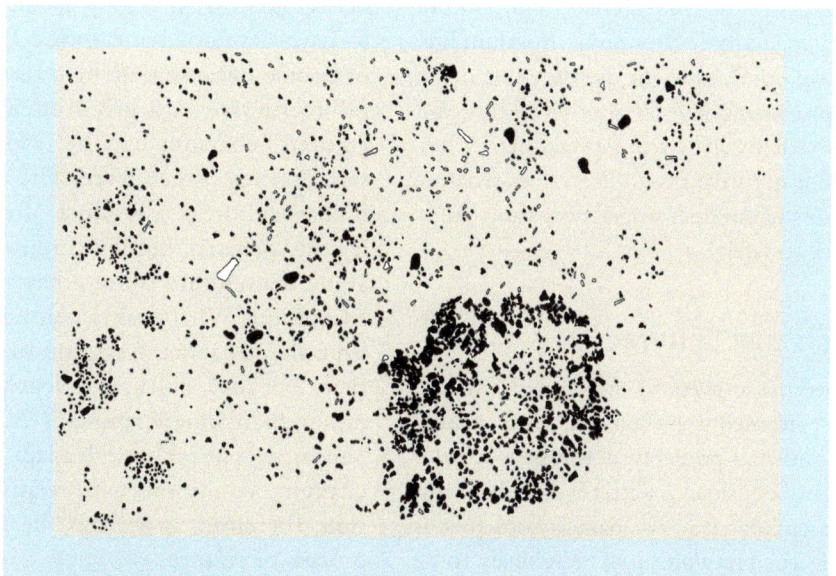

Figure 9–9 Olduvai "Hut"

A ring of stones and bones found in Bed I of Olduvai Gorge that Mary Leakey interpreted as the remains of an ancient hut.

The other was a circular area of dense debris surrounded by an area virtually without debris. Leakey suggested that the area lacking debris may represent the location of a ring of thorny brush with which early hominins surrounded their campsite in order to keep out predators—much like pastoralists living in the region do today (Leakey 1971). But archaeologists today are not so sure that these sites were home bases. For one thing, carnivores also frequented these sites. Places with meaty bones lying around may not have been so safe for hominins to use as home bases. Second, the animal remains at the sites had not been completely dismembered and butchered. If the sites had been hominin home bases, we would expect more complete processing of carcasses (Potts 1988).

If these sites were not home bases, what were they? Some archaeologists are beginning to think that these early sites with many animal bones and tools may just have been places where hominins processed food but did not live. Why would the hominins return to a particular site? Richard Potts suggested one possible reason—that hominins left caches of stone tools and stones for toolmaking at various locations to facilitate their food-collecting and food-processing activities (Potts 1988). Future research may tell us more about early hominin life. Did they have home bases, or did they just move from one processing site to another? How did they protect themselves from predators? They apparently did not have fire to keep the predators away. Did they climb trees to get away from predators or to sleep safely?

Stone Tools and Culture

Regardless of the answers to these questions, the presence of patterned stone tools means that these early hominins had probably developed culture. Archaeologists consider a pattern of behaviour, such as a particular way to make a tool that is shared and learned by a group of individuals, to be a sign of cultural behaviour. To be sure, toolmaking does not imply that early humans had anything like the complex cultures of humans today. Chimpanzees have patterns of tool use and toolmaking that appear to be shared and learned, but they do not have that much in the way of cultural behaviour.

What exactly makes human culture so different from other forms of animal behaviour? Anthropologists have spent more than a century trying to answer this question, and there is still no widely accepted answer. One thing is clear, however. Culture must be understood as a set of interrelated processes, not as a thing (Wolf 1984). What are the processes that make up culture? Let's consider some of the more important ones.

First, culture is learned and shared. That is the fundamental difference between culture and most other forms of animal behaviour. Culture is not a set of innate behaviours but rather a set of learned ones. Culture is something individuals acquire during their lifetimes as they mature and interact with others. Interaction is key here, because not only are cultural behaviours learned, they are learned through interaction with others and through education and shared experiences. Culture, then, is a social process, not an individual one.

Second, culture is generally adaptive. What this means is that most of the learned and shared behaviours that make up a culture are thought to have developed and spread through a group of people because they help that group of people to survive in a given environment. Thus, cultural behaviour may be favoured by natural selection just as genes are. The extent to which human culture is a product of natural selection is hotly debated, but few anthropologists would argue that culture is not a key aspect of human adaptation. What makes culture quite different from the behavioural systems of other animals is that, because culture is learned and shared rather than innate, humans can develop new behaviours quickly and adapt to diverse and changing conditions with relative ease. Adaptation, therefore, is perhaps the most significant process of culture.

Change is the third major process of culture, for culture is always changing. Culture change regularly occurs as new and beneficial means of adaptation are developed and shared. However, anthropologists also assume that when new behaviours are developed, they tend to become integrated within existing behaviours. That is, new behaviours that conflict with established ones may lead to one or the other changing. For example, a group of early humans could not have both scavenged meat and, at the same time, prohibited eating meat that they themselves did not kill. Such a situation would create a contradiction, and something would have to change. Working out contradictions between new, highly beneficial behaviours and established but less beneficial behaviours may be one of the reasons that cultures are so dynamic.

It seems clear that early hominins, like other primates, were social beings. It also seems clear from the archaeological record that early hominins were making and using stone tools. Tools are frequently found in discrete concentrations, and often in association with animal bones and other debris from activity. As has already been suggested, therefore, these concentrations may reflect campsites or small shelters, implying that home bases may have been a part of early hominin culture.

Whether they reflect home bases or not, these accumulations of tools and other artifacts suggest that the areas were being used by groups of individuals over periods of time. In such a situation, sharing of food is very likely. It seems counterintuitive to think that individuals would have purposely brought food to a common location only to keep it to themselves. While this is only speculation, it does not seem unreasonable to think that closely related individuals, such as families, would be more likely to associate and share food with one another than more distantly related individuals. This speculation is supported by the fact that when food-sharing takes place among chimpanzees it is usually among closely related individuals (Boyd and Silk 2000). Thus, the ancient locations of early hominin social activity may be evidence for family groups. If early *Homo* had home bases and families, those characteristics could have encouraged the development of learned and shared behaviours—in other words, culture. While we don't know for sure, such social activity is consistent with the archaeological record (Gowlett 2008).

Language

As discussed briefly in Chapter 7, the evidence for language capabilities among hominins comes from skeletal evidence like the increased flexion of the basicranium. Other evidence comes from endocasts that can give us clues as to the structure of the brain. Through the reconstruction of the skeletal anatomy associated with language in hominins, australopithecines appear to have had ape-like anatomy and brains that resemble the living apes in both size and external form—thus, there is no apparent evidence for spoken language (Lieberman 2002). Similarly, there is no strong evidence in support of language capabilities for *H. habilis*, with the exception of a 2-million-year-old endocast that shows a more developed frontal lobe and Broca's area—the area that is responsible for human speech (Tobias 1987).

However, some have argued that bipedalism, which allowed for the freeing of the hands, may have also provided the ability for increased communication by gestures among the earliest hominins—to a much greater extent than non-human primates (Corballis 1999). Merlin Donald, a researcher in the Department of Psychology at Queen's University, suggested that early forms of communication involved the whole body rather than just the hands and arms. There is debate about whether this form of "body language" is distinct from language proper, or whether it is a precursor to the development of spoken language (Corballis 1999). The earliest hominins appear not to have developed spoken language capabilities, although there may be evidence for selection favouring those features that would be important for spoken language in later hominins.

In the next chapter we will discuss the appearance of *H. erectus*, the first hominin to leave Africa, and early *H. sapiens* populations, including Neandertals.

SUMMARY AND REVIEW

TRENDS IN HOMININ EVOLUTION

9.1 Identify the main trends in hominin evolution.

- Physical changes in early hominins that led to the evolution of our genus, *Homo*, include the expansion of the brain, the widening of the female pelvis to allow birth of bigger-brained babies, and the reduction of the face, teeth, and jaws.
- Increased brain size may be linked to the emergence of stone toolmaking and to life in complex social groups. Expansion of the brain and reduction of the face occurred at about the same time and were probably related.

What factors may have led to the evolution of bipedalism in hominins?

THE TRANSITION TO HOMININS

9.2 Describe the fossils that chronicle the transition from hominoids to hominins.

- The fossil record between 8 and 6 million years ago is relatively sparse, making it difficult to pinpoint the transition from hominoids to hominins.
- Transitional species, and possibly the first hominins, include *Sahelanthropus* (7 million years ago), *Orrorin* (5.8 to 6 million years ago), and *Ardipithecus* (5.8 to 4.4 million years ago).
- At least six later species of early hominins have been classified into two types: australopithecines and paranthropoids. The number of suggested species for each type indicates that diversity was prevalent after 4 million years ago, perhaps reflecting an adaptive radiation (a dispersal and then divergence) resulting from adaptations of bipedal hominins to dynamic environmental conditions.

A. anamensis

- Likely ancestral to *A. afarensis*.
- Has a shallow, U-shaped palate and large back (anterior) teeth.
- New (derived) features include a smaller canine crown, thick enamel, and adaptations toward bipedalism.

A. afarensis

- More derived features than *A. anamensis* and may be ancestral to later *Australopithecus* (*A. africanus*, *A. sediba*, *A. bahrelghazali*, *A. garhi*).
- Retains cranial crest, prognathic face, U-shaped palate, large back teeth, curved fingers, long arms, wide pelvis, and short legs.
- New (derived) features involve changes in teeth (canine size and root, smaller back teeth, larger front teeth) and bipedal features of postcranial skeleton.

A. africanus

- Many more derived features (no cranial crest, change in base of cranium, more parabolic-shaped dental arcade) but postcranium much like *A. afarensis*.
- May have a unique relationship to *Paranthropus* and/or *Homo*.

A. sediba

- Small body and brain, and long arms.
- Broad braincase, less robust facial features, and many features of pelvis are like *Homo*.
- Discoverers propose it may be ancestral to *Homo* or even *H. erectus*

Paranthropus

- Once thought to be a robust line of australopithecines. An evolutionary dead end.
- *P. aethiopicus* and *P. robustus* in East Africa and *P. boisei* in South Africa have larger teeth and jaws and are more muscular than australopithecines.

- Teeth and jaws adapted for higher bite force allowed them to eat tougher foods.

 *What skeletal evidence indicates that australopithecines were capable of climbing and moving in trees?*

ONE MODEL OF HUMAN EVOLUTION

9.3 Explain one model of the evolutionary relationships among hominins.

- The last common ancestor of our genus *Homo* was likely one of the australopithecines.
- Paranthropoids appear to represent an evolutionary lineage of hominins that became extinct about a million years ago.

 *What is the widely agreed-upon relationship between* **Homo habilis** *and modern humans?*

EARLY SPECIES OF *HOMO*

9.4 Describe the evidence for the early species of the genus *Homo*.

- Members of *Homo* have larger brains and bodies and smaller teeth and jaws than *Australopithecus* and other early hominins.
- Early *Homo* are sometimes divided into smaller- and larger-brained groups: the smaller is *H. habilis* (630–640 cc); the larger, *H. rudolfensis* (a third larger than *H. habilis*).
- Both groups are found in East and South Africa from 1.9 to 1.4 million years ago.
- *H. habilis* is associated with Oldowan tool industry.
- They scavenged for meat or possibly hunted small animals. The evolution of cultural behaviour also seems to have played a role in the physical changes seen in early *Homo*.

 *What postcranial changes in* **Homo** *would have been associated with their increased brain size?*

EARLY HOMININ CULTURES

9.5 Describe the tools, lifestyle, and language abilities of early hominins.

- The earliest identifiable stone tools found come from East Africa and date from about 2.5 million years ago but reveal little information about culture.
- Among later tools from Olduvai beds in Tanzania, flake tools predominate, but choppers are also common. These early stone tools are referred to as Oldowan.
- Archaeologists have found sites dating to about 2 million years ago with concentrations of stone tools and animal bones. Archaeologists have shown that Oldowan tools can be used for cutting hides, dismembering animals, whittling wood, and cutting branches.
- Hominins were likely cutting up animal carcasses shortly after 2 million years ago. Most sites in Olduvai Gorge appear to have been home bases or food-processing places.
- The presence of patterned stone tools and possible home bases suggests that early hominins had culture—a dynamic, adaptive process of learned, shared, and integrated behaviours and ideas.
- The early *Homo* brain was almost one-third larger than the australopithecine brain. Brain expansion may have required reduced maturity at birth and prolonged infant dependency, likely influencing cultural evolution.
- There is no strong fossil support that provides evidence for language in *H. habilis*.

 *How can we gain insights into language capabilities among hominins from skeletal remains?*

THINK ON IT

1. How could there have been more than one species of hominin living in East Africa at the same time?
2. What may have enabled australopithecines to survive in the face of many ground predators?
3. What differentiates human culture from other forms of animal behaviour?
4. What is the evidence for language among the earliest hominins?
5. What do palaeoanthropologists agree upon about hominin evolution?

Homo erectus and Archaic Homo sapiens

10

Tom McHugh/Science Source

LEARNING OBJECTIVES

10.1 Explain when and where *Homo erectus* evolved.

10.2 Describe the tool technologies associated with the Lower Palaeolithic.

10.3 Discuss the anatomical characteristics of the Neandertals and the relationship between Neandertals and *Homo sapiens*.

10.4 Describe the features of Middle Palaeolithic cultures.

In this chapter, we examine the expansion of early Palaeolithic populations out of Africa and their transition to Middle Palaeolithic Archaic *Homo sapiens*. The fossil remains of all hominins more than 2 million years old were found only in Africa. With the emergence of *Homo erectus*, we see the movement of hominin populations off the African continent. *Homo erectus* flourished in Africa, Europe, and Asia from over 1.5 million years ago.

In the Middle Palaeolithic we see changes in the fossil evidence that reflect the emergence of Archaic *Homo sapiens*. This chapter discusses the evidence and controversies surrounding this transition. Evidence shows that toolmaking skills became more sophisticated; hominins now cooked their foods and lived in caves and campsites. The first signs of funeral rituals and altruism appear in the archaeological record. The chapter ends with consideration of the relationship between Neandertals and modern humans.

Homo erectus

Homo erectus is the first hominin to be found outside of Africa, with fossil specimens found in both Europe and Asia, dating to about 2 million years ago. Prior to the emergence of *Homo erectus*, neither *Homo habilis* nor the australopithecines are known to have inhabited areas outside of the African continent. Evidence that *H. erectus* was the first hominin to leave Africa comes from a variety of finds distributed throughout the Old World (see Figure 10–1). Examples of *H. erectus* were found first in Java, later in China, and still later in Africa. Most palaeoanthropologists agree that some human ancestor moved from Africa to Asia at some point. Until recently it was assumed that it was *H. erectus* who moved, because *H. erectus* lived in East Africa about 1.6 million years ago but not until after about 1 million years ago in Asia (Rightmire 1988). Recent discoveries of *H. erectus* skulls in the Republic of Georgia have been dated to 1.7 million years ago (Gabunia et al. 2000). If these dates are

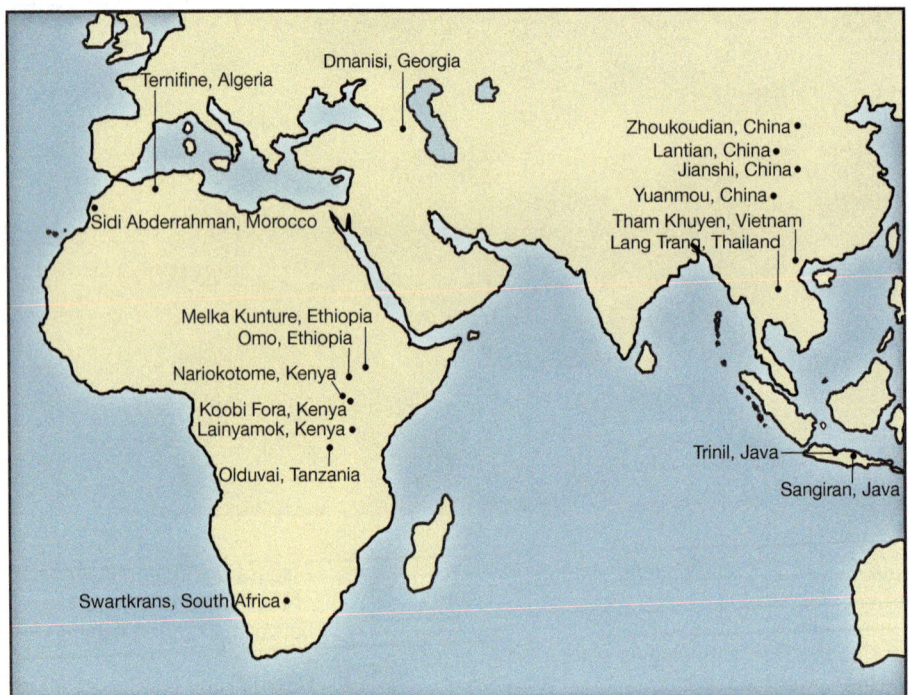

Figure 10–1 *Homo erectus* Sites

Source: Ciochon RL, Fleagle JG, editors. 1993. The human evolution source book. Englewood Cliffs, NJ: Prentice Hall. p. xi.

CURRENT RESEARCH AND ISSUES

The First Migrants

Hominins evolved in Africa, yet today hominins are found on every continent. Who were the first hominins to leave Africa, and when did they first leave? For many years the clear answer was that *Homo erectus* were the first to leave Africa, and they did so perhaps 700 000 to 1 million years ago. In recent years, new findings and sources of evidence have led scholars to question this established answer.

The first new information came from geochemist Carl Swisher, who in the mid-1990s re-dated the Java sites where *Homo erectus* fossils had been found and determined they dated to perhaps 1.8 million years ago. Since the earliest *H. erectus* fossils in Africa share a similar date, this created a problem—how did *H. erectus* appear in Java at about the same time they appeared in Africa? As this question was being pondered, a remarkable set of new *H. erectus* fossils were being uncovered in Dmanisi, Georgia. Dated at 1.7 million years ago, these fossils made it clear that *H. erectus* left Africa almost as soon as they had evolved. The discovery of a *Homo habilis*–like fossil at Dmanisi, and of Oldowan-like tools at Riwat, Pakistan, and Longgupo, China, suggested that *H. habilis* may have been the first to leave Africa and *H. erectus* followed a path their predecessors blazed. If they were following an earlier migration, it could explain how *H. erectus* were able to move so quickly across Asia.

A more unusual source of information on when hominins first left Africa comes from the parasites that accompanied them. All hominoids are plagued by lice, but humans host a distinct species, *Pediculus humanus*. Geneticist David Reed and his colleagues found that *P. humanus* diverged from other lice about 5.6 million years ago—about the time the first hominins appeared. More interesting, however, Reed and colleagues discovered that there are two subspecies of *P. humanus* that appear to have diverged about 1.2 million years ago. One subspecies is found worldwide today; the other is restricted to the New World. Reed and colleagues suggested this is evidence that at least some hominin migrants (probably *H. erectus*) became isolated in Asia by at least 1.2 million years ago, where their lice diverged from that of other hominin populations, only to be picked up much later by modern human migrants who ended up colonizing the New World.

So, who were the first hominin migrants? They may have been *H. habilis*, or they may have been very early *H. erectus*. When did the first hominin migrations out of Africa take place? Probably slightly less than 2 million years ago, but once these hominins left, they moved quickly, and they moved long distances. By 1.6 million years ago *H. erectus* was in both western and southern Asia, and by 1.2 million years ago their populations had moved far enough to have become isolated from one another. Whether or not they were the first migrants out of Africa, *H. erectus* migrated fast, far, and for life.

Sources: Reed D, Smith V, Hammond S, Rogers A, Clayton D. 2004. Genetic analysis of lice supports direct contact between modern and archaic humans. PLoS Biology. 2(November):1972–1983.

Tattersall I. 1997. Out of Africa again . . . and again? Scientific American. 276(April): 60–68.

---

accurate, then these specimens would represent some of the earliest hominins outside of the African continent (see Current Research and Issues, "The First Migrants"). One well-preserved skull from Dmanisi has features that are reminiscent of *H. habilis*—a capacity of only about 600 cc, relatively large canines, and a relatively thick brow ridge (Gabunia et al. 2000). While the excavator classes these remains as *H. erectus*, it does make one wonder if *H. habilis* or transitional species between *H. habilis* and *H. erectus* individuals were the first to leave Africa.

Nevertheless, for reasons that still remain speculative, *H. erectus* is thought to be the first hominin to move out of Africa. As we have mentioned, all these specimens from the Old World are broadly classed as *H. erectus*. However, some suggest that the African version appears to have a larger cranial capacity and smaller facial bones. Thus, an alternative scheme has been proposed in which the African remains are classed as *Homo ergaster*, with the East Asian forms remaining *H. erectus*, and later European specimens being classed

> *Homo ergaster:* classification given by some for *Homo erectus* remains from Africa.

CURRENT RESEARCH AND ISSUES

Ancestors of the Hobbit

In 2014, a team of researchers working at Mata Menge, close to the Liang Bua site on the Indonesian island of Flores where *Homo floresiensis* was initially discovered, made some new finds. They uncovered a partial jaw, part of a skull, and six teeth belonging to three individuals. It might not seem like much, but these fossils provided new insights into the probable ancestors of *H. floresiensis*.

Using radiometric dating, the researchers arrived at an age estimate of 700 000 years for the remains. When compared with the age estimates of the previously excavated *H. floresiensis* remains and stone tools, this date suggests that these hominins inhabited Flores for hundreds of millennia.

Furthermore, analysis of the newly discovered remains indicates that the Mata Menge hominins were substantially smaller than the later Liang Bua individuals.

The age of the remains, combined with their apparently diminutive size, suggests that rather than being dwarfed by some rare disease or deformity, as has been proposed for the older *H. floresiensis* remains, small size was an established characteristic of these hominins. It also suggests that *H. floresiensis*' ancestors shrank rapidly after reaching the island from either Africa or Southeast Asia.

Alternative interpretations have been proposed. It is possible the *H. floresiensis* evolved from smaller-brained species, such as *Homo habilis* or one of the *Australopithecus* species. It has also been proposed that the partial jawbone and skull piece found at Mata Menge came from an unusually small individual. Though the discovery of these new remains provided exciting new ideas about the miniature hominins of Flores, more fossils are needed to fully unravel their evolutionary story.

Sources: Brumm A, van den Bergh GD, Storey M, Kurniawan I, Alloway BV, Setiawan R, Setiyabudi E, Grün R, Moore MW, Yurnaldi D, Puspaningrum MR. 2016. Age and context of the oldest known hominin fossils from Flores. Nature. 534:249–253.

van den Bergh GD, Yousuke K, Kurniawan I, Kono RT, Brumm A, Setiyabudi E, Aziz F, Morwood MJ. 2016. *Homo floresiensis*-like fossils from the Early Middle Pleistocene of Flores. Nature. 534:245–248.

---

as *Homo heidelbergensis*. Other palaeoanthropologists think that the finds in Europe thought to be *H. erectus* are actually early examples of *H. sapiens*, as are some of the finds in southern Africa and the Near East that were previously thought to be *H. erectus* (Rightmire 1985; Wolpoff and Nkini 2001). Kramer (1993) suggested that the variation seen in specimens of *H. erectus* was within the range expected of a single species. However, a recent analysis of 3D geometry of landmarks of the temporal bone by Terhune et al. (2007) suggested that there is more variation present within the known *Homo erectus* specimens than one might expect for a single species. Further, they argued that *Homo ergaster* specimens seem to be distinctive from other *Homo erectus* fossil specimens. This is consistent with earlier arguments by Wood and Collard (1999), who argued that *H. ergaster* represents the ancestor to the modern human lineage.

There is also the question of the recently discovered *Homo floresiensis*, a diminutive hominin that has been suggested by some to be a miniature form of *Homo erectus* which evolved only on the isolated island of Flores, Indonesia (see Current Research and Issues, "Ancestors of the Hobbit," for recent insights into the evolution of *H. floresiensis*).

The Discovery in Java and Later Finds

In 1891, Eugène Dubois, a Dutch anatomist digging in Java, found what he called *Pithecanthropus erectus*, meaning "erect ape man." (We now refer to this hominin as *Homo erectus*.) The discovery was not the first human-like fossil found; Neandertals, which we discuss later in the chapter, were known many years earlier. However, no one was certain, not even Dubois himself, whether the fossil he found in Java represented an ape or a human.

The actual find consisted of a cranium and a thigh bone. For many years it was thought that the fragments were not even from the same animal. The skull was too large to be that of a modern ape but was smaller than that of an average human, having a cranial capacity between the average ape's 500 cc and the average modern human's 1300 cc or more. The thigh bone, however, matched that of a modern human. Did the two fragments in fact belong together? The question was resolved many years later by fluorine analysis. As mentioned in Chapter 2, if fossils from the same deposit contain the same amount of fluorine, they are the same age. The skull fragment and thigh bone found by Dubois were tested for fluorine content and found to be the same age.

A discovery by G.H.R. von Koenigswald in the mid-1930s, also in Java, not only confirmed Dubois's earlier speculations and extended our knowledge of the physical characteristics of *H. erectus* but also gave us a better understanding of this early human's place in time. Since then, many more *H. erectus* fossils have been found in Java. However, dating of *H. erectus* remains in Java is unclear, with estimates from more than 1 million years old (Rightmire 1990; Swisher et al. 1994) to less than 55 000 years old (Swisher et al. 1996).

Between the times of Dubois's and von Koenigswald's discoveries, Davidson Black, a Canadian anatomy professor teaching in Peking (now Beijing), China, set out to investigate a large cave at nearby Zhoukoudian where a fossilized tooth had been found. Davidson Black was born in Toronto in 1884. He obtained a medical degree in 1906 from the University of Toronto, after which he studied comparative anatomy and began working as an anatomy instructor in 1909. In 1919 Black accepted an invitation to work at the Peking Union Medical College in China. At that time, it was widely believed that the earliest humans evolved in Asia, and Black saw the position as an opportunity to search for early human ancestors. He searched unsuccessfully for the remains of early hominins in northern China, and later in Thailand. However, in 1926, while planning a journey to central Asia, he heard of two human fossil teeth that had been found near Peking. In 1927, with the aid of the Rockefeller Foundation, he began a large excavation there.

Confident that the tooth came from a hitherto unknown hominin genus, he obtained funds to excavate the area extensively. In 1927, Birger Bohlin, a member of Black's team, discovered another fossil hominin tooth at Dragon Bone Hill in Zhoukoudian, 48 kilometres from Beijing. He recognized immediately the evolutionary importance of the specimen, from which he inferred the existence of a previously unknown hominin genus and species—*Sinanthropus pekinensis*. While Black was travelling in 1928 trying to convince others of the find's validity, a portion of lower jaw with three teeth in place was found. Finally, in 1929, Black got the evidence he was looking for when the first "Peking Man" skull was discovered. A second skull was also discovered in 1929, but only recognized in 1930. Later excavations yielded 14 skullcaps, several mandibles, facial bones and limb bones, and the teeth of about 40 individuals. The Zhoukoudian hominin fossils are dated to the Middle Pleistocene, from about 900 000 to 130 000 years ago, although a more exact date has not been determined. Black died in 1934, and his work was carried on by Franz Weidenreich. Dubois never acknowledged the relationship between the *H. erectus* finds from Java and those from China.

It was not until the 1950s that *H. erectus* fossils were uncovered in northern Africa. Many finds since then have come from East Africa, particularly from two sites—Olduvai Gorge in Tanzania and the Lake Turkana region of Kenya. An almost complete skeleton of a boy was found at Nariokotome, on the western side of Lake Turkana, dating from about 1.6 million years ago. The Olduvai finds are from about 1.2 million years ago (Rightmire 2000).

The oldest known specimen of *H. erectus*, KNM-ER 3733, is a cranium found by Richard Leakey in 1975 on the shore of Lake Turkana, Kenya, that dates to about 1.78 million years ago (Feder and Park 1997:241). The specimen, with pronounced brow ridges and a *sagittal keel* (a pronounced flattening of the skull toward the midline) has a cranial capacity of about 850 cc. Leakey later found a similar specimen named KNM-ER 3883. It is somewhat less complete, being slightly more rugged in appearance and with a slightly smaller cranial capacity. It has been suggested that 3883 is a male and 3733 is a female (Tobias 1994; Feder and Park 1997).

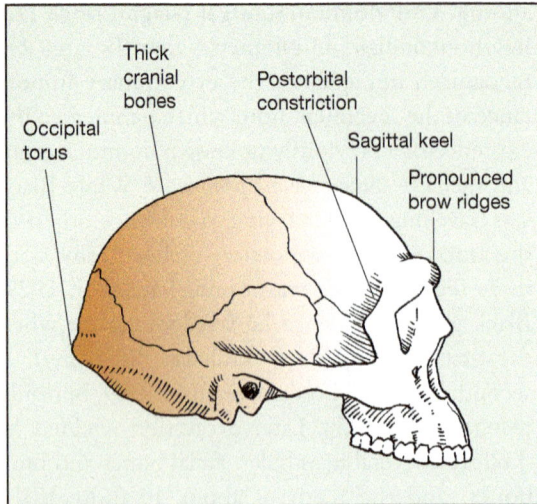

Figure 10–2
Homo erectus Features

Physical Characteristics of *Homo erectus*

The *H. erectus* skull generally is long, low, and thickly walled, with a flat frontal area and prominent brow ridges. It has a pronounced **sagittal keel** running along the crest of the skull. There is also a ridge of bone running horizontally along the back of the skull called the **occipital torus**, which adds to the skull's overall long shape (see Figure 10–2).

Compared with *H. habilis*, *H. erectus* had relatively small teeth. *H. erectus* was the first hominin to have third molars that were smaller than the second or first molars, as in modern humans. The molars also had an enlarged pulp cavity, called **taurodontism**, which may have allowed teeth to withstand harder use and wear than the teeth of modern humans. However, the *H. erectus* jaw was lighter and thinner than in either early *Homo* or the australopithecines, and the face was less **prognathic**, or forward thrusting, in the upper and lower jaw.

The brain, averaging 895 cc to 1040 cc, was larger than that found in any of the australopithecines or *H. habilis* but smaller than the average brain of a modern human (Tobias 1994; Rightmire 2000). While the increased brain size could be related to an increase in overall body size, the skull was proportioned differently—suggesting that the brain, too, was structured differently than the *H. habilis* brain.

Homo erectus had a prominent, projecting nose, in contrast to the australopithecines' flat, nonprojecting noses (Franciscus and Trinkaus 1988). From the neck down, *H. erectus* was practically indistinguishable from *H. sapiens*, although the *femoral cortex*—the thick dense bone that forms the shaft of the thigh bone—is very thick. In general, their ability to walk upright and manipulate objects was fully modern. In contrast to the much smaller australopithecines and *H. habilis*, who lived in East Africa around the same time, *H. erectus* was comparable to modern humans in size.

The discovery of KNM-WT 15000 by the Leakey team at Nariokotome, on the west side of Lake Turkana, is important because it is the nearly complete remains of an adolescent. The remains date to about 1.6 million years ago. At this time, the Nariokotome region was probably open grassland, with trees mostly along rivers (Feibel and Brown 1993). *Homo erectus* in East Africa was similar in size to Africans today who live in a similarly open, dry environment (Ruff and Walker 1993). Reconstruction of KNM-WT 15000 suggests that he was 1.6 metres tall when he died at between 11 and 12 years of age; the researchers estimate that he would have been 1.85 metres tall if he had lived to maturity (Brown et al. 1985). This is important because in most other animals, a 12-year-old would be fully grown. This specimen may provide evidence for a prolonged developmental period in *H. erectus*. This is also supported by analyses of

---

Sagittal Keel: an inverted V-shaped ridge running along the top of the skull in *Homo erectus*.
Occipital Torus: a ridge of bone running horizontally across the back of the skull in apes and some hominins.

Taurodontism: having teeth with an enlarged pulp cavity.
Prognathic: a physical feature that is sticking out or pushed forward, such as the faces in apes and some hominin species.

H. erectus hipbones that have suggested that *H. erectus* babies would have smaller heads relative to adult brain size. The implication is that, like modern humans, *H. erectus* babies would have been more immature when they were born so as to allow the head to pass through the bipedal pelvic outlet (Bogin 1997; Nelson and Thompson 1999). The partial skull fragment of the Mojokerto (Perning I) child, discovered in Java in 1936, has been assigned to a number of taxa, but is now believed to be a juvenile *H. erectus* (Anton 1997).

Those scholars who group the African populations into a distinct species, *H. ergaster*, point to several differences between them and other *H. erectus* populations. The cranial proportions differ in *H. ergaster*; the brow ridge is thinner and is arched above each of the eye sockets; the eye sockets are more rounded; and the face is oriented more vertically.

On the other hand, some scholars believe that the differences between *H. erectus* and modern humans are not large enough to call us different species, and argue that *H. erectus* populations should be lumped into *H. sapiens* (Wolpoff et al. 1994).

Homo floresiensis

Whether or not there are distinct African and Asian species of *Homo erectus*, some scholars have suggested that *Homo floresiensis* is a distinct species that is closely related to *Homo erectus*. *H. floresiensis* has been found only on the Indonesian island of Flores, and only a handful of individuals have been located to date. All are tiny (they stood perhaps just under one metre tall) and have very small brains, on the order of 380 cc (Brown et al. 2004; Morwood et al. 2004).

How might a miniature version of *H. erectus* have evolved? The answer is that both dwarfism and gigantism are common phenomena in isolated populations. Dwarfism appears to be an adaptation that occurs when there are few predators—a species in isolation can become smaller, and have a large population, if there are no predators threatening them. This may be what happened on Flores (Wong 2005; Weston and Lister 2009). It is interesting that the island also hosted a number of dwarf species in addition to *H. floresiensis*, including a dwarf elephant that appears to have been one of the favourite foods of *H. floresiensis*. Originally it was thought that *H. floresiensis* may have survived until as recently as 12 000 years ago—well into the time period when modern humans were living in Indonesia. However, recent dating has suggested that the species went extinct by 50 000 years ago, or around the time that modern humans reached Australia (Sutikna et al. 2016). The structure of the brain seems closely related to that of *H. erectus*, as do the structures of the skull (Falk et al. 2005). In other words, *H. floresiensis* appears to be a tiny version of *H. erectus*. *H. floresiensis* even made tools that look similar to those made by *H. erectus*, and in

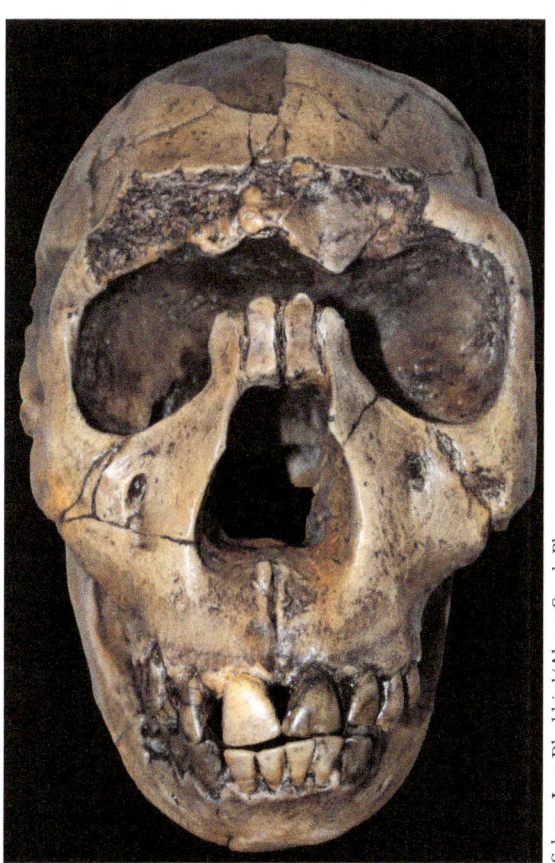

The skull of a *Homo erectus/ergaster* boy found at Nariokotome, Kenya. Though an adolescent when he died, he already stood at 1.65 metres tall.

Homo floresiensis: a distinct species closely related to *Homo erectus* and found only on the Indonesian island of Flores. They are tiny, with cranial capacities of about 380 cc.

some cases the tools look even more sophisticated. Martin and colleagues (2006), for example, suggested that the most likely explanation is that the remains represent a microcephalic *Homo sapien*. However, Matt Tocheri of Lakehead University and his colleagues examined the wrist bones of *H. floresiensis*. A 3D analysis of the wrist bones of this and other hominins clearly demonstrates the primitive nature of the wrist of *H. floresiensis* and that it does not yet possess the structures we see in an anatomically modern wrist (Tocheri et al. 2007; Orr et al. 2013). The skeleton of *H. floresiensis* is that of a biped (Brown et al. 2004; Morwood et al. 2005; Jungers et al. 2009b). However, analysis of the foot suggests a mode of bipedalism that is different from that of modern hominins (Jungers et al. 2009a).

The Evolution of *Homo erectus*

The evolution of *H. erectus* reflects a continuation of the general evolutionary trends we discussed previously. The brain continued to expand, its capacity increasing more than a third over that of the early *Homo* brain (just as the early *Homo* brain's capacity had increased more than a third over that of the australopithecines). The face, teeth, and jaws continued to shrink, moving toward a more modern form. An increasing use and variety of tools may have led to a further development of the brain. *Homo erectus* was eating and probably cooking meat, and this may have led to further reduction in the teeth and jaws.

One additional change in *H. erectus* is an apparent reduction in the extent of sexual dimorphism to almost modern levels. Recall that the australopithecines and early *Homo* were quite sexually dimorphic. *Homo erectus* does not appear to be as sexually dimorphic as these earlier hominins. What might have caused this change? In other primates, sexual dimorphism appears to be linked to social systems in which males are at the top of dominance hierarchies and dominant males control sexual access to multiple females. In contrast, lack of sexual dimorphism seems most pronounced in the few primates and other animals where *pair bonding* exists—that is, where one male and one female form a breeding pair that last for a long period of time (Fleagle 1999; Langdon 2005). Could pair bonding have developed in *H. erectus*? It seems possible.

Recall that early *Homo* may have established some of the basic elements of human culture, including home bases or meeting places, family groups, and sharing. Another basic element of recent human culture, one that is present in all known cultures, is *marriage*. Marriage is a socially recognized sexual and economic bond between two individuals that is intended to continue throughout the lifetimes of the individuals and to produce socially accepted children. It is a pair bond with a set of behaviours, expectations, and obligations that extend beyond the pair to those individuals' families. With marriage, then, the competition between males for access to females may have diminished, lessening the importance of sexual dimorphism. But why might this kind of bond have developed in *Homo erectus*?

In animal species where females can feed themselves and their babies after birth, pair bonding is rare. But in species where females cannot feed both themselves and their babies, pair bonding is common. Why? We think it is because a pair bond provides the best solution to the problem of incompatibility between a mother's feeding requirements and tending a newborn baby. A male partner can bring food and/or watch the newborn while the mother gets food (Ember and Ember 1979;

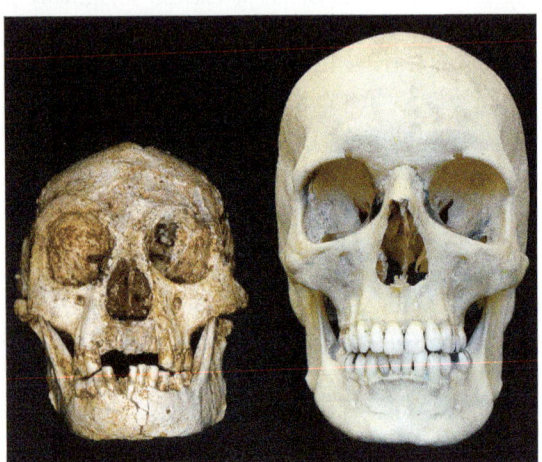

The skull of the dwarf species *Homo floresiensis* next to that of a modern human. Note how small it is in comparison.

Lovejoy 1981). But most primates lack pair bonding. This may be because primate infants are able to cling to their mother's fur soon after birth, so that the mother's hands are free to forage. Human infants demonstrate a residual form of this innate ability to cling during their first few weeks of life. This is called the *Moro reflex*. If a human infant feels it is falling backward, it will automatically stretch out its arms and clench its fists (Clayman 1989).

We have no way of knowing if *Homo erectus* had fur like other primates, but we think probably not because, as we will discuss, we think they may have worn clothing. The brain in *Homo erectus* may also have already expanded enough that *Homo erectus* infants, like modern human infants, could not adequately support their heads even if they could hold on to their mother's fur. In any case, when early hominins began to depend on scavenging and hunting for food (and for skins to be used in clothing), it would have been difficult and hazardous for a parent with a newborn baby to engage in these activities with a baby along.

Another important aspect of the evolution of *Homo erectus* was the movement of populations out of eastern and southern Africa. As with the lessening of sexual dimorphism, it seems likely that cultural innovations were the key to allowing *Homo erectus* to move into new environments. Why? Because upon entering new environments *Homo erectus* would have been faced with new (and generally colder) climatic conditions, new and different sources of raw material for tools, and new plants and animals to rely on for food. All animals adapt to such changes through natural selection, but natural selection typically takes a relatively long time and requires physical changes in the adapting organisms. *Homo erectus* was able to adapt to new environments very quickly and without apparent physical changes. This suggests that the primary mechanisms of adaptation for *Homo erectus* were cultural rather than biological.

What cultural adaptations might *Homo erectus* have made? Fire might have been the crucial cultural adaptation to colder climates. As we will discuss, there is tantalizing evidence that *Homo erectus* used fire (see Current Research and Issues, "Inside the Zhoukoudian Cave" for a discussion of the potential use of fire by *H. erectus*). But fire can only warm people when they are stationary; it doesn't help when people are out collecting food. To be mobile in colder climates, *Homo erectus* may have begun to wear animal furs for warmth. Some *Homo erectus* tools look like the hide-processing tools used by more recent human groups (Bordes 1968), and it seems unlikely that *Homo erectus* could have survived in the colder locations where they have been found, in eastern Europe and Asia, without some form of clothing. And if *Homo erectus* was wearing furs for warmth, they must have been hunting. *Homo erectus* could not have depended on scavenging to acquire skins—the skin is the first thing predators destroy when they dismember a carcass. *Homo erectus* needing skins would have had to kill fur-bearing animals themselves if they wanted intact skins and furs for clothing.

As we mentioned earlier, fossil remains themselves cannot provide evidence for whether or not *H. erectus* was hairless. But scientists have found that the genes of modern peoples may offer clues to when our ancestors became hairless. For example, one of the primary genes responsible for hair and skin colour, called MC1R, demonstrates uniformity among modern dark-skinned African populations but diversity among non-Africans. Alan Rogers and colleagues (2004) recently argued that the uniformity in this gene among Africans demonstrates recent, powerful selective pressure in favour of darker skin, and that protection against the tropical sun after the loss of body hair is the likely reason. When did this selective pressure start? Rogers and colleagues estimate it was at least 1.2 million years ago (Rogers et al. 2004).

It is interesting to consider that in eastern Africa, *Homo erectus* coexisted with at least one other species of hominin (*P. boisei*), and possibly with as many as three others (*P. boisei*, *A. africanus*, and *H. habilis/rudolfensis*). Why did *Homo erectus* survive and flourish while these other species went extinct? Again, culture may be the answer. *P. boisei* seems to have been a specialized grasslands species. Their large molars and powerful dental architecture would have

CURRENT RESEARCH AND ISSUES

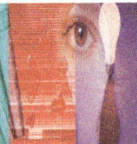

Inside the Zhoukoudian Cave

The Zhoukoudian cave site in Fangshan District, near Beijing, China, was excavated in the 1920s by Swedish geologist Johan Gunnar Andersson with several Chinese archaeologists, including the father of Chinese archaeology, Pei Wenzhong. In 1929, Pei unearthed the skullcap of Peking Man (since renamed Beijing Man), the second *Homo erectus* skull ever found.

In the following years, the multiple layers at the site produced remains from more than 40 *H. erectus pekinensis* individuals, along with stone tools and plant and animal remains. Many of these layers have since been dated, providing evidence that *H. e. pekinensis* first occupied the site more than 770 000 years ago and perhaps up until 230 000 years ago. The climate in North China 770 000 years ago would have made for cold living conditions. Tools at the site suggest that *H. e. pekinensis* was technologically advanced. But did they control fire? Charred animal bones and stones found at the site, along with possible evidence of hearths, suggest they did.

However, some analyses have cast doubt on the assertion of controlled fire at the Zhoukoudian cave site, citing the absence of siliceous aggregate (an insoluble phase of burned ash) in the ash remains recovered from the site, which calls into question whether it was in fact ash. It has been proposed that the presumed ash layers were actually sediments that had washed into the site from the surrounding hillsides. More recently, however, researchers have detected clear chemical evidence of ash from samples collected from the site, providing strong evidence that *H. e. pekinensis* did indeed control fire.

Sources: Goldberg, P, Weiner S, Bar-Yosef O, Xu Q, Liu J. 2001. Site formation processes at Zhoukoudian, China. Journal of Human Evolution. 41:483–530.

Norton CJ, Xing G. 2008. Zhoukoudian upper cave revisited. Current Anthropology. 49:732–745.

Shen G, Xing G, Bin G, Granger DE. 2009. Age of Zhoukoudian *homo erectus* determined with 26Al/10Be burial dating. Nature. 458:198–200.

Zhong M, Shi C, Gao X, Wu X, Chen F, Zhang S, Zhang X, Olsen JW. 2014. On the possible use of fire by *homo erectus* at Zhoukoudian, China. Chinese Science Bulletin. 59:335–343.

---

allowed them to eat hard grass seeds and other coarse materials that other hominins could not chew. However, they had to compete with the many other grassland animals that also relied on these plants but reproduced faster and had speed to help them escape from predators. Early *Homo* was apparently a tool user and relied at least in part on scavenging and hunting, but compared to *Homo erectus*, early *Homo* technology was crude and early *Homo* populations may not have been as well organized to scavenge and hunt and to defend themselves against predators. These differences in culture may have provided advantages to *Homo erectus* that drove early *Homo* to extinction.

This scenario, just like the one we suggested for the evolution of early *Homo*, is a "just-so" story that may or may not be true. But it does fit the facts we now have about *Homo erectus* and the area in which it evolved. Regardless of this story's particular details, there seems no doubt that the development of a more complex culture was vital to the evolution of *Homo erectus*.

Lower Palaeolithic Culture

The archaeological finds of tools and other cultural artifacts dating from 1.8 million years ago to about 200 000 years ago are assumed to have been produced by *H. erectus*. Unfortunately, fossils are not usually associated with these materials. Therefore, it is possible that some of the tools were produced by hominins other than *H. erectus*, such as *H. habilis* earlier and *H. sapiens* later. *Homo erectus* continued to use the Oldowan chopper tool technology, but also developed a more sophisticated tool tradition called **Acheulian**. The Acheulian tool assemblages

> **Acheulian:** a stone toolmaking tradition dating from 1.5 million years ago. Compared with the Oldowan tradition, Acheulian assemblages have more large tools created according to standardized designs or shapes. One of the most characteristic and prevalent tools in the Acheulian tool kit is the so-called hand axe, which is a teardrop-shaped, bifacially flaked tool with a thinned, sharp tip. Other large tools may have been cleavers and picks.

dating from 1.5 million years ago to more than a million years later are very similar to each other. *Homo erectus* is the only hominin that spans the entire period, so it is conventionally assumed that *H. erectus* was responsible for most if not all of the Acheulian tool assemblages we describe below (Phillipson 1993:57; Klein 2009: 377, 391).

The Acheulian Tool Tradition

The Acheulian stone toolmaking tradition was named after the site at St. Acheul, France, where the first examples were found. However, the oldest Acheulian tools, dating back about 1.5 million years, have been recovered from East Africa, on the Peninj River, Tanzania (Schick and Toth 1994). In contrast to Oldowan, the Acheulian tools were larger, with a set of typical designs or shapes. Oldowan tools have sharp edges, made by a few blows. Acheulian toolmakers shaped the stone by knocking more flakes off most of the edges. Many of these tools were made from very large flakes that had been struck from very large cores or boulders. One of the most characteristic and prevalent tools in the Acheulian tool kit is the so-called hand axe, which is a teardrop-shaped, bifacially flaked tool with a thinned, sharp tip. Other large tools resemble cleavers and picks. There were also many other kinds of flake tools, such as scrapers with a wide edge. Early Acheulian tools appear to have been made by blows with a hard stone, but later tools are wider and flatter and may have been made with a soft "hammer" of bone or antler (Schick and Toth 1994; Whittaker 1994). This soft hammer technique of making stone tools was an important innovation. Tools made by a hard hammer technique, rock against rock, have limits in terms of their sharpness and form, because only large and thick flakes can be made with a hard hammer technique (unless the flintknapper is very skillful and the stone being used has unique qualities). Flakes created by soft hammer flaking are much thinner and longer than hard hammer flakes, and the flintknapper generally has better control over their size and shape. This means that thinner and sharper tools can be made, as well as tools with complex shapes. Hand axes can be made with either technique, as their shape is simple, but those made using a soft hammer have much thinner and sharper edges (Bordes 1968; Whittaker 1994).

Were hand axes made for chopping trees, as their name suggests? We cannot be sure what they were used for, but experiments with Acheulian hand axes suggest that they are not good for cutting trees; they seem more suited for butchering large animals (Schick and Toth 1994; Whittaker 1994). Lawrence Keeley microscopically examined some Acheulian hand axes, and the wear on them is consistent with animal butchery. The picks may have been used for woodworking, particularly hollowing and shaping wood, and they are also good for digging (Schick and Toth 1994:260).

Acheulian tools are found widely in Africa, Europe, and western Asia, but bifacial hand axes, cleavers, and picks are not found as commonly in eastern and southeastern Asia. Because *H. erectus* has been found in all areas of the Old World, it is puzzling why the tool traditions seem to differ from west to east. Older arguments suggested differences in technological sophistication between eastern and western populations. However, some archaeologists have suggested that large bifacial tools may be lacking in eastern and southeastern Asia because *H. erectus* there had a better material for making tools—bamboo. Bamboo is used today in Southeast Asia for many purposes, including the making of

An Acheulian hand axe. Lawrence Keeley examined the edge wear on hand axes to determine how they were used.

incredibly sharp arrows and sticks for digging and cutting. Geoffrey Pope showed that bamboo is found in those areas of Asia where hand axes and other large bifacial tools are missing (Pope 1989; Ciochon et al. 1990). Recent evidence shows the presence of Acheulian hand axes over 800 000 years ago in southern China (Yamei et al. 2000).

Big-Game Eating

Some of the Acheulian sites have produced evidence of big-game eating. F. Clark Howell, who excavated sites at Torralba and Ambrona, Spain, found a substantial number of elephant remains and unmistakable evidence of human presence in the form of tools. These sites are situated strategically on two hilltops flanking a mountain pass. Howell suggested that the humans at those sites used fire to frighten elephants into muddy bogs, from which they would be unable to escape (Howell 1966). To hunt elephants in this way, the humans would have had to plan and work co-operatively in fairly large groups.

But do these finds of bones of large and medium-sized animals, in association with tools, tell us that the humans definitely were big-game hunters? Some archaeologists who have reanalyzed the evidence from Torralba think that the big game may have been scavenged. Because the Torralba and Ambrona sites are near ancient streams, many of the elephants could have died naturally, their bones accumulating in certain spots because of the flow of water (Binford 1987; Klein 1987). It is still unclear whether *H. erectus* deliberately butchered different kinds of game. While different types of tools are found with different types of animal (Freeman 1994; Klein 2009), reanalysis by Pat Shipman and Jennie Rose of the cut marks on the remains has cast new doubt on this evidence. Over 95 percent of the bones present were too poorly preserved to clearly identify stone tool cut marks. Of those that could be clearly identified, only 16 cut marks have been confirmed on four bones (Shipman and Rose 1983). Thus, whether the humans hunted big game at Torralba and Ambrona is debatable; all we can be sure of, as of now, is that they consumed big game and probably hunted smaller game.

Other sites that may represent evidence of co-operative hunting include BK II in Tanzania, which dates to at least 400 000 years ago. Here there are the remains of wild cattle that may have been driven into the swamp and then killed and butchered by *H. erectus* (Howell 1966; Butzer 1982a). At Olorgesailie in Kenya, there is possible evidence of co-operative hunting by *H. erectus*. On the lake edge at this site more than 60 individuals of extinct baboons have been excavated. K/Ar dates for this site suggest it may be as old as 700 000 to 900 000 years (Isaac 1977). It is worth noting that these are not the savannah baboons with which we are familiar today, but rather an extinct "giant" baboon, *Theropithecus oswaldi*, which could be as big as a female gorilla. Given an animal of this size and power, the argument for some sort of co-operative hunting is strengthened that much more. At both these sites the animal remains have been excavated in association with cobbles and stone tools.

Control of Fire

Because *H. erectus* was the first hominin to be found throughout the Old World and in areas with freezing winters, most anthropologists presume that *H. erectus* had learned to control fire, at least for warmth. There is archaeological evidence of fire in some early sites, but fires can be natural events. Thus, whether fire was under deliberate control by *H. erectus* is difficult to establish.

Suggestive but not conclusive evidence of the deliberate use of fire comes from Wonderwerk Cave in South Africa, dated to over 1.7 million years ago (Beaumont 2011), and from the Swartkans cave in South Africa, dated to between 1.5 and 1 million years ago (Brain and Sillen 1988). Possible evidence of human control of fire, dating from nearly 500 000 years ago, comes from the cave at Zhoukoudian in China where *H. erectus* fossils have been found (Klein 1989:171). In that cave are thousands of splintered and charred animal bones, apparently the remains of meals. There are also layers of ash, suggesting human control of fire. But recent analysis raises questions about these finds. The most serious problem is that human remains, tools, and ash rarely occur together in the same layers. In addition, there are no hearths at the Zhoukoudian site. Fires can spontaneously occur with heavy accumulation of organic matter, so clear evidence of human control of fire is still not definitely attested. Even the inference that humans brought the animals to the cave for butchering is only possibly a correct guess. Throughout the cave there is evidence of hyenas and wolves, and they, not the humans, may have brought many of the animal parts to the cave (Binford and Ho 1985).

More persuasive evidence of human control of fire, dating from nearly 800 000 years ago, comes from the site of Gesher Benot Ya'aqov in Israel. Here researchers found evidence of burned seeds, wood, and stone, as well as concentrations of burned items suggestive of hearths (Goren-Inbar et al. 2004; Alperson-Afil et al. 2009).

Better evidence of the deliberate use of fire comes from Europe somewhat later. Unfortunately, the evidence of control of fire at these European sites is not associated with *H. erectus* fossils either, so the link between deliberate use of fire and *H. erectus* cannot be definitely established yet (Binford and Ho 1985). The lack of clear evidence does not, of course, mean that *H. erectus* did not use fire. After all, *H. erectus* did move into cold areas of the world, and it is hard to imagine how that could have happened without the deliberate use of fire. Such a move is also hard to imagine if *H. erectus* were relatively hairless and did not get warm skins and furs from hunting.

Clothing, therefore, may have been necessary, but fire might have been even more important, and not only for warmth. Cooking would be possible. The control of fire was a major step in increasing the energy under human control. Cooking made all kinds of food (not just meat) more safely digestible and therefore more usable (Leonard 2002; Wrangham 2009). Fires would also have kept predators away, a not inconsiderable advantage given that there were a lot of them around.

Campsites

Acheulian sites were usually located close to water sources, lush vegetation, and large stocks of herbivorous animals. Some camps have been found in caves, but most were in open areas surrounded by rudimentary fortifications or windbreaks. Several African sites are marked by stony rubble brought there by *H. erectus*, possibly for the dual purpose of securing the windbreaks and providing ammunition in case of a sudden attack (Clark 1970).

The presumed base campsites display a variety of tools, indicating that the camps were the centre

Homo erectus ate—and probably hunted—large game animals, and probably also learned to control fire.

of many group functions. More specialized sites away from camp have also been found. These are marked by the predominance of a particular type of tool. For example, a butchering site in Tanzania contained dismembered hippopotamus carcasses and rare heavy-duty smashing and cutting tools. What appear to have been workshops are another kind of specialized site encountered with some regularity. They are characterized by tool debris and are located close to a source of natural stone suitable for toolmaking (Clark 1970).

A camp has been excavated at the Terra Amata site near Nice, on the French Riviera. The camp appears to have been occupied in late spring or early summer, judging by the pollen found in fossilized human feces. The excavator described stake holes driven into the sand, associated with parallel lines of stones, presumably marking the spots where the people constructed huts of roughly 4.5 metres by 9 metres (see Figure 10–3). A basic feature of each hut was a central hearth that seems to have been protected from drafts by a small wall built just outside the northeast corner of the hearth. The evidence suggests that the Terra Amata occupants gathered seafood such as oysters and mussels, did some fishing, and hunted in the surrounding area. The animal remains suggest that they obtained both small and large animals, but mostly got the young of larger animals such as stags, elephants, boars, rhinoceroses, and wild oxen. Some of the huts contain recognizable toolmakers' areas, scattered with tool debris; occasionally, the impression of an animal skin shows where the toolmaker actually sat (de Lumley 1969). The site at Terra Amata, which is geologically dated between 400 000 and 200 000 years ago, has been interpreted as possibly one of the earliest identified hominin shelters (de Lumley 1969).

Religion and Ritual

Did *H. erectus* take part in rituals? Did *H. erectus* have religion? The data we have to answer these questions are limited, but there are some hints that ritual may have been part of Lower Palaeolithic culture.

Figure 10–3 A Reconstruction of the Oval Huts Built at Terra Amata
These huts were approximately 4.5 metres by 9 metres.

Source: Illustrations by Eric Mose, Copyright © 1969

Remains of red ochre (oxidized clay) have been found on a number of Lower Palaeolithic sites (Dickson 1990; Klein 2009). This may be significant because in many later cultures, even modern ones, red ochre has been used in rituals of various types to represent blood, or more generally, life. Ochre seems to be particularly important in burial rituals, and human remains sprinkled with red ochre have been found in many parts of the world and dating back as far as the Middle Palaeolithic (about 200 000 years ago). However, there is no evidence to suggest that *H. erectus* buried their dead, nor any evidence that red ochre was used in rituals. It may have been used for body decoration, or simply for protection against insects or sunburn.

More significant, and even more controversial, is the suggestion made by the excavators of Zhoukoudian in northern China that some of the *H. erectus* remains there showed evidence of ritual cannibalism (Dickson 1990; Tattersall and Schwartz 2000). The foramen magnum of some specimens had been deliberately enlarged and the facial bones had been deliberately broken away from the cranium on others. A possible reason may have been to remove the brain for ritual consumption. Ritual cannibalism has been widely reported among living peoples, so its presence among ancient peoples is not impossible. But scholars have pointed out that the parts of the skull that seem to have been purposely enlarged to remove the brain are those that are also the weakest points of the skull, and may have broken away because of decay or disturbance over time. Therefore, at this time we cannot say with any certainty what role, if any, religion or ritual played in Lower Palaeolithic culture.

Language

We use the same skeletal evidence to determine whether *H. erectus* had developed language that we used to examine language development in earlier hominins. As noted earlier, while an increased cranial capacity in *H. erectus* could be related to an increase in overall body size, it appears that the skull was proportioned differently than in earlier hominins. This suggests a remodelling of the brain, in particular the differential growth of the frontal and posterior portion of the brain. In other words, the *H. erectus* brain is more similar in form to the modern brain. Analysis of endocasts of *H. erectus* specimens from Ngandong and Sangiran in Java suggested that hemispheric specialization—the idea that the right and left halves of the brain control different aspects of behaviour, as in modern humans—is present in *H. erectus* (Holloway 1980, 1981). This was interpreted by some to suggest that by 1.7 million years ago *H. erectus* would have possessed linguistic skills and the ability to manipulate symbols (Holloway 1980, 1981). MacLarnon and Hewitt (2004) suggested that *H. erectus* did not have anatomical evidence in support of the level of breath control seen in modern humans, and would therefore have had quite restricted speech capabilities. Other evidence from the basicranial remains of *H. erectus* supports a capability for language. It is suggested that *H. erectus* had the ability for language at the level of a modern 6-year-old (Laitman and Heimbuch 1984). However, recent studies of the Mojokerto child suggested some differences. Balzeau and colleagues' (2005) study of the Mojokerto endocast suggested that there are differences in development of the frontal lobes. Coqueugniot and co-workers (2004) suggested that the relative brain development of the specimen is more like that of apes than modern humans, and therefore the cognitive abilities of *H. erectus* were not the same as *H. sapiens*. Recent reanalyses of the cranial growth of *Homo erectus* by O'Connell and DeSilva suggested that the Mojokerto individual falls between the chimpanzee and human developmental averages (though within the range of both species), and thus *H. erectus* represents an important step in brain evolution from apes to humans (O'Connell and DeSilva 2013).

Archaic *Homo sapiens*

The cultures of early hominins are traditionally classified as Lower Palaeolithic or early Stone Age. In this section we discuss the fossil evidence as well as the controversies about the transition from *H. erectus* to Archaic *Homo sapiens*, which may have begun 500 000 years ago. We also discuss what we know archaeologically about Middle Palaeolithic cultures of the early *H. sapiens* that lived between about 300 000 and 40 000 years ago.

Most palaeoanthropologists agree that *H. erectus* evolved into *H. sapiens*, but they disagree about how and where the transition occurred. There is also disagreement about how to classify some fossils from 400 000 to about 200 000 years ago that have a mix of *H. erectus* and *H. sapiens* traits (Stringer 1985). A particular fossil might be called *H. erectus* by some anthropologists and "Archaic" *Homo sapiens* by others. As we shall see, still other anthropologists see so much continuity between *H. erectus* and *H. sapiens* that they think it is completely arbitrary to call them different species. According to these anthropologists, *H. erectus* and *H. sapiens* may just be earlier and later varieties of the same species and therefore all should be called *H. sapiens*. (*Homo erectus* would then be *H. sapiens erectus*.)

There seems to be a fair degree of homogeneity in *H. erectus* specimens, both geographically and temporally, over the 1 million years or so of their successful existence. While there are regular anatomical changes over time, like a reduction in the size of the rear teeth, an associated decrease in the size of the face and lower jaw, and an increase in incisor size, other features remain relatively constant. Similarly, there is also a small increase in cranial capacity over time, but for the most part, even this feature is relatively consistent. Archaeologically, the Acheulian tool kit also seems to remain relatively consistent over time, although later hand axes do appear to be more refined than earlier ones. However, around 400 000 years ago there is a substantial increase in cranial capacity in the fossil hominin record. These new specimens are classed as early *Homo sapiens*. These early *H. sapiens* are not exactly like anatomically modern humans, so they are distinguished as **Archaic *Homo sapiens***. While modern people are classed in the subspecies *sapiens* (that is, ***Homo sapiens sapiens***), Archaic *H. sapiens* are believed to represent one or several ancient and extinct subspecies.

Archaic *H. sapiens* fossils have been found in Africa, Europe, and Asia. In recent years some scholars have suggested that the "transitional" fossils share common traits and may actually represent a separate species—***Homo heidelbergensis***, named after a jaw found in 1907 in the village of Mauer near Heidelberg, Germany (Rightmire 1998; Fleagle 1999). For example, a specimen from the Broken Hill mine in Zambia, Africa, dates from about 200 000 years ago. Its mixed traits include a cranial capacity of over 1200 cc (well within the range of modern *H. sapiens*), together with a low forehead and large brow ridges, which are characteristic of earlier *H. erectus* specimens (Rightmire 1984:303). The most extensive collection of fossil remains from a single site comes from Atapuerca, Spain (Arsuaga et al. 1993; Bermúdez de Castro and Nicolás 1997). Other fossils with mixed traits have been found at Bodo, Hopefield, Ndutu, Elandsfontein, and Rabat in Africa; Heidelberg, Bilzingsleben, Petralona, Arago, Steinheim, and Swanscombe in Europe; and Dali and Solo in Asia. New evidence from the site of Atapuerca, dating to over 750 000 years ago, has been used to propose a new species, ***Homo antecessor***, that represents the last common ancestor to Neandertals and modern humans (Bermúdez de Castro et al. 1997; Arsuaga et al. 1999; Carretero et al. 1999). Somewhat older remains from Ceprano, Italy, have also been suggestive of a transition between *H. erectus* and later *H. heidelbergensis* (Manzi et al. 2001). Most recently, Lee Berger and colleagues (2015; Dirks et al. 2015) reported on a new species of extinct hominid from South Africa, *Homo naledi*. While the fossils have yet to be dated, they represent an interesting combination of skeletal features. Its postcranial body is similar to that of a small-bodied human (Berger et al. 2015), though its cranial

---

Archaic *Homo sapiens*: specimens of early *Homo sapiens* that are not exactly like anatomically modern humans are distinguished as Archaic *Homo sapiens*. Neandertals are a specific group of Archaic *Homo sapiens*.

***Homo sapiens sapiens*:** modern-looking humans, undisputed examples of which appeared about 50 000 years ago; may have appeared earlier.

***Homo heidelbergensis*:** classification given by some for *Homo erectus* remains from Europe.

***Homo antecessor*:** a proposed last common ancestor between Neandertals and modern humans.

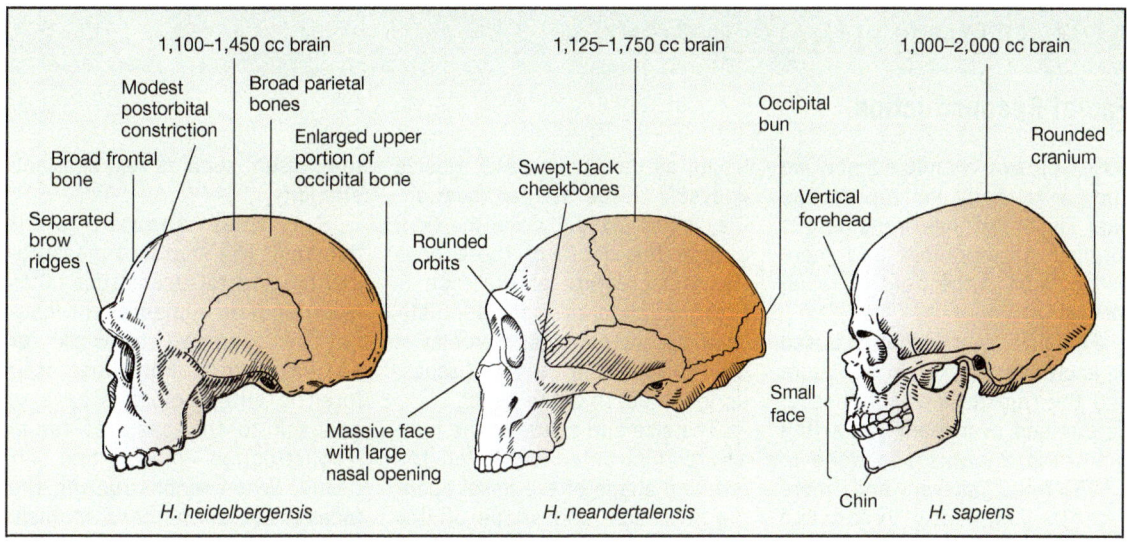

Figure 10–4 Comparison of the Crania of *Homo heidelbergensis*, *Homo neandertalensis*, and *Homo sapiens*, showing important differences

capacity more closely resembles an australopithecine's (Berger et al. 2015). While its wrist shows morphological features consistent with manual manipulation in *H. sapiens*, its long fingers are indicative of substantial grasping and climbing (Kivell et al. 2015). We will have to wait as more information on the dates for these remains becomes available to better understand its place in human evolution.

H. heidelbergensis differs from *H. erectus* in having smaller teeth and jaws, a much larger brain (on the order of 1300 cc), a skull that lacks a sagittal keel and occipital torus, a brow ridge that divides into separate arches above each eye, and a more robust skeleton. *H. heidelbergensis* differs from *H. sapiens* in retaining a large and prognathic face with relatively large teeth and jaws, a brow ridge, and a long, low cranial vault with a sloping forehead, and in its more robust skeleton (Fleagle 1999; Rightmire 1998).

Many scholars question whether *H. heidelbergensis* represents one or several species of Middle Pleistocene hominin, or whether it is indeed a separate species at all. Many would argue that *H. heidelbergensis* should be considered an Archaic *H. sapiens*. As noted, some scholars also argue that *H. erectus* should be included in the *H. sapiens* species (see Figure 10–4).

Neandertals

There may be disagreement about how to classify the mixed-trait fossils from 500 000 to 200 000 years ago, but there is hardly any disagreement about the fossils that are less than 200 000 years old. Nearly all anthropologists agree that they were definitely *H. sapiens*. These early definite *H. sapiens* did not look completely like modern humans, but they were not so different from us either—not even the ones called **Neandertals**, after the valley in Germany where the first evidence of them was found. Somehow through the years the Neandertals have become the victims of their cartoon image, which usually misrepresents them as burly and more ape than human. Actually, they might go unnoticed in a cross-section of the world's population today (see Applied Anthropology, "Facial Reconstruction").

In 1856, three years before Darwin's publication of *The Origin of Species*, a skullcap and other fossilized bones were discovered in a cave in the Neander Valley (*Tal* is the German word for "valley"), near Düsseldorf, Germany. The fossils in the Neander Valley were the first that scholars could tentatively consider

> **Neandertal:** the common name for the species *Homo neandertalensis*.

APPLIED ANTHROPOLOGY

Facial Reconstruction

Have you ever wondered how we know what early humans looked like? The answer lies in the field of forensic anthropology and more particularly in the field of facial reconstruction.

Facial reconstruction is based on knowledge of skull musculature and the thickness of soft tissue, determined over many years (the first such analysis was done in 1895) from cadavers and, more recently, magnetic resonance images of living people. From these measurements, forensic anthropologists have established a standard set of 21 to 34 locations on the skull where the average soft tissue thicknesses are known. The first step in facial reconstruction is to mark these locations on a cast of the skull to be reconstructed, using pegs that are the same length as the thickness of muscle and soft tissue at that location. Clay is then used to cover the skull cast to the depth of these pegs (the musculature of the face is first modelled in more sophisticated reconstructions, then clay is used to represent the soft tissues, up to the depth of the pegs).

The size and shape of the nose are reconstructed based on the size and shape of the nasal opening. The size and shape of lips and ears are more difficult to determine, and the skull itself can tell the forensic anthropologist almost nothing about hair or eye colour, whether the person had facial hair, or how the person's hair was cut. Those aspects of facial reconstruction require some artistic intuition, and it is helpful to know something about the person, such as sex, age, and ethnicity.

But what about ancient humans? The standard measurements used to reconstruct faces from modern human skulls cannot be assumed to work for ancient skulls. For those, the forensic anthropologists have to go back to the basis of facial reconstruction—muscle and soft tissue. When reconstructing the faces of ancient humans, forensic anthropologists begin with a careful reconstruction of skull musculature, often aided by the comparative anatomy of modern great apes. Once the muscles are in place, glands, fatty tissue, and skin are added, and the face begins to take shape.

Though based on study of the likely muscular anatomy in fossils and the comparative anatomy of modern humans and great apes, it is important to realize that the reconstruction of ancient faces is in part an artistic exercise. This is why reconstructions vary in the ways they depict ancient humans. We need to keep in mind when we look at reconstructions that they are educated, perhaps biased, guesses, and not necessarily true depictions of ancient people.

Sources: DeGreef S, Willems G. 2005. Three-Dimensional Cranio-Facial Reconstruction in Forensic Identification: Latest Progress and New Tendencies in the 21st Century. Journal of Forensic Sciences. 50:12–17.

Moser S. 1998. Ancestral Images: The Iconography of Human Origins. Ithaca, NY: Cornell University Press.

Prag J, Neave R. 1997. Making Faces: Using Forensic and Archaeological Evidence. College Station: Texas A&M University Press.

Reconstructions of ancient hominins.

Early renditions of Neandertals portrayed them as brutish and very non-human-like.

an early hominin. (The fossils classified as *H. erectus* were not found until later in the 19th century, and the fossils belonging to the genus *Australopithecus* not until the 20th century.) After Darwin's revolutionary work was published, the Neandertal find aroused considerable controversy. A few evolutionist scholars, such as Thomas Huxley, thought that the Neandertal was not that different from modern humans.

Others dismissed the Neandertal as irrelevant to human evolution; they saw it as a pathological freak, a peculiar, disease-ridden individual. However, similar fossils turned up later in Belgium, Yugoslavia, France, and elsewhere in Europe, which meant that the original Neandertal find could not be dismissed as an oddity (Spencer 1984).

The predominant reaction to the original and subsequent Neandertal-like finds was that the Neandertals were too "brutish" and "primitive" to have been ancestral to modern humans. This view prevailed in the scholarly community until well into the 1950s. A major proponent of this view was French anatomist Marcellin Boule, who claimed between 1908 and 1913 that the Neandertals would

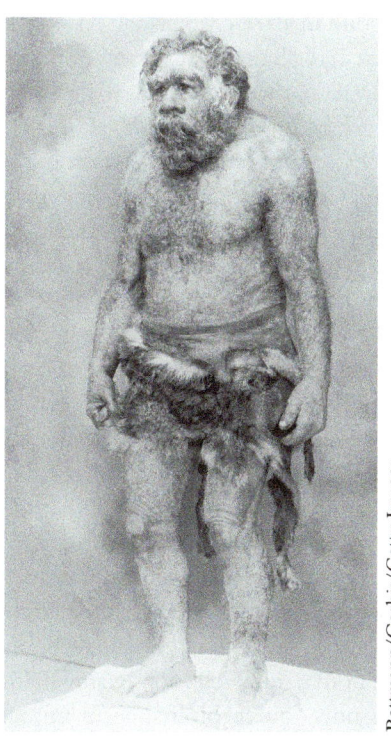

Boule's reconstruction of Neandertal (left) as displayed at Chicago's Field Museum in 1929, and a more recent construction (right). The recent reconstruction makes Neandertal seem more like modern humans.

not have been capable of complete bipedalism. Boule's reconstruction of the La Chapelle-aux-Saints Neandertal remains emphasized the minor differences rather than the remarkable similarities between the Neandertal and modern skeletons. Further, Boule's reconstruction was based on an older male, who suffered from severe arthritis. Despite the fact that Boule seemed to have ignored two other healthy skeletons on which to reconstruct the Neandertals, Boule's biased view was maintained in popular culture for a considerable time.

Since the 1950s, however, a number of studies have disputed Boule's claim, and it is now generally agreed that the skeletal traits of the Neandertals are completely consistent with bipedalism. Perhaps more important, when the much more ancient australopithecine and *H. erectus* fossils were accepted as hominins in the 1940s and 1950s, anthropologists realized that the Neandertals did not look that different from modern humans—despite their sloping foreheads, large brow ridges, flattened braincases, large jaws, and nearly absent chins (Trinkaus 1985). After all, they did have larger brains (averaging more than 1450 cc) than modern humans (slightly more than 1300 cc) (Stringer 1988b). Some scholars believe that the large brain capacity of Neandertals suggests that they were capable of the full range of behaviour characteristic of modern humans. Their skeletons did, however, attest to one behavioural trait markedly different from most modern humans: Neandertals had much more robust and more heavily muscled bodies (Trinkaus and Shipman 1993).

It took almost 100 years for scholars to accept the idea that Neandertals were not that different from modern humans and therefore should be classified as *Homo sapiens neandertalensis*. As we shall discuss later, though, there is still debate over whether the Neandertals in western Europe were ancestral to modern-looking people who lived later in western Europe, after about 40 000 years ago. In any case, Neandertals lived in other places besides western Europe. A large number of fossils from central Europe strongly resemble those from western Europe, although some features, such as a projecting midface, are less pronounced (Smith 1984:187). Neandertals have also been found in southwestern Asia (Israel, Iraq) and Central Asia (Uzbekistan). One of the largest collections of Neandertal fossils comes from Shanidar Cave in the mountains of northeastern Iraq, where Ralph Solecki unearthed the skeletons of nine individuals (see site 31 in Figure 10–5) (Trinkaus 1984).

The Neandertals have received a great deal of scholarly and popular attention, probably because they were the first premodern humans to be found. We now know, though, that other premodern *H. sapiens*, some perhaps older than Neandertals, lived elsewhere in the Old World—in East, South, and North Africa, as well as in Java and China (Smith and Spencer 1984). These other premodern, but definite, *H. sapiens* are sometimes considered Neandertal-like, but more often they are named after the places where they were first found, as indeed the original Neandertal was. For example, the cranium from China called *Homo sapiens daliensis* was named after the Chinese locality, Dali, in which it was found in 1978 (Xinzhi and Maolin 1985).

What has changed scholars' opinions of the Neandertals so that they are now most commonly seen as not belonging to the *H. sapiens* group?

In 1997, a group of researchers from the United States and Germany published findings that forced a reconsideration of the Neandertals and their relationship to modern humans. These scholars reported that they had been able to extract DNA from the original Neandertal specimen found in 1856 (Krings et al. 1997, 1999). The DNA they extracted was not nuclear DNA—the material that makes up the human genome. Rather, it came from a tiny structure found in all eukaryotic cells (that is, cells with a membrane-bound nucleus and DNA in the chromosomes) called *mitochondria*. Mitochondria produce enzymes needed for energy production, and they have their own DNA, which replicates when a cell replicates but is not thought to be under any pressure from natural selection (Cann 1988).

The only source of change in mitochondrial DNA (usually referred to as mtDNA) is random mutation. Mitochondrial DNA is inherited only

Homo sapiens neandertalensis: a variety of early *Homo sapiens*.

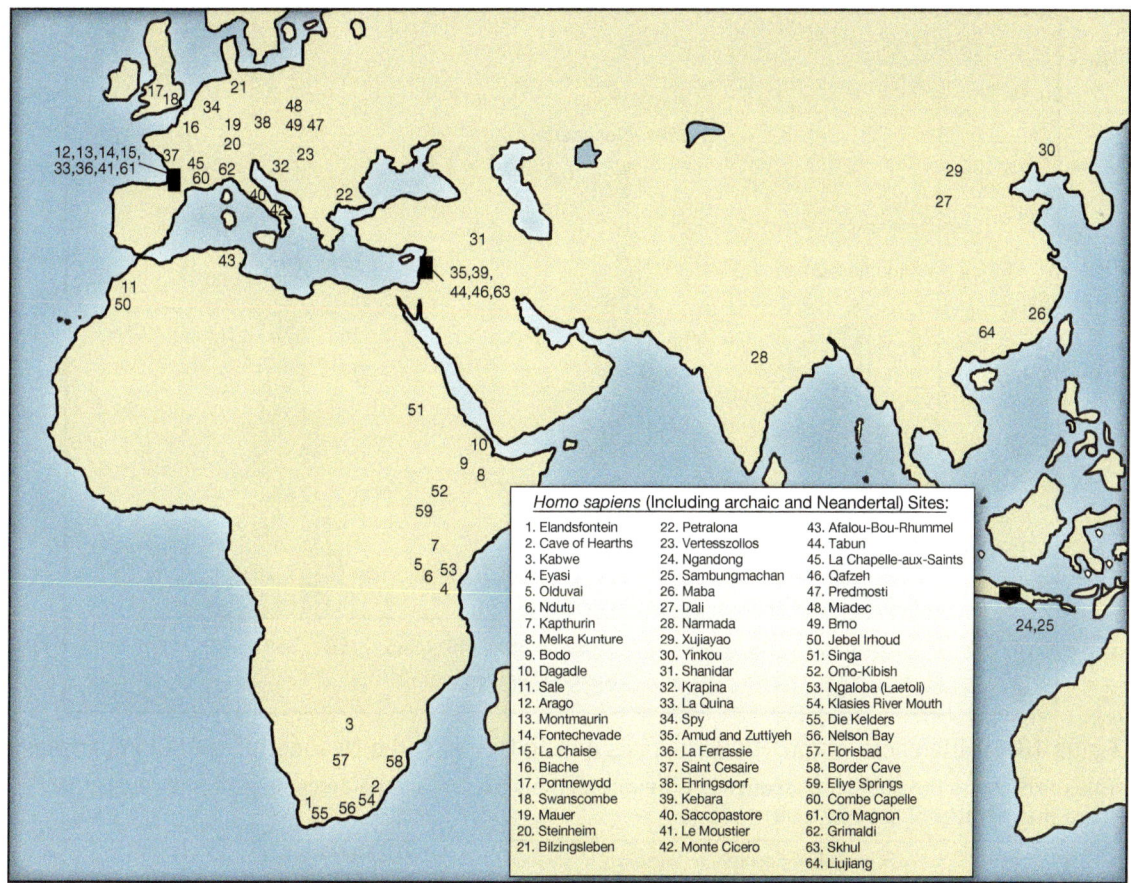

Figure 10–5 *Homo sapiens* Sites

Source: Ciochon RL, Fleagle JG, editors. 1993. The human evolution source book. Englewood Cliffs, NJ: Prentice Hall. p. xi.

from mothers in animals; it is not carried into an egg cell by sperm, but is left with the sperm's tail on the outside of the egg. These unique characteristics make it possible to use mtDNA to measure the degree of relatedness between two species, and even to say how long ago those species diverged (Cann 1988). The longer two species have been separated, the more differences there will be in their mtDNA, which is thought to mutate at a fairly constant rate of about 2 percent per million years. Thus, the number of differences between the mtDNA of two organisms can be converted into an estimated date in the past when those organisms stopped being part of the same breeding population. While controversy remains over many of the details of how and why mtDNA mutates and about its accuracy for determining absolute dates of divergence, most scholars agree that it is a powerful tool for examining relative degrees of relatedness between species (Vigilant et al. 1991).

How similar is Neandertal mtDNA to modern human DNA? Not as similar as many scholars would have expected. Among individual modern humans, there were usually five to ten differences in the sequence of mtDNA examined by the U.S. and German researchers. Between modern humans and the Neandertal specimen, there tended to be about 25 differences—more than three times that among modern humans (see Figure 10–6). This suggested to the researchers that the ancestors of modern humans and the Neandertal must have diverged about 600 000 years ago (Krings et al. 1997, 1999). If the last common ancestor of ours and the Neandertal lived that long ago, the Neandertal would be a much more distant relative than previously thought. This research has since been

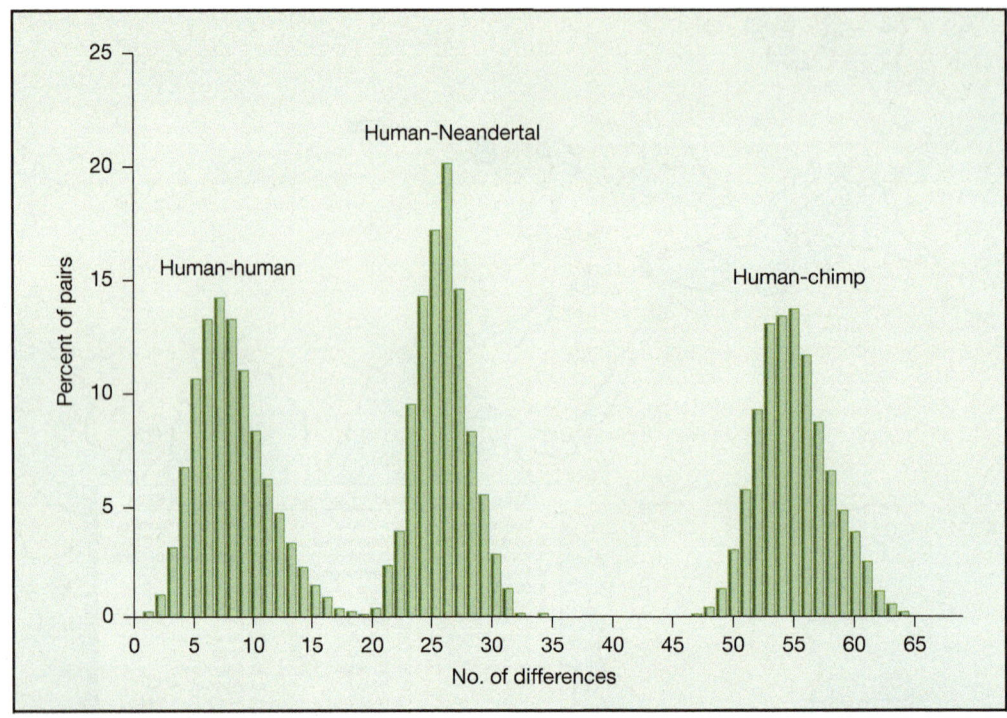

Figure 10–6 Differences in mtDNA Sequences among Humans, the Neandertal, and Chimpanzees
The x-axis shows the number of sequence differences; the y-axis shows the percentage of individuals that share that number of sequence differences.

Source: Krings M, Stone A, Schmitz RW, Krainitzki H, Stoneking M, Paabo S. 1997. Neandertal DNA sequences and the origin of modern humans. Republished with permission of Elsevier Science Inc.; permission conveyed through Copyright Clearance Center, Inc.

replicated with mtDNA from other Neandertal fossils (Ovchinnikov et al. 2000; Scholz et al. 2000), although some have been critical of earlier studies. For example, Gutiérrez and colleagues (2002) argued that the overlap of modern and Neandertal DNA is greater than earlier studies suggested. More recent analyses have been more conservative in their interpretations, arguing that the lack of Neandertal DNA in modern humans does not rule out some genetic contribution (Cooper et al. 2004; Serre et al. 2004). This is consistent with Trinkaus's (2007) most recent arguments based on morphological variation in the fossil record.

But mtDNA is only part of the story. After their success in sequencing mtDNA, anthropological geneticist Svante Pääbo and his colleagues began trying to recover and sequence nuclear DNA from Neandertals. After several setbacks, Pääbo and collaborators successfully sequenced the nuclear DNA from two female Neandertals (Krings et al. 1997). Analysis of the Neandertal DNA found that Neandertals and modern humans have identical versions of several genes that were thought to be found only in modern humans, and that the two species occasionally interbred (Krause et al. 2007). Neandertals also had fair skin, and at least some had red hair (Lalueza-Fox et al. 2007).

However, some significant differences between Neandertal and modern human nuclear DNA have also been identified. For example, Neandertals apparently lack the modern human version of microcephalin, a gene that is associated with brain development (Burbano et al. 2010). And initial analyses of the nuclear DNA suggested that the ancestral modern human and Neandertal populations split more than a half million years ago (Serre et al. 2004; Hodgson and Driscoll 2008).

Recent archaeological findings from Europe and the Near East may also indicate that Neandertals and the modern human were different

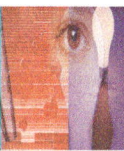

CURRENT RESEARCH AND ISSUES

Neandertal Growth and Development

One of the reasons many scholars think the Neandertals did not belong to the *Homo sapiens* species is that their material culture was less sophisticated than that of early modern humans who lived at the same time. Since much of contemporary human behaviour is dependent on learning that takes place during our long period of infant dependency, could it be that Neandertals matured more rapidly than modern humans and thus had a shorter period in which to learn cultural behaviours?

Palaeoanthropologist Nancy Minugh-Purvis decided to test this idea by examining growth and development of the skull and face in Neandertals. Minugh-Purvis's study of Neandertal growth and development was feasible largely because Neandertals may have buried their dead. Juvenile and infant skeletons are rare in the archaeological record and often do not preserve well. In juveniles and infants, many of the bones are still growing and thus are relatively delicate. They are also smaller than adult bones, and a wider variety of scavengers can consume them. But because Neandertals may have buried their dead, a number of well-preserved juvenile and infant skeletons are available for study. Indeed, Minugh-Purvis was able to locate more than 100 Neandertal skeletons, ranging in age from newborn to young adult.

To chart the way the skull and face of Neandertals grew from infancy to adulthood, Minugh-Purvis measured the available fossils on a set of standard anthropometric indices—indices that are widely used in physical anthropology to compare the size and shape of bones. She found that newborn Neandertals and modern humans do not differ very much, but that Neandertal infants tend to have thicker cranial bones than modern humans and perhaps heavier musculature. Many of the more striking features of adult Neandertals—a large face with a protruding nose, brow ridges, and a long skull—are not present in infants. These typical Neandertal characteristics begin to appear in children. For example, a 4-year-old Neandertal from the site of Engis, Belgium, already had brow ridges. A 7-year-old from the site of La Quinta in France had not only brow ridges but also a large, protruding nose and face and a long skull. Finally, a 10-year-old from the site of Teshik-Tash in Uzbekistan had all the typical Neandertal features, and is basically identical to an adult Neandertal except in size. A reanalysis of the Le Moustier 1 by Thompson and Illerhaus suggested that growth in facial height occurred at a faster rate than prognathism during the adolescent period.

In short, Neandertals are born similar to modern humans, but by the age of about 10 have developed all the striking physical features that differentiate Neandertals from modern humans. What does this tell us about Neandertal growth and development? Minugh-Purvis suggested that it was much like our own. Indeed, she argued that many of the physical differences between the Neandertal face and skull and those of modern humans might be due not to genetic differences but rather to behavioural ones. Neandertal teeth show wear patterns that suggest they were used as tools, particularly to hold objects while working on them with the hands. The teeth and jaws were apparently placed under tremendous stress from these uses. Minugh-Purvis suggested that the prognathic face and heavy musculature may be a result of the teeth and jaws being used as tools from a young age, rather than from developmental differences between modern humans and Neandertals.

However, there are other differences between Neandertals and modern humans that cannot be explained by behaviour. The overall picture that appears from Minugh-Purvis's study is that Neandertals did indeed mature slightly faster than modern humans. Thompson and Nelson also examined several fossils, arguing that Neandertals exhibited either slow growth in height or more rapid dental development than modern humans. But was their maturation fast enough to account for the lack of cultural development among the Neandertals? Did Neandertals grow so fast they had no time to learn? Minugh-Purvis suggested the differences are not that significant, and that other factors must be sought to explain the differences in cultural development between Neandertals and modern humans.

Sources: Minugh-Purvis N. 2002. Neandertal Growth: Examining Developmental Adaptations in Earlier *Homo sapiens*. In: Peregrine PN, Ember CR, Ember M, editors. Physical Anthropology: Original Readings in Method and Practice. Upper Saddle River, NJ: Prentice Hall. Also in: Ember CR, Ember M, editors. 2003. New Directions in Anthropology. Upper Saddle River, NJ: Prentice Hall. CD-ROM.

Stringer C, Gamble C. 1993. In Search of the Neanderthals. New York: Thames and Hudson.

Thompson JL, Illerhaus B. 1998. A New Reconstruction of the Le Moustier 1 Skull and Investigation of Internal Structures Using 3-D-muCT Data. Journal of Human Evolution. 35:647–665.

Thompson JL, Nelson AJ. 2000. The Place of Neandertals in the Evolution of Hominid Patterns of Growth and Development. Journal of Human Evolution. 38:475–495.

Trinkaus E. 1987. The Neandertal Face: Evolutionary and Functional Perspectives on a Recent Hominid Face. Journal of Human Evolution. 16:429–443.

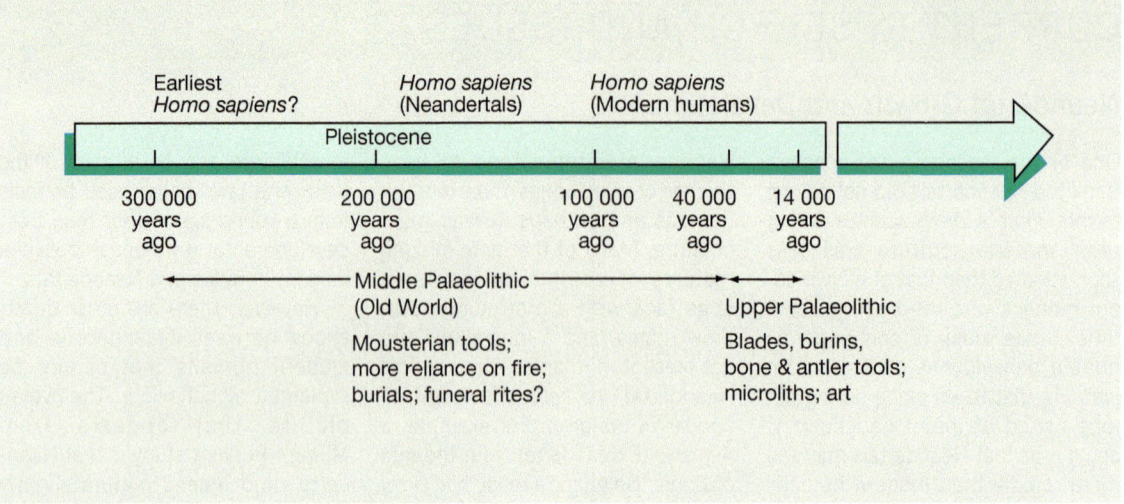

Figure 10–7 An Evolutionary Timeline

species. It has been known for decades that both modern human and Neandertal fossils are found in the same locations in parts of the Levant, but recent improvements in dating technology and newly discovered fossils have even more clearly demonstrated that the two kinds of hominin coexisted. In fact, several caves in the Mount Carmel region of Israel contain evidence of both modern human and Neandertal occupations. The fact that these two groups of hominins co-inhabited the Near East for perhaps as much as 30 000 years and did not interbreed or share much in the way of tool technology strongly suggests that the two are different species (Tattersall 1999; Gibbons 2001). In addition, finds in Europe seem to corroborate that assessment. As early modern humans began moving into Europe, they appear to have displaced populations of Neandertals already living there. Sites with tools thought to be associated with Neandertals become less frequent throughout Europe as sites with tools thought to be associated with modern humans expand their range (Mellars 1996). Significantly, the area of Europe (Iberia) last colonized by modern humans contains the very latest Neandertal fossils yet found, dating to some 30 000 years ago (Mellars 1998).

With all this evidence pointing to Neandertals not being part of the modern human species, why is there an ongoing debate? In part, this is because none of the evidence is conclusive, and much of it can be interpreted in alternative ways. There is also evidence suggesting that Neandertals were not all that different physically from modern humans (see Current Research and Issues, "Neandertal Growth and Development"). Perhaps more important, however, Neandertal culture, typically referred to as Middle Palaeolithic after the predominant tool technology, has some features that make it seem similar to the culture of early modern humans.

Middle Palaeolithic Cultures

The period of cultural history associated with the Neandertals is traditionally called the **Middle Palaeolithic** in Europe and the Near East and dates from about 300 000 years ago to about 40 000 years ago (Strauss 1989). For Africa, the term *Middle Stone Age* is used instead of *Middle Palaeolithic*. The tool assemblages from this period are generally referred to as *Mousterian* in Europe and the Near East and as *post-Acheulian* in Africa. (See the timeline in Figure 10–7.)

Tool Assemblages

The Mousterian.
The Mousterian type of tool complex is named after the tool assemblage found

> **Middle Palaeolithic:** the time period of the Mousterian stone tool tradition.

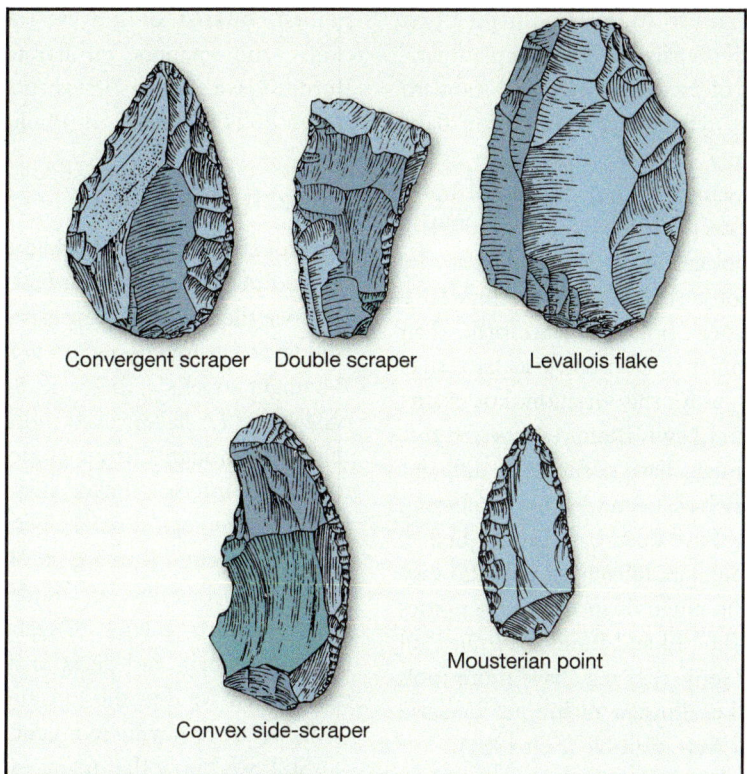

Figure 10–8 A Typical Mousterian Tool Kit

A Mousterian tool kit emphasized sidescrapers (1–4), notches (5), points (6), and sawtoothed denticulates (7). How these stone artifacts were actually used is not known, but the points may have been joined to wood shafts, and denticulates could have been used to work wood. The tools illustrated here are from Mousterian sites in western Europe.

Source: Klein RG. June 1974. Ice-age hunters of the Ukraine. Scientific American. 96–105. Reprinted with permission of Nelson H. Prentiss.

in a rock shelter at Le Moustier in the Dordogne region of southwestern France. Compared with an Acheulian assemblage, a **Mousterian tool assemblage** has a smaller proportion of large core tools such as hand axes and cleavers and a bigger proportion of small flake tools such as scrapers (Schick and Toth 1994). Although many flakes struck off from a core were used "as is," the Mousterian is also characterized by flakes that were often altered or "retouched" by striking small flakes or chips from one or more edges (see Figure 10–8) (Klein 2009). Studies of the wear on scrapers suggest that many were used for scraping hides or working wood. The fact that some of the tools, particularly projectile points, were thinned or shaped on one side suggests that they were hafted or attached to a shaft or handle (Schick and Toth 1994; Whittaker 1994).

Toward the end of the Acheulian period, toolmakers developed a technique to produce flake tools of a predetermined size instead of simply chipping flakes away from the core at random. In

> **Mousterian Tool Assemblage:** named after the tool assemblage found in a rock shelter at Le Moustier in the Dordogne region of southwestern France. Compared with an Acheulian assemblage, the Middle Palaeolithic (40 000–300 000 years ago) Mousterian has a smaller proportion of large core tools such as hand axes and cleavers and a bigger proportion of small flake tools such as scrapers. Flakes were often altered or "retouched" by striking small flakes or chips from one or more edges.

this **Levalloisian method**, the toolmaker first shaped the core and prepared a "striking platform" at one end. Flakes of predetermined and standard sizes could then be detached by percussion flaking. Although some Levallois flakes date as far back as 400 000 years ago, they are found more frequently in Mousterian tool kits (Klein 2009).

The tool assemblages in particular sites may be characterized as Mousterian, but one site may have more or fewer scrapers, points, and so forth, than another site. A number of archaeologists have suggested possible reasons for this variation. For example, Sally Binford and Lewis Binford suggested that different activities might have occurred in different sites. Some sites may have been used for butchering and other sites may have been base camps; hence, the kinds of tools found in different sites should vary as a reflection of the range of specialized activities carried out there (Binford and Binford 1969). Paul Fish suggested that some sites may have more tools produced by the Levalloisian technique because larger pieces of flint were available (Fish 1981).

The Middle Stone Age in Africa.
Like Mousterian tools, many of the post-Acheulian tools in Africa during the Middle Stone Age were struck off prepared cores in the Levalloisian way.

The assemblages consist mostly of various types of flake tools. A well-described sequence of such tools comes from the area around the mouth of the Klasies River on the southern coast of South Africa. This area contains rock shelters and small caves in which early and later *H. sapiens* lived. The oldest cultural remains in one of the caves may date back 120 000 years (Butzer 1982b). These earliest tools include parallel-sided flake **blades** (probably used as knives), pointed flakes (possibly spear points), **burins** or gravers (chisel-like incising tools), and scrapers. Similar tools discovered at Border Cave, South Africa, may have been used almost 200 000 years ago (Phillipson 1993).

Homesites

Most of the excavated Middle Palaeolithic homesites in Europe and the Near East are located in caves and rock shelters. The same is true for the excavated Middle Stone Age homesites in sub-Saharan Africa. We might conclude, therefore, that Neandertals and other early *H. sapiens* lived mostly in caves or rock shelters, although this conclusion could be incorrect. Caves and rock shelters may be overrepresented in the archaeological record because they are more likely to be found than are sites that originally were in the open but now are hidden by thousands of years, and many metres, of sediment. **Sediment** is the dust, debris, and decay that accumulates over time; when we dust the furniture and vacuum the floor, we are removing sediment.

Still, we know that many early *H. sapiens* lived at least part of the year in caves. This was true, for example, along the Dordogne River in France. The river gouged deep valleys in the limestone of that area. Below the cliffs are rock shelters with overhanging roofs and deep caves, many of which were occupied during the Middle Palaeolithic. Even if the inhabitants did not stay all year, the sites do seem to have been occupied year after year (Binford 1973). Although there is evidence of some use of fire in earlier cultures, Middle Palaeolithic humans seem to have relied more on fire. There are thick layers of ash in many rock shelters and caves, and also evidence that hearths were used to increase the efficiency of the fires (Balter 2009).

Levalloisian Method: a method that allowed flake tools of a predetermined size to be produced from a shaped core. The toolmaker first shaped the core and prepared a "striking platform" at one end. Flakes of predetermined and standard sizes could then be knocked off. Although some Levallois flakes date from as far back as 400 000 years ago, they are found more frequently in Mousterian tool kits.
Blade: a thin flake whose length is usually more than twice its width. In the blade technique of toolmaking, a core is prepared by shaping a piece of flint with hammer stones into a pyramidal or cylindrical form. Blades are then struck off until the core is used up.
Burin: a chisel-like stone tool used for carving and for making such artifacts as bone and antler needles, awls, and projectile points.
Sediment: the dust, debris, and decay that accumulates over time.

Archaeologist Hilary Deacon at the mouth of the Klasies River in South Africa, where early modern humans have been found.

Quite a few homesites of early *H. sapiens* were in the open. In Africa, open-air sites were located on floodplains, at the edges of lakes, and near springs (Klein 1977, 2009). Many open-air sites have been found in Europe, particularly eastern Europe. The occupants of the well-known site at Moldova in western Russia lived in river-valley houses framed with wood and covered with animal skins. Bones of mammoths (huge elephants now extinct) surround the remains of hearths and were apparently used to help hold the animal skins in place. Even though the winter climate near the edge of the nearby glacier was cold at that time, there would still have been animals to hunt because the plant food for the game was not buried under deep snow.

The hunters probably moved away in the summer to higher land between the river valleys. In all likelihood, the higher ground was grazing land for the large herds of animals the Moldova hunters depended on for meat. In the winter river-valley sites, archaeologists have found skeletons of wolf, arctic fox, and hare with their paws missing. These animals probably were skinned for pelts that were made into clothing (Klein 1974).

Getting Food

How early *H. sapiens* got their food probably varied with their environment. In Africa, they lived in savannah and semi-arid desert. In western and eastern Europe, they had to adapt to cold; during periods of increased glaciation, much of the environment was steppe grassland and tundra.

The European environment during this time was much richer in animal resources than the tundra of northern countries is today. Indeed, the European environment inhabited by Neandertals abounded in game, both big and small. The tundra and alpine animals included reindeer, bison, wild oxen, horses, mammoths, rhinoceroses, and deer, as well as bears, wolves, and foxes (Bordes 1961). Some European sites have also yielded bird and fish remains. For example, people in a summer camp in northern Germany apparently hunted swans and ducks and fished for perch and pike (Patterson 1981). Little, however, is known about the particular plant foods the European Neandertals may have consumed; the remains of plants are unlikely to survive thousands of years in a non-arid environment.

In Africa, too, early *H. sapiens* got food in different ways. For example, we know that the people living at the mouth of the Klasies River in South Africa ate shellfish as well as meat from small grazers such as antelopes and large grazers such as eland and buffalo (Klein 2009; Phillipson 1993). But archaeologists disagree about how the Klasies River people got their meat when they began to occupy the caves in the area.

Richard Klein argued that they hunted the large as well as small game. Klein speculated that because the remains of eland of all ages have been found in Cave 1 at this site, the people there probably hunted the eland by driving them into corrals or other traps, where animals of all ages could be killed. Klein thought that buffalo were hunted differently. Buffalo tend to charge attackers, which would make it difficult to drive them into traps. Klein suggested that, because bones from mostly very young and very old buffalo were found in the cave, the hunters were able to stalk and kill only the most vulnerable animals (Klein 1983, 2009).

Lewis Binford speculated that the Klasies River people hunted only small grazers and scavenged the eland and buffalo meat from the kills of large carnivores. He argued that sites should contain all or almost all of the bones from animals that were hunted. According to Binford, since more or less complete skeletons were found only from small animals, the Klasies River people were not at first hunting all the animals they used for food (Klein 1983; Binford 1984).

But there is new evidence suggesting that people were hunting big game as much as 400 000 years ago. Wooden spears that old were recently found in Germany in association with stone tools and the butchered remains of more than 10 wild horses. The heavy spears resemble modern aerodynamic javelins, which suggests they would have been thrown at large animals such as horses, not at small animals. This new evidence strongly suggests that hunting, not just scavenging, may be older than archaeologists used to think (Wilford 1997).

The extent and level of hominin hunting during the Middle Palaeolithic has been widely debated. There is a growing realization of the importance of faunal analyses for reconstructing complex behaviour in Middle Palaeolithic hominin populations. Dr. Ariane Burke is an archaeologist at the Université de Montréal. Much of her research has focused on the analysis of faunal remains from Middle Palaeolithic sites in western Crimea in Ukraine. This research has enabled Burke to develop a hypothesis of land use and resource exploitation among Neandertal populations in the Crimea.

One of the issues emerging from this kind of research is that Neandertal resource strategies (getting food and using the land) are far more complicated than previously thought. In particular, recent research from a variety of areas in the Old World has emphasized the importance of Neandertal flexibility in their food-gathering activities in response to changes in the seasons and possible different sources of food. For example, studies have implied a mixture of both seasonally focused hunting of specific animals, intermixed with opportunistic hunting of animals that are encountered unintentionally. Further, periods of climatic crisis show a greater variety of foods being utilized by Neandertal populations, which suggests flexibility in hunting strategies during these hard times (Burke 2000). In contrast, stable isotope analysis of Neadertal remains by Richards and colleagues (2001) suggested a diet focused primarily on terrestrial sources.

Burke and others (see Burke 2000), through research at a variety of Middle Palaeolithic sites, have begun to challenge the traditional notion of a lack of forethought and planning among Neandertal populations. The capacity for complex planning is abundantly demonstrated by Middle Palaeolithic patterns of land-use and subsistence strategies. This, of course, is important with respect to defining "modern" humans. The idea of a "Neandertal niche"—whereby Neandertals were overspecialized to very specific environmental conditions—implies that Middle Palaeolithic populations were biologically and culturally distinct from anatomically modern Upper Palaeolithic populations. Renewed research in this area brings a greater understanding of what it is to be truly "modern," and helps us to understand both the evolution of modern cultures and why Neandertal populations disappeared.

Funeral Rituals?

Some Neandertals were deliberately buried. At Le Moustier, the skeleton of a boy 15 or 16 years old was found with a beautifully fashioned stone axe near his hand. Near Le Moustier, graves of five other children and two adults, apparently interred together in a family plot, were discovered. These finds, along with one at Shanidar Cave in Iraq, have aroused speculation about the possibility of funeral rituals.

The evidence at Shanidar consists of pollen around and on top of a man's body. Pollen analysis suggests that the flowers included ancestral forms of modern grape hyacinths, bachelor's buttons, hollyhocks, and yellow flowering groundsels. John Pfeiffer speculated about this find:

> A man with a badly crushed skull was buried deep in the cave with special ceremony. One spring day about 60 000 years ago, members of his family went out into the hills, picked masses of wild flowers, and made a bed of them on the ground, a resting place for the deceased. Other flowers were

HOMO ERECTUS AND ARCHAIC HOMO SAPIENS

As this reconstruction illustrates, Neandertals may have been the first humans to purposely bury their dead.

Luigi Galante/DK Images

probably laid on top of his grave; still others seem to have been woven together with the branches of a pine-like shrub to form a wreath. (Pfeiffer 1978)

Can we be sure? Not really. All we really know is that there was pollen near and on top of the body. It could have been deposited there because humans put flowers in the grave, or perhaps through other, even accidental, reasons. Some scholars argued that other Shanidar burials are actually the remains of people who were trapped under rockfalls within the cave and killed—they were not deliberately buried at all, but rather buried accidentally (Trinkaus 1984; Klein 2009:572).

Neandertals may have taken part in other rituals as well, but, as with funeral rituals, the evidence is ambiguous. At Drachenloch cave in the Swiss Alps, for example, a stone-lined pit holding the stacked skulls of seven cave bears was found in association with a Neandertal habitation. Why preserve these skulls? One reason might be for rituals intended to placate or control bears. Cave bears were enormous—some nearly 2.7 metres tall—and competed with Neandertals for prime cave-living sites. Perhaps the Neandertals preserved the skulls of bears they killed in the cave as a way of honouring or appeasing either the bears or their spirits. But, as with funeral rituals, the evidence is not completely persuasive. In our own society some may hang a deer or moose head on the wall without any associated ritual. At this point we cannot say for certain whether or not Neandertals engaged in ritual behaviour (Chase and Dibble 1987; Klein 2009).

Altruism

Another aspect associated with Neandertals is the evidence for **altruism**—the concept of caring for and sustaining members of the group who may no longer contribute to the group's survival. The interpretation of altruism among the Neandertals comes from the La Chapelle-aux-Saints and the Shanidar I skeletons that implicitly demonstrate the Neandertals' capacity to care for the sick and aged. For example, the La Chapelle-aux-Saints finds included the remains of a middle-aged male suffering from arthritis. Whether or not this individual could care for himself has been debated, and while it is probable that he was able to interact with the group until his death, it is possible that his survival was in part due to the aid of other members of the group. Better evidence comes from the Shanidar I remains, which include the skeleton of an individual with healed injuries that would have left him blind with a paralyzed right arm (Trinkaus 1983). In this case it certainly seems likely that the individual's survival, at least during the period of recovery from his injuries, would have been possible only with the support of other members of the group (Trinkaus 1983).

Cannibalism

Another area of interest for Neandertals that has re-emerged in the news is the possibility of cannibalism. Recent research by Tim White and colleagues suggested that the site of Moula-Guercy—a Neandertal cave site in France dating to 100 000 years ago—contains evidence of cannibalism. The site includes 78 bone fragments representing the remains of at least six individuals including two adults, two adolescents, and two young children. Tim White suggested that the cut marks on these

Altruism: the concept of caring for and sustaining members of the group who may no longer contribute to the group's survival.

bones could have been caused by sharp flints, and that the skulls were smashed and long bones broken open, presumably to extract the marrow. Further, there was no evidence of animals gnawing on the bones (Defleur et al. 1999).

Language

Recall from earlier discussions that the basicranium of the australopithecines is ape-like while that of *H. erectus* is more reminiscent of modern humans. Similarly, the basicranium of Archaic *H. sapiens* appears modern, with specimens from Petralona, Steinheim, Kabwe, and other sites implying a modern ability for language by about 250 000 years ago (Laitman and Heimbuch 1984). However, there is ongoing debate as to whether Neandertals may have been different. Neandertal specimens do show a greater degree of flexion of the basicranium than those of *H. erectus*, but less so than other Archaic *H. sapiens*. This has led some researchers to suggest that Neandertals had a more constricted range of vocalization than other Archaic populations. This notion has been challenged from an analysis of a fully modern-looking hyoid bone from Kebara, Israel (Arensburg et al. 1990).

Evolutionary Relations

One of the primary questions concerning the Neandertals is, What is their evolutionary relationship to modern humans? For a long time it was assumed that modern *H. sapiens* had evolved directly from Archaic populations like Neandertals. However, as we have already discussed, new evidence has emerged from molecular anthropology, implying that this is likely not the case. We also now know from the archaeological record that some Neandertal populations lived at the same time and in some cases in the same place as anatomically modern humans. The question now becomes, What is the evolutionary relation of Neandertals to modern human populations? In the next chapter, we will discuss in further detail the three prevailing models of the origins of modern humans. Regardless of the model, it is clear that the Neandertals disappear from the archaeological record and are replaced, either biologically or culturally, by anatomically modern humans. Whether or not Neandertal genes are incorporated into the modern human genome remains to be debated.

The Denisovans

While there remain many unanswered questions about the Neandertals and their culture, a recent find in Siberia has created a new mystery, in this case involving a potentially new species of hominin living contemporaneously with the Neandertals and modern humans—the **Denisovans**. Surprisingly, this new hominin species is known from only one site, Denisova Cave in the Altai region of southern Siberia, and through only a single molar and several fragmentary bones. How can a new species be defined through such a tiny amount of evidence? The answer is that the Denisovan finds were subjected to a new DNA recovery process, and the results were spectacular. We now have the most complete genetic picture of any ancient human, and it is different from either ancient modern humans or Neandertals (Gibbons 2012).

Who were the Denisovans? It's a difficult question to answer with so little information, but we do know several things. The Denisovans were neither Neandertals nor modern humans but a separate species that was more closely related to Neandertals than to modern humans. They appear to have separated from our lineage about 1 million years ago (Krause et al. 2010) and from Neandertals before 430 000 years ago (Meyer et al. 2016). If artifacts associated with the Denisovan remains were made by the Denisovans (both Neandertals and modern humans lived in the cave after Denisovans), they fashioned Middle Palaeolithic–style tools, but the stratigraphy of the cave makes this conclusion uncertain. Far less uncertain is the contribution of Denisovans to the modern human genome—people in Melanesia can count 4 percent to 6 percent of their DNA as coming from the Denisovans (Reich et al. 2010).

> **Denisovans:** a group of Siberian hominins contemporary with Neandertals and modern humans who all share a common ancestor based on DNA analysis.

SUMMARY AND REVIEW

HOMO ERECTUS

10.1 Explain when and where *Homo erectus* evolved.

- *Homo erectus* first appear 1.8 to 1.9 million years ago in Africa and persist until about 100 000 years ago.
- The species is divided into *H. ergaster* in Africa, *H. antecessor* in Europe, and *H. erectus* in Asia, based upon cranial anatomy.
- *Homo floresiensis* is a dwarf species related to *Homo erectus* found only on the Indonesian island of Flores.
- *Homo erectus* has a larger brain than *H. habilis*, a low skull with prominent brow ridges, and tooth and jaw size smaller than earlier species. There is an increase in sexual dimorphism.
- The teeth suggest a diet different from australopithicenes and later *H. sapiens*.
- *H. erectus* adapted to new environments quickly without significant physical changes, suggesting the species' primary mechanisms of adaptation were cultural.

 *What factors may have led to reduced sexual dimorphism in* **Homo erectus?**

LOWER PALAEOLITHIC CULTURE

10.2 Describe the tool technologies associated with the Lower Palaeolithic.

- Lower Palaeolithic tools from 1.6 million to around 200 000 years ago were likely made by *H. erectus*.
- Initially, *H. erectus* made tools of the Oldowan industry—just like *H. habilis* and perhaps some australopithecines—but 1.6 million years ago they invented a new industry, the Acheulian.
- The Acheulian tool tradition includes small flake tools, but larger bifacial hand axes and cleavers are characteristic of the Acheulian tool kit.
- Acheulian tools have a longer cutting edge and are easier to hold than flakes. They could have been adapted to process animal carcasses.
- *H. erectus* ate meat from big game but there is no evidence that they hunted larger animals.
- *H. erectus* likely used fire in colder areas but direct evidence for the controlled use of fire is controversial.
- Some scholars have suggested that Archaic *H. sapiens* be called *Homo heidelbergensis*, but they may not form a cohesive species. Whatever their name, the early *H. sapiens* from about 800 000 to 200 000 years ago seem to be ancestral to Neandertals in Europe and modern humans in Africa.

 *What is the significance of red ochre found at Lower Palaeolithic sites?*

NEANDERTALS

10.3 Discuss the anatomical characteristics of the Neandertals and the relationship between Neandertals and *Homo sapiens*.

- Neandertals are genetically distinct from modern humans and evolved in Europe around 500 000 years ago.
- The last Neandertals existed until 30 000 years ago, overlapping in time with and living in the same areas as modern humans. A draft sequence of the Neandertal genome has demonstrated that they contributed DNA to modern humans outside of Africa, most importantly to our immune system.
- Neandertals lived over much of Europe and Asia; most lived around the Mediterranean, but fossils have been found across the Near East, in Uzbekistan and as far east as Siberia.
- Neandertals have large, low braincases; wide, long noses; large, double-arched brow ridges; and no chin.

 *How has DNA analysis of Neandertals changed our understanding of their relationship with modern humans?*

MIDDLE PALAEOLITHIC CULTURES

10.4 Describe the features of Middle Palaeolithic cultures.

- The Middle Palaeolithic in Europe and the Near East dates from 300 000 to 40 000 years ago.
- The Mousterian industry (Europe and Near East) and the Middle Stone Age industry (Africa) consist of flaked tools and fewer hand axes and cleavers.
- Middle Palaeolithic (Middle Stone Age) tools were prepared-core technologies. Both hard and soft hammer techniques and bone tools were used in multiple steps to release a flake with specific characteristics from a core (Levallois technique).
- Middle Palaeolithic humans lived at least part of the year in caves and seemed to have relied more on fire than earlier species. Some Mousterian sites show signs of intentional burial.

 *How does the Levalloisian method compare with the Acheulian tool industry?*

THINK ON IT

1. *Homo erectus* lived in many places in the Old World. What enabled them to spread so widely?
2. Why do you think Neandertals became extinct?
3. Archaic *H. sapiens* including Neandertals show evidence of some key cultural differences from earlier hominins. What are they, and how might they have developed? Did Neandertals have the capacity for symbolic behaviour?
4. What are some of the differences among *H. erectus*, *H. sapiens*, Denisovans, and Neandertals?

Tom McHugh/Science Source

Part IV Modern Humans

Modern *Homo Sapiens* 11

Album/Oronoz/Newscom

LEARNING OBJECTIVES

11.1 Evaluate the theories have been proposed to explain the origins of modern humans.

11.2 Describe Upper Palaeolithic tools and culture.

11.3 Discuss the different scenarios used to explain the migration of humans into the New World.

Until recently, palaeoanthropologists thought that modern-looking people evolved about 50 000 years ago in Europe. Now we know that they appeared earlier. Recent finds in southern Africa and elsewhere indicate the presence of modern-looking people perhaps as much as 100 000 or even 200 000 years ago. In this chapter we examine the major theories regarding the emergence of anatomically modern humans. The two major theories involve the question, Did modern humans evolve from a single population in a single location, or did they evolve from multiple locations throughout the Old World?

We examine evidence from various sources—fossils, genetics, and archaeological discoveries—to better understand this period. We also discuss the movement of modern human populations into the New World.

The Emergence of Modern Humans

The skeletal resemblances between Archaic humans and recent people are so great that most palaeoanthropologists consider them all to be "anatomically modern humans," *Homo sapiens sapiens*. One palaeoanthropologist, Christopher Stringer, characterized anatomically modern humans, *H. sapiens sapiens*, as having "a domed skull, a chin, small eyebrows, brow ridges, and a rather puny skeleton" (Stringer 1985). Some of us might not like to be called puny, but except for our larger brain, most modern humans definitely are small compared with *H. erectus* and even with earlier forms of our own species, *H. sapiens*. This smallness is true in many respects, including our thinner and lighter bones as well as our smaller teeth and jaws.

Cro-Magnon humans, who appeared in western Europe about 35 000 years ago, were once thought to be the earliest specimens of modern humans, or *H. sapiens sapiens*. The Cro-Magnons are named after the rock shelter in France where their remains were first found in 1868 (Stringer et al. 1984). As of now, the oldest known fossils classified as *H. sapiens sapiens* came from Africa.

Some of these fossils, discovered in one of the Klasies River Mouth caves, are possibly as old as 100 000 years (Singer and Wymer 1982). Other modern-looking fossils of about the same age have been found in Border Cave in South Africa, and a find at Omo in Ethiopia may be an early *H. sapiens sapiens* (Bräuer 1984; Rightmire 1984). Remains of anatomically modern humans found at two sites in Israel, at Skhul and Qafzeh, which used to be thought to date back 40 000 to 50 000 years, may be 90 000 years old (Valladas et al. 1988; Schwarcz and Grun 1992). There are also anatomically modern human finds in Borneo, at Niah, from about 40 000 years ago and in Australia, at Lake Mungo, from about 30 000 years ago (Stringer et al. 1984).

These modern-looking humans differed from the Neandertals and other early *H. sapiens* in that they had higher, more bulging foreheads, thinner and lighter bones, smaller faces and jaws, chins, and slight bone ridges (or no ridges at all) over the eyes and at the back of the head.

Theories about the Origins of Modern Humans

Three hypotheses about the origins of modern humans continue to be debated among anthropologists. We will first consider the **single-origin hypothesis**. This suggests that modern humans emerged in just one part of the Old World (Africa is generally thought to be the place of origin for modern humans) and then spread to other parts, replacing Neandertals and other premodern *H. sapiens*.

Single-Origin Hypothesis. According to the single-origin hypothesis, the Neandertals and Denisovans did not evolve into modern humans. Instead, anatomically modern humans evolved in a limited geographic area.

Neandertals became extinct after 30 000 years ago because they were replaced by modern humans (we do not know yet when Denisovans

Single-Origin (or Replacement) Hypothesis: the theory that anatomically modern humans evolved in a single region, Africa, and then replaced all existing Archaic populations in other regions of the world.

became extinct). The presumed place of origin of the first modern humans has varied over the years as new fossils have been discovered. When earlier *Homo sapiens* were found in Africa, palaeoanthropologists postulated that modern humans emerged first in Africa and then moved to the Near East and from there to Europe and Asia. Single-origin theorists think that the originally small population of *H. sapiens* had some biological or cultural advantage, or both, that allowed them to spread and replace Neandertals, Denisovans, and other hominins. The main evidence for the single-origin theory comes from the genes of living peoples.

In 1987, Rebecca Cann and her colleagues presented evidence that the mtDNA from people in the United States, New Guinea, Africa, and East Asia showed differences consistent with a common ancestor living only 200 000 years ago. Cann and colleagues further claimed that because the amount of variation among individuals was greatest in African populations, the common ancestor of all lived in Africa (Cann et al. 1987). (It is generally the case that people living in a homeland exhibit more variation than any emigrant descendant population.) Thus was born what the media called the "mitochondrial Eve" and the "Eve hypothesis" for the origins of modern humans. Of course, there wasn't just one "Eve"—there must have been more than one of her generation with similar mtDNA.

There were many problems with early mtDNA studies, but those problems have been addressed over the years, and new and better mtDNA analyses have been performed. Most scholars now agree that the mtDNA of modern humans shows a remarkably small degree of variation (in fact, less than half the variation found in most chimpanzee populations), which strongly suggests that we all share a very recent, common ancestry (Vigilant et al. 1991). More detailed analyses of mtDNA diversity in modern humans have allowed scholars to identify the ancestral roots of contemporary populations around the world, and these analyses also point to modern human origins in East Africa and a subsequent spread out of that region (see Figure 11–1) (Gibbons 2011).

Evidence for an East African origin of modern humans and the subsequent expansion also comes from research on variation in the Y chromosome. The Y chromosome is the chromosome that determines whether a person is male. A female inherits an X chromosome from both her mother

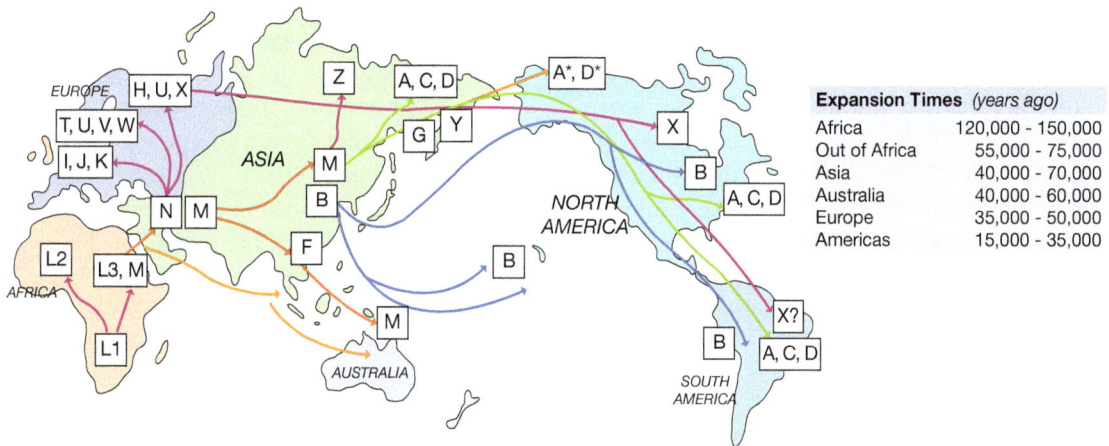

Figure 11–1 Mitochondrial Evidence for a Single Origin of Modern Humans

This map shows the current location and suspected origin of mitochondrial DNA haplogroups in modern human populations. A haplogroup reflects a population that shares a unique mutation in their mtDNA. Such mutations, their age as determined by the molecular clock, and their relationship to other haplogroups that suggest a shared ancestral homeland provide strong evidence for an African origin of modern humans.

and father, whereas a male inherits an X chromosome from his mother and a Y chromosome from his father. Only men have a Y chromosome, and because there is only one copy in any given man, the Y chromosome is the only nuclear chromosome that, like mtDNA, does not undergo recombination. Although the Y chromosome can be affected by selection, it is thought that most variation in the Y chromosome, like variation in mtDNA, is caused by random mutations. Variation in the Y chromosome can therefore be analyzed in much the same way as variation in mtDNA (Hammer and Zegura 1996).

The results of research on variation in the Y chromosome mirror those on variation in mtDNA to a remarkable extent. Analysis of Y chromosome variation points to Africa as the source of modern humans and suggests an exodus from Africa of modern humans. One of the major differences between mtDNA studies and those employing the Y chromosome is in the dating of the most recent common ancestor. As noted previously, studies of mtDNA suggest the most recent common ancestor lived about 200 000 years ago, whereas studies of the Y chromosome suggest the most recent ancestor lived only about 100 000 years ago (Hammer and Zegura 2002). Additional research, including new research on variation in nuclear DNA, may help to resolve these differences. For now, however, it seems clear that the modern human gene pool has a single, and fairly recent, origin in Africa (Cavalli-Sforza and Feldman 2003). The *Homo sapiens* skeletal material from Ethiopia, Africa, in the time range of 150 000 to 200 000 years ago further supports the single-origin theory (Stringer 2003). However, such evidence does not necessarily contradict the validity of the multiregional theory of human origins.

Multiregional Hypothesis. The second hypothesis has been called the **multiregional hypothesis**.

> **Multiregional Hypothesis:** the theory that anatomically modern humans evolved *in situ* in a variety of different regions around the world.

This suggests that modern humans evolved in various parts of the Old World after *H. erectus* spread out of Africa. According to the multiregional hypothesis, *H. erectus* populations in various parts of the Old World gradually evolved into anatomically modern-looking humans. This hypothesis supports the idea of gradual, "in place" evolution of regional populations of ancient hominins into modern humans. If this hypothesis is correct, we should be able to trace regional morphological traits through the evolutionary record, and we should see the simultaneous evolution toward anatomically modern humans in Europe, Asia, and Africa. It is also assumed that there is sufficient gene flow—movement of genetic material among populations—to maintain a single species.

To explain why human evolution would proceed gradually and in the same direction in various parts of the Old World, multiregional theorists point to cultural improvements in cutting-tool and cooking technology that occurred all over the Old World. These cultural improvements may have relaxed the prior natural selection for heavy bones and musculature in the skull. The argument is that unless many plant and animal foods were cut into small pieces and thoroughly cooked in hearths or pits that were efficient thermally, they would be hard to chew and digest. Thus, people previously would have needed robust jaws and thick skull bones to support the large muscles that enabled them to cut and chew their food. However, robust bone and muscle would no longer be needed after people began to cut and cook more effectively (Trinkaus 1986).

Continuity is the main evidence multiregional theorists use to support their position. In several parts of the world, there seem to be clear continuities in distinct skeletal features between *Homo erectus* and *Homo sapiens*. For example, *Homo erectus* fossils from China tend to have broader faces with more horizontal cheekbones than specimens from elsewhere in the world, traits that also appear in modern Chinese populations (Frayer et al. 1993; Wolpoff 1999). Southeast Asia provides more compelling evidence, according to multiregional theorists. There, a number of traits—relatively thick cranial bones, a receding forehead, an unbroken brow ridge, facial prognathism, relatively large cheekbones, and relatively large molars—appear to persist from *Homo erectus* through modern populations (Wolpoff 1999; Frayer et al. 1993). But others suggested that these traits cannot be used to establish a unique continuation from *Homo erectus* in Southeast Asia because these traits are found in modern humans all over the world. And still others argued that the traits are not as similar as the multiregional theorists claim (Lieberman 1995).

Assimilation Theory. The assimilation theory, which is perhaps the most widely supported of the three theories of modern human origins today, suggests that while there may have been replacement of one population by another, interbreeding between early modern humans who spread out of Africa and populations encountered in North Africa, Europe, and Asia also contributed to the emergence of modern humans (Eswaran 2002). Genetic data provide the strongest support for the assimilation theory. Not only does it appear that modern human nuclear DNA contains from 1 percent to 6 percent of Neandertal and Denisovan nuclear DNA, but some of that DNA provided important benefits to modern humans. For example, it appears that an important part of the modern human immune system, human leukocyte antigens (HLA), were inherited from Neandertals and Denisovans (Abi-Rached et al. 2011). Presumably, these antigens provided unique benefits to modern humans and so were transmitted throughout the human population despite their introduction through what appears to be a very low level of interbreeding.

Genetic Evidence

The single-origin (sometimes called the "out of Africa" or "replacement") hypothesis first emerged

> **Assimilation Theory:** a variation on the replacement theory that suggests modern human populations that evolved in Africa interbred and replaced populations they encountered in North Africa, Europe, and Asia.

from studies where diversity in mitochondrial DNA (mtDNA) in modern human populations was used for estimating the timing of divergence between various regional populations. The question of modern human relations is based on the notion that mtDNA is inherited from the mother only and that mutation rates remain constant over time. The single-origin hypothesis implies little genetic diversity among modern populations, whereas the multiregional hypothesis implies greater genetic diversity since the genetic makeup of populations in different regions would change relatively independently of one another. Early studies of mtDNA demonstrated that the greatest variation was in African populations, implying that they represented the oldest modern human lineage. Using this information as a "molecular clock" (see Chapter 8), the time of "divergence" for modern humans from their Archaic ancestral population was estimated at about 200 000 years ago (Cann et al. 1987). However, a reanalysis of the mtDNA data from the original study that suggested this "Eve" hypothesis is more critical, showing that the computer models could support either model (Excoffier and Langaney 1989; Stoneking 1994; Ayala 1995).

Additional genetic evidence continues to corroborate the mtDNA studies. For example, the analysis of microsatellite segments of nuclear DNA imply an African origin of modern humans from about 150 000 years ago (Seielstad et al. 1999). Like the original mtDNA support for the "Eve" hypothesis, Y-chromosome studies (genetic material passed from males to males only) have implied a common male ancestor to modern living populations who lived about 270 000 years ago (Dorit et al. 1995).

Another issue to keep in mind for these studies, however, is the concept of *genetic bottlenecks* in human evolution. Genetic bottlenecks, which can result from *demographic collapse*, can make human populations appear evolutionarily "younger" than they actually are. The reason is that demographic collapse results in the subsequent populations descending from a reduced gene pool, and therefore showing reduced genetic diversity from a relatively recent period (Harpending et al. 1998). Just as the term *demographic collapse* implies, imagine a wine bottle filled with pebbles of various colours. If you were asked to pick any coloured pebble from that bottle, you could choose from a wide range. However, if you were asked to choose from only those colours that fall though the neck of the bottle immediately after tipping it over, your current selection, despite the original diversity of the bottle's contents, would be severely limited by the reduced flow of pebbles through the constricted neck of the bottle. Thus, the term *genetic bottleneck* refers to a rapid reduction in gene flow. Genetic bottlenecks among hominoid groups have been implied by various studies, and in some cases may be the result of infectious disease (Harpending et al. 1998). In general, though, the molecular anthropological data continue to provide support for the "out of Africa" hypothesis, although the question now remains as to the degree of gene flow and local evolution in other areas. To address this, we must look more closely at the fossil evidence.

Fossil Evidence

As we noted earlier, the oldest known fossils attributed to anatomically modern humans come from Africa. Sites that are dated to around 100 000 years ago include the Klasies River Mouth, the Border Cave in South Africa, and Omo in Ethiopia (Singer and Wymer 1982; Bräuer 1984; Rightmire 1984). Found at the Klasies River Mouth, a modern upper jaw and a lower jaw (mandible) with distinct chin have been dated to 90 000 years ago (Grün et al. 1990).

From the Border Cave we have a near complete cranium, a mandible, and partial infant skeleton dating between 60 000 and 80 000 years ago (Grün et al. 1990). The Omo 1 skull dates to 130 000 years ago, and the Mumba teeth have been dated as 110 000 years old (Feder and Park 1997:310). More transitional specimens have been found at the sites of Florisbad, Jebel Irhoud, Omo (Omo 2), and Ngaloba (Laetoli Hominin 18) (Smith et al. 1989). These specimens all have larger, more rounded crania and smaller brow ridges than do older African Archaic populations and are somewhat older than the modern-looking material discussed above.

The Cro-Magnon fossils discovered in 1868 in France remain the oldest evidence of anatomically modern populations in western Europe. They have modern-looking skulls with vertical foreheads, small brow ridges, and a large cranial capacity. Cro-Magnons date to less than 30 000 years ago, and until recently there have been no intermediate forms observed in western Europe. In 1999, a multinational team of anthropologists published the discovery of an early Upper Palaeolithic human burial from Portugal. They argued that this provided evidence of a transitional Neandertal–early modern human, a conclusion that remains debated (Duarte et al. 1999; Tattersall and Schwartz 1999). The remains are that of a young child (approximately 4 years old) with an associated date of about 24 500 years ago. The skeleton presents a "mosaic of European early modern human and Neandertal features" (Duarte et al. 1999; Tattersall and Schwartz 1999). In eastern Europe, however, there is some evidence that has been interpreted as being transitional (Neandertal to modern). Material found in the Czech Republic dates to between 35 000 and 45 000 years ago (Omoto and Tobias 1998). More recently, radiocarbon dates taken directly on Neandertal remains from the sites of Vindija and Velika Pećina in Croatia have suggested that this group of Archaic *H. sapiens* may have survived until as recently as 28 000 to 29 000 years ago (Smith et al. 1999), although re-dating of these remains places them slightly earlier at 32 000 to 33 000 years ago (Higham et al. 2006).

Based on the range of recent dates we have noted, it seems clear that both Neandertals and modern humans (*H. sapiens sapiens*) coexisted in Europe and the Near East for at least 20 000 years, and maybe as long as 60 000 years. But what happened to the Neandertals? Three answers have generally been considered. First, they interbred with modern humans and the unique Neandertal characteristics slowly disappeared from the interbreeding population. Second, they were killed off by modern humans. Third, they were driven to extinction due to competition with modern humans.

The interbreeding scenario seems the most probable, yet evidence supporting it is weak. If modern humans and Neandertals interbred, we should be able to find "hybrid" individuals in the fossil record. In fact, a group of scholars argued that an Upper Palaeolithic skeleton from Portugal demonstrates a combination of modern human and Neandertal features (Duarte et al. 1999). The finding remains controversial, however, because it is a child's skeleton (approximately 4 years old) and its Neandertal-like features have not been corroborated by other scholars. More significantly, if the interbreeding hypothesis is correct, then the mtDNA analysis we have discussed several times in this chapter must be wrong. On the other hand, recent research on Neandertal tools suggests that some Neandertal groups adopted new techniques of tool manufacture that are thought to be uniquely associated with modern humans (Bahn 1998). If Neandertals were learning from modern humans, then the idea that they could have interbred and perhaps been absorbed within the modern human population gains credibility. Trinkaus (2007) suggested that the presence of morphological features seen in early European specimens can best be explained by some level of assimilation of Neandertal populations by modern humans.

The genocide scenario, that modern humans killed off Neandertals, has appeal as a sensational story, but little evidence. Not a single "murdered" Neandertal has ever been found, and one might wonder, in a fight between the powerful Neandertals and the more gracile modern humans, who might get the better of whom.

Finally, it may have been that Neandertals simply could not compete with modern humans. Physical anthropologist Erik Trinkaus argued, based on both physical characteristics of the Neandertal skeleton and their apparent patterns of behaviour, that Neandertals were less efficient hunters and gatherers than modern humans (Trinkaus 1986). If this is true, a modern human group would have been able to live and reproduce more easily than a Neandertal group in the same territory, and this would likely drive the Neandertals away. When there were no new territories to run to, the Neandertals would go extinct— precisely what the archaeological record seems to suggest (Klein 2003). However, as we discussed in the last chapter, archaeological evidence has suggested that Neandertal hunting strategies were more complex than previously demonstrated (Burke 2000). Thus, it remains that some additional cultural forces were being selected for in anatomically modern humans.

In southwest Asia anatomically modern specimens have been excavated from regions where Neandertals have also been discovered. Modern remains from Skhul and Qafzeh in Israel predate Neandertal remains discovered there (Stringer 1988a). Similarly, some have argued that fossils from the Levant show Neandertals lived there at the same time as anatomically modern human populations from about 120 000 years ago, although others use the same evidence to suggest a continuum, rather than distinct populations (Corruccini 1992; Sohn and Wolpoff 1993). In East Asia there does appear to be some continuity in regional traits from *H. erectus* to Archaic to modern populations. Traits like shovel-shaped incisors, extra cranial sutures, and a mandibular torus that are more common in modern populations from this area seem to imply at least some level of long-term regional continuity.

The fossil evidence does seem to suggest the presence of anatomically modern populations in many areas that would be suggestive of the single-origin model. However, despite many areas having overlap between both Archaic and anatomically modern populations, other regions like eastern Europe show evidence of transitional forms that would seem to support the multiregional hypothesis.

Cultural Evidence

Artifacts found in association with early modern sites do seem to be more sophisticated than other assemblages of the same period from Europe and Asia, including the blade technology. Sites from southern Africa dating to 90 000 years ago have shown worked bone, harpoons, and other tools that are not seen at Archaic sites anywhere (Yellen et al. 1995). Outside of Africa, however, the evidence is problematic. In areas like the Middle East there are few differences in the tool assemblages of Neandertal and Archaic populations from those associated with early modern populations in Africa and southwest Asia (Thorne and Wolpoff 1992). In Europe, others see a clear increase in sophistication of later Mousterian tools after Neandertals came into contact with modern populations and their more sophisticated tool technology, called Aurignacian. **Aurignacian tools**—a stone tool technology that began in Europe around 35 000 years ago—included the production of long, narrow blade tools.

Upper Palaeolithic Cultures

The period of cultural history in Europe, the Near East, and Asia known as the **Upper Palaeolithic** dates from about 40 000 years ago to the period known as the **Mesolithic** (about 14 000 to about 10 000 years ago, depending on the area). In Africa, the cultural period comparable to the Upper Palaeolithic is known as the Later Stone Age and may have begun much earlier. To simplify terminology, we use the term *Upper Palaeolithic* in referring to cultural developments in all areas of the Old World during this period.

In many respects, lifestyles during the Upper Palaeolithic were similar to lifestyles before. People were still mainly hunters and gatherers and fishers who probably lived in highly mobile bands. They made their camps out in the open in skin-covered huts and in caves and rock shelters, and continued to produce smaller and smaller stone tools.

The Upper Palaeolithic is also characterized by a variety of new developments. One of the most striking is the emergence of art—painting on cave walls and stone slabs and carving tools, decorative objects, and personal ornaments out of bone, antler, shell, and stone. (Perhaps for this, as well as other purposes, people began to obtain materials from distant sources.) Because more archaeological sites date from the Upper Palaeolithic than from any previous period and some Upper Palaeolithic sites seem larger than any before, many archaeologists think that the human population increased considerably during the Upper Palaeolithic (White 1982). At the same time, new inventions, such as the bow and arrow, the spear-thrower, and tiny replaceable blades that could be fitted into handles, appear for the first time (Strauss 1982).

The Last Ice Age

The Upper Palaeolithic world had an environment very different from today's. The earth was gripped by the last ice age, with glaciers covering Europe as far south as Berlin and Warsaw, and North America as far south as Chicago. To the south of these glacial fronts was a tundra zone extending in Europe to the Alps and in North America to the Ozarks, Appalachians, and well out onto the Great Plains (see Figure 11–2). Environmentally, both Europe and North America probably resembled contemporary Siberia and northern Canada. Elsewhere in the world conditions were not as extreme, but were still different from conditions today (Dawson 1992).

Aurignacian Tools: a stone tool technology associated with modern humans that began in Europe around 35 000 years ago. It includes the production of long, narrow blade tools.

Upper Palaeolithic: the period associated with the emergence of modern humans and their spread around the world.

Mesolithic: the archaeological period in the Old World beginning about 12 000 B.C. Humans were starting to settle down in semipermanent camps and villages as people began to depend less on big game (which they used to have to follow over long distances) and more on relatively stationary food resources such as fish, shellfish, small game, and wild plants rich in carbohydrates, proteins, and oils.

Figure 11–2 The Extent of Glaciation during the Upper Palaeolithic

For one thing, the climate was different. Average annual temperatures were as much as 10 degrees Celsius below today's, and changes in ocean currents would have made temperature contrasts (that is, the differences between summer and winter months) more extreme as well. The changing ocean currents also changed weather patterns, and Europe experienced heavy annual snowfall. Not all the world was cold, however; still, the presence of huge ice sheets in the north changed the climate throughout the world. North Africa, for example, appears to have been much wetter than today, and South Asia was apparently drier. And everywhere the climate seems to have been highly variable.

The plants and animals of the Upper Palaeolithic world were adapted to these extreme conditions. Among the most important, and impressive, were the large game animals collectively known as *Pleistocene megafauna* (Martin and Wright 1967). These animals, as their name suggests, were huge compared with their contemporary descendants. In North America, for example, giant ground sloths stood some 2.5 to 3 metres tall and weighed a few thousand kilograms. Siberian mammoths were the largest elephants ever to live—some standing more than 4 metres tall. In East Asia, species such as the woolly rhinoceros and giant deer were present.

Upper Palaeolithic Europe

With the vast supplies of meat available from megafauna, it is not surprising that many Upper Palaeolithic cultures relied on hunting, and this was particularly true of the Upper Palaeolithic peoples of Europe, on whom we focus here. Their way of life represents a common pattern throughout the Old World. But as people began to use more diverse resources in their environments, the use of local resources allowed Upper Palaeolithic groups in much of the Old World to become more sedentary than their predecessors. They also began to trade with neighbouring groups in order to obtain resources not available in their local territories (Mellars 1994).

As was the case in the known Middle Palaeolithic sites, most of the Upper Palaeolithic remains that have been excavated were situated in caves and rock shelters. In southwestern France, some groups seem to have paved parts of the floor of the shelter with stones. Tent-like structures were built in some caves, apparently to keep out the cold (Patterson 1981). Some of what were formerly open-air sites have also been excavated.

The site at Dolní Věstonice in what is now the Czech Republic dates to about 25 000 years ago. It is one of the first for which there is an entire settlement plan (Klima 1962). The settlement seems to have consisted of four tent-like huts, probably made from animal skins, with a great open hearth in the centre. Around the outside were mammoth bones, some rammed into the ground, which suggests that the huts were surrounded by a wall. All told, there were bone heaps from about 100 mammoths. Each hut probably housed a group of related families—about 20 to 25 people. (One hut was approximately 8 by 14 metres and had five hearths distributed inside it, presumably one for each family.) With 20 to 25 people per hut, and assuming that all four huts were occupied at the same time, the population of the settlement would have been 100 to 125.

Up a hill from the settlement was a fifth and different kind of hut. It was dug into the ground and contained a bake oven and more than 2300 small, fired fragments of animal figurines. There were also some hollow bones that may have been musical instruments. Another interesting feature of the settlement was a burial find of a woman with a disfigured face. She may have been a particularly important personage, because her face was found engraved on an ivory plaque near the central hearth of the settlement.

Upper Palaeolithic Tools

Upper Palaeolithic toolmaking appears to have had its roots in the Mousterian and post-Acheulian traditions, because flake tools are found in many Upper Palaeolithic sites. The Upper Palaeolithic, however, is characterized by a preponderance of blades; there were also burins, bone and antler tools, and *microliths* (see Figure 11–3).

In addition, two new techniques of toolmaking appeared—*indirect percussion* and *pressure flaking*. Blades were found in Middle Palaeolithic assemblages, but they were not widely used until the Upper Palaeolithic. Although blades can be made in a variety of ways, **indirect percussion** using a hammer-struck punch was commonly used in the Upper Palaeolithic. After shaping a core into a pyramidal or cylindrical form, the toolmaker put a punch of antler or wood or another hard material into position and struck it with a hammer. Because the force was directed, the toolmaker was able to strike off consistently shaped blades, which were more than twice as long as they were wide (Schick and Toth 1994; Whittaker 1994) (see Figure 11–4).

The Upper Palaeolithic is also noted for the production of large numbers of bone, antler, and ivory tools; needles, awls, and harpoons made of bone appear for the first time (Whittaker 1994). The manufacture of these implements may have been made easier by the development of many varieties of burins. Burins are chisel-like stone tools used for carving (see Figure 11–3); bone and

> **Indirect Percussion:** a toolmaking technique common in the Upper Palaeolithic. After shaping a core into a pyramidal or cylindrical form, the toolmaker could put a punch of antler or wood or another hard material into position and strike it with a hammer. Using a hammer-struck punch enabled the toolmaker to strike off consistently shaped blades.

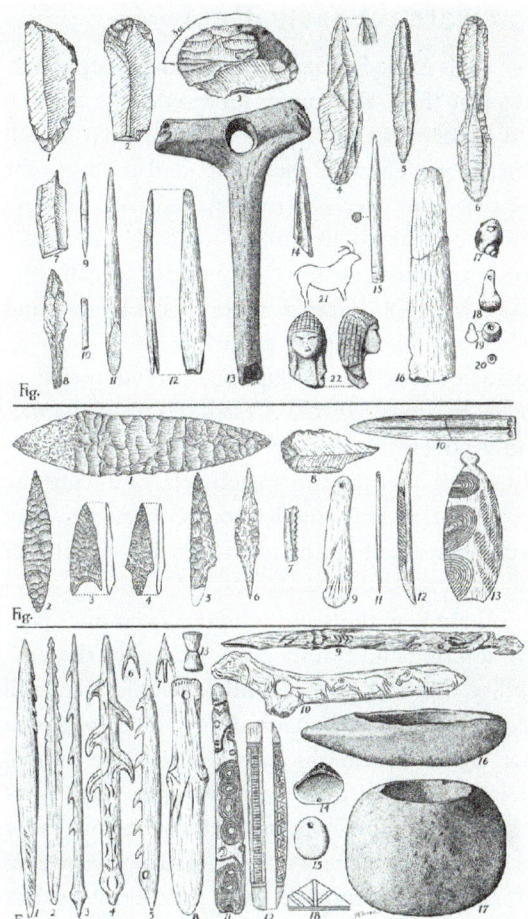

Figure 11–3 Upper Palaeolithic Tools

Upper Palaeolithic peoples made a much wider variety of tools than their predecessors.

Source: Reprinted with permission of the American Museum of Natural History

Figure 11–4 Percussion Flaking

One way to remove blades from a core is to hit them with a punch using indirect percussion. The object being struck is the punch, which is made of bone or horn.

Source: Fagan BM. 1972. In the beginning. Boston: Little, Brown. p. 195.

antler needles, awls, and projectile points could be produced with them (Bordaz 1970). Burins have been found in Middle and Lower Palaeolithic sites but are present in great number and variety only in the Upper Palaeolithic.

Pressure flaking also appeared during the Upper Palaeolithic. Rather than using percussion to strike off flakes as in previous technologies, pressure flaking works by employing pressure with a bone, wood, or antler tool at the edge of the tool to remove small flakes. Pressure flaking would usually be used in the final stages of retouching a tool (Whittaker 1994).

As time went on, all over the Old World smaller and smaller blade tools were produced. The very tiny ones, called **microliths**, were often hafted or fitted into handles, one blade at a time

> **Pressure Flaking:** toolmaking technique whereby small flakes are struck off by pressing against the core with a bone, antler, or wood tool.
> **Microlith:** a small, razor-like blade fragment that was probably attached in a series to a wooden or bone handle to form a cutting edge.

or several blades together, to serve as spears, adzes, knives, and sickles. The hafting required inventing a way to trim the blade's back edge so that it would be blunt rather than sharp. In this way the blades would not split the handles into which they might be inserted; the blunting would also prevent the users of an unhafted blade from cutting themselves (Phillipson 1993).

Some archaeologists think that the blade technique was adopted because it made for more economical use of flint. André Leroi-Gourhan of the Musée de l'Homme in Paris calculated that with the old Acheulian technique, a 1-kilogram lump of flint yielded 40 centimetres of working edge and produced only two hand axes. If the more advanced Mousterian technique were used, a lump of equal size would yield 1.8 metres of working edge. The indirect percussion method of the Upper Palaeolithic would yield as much as 22.8 metres of working edge (Bordaz 1970). With the same amount of material, a significantly greater number of tools could be produced. Getting the most out of a valuable resource may have been particularly important in areas lacking large flint deposits.

Jacques Bordaz suggested that the evolution of toolmaking techniques, which continually increased the amount of usable edge that could be derived from a lump of flint, was significant because people could then spend more time in regions where flint was unavailable. Another reason for adopting the blade toolmaking technique may have been that it made for easy repair of tools. For example, the cutting edge of a tool might consist of a line of razor-like microliths set into a piece of wood. The tool would not be usable if just one of the cutting edge's microliths broke off or was chipped. If, however, the user carried a small, prepared core of flint from which an identical-sized microlith could be struck off, the tool could be repaired easily by replacing the lost or broken microlith. A spear whose point was lost could be similarly repaired. Thus, the main purpose of the blade toolmaking technique may not have been to make more economical use of flint, but rather to allow easy replacement of damaged blades (Clark 1977).

How Were the Tools Used?

The tools made by Upper Palaeolithic people suggest that they were much more effective hunters and fishers than their predecessors (Klein 1994). During the Upper Palaeolithic, and probably for the first time, spears were launched with a spear-thrower rather than thrown with the arm. We know this because bone and antler **atlatls** (the Aztec word for "spear-thrower") have been found in some sites. A spear propelled off a grooved board could be sent through the air with increased force, causing it to travel farther and hit harder, and with less effort by the thrower. The bow and arrow was also used in various places during the Upper Palaeolithic, and harpoons, used for fishing and perhaps for hunting reindeer, were invented at this time.

These new tools and weapons for more effective hunting and fishing do not rule out the possibility that Upper Palaeolithic people were still scavenging animal remains. Olga Soffer suggested that Upper Palaeolithic people may have located their settlements near places where many mammoths died naturally in order to use the bones for building (see Figure 11–5). For example, in Moravia the mammoths may have come to lick deposits of calcite and other sources of magnesium and calcium, particularly during the late spring and early summer when food resources were short and mortality was high. Consistent with the idea that humans may not have killed all the enormous mammoths found there is the fact that in some places there are few human-made cut marks on mammoth bones. For example, at Dolní Věstonice, where bones of 100 mammoths were found, few bones show cut marks from butchering and few bones were found inside the huts. In contrast, the living floors are littered with bison, horse, and reindeer bones, suggesting that these other animals were deliberately killed and eaten by humans. If the people had actually killed all the mammoths that we find the remains of, why would they have hunted so many other animals (Soffer 1993)?

Atlatl: Aztec word for "spear-thrower."

Figure 11–5 Mammoth Shelters

Here we see the type of mammoth-bone shelters constructed about 15 000 years ago on the East European Plain. Often mammoth skulls formed part of the foundation for the tusk, long bone, and wooden frame, covered with hide. As many as 95 mammoth mandibles were arranged around the outside in a herringbone pattern.

Upper Palaeolithic Art

The earliest discovered traces of art are beads and carvings, and then paintings, from Upper Palaeolithic sites. We might expect that early artistic efforts were crude, but the cave paintings of Spain and southern France show a marked degree of skill. So do the naturalistic paintings on slabs of stone excavated in southern Africa. Some of those slabs appear to have been painted as much as 28 000 years ago, which suggests that painting in Africa is as old as painting in Europe (Phillipson 1993). In fact, painting may be even older than that. The early Australians may have painted on the walls of rock shelters and cliff faces at least 30 000 years ago and maybe as much as 60 000 years ago (Morell 1995).

Peter Ucko and André Rosenfeld identified three principal locations of paintings in the caves of western Europe: (1) in obviously inhabited rock shelters and cave entrances—art as decoration or "art for art's sake"; (2) in "galleries" immediately off the inhabited areas of caves; and (3) in the inner reaches of caves, whose difficulty of access has been interpreted by some as a sign that magical-religious activities were performed there (Ucko and Rosenfeld 1967).

The subjects of the paintings are mostly animals. The paintings rest on bare walls, with no backdrops or environmental trappings. Perhaps, like many contemporary peoples, Upper Palaeolithic men and women believed that the drawing of a human image could cause death or injury. If that were indeed their belief, it might explain why human figures are rarely depicted in cave art. Another explanation for the focus on animals might be that these people sought to improve their luck at hunting. This hypothesis is suggested by evidence of chips in the painted figures, perhaps made by spears thrown at the drawings.

A piece of three-dimensional Upper Palaeolithic art from France. This depiction of a bison licking itself is both accurate and beautifully executed, clearly showing the skill of Upper Palaeolithic artists.

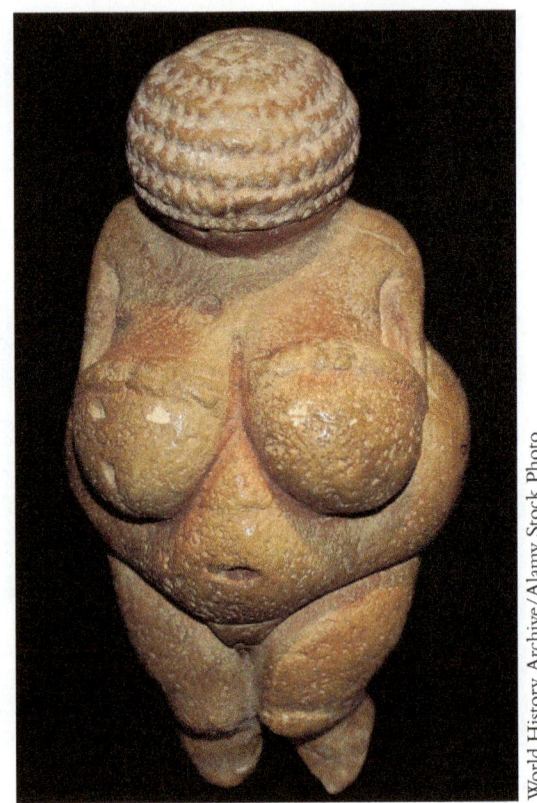

The Venus of Willendorf, one of the most famous Venus figurines.

However, if hunting magic was the chief motivation for the paintings, it is difficult to explain why only a few show signs of having been speared. Perhaps the paintings were inspired by the need to increase the supply of animals. Cave art seems to have reached a peak toward the end of the Upper Palaeolithic period, when the herds of game were decreasing.

The particular symbolic significance of the cave paintings in southwestern France is more explicitly revealed, perhaps, by the results of Patricia Rice and Ann Paterson's statistical study (Rice and Paterson 1985, 1986). The data suggest that the animals portrayed in the cave paintings were mostly the ones that the painters preferred for meat and for materials such as hides. For example, wild cattle (bovines) and horses are portrayed more often than we would expect by chance, probably because they were larger and heavier (meatier) than the other animals in the environment. In addition, the paintings mostly portray animals that the painters may have feared the most because of their size, speed, natural weapons such as tusks and horns, and unpredictability of behaviour. That is, mammoths, bovines, and horses are portrayed more often than deer and reindeer. Thus, the paintings are consistent with the idea that "the art is related to the importance of hunting in the economy of Upper Palaeolithic people" (Rice and Paterson 1985:98). Consistent with this idea, according to the investigators, is the fact that the art of the cultural period that followed the Upper Palaeolithic also seems to reflect how people got their food. However, in that period, when getting food no longer depended on hunting large game (because they were becoming extinct), the art ceased to focus on portrayals of animals.

Upper Palaeolithic art was not confined to cave paintings. Many shafts of spears and similar objects were decorated with figures of animals. Alexander Marshack had an interesting interpretation of some of the engravings made during the Upper Palaeolithic. He suggested that as far back as 30 000 B.C., hunters may have used a system of notation, engraved on bone and stone, to mark the phases of the moon. If this is true, it would mean that Upper Palaeolithic people were capable of complex thought and were consciously aware of their environment (Marshack 1972). In addition, figurines representing the human female in exaggerated form have been found at Upper

Palaeolithic sites. Called *Venuses*, these figurines portray women with broad hips and large breasts and abdomens. It has been suggested that the figurines were an ideal type or an expression of a desire for fertility. Most of these figurines were made during the Gravettian period from about 25 000 to 23 000 years ago. Clive Gamble argued that the Venus figurines were religious in nature. As such, their presence in the archaeological record implies a widespread belief system shared between geographically isolated groups. From her analysis of the shape, size, and form of almost 200 figurines, Patricia Rice concluded that the figurines reflect a distribution of ages similar to the demographic profiles seen in contemporary foraging groups. A number of questions remain unanswered, however, particularly regarding the general featureless style of the figures. LeRoy McDermott suggested they are a reflection of how a woman represents herself through self-observation, including the absence of anatomical features and distortions in the bodily proportions. However, more recent exploration of these artifacts by Soffer and colleagues suggested that a variety of aspects of these figurines have been missed or misinterpreted by past investigations. In particular, these researchers argued that a number of the figurines are depicted wearing clothing that demonstrates considerable craftsmanship and knowledge of woven fabric (Marshack 1972). In addition to the Venus figurines, there are other depictions of women in Upper Palaeolithic art.

In a survey of Upper Palaeolithic art, Jean-Pierre Duhard (1993) found that all shapes and sizes of women, as well as all age ranges, were present. Indeed, he argued that a range of female body types can be seen. One engraved figure from Gönnersdorf cave on the Rhine River, for example, depicts four women. Three are the same size, but one is smaller and has small breasts—she may be an adolescent. Of the three larger figures, one appears to have a child tied to her back, and she also has large, rounded breasts, as opposed to the flat and pointed breasts of the other two. Duhard argued that this is an accurate depiction of four women, one with a child she is breast-feeding.

Duhard (1993) suggested that women's roles as mothers may have given them a privileged status in Upper Palaeolithic life, which may be why that status is the most frequently depicted subject in Upper Palaeolithic art. In a similar way, Patricia Rice (1981) argued that Venus figurines accurately reflect the social importance of women in Upper Palaeolithic society. She demonstrated that a range of body types and ages are represented in Venus figurines, and argued that, since the Venuses depict real women of all ages, not just pregnant women, they should be seen as symbols of "womanhood" rather than "motherhood." The wide distribution of Venus figurines and their apparent importance to Upper Palaeolithic peoples reflect, according to Rice, the recognized importance of women in Upper Palaeolithic society.

Arguing along similar lines, Soffer et al. (2000) examined the clothing worn by some Venus figures. They showed that woven items are the most frequently depicted, and argued that, since these woven items would have been highly valued in Upper Palaeolithic society, their presence on some Venus figurines suggests that some women held positions of high status in Upper Palaeolithic society.

Duhard also argued that while depictions of women are common in Upper Palaeolithic art, similar depictions of men and children are comparatively rare. He suggested this disparity may reflect women's status in Upper Palaeolithic societies. Most depictions of women show them in some motherhood role—pregnant, in childbirth, or carrying an infant (and perhaps walking with older children).

The controversies surrounding Venus figurines provide insight into a basic problem in archaeology: there is often little or no evidence available that allows us to accept or reject a particular interpretation. Rather, in most cases, we have to balance data and interpretation to come to an informed judgment, recognizing that our judgment will likely change with new data.

Language

When did hominins acquire language? It is a notoriously difficult question to answer archaeologically.

Some scholars have argued that *Homo erectus* must have had language to develop the broadly shared Acheulean tool tradition. Others have suggested that the modern FOXP2 gene is directly associated with language, and because Neandertals and modern humans share the same gene, Neandertals must have had language. But none of this is direct evidence of language (see Current Research and Issues, "How Did Spoken Language Emerge?" for theories on the origins of language in our ancestors).

If we think of language as a system of shared symbols (whether vocal or written), then the

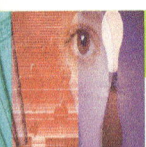

CURRENT RESEARCH AND ISSUES

How Did Spoken Language Emerge?

The origins of spoken language are largely a mystery, owing to the fact that no written or fossil record of its emergence was left behind. Intuitively, one might expect that language was a natural extension of the sounds our ancestors produced. Danish linguist Otto Jespersen had two theories about the vocal origins of human speech. His "bow-wow" theory suggested that early humans formed their first words by imitating the sounds they heard in nature, and eventually they began using those sounds to refer to the objects making them. However, critics of this theory noted that this process fails to supply words for silent objects, abstract concepts, and most parts of speech. Jespersen also proposed the similar "pooh-pooh" theory, which posits that speech developed from instinctive vocalizations uttered when experiencing certain emotions, like sighs of pleasure or moans of pain, and that these sounds eventually came to have certain emotional connotations. Most of the objections to the "bow-wow" hypothesis apply here as well.

A separate theory holds that the first step toward language was the evolution of bipedalism. Walking on two legs would have freed up the upper limbs, making them available for gesturing; many researchers believe it was this gestural communication that paved the way for spoken language. After all, children use gestures to communicate before they learn to speak, and studies have shown that the same neural structures in the brain underlie both verbal and gestural communication. What would have triggered the shift in early *Homo* from gestures to spoken language? With the advent of toolmaking, spoken language may have been the only available means of communication while one's hands were busy fashioning tools. Another possibility is that for early toolmaking technology to successfully spread, the capacity to teach, along with some form of spoken language (or protolanguage), was required.

Whether the vocal or gestural theories hold true, it wasn't until certain genetic changes occurred and specialized structural anatomy evolved that speech would have been possible. More than 100 000 years ago our ancestors' mouths began getting smaller and their tongues became more flexible, while their necks grew longer. Additionally, the hyoid bone (the only bone in the body not connected to any other) was well positioned to support the root of the tongue in early modern humans and Neandertals. Though other animal species have their own versions of this bone, the one present in members the genus *Homo* is the only version that is correctly positioned to enable speech. In addition, the FOXP2 gene, sometimes referred to as the "language gene," appears to be necessary for human speech as mutations in this gene result in severe speech impairments. Astonishingly, only three mutations differ between the mice and human versions of the gene, while only two mutations separate the chimpanzee version from ours. The human form appears to have arisen within the past 200 000 years, corresponding to the emergence of bipedalism and, perhaps, the beginnings of the transition from gestural to vocal communication in humans.

Sources: Aitchiso J. 1996. The Seeds of Speech: Language Origin and Evolution. Cambridge: Cambridge University Press.

Arbib MA, Liebal K, Pika S. 2008. Primate Vocalization, Gesture, and the Evolution of Human Language. Current Anthropology. 49:1053–1076.

Hauser MD, Chomsky N, Tecumseh Fitch W. 2002. The Faculty of Language: What Is It, Who Has It, and How Did It Evolve? Science. 298:1569–1579.

Lieberman P, McCarthy R. 2007. Tracking the Evolution of Language and Speech: Comparing Vocal Tracts to Identify Speech Capabilities. Expedition: The Magazine of the University of Pennsylvania. 49:15–20.

Morgan TJH, Uomini NT, Rendell LE, Chouinard-Thuly L, Street SE, Lewis HM, Cross CR, Evans C, Kearney R, de la Torre I, Whiten A, Laland KN. 2015. Experimental Evidence for the Co-evolution of Hominin Tool-Making Teaching and Language. Nature Communications. 6:6029.

emergence of symbolic art in the Upper Palaeolithic may be taken as direct archaeological evidence of language. Indeed, palaeoanthropologist Richard Klein sees the rapid emergence of art and ritual in the Upper Palaeolithic as evidence of the emergence of the modern human brain. He believes that around 50 000 years ago some key mutation occurred that unlocked our big brain's potential for abstract and symbolic thought. But evidence for complex human cognition pre-dates 50 000 years ago elsewhere, in southern Africa. For example, at Blombos Cave, 70 000 to 75 000 years ago, there is substantial evidence for engraving bone, decorating with ochre, creating shell-bead necklaces, and pressure flaking lithic artifacts long before such evidence occurs in Europe (D'Errico et al. 2001, 2005; Henshilwood et al. 2001, 2009, 2011; Mourre et al. 2010).

Whenever and wherever it happened, the potential for abstract and symbolic thought is important for the evolution of complex cultural life as we know it today. As Klein explained,

This is because it permitted its possessors to extract far more energy from nature and to invest it in society. It also allowed human populations to colonize new and challenging environments. Possibly the most critical aspect of the neural change was that it allowed the kind of rapidly spoken phonemic language that is inseparable from culture as we know it today. (Klein and Edgar 2002:24; see also Klein 2009:650–653).

For now, all we can say is that the symbolic aspects of culture blossomed during the Upper Palaeolithic and set the stage for the complex cultural life we follow today. The emergence of language may well have been a key aspect of the Upper Palaeolithic cultural fluorescence.

Upper Palaeolithic Cultures in Africa and Asia

Europe was not the only region where Upper Palaeolithic peoples thrived. In North Africa, for example, Upper Palaeolithic peoples hunted large animals on the grasslands that covered the region

Paintings in the "Hall of Bulls" at Lascaux in France. Cave paintings like this demonstrate the remarkable skill of Upper Palaeolithic artists.

during that period. They lived in small communities located within easy access to water and other resources, and moved regularly, probably to follow the animal herds. Trade took place between local groups, particularly for high-quality stone used in making tools (Hawkins and Kleindienst 2001). In eastern and southern Africa, a way of life known as the Later Stone Age developed that persisted in some areas until very recently. People lived in small, mobile groups, hunting large animals and collecting a wide variety of plant foods. Interaction was common among these bands. Among their ethnographically known descendants, individuals would regularly switch their membership from one band to another (Peregrine 2001).

In South Asia the Upper Palaeolithic saw an increasingly sedentary lifestyle developing along the banks of freshwater streams. The Upper Palaeolithic peoples in South Asia combined hunting, fishing, and gathering with seasonal movements to exploit seasonally abundant resources (Jayaswal 2002). In East and Southeast Asia ocean resources became vital to coastal-dwelling peoples, while those inland lived primarily in caves, hunting and collecting broadly in the local environment. Many of these sites appear to have been occupied for long periods of time, suggesting some degree of sedentism. During the Upper Palaeolithic, peoples from Asia also populated Australia, New Guinea, and some of the islands of western Melanesia, clearly demonstrating the ability of these peoples to navigate on the sea and to use its resources (Peregrine and Bellwood 2001).

The Earliest Humans in the New World

So far in this chapter we have dealt only with the Old World—Africa, Europe, and Asia. What about the New World—North and South America? How long have humans lived there, and what were their earliest cultures like?

Because only *H. sapiens sapiens* fossils have been found in North and South America, migrations of humans to the New World had to have taken place sometime after the emergence of *H. sapiens sapiens*. When exactly these migrations occurred is subject to debate, particularly about when people got to areas south of Alaska (see Applied Anthropology, "Who Were the First North Americans?"). At the Old Crow site on the Porcupine River in Yukon Territory, a possible early human occupation site has been dated to between 12 000 and 27 000 years ago (Morlan et al. 1990). If the site is indeed that old, it represents the oldest known human habitation site in the New World. Nearby, the Bluefish Caves site in Yukon Territory revealed the faunal remains of mammoth, horse, bison, and caribou. Stone tools, including some microblades, were discovered at the site. Radiocarbon dating on bone collagen from the faunal remains suggests a date of between 15 000 and 12 000 years ago (Harington and Cinq-Mars 1995; Burke and Cinq-Mars 1998). Because of a lack of archaeological evidence in the northwest Arctic, the prevailing view has been that humans were not present south of Alaska until after 15 000 years ago. However, evidence from an archaeological site called Monte Verde in Chile suggests that modern humans might have been living in southern South America at least 12 500 years ago, and maybe as much as 33 000 years ago. The Monte Verde site contains more than 700 stone tools, the remains of hide-covered huts, and a child's footprint next to a hearth (McDonald 1998).

The people there may or may not have hunted big game, but just a little while later there were people living in the tropical rain forest of the Amazon basin in what is now Brazil who were definitely not hunters of mammoths and other big game, as their contemporaneous North American counterparts were. In other words, it looks like the earliest inhabitants of the New World—in what is now Chile and Brazil, and in North America—varied in culture. The people in the Amazon lived by collecting fruits and nuts, fishing, and hunting small game. They lived in caves with painted art on the walls and left 30 000 stone chips from making tips of spears, darts, or harpoons (Gibbons 1995; Roosevelt et al. 1996).

And there are other possible sites of early occupation (Goebel et al. 2008). For example, the Cactus Hill site in Virginia, the Gault site in Texas, and the Shriver site in Missouri all contain a stratum of blades and other stone tools below a Palaeo-Indian stratum containing Clovis tools (described later in this chapter). Meadowcroft Rockshelter in western Pennsylvania contains the most carefully reported pre-Clovis occupation in North America (Dillehay 2000). In the bottom third of a stratum that seems to date from 19 600 years to 8000 years ago, the Meadowcroft site shows clear signs of human occupation—a small fragment of human bone, a spearpoint, and chipped knives and scrapers. If the dating is accurate, the tools would be about 12 800 years old. Perhaps the most surprising physical evidence for early people in the Americas comes from the Paisley Caves in southern Oregon. Here, human coprolites (dried feces) have been found and dated to 14 400 years ago (Gilbert et al. 2008). Stone tools dating to about 13 000 years ago have also been found (Jenkins et al. 2012).

On the basis of similarities in biological traits such as tooth forms and blood types, and on possible linguistic relationships, anthropologists agree that North American Indigenous people originally came from Asia. The traditional assumption is that they came to North America from Siberia, walking across a land bridge (Beringia) that is now under water (the Bering Strait) between Siberia and Alaska. The ice sheets or glaciers that periodically covered most of the high latitudes of the world contained so much of the world's water (the ice sheets were thousands of metres thick in some places) that **Beringia** was dry land in various periods (see Figure 11–6). For example, there was a land bridge for a while until the last 10 000 years or so. Since then, the glaciers have mostly melted, and the Bering "bridge" has been completely covered by a higher sea level.

It was geologically possible for humans to have walked into the New World at various times, and

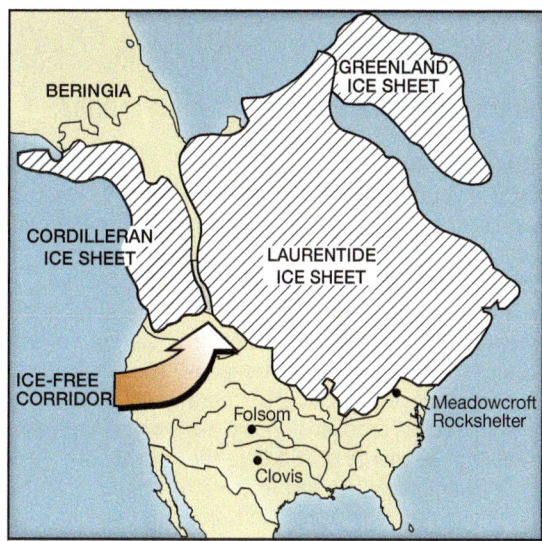

Figure 11–6 Beringia and the Ice Sheets

Source: Meltzer DK. 1993. Pleistocene peopling of the Americas. Evolutionary Anthropology. Vol. 1. Copyright © 1993. John Wiley and Sons, Inc.

they could have travelled by boat, too, as coastal areas of Alaska were ice-free by at least 16 000 years ago (Meltzer 2009). Parts of the Beringia land bridge were exposed from about 60 000 years to 25 000 years ago. Not until between 20 000 years and 18 000 years ago was the land bridge at its maximum, and it was finally inundated about 10 000 years ago. An ice-free corridor between the Laurentide and Cordilleran ice sheets may have been present after 25 000 years ago, but that corridor is not likely to have supported big game, and permitted humans to hunt enough for sustenance, until after about 14 000 years ago (Hoffecker et al. 1993). Thus, it is likely that humans didn't arrive in the New World over land until after 14 000 years ago, but they could have arrived by a coastal route in boats much earlier, and certainly after 16 000 years ago (Pringle 2011).

According to the comparative linguists Joseph Greenberg and Merritt Ruhlen, there were three waves of migration into the New World (Greenberg and Ruhlen 1992). They compared hundreds of languages in North and South America, grouping them into three different language families. Because each of these language families has a closer relationship to

---

Beringia: the land mass that is now under water (the Bering Strait) between Siberia and Alaska.

APPLIED ANTHROPOLOGY

Who Were the First North Americans?

The most widely accepted model for how humans entered the New World is by walking across Beringia, which joined Asia and North America at the end of the last ice age, when sea levels were lower than today. There is good evidence to support this model, both archaeological and geological. But there are also some problems. There are sites that appear to date before the time when glacial ice had retreated far enough to allow access to North America. There are also South American sites that appear to be older than the oldest North American ones, which seems contradictory to a model based on humans moving into the New World from north to south. Humans may have travelled to North America by boat along the glaciated coastline of the Bering Sea.

Though most of Canada was covered in ice sheets during the last ice age, Old Crow Flats and Basin in Canada's northern Yukon was one of the areas untouched by glaciation. The area contains evidence of human habitation dating about 12 000 years ago. Additionally, fluted points and flakes and microblades discovered at the Bluefish Caves in northeast Yukon indicate humans occupied the area between 25 000 and 12 000 years ago. However, there are no human bones in Canada that lend direct support to the Beringia model.

An alternative model for human entry into the New World, which solves some of the problems with the Beringia model, suggests that some people came to the New World from Asia by boat. These people would have moved along the sea edge of the glaciers, subsisting on fish and sea mammals. Once past the glaciers, they either would have moved farther down the coast, perhaps all the way to the tip of South America, or proceeded inland into North America. Small groups of people may have made such voyages on many occasions, and it may be that none established communities that lasted more than a few generations.

Some scholars posit that the few very early archaeological sites may be the remnants of these early explorers. The small numbers would leave only a small archaeological record, so it is not surprising that more material has not been found. The fact that early occupations at a number of sites are separated from later occupations by soil showing no signs of human presence may also be evidence that these early explorers were present but died out. Additional support for the coastal migration model has recently come from archaeological explorations of ancient coastlines now lying deep beneath the Bering Sea. Archaeologists have found stone tools in locations that would have been coastal during the last ice age.

Skeletons of very early North Americans also suggest there may have been early populations that died out, as many appear more similar to East Asians than to contemporary Indigenous North Americans in their skeletal features. If the colonization of the Americas was not as simple as the Beringia model suggests, how are archaeologists to determine descendant groups? What if no descendants remain? Current historic preservation laws make the situation difficult, and a number of lawsuits have tested the question of whether or not the first North Americans were directly ancestral to contemporary Indigenous peoples. The most well known of these legal cases involved a 9300-year-old skeleton found along the Columbia River near Kennewick, Washington. After a nearly decade-long legal battle, a federal court decided that the skeleton was not "Native American" under current laws. Other cases are pending, and the U.S. Congress may step in to clarify the legal status of the first Americans. Canada has a similar policy of repatriation of human remains to Indigenous communities, but it has not officially passed into legislation.

Sources: Dillehay T. 2000. The Settlement of the Americas. New York: Basic Books.

MacDowell LS. 2012. An Environmental History of Canada. Vancouver: UBC Press. p. 14.

Powell J. 2005. The First Americans. New York: Cambridge University Press.

Thomas DH. 2000. Skull Wars. New York: Basic Books.

an Asian language family than to the other New World language families, it would appear that three different migrations came out of Asia. The first arrivals spoke a language that diverged over time into most of the languages found in the New World—the Amerind family of languages; the speakers of these related languages came to occupy all of South and Central America as well as most of North America. Next came the ancestors of the people who speak languages belonging to the Na-Dené family, which today includes Haida on the northwest coast of Canada, Navaho and Apache in the southwestern

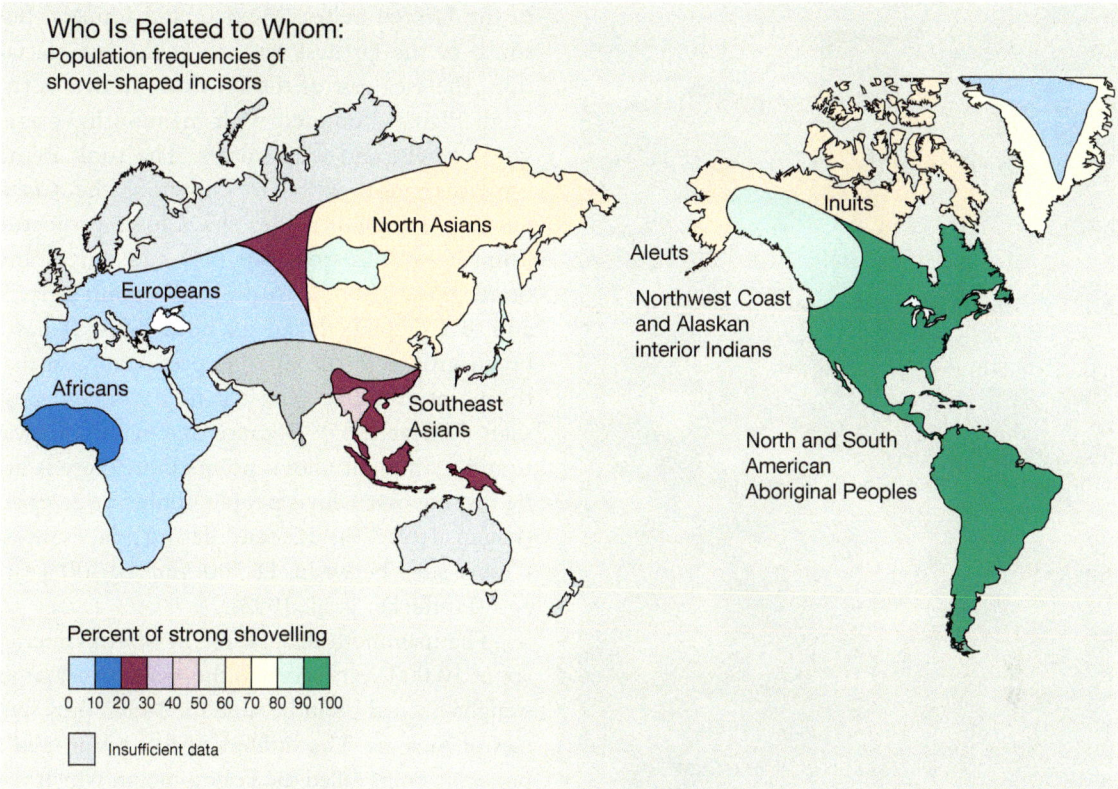

Figure 11–7 Who Is Related to Whom? Population Frequencies of Shovel-Shaped Incisors

Inuit and Aleut, speakers of Na-Dené languages, and other Indigenous language groups differ in the frequency of shovel-shaped incisors. These genetic differences seem to reflect three waves of migration into the New World.

Source: Based on data from Turner II CG. January 1987. Telltale Teeth. Natural History 8.

United States, and various Athapaskan languages. Finally, perhaps 4000 years ago, came the ancestors of Inuit and Aleut (the latter came to occupy the islands southwest of Alaska and the adjacent mainland), who speak languages belonging to the Inuit-Aleut family.

Christy Turner's study of New World teeth supports the Greenberg and Ruhlen proposal of three separate migrations. Turner looked at the proportions of shovel-shaped incisors, a common Asian trait, in New World populations. The varying proportions fall into three distinct groupings, the same three suggested by the linguists (Turner II 1989) (see Figure 11–7). In contrast, genetic analysis suggests that Inuit-Aleut may have split from Na-Dené in the New World (Szathmáry 1993). In their study of mtDNA, Rubicz and colleagues (2004) also suggested that the Aleut represent a distinct wave of migration across Beringia. Schurr and Sherry's (2004) analysis of mtDNA and Y chromosome data suggested a migration from Siberia into the New World around 15 000 to 20 000 years ago. Current recent genetic analyses generally support the three-wave migration model but also suggest that the peopling of the New World may have been even more complicated (Reich et al. 2012). There could have been four separate migrations from the Old World, from different regions of Asia (McDonald 1998; Turner 2005).

The Palaeo-Indians

Archaeological remains of early New World hunters, called *Palaeo-Indians*, have been found

A jury of visiting archaeologists at the Monte Verde site in Chile confirmed that modern humans arrived in southern South America at least 12 500 years ago.

in the United States, Mexico, and Canada. Just south of the farthest reaches of the last glaciation, the area east of the Rockies known as the High Plains abounded with mammoths, bison, wild camels, and wild horses. The tools found with mammoth kills are known as the *Clovis complex*, which includes the Clovis projectile point as well as stone scrapers and knives and bone tools. The Clovis projectile point is large and leaf-shaped, flaked on both sides. It has a broad groove in the middle, presumably so that the point could be attached to a wooden spear shaft (Wheat 1967). Because one mammoth was found with eight Clovis points in it, there is little dispute that Clovis people hunted large game (Fagan 1991:79). Recent dating places most Clovis sites between 11 200 and 10 900 years ago (Hoffecker et al. 1993).

The mammoth disappeared in North America about 10 000 years ago, and the now extinct large, straight-horned bison became the largest prey species of humans. The hunters of that bison used a projectile point called the Folsom point, which was much smaller than the Clovis point. Tools are also found with many other kinds of animal remains, including wolf, turtle, rabbit, horse, fox, deer, and camel, so the bison hunters obviously depended on

Both Clovis and pre-Clovis stone tools have been found at the Cactus Hill site in Virginia. Now a number of sites suggest humans were present in North America shortly before the Clovis culture emerged.

other animals as well (Jennings 1968). In the Rio Grande valley, the Folsom toolmakers characteristically established a base camp on low dune ridges overlooking both a large pond and broad, open grazing areas. If we assume that the pond provided water for the grazing herds, the people in the camp would have been in an excellent position to watch the herds (Judge and Dawson 1972).

As the climate of what is now the American Southwest became drier, the animals and the cultural adaptations changed somewhat. About 9000 years ago the earlier straight-horned bison variety became extinct and was replaced by smaller modern forms (Wheat 1967). Base camps began to be located farther from ponds and grazing areas and closer to streams. If the ponds were no longer reliable sources of water during these drier times, the animals probably no longer frequented them, which would explain why the hunters had to change the sites of their base camps. Not that much is known about the plant foods these people may have exploited, but on the desert fringes plant gathering may have been vital. In Nevada and Utah, archaeologists have found milling stones and other artifacts for processing plant food (Fagan 1989).

The Olsen-Chubbuck site, a kill site excavated in Colorado, shows the organization that may have been involved in hunting bison (Wheat 1967). In a dry gulch dated to 6500 B.C. were the remains of 200 bison. At the bottom were complete skeletons and at the top, those of completely butchered animals. This find clearly suggests that hunters deliberately stampeded the animals into a natural *trapùan arroyo*, or steep-sided dry gully. The animals in front were probably pushed by the ones behind into the arroyo. Joe Wheat estimated that the hunters might have obtained 25 000 kilograms of meat from this one kill. If we judge from the habits of 19th-century Plains peoples, who could prepare bison meat to last a month, and estimate that each person would eat half a kilogram a day, the kill at the Olsen-Chubbuck site could have fed more than 1800 people for a month (they probably did not all live together throughout the year).

The hunters must have been highly organized, not only for the stampede itself, but also for butchering. It seems that the enormous carcasses had to be dragged to flat ground for that job. In addition, the 25 000 kilograms of meat and hides had to be carried back to camp (Wheat 1967). Since a dead bison is too bulky and heavy to move whole, the kill site is usually the scene of primary butchering. This involves cutting manageable portions off the carcass and removing them for secondary butchering and processing elsewhere. The low-value portions of the skeleton are abandoned in the "kill floor," perhaps to be exposed later by the archaeologist. In this case they are overlying the unbutchered animals that got trampled under by the stampede into the trap. There are important social implications associated with all the processes required for an undertaking of this magnitude. In particular it requires large groups and thorough political integration to organize these kills and subsequently distribute the meat and hides among participants.

The "river of bones" at the Olsen-Chubbuck site. These are the remains of bison that Palaeo-Indian hunters stampeded into an arroyo.

Although big game may have been most important on the High Plains, other areas show different adaptations. For example, Palaeo-Indian people in woodland regions of what is now the United States seem to have depended more heavily on plant food and smaller game. In some woodland areas, fish and shellfish may have been a vital part of the diet (Fagan 1989). On the Pacific coast, some Palaeo-Indian people developed food-getting strategies more dependent on fish (Fagan 1991). And in other areas, the lower Illinois River valley being one example, Palaeo-Indian people who depended on game and wild vegetable foods managed to get enough food to live in permanent villages of perhaps 100 to 150 people (Fagan 1989).

As the climate became warmer and drier, the flora and fauna of North America changed. Megafauna, as elsewhere in the world, went extinct, and were replaced by smaller mammals, particularly deer. The availability of meat was greatly reduced—hunters could count on coming home with kilograms, not tonnes, of meat. Warmer-adapted plants replaced cold-adapted plants, and were used for food to replace the meat that was no longer available. Warmer-adapted plants had advantages as food resources for humans over cold-adapted ones because edible seeds, fruits, and nuts were more common, and often more plentiful and accessible, on the warmer-adapted plants. Thus a much greater diversity of plants and animals came to be used by the Archaic peoples (Daniel 2001).

The Archaic peoples of North America began to follow a more sedentary lifestyle. Two forms of Archaic settlement appear to have been typical. One was a residential base camp, which would have been inhabited seasonally by several, probably related families. The other was a special-purpose camp, which would have been a short-term habitation near a particular resource or perhaps used by a group of hunters for a short period (Sassaman 1996). On the Atlantic coast, for example, individual groups apparently moved seasonally along major river valleys, establishing summer base camps in the piedmont and winter camps near the coast. Special-purpose camps were created year-round as groups went out from the base camp to hunt and collect particular resources, such as stone for making tools (Sassaman 1996).

One of the innovations of the Archaic peoples was the development of ground stone woodworking tools. Axes, adzes, and tools for grinding seeds and nuts become more and more common in the tool kit (Brown 1983). This probably reflects the emergence of greater areas of forest following the retreat of the glaciers from North America, but it also demonstrates a greater reliance on forest products and, most likely, a greater use of wood and wood products. Fish and shellfish also came to be relied upon in some areas, and this too reflects the adjustment made by the Archaic peoples to the changing conditions they faced at the end of the last ice age.

Early Arctic Populations

The **Palaeo-Arctic tradition** represents the first undisputed cultural development in the Arctic, after the more tentative early occupation sites associated with the peopling of the New World. The earliest well-documented Palaeo-Arctic sites are dated from 8000 B.C. to 5000 B.C., and are identified by stone tools, including microblades and small bifaces—no bone artifacts have been found (McGhee 1996). The Palaeo-Arctic tradition is present throughout Alaska, east into the southwestern Yukon, and south to Haida Gwaii in British Columbia. Following the Palaeo-Arctic tradition comes the **Arctic Small Tool tradition**, representing the first humans to move into the eastern Canadian Arctic and Greenland. In Alaska the Arctic Small Tool tradition evolved into the *Norton tradition*, while in the eastern Arctic it became the

> **Palaeo-Arctic Tradition:** the first undisputed cultural development in the Arctic, after the more tentative early occupation sites associated with the peopling of the New World. The earliest well-documented Palaeo-Arctic sites occur from 8000 B.C. to 5000 B.C.
>
> **Arctic Small Tool Tradition:** culture that follows the Palaeo-Arctic tradition, representing the first humans to move into the eastern Canadian Arctic and Greenland. In Alaska the Arctic Small Tool tradition evolved into the Norton tradition, while in the eastern Arctic it became the Dorset culture.

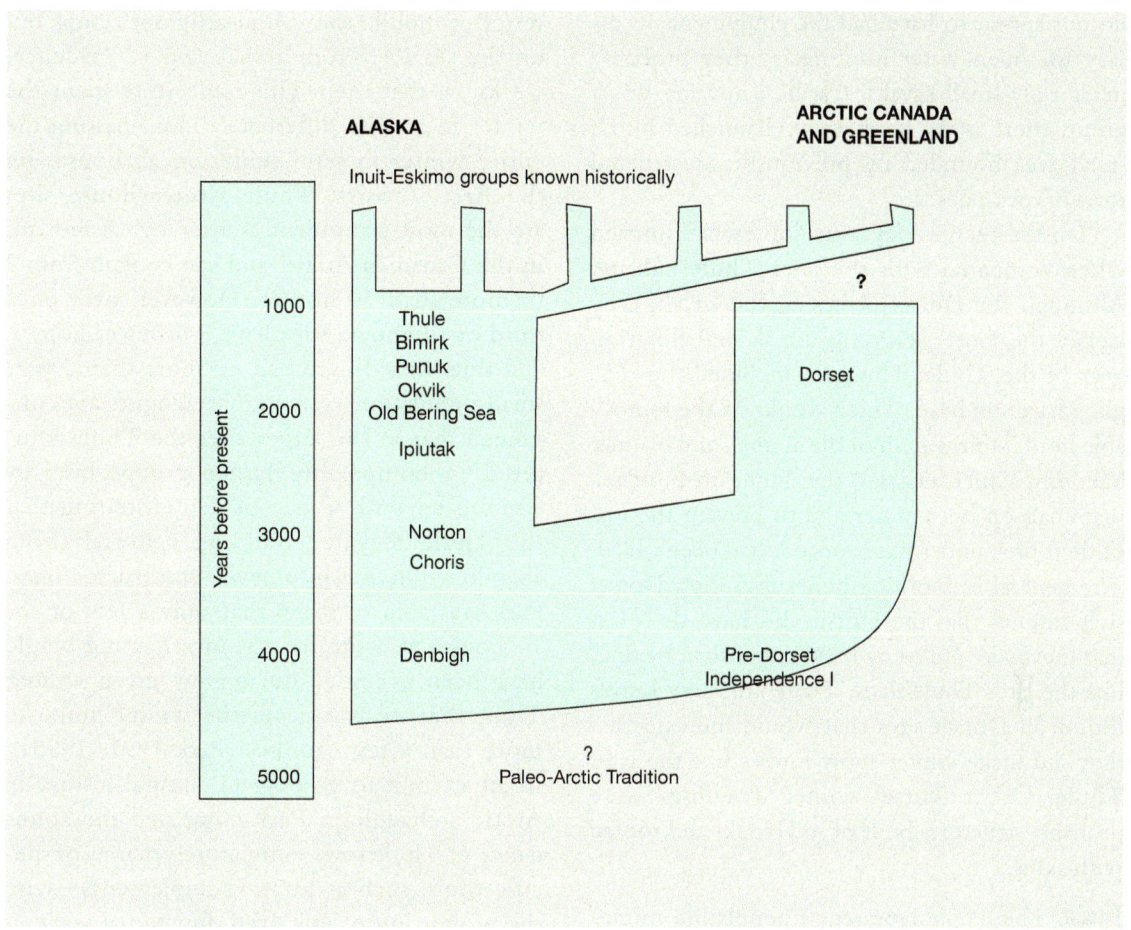

Figure 11–8 A Model of the Cultural Relationships between Early Arctic Peoples in North America

This model, proposed by Robert Park, shows the relationship between modern Inuit populations and a variety of archaeologically defined Arctic populations over the past 5000 years. In particular note that it is the Thule rather than the Dorset tradition that is the precursor to modern Arctic populations.

Source: Robert Park's webpage (http://anthropology.uwaterloo.ca/park.html). Reprinted with permission of Robert Park.

Dorset culture. The later Thule tradition developed from the Norton tradition in the area around Bering Strait and subsequently spread throughout the entire Arctic region with the exception of the Aleutian Islands (see Figure 11–8).

Arctic Small Tool Tradition

The Arctic Small Tool tradition represents a widespread phenomenon in the North American Arctic that occurred between approximately 2000 B.C. and 800 B.C. It is characterized by finely made microblades, burins, scrapers, and blades, and, more important, the bow and arrow. The Arctic Small Tool tradition does not appear to be related to the preceding Palaeo-Arctic tradition, but is most likely the product of a rapid migration of people from eastern Siberia.

Dorset. The Dorset culture was an incredibly stable Arctic culture, surviving longest in the eastern Arctic regions (Maxwell 1985; McGhee 1996). The Dorset subsistence pattern depended mostly on seal, caribou, muskox, and fish, but bones of walrus, polar bear, and some bird species have also been found (Maxwell 1985; McGhee 1996). Seal was probably primarily hunted on the sea ice or by hunting along the edge of ice floes; the Dorset do not appear to have had the equipment necessary for open-water hunting, as they probably made only small kayaks. Caribou hunting was a group effort as the herds were channelled into a small area bounded by previously constructed rows of rock piles.

Dorset technology was somewhat limited when compared with the later Thule culture. Although the Dorset possessed the kayak, they lacked the larger seagoing umiak and flotation gear of the Thule. This gear included the toggling harpoon head, which would fix the removable head into the flesh of the animal, and bladder balloons, which enabled the Thule to hunt sea mammals on open water and to prevent the loss of their prey under water once it had been killed. The general lack of dog bones found on Dorset sites implies that the Dorset did have sleds but that they were pulled by hand rather than by dogs like the later Thule sleds. There are snow knives found on Dorset sites that would indicate that they did make winter snow houses like the later Thule. Other Dorset winter dwellings were probably structures built of sod blocks and roofed with skins.

Thule. The Thule represent a population migration from Alaska that brought with it a whole new technology. This technology included the use of metals including iron (the Dorset had used some cold-worked copper), which came through contact with Siberia in their Alaskan homeland (Maxwell 1985; McGhee 1996). In the west, some Thule groups also used crude ceramics, but in the eastern Arctic soapstone was utilized for bowls and cooking pots. Modern Inuit are descended from the Thule population (Park 1993, 2000).

From historic records we know that when Europeans arrived in the Arctic, large groups of Inuit would spend the winter together in a series of mobile snow-house (igloo) camps out on the sea ice. From archaeological evidence, we know that their Thule ancestors spent the winter in a quite different fashion, passing the entire winter in semi-subterranean houses on the Arctic coasts. Thule winter house sites are the most prominent archaeological remains in the Canadian Arctic, and can contain from 2 to more than 50 houses. However, over one-third of all known sites have 3 or fewer houses, and thus would have had no more than a very small population. Some archaeologists are convinced that at the larger sites the Thule wintered in comparably larger groups but, by coming up with a way of demonstrating that the Thule recycled building materials from abandoned houses into newly constructed ones, Park was able to show that only a few of the 14 houses at a site he was investigating would have been occupied during any given winter. Thus, the site was never the winter home to more than a few families (Park 1997, 1998a). In an attempt to go beyond cultural history in Arctic archaeology, Park compared the abundance of Thule toys—miniature versions of specific tools, such as hunting implements—with the proportion of full-sized, functional versions of the same types. He found that the miniature and full-sized versions of several classes of artifacts occurred in strikingly similar proportions, but with a few significant exceptions. Studying these patterns allowed him to explore differences in gender roles between children and adults in Thule culture. He was able to demonstrate that the historic Inuit practice of treating children as "miniature adults" was practised by the Thule people as well. Intriguingly, there are hints that children in the Dorset culture did not have the same types of toys, suggesting that the experience of childhood may have been different in that earlier culture (Park 1998b)

SUMMARY AND REVIEW

THE EMERGENCE OF MODERN HUMANS

11.1 Evaluate the theories have been proposed to explain the origins of modern humans.

- The replacement or single-origin theory suggests that modern humans originated one part of the Old World, likely Africa, and then spread to other parts, completely replacing all other hominin species. This theory suggests that anatomically distinct hominin species and modern humans should occur in each region and they should overlap in time. There should be little or no gene flow between modern humans and earlier hominins, and no continuity in behaviour between earlier *H. sapiens* and modern humans.

- The multiregional theory suggests that *Homo erectus* populations in each part of the Old World evolved into anatomically modern humans. There should be a genetic contribution from archaic *H. sapiens* to modern populations in a region and gene flow between regions. There should be intermediate fossil forms between *Homo erectus* and modern humans in each region, and continuity in behaviour from earlier *H. sapiens* to later modern humans.

- The assimilation theory is a variation on the replacement theory. It suggests there was replacement of hominin species in the Old World by modern human populations that evolved in Africa and that there was interbreeding between the migrating populations from Africa and those they encountered in North Africa, Europe, and Asia.

- Ancient DNA studies suggest fossil *H. sapiens* of Europe are more similar to living humans than fossil Neandertals of the same age.

- The last common ancestor for all modern humans is from 800 000 to 200 000 years ago.

- Anatomically, modern humans are defined relative to archaic *H. sapiens* and Neandertals by the presence of a chin, reduced facial and brow size, a canine fossa, a large globular braincase with parallel sides, a distinct mastoid process, and a more gracile postcranial skeleton.

- Earliest modern humans appeared in Africa about 195 000 years ago and in the Near East 100 000 years ago, and by 50 000 years ago had spread to the islands of Southeast Asia and Australia.

How do mitochondrial and Y chromosomal DNA each shed light on the origin of modern humans?

UPPER PALAEOLITHIC CULTURES

11.2 Describe Upper Palaeolithic tools and culture.

- The climate became more temperate at the end of the last ice age around 14 000 years ago. Animals adapted to the ice age became extinct and new plants better adapted to warmer climates provided new food sources.

- In northern Europe, Upper Palaeolithic people adapted to the new climate by shifting from hunting big game to small game, and they developed new stone tools to chop down trees and work the wood into shelters and canoes.

- Around the world, people began to experiment with new ways of tending plants and interacting with animals.

- Upper Palaeolithic humans were hunters, gatherers, and fishers who lived in highly mobile bands. They made their camps in the open and in caves and rock shelters.

- During this time people began to trade among each other and there was significant population growth.

- Modern humans showed abundant evidence for symbolic behaviour, represented by personal ornaments, portable art, cave art, and burials that often had grave goods.

 *What explanations have been proposed for the focus on animals in Upper Palaeolithic art?*

THE EARLIEST HUMANS IN THE NEW WORLD

11.3 Discuss the different scenarios used to explain the migration of humans into the New World.

- The earliest remains of people living in North America date to about 14 000 years ago and in South America to about 12 500 years ago.

- The dominant opinion is that humans migrated to the New World by boat down the coast or across a land bridge between Siberia and Alaska in what is now the Bering Strait.

- These early "Palaeo-Indian" people had diverse lifestyles—some hunted and followed herds, other relied on fish and shellfish, and some lived a semi-sedentary life along rivers.

- The late dispersal of modern humans to the Americas and the Pacific reflects the heavy direct and indirect influence that modern people have on the ecosystems they move into.

- The Palaeo-Arctic tradition represents the first undisputed cultural development in the Arctic. This was followed by the Arctic Small Tool tradition, and then the Dorset and Thule cultures.

 *What is the significance of the Monte Verde site in Chile in terms of understanding early human migration in the Americas?*

THINK ON IT

1. If the single-origin or "out of Africa" hypothesis is correct, by what mechanisms could one group of *H. sapiens* have been able to replace another?

2. If modern human traits emerged in *H. erectus* populations in different areas more or less at the same time, what mechanisms would account for similar traits emerging in different regions?

3. Upper Palaeolithic cave paintings arouse our imaginations. We have described some research that tested ideas about what these paintings might mean. Can you think of other ways to understand the significance of cave art?

4. The peopling of the New World continues to be debated by archaeologists. Different kinds of evidence can be used to understand how various populations are related to one another in the New World. Given the different kinds of evidence available, why is there so much debate regarding this issue?

5. How do the Dorset and Thule traditions differ from one another?

Origins of Food Production and Settled Life

12

Peter Giovannini/Age Fotostock

LEARNING OBJECTIVES

12.1 Explain the difference between foragers, horticulturalists, and agriculturalists.

12.2 Explain the relationship between broad-spectrum collecting, sedentism, and population growth in terms of pre-agricultural developments.

12.3 Discuss the domestication of plants and animals in the Near East, Mesoamerica, and elsewhere in the world.

12.4 Evaluate theories for why food production developed.

12.5 Critically analyze the consequences of food production.

Toward the end of the Upper Palaeolithic, people seem to have obtained most of their food from hunting migratory herds of large animals, such as wild cattle, antelope, bison, and mammoths. These hunter-gatherers were probably highly mobile in order to follow the migrations of the animals. Beginning about 14 000 years ago, people in some regions began to depend less on big-game hunting and more on relatively stationary food resources, such as fish, shellfish, small game, and wild plants (see Figure 12–1). In some areas, particularly Europe and the Near East, the exploitation of local, relatively permanent resources may account for an increasingly settled way of life. The cultural period in Europe and the Near East during which these developments took place is called the *Mesolithic*. Other areas of the world show a similar switch to what is called *broad-spectrum* food collecting, but they do not always show an increasingly settled lifestyle.

We see the first clear evidence of a changeover to food production—the cultivation and domestication of plants and animals—in the Near East, in about 8000 B.C. (Miller 1992; Scarre 2012). This shift, called the *Neolithic revolution*, occurred, probably independently, in other areas of the Old and New Worlds within the next few thousand years. In the Old World there were independent centres of domestication in China, Southeast Asia (what is now Malaysia, Thailand, Cambodia, and Vietnam), and Africa by around 6000 B.C. (MacNeish 1991; Crawford 1992; Bellwood 2005; Phillipson 2005). In the New World there were centres of cultivation and domestication in the highlands of Mesoamerica (about 7000 B.C.), the central Andes around Peru (about 7000 B.C.), and the Eastern Woodlands of North America

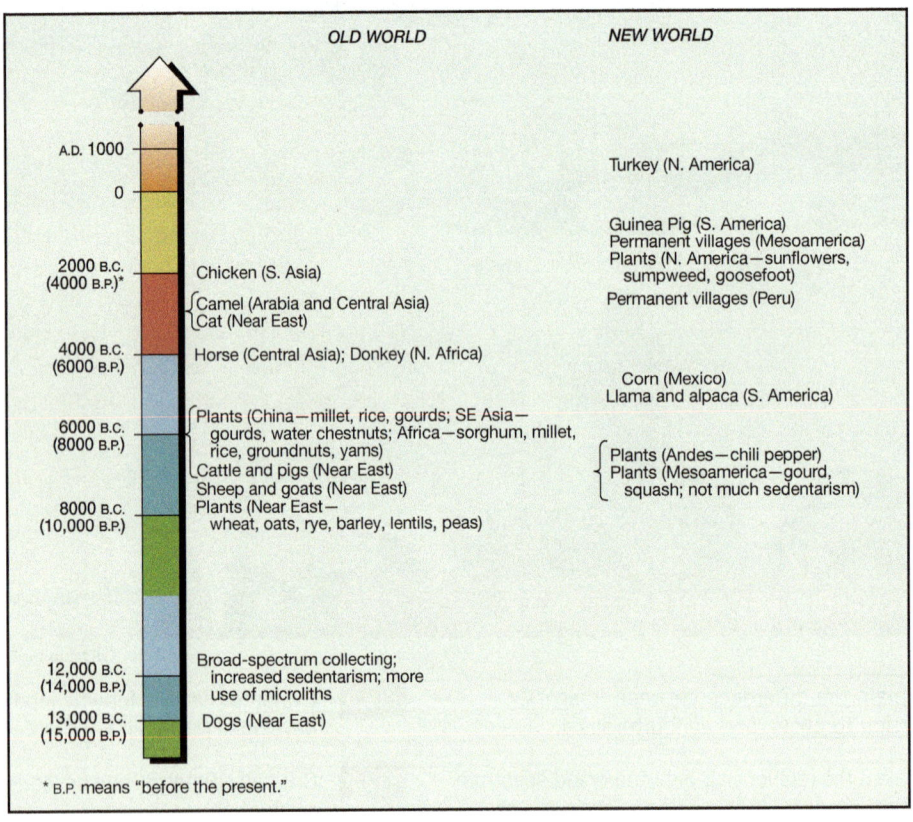

Figure 12–1 The Evolution of Domestication

Source: Dates for animal domestication are from Clutton-Brock J. 1992. Domestication of animals. In: Jones J, Martin R, Pilbeam D, editors. The Cambridge Encyclopedia of Human Evolution. New York: Cambridge University Press. p. 384. Copyright © 1992.

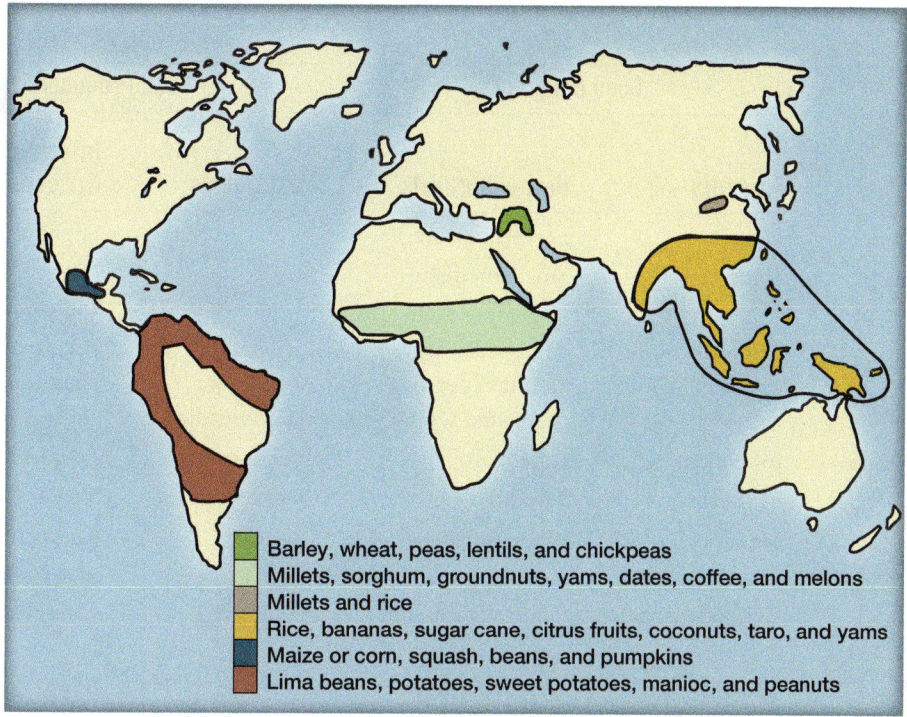

Figure 12–2 Original Locations of the World's Main Food Crops
The world's main food crops were originally domesticated in different regions.

Source: Hole F. 1992. Origins of agriculture. In: Jones S, Martin R, Pilbeam D, editors. The Cambridge Encyclopedia of Human Evolution. New York: Cambridge University Press p. 376.

(about 2000 B.C.) (Flannery 1986; Pearsall 1992; Smith 1992a). Most of the world's major food plants and animals were domesticated well before 2000 B.C. Also developed by that time were techniques of plowing, fertilizing, fallowing, and irrigation (Hole 1992). Figure 12–2 shows the regions of the world that domesticated today's main food crops.

In this chapter we discuss what is believed about the origins of food production and settled life, called **sedentism**—how and why people in different places may have come to cultivate and domesticate plants and animals and to live in permanent villages. Agriculture and a sedentary life did not necessarily go together. In some regions of the world, people began to live in permanent villages before they cultivated and domesticated plants and animals, whereas in other places people planted crops without settling down permanently. Much of our discussion focuses on the Near East and Europe, the areas we know best archaeologically for the developments leading to food production and settled life. As much as we can, however, we try to indicate how data from other areas appear to suggest patterns different from, or similar to, those in Europe and the Near East.

Food Collection and Production

Food collection may be generally defined as all forms of **subsistence technology** in which

Sedentism: settling in a single, permanent location.
Food Collection: all forms of subsistence technology in which food-getting is dependent on naturally occurring resources—wild plants and animals.

Subsistence Technology: the methods humans use to procure food.

Table 12–1 Variation in Food-Getting and Associated Features

	Food Collectors		Food Producers	
	Foragers	Horticulturalists	Pastoralists	Intensive Agriculturalists
Population density	Lowest	Low–moderate	Low	Highest
Maximum community size	Small	Small–moderate	Small	Large (towns and cities)
Nomadism/permanence of settlements	Generally nomadic or seminomadic	More sedentary: communities may move after several years	Generally nomadic or seminomadic	Permanent communities
Food shortages	Infrequent	Infrequent	Frequent	Frequent
Trade	Minimal	Minimal	Very important	Very important
Full-time craft specialists	None	None or few	Some	Many (high degree of specialization)
Individual differences in wealth	Generally none	Generally minimal	Moderate	Considerable
Political leadership	Informal	Some part-time political officials	Part- and full-time political officials	Many full-time political officials

food-getting is dependent on naturally occurring resources, that is, wild plants and animals. Although this was the way humans got their food for most of human history, the few remaining food collectors in the world today, also referred to as **foragers**, live in what have been called the *marginal areas* of the earth—deserts, the Arctic, and dense tropical forests—habitats that do not allow easy exploitation by modern agricultural technologies.

Anthropologists are interested in studying the relatively few food-collecting societies still available for observation because these groups may help us understand some aspects of human life in the past when all people were foragers (see Table 12–1). Ethnographic analogy from contemporary or recent historic hunter-gatherer and foraging populations can also provide us with models for prehistoric populations (Fix 1977; Howell 1979; Ray and Roth 1984; Borgerhoff Mulder 1992; Early and Peters 1992). The basic premise underlying ethnographic data is that recent foragers and hunter-gatherers are like prehistoric populations in the same kinds of environments in terms of the ways in which they get food and therefore similar in terms of demographic structure, mobility patterns, social networks, and so forth. However, the range of fertility (the number of births per mother) and mortality among different hunter-gatherer, forager, and sedentary populations is so diverse that ethnographic analogy from subsistence base and mobility is extremely problematic (Harpending and Pennington 1991; Pennington and Harpending 1991; Pennington 1992).

We must be cautious in drawing inferences about the past from our observations of contemporary food collectors for three reasons. First, early foragers lived in almost all types of environments, including some very bountiful ones. Therefore, what we observe among recent and contemporary food collectors may not be comparable to what would have been observable in more favourable environments in the past (Ember 1978). Second, contemporary foragers are not relics of

Foragers: people who subsist on the collection of naturally occurring plants and animals. Also referred to as *hunter-gatherers.*

the past. Like all contemporary societies, they have evolved and are still evolving. Indeed, recent research has suggested considerable variation in economic behaviour as well as in social structure in foraging groups that share common ancestry. This implies that recent foragers have responded to differences in local environmental conditions (Kent 1996). Third, recent and contemporary foragers have been interacting with kinds of societies that did not exist until after 10 000 years ago—agriculturalists, pastoralists (groups who maintain and/or follow grazing herd animals), and intrusive powerful state societies (Schrire 1984; Myers 1988). So what we see in intersociety relations recently may be different from intersociety relations in the past. As a result, we must be careful not to automatically assume that similar subsistence strategies necessarily reflect social or cultural similarities between past and present societies.

Beginning about 10 000 years ago, certain peoples in widely separated geographic locations made the revolutionary changeover to **food production**. That is, they began to cultivate and then domesticate plants and animals. (Domesticated plants and animals are different from the ancestral wild forms.) With domestication of these food sources, people acquired control over certain natural processes, such as animal breeding and plant seeding. Today, most peoples in the world depend for their food on some combination of domesticated plants and animals.

Horticulture

The word **horticulture** may conjure up visions of people with "green thumbs" growing orchids and other flowers in greenhouses. To anthropologists, though, the word means the growing of crops of all kinds with relatively simple tools and methods, in the absence of permanently cultivated fields. The tools are usually hand tools, such as the digging stick or hoe, not plows or other equipment pulled by animals or tractors. Nor do the methods used include fertilization, irrigation, or other ways to restore soil fertility after a growing season.

There are two kinds of horticulture. The more common one involves a dependence on **shifting cultivation**. The land is worked for short periods and then left idle for some years. During the years when the land is not cultivated, wild plants and brush grow up; when the fields are later cleared by **slash-and-burn techniques**, nutrients are returned to the soil. The other kind of horticulture involves a dependence on long-growing tree crops. The two kinds of horticulture may be practised in the same society, but in neither case is there permanent cultivation of field crops.

Most horticultural societies do not rely on crops alone for food. Many also hunt or fish; a few are nomadic for part of the year. For example, the northern Kayapo of the Brazilian Amazon leave their villages for as long as three months at a time to trek through the forest in search of game. The entire village participates in a trek, carrying large quantities of garden produce and moving their camp every day (Werner 1978). Other horticulturalists raise domestic animals, but these are usually not large animals, such as cattle and camels (Anonymous 1967). More often than not, the animals raised by horticulturalists are smaller ones, such as pigs, chickens, goats, and sheep.

In most horticultural societies, simple farming techniques have tended to yield more food from a given area than is generally available to food collectors. Consequently, horticulture is able to support larger, more densely populated communities. The way of life of horticulturalists is more sedentary than that of food collectors, although

---

Food Production: the form of subsistence technology in which food-getting is dependent on the cultivation and domestication of plants and animals.
Horticulture: plant cultivation carried out with relatively simple tools and methods; nature replaces nutrients in the soil, in the absence of permanently cultivated fields.

Shifting Cultivation: a type of horticulture in which the land is worked for short periods and then left to regenerate for some years before being used again.
Slash-and-Burn Techniques: a form of shifting cultivation in which the natural vegetation is cut down and burned off. The cleared ground is used for a short time and then left to regenerate.

communities may move after some years to farm a new series of plots. (Some horticulturalists have permanent villages because they depend mostly on food from trees that keep producing for a long time.) In contrast with most recent food-collecting groups, horticultural societies exhibit the beginnings of *social differentiation*. For example, some individuals may be part-time craft workers or part-time political officials, and certain members of a kin group may have more status than other individuals in the society.

Intensive Agriculture

People engaged in **intensive agriculture** use techniques that enable them to cultivate fields permanently. Essential nutrients may be put back in the soil through the addition of fertilizers, which may be organic material (most commonly dung from humans or other animals) or inorganic (chemical) fertilizers. There are, however, other ways to restore nutrients. The Luo of western Kenya plant beans around corn plants. Bacteria growing around the roots of the bean plant replace lost nitrogen, and the corn plant conveniently provides a pole for the bean plant to wind around as it grows. Some intensive agriculturalists use irrigation from streams and rivers to ensure an adequate supply of waterborne nutrients. Crop rotation—using different fields from year to year—and plant stubble that has been plowed under also restore nutrients to the soil.

Pre-agricultural Developments

The Near East

In the Near East there seems to have been a shift from mobile big-game hunting to the utilization of a broad spectrum of natural resources near the end of the Palaeolithic (Binford 1971; Scarre 2012). There is evidence that people subsisted on a variety of resources, including fish, molluscs, and other water life; wild deer, sheep, and goats; and wild grains, nuts, and legumes (Flannery 1973a; Scarre 2012). The increased utilization of stationary food sources such as wild grain may partly explain why some people in the Near East began to lead more sedentary lives during the Mesolithic.

Even today, a traveller passing through the Anatolian highlands of Turkey and other mountainous regions in the Near East may see thick stands of wild wheat and barley growing as densely as if they had been cultivated (Lev-Yadun et al. 2000). Wielding flint sickles, Mesolithic people could easily have harvested a bountiful crop from such wild stands. Just how productive these resources can be was demonstrated in a field experiment duplicating prehistoric conditions. Using the same kind of flint-blade sickle that a Mesolithic worker would have used, researchers were able to harvest a little over 1 kilogram of wild grain in an hour. A Mesolithic family of four, working only during the few weeks of the harvest season, probably could have reaped more wheat and barley than they needed for the entire year (Harlan 1967).

The amount of wild wheat harvested in the experiment prompted Kent Flannery to conclude, "Such a harvest would almost necessitate some degree of sedentism—after all, where could they go with an estimated metric ton of clean wheat?" (Flannery 1971). Moreover, the stone equipment used for grinding would have been a clumsy burden to carry. Part of the harvest would probably have been set aside for immediate consumption, ground, and then cooked either by roasting or boiling. The rest of the harvest would have been stored to supply food for the remainder of the year. A grain diet, then, could have been the impetus for the construction of roasters, grinders, and storage pits by some Mesolithic people, as well as for the construction of solid, fairly permanent housing. Once a village was built, people may have been reluctant to abandon it. We can visualize the earliest pre-agricultural settlements clustered around such naturally rich regions, as archaeological evidence indeed suggests they were.

> **Intensive Agriculture:** food production characterized by the permanent cultivation of fields and made possible by the use of the plow, draft animals or machines, fertilizers, irrigation, water-storage techniques, and other complex agricultural techniques.

The Natufians of the Near East. Eleven thousand years ago the Natufians, a people living in the area that is now Israel and Jordan, inhabited caves and rock shelters and built villages on the slopes of Mount Carmel in Israel. At the front of their rock shelters they hollowed out basin-shaped depressions in the rock, possibly for storage pits. Examples of Natufian villages are also found at the Eynan site in Israel.

Eynan is a stratified site containing the remains of three villages in sequence, one atop another. Each village consisted of about 50 circular pit houses. The floor of each house was sunk a few metres into the ground, so that the walls of the house consisted partly of earth, below ground level, and partly of stone, above ground level. Pit houses had the advantage of retaining heat longer than houses built above the ground. The villages appear to have had stone-paved walks; circular stone pavements ringed what seem to be permanent hearths; and the dead were interred in village cemeteries.

The tools suggest that the Natufians harvested wild grain intensively. Sickles recovered from their villages have a specific sheen, which experiments have shown to be the effect of flint striking grass stems, as the sickles would have been used in the cutting of grain. The Natufians are the earliest Mesolithic people known to have stored surplus crops. Beneath the floors of their stone-walled houses, they constructed plastered storage pits. In addition to wild grains, the Natufians exploited a range of other resources (Mellaart 1961; Watkins 2009). The remains of many wild animals are found in Natufian sites; Natufians appear to have concentrated on hunting gazelle, which they would take by surrounding whole herds (Henry 1989; Watkins 2009).

The Natufians, as well as food collectors in other areas at the time, show many differences as compared with food collectors in earlier periods (Brown and Price 1985; Bellwood 2005). Not only was Natufian food collection based on a more intensive use of stationary resources, such as wild grain, but the archaeological evidence suggests increasing social complexity. Natufian sites were, on average, five times larger than those of their predecessors. Communities were now occupied for most of the year, if not year-round. Burial patterns suggest more social differences between people. Although wild cereal resources appear to have enabled the Natufians to live in relatively permanent villages, their diet seems to have suffered. Their tooth enamel shows signs of nutritional deficiency, and their stature declined over time (Henry 1989, 1991; Olszewski 1991).

Hayonim, one of the many caves in which the Natufians built relatively permanent settlements. Archaeologists are at work at the site.

Europe

After about 10 000 years ago in Europe, the glaciers began to disappear. With their disappearance came other environmental changes. The melting of the glacial ice caused the oceans to rise, and, as the seas moved inland, the waters inundated some of the richest fodder-producing coastal plains, creating islands, inlets, and bays. Other areas, particularly in Scandinavia, were opened up for human occupation as the glaciers retreated and the temperatures rose (Collins 1976). The cold, treeless plains, tundra, and grasslands eventually gave way to dense mixed forests, mostly birch, oak, and pine, and the mammoths became extinct. The warming waterways gradually cleared of glacial sediment, and began to be filled with fish and other aquatic resources (Chard 1969).

Archaeologists believe that these environmental changes induced some populations in Europe to alter their food-getting strategies. When the tundra and grasslands disappeared, hunters could no longer obtain large quantities of meat simply by remaining close to large migratory herds of animals, as they probably did during Upper Palaeolithic times. Even though deer and other game were available, the number of animals per square kilometre (density) had decreased, and it became more difficult to stalk and kill animals sheltered in the thick woods. Thus, in many areas of Mesolithic Europe people seem to have turned from a reliance on big-game hunting to the intensive collecting of wild plants, molluscs, fish, and small game to make up for the extinction of the mammoths and the northward migration of the reindeer.

The Maglemosian Culture of Northern Europe.

Some adaptations to the changing environment can be seen in the cultural remains of the settlers in northern Europe who are called Maglemosians by archaeologists. Their name derives from the peat bogs (*magle mose* in Danish means "great bog") where their remains have been found.

To deal with the new, more forested environment, the Maglemosians made stone axes and adzes to chop down trees and form them into various objects. Large timber appears to have been split for houses; trees were hollowed out for canoes; and smaller pieces of wood were made into paddles. The canoes presumably were built for travel and perhaps for fishing on the lakes and rivers that abounded in the postglacial environment.

We do not know to what extent the Maglemosians relied on wild plant foods, but there were a lot of different kinds available, such as hazelnuts. However, we do know many other things about the Maglemosians' way of life. Although fishing was fairly important, as suggested by the recovery of fish hooks and the frequent occurrence of bones from pike and other fish, these people apparently depended mainly on hunting for food. Game included elk, wild ox, deer, and wild pig. In addition to many fishing implements and the adzes and axes, the Maglemosians' tool kit included the bow and arrow. Some of their tools were ornamented with finely engraved designs. Ornamentation independent of tools also appears in amber and stone pendants and small figurines such as the head of an elk (Clark 1975).

Like the Maglemosian finds, many of the European Mesolithic sites are along lakes, rivers, and marine shorelines. But these sites probably were not inhabited year-round; there is evidence that at least some groups moved seasonally from one place of settlement to another, perhaps between the coast and inland areas (Petersen 1973). Finds such as kitchen middens with piles of shells that centuries of Mesolithic seafood-eaters had discarded and remains of fishing equipment, canoes, and boats indicate that Mesolithic people depended much more heavily on fishing than had their ancestors in Upper Palaeolithic times. The very fact that this domestic waste accumulated in middens is indicative of the growing degree of sedentism associated with the Mesolithic.

Mesoamerica

A similar shift toward more broad-spectrum hunting and gathering occurred in the New World at the end of the Palaeo-Indian period, about 10 000 years ago. Climate change seems to have been vital here, too, as it was in the Old World. The retreat of glacial ice from North America and overall warmer and wetter climate brought dramatic changes to plant and animal communities throughout North America and Mesoamerica. Pleistocene megafauna, such as mammoths, mastodon, rhinoceros, giant ground sloth, and others, as well as a variety of smaller game animals, such as the horse, all went extinct in a relatively short period of time (Martin and Wright 1967). Hunting strategies shifted toward a broader range of game species, particularly deer, antelope, bison, and small mammals. At the same time, deciduous woodlands and grasslands expanded, providing a range of new plants to exploit. Ground-stone woodworking tools such as axes and adzes first appeared, as did nut-processing tools such as mortars and pestles. Shellfish began to be exploited in some areas. Throughout North America and Mesoamerica people began to expand the range of plants and animals they relied upon (Brown 1985; Keuhn 1998).

The Archaic Peoples of Highland Mesoamerica.

In Highland Mesoamerica, that is, the mountainous regions of central and southern Mexico, we also see a shift from big-game hunting to a broader use of resources, in part due to a change in climate more like today's. Altitude became an important factor in the hunting and collecting regime, as different altitudes have different plant and animal resources. Valleys tend to have scrubby, grassland vegetation, whereas foothills and mountains have "thorn forests" of cactuses and succulents giving way to oak and pine forests at higher altitudes, where there is more moisture. This vertical zonation means that a wide range of plants and animals were available in relatively close proximity—different environments were close by—and the Archaic peoples took advantage of these varied conditions to hunt and collect a range of resources (Marcus and Flannery 1996).

About 8000 years ago the Archaic peoples in Mesoamerica appear to have moved seasonally between communities of two different sizes: camps with 15 to 30 residents (*macrobands*) and camps with only 2 to 5 residents (*microbands*). Macroband camps were located near seasonally abundant resources, such as acorns or mesquite pods. Several families would have come together when these resources were in season, both to take advantage of them and to work together to harvest them while they were plentiful, to perform rituals, and simply to socialize. Microband camps were also inhabited seasonally, probably by a single family, when groups were not assembled into macroband camps. Remains of these microband camps are often found in caves or rock shelters from which a variety of environments could be exploited by moving either upslope or downslope from the campsite (Marcus and Flannery 1996).

Unlike the Natufians of the Near East, there is no evidence of social differences among the Archaic peoples of Highland Mesoamerica. The largest social unit, the macroband camp, was probably composed of related family groups, and leadership in these groups was probably informal. There is little evidence of ritual behaviour beyond the presence of what may have been a ceremonial dance floor at Gheo-Shih, a macroband campsite in the Valley of Oaxaca. In short, lifestyles remained much like the simple and egalitarian ones of the Palaeo-Indians, despite the transition to a much broader strategy of food collection.

Other Areas

People in other areas of the world also shifted from hunting big game to collecting many types of food before they apparently began to practise agriculture. The still sparse archaeological record suggests that such a change occurred in Southeast Asia, which may have been one of the important centres of original plant and animal domestication (Balter 2007; Jones and Liu 2009). The faunal remains recovered from inland sites in the region indicate that many different sources of food were being exploited from the same base camps. For example, these base camps yield the remains of animals from high mountain ridges as well as lowland river valleys, birds and primates from nearby forests, bats from caves, and fish from streams. The few coastal sites indicate that many kinds of fish and shellfish were collected and that animals such as deer, wild cattle, and rhinoceros were hunted (Gorman 1970; Higham 2009). As in Europe, the pre-agricultural developments in Southeast Asia probably were responses to changes in the climate and environment, including a warming trend, more moisture, and a higher sea level (Chang 1970; Gorman 1970).

In Africa, too, the pre-agricultural period was marked by a warmer, wetter environment. The now numerous lakes, rivers, and other bodies of water provided fish, shellfish, and other resources that apparently allowed people to settle more permanently than they had before. For example, there were lakes in what is now the southern and central Sahara Desert, where people fished and hunted hippopotamuses and crocodiles. This pattern of broad-spectrum food-collecting seems also to have been characteristic of the areas both south and north of the Sahara (Clark 1970; Connah 2009). One area showing increased sedentism is the Dakhleh Oasis in the Western Desert of Egypt.

Between 9000 and 8500 years ago, the inhabitants lived in circular stone huts on the shores of rivers and lakes. Bone harpoons and pottery are found there and in other areas from the Nile Valley through the central and southern Sahara westward to what is now Mali. Fishing seems to have allowed people to remain along the rivers and lakes for much of the year (Phillipson 1993).

At about the same time in the Americas, people were beginning to exploit a wide variety of wild food resources. For example, evidence from present-day Alabama and Kentucky shows that, by about 5000 B.C., people had begun to collect freshwater mussels as well as wild plants and small game. In the Great Basin of what is now the United States, people were beginning to spend longer and longer periods each year collecting the wild resources around and in the rivers and glacial lakes (Patterson 1973).

Why Did Broad-Spectrum Collecting Develop?

It is apparent that the pre-agricultural switch to broad-spectrum collecting was fairly common throughout the world. Climate change was probably at least partly responsible for the exploitation of new sources of food. For example, the worldwide rise in sea level may have increased the availability of fish and shellfish. Changes in climate may have also been partly responsible for the decline in the availability of big game, particularly the large herd animals (Gill et al. 2009). In addition, it has been suggested that another possible cause of that decline was human activity, specifically overkilling of some of these animals (Alroy 2001). The evidence suggesting overkill is that the extinction in the New World of many of the large Pleistocene animals, such as the mammoth, coincided with the movement of humans from the Bering Strait region to the southern tip of South America (Martin 1973).

The overkill hypothesis has been largely discredited on the basis of the breadth of extinctions that includes bird as well as mammal species in the Americas. An enormous number of bird species also became extinct during the last few thousand years of the North American Pleistocene, and it is difficult to argue that human hunters caused all those extinctions. Because the bird and mammal extinctions occurred simultaneously, it is likely that most or nearly all the extinctions were due to climatic and other environmental changes (Grayson 1977, 1989; Guthrie 1984; Marshall 1984; Barnosky et al. 2004). Then again, the example of the New Zealand moas, which went extinct soon after humans colonized the islands, may be instructive. Moas had low reproductive rates; computer simulations suggest their population would have been very sensitive to increases in adult mortality. Because many large animals have low reproductive rates like moas, human overhunting may have been responsible for their extinction (Holdaway and Jacomb 2000).

The decreasing availability of big game may have stimulated people to exploit new food resources, but they may have turned to a broader spectrum of resources for another reason—population growth (see Figure 12–3). As Mark Cohen noted, hunter-gatherers were "filling up" the world, and they may have had to seek new, possibly less desirable sources of food (Cohen 1977a). (We might think of shellfish as more desirable than mammoths, but only because we don't have to do the work to get such food. A lot of shellfish have to be collected, shelled, and cooked to obtain about the same amount of protein obtainable from one large animal.) Consistent with the idea that the world was filling up around this time is the fact that not until after 30 000 years ago did hunter-gatherers begin to move into previously uninhabited parts of the world, such as Australia and the New World (Cohen 1977a; Hassan 1981; Bailey et al. 1989).

Broad-spectrum collecting may have involved exploitation of new sources of food, but that does not necessarily mean that people were eating better. A decline in stature often indicates a poorer diet. During the Mesolithic, height apparently declined by as much as 5 centimetres in many parts of the Old World (Greece, Israel, India, and northern and western Europe) (Cohen 1989). This decline may have been a result of decreasing nutrition, but it could also be that natural selection for greater height was relaxed because leverage for throwing projectiles such as spears was not so favoured after the decline of big-game hunting. (Greater limb-bone

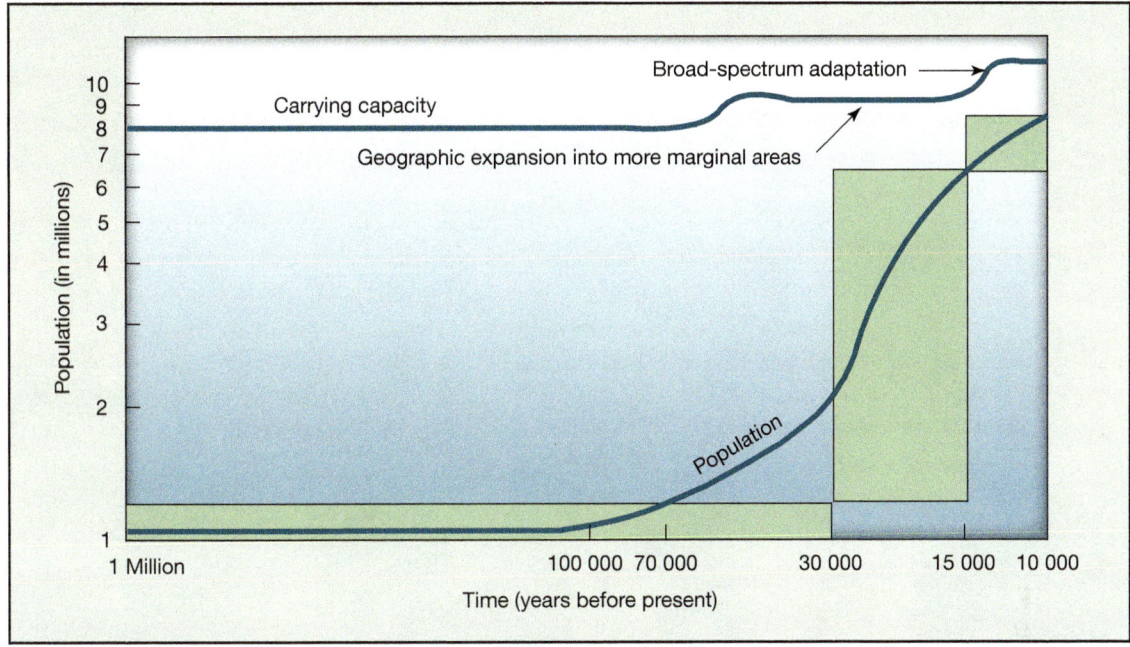

Figure 12–3 Reconstructed Increases in World Population and Carrying Capacity for Humans during the Pleistocene

Estimates of human population suggest that substantial increases preceded the movement of humans into more marginal areas. Further population increase preceded the emergence of broad-spectrum collecting.

Source: Adapted from Hassan FA. 1981. Demographic archaeology. New York: Academic Press. p. 207.

length, and therefore greater height, would enable you to throw a spear with more force and farther [Frayer 1981].) In other areas of the world, such as Australia and what is now the midwestern United States, skeletal evidence also suggests a decline in the general level of health with the rise of broad-spectrum collecting (Cohen 1989).

Broad-Spectrum Collecting and Sedentism

Does the switch to broad-spectrum collecting explain the increasingly sedentary way of life we see in various parts of the world in pre-agricultural times? The answer seems to be both yes and no. In some areas of the world—some sites in Europe, the Near East, Africa, and Peru—settlements became more permanent. In other areas, such as the semi-arid highlands of Mesoamerica, the switch to broad-spectrum collecting was not associated with increasing sedentism. Even after the highland Mesoamericans began to cultivate plants, they still did not live in permanent villages (Flannery 1973b). The question is why.

It would seem that it is not simply the switch to broad-spectrum collecting that accounts for increasing sedentism in many areas. Rather, a comparison of settlements on the Peruvian coast suggests that the more permanent settlements were located nearer (within 6 kilometres) than were temporary settlements to most, if not all, of the diverse food resources exploited during the year. The community that did not have a year-round settlement seems to have depended on more widely distributed resources. What accounts for sedentism may thus be the nearness (Patterson 1971) or the high reliability and yield (Harris 1977; Johnson 1977) of the broad-spectrum resources, rather than the broad spectrum itself.

Sedentism and Population Growth

Although some population growth undoubtedly occurred throughout the hunting and gathering

A group of !Kung women heading out to collect plant foods. On some days women will walk several miles to find the plants they want to harvest. Spacing births an average of four years apart helps to ensure that a woman will not have to carry more than two children at a time.

phase of world history, some anthropologists have suggested that populations would have increased dramatically when people began to settle down. The evidence for this suggestion comes largely from a comparison of recent nomadic and sedentary !Kung populations.

The settling down of a nomadic group may reduce the typical spacing between births (Lee 1972; Sussman 1972). Nomadic !Kung have children about every four years; in contrast, recently settled !Kung have children about every three years. Why might birth spacing change with settling down? There are several possibilities.

Regulating the spacing of childbirths can occur in a number of ways. One way, if effective contraceptives are not available, is prolonged sexual abstinence after the birth of a child—the post-partum sex taboo—that is common in recent human societies. Another way is abortion or infanticide (Harris 1977). Nomadic groups may be motivated to have children further apart because of the problem of carrying small children. Carrying one small child is difficult enough; carrying two might be too burdensome. Thus, sedentary populations could have children spaced more closely because carrying children would not always be necessary.

It is possible that intensive collectors and early horticulturalists may have seen advantages to having larger families (more individuals could contribute to labour). It may be that women, who were likely doing much of the plant foraging and early horticulture, saw an advantage from having more children as a means of improving the efficiency of the group.

Although some nomadic groups may have deliberately spaced births by abstinence or infanticide, there is no evidence that such practices explain why there is typically four years between births among nomadic !Kung. There may be another explanation, involving an unintended effect of how babies are fed. Nancy Howell and Richard Lee suggested that the presence of baby foods other than mother's milk may be responsible for the decreased birth spacing in sedentary agricultural !Kung groups (Howell 1979; Lee 1979). It is now well established that the longer a mother nurses her baby without supplementary foods, the longer it is likely to be before she starts ovulating again. Nomadic !Kung women have little to give their babies in the way of soft, digestible food, and the babies depend largely on mother's milk for two to three years. Sedentary !Kung mothers can, however, give their babies soft foods such as cereal (made from cultivated grain) and milk from domesticated animals. Such changes in feeding practices may shorten birth spacing by shortening the interval between birth and the resumption of ovulation. In pre-agricultural sedentary communities, it is possible that baby foods made from wild grains might have had the same effect. For this reason alone, therefore, populations may have grown even before people started to farm or herd.

Another reason sedentary !Kung women may have more babies than nomadic !Kung women has to do with the ratio of body fat to body weight. Some investigators suspect that a critical minimum of fat in the body may be necessary for ovulation. A sedentary !Kung woman may have more fatty tissue than a nomadic !Kung woman, who walks many kilometres daily to gather wild plant foods, often carrying a child around with her. Thus, sedentary !Kung women might resume ovulating sooner after the birth of a baby and so may be likely for that reason alone to have more closely spaced children. If some critical amount of fat is necessary for ovulation, that would explain why in our own society many women who have little body fat—long-distance runners, gymnasts, and ballet dancers are examples—do not ovulate regularly (Howell 1979; Frisch 1980).

Microlithic Technology

Technologically, pre-agricultural cultures did not differ radically from Upper Palaeolithic cultures (Phillipson 1993; Scarre 2012). However, the trend toward smaller and lighter tools continued. Microliths, small blades 1.2 centimetres to 5 centimetres long, which were made in late Upper Palaeolithic times, were now used in quantity. In place of the one-piece flint implement, Mesolithic peoples in Europe, Asia, and Africa equipped themselves with composite tools—that is, tools made of more than one material.

Microliths, too small to be used one at a time, could be fitted into grooves in bone or wood to form arrows, harpoons, daggers, and sickles. A sickle, for example, was made by inserting several microliths into a groove in a wooden or bone handle. The blades were held in place by resin. A broken microlith could be replaced like a blade in a modern razor. Besides being adaptable for many uses, microliths could be made from many varieties of available stone; Mesolithic people were no longer limited to flint. Since they did not need the large flint nodules to make large core and flake tools, they could use small pebbles of flint to make the small blades (Semenov 1970; Whittaker 1994).

A sickle made with microliths.

The Domestication of Plants and Animals

Neolithic means "of the new Stone Age"; the term originally signified the cultural stage in which humans invented pottery and stone tools with ground edges. We now know, however, that both were present in earlier times, so we cannot define a Neolithic state of culture on the basis of the presence of pottery and ground-stone tools. At present, archaeologists generally define the Neolithic in terms of the presence of domesticated plants and animals. In this type of culture, people began to produce food rather than merely collect it.

The line between food-collecting and food-producing occurs when people begin to plant crops and to keep and breed animals. How do we know when this transition occurred? In fact, archaeologically we do not see the beginning of food production; we can see signs of it only after plants and animals show differences from their wild varieties. When people plant crops, we refer to the process as *cultivation*. It is only when the crops cultivated and the animals raised are modified—and become different from wild varieties—that we speak of plant and animal **domestication**. A domesticated plant or animal is one that depends upon human intervention for its continued survival.

We know, in a particular site, that domestication occurred if plant remains have characteristics different from those of wild plants of the same types. For example, wild grains of barley and wheat have a fragile **rachis**—the seed-bearing part of the stem—which shatters easily, releasing the seeds. Domesticated grains have a tough rachis, which does not shatter easily. Similarly, domesticated plants tend to have larger seeds than their wild ancestors. In addition, plants found in areas for which there is no naturally growing ancestral form are assumed to have been brought there by humans, and are therefore, by definition, domesticates.

How did the domesticated plants get to be different from the wild varieties? Artificial or human selection, deliberate or accidental, obviously was required. Consider how the rachis of wheat and barley may have changed. As we said, when wild grain ripens in the field, the rachis shatters easily, scattering the seed. This trait is selectively advantageous under wild conditions; it is nature's method of propagating the species. Plants with a tough rachis, therefore, have only a slight chance of reproducing themselves under natural conditions, but they are more desirable for maximizing yield during harvesting. When humans arrived with sickles and flails to collect the wild stands of grain, the seeds harvested probably contained a high proportion of tough-rachis mutants, because these could best withstand the rough treatment of harvest processing. If planted, the harvested seeds would be likely to produce tough-rachis plants (see Figure 12–4). If in each successive harvest seeds from these plants were the least likely to be lost, tough-rachis plants would come to predominate (Zohary 1969).

Domesticated species of animals also differ from the wild varieties. For example, the horns of wild goats in the Near East are shaped differently from those of domesticated goats (Flannery 1965). Differences in physical characteristics may not be the only indicators of domestication. Some archaeologists believe that imbalances in the sex and age ratios of animal remains at particular sites also suggest that domestication had occurred. For example, at Zawi Chemi Shanidar in Iraq, the proportion of young to mature sheep remains was much higher than the ratio of young to mature sheep in wild herds. One possible inference to be drawn is that the animals were domesticated, the adult sheep being saved for breeding purposes

---

Neolithic: originally meaning "the new Stone Age," now meaning the presence of domesticated plants and animals. The earliest evidence of domestication comes from the Near East about 8000 B.C.

Domestication: modification or adaptation of plants and animals for use by humans. When people plant crops, we refer to the process as *cultivation*. It is only when the crops cultivated and the animals raised have been modified—are different from wild varieties—that we speak of plant and animal domestication.

Rachis: the seed-bearing part of a plant. In the wild variety the rachis shatters easily, releasing the seeds. Domesticated grains have a tough rachis, which does not shatter easily.

Figure 12–4 Seed Heads of Wild and Domesticated Wheat

Note the larger and more numerous seeds on domesticated wheat.

Source: Feder KL. The past in perspective. Reprinted by permission of the author.

while the young were eaten. (If mostly young animals were eaten, and only a few animals were allowed to grow old, most of the bones found in a site would be from the young animals that were killed regularly for food [Flannery 1965; Collier and White 1976].)

Domestication in the Near East

For some time most archaeologists have thought that the arc of land stretching up from Israel and the Jordan Valley through southern Turkey and then downward to the western slopes of the Zagros Mountains in Iran (see Figure 12–5) was one of the earliest centres of plant and animal domestication. We know that several varieties of domesticated wheat were grown there after about 8000 B.C., as were oats, rye, barley, lentils, peas, and various fruits and nuts (apricots, pears, pomegranates, dates, figs, olives, almonds, and pistachios) (MacNeish 1991; Hole 1992; Zeder 2011). It appears that the first animals were domesticated in the Near East. Dogs were first domesticated before the rise of agriculture, around 10 000 B.C., goats and sheep around 7000 B.C., and cattle and pigs around 6000 B.C. (Clutton-Brock 1988; Chessa et al. 2009; Zeder 2011), though recent genomic studies of dogs suggested a Central Asian origin (Savolainen et al. 2002; Shannon et al. 2015).

Let us look at two early Neolithic sites in the Near East to see what life there may have been like after people began to depend on domesticated plants and animals for food.

Ali Kosh. At the stratified site of Ali Kosh in what is now southwestern Iran (see Figure 12–5), we see the remains of a community that started out around 7500 B.C. living mostly on wild plants and animals. Over the next 2000 years, until about 5500 B.C., agriculture and herding became increasingly important. After 5500 B.C. we see the appearance of two innovations—irrigation and the use of domesticated cattle—that seem to have stimulated a minor population explosion during the following millennium.

From 7500 to 6750 B.C., the people at Ali Kosh cut small slabs of raw clay out of the ground to build small multiroom structures. The rooms excavated by archaeologists are small, seldom more than 2.1 metres by 3 metres, and there is no evidence that the structures were definitely houses where people actually spent time or slept. Instead, they may have been storage rooms. On the other hand, house rooms of even smaller size are known in other areas of the world, so it is possible that the people at Ali Kosh in its earliest phase were actually living in those tiny, unbaked "brick" houses. There is a bit of evidence that the people at Ali Kosh may have moved over the course of the summer with their goats to nearby mountain valleys (just a few days' walk away), perhaps in search of more grassy habitats.

We have a lot of evidence about what the people at Ali Kosh ate. They got some of their food from cultivated emmer wheat and a barley variety. However, a considerable amount of protein was derived from domesticated goats. We know the goats were domesticated because wild goats do not seem to have lived in the area. Also, the fact that virtually no bones from elderly goats were

Figure 12–5 Early Agricultural Settlements in the Near East
Modern cities are represented by a dot, early settlements by a square. The yellow colour indicates the area of early agricultural settlement.

---

found in the site suggests that the goats were domesticated and herded rather than hunted. Moreover, it would seem from the horn cores found in the site that mostly young male goats were eaten, suggesting that the females were kept for breeding and milking. Despite all these signs of deliberate food production, there is an enormous amount of evidence—literally tens of thousands of seeds and bone fragments—that the people at the beginning of Ali Kosh depended mostly on wild plants (legumes and grasses) and wild animals (including gazelles, wild oxen, and wild pigs). They also collected fish, such as carp and catfish, and shellfish, such as mussels, as well as waterfowl that visited the area during part of the year.

The flint tools used during this earliest phase at Ali Kosh were varied and abundant. Finds from this period include tens of thousands of tiny flint blades, some only a few millimetres wide. About 1 percent of the chipped stone found by archaeologists was obsidian, or volcanic glass, which came from what is now eastern Turkey, several hundred kilometres away. Thus, the people at Ali Kosh during its earliest phase definitely had some kind of contact with people elsewhere. This contact is also suggested by the fact that the emmer wheat they cultivated did not have a wild relative in the area.

From 6750 to 6000 B.C., the people increased their consumption of cultivated food plants; 40 percent of the seed remains in the hearths and refuse areas were now from emmer wheat and barley. The proportion of the diet coming from wild plants was much reduced, probably because the cultivated plants have the same growing season and grow in the same kind of soil as the wild plants. Grazing by the goats and sheep that were kept may also have contributed to the reduction of wild plant foods in the area and in the diet. The village may or may not have become larger, but the multiroom houses definitely had. The rooms were now larger than 3 metres by 3 metres; the walls were much thicker; and the clay-slab bricks were now held together by a mud mortar. Also, the walls now often had a coat of smooth mud plaster on both sides. The stamped-mud house floors were apparently covered with rush or reed mats (you can see the imprints of them). There were courtyards with domed brick ovens and brick-lined roasting pits. Understandably, considering the summer heat in the area, none of the ovens found were inside a house.

Even though the village probably contained no more than 100 individuals, it participated in an extensive trading network. Seashells were probably obtained from the Persian Gulf, which is some distance to the south; copper may have come from what is now central Iran; obsidian came from eastern Turkey; and turquoise somehow made its way from what is now the border between Iran and Afghanistan. Some of these materials were used as ornaments worn by both sexes—or so it seems from the remains of bodies found buried under the floors of houses.

After about 5500 B.C., the area around Ali Kosh began to show signs of a much larger population, apparently made possible by a more complex agriculture employing irrigation and plows drawn by domesticated cattle. Over the next thousand years, by 4500 B.C., the population of the area probably tripled. This population growth was apparently part of the cultural developments that culminated in the rise of urban civilizations in the Near East (Hole et al. 1969), as we will see in the next chapter.

Population growth may have occurred in and around Ali Kosh but did not continue in all areas of the Near East after domestication. For example, one of the largest early villages in the Near East, 'Ain Ghazal (on the outskirts of what is now Amman, Jordan), suffered a decline in population and standard of living over time, perhaps because the environment around 'Ain Ghazal could not permanently support a large village (Simmons et al. 1988).

Çatal Hüyük. On a windswept plateau in the rugged, mountainous region of southern Turkey stand the remains of a mud-brick town known as Çatal Hüyük (see Figure 12–5). *Hüyük* is the Turkish word for a mound formed by a succession of settlements, one built on top of another.

About 5600 B.C., Çatal Hüyük was an adobe town. Some 200 houses have been excavated, and they are interconnected in pueblo fashion (each flat-roofed structure housed a number of families). The inhabitants decorated the walls of the houses with imaginative murals, and their shrines with symbolic statuary. The murals depict what seem to be religious scenes and everyday events. Archaeologists peeling away frescoes found layer upon layer of murals, indicating that old murals were plastered over to make way for fresh paintings. Several rooms are believed to have been shrine rooms. They contain many large bull murals and clay bull figurines and have full-sized clay heads of cattle on the walls. Other "shrine-room" murals depict scenes of life and death, painted in red and black, respectively. Clay statuettes of a pregnant woman and of a bearded man seated on a bull have also been found in these rooms.

Farming was well advanced at Çatal Hüyük. Lentils, wheat, barley, and peas were grown in quantities that produced a surplus. Archaeologists were astonished at the richly varied handicrafts, including beautifully carved wooden bowls and boxes that the people of the town produced. These people also had obsidian and flint daggers, spearheads, lance heads, scrapers, awls, and sickle blades. Bowls, spatulas, knives, ladles, and spoons were made from bone. The houses contained belt hooks,

Excavation in one of the pueblo-like structures of Neolithic Çatal Hüyük.

toggles, and pins carved from bone. Evidence also suggests that men and women wore jewellery fashioned from bone, shell, and copper and that they used obsidian mirrors (Mellaart 1964).

Since Çatal Hüyük is located in a region with few raw materials, the town evidently depended on exchange with other areas to secure the rich variety of materials it used. Shells were procured from the Mediterranean, timber from the hills, obsidian from 80 kilometres away, and marble from western Turkey.

Domestication in Mesoamerica

A very different pattern of domestication is seen in Mesoamerica. Here the semi-nomadic Archaic hunting-and-gathering lifestyle persisted long after people first domesticated plants (Flannery 1986; Pringle 1998). How can this be? Don't people have to settle near their crops to take care of them? Once they have domesticated plants, don't they stop collecting wild plants? The answer is no. In Mesoamerica, people sowed a variety of plants, but after doing so they went on with their seasonal rounds of hunting and gathering, and came back later to harvest what they had sown. Many of the early domesticates in Mesoamerica were not basic to subsistence, even if they were highly desirable. Domestication may have been a way for Archaic peoples to make desirable plants more common in their environment. For example, one of the first domesticates was the bottle gourd. These were not eaten but were used to carry water. Joyce Marcus and Kent Flannery hypothesized that the bottle gourd was domesticated by people deliberately planting them in areas where they did not grow naturally, so that as groups moved through those areas, they always had access to gourds for carrying water (Marcus and Flannery 1996).

Bottle gourds are only one of many early domesticates from Highland Mesoamerica. Others include tomatoes, cotton, a variety of beans and squashes, and, perhaps most importantly, maize. The earliest domesticated form of maize (corn), dating from about 5900 B.C. has been found in Tehuacán, Mexico (Farnsworth et al. 1985). Recent research by Piperno and colleagues (2009) that looked at starch residues in the grinding stones and chipped tools from the Balsas River Valley of southwestern Mexico suggested maize was present by 6700 B.C.

Genetic studies of maize show that it was domesticated from teosinte, a tall wild grass that still grows widely in Mexico (see Figure 12–6) (Flannery 1986; Staller et al. 2006). Indeed, these genetic studies suggest that changes occurred in only two genes, one related to the kernel glumes (outer casing), and one related to the stalk shape (Fedoroff 2003). The genes of modern corn were already established 4000 to 6000 years ago.

Teosinte is quite different from maize in several important ways, but small genetic changes led to major phenotypic changes. The genetic malleability of maize may be one reason it has become one of the most important domesticated crops on earth. Teosinte stalks do look a lot like maize, but teosinte has a "spike" to which 7 to 12 individual seeds are attached in a single row, unlike the maize cob, which has many seeds in many rows. Each teosinte seed has its own brittle shell, whereas the entire maize cob is covered with a tough husk. However, early maize was also considerably different from modern maize. The oldest maize cobs—dating to about 7000 years ago—are tiny, only about 3 centimetres long. They have only a half-dozen rows of seeds, and each seed is tiny. One interesting fact about both ancient and modern maize is that it is almost completely dependent on humans to reproduce—the shift from seeds with brittle coats to cobs with a tough husk meant that someone had to open the husk without damaging the seeds in

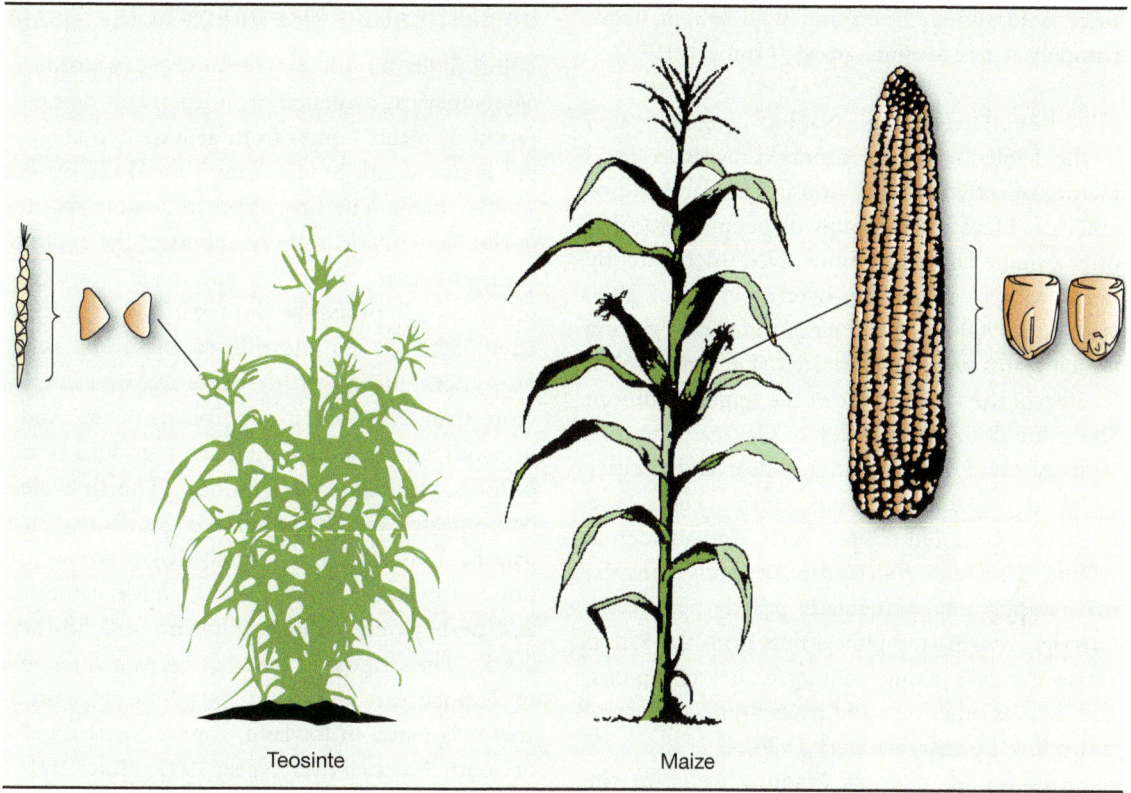

Figure 12–6 Teosinte Plant and Seeds and Maize Plant, Cob, and Kernels

Note how much larger the domesticated maize cob and kernels are compared with the teosinte spike and seeds.

Source: Feder KL. The past in perspective. Reprinted by permission of the author.

order for them to be dispersed and reproduce (Flannery 1986; Marcus and Flannery 1996).

Like maize and the bottle gourd, beans and squash were probably domesticated by simple manipulation of wild varieties. Runner beans, for example, grow naturally in the soils on the slopes outside of rock shelters and caves. It is not a stretch of the imagination to envision Archaic peoples harvesting these beans (for their roots to begin with—non-domestic runner bean seeds are tiny and probably were not eaten) and selectively planting those with desired qualities, like large seeds. Similarly, only the seeds of wild squashes were likely eaten by Archaic peoples, as the flesh of wild squashes often has an unattractive smell and taste. But they may have selectively planted mutants with good-tasting flesh and larger seeds, eventually producing the domestic varieties over time (Marcus and Flannery 1996).

People who lived in Mesoamerica, Mexico, and Central America are often credited with the invention of planting maize, beans, and squash together in the same field. This planting strategy provides some important advantages. Maize takes nitrogen from the soil; beans, like all legumes, put nitrogen back into the soil. The maize stalk provides a natural pole for the bean plant to twine around, and the low-growing squash can grow around the base of the tall maize plant. Beans supply people with the amino acid lysine, which is missing in maize. Thus, maize and beans together provide all the essential amino acids that humans need to obtain from food. Whether teosinte was or was not the ancestor of maize, it may have provided the model for this unique combination since wild runner beans and wild squash occur naturally where teosinte grows (Flannery 1986).

Guilá Naquitz. The Guilá Naquitz cave, excavated in the 1960s by Kent Flannery, provides a good picture of early domestication in Highland Mesoamerica. Here small groups of people, probably only a single family at a time, lived intermittently (and probably seasonally) over a period of 2000 years (ca. 8900 B.C.–6700 B.C.), the period during which plants were domesticated. The cave itself is located in the thorn forest of the upper piedmont above the floor of the Valley of Oaxaca. The residents of Guilá Naquitz hunted deer and peccary (a wild pig-like animal) with spears and spear-throwers, and trapped small animals such as rabbits. They also collected plant foods from the surrounding area, particularly prickly pear fruits, cherries, acorns, and piñon nuts from the forests above the cave, along with agave hearts, onions, and various other nuts and fruits from a variety of thorn forest plants (Flannery 1986).

Also found in Guilá Naquitz cave are the remains of domesticated plants, including bottle gourd and several varieties of squashes. How did these come to be in the cave? Were the inhabitants planting fields of squashes? Probably not in the way one thinks of planting a field today. Squashes are common wild plants in Highland Mesoamerica, and thrive in disturbed soils such as those outside of caves. It may be that the inhabitants of the Guilá Naquitz cave knew squashes would grow easily near their cave, and so actively planted some with better-tasting flesh or larger seeds than those that might naturally grow there (Flannery 1986). Domestication and the use of domesticated plants would be rather informal—a supplement to a diet already rich in animal and plant species. This picture seems much different from that at Near Eastern sites such as Ali Kosh and Çatal Hüyük. Domestication in Guilá Naquitz appears to have been accomplished by hunters and gatherers who supplemented their basic diet with some desired plants (squashes with tasty flesh, for example); there was no "revolution" that enabled the people to rely on domesticated plants.

Domestication Elsewhere in the World

South America and North America. Outside of Mesoamerica, evidence of independent domestication of plants comes from at least two areas in the New World: South America and the eastern United States. The first plants to be domesticated in the New World were members of the cucurbit family, including the bottle gourd and a variety of squashes, all probably domesticated sometime after 7500 B.C. In addition to these and other plants domesticated in Mesoamerica, we can trace more than 200 domesticated plants to the Andes in South America, including potatoes, lima beans, peanuts, amaranth, and quinoa. The first clear domesticates were squashes and gourds that may date back to 8000 B.C., which makes domestication in the Andes about as old as in Mesoamerica, and perhaps even older (Piperno and Stothert 2003). The origins of the root crops manioc and sweet potato are less certain, but those crops probably originated in lowland tropical forest regions of South America (MacNeish 1991; Hole 1992).

Many of the plants grown in North America, such as corn, beans, and squash, were apparently introduced from Mesoamerica. However, at least three seed plants were probably domesticated independently in North America at an earlier time—sunflowers, sumpweed, and goosefoot. Sunflowers and sumpweed contain seeds that are highly nutritious in terms of protein and fat; goosefoot is high in starch and similar to corn in food value (Smith 1992b). Sumpweed is an unusually good source of calcium, rivalled only by greens, mussels, and bones. It is also a very good source of iron (better than beef liver) and thiamine (Asch and Asch 1978). These plants may have been cultivated in the area of the plains around the lower Ohio, Tennessee, and mid-Mississippi River valley beginning around 2000 B.C. (corn was introduced about A.D. 200). At the same time people were domesticating squashes, the wild bees that collected pollen from their flowers became domesticated as they followed the spread of these crops farther northeast into areas where neither the squash nor the bees were native (Bischoff et al. 2009). All the pre-corn domesticates are nutritionally superior to corn, so why did North American agriculturalists switch to a reliance on corn in the last 1000 years (Smith 1992a, 1992b)? In archaeologist Bruce Smith's words, "With the exception of the sunflower, North American seed crops are not exactly household words" (Smith 1992b). Crop yields of corn would have had to be quite high to surpass the yields of those other crops, so perhaps the crucial factors were the time of harvest and the amount of effort required. Goosefoot, for example, was comparable to corn nutritionally. Harvesting and preparing it for storage, though, took a lot of work and had to be done during the fall, the time of year when deer could be hunted intensively. So perhaps the incompatibility of goosefoot production and deer hunting and the ease of harvesting corn and preparing it for storage explain the switch to corn (Smith 1992b). Maize consumption elsewhere in North America was likely more extensive than previously suspected. For instance, in the subarctic boreal forest and lower Great Lakes, maize residue has been identified in pottery dating from as early as A.D. 500 (Boyd and Surette 2010). Its importance may have been largely social rather than dietary, and it may have be used in gift giving to maintain alliances over large territories (Boyd and Surette 2010).

On the whole, domestic animals were less important economically in the New World than they were in many parts of the Old World. In North America, dogs and turkeys were the main domesticated animals before the arrival of the Spaniards. Dogs in North and South America probably accompanied the first colonizers of the Americas, as all domesticated dogs appear to be descended from a common Asian ancestor (Savolainen et al. 2002). Domesticated turkeys from about A.D. 500 have been found in pueblos in the American Southwest (Clutton-Brock 1988). Their feathers were used for arrows, ornaments, and weaving, and their bones for tools, but they do not seem to have been used frequently for food. However, turkeys were an important food in Mexico, where they may have been independently domesticated, and in Central America. When Cortés came to Mexico in 1519, he found domesticated turkeys in great quantities (Crawford 1984).

The Spanish also noted the importance of stingless bees to the Maya, who used their honey for both food and medicinal purposes (Cortopassi-Laurino et al. 2006:276). These bees were in fact so revered by the Maya that there was a recognized god of honey.

The central Andes was the only part of the New World where domesticated animals were a significant part of the economy. Used for meat, transportation, and wool, llamas and alpacas (members of the camel family) were domesticated as early as 5000 B.C. in the Andes (Clutton-Brock 1988; Browman et al. 2009:343). Guinea pigs, misnamed because they are neither pigs nor from Guinea, are rodents that were domesticated in the Andes sometime later. They were an important source of food even before domestication (Müller-Haye 1984; Browman et al. 2009:343). Since they were domesticated, they have been raised in people's dwellings.

Animal domestication in the New World differed from that in the Old World because different wild species were found in the two hemispheres. The Old World plains and forests were the homes for the wild ancestors of the cattle, sheep, goats, pigs, and horses we know today. In the New World, the Pleistocene herds of horses, mastodons, mammoths, and other large animals were long extinct, allowing few opportunities for domestication of large animals (Wenke and Olszewski 2007:262).

East Asia. The archaeological record for the domestication of seed crops is better known than for soft-flesh crops because the latter do not preserve well. The earliest clear evidence of cereal cultivation outside the Near East is from China. Late in the sixth millennium B.C. in North China there were sites where foxtail millet was cultivated. Storage pits, storage pots, and large numbers of grinding stones suggest that millet was an enormously important item in the diet. The wild-animal bones and the hunting and fishing tools that have been found suggest that people still depended on hunting and fishing somewhat, even though domesticated pigs (as well as dogs) were present. In South China, from about the same time, archaeologists found a village by the edge of a small lake where people cultivated rice, bottle gourds, water chestnuts, and the date-like fruit called jujube. The people in south China also raised water buffalo, pigs, and dogs. And, as in the north China sites, some of their food came from hunting and fishing (Chang 1981; MacNeish 1991; Cohen 2011).

Mainland Southeast Asia may have been a place of domestication as early as the Near East was. The dating of domestication in Southeast Asia is not yet clear; the dates of the oldest site with probable domesticates—Spirit Cave in northwest Thailand—range from about 9500 B.C. to 5500 B.C. Some of the plants found at Spirit Cave are not clearly distinguishable from wild varieties, but others, such as gourds, betel nut, betel leaf, and water chestnut, were probably domesticates (MacNeish 1991).

Most of the early cultivation in mainland Southeast Asia seems to have occurred in the plains and low terraces around rivers, although the main subsistence foods of early cultivators were probably the fish and shellfish in nearby waters. The first plants to be domesticated probably were not cereal grains, as they were in the Near East. Indeed, some early cultivated crops may not have been used for food at all. In particular, bamboo may have been used to make cutting tools and for a variety of building purposes, and gourds were probably used as containers or bowls. We do not know yet exactly when rice was first domesticated, but there is definite evidence of cultivated rice in the Yangzi Valley in China around 6500 to 6000 B.C. (Higham and Lu 1998).

Bananas and taro may have been first domesticated in New Guinea. Recent analyses of soils from archaeological deposits at Kuk Swamp have identified phytoliths (small silica crystals formed between plant cells that are unique to particular species of plants) from bananas and taro dating from almost 7000 years ago (Denham et al. 2003; Neumann 2003). Archaeologists have known that agricultural fields with soil mounds and irrigation features have a long history in New Guinea, dating back as far as 10 000 years. The new findings of very early taro and banana cultivation suggest that New Guinea may have been the location where these plants were first domesticated. Other major food plants were domesticated first in Southeast Asia, including root crops, such as taro and yams, and tree crops, such as breadfruit, coconuts, and bananas (MacNeish 1991; Hole 1992).

Africa. Some plants and animals were domesticated first in Africa. Most of the early domestications probably occurred in the wide, broad belt of woodland-savannah country south of the Sahara and north of the equator. Among the cereal grains, sorghum was probably first domesticated in the central or eastern part of this belt, bulrush millet and a kind of rice (different from Asian rice) in the western part, finger millet in the east, and tef,

A farmer threshing his sorghum crop in Sudan. Sorghum is one of several plant species domesticated in Africa.

enset, and noog in the Horn of Africa. Groundnuts (peanuts) and yams were first domesticated in West Africa (Phillipson 1993; Connah 2009). We do know that farming became widespread in the northern half of Africa after 6000 B.C.; investigators continue to debate whether the earliest crops grown there were indigenous or borrowed from the Near East. There is little doubt, however, that some of the plant foods were first domesticated in sub-Saharan Africa because the wild varieties occur there (MacNeish 1991; Phillipson 1993). Many of the important domestic animals in Africa today—cattle, sheep, and goats—probably were domesticated first in the Near East; most likely the donkey and guinea fowl were first domesticated in Africa (Clutton-Brock 1988).

Why Did Food Production Develop?

We know that an economic transformation occurred in widely separate areas of the world beginning after about 10 000 years ago, as people began to domesticate plants and animals. The question is, Why did domestication occur? And why did it occur independently in many different places within a period of a few thousand years? Considering that people depended only on wild plants and animals for millions of years, the differences in exactly when domestication first occurred in different parts of the world seem small. The spread of domesticated plants seems to have been more rapid in the Old World than in the New World, perhaps because the Old World spread was more along an east–west axis (except for the spread to sub-Saharan Africa), whereas the New World spread was more north–south. Spreading north and south may have required more time to adapt to variation in day lengths, climates, and diseases (Diamond 1997). (Figure 12–1 on page 292 shows a timeline for domestication of plants and animals in the Old and New Worlds.)

There are many theories of why food production developed; most have tried to explain the origin of domestication in the area of early agriculture. Theories that explain the origins of food production can be divided into two kinds: "push models," which argue that hunter-gatherers were forced into farming by some kind of stressor, such as environmental change or population pressure, and "pull models," which argue that hunter-gatherers were drawn to the benefits of the new farming lifestyle (Stark 1986). Most archaeologists think that, at least initially, certain conditions must have pushed people to switch from collecting to producing food, as opposed to food production being a voluntary choice.

Popular in the 1950s, Gordon Childe's theory was that a drastic change in climate caused domestication in the Near East (MacNeish 1991). According to Childe, the postglacial period was marked by a decline in summer rainfall in the Near East and northern Africa. As the rains decreased, people were forced to retreat into shrinking pockets, or oases, of food resources, which were surrounded by desert. The lessened availability of wild resources provided an incentive for people to cultivate grains and to domesticate animals, according to Childe.

Robert Braidwood criticized Childe's theory for two reasons. First, Braidwood believed that the climate changes may not have been as dramatic as Childe had assumed, and therefore the "oasis incentive" may not have existed. Second, the climatic changes that occurred in the Near East after the retreat of the last glaciers had probably occurred at earlier interglacial periods too, but there had never been a similar food-producing revolution before. Hence, according to Braidwood, there must be more to the explanation of why people began to produce food than simply changes in climate (Braidwood 1960).

Braidwood and Gordon Willey claimed that people did not undertake domestication until they had learned a great deal about their environment and until their culture had evolved enough for them to handle such an undertaking: "Why did incipient food production not come earlier? Our only answer at the moment is that culture was not ready to achieve it" (Braidwood and Willey 1962).

Most archaeologists now think we should try to explain why people were not "ready" earlier to achieve domestication. Both Lewis Binford and

Kent Flannery suggested that some change in external circumstances must have induced or favoured the changeover to food production (Binford 1971; Flannery 1971). As Flannery pointed out, there is no evidence of a great economic incentive for hunter-gatherers to become food producers. In fact, some contemporary hunter-gatherers may actually obtain adequate nutrition with far less work than many agriculturalists. So what might push food collectors to become food producers?

Binford and Flannery thought that the incentive to domesticate animals and plants might have been a desire to reproduce what was wildly abundant in the most bountiful or optimum hunting and gathering areas. Because of population growth in the optimum areas, people might have moved to surrounding areas containing fewer wild resources. It would have been in those marginal areas that people might have first turned to food production in order to reproduce what they used to have.

The Binford-Flannery model seems to fit the archaeological record in the Levant, the southwestern part of the earliest agriculture, where population increase did precede the first signs of domestication (Wright 1971). However, as Flannery admitted, in some regions, such as southwestern Iran, the optimum hunting-gathering areas do not show population increase before the emergence of domestication (Flannery 1986).

The Binford-Flannery model focuses on population pressure in a small area as the incentive to turn to food production. Mark Cohen theorized it was population pressure on a global scale that explains why so many of the world's peoples adopted agriculture within the span of a few thousand years (Cohen 1977a, 1977b). He argued that hunter-gatherers all over the world gradually increased in population so that by about 10 000 years ago the world was more or less filled with food collectors. Thus, people could no longer relieve population pressure by moving to uninhabited areas. To support their increasing populations, they would have had to exploit a broader range of less desirable wild foods; that is, they would have had to switch to broad-spectrum collecting, or they would have had to increase the yields of the most desirable wild plants by weeding, protecting them from animal pests, and perhaps deliberately planting only the most productive among them. Cohen thought that people might have tried a variety of these strategies but would generally have ended up depending on cultivation because that would have been the most efficient way to allow more people to live in one place.

Recently, some archaeologists have returned to the idea that climatic change (not the extreme variety that Childe envisaged) might have played a role in the emergence of agriculture. It seems clear from the evidence now available that the climate of the Near East about 13 000 to 12 000 years ago became more seasonal: the summers got hotter and drier than before and the winters became colder. These climatic changes may have favoured the emergence of annual species of wild grain, which archaeologically we see proliferating in many areas of the Near East (Byrne 1987; Henry 1989; Blumler and Byrne 1991; McCorriston and Hole 1991). People such as the Natufians intensively exploited the seasonal grains, developing an elaborate technology for storing and processing the grains and giving up their previous nomadic existence to do so. The transition to agriculture may have occurred when sedentary foraging no longer provided sufficient resources for the population. This could have happened because sedentism led to population increase and therefore resource scarcity (Henry 1989), or because local wild resources became depleted after people settled down in permanent villages (McCorriston and Hole 1991). In the area of Israel and Jordan where the Natufians lived, some of the people apparently turned to agriculture, probably to increase the supply of grain, whereas other people returned to nomadic food collection because of the decreasing availability of wild grain (Henry 1989).

Change to a more seasonal climate might also have led to a shortage of certain nutrients for food collectors. In the dry seasons certain nutrients would have been less available. For example, grazing animals get lean when grasses are not plentiful, so meat from hunting would have been in short supply in the dry seasons. Although it may seem surprising, some recent hunter-gatherers have starved when they had to rely on lean meat. If they could have somehow increased their carbohydrate or fat intake, they might have been more likely to get through the periods of lean game (Speth and Spielmann 1983). So it is possible that some wild-food collectors in the past thought of planting crops to get them through the dry seasons when hunting, fishing, and gathering did not provide enough carbohydrates and fat for them to avoid starvation.

Mesoamerica presents a very different picture, because the early domesticates were not important to subsistence. Theories about population pressure and nutrient shortage don't seem to fit Mesoamerica well. However, there were apparently shortages of desired plants, such as bottle gourds, and domestication may well have occurred as humans actively sowed these desired plants. The difference between this model and the ones described earlier is that humans in Mesoamerica were apparently not forced into domestication by climate change or population pressure, but actively turned to domestication to obtain more of the most desired or useful plant species. The most interesting case is maize, which only became a staple food some 2500 or more years after it was first domesticated. Why did it become a staple? Probably both because it was a suitable staple crop (especially when intercropped with beans and squash, as discussed earlier) and because people liked it, so they grew it in large quantities. Over time, and perhaps because of conflict, population pressure, and other forces similar to those that apparently led to domestication in the Near East, people in Mesoamerica and later North and South America came to rely on maize as their dietary mainstay.

Consequences of the Rise of Food Production

We know that intensive agriculture (permanent rather than shifting cultivation) probably developed in response to population pressure, but we do not know for sure that population pressure was even partly responsible for plant and animal domestication in the first place. Still, population growth certainly accelerated after the rise of food production (see Figure 12–7). There were other consequences too. Paradoxically, perhaps, health seems to have declined. Material possessions, though, became more elaborate (see Applied Anthropology, "The Archaeology of Environmental Collapse").

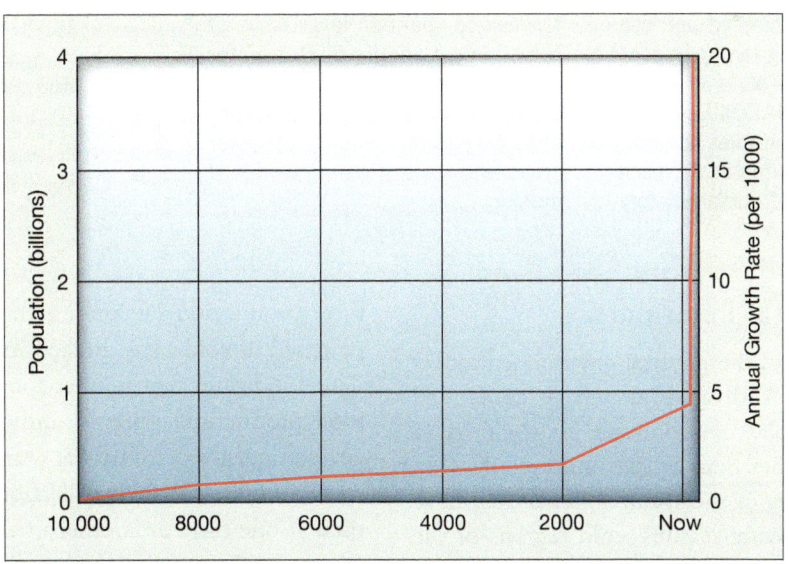

Figure 12–7 Population Growth since 10 000 Years Ago
The rate of population growth accelerated after the emergence of farming and herding 10 000 years ago. The rate of growth has accelerated even more dramatically in recent times.

Source: Reproduced with permission. Copyright © (1974). Scientific American, a division of Nature America, Inc. All rights reserved.

APPLIED ANTHROPOLOGY

The Archaeology of Environmental Collapse

In *The Life of Reason*, philosopher George Santayana (1905) wrote, "Those who cannot remember the past are condemned to repeat it" (p. 284). Archaeologists have long sought to provide a way for government agencies to remember the past so that mistakes will not be repeated. Today, the world's governments are struggling with problems of environmental degradation and global warming, but this is nothing new to archaeologists. Societies have routinely damaged or even destroyed their environments and either developed solutions or collapsed.

In the 1990s, the European Union (EU) decided that an archaeological perspective might help them to better understand the problem of land degradation within Europe. A team of archaeologists, geographers, environmental scientists, and others developed the ARCHAEOMEDES project for the EU, with the expressed purpose of developing a long-term perspective on the problem of land degradation. The ARCHAEOMEDES team completed case studies on four situations of land degradation spanning the range of human history in Europe from the Bronze Age to the present.

One example is the Rhône Valley of southeastern France. During the first few centuries A.D., the Rhône experienced a major period of Roman colonization. Hundreds of new towns emerged, transportation and water management systems were put in place, and thousands of acres were brought into agricultural production. Much of the agricultural production was market-oriented, particularly olive oil and wine. But, by the fifth century A.D., much of the region had been deserted, and agricultural land had been degraded (mainly by erosion) to the point that some has not yet recovered. What happened?

The ARCHAEOMEDES team found that the answer was complex. Minor climatic fluctuations increased the amount of rainfall and runoff from the Alps, causing periodic floods that forced farmers to abandon large parts of the Rhône floodplain. But water control systems the Romans put in place exacerbated the problem, extending flooding to other areas and fostering high levels of erosion.

The ARCHAEOMEDES team concluded that the environmental crisis of the first centuries A.D. in the Rhône Valley were largely political and economic in their origins. The changes Roman colonists imposed on the Rhône Valley triggered land degradation because the infrastructure could only be sustained during good times. When too much rain fell, flooding could not be controlled, and the system collapsed. The lesson seems clear. The environment itself did not collapse; human alterations to the environment could not adapt to "normal" fluctuations in the climate and sparked an environmental crisis. It is a lesson the ARCHAEOMEDES team hopes European governments will take to heart.

Sources: Redman CL. 1999. Human Impact on Ancient Environments. Tucson: University of Arizona Press.

Van der Leeuw S. 1999. The Archaeomedes Project: Understanding the Natural and Anthropogenic Causes of Desertification and Land Degradation. Luxembourg: European Union.

Van der Leeuw S, Favory F, Girardot JJ. 2004. The Archaeological Study of Environmental Degradation: An Example from Southeastern France. In: Redman C, James SR, Fish P, Rogers JD. The Archaeology of Global Change. Washington, DC: Smithsonian. pp. 112–129.

Environmental Restraints

How much does the physical environment affect food-getting? Anthropologists have concluded that the physical environment by itself has a restraining, rather than a determining, effect on the major types of subsistence. Since they have very short growing seasons, cold regions of the earth are not particularly conducive to the growing of plants. No society we know of has practised agriculture in the Arctic; instead, people who live there rely primarily on animals for food. Nevertheless, both food collection (as among Inuit) and food production (as among the Lapps) can be practised in cold areas. Indeed, cross-cultural evidence indicates that neither food collection nor food production is significantly associated with any particular type of habitat (Anonymous 1967).

We know that food collection has been practised at one time or another in almost all areas of the earth. The physical environment does seem to have some effect on what kind of food collection is practised, that is, on the extent to which food collectors will depend on plants, animals, or fish. Farther away from the equator, food collectors depend much less on plants for food and much more on animals and fish (Binford 1990; Low 1990). Lewis Binford argued that fishing becomes increasingly important in cold climates because food collectors need non-portable housing in severe winters to protect themselves from the cold. Therefore, they cannot rely on large animals, which usually have to feed themselves by moving over considerable distances in the winter. Fishing is more localized than hunting, and therefore food collectors who rely on fishing can stay in their non-portable houses in winter (Binford 1990).

When we contrast horticulture and intensive agriculture, the physical environment appears to explain some of the variation. Approximately 80 percent of all societies that practise horticulture or simple agriculture are in the tropics, whereas 75 percent of all societies that practise intensive agriculture are not in tropical forest environments (Anonymous 1967). Tropical forests have abundant rainfall. Despite the attractiveness of lush vegetation and brilliant colouring, tropical forest lands do not usually offer favourable environments for intensive agriculture. Perhaps this is because the heavy rainfall quickly washes away certain minerals from cleared land. Also, the difficulty of controlling insect pests and weeds, which abound in tropical forests (Carneiro 1968; Janzen 1973), may make intensive agriculture less productive.

Whatever the reasons for the switch to food production, we still need to explain why food production has supplanted food collection as the primary mode of subsistence. We cannot assume that collectors would automatically adopt production as a superior way of life once they understood the process of domestication. After all, as we have noted, domestication may entail more work and provide less security than the food-collecting way of life.

The spread of agriculture may be linked to the need for territorial expansion. As a sedentary, food-producing population grew, it may have been forced to expand into new territory. Some of this territory may have been vacant, but much of it was probably already occupied by food collectors. Although food production is not necessarily easier than collection, it is generally more productive per unit of land. Greater productivity enables more people to be supported in a given territory. In the competition for land between the faster-expanding food producers and the food collectors, the food producers may have had a significant advantage: they had more people in a given area. Thus, the foraging groups may have been more likely to lose out in the competition for land. Some groups may have adopted cultivation, abandoning the foraging way of life in order to survive. Other groups, continuing as food collectors, may have been forced to retreat into areas not desired by the cultivators. Today, as we have seen, the small number of remaining food collectors inhabit areas not particularly suitable for cultivation—dry lands, dense tropical forests, and polar regions.

Just as prior population growth might account for the origins of domestication, so would further population growth and ensuing pressure on resources at least partly explain the transformation of horticultural systems into intensive agricultural systems at later periods. However, just as the environment can affect the mode of subsistence, so, too, can the mode of subsistence affect the environment. We are all too familiar with the destruction of the world's tropical rain forests. It is estimated that 31 million hectares of global rain forest are destroyed each year. However, all human behavioural patterns associated with subsistence affect the environment (see Applied Anthropology, "The Effect of Food Production on the Environment"). Some environments may make it difficult to adopt certain subsistence practices. For example, intensive agriculture cannot supplant horticulture in some tropical environments and horticulture continues to be practised in these regions.

Accelerated Population Growth

As we have seen, sedentism (even before the rise of food production) may have increased the rate of human population growth. But population growth definitely accelerated after the emergence of farming and herding, possibly because the spacing between births was reduced and therefore fertility increased. Increased fertility may have been an advantage, because of the greater value of children in farming and herding economies; there is evidence from recent population studies that fertility

APPLIED ANTHROPOLOGY

The Effect of Food Production on the Environment

Many people are now aware of industrial pollution—the dumping of industrial wastes in the ground or into rivers, the spewing of chemicals into the air through smokestacks—but we don't often realize how much humans have altered the environment by the ways they collect and produce food. Consider irrigation. There are various ways to capture water for irrigation. Water can be channelled from rivers; rainwater can be caught in terraces carved out of hillsides; ancient water can be pumped up from vast underground reservoirs called aquifers. But not all of the water drawn for irrigation seeps into the ground. Much of it evaporates, leaving behind minerals and salts. And the more a piece of land has been irrigated, the saltier the ground becomes. Eventually, the soil becomes too salty to grow crops effectively.

Some archaeologists have suggested that the accumulation of toxic salts in the soil at least partly explains the doom or decline of various groups in the past. For example, salinization may have contributed to the decline of the earliest city-states in Mesopotamia, present-day southern Iraq, and southwestern Iran. The Hohokam farmers who lived in what is now Arizona had about 240 kilometres of canals for irrigation; some of their ditches were 4.5 metres deep and 7.6 metres wide. In fact, their irrigation networks were comparable to those that served the Aztecs in pre-Columbian Mexico City. The Hohokam seem to have vanished around A.D. 1400, perhaps because the salty soil poisoned their crops. Today much of the soil is still too salty for cultivation.

The lessons of history may not have been learned yet. The San Joaquin Valley of California, perhaps the most productive agricultural area in the world, now has a serious salinization problem. One solution in many of the areas of the Great American Desert is to pump water up from underground. Indeed, in many places there is a great deal of water underground. The pumping solution, if it is a solution, is only a short-term fix, though, for the huge Ogallala aquifer is also the fastest-disappearing aquifer. The only question is how long it will take to disappear totally. Salinization is also a major problem for farmers in the Canadian prairies, where it limits crop growth by blocking the crops' ability to take up water. However, management efforts such as reduction in summer fallow—the practice of leaving land bare during the growing season—and increased use of permanent soil-cover crops have reduced the prairie-wide risk of salinization.

Too many people raising too many animals can also have serious effects on the environment. We can easily imagine how the possibility of profit might inspire people to try to raise more animals than the land will support. For example, 300 years ago the Great American Desert looked like a vast grassland. It supported large herds of buffalo, which in the next 200 years were all but exterminated by overhunting. The white settlers soon discovered they could raise cattle and sheep on this grassland, but many parts of it were overgrazed. It took the swirling dust storms of the 1930s to make people realize that overgrazing as well as poor farming practices could be disastrous. These problems are not new. The Norse colonized Greenland and Iceland around A.D. 800, but overgrazing of pasture undoubtedly contributed to soil erosion and the disappearance or decline of the colonies by A.D. 1500.

Are environmental problems associated only with food production? Although food producers may be the worst offenders, there is reason to think that foragers may also have sometimes overfished, overgathered, or overhunted. For example, some scholars suspect that the movement of humans into the New World was mainly responsible for the disappearance of the mammoth. Unfortunately, there is little evidence that humans have been good conservers in the past. That does not mean that humans cannot do better in the future—but they have to want to.

Sources: Dirks R. 1998. Hunger and Famine. In: Ember CR, Ember M, Peregrine PN, editors. Research Frontiers in Anthropology. Upper Saddle River, NJ: Prentice Hall.

Plundering Earth Is Nothing New. 12 June 1994. Los Angeles Times News Service as reported in the New Haven Register. pp. A18–19.

Reisner M. 1993. Cadillac Desert: The American West and Its Disappearing Water. Revised edition. New York: Penguin.

Wiebe BH, Eilers RG, Eilers WD, Brierley JA. 2007. Application of a Risk Indicator for Assessing Trends in Dryland Salinization Risk on the Canadian Prairies. Canadian Journal of Soil Science. 87:213–224.

---

rates are higher where children contribute more to the economy (Kasarda 1971; White 1973). Not only may parents desire more children to help with chores, but the increased workload of mothers may also (inadvertently) decrease birth spacing. The busier a mother is, the less frequently she may nurse and the more likely her baby will be given supplementary food by other caretakers such as older siblings (Ember 1983). Less frequent nursing (Konner and Wortman 1980) and greater reliance on other food may result in the earlier resumption of ovulation after the birth of a baby. (Farmers and herders are likely to have animal milk to feed to babies, and also cereals that have been transformed by cooking into soft, mushy porridges.) Therefore, the spacing between births may have decreased (and the number of births per mother, in turn, increased) when mothers got busier after the rise of food production.

Declining Health

Although the rise of food production may have led to increased fertility, this does not mean that health generally improved. In fact, it appears that health declined at least sometimes with the transition to food production. The two trends may seem paradoxical, but rapid population growth can occur if each mother gives birth to a large number of babies, even if many of them die early because of disease or poor nutrition.

The evidence that health may have declined sometime after the rise of food production comes from studies of the bones and teeth of some prehistoric populations, before and after the emergence of food production. Nutritional and disease problems are indicated by such features as incomplete formation of tooth enamel, non-accidental bone lesions (incompletely filled-in bone), reduction in stature, and decreased mean age at death.

In a review of the impact of agriculture, Clark Larsen referred to a variety of studies that have observed lower mean ages at death for agricultural populations as compared with earlier hunter-gatherer samples (Larsen 1995). This, he noted, has been interpreted as a reflection of increased mortality and decreased life expectancy associated with the shift to agriculture. This hypothesis was the central focus of the 1984 volume of papers *Palaeopathology at the Origins of Agriculture* (Cohen and Armelagos 1984a), in which osteological evidence for demographic patterns and indicators of health were presented for several regions of the world. Many of the prehistoric populations that were studied relied heavily on agriculture and seemed to show less adequate nutrition and higher infection rates than populations living in the same areas before agriculture. Some of the agricultural populations were of shorter stature and had lower life expectancies (Cohen and Armelagos 1984b; Roosevelt 1984; Cohen 1987; Wood et al. 1992; Cohen 1998). The general conclusions drawn from studies throughout the 1970s and 1980s was that the shift to an agricultural subsistence and economy was associated with increases in mortality and the prevalence of infectious diseases. However, for populations that were undergoing moderate growth or decline, the effects of changes in mortality were negligible, while the effects of birth rate, and therefore fertility, were significant (Larsen 1995). As discussed in Chapter 3, this is critical since life expectancy derived from skeletal samples depends on the simple assumption of mean age at death being approximately equivalent to life expectancy at birth.

Given these arguments, the observed decline in mean age at death among agricultural populations in the archaeological record is more likely a reflection of their rapid population growth (Howell 1986). The extent to which fertility and mortality increased or decreased with a shift to agriculture is a key question, which as yet remains unsolved (Johansson and Horowitz 1986). However, given the wide range of ecological conditions in which various populations adopted agricultural practices, there may have been a similarly broad spectrum of demographic responses to this shift with respect to mortality and fertility (Jackes et al. 1997a, 1997b).

Understanding the biological impact of the Mesolithic–Neolithic transition is in fact not an easy task. Most of the evidence for apparent health declines associated with agriculture comes from Nubia in the Nile Valley and from the American Southwest. However, examining this question is difficult since regions with reasonably large samples of Mesolithic skeletons followed immediately by large, well-preserved Neolithic samples are fairly rare (Jackes et al. 1997a, 1997b). Mary Jackes, David Lubell, and Chris Meiklejohn studied large samples of Mesolithic and Neolithic skeletal material from central and southern Portugal (Jackes et al. 1997a, 1997b). In their study of three Mesolithic and eight Neolithic sites, these researchers observed little increase in rates of skeletal infection over this period. They didn't find this surprising, however, since the

Mesolithic populations showed evidence of being relatively sedentary, and the Neolithic populations continued to show some evidence of seasonal foraging (Jackes et al. 1997a, 1997b). Despite this continuity, there was some apparent increase in fertility and population growth in the Neolithic period. In contrast to the evidence from the Near East, they concluded from their study that there was "no evidence that the comfortable way of life of the Portuguese Mesolithic was replaced by a wretched and unhealthy Neolithic existence" (Jackes et al. 1997a).

The question of a decline in health associated with earlier agricultural populations remains a topic of debate. Greater malnutrition can result from an overdependence on a few dietary staples that lack some necessary nutrients. Overdependence on a few sources of food may also increase the risk of famine because the fewer the staple crops, the greater the danger to the food supply posed by a weather-caused crop failure. However, some or most nutritional problems may be the result of social and political factors, particularly the rise of different socio-economic classes of people and unequal access, between and within communities, to food and other resources (Roosevelt 1984). Social stratification or considerable socio-economic inequality seems likely to have developed after the rise of food production. The effects of stratification and political dominance from afar on the general level of health may be reflected in the skeletal remains of prehistoric people who died in what is now Illinois between A.D. 950 and 1300, the period spanning the changeover in that region from hunting and gathering to agriculture. The agricultural people living in the area of Dickson Mounds—burial sites named after the doctor who first excavated them—were apparently in much worse health than their hunter-gatherer ancestors. Curiously, archaeological evidence suggests that they were still also hunting and fishing. A balanced diet was apparently available, but who was getting it? Possibly it was the elite at Cahokia, 177 kilometres away, where perhaps 15 000 to 30 000 people lived, who were getting most of the meat and fish. The individuals near Dickson Mounds who collected the meat and fish may have acquired luxury items such as shell necklaces from the Cahokia elite, but many of the people buried at Dickson Mounds clearly did not benefit nutritionally from the relationship with Cahokia (Goodman et al. 1984a; Goodman and Armelagos 1985; Cohen 1998).

The Elaboration of Material Possessions

Every society makes use of a technology to convert raw materials to food and other goods. **Technology** includes tools, constructions (such as fish traps), the required skills (such as how and where to set up a fish trap), and also the political organization required to extract, process, and redistribute resources. Societies vary considerably in their technologies and in the way access to technology is allocated. For example, food collectors and pastoralists typically have fairly small tool kits. They must limit their tools, and their material possessions in general, to what they can comfortably carry with them, or to those that can be expediently manufactured at the place where they are needed.

As this reconstruction shows, transforming grain into flour was a "daily grind," putting a great deal of stress on the lower back and knees of women. Studies of Neolithic skeletons of women show marks of stress on bone and arthritis, probably reflecting their long hours of work at the grinding stone.

Museo Archeologico, Florence, Italy/Bridgeman Images

Technology: constructions such as traps, skills required to use these constructions, and the organizations needed to extract, process, and redistribute resources.

The tools most needed by food collectors are weapons for the hunt, digging sticks, and receptacles for gathering and carrying. Andaman Islanders used bows and arrows for hunting game and large fish. Australian Aborigines developed two types of boomerangs: a heavy one for a straight throw in killing game and a light, returning one for playing games or for scaring birds into nets strung between trees. The Semang of Malaya used poisoned darts and blowguns. The Mbuti Pygmies of the Congo River basin still trap elephants and buffalo in deadfalls and nets. Of all food collectors, Inuit probably had the most sophisticated weapons, including harpoons, compound bows, and ivory fish hooks. Yet Inuit also had relatively fixed settlements with available storage space and dog teams and sleds for transportation (Service 1979).

Societies with intensive agriculture and industrialized societies are likely to have tools made by specialists, which means that tools must be acquired by trade or purchase. Probably because complex tools have greater value, they are less likely than simple tools to be shared except by those who contributed to their production.

In the more permanent villages that were established after the rise of food production about 10 000 years ago, houses became more elaborate and comfortable, and construction methods improved. The materials used in construction depended on whether timber or stone was locally available or whether a strong sun could dry mud bricks. Modern architects might find to their surprise that bubble-shaped houses were known long ago in Neolithic Cyprus. Families in the island's town of Khirokitia made their homes in large, domed, circular dwellings shaped like beehives and featuring stone foundations and mud-brick walls. Often, more space was created by dividing the interior horizontally and firmly propping a second floor on limestone pillars.

Sizable villages of solidly constructed, gabled wood houses were built in Europe on the banks of the Danube and along the rims of Alpine lakes (Clark and Piggott 1965). Many of the gabled wooden houses in the Danube region were long, rectangular structures that apparently sheltered several family units. In Neolithic times these longhouses had doors, beds, tables, and other furniture

Sophisticated ceramics like this 5000-year-old Chinese funeral urn first appeared in the Neolithic era as part of the elaboration of material possessions.

that closely resembled those in modern-day societies. We know the people had furniture because miniature clay models have been found at their sites. Several of the chairs and couches seem to be models of padded and upholstered furniture with wooden frames, indicating that Neolithic European artisans were creating fairly sophisticated furnishings (Clark and Piggott 1965). Such furnishings were the result of an advanced tool technology put to use by a people who, because they were staying in one area, could take time to make and use furniture.

For the first time, apparel made of woven textile appeared. This development was not simply the result of the domestication of flax (for linen), cotton, and wool-growing sheep. These sources of fibre alone could not produce cloth. It was the development by Neolithic society of the spindle and loom for spinning and weaving that made textiles possible. True, textiles can be woven by hand without a loom, but to do so is a slow, laborious process, impractical for producing garments.

The pottery of the early Neolithic was similar to the plain earthenware made by some Mesolithic groups and included large urns for grain storage, mugs, cooking pots, and dishes. To improve the retention of liquid, potters in the Near East may have been the first to glaze the earthenware's porous surface. Later, Neolithic ceramics became more artistic. Designers shaped the clay into graceful forms and painted colourful patterns on the vessels.

It is probable that virtually none of these architectural and technological innovations could have occurred until humans became fully sedentary. Nomadic hunting-and-gathering peoples would have found it difficult to carry many material goods, especially fragile items such as pottery. It was only when humans became fully sedentary that these goods would have provided advantages, enabling villagers to cook and store food more effectively and to house themselves more comfortably.

There is also evidence of long-distance trade in the Neolithic, as we have noted. Obsidian from southern Turkey was exported to sites in the Zagros Mountains of Iran and to what are now Israel, Jordan, and Syria in the Levant. Great amounts of obsidian were exported to sites about 300 kilometres from the source of supply; more than 80 percent of the tools used by residents of those areas were made of this material (Renfrew 1969). Marble was sent from western to eastern Turkey, and seashells from the coast were traded to distant inland regions. Such trade suggests a considerable amount of contact among various Neolithic communities.

About 3500 B.C., cities first appeared in the Near East. These cities had political assemblies, kings, scribes, and specialized workshops. The specialized production of goods and services was supported by surrounding farming villages, which sent their produce to the urban centres. A dazzling transformation had taken place in a relatively short time. People had not only settled down but also become "civilized," or urbanized. (The word *civilized* literally means to make "citified" [Anonymous 1988].) Urban societies seem to have developed first in the Near East and somewhat later around the eastern Mediterranean, in the Indus Valley of northwestern India, in northern China, and in Mexico and Peru. In the next chapter we turn to the rise of these earliest civilizations.

SUMMARY AND REVIEW

FOOD COLLECTION AND PRODUCTION

12.1 **Explain the difference between foragers, horticulturalists, and agriculturalists.**

- Food collection is defined as all forms of subsistence technology in which food-getting is dependent on naturally occurring resources. Food collectors are referred to as *foragers*.

- Beginning around 10 000 years ago, populations began to cultivate and later domesticate plants and animals, a process known as *food production*.

- In horticulture, plant cultivation is carried out with relatively simple tools and methods; nature replaces nutrients in the soil in the absence of permanently cultivated fields.

- Intensive agriculture is characterized by the permanent cultivation of fields and the use of complex agricultural techniques.

 *How are slash-and-burn techniques used in land cultivation?*

PRE-AGRICULTURAL DEVELOPMENTS

12.2 **Explain the relationship between broad-spectrum collecting, sedentism, and population growth in terms of pre-agricultural developments.**

- Before plants and animals were domesticated in many parts of the world there seems to have been a shift to less dependence on big-game hunting and greater dependence on broad-spectrum collecting.

- The broad spectrum of resources frequently included aquatic resources, such as fish and shellfish, and a variety of wild plants, deer, and other game.

- Climatic changes may have been partly responsible for the shift to broad-spectrum collecting.

- Broad-spectrum collecting is associated with more permanent communities in some parts of the world—such as the Near East, Europe, Africa, and Peru. In others—like areas of Mesoamerica—the domestication of plants and animals may have preceded permanent settlements.

 *Why do sedentary !Kung women have more babies than nomadic !Kung women?*

THE DOMESTICATION OF PLANTS AND ANIMALS

12.3 Discuss the domestication of plants and animals in the Near East, Mesoamerica, and elsewhere in the world.

- *Domestication* refers to changes in plants and animals that make them more useful to humans.
- The earliest evidence for domestication is in the Near East about 8000 B.C. There are likely other independent centres of domestication elsewhere in the Old World—China, Southeast Asia (now Malaysia, Thailand, Cambodia, and Vietnam), New Guinea, and Africa—around or after 6000 B.C.
- In the New World, early areas of cultivation and domestication are found in the highlands of Mesoamerica (ca. 7000 B.C.), the Central Andes around Peru (around the same time, but maybe even earlier), and the Eastern Woodlands of North America (ca. 2000 B.C.).
- Humans selected certain plants and animals—deliberately or accidentally—because they had characteristics more advantageous for our use: plants with a tougher rachis hold seeds longer and are more desirable for planting; smaller sheep, goats, and cattle are easier to manage than larger ones common in wild herds. Many of these characteristics made it more difficult for plants and animals to reproduce without human assistance: plants that do not easily drop their seeds or small male goats are less likely to propagate their species.
- When comparing wild versus domesticated plants, archaeologists look for differences in the fragility of rachis (stems), the size of seeds, and the presence of naturally growing ancestors in the region.
- When comparing wild versus domesticated animals, archaeologists look for differences in physical characteristics (e.g., horn shape), the size of animals, and the demography (age–sex composition) of herds.

 *How did people maintain a semi-nomadic hunting-and-gathering lifestyle in Mesoamerica?*

WHY DID FOOD PRODUCTION DEVELOP?

12.4 Evaluate theories for why food production developed.

- Theories that explain the origins of food production are controversial. They can be divided into two kinds: "push models," which argue hunter-gatherers were forced into farming by some kind stressor, such as environmental change or population pressure, and "pull models," which argue hunter-gatherers were drawn to the benefits of the new farming lifestyle.
- More archaeologists think that—at least initially—certain conditions must have pushed people to switch from collecting to producing food, as opposed to food production being a voluntary choice.
- Another cause may have been global population growth; as people moved to fill most of the world's best habitable regions, people were forced to use a broader spectrum of wild resources and to produce more than what nature could offer by domesticating plants and animals.
- Another possible cause could be environmental. As summers became hotter and winters colder 10 000 years ago, some people began to favour sedentism in places with vast stands of wild grain; with an abundance of food nearby, populations grew, forcing people to plants crops and raise animals to feed themselves.
- Neither climate change nor population pressure led to domestication in Mesoamerica.

Instead, people turned to domestication to produce more of the most desired and useful plants found in nature.

- One cause of food production might have been population growth in regions with many wild resources. Large populations then pushed people to live in marginal areas and re-create the abundance of resources they once knew.

 *Why might the spread of domesticated plants have been more rapid in the Old World than in the New World?*

CONSEQUENCES OF THE RISE OF FOOD PRODUCTION

12.5 Critically analyze the consequences of food production.

- Whatever the reasons for the development of food production, it seems to have had important consequences for human life, including the following.

- Accelerated population growth: Plant and animal domestication led to substantial increases in population.
- Settling down: A greater reliance on agriculture led to an increase in sedentism in many areas.
- Declining health: Populations that relied heavily on agriculture were less healthy compared with earlier foraging people. Grains were high in carbohydrates and led to tooth decay (dental caries); population crowding and close proximity to herd animals led to new infectious diseases.
- Elaboration of material possessions: In more permanent villages, houses and furnishings became more elaborate, people began to make textiles and to paint pottery, long-distance trade seemed to increase, and political assemblies formed.

 *What might account for the observed decline in mean age at death among agricultural populations in the archaeological record?*

THINK ON IT

1. What were some of the pre-agricultural developments in the Near East and Mesoamerica that might have led to agriculture?
2. How do domesticated sheep, goats, and cattle differ from their wild counterparts?
3. Why might foragers be less likely then intensive agriculturalists to suffer from food shortages?
4. Compare two theories for the origins of agriculture. What are the strengths and weaknesses of each theory?
5. What have been some of the consequences of food production?

Origins of Cities and States

13

Will & Deni McIntyre/Science Source

LEARNING OBJECTIVES

13.1 Explain how archaeologists infer that a particular people in the past had social classes, cities, or a centralized government.

13.2 Describe the emergence of cities and states in Sumer.

13.3 Describe the emergence of cities and states in Mesoamerica.

13.4 Describe the first cities and states in other areas of the world.

13.5 Evaluate the major theories about the origin of the state.

13.6 Identify and explain consequences of state formation.

13.7 Discuss explanations for the decline and collapse of states.

From the time agriculture first developed until about 6000 B.C., people in the Near East lived in fairly small villages. There were few differences in wealth and status from household to household, and apparently there was no governmental authority beyond the village. There is no evidence that these villages had any public buildings or craft specialists or that one community was very different in size from its neighbours. In short, these settlements had none of the characteristics we commonly associate with "civilization."

Sometime around 6000 B.C., in parts of the Near East—and at later times in other places—a great transformation in the quality and scale of human life seems to have begun. For the first time we can see evidence of differences in status between households. For example, some were much bigger than others. Communities began to differ in size and to specialize in certain crafts, and there are signs that some political officials had acquired authority over several communities, that what anthropologists call "chiefdoms" had emerged.

Somewhat later, by about 3500 B.C., we can see many, if not all, of the conventional characteristics of **civilization**: the first inscriptions, or writing; cities; many kinds of full-time craft specialists; monumental architecture; great differences in wealth and status; and the kind of strong, hierarchical, centralized political system we call the **state**.

This type of transformation has occurred many times and in many places in human history. The most ancient civilizations arose in the Near East around 3500 B.C., in northwestern India after 2500 B.C., in northern China around 1750 B.C., in the New World (Mexico and Peru) just over 2000 years ago, and in tropical Africa somewhat later (Connah 1987; Wenke and Olszewski 2007). At least some of these civilizations evolved independently of the others—for example, those in the New World and those in the Old World.

Why did they do so? What conditions favoured the emergence of centralized, state-like political systems? What conditions favoured the establishment of cities? We ask this last question separately, because archaeologists are not yet certain that all the ancient state societies had cities when they first developed centralized government. In this chapter we discuss some of the things archaeologists have learned or suspect about the growth of ancient civilizations. Our discussion focuses primarily on the Near East and Mexico because archaeologists know the most about the sequences of cultural development in those two areas (see Figure 13–1).

Archaeological Inferences about Civilization

The most ancient civilizations have been studied by archaeologists rather than historians because those civilizations evolved before the advent of writing. How do archaeologists infer that a particular people in the preliterate past had social classes, cities, or a centralized government?

It appears that the earliest Neolithic societies were **egalitarian societies**; that is, people did not differ much in wealth, prestige, or power. Differences in prestige and social power that existed in the Neolithic were conferred upon individuals as a function of respect (status) that was earned through a lifetime of demonstrated skills and accomplishments. This status was not transferable to descendants. Some later societies show signs of social inequality, indicated by burial finds. Archaeologists generally assume that inequality in death reflects inequality in life, at least in status and perhaps also in wealth

Civilization: urban society, from the Latin word for "city-state."
State: a political unit with centralized decision making affecting a large population. Most states have cities with public buildings; full-time craft and religious specialists; an "official" art style; a hierarchical social structure topped by an elite class; and a governmental monopoly on the legitimate use of force to implement policies.

Egalitarian Society: a society in which all persons of a given age-sex category have equal access to economic resources, power, and prestige.

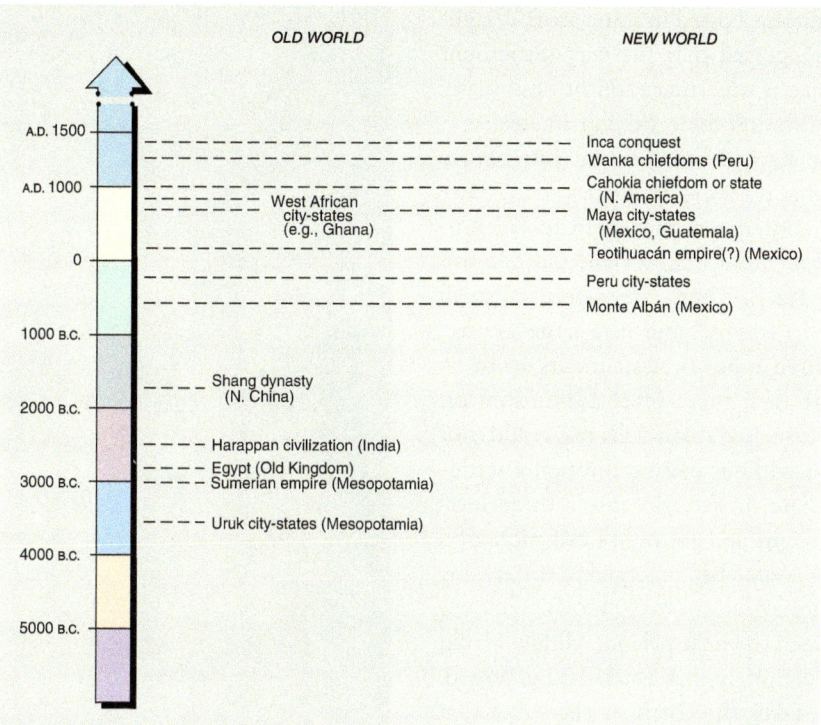

Figure 13–1 The Emergence of Civilization

and power. Thus, we can be fairly sure that a society had differences in status if only some people were buried with special objects, such as jewellery or pots filled with food. Further, we can be fairly sure that high status was assigned at birth rather than achieved in later life if we find noticeable differences in children's tombs. For example, some (but not all) child burials from as early as 5500 to 5000 B.C. at Telles-Sawwan in Iraq, and from about 800 B.C. at La Venta in Mexico, are filled with statues and ornaments, suggesting that some children had high status from birth (Flannery 1972; Wenke and Olszewski 2007). However, burials indicating differences in status do not necessarily mean a society had significant differences in wealth. It is only when archaeologists find other substantial differences, as in house size and furnishings, that we can be sure the society had different socio-economic classes of people.

Some archaeologists think that states first evolved around 3500 B.C. in Greater Mesopotamia, the area now shared by southern Iraq and southwestern Iran. Archaeologists do not always agree on how a state should be defined, but most think that hierarchical and centralized decision making affecting a substantial population is the key criterion. Other characteristics are usually, but not always, found in these first states. They usually have cities with a substantial part of the population not involved directly in the collection or production of food (which means that people in cities are heavily dependent on people elsewhere); full-time religious and craft specialists; public buildings; and often an official art style. There is a hierarchical social structure topped by an elite class from which the leaders are drawn (Flannery 1972; Redman 1978).

How can archaeologists tell, from the information provided by material remains, whether a society was a state or not? This depends in part on the individual criteria for a state. For example, Henry Wright and Gregory Johnson defined a state as a centralized political hierarchy with at least three levels of administration (Wright and Johnson 1975). How might archaeologists infer that such a hierarchy existed in some area? Wright and Johnson suggested that the way settlement sites differ in size is one indication of how many levels of administration there were in an area.

During the Early Uruk period (just before 3500 B.C.) in what is now southwestern Iran, there were some 50 settlements that seem to fall into three groups in terms of size (Wright and Johnson 1975; Johnson 1987). There were about 45 small villages, 3 or 4 "towns," and one large centre, Susa. These three types of settlements seem to have been part of a three-level administration hierarchy, since many small villages could not trade with Susa without passing through a settlement intermediate in size. Because a three-level hierarchy is Wright and Johnson's criterion of a state, they think a state had emerged in the area by early Uruk times.

Evidence from the next period, Middle Uruk, suggests more definitely that a state had emerged. This evidence takes the form of clay seals that were apparently used in trading (Wright and Johnson 1975). *Commodity sealings* were used to keep a shipment of goods tightly closed until it reached its destination, and *message sealings* were used to keep track of goods sent and received. The clay seals found in Susa include many message seals and *bullae*, clay containers that served as bills of lading for goods received. The villages, in contrast, had few message seals and *bullae*. Again, this finding suggests that Susa administered the regional movement of goods and that Susa was the "capital" of the state.

Let us turn now to the major features of the cultural sequences leading to the first states in southern Iraq.

Cities and States in Sumer

Farming communities older than the first states have not been found in the arid lowland plains of southern Iraq—the area known as Sumer, where some of the earliest cities and states developed. Perhaps silt from the Tigris and Euphrates rivers has covered them. Or, as has been suggested, Sumer may not have been settled by agriculturalists until people learned how to drain and irrigate river-valley

Reconstruction of the burial of a prehistoric Peruvian king, known as the "Lord of Sipan." Note the carefully laid-out wood tomb and the ornate cloth and gold items buried with the individual. Archaeologists assume that such special treatment indicates elite status.

soils otherwise too wet or too dry for cultivation. At any rate, small communities depending partly on agriculture had emerged in the hilly areas north and east of Sumer early in the Neolithic. Later, by about 6000 B.C., a mixed herding-farming economy developed in those areas.

The Formative Era

Elman Service (1975) called the period from about 5000 to 3500 B.C. the *formative era*, for it saw the coming together of many changes that seem to have played a part in the development of cities and states. Service suggested that with the development of small-scale irrigation, lowland river areas began to attract settlers. The rivers provided not only water for irrigation but also molluscs, fish, and water birds for food, and they provided routes by which to import needed raw materials, such as hardwood and stone that were lacking in Sumer.

Changes during this period suggest an increasingly complex social and political life. Differences in status are reflected in the burial of statues and ornaments with children. Different villages specialized in the production of different goods—pottery in some, copper and stone tools in others (Flannery 1972; Matthews 2009). Temples were built in certain places that may have been centres of political as well as religious authority for several communities (Service 1975; Matthews 2009). Furthermore, some anthropologists think that **chiefdoms**, each having authority over several villages, had developed by this time (Flannery 1972; Service 1975).

Sumerian Civilization

By about 3500 B.C., there were quite a few cities in the area of Sumer. Most were enclosed in a fortress wall and surrounded by an agricultural area. About 3000 B.C., all of Sumer was unified under a single government. After that time, Sumer became an empire, with great urban centres. Imposing temples, commonly set on artificial mounds, dominated the cities. In the city of Warka the temple mound was about 45 metres high. The empire was very complex and included an elaborate system for the administration of justice, codified laws, specialized government officials, a professional standing army, and even sewer systems in the cities. Among the many specialized crafts were brick making, pottery, carpentry, jewellery making, leatherworking, metallurgy, basket making, stonecutting, and sculpture. Sumerians learned to construct and use wheeled wagons, sailboats, horse-drawn chariots, and spears, swords, and armour of bronze (Kramer 1963).

As economic specialization developed, social stratification became more elaborate. Sumerian documents describe a system of social classes: nobles, priests, merchants, craft workers, metallurgists,

> **Chiefdom:** a political unit, with a chief at its head, integrating more than one community but not necessarily the whole society or language group.

A partially restored ziggurat, or temple tower, in what was the Sumerian city of Ur in 2100 B.C.

Examples of two of the earliest writing systems on earth. In the centre is a cuneiform tablet and below is a section of a hieroglyphic panel.

bureaucrats, soldiers, farmers, free citizens, and slaves. Slaves were common in Sumer; they often were captives, brought back as the spoils of war.

We see the first evidence of writing around 3000 B.C. The earliest Sumerian writings were in the form of ledgers containing inventories of items stored in the temples and records of livestock or other items owned or managed by the temples. Sumerian writing had wedge-shaped characters, or **cuneiform**, formed by pressing a stylus against a damp clay tablet. For contracts and other important documents, the tablet was fired to create a virtually permanent record. Egyptian writing, or **hieroglyphics**, appeared about the same time. Hieroglyphics were written on rolls woven from papyrus reeds, from which our word *paper* derives.

Cities and States in Mesoamerica

Cities and states emerged in Mesoamerica—now Mexico and Central America—later than they did in the Near East. The later appearance of civilization in Mesoamerica may be linked to the later emergence of agriculture in the New World, as we saw in the last chapter, and possibly to the near absence of large animals such as cattle and horses that could be domesticated (Diamond 1989). We focus primarily on the developments that led to the rise of the city-state of Teotihuacán, which reached its height almost 2000 years ago. Teotihuacán is located in a valley of the same name, which is the northeastern part of the larger Valley of Mexico.

The Formative Period

The formative period in the area around Teotihuacán (1000–300 B.C.) was characterized initially by small, scattered farming villages on the hilly slopes just south of the Teotihuacán Valley.

> **Cuneiform:** wedge-shaped writing invented by the Sumerians around 3000 B.C.
> **Hieroglyphics:** "picture writing," as in ancient Egypt and in Mayan sites in Mesoamerica (Mexico and Central America).

There were probably a few hundred people in each hamlet, and each of these scattered groups was probably politically autonomous. After about 500 B.C., there seems to have been a population shift to settlements on the valley floor, probably in association with the use of irrigation. Between about 300 and 200 B.C., small "elite" centres emerged in the valley; each had an earthen or stone raised platform. Residences or small temples of poles and thatch originally stood on these platforms. That some individuals, particularly those in the elite centres, were buried in special tombs supplied with ornaments, headdresses, carved bowls, and a good deal of food indicates some social inequality (Helms 1975; Sanders et al. 1979). The various elite centres may indicate the presence of chiefdoms.

The City and State of Teotihuacán

About 150 B.C. no more than a few thousand people lived in scattered villages in the Teotihuacán Valley. In A.D. 100 there was a city of 80 000. By A.D. 500, well over 100 000 people, or approximately 90 percent of the entire valley population, seem to have been drawn or coerced into Teotihuacán (Millon 1967; Wenke and Olszewski 2007).

The layout of the city of Teotihuacán, which shows a tremendous amount of planning, suggests that from its beginning the valley was politically unified under a centralized state. Mapping has revealed that the streets and most of the buildings are laid out in a grid pattern, where each grid square measures 57 square metres. Residential structures are often squares of this size, and many streets are spaced apart according to multiples of the basic unit. Even the river that ran through the centre of the city was channelled to conform to the grid pattern. Perhaps the most outstanding feature of the city is the colossal scale of its architecture. Two pyramids dominate the metropolis, the so-called Pyramid of the Moon and the Pyramid of the Sun. At its base the latter is as big as the great Pyramid of Cheops in Egypt.

The city of Teotihuacán, which had its peak in A.D. 500, was a planned city built on a grid pattern. At the centre was the Pyramid of the Sun, seen in the background on the left here.

The thousands of residential structures built after A.D. 300 follow a standard pattern. Narrow streets separate the one-storey buildings, each of which has high, windowless walls. Patios and shafts provide interior light. The layout of rooms suggests that each building consisted of several apartments; more than 100 people may have lived in one of these apartment compounds. There is variation from compound to compound in the size of rooms and the elaborateness of interior decoration, suggesting considerable variation in wealth (Millon 1976).

Like any major city, Teotihuacán attracted migrants from the surrounding areas. Researchers at Western University in Ontario are currently examining the question of how migrant populations maintained their ethnic identity within Teotihuacán. Around A.D. 200, a small population of about 1000 Zapotecs emigrated from the Valley of Oaxaca, 400 kilometres southeast of Teotihuacán (Spence 1992). These people settled in an enclave (Tlailotlacan) at the edge of the city, maintaining their identity for over 500 years (Spence 1992).

When the Temple of Quetzalcoatl in Teotihuacán was built in A.D. 200, more than 200 individuals were sacrificed. A collaborative effort between Mike Spence at Western University and Mexican physical anthropologists is being undertaken to conduct an osteological analysis of 160 skeletons associated with this event. Using a variety of methods including analysis of ancient DNA, stable isotopes, and skeletal traits, anthropologists hope to be able to paint a clear picture of the health and nutrition, origin, and relationships of those who died.

At the height of its power (A.D. 200–500), the metropolis of Teotihuacán encompassed an area larger than imperial Rome (Millon 1967). Much of Mesoamerica seems to have been influenced by Teotihuacán. Archaeologically, its influence is suggested by the extensive spread of Teotihuacán-style pottery and architectural elements. Undoubtedly, large numbers of people in Teotihuacán were engaged in production for and the conduct of long-distance trade. Perhaps 25 percent of the city's population worked at various specialized crafts, including the manufacture of projectile points and cutting and scraping tools from volcanic obsidian. Teotihuacán was close to major deposits of obsidian, which was apparently in some demand over much of Mesoamerica. This fine-grained volcanic stone was used to produce a variety of items in Teotihuacán (projectile points, knives, scrapers, drills, figurines, etc.) that were distributed at times over distances of more than 1000 kilometres (Spence 1996). Materials found in graves indicate that there was an enormous flow of foreign goods into the city, including precious stones, feathers from colourful birds in the tropical lowlands, and cotton (Helms 1975; Weaver 1993).

The City of Monte Albán

Teotihuacán probably was not the earliest city-state in Mesoamerica: there is evidence of political unification somewhat earlier, about 500 B.C., in the Valley of Oaxaca, in southern Mexico, with the city of Monte Albán at its centre. Monte Albán presents an interesting contrast to Teotihuacán. Whereas Teotihuacán seems to have completely dominated its valley, containing almost all its inhabitants and craftspeople, Monte Albán did not. The various villages in the Valley of Oaxaca seem to have specialized in different crafts, but Monte Albán did not monopolize craft production. After the political unification of the valley, cities and towns other than Monte Albán remained important; the population of Monte Albán grew only to 30 000 or so. Unlike Teotihuacán, Monte Albán was not an important commercial or market centre, it was not laid out in a grid pattern, and its architecture was not much different from that of other settlements in the valley (Blanton 1981; Marcus 1983; Wenke and Olszewski 2007).

Monte Albán did not have the kinds of resources that Teotihuacán had. It was located on top of a mountain in the centre of the valley, far from either good soil or permanent water supplies that could have been used for irrigation. Even finding drinking water must have been difficult. No natural resources for trade were nearby, nor is there much evidence that Monte Albán was used as a ceremonial centre. Because the city was at the top of a steep mountain, it is unlikely that it could have been a central marketplace for valley-wide trade.

Why, then, did Monte Albán rise to become one of the early centres of Mesoamerican civilization? Richard Blanton suggested it might have originally been founded in the late formative period (500–400 B.C.) as a neutral place where representatives of the different political units in the valley could reside to coordinate activities affecting the whole valley. Thus, Monte Albán may have been like the cities of Brasília; Washington, D.C.; and Athens, all of which were originally founded in "neutral," non-productive areas. Such a centre, lacking obvious resources, would not, at least initially, threaten the various political units around it. Later it might become a metropolis dominating a more politically unified region, as Monte Albán came to do in the Valley of Oaxaca (Blanton 1976; Blanton 1978).

Other Centres of Mesoamerican Civilization

In addition to Teotihuacán and Oaxaca, there were other Mesoamerican state societies, which developed somewhat later. For example, there are a number of centres with monumental architecture, presumably built by speakers of Mayan languages, in the highlands and lowlands of modern-day Guatemala and the Yucatán Peninsula of modern-day Mexico. On the basis of surface appearances, the Mayan centres do not appear to have been as densely populated as Teotihuacán or Monte Albán. It is now evident, though, that these other Mayan centres were more densely populated and more dependent on intensive agriculture than was once thought (Turner 1970; Harrison and Turner 1978; Coe 2011), and recent translations of Mayan picture writing indicate a much more developed form of writing than previously thought (Houston 1988; Coe 2011). It is apparent now that Mayan urbanization and cultural complexity were underestimated by earlier archaeologists because of the dense tropical forest that now covers much of the area of Mayan civilization.

The First Cities and States in Other Areas

So far we have discussed the emergence of cities and states in southern Iraq and Mesoamerica whose development is best, if only imperfectly, known archaeologically. But other state societies probably arose more or less independently in many other areas of the world as well (see Figure 13–2). We say "independently" because such states seem to have emerged without colonization or conquest by other states.

Almost at the same time as the Sumerian empire, the great dynastic age was beginning in the Nile Valley in Egypt. The Old Kingdom, or early dynastic period, began about 3100 B.C., with a capital at Memphis. The archaeological evidence from the early centuries is limited, but most of the population appears to have lived in largely self-sufficient villages. Many of the great pyramids and palaces were built around 2500 B.C. (Bard 2008).

Elsewhere in Africa, states also arose. In what is present-day Ethiopia, the Axum (or Aksum) state evolved beginning sometime early in the 1st millennium A.D., and ultimately became a centre of trade and commerce between Africa and the Arabian Peninsula. Among the unique accomplishments of the Axum state were multistorey stone residences built in a singular architectural style. Axum is also notable as being perhaps the first officially Christian state in the world (Connah 1987, 2009).

In sub-Saharan Africa, by A.D. 800, the savannah and forest zones of western Africa had a

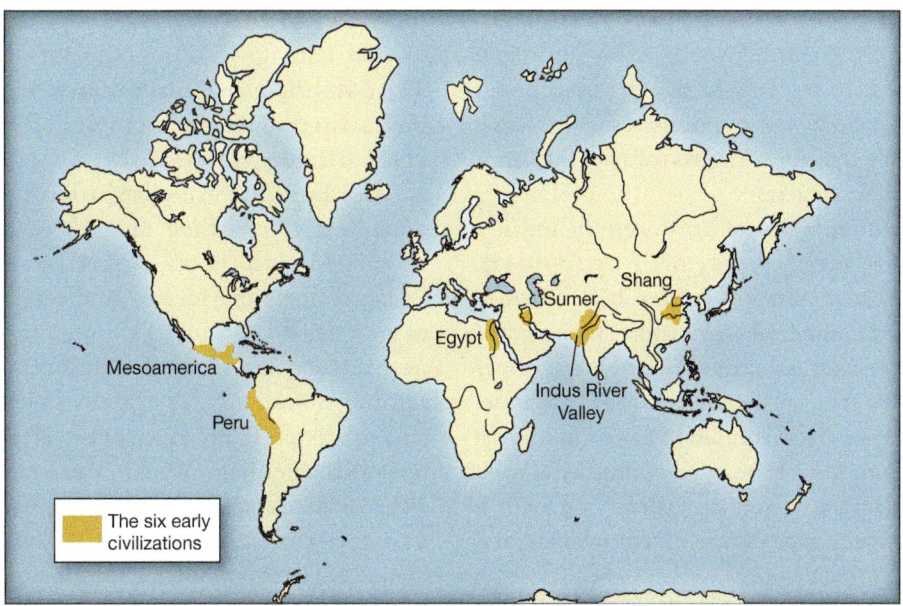

Figure 13–2 Six Early Civilizations

Source: "Map of the Six Early Civilization," from Service ER. 1975. The origins of the state and civilization: The process of cultural evolution. Copyright © 1975. W.W. Norton & Company, Inc. Used by permission of W.W. Norton & Company, Inc.

Artist's reconstruction of the ancient city of Harappa. Despite large public works like this water control system, there was little display of grandeur at Harappa. Unlike many ancient civilizations, all Harappan cities were laid out according to the same plan.

succession of city-states. One of them was called Ghana, and it became a major source of gold for the Mediterranean world, as did other states in what came to be known as the "Gold Coast" (Fagan 1989:428). In the Congo River basin, a powerful kingdom had evolved by A.D. 1200, with cities described as having tens of thousands of residences and a king who was recognized as an equal by the Portuguese king in the early 1500s (Connah 1987, 2009). Farther south, states apparently arose in several areas early in the 2nd millennium A.D. One of these was responsible for the large, circular stone structures known today as the Great Zimbabwe (Vogel 2002).

In the Indus Valley of northwestern India, a large state society had developed by 2300 B.C. This Harappan civilization did not have much in the way of monumental architecture, such as pyramids and palaces, and it was also unusual in other respects. The state apparently controlled an enormous territory—over a million square kilometres. There was not just one major city but many, each built according to a similar pattern and with a municipal water and sewage system (Wenke and Olszewski 2007).

The Shang dynasty in northern China (1750 B.C.) has long been cited as the earliest state society in East Asia. Research has suggested that an even earlier one, the Xia dynasty, may have emerged in the same general area by 2200 B.C. (Chang 1981). In any case, the Shang dynasty had all the earmarks of statehood: a stratified, specialized society; religious, economic, and administrative unification; and a distinctive art style (Chang 1986; Wenke and Olszewski 2007).

In South America, a group of distinct state societies may have emerged as early as 2500 B.C. in the Supe and Pativilca valleys north of Lima, Peru. The valley contains a group of large cities that seem to have been interdependent—cities on the coast supplied inland cities with fish, while inland cities served as political and economic centres. The cities contain plaza areas and large pyramids, which are thought to be temple structures (Solis et al. 2001; Haas et al. 2004). After 200 B.C. the major river valleys leading from the Andes to the sea witnessed the development of a complex agricultural system dependent on irrigation. The separate, but similar, states participated in a widespread system of religious symbols and beliefs called Chavín. The various states included the well-known Moche state, creators of some of the most remarkable effigy ceramics ever known, and the Nazca state, the people of which constructed a huge landscape of intaglios (inscribed images and lines) on the hard ground of highland deserts. By A.D. 700, these regional states were integrated into a large, militaristic empire called Wari or Huari (Lumbreras 1974).

And in North America, a huge settlement, with over 100 earthen mounds (one of them, Monk's Mound, is the largest pre-Columbian structure north of Mexico), and covering an area of more than 13 square kilometres, developed near present-day St. Louis, Missouri, late in the 1st millennium A.D. The site is called Cahokia, and it was certainly the centre of a large and powerful chiefdom. Whether it had achieved a state level of organization is controversial (see Current Research and Issues, "Was Cahokia a State?"). There is evidence for religious and craft specialists and there is clear social stratification, but whether or not the leaders of Cahokian society were able to govern by force is still unclear (Fowler 1975).

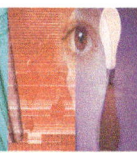

CURRENT RESEARCH AND ISSUES

Was Cahokia a State?

Cahokia was the largest community to develop in the pre-Columbian Americas north of Mexico, but scholars are not sure if it was a complex chiefdom or a simple state. What factors suggest a state? Factors suggesting that it was a state include its size—the core community covered over 13 square kilometres and included more than 100 earthen mounds. The largest of these mounds was the largest human-made construction in the Americas north of Mexico until the Empire State Building was completed in 1931. The population of Cahokia was at least 10 000 people and may have been more like 15 000. There were also elites—one buried on a blanket decorated with over 20 000 shell beads and surrounded by over 100 other individuals who appear to have been sacrificed at the time of the elite individual's death. Cahokia also engaged in long-distance trade that stretched from the Gulf of Mexico to the Great Lakes and from the Appalachians to the Black Hills. There were a number of smaller communities in the Cahokia region, and some scholars have suggested a four-level settlement hierarchy was present. Four-level hierarchies indicate the presence of states. With all this evidence suggesting a state, why is there any controversy?

So why do most scholars not think Cahokia was a state? Largely because the evidence is lacking on a number of points. There is no evidence of leaders able to control the population by force. There was no standing army, no obvious administrative bureaucracy, and no obvious administrative control over the economy. While there was an obvious elite who controlled access to prestige goods (and for whom human sacrifices may have been made upon their deaths), it is not clear that these elites had political power over the entire society or controlled an all-encompassing bureaucracy. The settlement hierarchy, too, may have been informal, rather than administrative, and trade may have been carried out by individuals without any government regulation. In short, most scholars think that while Cahokia was clearly a complex social and economic entity, it was not a true state.

Regardless of whether Cahokia was actually a state, it demonstrates the difficulty of interpreting political and economic organization from the archaeological record.

An embossed copper plate depicting an elite like those who lived at Cahokia.

Sources: Milner GR. 1998. The Cahokia Chiefdom: The Archaeology of a Mississippian Society. Washington, DC: Smithsonian Institution Press.

O'Brien P. 1989. Cahokia: The Political Capital of the "Ramey" State? North American Archaeologist. 10(4):275–292.

Pauketat T. 2004. Ancient Cahokia and the Mississippians. Cambridge: Cambridge University Press.

Theories about the Origin of the State

We have seen that states developed in many parts of the world. Why did they evolve when and where they did? A number of theories have been proposed to explain the origins of the state. We consider those that have been discussed frequently by archaeologists (Cohen and Service 1978; Wenke and Olszewski 2007).

Irrigation

Irrigation seems to have been important in many of the areas in which early state societies developed. Irrigation made the land habitable or productive in parts of Mesoamerica, southern Iraq, the Nile Valley, and other areas. It has been suggested that the labour and management needed for the upkeep of an irrigation system led to the formation of a political elite, in effect, the overseers of the system, who also eventually became the governors of the society (Wittfogel 1957). Proponents of this view believe that both the city and civilization were outgrowths of the administrative requirements of an irrigation system.

Critics note that this theory does not seem to apply to all areas where cities and states may have emerged independently. For example, in southern Iraq, the irrigation systems serving the early cities were generally small and probably did not require extensive labour and management. Large-scale irrigation works were not constructed until after cities had been fully established (Adams 1960; Wright 1986). Thus, irrigation could not have been the main stimulus for the development of cities and states in Sumer. Even in China, for which the irrigation theory was first formulated, there is no evidence of large-scale irrigation as early as Shang times (Wheatley 1971).

Although large-scale irrigation may not always have preceded the emergence of the first cities and states, even small-scale irrigation systems could have resulted in unequal access to productive land and so may have contributed to the development of a stratified society (Adams 1960). In addition, irrigation systems may have given rise to border and other disputes between adjacent groups, thereby prompting people to concentrate in cities for defence and stimulating the development of military and political controls (Adams 1981). Finally, as Robert Adams and Elman Service both suggested, the main significance of irrigation, either large- or small-scale, may have been its intensification of production, a development that in turn may have indirectly stimulated craft specialization, trade, and administrative bureaucracy (Service 1975; Adams 1981).

Population Growth, Circumscription, and War

Robert Carneiro suggested that states may emerge because of population growth in an area that is physically or socially limited. Competition and warfare in such a situation may lead to the subordination of defeated groups, who are obliged to pay tribute and to submit to the control of a more powerful group (Sanders and Price 1968; Carneiro 1970). Carneiro illustrated his theory by describing how states may have emerged on the northern coast of Peru.

After the people of that area first settled into an agricultural village life, population grew at a slow, steady rate. Initially, new villages were formed as population grew. However, in the narrow coastal valleys—blocked by high mountains, fronted by the sea, and surrounded by desert—this splintering-off process could not continue indefinitely. The result, according to Carneiro, was increasing land shortage and warfare between villages as they competed for land. Since the high mountains, the sea, and the desert blocked any escape for losers, the defeated villagers had no choice but to submit to political domination. In this way, chiefdoms may have become kingdoms as the most powerful villages grew to control entire valleys. As chiefs' power expanded over several valleys, states and empires may have been born.

Carneiro noted that physical or environmental circumscription may not be the only kind of barrier that gives rise to a state. Social circumscription may be just as important. People living at the centre of a high-density area may find that their migration is blocked by surrounding settlements just as effectively as it could be by mountains, sea, and desert.

Marvin Harris suggested a somewhat different form of circumscription. He argued that the first states with their coercive authority could emerge only in areas that supported intensive grain agriculture (and the possibility of high food production) and were surrounded by areas that could not support intensive grain agriculture. So people in such areas might tolerate the coercive authority of a state because they would suffer a sharp drop in living standards if they moved away (Harris 1979; Wenke 1990).

Carneiro suggested that his theory applies to many areas besides the northern coast of Peru, including southern Iraq and the Indus and Nile valleys. Although there were no geographic barriers in areas such as northern China or the Mayan lowlands on the Yucatán Peninsula, the development of states in those areas may have been the result of social circumscription. Carneiro's theory seems to be supported for southern Iraq, where there is archaeological evidence of population growth, circumscription, and warfare (Young, Jr. 1972). And there is evidence of population growth before the emergence of the state in the Teotihuacán Valley (Sanders and Price 1968).

Population growth does not necessarily mean population pressure though. For example, the populations in the Teotihuacán and Oaxaca valleys apparently did increase prior to state development, but there is no evidence that they had even begun to approach the limits of their resources. More people could have lived in both places (Brumfiel 1976; Blanton et al. 1981; Feinman et al. 1985). Nor is population growth definitely associated with state formation in all areas where early states arose. For example, according to Wright and Johnson, there was population growth long before states emerged in southwestern Iran, but the population apparently declined just before the states emerged (Wright and Johnson 1975; Carneiro 1988; Hole 1994).

In addition, Carneiro's circumscription theory leaves an important logical question unanswered: Why would the victors in war let the defeated populations remain and pay tribute? If the victors wanted the land so much in the first place, why wouldn't they try to exterminate the defeated and occupy the land themselves, which has happened many times in history?

Local and Long-Distance Trade

It has been suggested that trade was a factor in the emergence of the earliest states (Polanyi et al. 1957; Sanders 1968). Wright and Johnson theorized that the organizational requirements of producing items for export, redistributing the items imported, and defending trading parties would foster state formation (Wright and Johnson 1975). Does the archaeological evidence support such a theory?

In southern Iraq and the Mayan lowlands, long-distance trade routes may indeed have stimulated bureaucratic growth. In the lowlands of southern Iraq, as we have seen, people needed wood and stone for building, and they traded with highland people for those items. In the Mayan lowlands, the development of civilization seems to have been preceded by long-distance trade.

Farmers in the lowland regions traded with people in faraway places in order to obtain salt, obsidian for cutting blades, and hard stone for grinding tools (Rathje 1971). In southwestern Iran, long-distance trade did not become very important until after Susa became the centre of a state society, but short-distance trade may have played the same kind of role in the formation of states.

Kwang-chih Chang put forward a similar theory for the origin of states in China. He suggested that Neolithic societies in the Yellow River valley developed a long-distance trade network, which he called an *interaction sphere*, by about 4000 B.C. Trade spread cultural elements among the societies in the interaction sphere, so that they came to share some common elements. Over time, these societies came to depend on each other both as trade partners and as cultural partners, and around 2000 B.C. they unified into a single political unit under the Shang dynasty (Chang 1986). Thus, Chang saw political unification in China as an outgrowth of a pre-existing system of trade and cultural interaction.

The Various Theories: An Evaluation

Why do states form? As of now, no one theory seems to fit all the known situations. The reason may be that different conditions in different places may have favoured the emergence of centralized government. After all, the state, by definition, implies an ability to organize large populations for a collective purpose. In some areas, this purpose may have been the need to organize trade with local or far-off regions. In other cases, the state may have emerged as a way to control defeated populations in circumscribed areas. In still other instances, a combination of factors may have fostered the development of the state type of political system (Brumfiel 1983).

The Consequences of State Formation

We have considered several areas where states arose, as well as a number of theories to explain the origin of states. But what were the consequences for the people living in those societies? The consequences seem to have been dramatic.

One of the ways states change the lifestyles of people is by allowing for larger and denser populations (Johnson and Earle 2000). As we have already seen, agriculture itself gives populations the potential to grow, and the development of a state only furthers that potential. Why? Because a state is able to build infrastructure—irrigation systems, roadways, markets—that allows both the production and distribution of agricultural products to become more efficient. States are able to coordinate information as well, and can use that information to manage agricultural production cycles and to anticipate or manage droughts, blights, or other natural disasters. States are also able to control access to land (through laws and a military) and thus can both maintain farmers on the land and prevent others (from either within or outside of the state) from removing the farmers or interfering with their ability to produce food.

With increased efficiency of agricultural production and distribution, states also allow many (if not most) people in the society to be relieved of food production. These people are freed to become craftspeople, merchants, and artists, as well as bureaucrats, soldiers, and political leaders. People may also live apart from agricultural fields, and thus cities with dense populations can arise. Cities can also arise in locations that are not suited to agriculture but that perhaps are suited to trade (such as the cities on rivers in southern Mesopotamia) or defence (such as on top of a mountain, as in the case of Monte Albán). Art, music, and literature often flourish in such contexts, and these too are often consequences of the rise of states. Organized religion also often develops after states appear. Thus, all the hallmarks we associate with civilization can be seen as resulting from the evolution of states (Childe 1950).

The development of states can have many negative impacts as well (see Perspectives on Gender, "Effects of Imperialism on Women's Status"). When states develop, people become governed by force and are no longer able to say no to their leaders. Police and military forces can become instruments of oppression and terror (Service 1975). On a less obvious level, the class stratification of states creates differences in access to resources and an underclass of poor, uneducated, and frequently unhealthy people. Health issues are exacerbated by the concentration of people in cities, an environment in which epidemic diseases can flourish (Diamond 2003). Without direct access to food supplies, people in cities also face the threat of malnutrition or outright starvation if food production and distribution systems fail (Dirks 1993).

All states appear to be expansionistic, and the emergence of state warfare and conquest seems one of the most striking negative impacts of the evolution of states. In fact, more human suffering can probably be linked to state expansion than to any other single factor. Why do states expand? One basic reason may be that they are simply able to. States have standing armies ready to fight or be sent to conquer enemies. Another reason for state expansion might be related to the threat of famine and disease, which is more likely with intensive agriculture (Johnson and Earle 2000). A third answer to the question of why states tend to expand might be that belligerence is simply part of the nature of states. States often arise through military means, and it may be vital to the continuation of some states that military power be continually demonstrated (Ferguson and Whitehead 1992). Regardless of the causes, war and conquest are the consequences of state formation. Often, too, defeat in war is the fate of states.

The Decline and Collapse of States

All of the most ancient states collapsed eventually. None of them maintained their power and influence into historic times. Why? Might the reasons for their fall tell us something about why they rose in the first place? For example, if a particular factor was partly responsible for the rise of an ancient state, its disappearance or deterioration may partly explain the decline of that state. Then again, the reasons for the decline of states may be quite different from the reasons for the growth of states.

One suggested explanation for state development, environmental conditions, is perhaps relevant to the decline and collapse of states. If states originally arose where the environment was conducive to intensive agriculture and harvests big enough to support social stratification, political officials, and a state type of political system, then perhaps environmental degradation—declining soil productivity, persistent drought, and the like—contributed to the collapse of ancient states. Archaeologist Harvey Weiss (Weiss et al. 1993) suggested that persistent drought helped to bring about the fall of the ancient Akkadian empire, in the Near East. By 2300 B.C., the Akkadians had established an empire stretching 1300 kilometres from the Persian Gulf in what is now Iraq to the headwaters of the Euphrates River in what is now Turkey. A century later the empire collapsed. Weiss contended that a long-term drought brought the empire down, as well as other civilizations that existed at that time too. Many archaeologists doubted there was such a widespread drought, but evidence recently presented at a meeting of the American Geophysical Union indicates that the worst dry spell of the past 10 000 years began just as the Akkadians' northern stronghold was being abandoned. The evidence of the drought—windblown dust in sediment retrieved from the bottom of the Persian Gulf—indicates that the dry spell lasted 300 years. Other geophysical evidence suggests that the drought was worldwide (Kerr 1998; Grossman 2002).

Environmental degradation may also have contributed to the collapse of Mayan civilization (Haug et al. 2003). The Mayans built large temple complexes in the lowland regions of Mexico and

The history of Ephesus, a former city lying in ruins in what is now western Turkey, illustrates the waxing and waning of states and empires. From about 1000 B.C. to 100 B.C. it was controlled by the Greeks, Lydians, Persians, Macedonians, and Romans, among others.

PERSPECTIVES ON GENDER

Effects of Imperialism on Women's Status

Archaeologists, particularly those who are women, have begun to pay attention to the gender implications of archaeological materials. Do the findings from excavated houses imply anything about what women and men did where they lived? What do the findings in houses and other places suggest about the division of labour by gender? Can archaeology tell us about women's status in the culture and how it may have changed over time? Research suggests that if you look for gender-related results, you often can find some. For example, archaeologist Cathy Costin studied the effects of Inca imperialism on women's status in a conquered area.

Costin participated in a research project that studied culture change in the Yanamarca Valley of highland Peru. The project focused on the development of chiefdoms among the Indigenous Wanka ethnic group between A.D. 1300 and 1470 and on the effects of the Inca conquest at the end of that period. According to the archaeology, most people before the Inca conquest were farmers, but some households specialized part time in the production of pottery, stone tools, and perhaps textiles. Documents written after the arrival of the Spaniards suggest that the Wanka had developed chiefdoms at about A.D. 1300, possibly as a result of intensified warfare among the various communities. A high level of conflict is inferred from the locations and configurations of the settlements: most people lived in fortified (walled) communities located on hills above the valley floor. According to the documentary sources, the Wanka chiefs had achieved their positions because of success as war leaders.

We know from documents that the Inca conquered the Wanka during the reign of the emperor Pachakuti (about A.D. 1470). The Wanka region became a province within the Inca empire, and bureaucrats from the capital at Cuzco came to govern the Wanka. The Inca conquerors, including military personnel, formed the highest class in the valley. The Wanka chiefs became vassals of the Inca state and imitators of Inca ways, using Inca-like pottery and building Inca-style additions to their homes. The economy of the valley became more specialized, apparently to meet the needs of the Inca. People in some villages still mostly farmed, but in other villages most households specialized in the production of pottery, stone tools, and other crafts. Skeletal remains indicate that the commoners became healthier and lived longer after the Inca conquest.

How did the Inca conquest affect the status of women? One key to an answer was suggested by the presence in the excavations of several thousand perforated round ceramic objects. They were spindle whorls, weights used in spinning to keep the thread tight and even. The thread (from llama and alpaca wool) was made into cloth, which became the major form of tax payment after the Inca took over. Each village had to produce a certain amount of cloth for the state tax collectors. The cloth collected was used to clothe

---

the Yucatán Peninsula beginning about A.D. 250, but after about A.D. 750 construction ceased, and by about A.D. 900 the temple complexes appear to have been all but abandoned. Lake sediments show that the region the Maya inhabited experienced an extended period of drought lasting between roughly A.D. 800 and A.D. 1000. The Maya, who depended on rainfall agriculture for subsistence, may not have been able to produce enough food in areas around temple complexes during this long period of drought to feed the resident populations. People would have been forced to move into less populated areas to survive, and the temple complexes would have slowly been abandoned (deMenocal 2001; Haug et al. 2003).

Environmental degradation may occur for other reasons than natural events. The behaviour of humans may sometimes be responsible. Consider the collapse of Cahokia, a city of at least 15 000 people that thrived for a while in the area where the Missouri and Mississippi rivers converge. In the 12th century A.D., Cahokia had large public plazas, a city wall constructed from some 20 000 logs, and massive mounds. But within 300 years only the mounds were left. Silt from flooding covered former croplands and settled areas. Geographers Neal Lopinot and Bill Woods (1993) suggested that overuse of woodlands for fuel, construction, and defence led to deforestation, flooding, and persistent crop failure. The

men serving in the army and to "pay" other government personnel. The burden of producing the cloth fell on the traditional spinners and weavers, who we know from the post-Spanish documents were females of all ages.

All excavated households, dated to just before the Inca conquest, had spindle whorls, indicating that the female occupants in all households spun and made cloth. More whorls were found the farther up the mountain the house was located, indicating that women who lived closer to the high grasslands, where the flocks of llamas and alpacas were kept, spun more thread than did women who lived farther down from the pastures. We might expect that elite women would do less work. But, to the contrary, the women in elite households seem to have produced more cloth than the women in commoner households; the elite households had twice as many whorls on average as the commoner households had.

After the Inca conquest, households appear to have produced twice the amount of thread they did before, because there are twice the number of recovered spindle whorls. There is no indication, archaeological or documentary, that the women were freed from other tasks to make more time for spinning, so it would appear that women had to work harder under Inca domination to produce thread and cloth. However, the producers do not appear to have benefited from the increased cloth production. Much if not most of the cloth produced was removed from the villages and taken to Inca storage facilities in the capital and redistributed from there.

In addition to working harder for the Inca, women seem to have fared worse than the men when it came to nutrition. Christine Hastorf's chemical analysis of bones from Inca-period graves suggests that women ate less maize (corn) than did men. It seems that the men were "eating out" more than women. Maize was often consumed as *chicha* beer, a key component of state-sponsored feasts, which were probably attended more by men than women. Men also worked more in state-organized agricultural and production projects, where they probably were rewarded with meat, maize, and *chicha* for their service to the state. However, more recent osteological data indicate that males may have actually been more nutritionally stressed than females, which could be attributed to the higher labour demands placed on males paired with insufficient caloric intake.

Sources: Brumfiel EM. 1992. Distinguished Lecture in Archeology: Breaking and Entering the Ecosystem—Gender, Class, and Faction Steal the Show. American Anthropologist. 94:551–567.

Costin CL. 1998. Cloth Production and Gender Relations in the Inka Empire. In: Ember CR, Ember M, Peregrine PN, editors. Research Frontiers in Anthropology. Upper Saddle River, NJ: Prentice Hall.

Gero JM, Conkey MW, editors. 1991. Engendering Archaeology: An Introduction to Women and Prehistory. Oxford: Basil Blackwell.

Hastorf C. 1991. Gender, Space, and Food in Prehistory. In: Gero JM, Conkey MW, editors. Engendering Archaeology: An Introduction to Women and Prehistory. Oxford: Basil Blackwell. pp. 132–163.

Williams JS, Murphy MS. 2013. Living and Dying as Subjects of the Inca Empire: Adult Diet and Health at Puruchuco-Huaquerones, Peru. Journal of Anthropological Archaeology. 32:165–179.

Monk's Mound at Cahokia.

APPLIED ANTHROPOLOGY

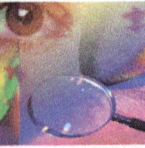

Predicting Societal Collapse

Nothing lasts forever. Every society we know of has at some point collapsed or been transformed into a new one. That is why societal collapse is a major theme in the study of human societies, especially the most complex ones.

Archaeologists and historians who study civilizations have attributed a range of factors that led to collapse: forces of nature (e.g., volcanoes, climate change leading to droughts and floods), population growth, overuse of resources, foreign invasions, civil war, or social decadence. Modern civilizations are not exempt, especially considering current trends in population growth and resource overuse.

Any one of these factors can make civilizations vulnerable to collapse. While one or more factors might apply to specific cases, the problem is that none are sufficient to explain collapse in a general sense. This is because many societies with fewer vulnerabilities than modern ones have failed, whereas other societies with more vulnerabilities have succeeded.

Unlike other disciplines, archaeology provides a rich source of data on social successes and collapses. Total collapse of a civilization is quite rare, but social transformation is exceedingly common, and may be quite necessary for long-term sustainability. Kathleen Morrison of the University of Chicago once wrote that these data may someday be used to understand the challenges of present-day societies, in much the same way that ecological data are used in climate change modelling.

Concerned that modern societies are becoming more unsustainable and more vulnerable to collapse, researchers from the University of Maryland and the University of Minnesota used archaeological data to develop a mathematical model that could provide signposts for detecting societal collapse.

Their model is called Human and Nature DYnamics, or HANDY for short, and it is based on predator–prey dynamics. The human population is the "predator," while the natural resources in the environment can be considered the "prey" of humans. When animal populations in nature surpass their threshold carrying capacity, they begin to decline due to starvation or migration. But this is not the case in human societies because humans have the capacity to build up surpluses, which they draw on when resources from the environment are depleted. However, these surpluses are not evenly distributed throughout society due to the presence of two distinct classes: "elites" and "commoners." With consideration of natural resources, accumulation of wealth, and the class structure of society, HANDY was well suited to analyze various social scenarios.

When societies had no "elites"—they were equitable and more egalitarian—collapse could be avoided, even when a high proportion of the population consisted of non-workers (e.g., students and disabled persons). However, collapse became increasingly likely after natural resources had been depleted, even though there were no "elites." In unequal societies, collapse was found to be almost inevitable. Importantly, this second scenario most closely matches our world today. Based on their implementation of the HANDY model, the researchers concluded that "collapse can be avoided and population can reach equilibrium if the per capita rate of depletion of nature is reduced to a sustainable level, and if resources are distributed in a reasonably equitable fashion" (Motesharrei et al. 2014:101).

Models of societal collapse like HANDY can have important implications for thinking about societal successes and failures both in the past and in the future. For instance, it can help explain why the Mayan civilization in Mexico collapsed while others around it did not. Environmental degradation, population expansion, warfare, and a decline in the power of kings all led to the collapse of Mayan civilization, while not far away, the city of Teotihuacán managed to support up to 100 000 people for over 400 years because people there used different social and economic strategies. Importantly, the model shows that economic inequality and economic unsustainability can independently lead to collapse. Combined, the effects can be catastrophic. Unless finite resources are distributed more equitably and population growth is kept in check, any society is vulnerable to collapse. To avoid failure, it must transform.

Sources: Morrison KD. 2006. Archaeology: Failure and How to Avoid It. Nature. 440(7085):752–754.

Motesharrei S, Rivas J, Kalnay E. 2014. Human and Nature Dynamics (HANDY): Modeling Inequality and Use of Resources in the Collapse or Sustainability of Societies. Ecological Economics. 101:90–102.

result was the abandonment of Cahokia. Timber depletion is also indicated by studies of charcoal from excavations in the area. Apparently the quality of wood used in construction declined over time, suggesting that choice trees became scarcer. Cahokia is just one example of degradation that may have been caused by human behaviour. Another example is the increasing saltiness of soils caused by evaporation of water from fields that have been irrigated over long periods of time, as in what is now southern Iraq (Anonymous 1996).

Civilizations may sometimes decline because human behaviour has increased the incidence of disease. For example, many lowland Mayan cities were abandoned between A.D. 800 and 1000. Explanations of this collapse have ranged from overpopulation to resource depletion. In fact, another factor may have been increasing incidence of yellow fever. The clearing of forests and the consequent increase of breeding sites for mosquitoes may have favoured the spread of the disease from areas farther south in Central America. Or the planting of particular trees by the Mayans in their urban areas may have increased the populations of co-resident monkeys who carried the disease (which mosquitoes transmitted to people) (Wilkinson 1995).

Another reason that some states have collapsed appears to be overextension. This is often one of the reasons given for the decline of the Roman Empire. By the time of its fall, beginning in the 2nd century A.D., the empire had expanded throughout the Mediterranean region and into northwestern Europe. That huge area may simply have been too large to administer. "Barbarian" incursions on the peripheries of the empire went unchecked because it was too difficult, and too costly, to reinforce these far-flung frontiers. Sometimes these incursions became wholesale invasions that were exacerbated by famines, plagues, and poor leadership. By the time the last Roman emperor of the West was deposed in A.D. 476, the empire had withered to virtually nothing (Tainter 1988).

Many other ideas have been put forward to explain collapse, ranging from catastrophes to almost mystical factors such as "social decadence," but, as with theories for the origin of states, no single explanation seems to fit all or even most of the situations. While it is still not clear what specific conditions led to the emergence or collapse of the state in each of the early centres of civilization, the question of why states form and decline is a lively focus of research today (see Applied Anthropology, "Predicting Societal Collapse" for a mathematical approach to understanding why certain societies fail). More satisfactory answers may come out of ongoing and future investigations.

SUMMARY AND REVIEW

ARCHAEOLOGICAL INFERENCES ABOUT CIVILIZATION

13.1 Explain how archaeologists infer that a particular people in the past had social classes, cities, or a centralized government.

- Archaeologists rather than historians have studied the most ancient civilizations because those civilizations evolved before the advent of writing.

- Archaeologists generally assume that burial finds reflecting inequality in death reflect inequality in life, at least in status and perhaps also in wealth and power.

- When archaeologists find other substantial differences, as in house size and furnishings, they can confirm that the society had different socio-economic classes of people.

- Archaeologists do not always agree on how a state should be defined, but most seem to agree that hierarchical and centralized decision making that affects a substantial population is the key criterion.
- Most states have cities with public buildings, full-time craft and religious specialists, an official art style, and a hierarchical social structure topped by an elite class from which the leaders are drawn.
- Most states maintain power with a monopoly on the use of force. The state uses force or the threat of force to tax its population and to draft people for work or war.

 *How can archaeologists infer a political hierarchy existed in a particular society?*

CITIES AND STATES IN SUMER

13.2 Describe the emergence of cities and states in Sumer.

- The earliest state societies are found in Mesopotamia—what is now southern Iraq.
- During the formative era, burial sites reveal differences in social status. Villages specialized in the production of particular goods, and temples may have been centres of political and religious authority for several communities. These centres may have developed into chiefdoms that had authority over several villages.
- The state of Sumer was unified under a single government around 3000 B.C.; it had writing, urban centres, imposing temples, codified laws, a standing army, wide trade networks, complex irrigation, and a high degree of craft specialization.

 *What are some of the earliest examples of Sumerian writing?*

CITIES AND STATES IN MESOAMERICA

13.3 Describe the emergence of cities and states in Mesoamerica.

- During the formative period, small, autonomous farming villages shifted from the hills to the bottom of the Teotihuacán Valley and likely used irrigation. Small "elite" centres emerged, each with a raised platform where temples and residences were built.
- The later state of Teotihuacán in the Valley of Mexico had a city laid out in a well-planned grid pattern. It influenced much of Mesoamerica; its style of pottery and architecture are found extensively and graves include many foreign goods.
- The earliest city-state developed in the Valley of Oaxaca with a capital at Monte Albán. Originally, the city may have been a neutral centre where different political units in the valley coordinated activities affecting the entire valley.
- Mayan state societies were densely populated and depended on intensive agriculture. New research shows that Mayan societies may have been more urban and complex than previously thought.

 *What evidence indicates that people in Teotihuacán were engaged in long-distance trade?*

THE FIRST CITIES AND STATES IN OTHER AREAS

13.4 Describe the first cities and states in other areas of the world.

- Cities and states arose early on in Africa, Asia, South America, and North America.
- In Africa, the earliest state was in the Nile Valley in Egypt by 3000 B.C. It was supported by a population that mainly lived in self-sufficient villages. The strong unified state of

the Old Kingdom built the pyramids as tombs for pharaohs—their divine kings. The later Axum state in Ethiopia was the centre of trade, with multistorey stone residences. A variety of city-states are found throughout sub-Saharan Africa.

- In central Asia, the Harappan civilization in the Indus Valley controlled an enormous territory; major cities were built on a similar pattern and had municipal water and sewage systems. The Shang dynasty in China was a stratified and specialized intraregional state society with religious, economic, and administrative unification and a distinctive art style.
- In South America, state societies in Peru had cities, plazas, and large pyramids, while those in the Andes had complex agricultural systems with irrigation, a widespread system of religious beliefs and symbols, and art.
- Cahokia, near present-day St. Louis, was the centre of a powerful chiefdom that had religious and craft specialists, and social stratification.

 *Why do scholars not think Cahokia was a state?*

THEORIES ABOUT THE ORIGIN OF THE STATE

13.5 Evaluate the major theories about the origin of the state.

- There are three major theories for the origin of the state.
- The irrigation theory suggests that the administrative needs of maintaining an extensive irrigation network caused state formation.
- The circumscription theory suggests that states emerge when competition and warfare in a circumscribed area lead to the subordination of defeated groups, which are then obliged to submit to the control of the most powerful group.
- Theories involving trade suggest that the organizational requirements of producing exportable items, redistributing imported ones, and defending trading parties foster state formation.
- No one theory explains the formation of every state. It is more likely that different organizational requirements in different areas favoured centralized government.

 *How might irrigation systems have resulted in stratified societies?*

THE CONSEQUENCES OF STATE FORMATION

13.6 Identify and explain consequences of state formation.

- Populations grow and become concentrated in cities.
- More efficient agriculture allows many people to stop farming; as a result, art, music, literature, and organized religion can develop and flourish.
- Military expansion and conquest often occurs and leaders have power over their own population, which for the first time includes an underclass of poor and unhealthy people.
- Epidemic disease and periodic famine affect the population, often resulting from dense populations and problems with food production and storage.

 *What positive effects and negative issues can arise in cities unsuited to agriculture?*

THE DECLINE AND COLLAPSE OF STATES

13.7 Discuss explanations for the decline and collapse of states.

- All ancient states eventually collapsed.
- Four reasons have been given to explain the collapse of a state—environmental degradation,

human behaviour that increases disease, depletion of resources, and internal conflict from mismanagement by leaders or mistreatment of people—but no single explanation seems to fit all the situations.

- Research into the collapse of states could have implications for the length of our modern state systems.

 *What factors might account for the decline of the Roman Empire?*

THINK ON IT

1. How do archaeologists infer that a particular people in the past had social classes, cities, or a centralized government?

2. As with the emergence of food production, the earliest cities and states developed within a few thousand years of each other. What might be the reasons?

3. How was Sumer after 3000 B.C. different from earlier societies in southern Iraq?

4. What economic and political features characterize Mesoamerican state societies?

5. What characteristics of states make them susceptible to collapse?

6. What factors might explain why certain civilizations of the past were more successful than others?

Part V Applied Anthropology

Applied Anthropology: Physical Anthropology and Archaeology

14

Twohumans/E+/Getty Images

LEARNING OBJECTIVES

14.1 Explain what applied anthropology is.

14.2 Explain the perspective that medical anthropology brings to understanding health.

14.3 Describe the field of environmental anthropology.

14.4 Describe the role of forensic anthropology in medical-legal cases.

14.5 Describe the field of nutritional anthropology.

14.6 Explain how archaeology can be used for understanding culture history.

14.7 Describe how landscape archaeology can have an impact on society.

The news on radio and television and in the newspapers makes us aware every day that social problems threaten people around the world. Every day we see how people in many parts of the world are jeopardized by a variety of social conditions from war to crime and family violence, from diseases like AIDS, from famine and poverty to political corruption.

Worldwide communication has increased our awareness of problems elsewhere, and we seem to be increasingly bothered by problems in our own society. For these two reasons, and perhaps also because we know more than we used to about human behaviour, we may be more motivated to try to solve those problems. We call them "social" problems not only because a lot of people worry about them but also because they have social causes or consequences, and their possible treatments or solutions require at least some changes in social behaviour. For example, a family of viruses may cause AIDS, but it is also a social problem because it is mostly transmitted by sexual contact with another person. Thus, the only ways to avoid it now—abstinence and "safe" sex—require changes in social behaviour. The lives of millions are at risk because of this global social problem.

Anthropology and most of the other social sciences have long been concerned with social problems. One way in which this concern is expressed is through "basic research" that tests theories about the possible causes of social problems. The results of such tests could suggest solutions to the problems if the causes, once discovered, can be reduced or eliminated. Another way to be concerned with social problems is to participate in or evaluate programs intended to improve people's lives. **Applied or practising anthropology** as a profession is explicitly concerned with making anthropological knowledge useful. Applied or practising anthropologists may be involved in one or more phases of a program: assembling relevant knowledge, developing plans, assessing the likely social and environmental impact of particular plans, implementing the program, and monitoring the program and its effects (Kushner 1991).

Clearly, theory testing and applied research may both be motivated by a desire to improve the quality of human life. However, it is often difficult to decide if a particular project is basic or applied. For example, consider a study of the possible causes of war; its results may suggest how the risk of war might be reduced. Is such a study basic or applied research?

This chapter has two major parts. The first deals with applied or practising anthropology, including types of application, the ethical issues involved in trying to improve people's lives, the difficulties in evaluating whether a program is beneficial, and the problems in instituting planned change. In the second part of the chapter, we present a variety of examples of applied research in physical anthropology and archaeology.

Applied and Practising Anthropology

Anthropologists care and worry about the people they study, just as they care and worry about family and friends back home. It is upsetting if most of the families in your place of fieldwork have lost many of their babies to diseases that could be eliminated by medical care. It is upsetting when outside political and economic interests threaten to deprive your fieldwork friends of their resources and pride. Anthropologists have usually studied people who are disadvantaged—by imperialism, colonialism, and other forms of exploitation—so it is no wonder that we feel protective about these people, among whom we have lived and who we have shared with in the field.

Nevertheless, caring is not enough to improve others' lives. We may need basic research that allows us to understand how a condition might be successfully treated. A particular proposed "improvement" might actually not be an improvement; well-meaning efforts have sometimes produced harmful consequences. Even if we know

---

Applied Anthropology: the branch of anthropology that concerns itself with applying anthropological knowledge to achieve practical goals, usually in the service of an agency outside the traditional academic setting. Also called *practising anthropology*.

that a change would be an improvement, there is still the problem of how to make it happen. The people to be affected may not want to change. Is it ethical to try to persuade them? On the other hand, is it ethical not to try? Applied anthropologists must take all of these matters into consideration in determining whether and how to act in response to a perceived need.

History of Applied Anthropology

In 1934, John Collier, the head of the United States Bureau of Indian Affairs, got legislation passed that provided protections for Native Americans: land could no longer be taken away, lost land was supposed to be restored, tribal governments would be formed, and loans would be made available to reservations. This opened the way toward recognition of the useful roles that anthropologists could play outside academic settings. Events in the 1940s encouraged more applied anthropology. In 1941, anthropologists founded the Society for Applied Anthropology and a new journal devoted to applied anthropology, now called *Human Organization* (Partridge and Eddy 1987). Following World War II, there was a lull of interest in the field, and it was not until the late 1970s that interest in applied anthropology began to flourish once more.

Applied anthropology in Canada developed much later than in the United States. Early applied work in Canada included a conference organized in 1939 by anthropologists and historians at the University of Toronto on the state of then contemporary Indigenous Canadian populations (Hedican 1995; Ervin 2000). Following this in 1947, Harry Hawthorne at the University of British Columbia arranged a meeting of British Columbia First Nations chiefs to discuss Indigenous life and the role of anthropologists in Indigenous welfare (Hedican 1995; Ervin 2000). In the early 1960s, 50 researchers across Canada conducted a nationwide survey of Indigenous people's quality of life, and made a series of recommendations to the federal government. At the same time, anthropological investigations on aspects of development in the Canadian Arctic and subarctic were being undertaken (Hedican 1995; Ervin 2000). In particular, researchers at McGill University examined in detail the impact of large development projects like the James Bay hydroelectric project in northern Quebec and the proposed Mackenzie Valley pipeline project in the Northwest Territories on the life of northern Indigenous peoples (Hedican 1995; Ervin 2000). Following this period, applied anthropology in Canada flourished in a variety of areas from Indigenous self-government and land claims to multiculturalism, mining, fishing, and medical anthropology (Hedican 1995; Ervin 2000).

Today anthropologists are interested in studying and solving problems in non-Indigenous society as well. Anthropologists who call themselves applied or practising anthropologists are usually employed in non-academic settings, working for government agencies, international development agencies, private consulting firms, public health organizations, medical schools, public interest law firms, community development agencies, charitable foundations, and even profit-seeking corporations. Indeed, there are more anthropologists working in non-academic than in academic settings (Frankel and Trend 1991). These practising anthropologists often work on specific projects that aim to improve people's lives, usually by trying to change behaviour or the environment, or they monitor or evaluate efforts by others to bring about change (Hackenberg 1988). Usually the problems and projects are defined by the employers or clients (the client is sometimes the "target" population), not by the anthropologists (Kushner 1991). However, anthropologists are increasingly called upon to participate in deciding exactly what improvements might be possible, as well as how to achieve them.

Anthropologists who work in applied fields come out of all sub-fields of anthropology, although most are from ethnology. They may work on public and private programs at home and abroad to provide improvements in agriculture, nutrition, mental and physical health, housing, job opportunities, transportation, education, and the lives of women or minorities. A frequent type of applied work is the "social impact" study required in connection with many programs funded by government or private agencies. For example, archaeologists are hired to study, record, and preserve "cultural resources" that will be disturbed or destroyed by construction projects. Applied anthropologists who were trained in physical anthropology may work in the area of medicine, public health, and forensic investigations.

Ethics of Applied Anthropology

Ethical issues always arise in the course of fieldwork, and anthropology as a profession has adopted certain principles of responsibility. Above all, an anthropologist's first responsibility is to those who are being studied; everything should be done to ensure that their welfare and dignity will be protected. Anthropologists also have a responsibility to those who will read about their research; research findings should be reported openly and truthfully (Anonymous 1990b). Since applied anthropology often deals with planning and implementing changes in some target population, ethical responsibilities can become complicated. Perhaps the most important ethical question is, Will the change truly benefit the target population?

In May 1946, the Society for Applied Anthropology established a committee to draw up a specific code of ethics for professional applied anthropologists. After many meetings and revisions, a statement on ethical responsibilities was finally adopted in 1948, and in 1983, the statement was revised (Anonymous 1990a). According to the code, the target community should be included as much as possible in the formulation of policy, so that people in the community may know in advance how the program will affect them. Perhaps the most important aspect of the code is the pledge not to recommend or take any action that is harmful to the interests of the community.

Ethical issues are often complicated. When physical anthropologists and archaeologists work with skeletal and even fossil materials, the ethical complications can become extremely complex. Consider the case of "Kennewick Man," a 9200-year-old skeleton found in July 1996 along the Columbia River in Washington state. Before the skeleton could be studied by anthropologists, the U.S. Army Corps of Engineers decided to turn the remains over to the Umatilla, as the remains were found on Corps land within their reservation. The physical anthropologists and archaeologists who wanted to study this very old skeleton faced an ethical quandary: a group claiming to be related to the individual did not want the study to be undertaken, but, without study, the group's claim of relationship could not be firmly established (Weiss 2001; Dalton 2005). The physical anthropologists and archaeologists filed a lawsuit under the Native American Protection and Repatriation Act of 1900, which provides absolute protection to Native American graves on federal land, and which makes it a felony to collect, possess, or transfer human remains of known affinity to an existing Native American culture, except if approved by the members of that culture.

At the core of the legal case was the question, To whom does this skeleton belong? If this is an individual who is related to contemporary Native Americans, then do the Umatilla get to speak for all Native American groups, even though 9000 years separate them? Or should other Native American groups, who may also be descended from this individual or his group, also have a say in what happens? If this is an individual who appears not to be related to contemporary Native Americans, then should the U.S. government decide what happens to his remains? Underlying these questions was a deeper struggle between anthropologists and Native Americans over historic preservation and whose wishes and ideas carry the most weight. Archaeologists and physical anthropologists feel ethical responsibilities that can be in conflict when dealing with human remains. As part of the archaeological record, archaeologists and physical anthropologists have an ethical responsibility to protect and preserve human remains. As anthropologists, they have the ethical responsibility to consult with and follow the wishes of local groups with whom they are working. The "Kennewick Man" case highlights this ethical conflict, for which there seems no easy answer.

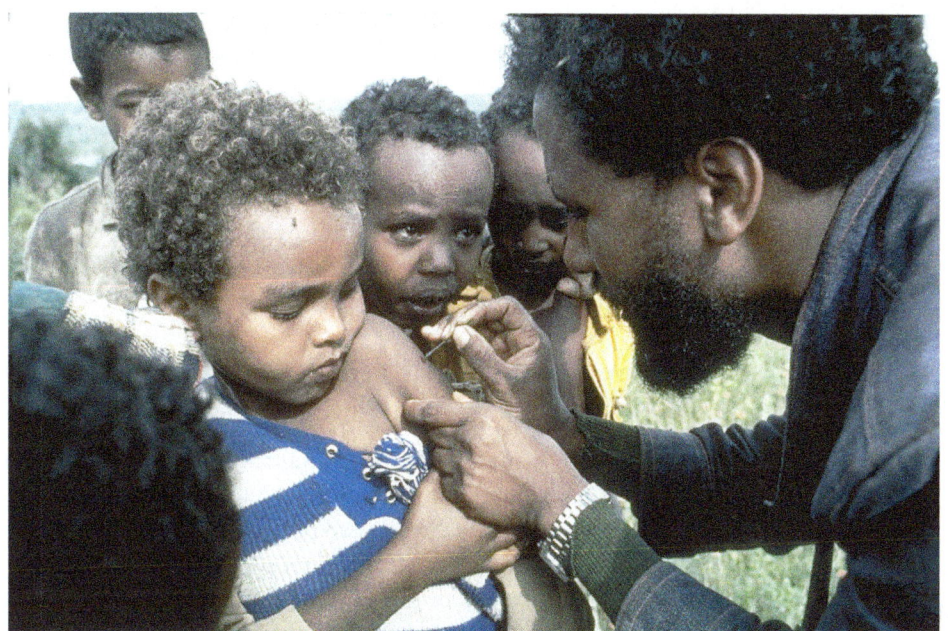

A medical worker in rural Ethiopia vaccinates children. Medical care without a subsequent reduction in births can have harmful consequences because of the increase in population.

For archaeology and physical anthropology, a number of professional organizations have implemented specific statements on ethics. The Canadian Archaeological Association has a statement of principles concerning ethical conduct in archaeological excavation and research. Both the Canadian Association for Physical Anthropology and the American Association of Physical Anthropologists have statements on ethical conduct in research, and the Canadian federal government, including the major grant-funding agencies, has statements on human rights, human subjects in research, and Indigenous rights with respect to research. A variety of museums also have policy statements on ethics. While no documents can cover all conceivable circumstances, the spirit of these policies is meant to guide individuals conducting and participating in applied research in archaeology or physical anthropology.

Evaluating the Effects of Planned Change

The decision as to whether a proposed change would benefit the target population is not always easy to make. In certain cases, as when improved medical care is involved, the benefits offered to the target group would seem to be unquestionable—we all feel sure that health is better than illness. However, this may not always be true. Consider a public health innovation such as inoculation against disease. Although it would undoubtedly have a beneficial effect on the survival rate of a population, a reduction in the mortality rate might have unforeseen consequences that would in turn produce new problems. For example, once the inoculation program is begun, the number of children surviving would probably increase. However, it might not be possible to increase the rate of food production, given the level of technology, capital, and land resources of the target population. Thus, the death rate, because of starvation, might rise to its previous level and perhaps even exceed it. The inoculation program would not affect the death rate; it might merely change the causes of death. This example shows that even if a program of planned change has beneficial consequences in the short run, a great deal of thought and investigation have to be given to its long-term effects.

In another example, Debra Picchi raised questions about the long-term effects on the Bakairi Indians of a program by the Brazil's National Indian Foundation (FUNAI) to produce rice with machine technology (Picchi 1991, 1998). The Bakairi of the Mato Grosso region largely practise slash-and-burn horticulture in gallery forests along rivers, with supplementary cattle raising, fishing, and hunting. In the early part of the 20th century their population had declined to 150 people and they were given a relatively small reserve. Some of it was gallery forest, but a larger part was parched and infertile (*cerrado*). When the Bakairi population began to increase, FUNAI introduced a scheme to plant rice on formerly unused *cerrado* land, using machinery, insecticides, and fertilizer. FUNAI paid the costs for the first year and expected that by the third year the scheme would be self-supporting. The project did not go so well because FUNAI did not deliver all the equipment needed and did not provide adequate advice. So only half the expected rice was produced. Still, it was more food than the Bakairi had previously, so the program should have been beneficial to them.

There were, however, unanticipated negative side effects. Nutritionally, to be sure, the Bakairi were growing an additional starchy food. But the use of the *cerrado* for agriculture reduced the area for grazing cattle, an important source of high-quality protein. So the now-mechanized agriculture has reduced the availability of animal protein. The mechanization also makes the Bakairi more dependent on cash for fuel, insecticides, fertilizer, and repairs. Since cash is hard to come by, only some individuals can be hired—usually men with outside experience who have the required knowledge of machinery. So the cash earned in the now-mechanized agriculture goes mainly to a relatively small number of people. It is debatable whether the new inequalities of income provide long-term effects that are beneficial to the Bakairi.

These failures were not the fault of anthropologists—indeed, most instances of planned change by governments and other agencies have begun without the input of anthropologists; however, applied anthropologists have played an important role in pointing out the problems with programs like these that fail to evaluate long-term consequences. Such evaluations are an important part of convincing governments and other agencies to ask for anthropological help in the first place. Ironically, failure experiences are learning experiences—applied anthropologists who study previous examples of planned change can often learn a great deal about what is likely or not likely to be beneficial in the long run.

Difficulties in Instituting Planned Change

Whether a program of planned change can be successfully implemented depends largely on whether the targeted population wants the proposed change and likes the proposed program. Before an attempt can be made at cultural innovation, the innovators must determine whether the target population is aware of the benefits of the proposed change. Lack of awareness can be a temporary barrier to solving the problem at hand. For example, health workers have often had difficulty convincing people that they were becoming ill as a result of a problem with their water supply because many people do not believe that disease can be transmitted by water. At other times, the target population is perfectly aware of the problem. A case in point involved Taiwanese women who were introduced to family-planning methods beginning in the 1960s. The women knew they were having more children than they wanted or could easily afford, and they wanted to control their birth rate. They offered no resistance—they merely had to be given the proper devices and instructions and the birth rate quickly fell to a more desirable, and more manageable, level (Niehoff 1966).

Resistance by Target Population.
Not all proposed change programs are beneficial to the target population. Sometimes resistance is rational. Applied anthropologists have pointed to cases where the judgment of the affected population has been better than that of the agents of change. One such example occurred during a Venezuelan government-sponsored program to give infants powdered milk. The mothers rejected the milk, even though it was free, on the grounds that it

implied that the mothers' milk was no good (Foster 1962). But who is to say that the resisting mothers were not in fact intuitively smart, reflecting an awareness that such a milk program would not benefit the children? Medical research now indicates quite clearly that mother's milk is far superior to powdered milk or formula. First, human milk best supplies the nutrients needed for human development. Second, it is now known that the mother, through her milk, is able to transmit antibodies (disease resistances) to the baby. Third, nursing delays ovulation and usually increases the spacing between births (Jelliffe and Jelliffe 1975).

The switchover to powdered milk and formula in many underdeveloped areas has been nothing short of a disaster, resulting in increased malnutrition and misery. For one thing, powdered milk must be mixed with water, but if the water and the bottles are not sterilized, more sickness is introduced. Then, too, if powdered milk has to be purchased, mothers without cash are forced to dilute the milk to stretch it. If a mother feeds her baby formula or powder for even a short time, the process is tragically irreversible, for her own milk dries up and she cannot return to breast-feeding even if she wants to.

As the Venezuelan example suggests, individuals may be able to resist proposed medical or health projects because acceptance is ultimately a personal matter. Large development projects planned by powerful governments or agencies are rarely stoppable, but even they can be resisted successfully. In the early 1990s, the Kayapo of the Xingu River region of Brazil were able to cancel a plan by the Brazilian government to build dams along the river for hydroelectric power. The Kayapo gained international attention when some of their leaders appeared on North American and European television and then successfully organized a protest in 1989 by members of several tribal groups. Their success seemed to come in part from their ability to present themselves to the international community as guardians of the rain forest—an image that resonated with international environmental organizations that supported their cause. Although to outsiders it might seem that the Kayapo want their way of life to remain as it was, the Kayapo are not opposed to all change. In fact, they want greater access to medical care, other government services, and manufactured goods from outside (Fisher 1994).

However, even if a project is beneficial to a population, it may still meet with resistance. Factors that may hinder acceptance can be divided roughly into three sometimes overlapping categories: *cultural*, *social*, and *psychological* barriers.

Cultural barriers are shared behaviours, attitudes, and beliefs that tend to impede the acceptance of an innovation. For example, members of different societies may view gift giving in different ways. Particularly in commercialized societies, things received for nothing are often believed to be worthless. When the government of Colombia instituted a program of giving seedling orchard

Breast-feeding is now known to be better for the health of the baby. In many countries, breast-feeding in public is perfectly acceptable, as among the Huastec of Mexico.

trees to farmers in order to increase fruit production, the farmers showed virtually no interest in the seedlings, many of which proceeded to die of neglect. When the government realized that the experiment had apparently failed, it began to charge each farmer a nominal fee for the seedlings. Soon the seedlings became immensely popular and fruit production increased (Foster 1962). The farmers' demand for the seedlings may have increased because they were charged a fee and therefore came to value the trees. The market demand for fruit may also have increased.

It is important for agents of change to understand the shared beliefs and attitudes of a target population. First, local cultural concepts or knowledge can sometimes be used effectively to enhance educational programs. For instance, in a program in Haiti to prevent child mortality from diarrhea, change agents used the terminology for traditional herbal tea remedies (*rafrechi*, or cool refreshment) to identify the new oral rehydration therapy, which is a very successful medical treatment. In local belief, diarrhea is a "hot" illness and appropriate remedies must have cooling properties (Coreil 1989). Second, even if local beliefs are not helpful to the campaign, not paying attention to contrary beliefs can undermine the campaign. However, uncovering contrary beliefs is not easy, particularly when they do not emerge in ordinary conversation (see Applied Anthropology, "Exploring Why an Applied Project Didn't Work").

The acceptance of planned change may also depend on social factors. Research suggests that acceptance is more likely if the change agent and the target (or potential adopter) are similar socially. But change agents may have higher social status and more education than the people they are trying to influence. So change agents may work more with higher-status individuals because they are more likely to accept new ideas. If lower-status individuals also have to be reached, change agents of lower status may have to be employed (Rogers 1983).

Finally, acceptance may depend on psychological factors—that is, how the individuals perceive both the innovation and the agents of change. In the course of trying to encourage women in the southeastern United States to breast-feed rather than bottle-feed their infants, researchers discovered a number of reasons why women were reluctant to breast-feed their infants, even though they heard it was healthier. Many women did not have confidence that they would produce enough milk for their babies; they were embarrassed about breast-feeding in public; and their family and friends had negative attitudes (Bryant and Bailey 1990:32). In designing an educational program, change agents may have to address such psychological concerns directly. A survey of young adults in Canada by Spurles and Babineau (2011) showed that while almost all of those interviewed showed a desire to have any future children breast-fed, nearly two-thirds expressed restrictive notions of breast-feeding in public. While the survey was small, it led the investigators to suggest that ongoing dialogue about breast-feeding in public spaces, as well as the health benefits of breast-feeding, would be beneficial.

Discovering and Utilizing Local Channels of Influence. In planning a project involving cultural change, the administrator of the project should determine the normal channels of influence in the population. In most communities, there are pre-established networks for communication, as well as persons of high prestige or influence who are looked to for guidance and direction. An understanding of such channels of influence is extremely valuable when deciding how to introduce a program of change. In addition, it is useful to know at what times, and in what sorts of situations, one channel is likely to be more effective in spreading information and approval than another.

An example of the effective use of local channels of influence occurred when an epidemic of smallpox broke out in the Kalahandi district of the state of Orissa in India in the 1940s. The efforts of health workers to vaccinate villagers against the disease were consistently resisted. The villagers, naturally suspicious and fearful of these strange men with their equally strange medical equipment, were unwilling to offer themselves, and particularly their babies, to the peculiar experiments

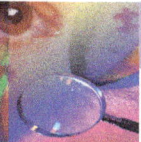

APPLIED ANTHROPOLOGY

Exploring Why an Applied Project Didn't Work

When applied projects do not succeed, it is important for researchers to try to understand why. Part of the problem may be that the intended recipients' ideas about how things work may be very different from the researchers' ideas. Consider the following example.

In Guatemala, village healthcare workers were not only testing people for malaria, but also offering free antimalarial drugs. Yet, only 20 percent of people with malaria symptoms took advantage of the free treatment. More surprisingly, most people with symptoms spent the equivalent of a day's wages to buy an injection that was not strong enough to be effective. Why?

Finding the answer was not easy. First, researchers designed interviews to elicit folk concepts about illness—kinds of illnesses, their symptoms, their causes, and how they were treated. They conducted interviews with a random sample of households to check on what illnesses people had and what they did about them. Then they asked people to consider different hypothetical scenarios (vignettes), with different types of people and different degrees of severity of illness, to find out what treatment they would choose for these other people. All of these methods were well thought out, but the answers still did not predict what people actually did when they thought they had malaria. Finally, the researchers devised precise comparisons of the kinds of pills passed out by health-care workers and the pills and ampoules for injections sold by the drugstore. They compared them two at a time, varying dosages and brands. People did think that more pills were more effective, as indeed they were, but they thought that the colourfully wrapped store-bought pill was more effective than the equivalent white unwrapped free pill, even though it was not. They also thought that one store-bought ampoule used for injections, for which they would pay a day's wages, was more effective than four pills of any kind. In fact, one ampoule was equivalent to only one pill.

Applied researchers often use such trial-and-error methods to find out how to get the information they need. Methods that work in one field setting don't always work in others. To get the information needed, researchers must sometimes let the subjects structure their own answers. At other times, as in this case, they may have to make very specific comparisons to get predictive answers. The people in the Guatemala study didn't believe that the free pills were strong enough to work, so they didn't use them. More research would be needed to uncover why they did not believe the free pills were effective. Was it because they were free? Was it because the store-bought drugs were attractively packaged? Or was there a belief that injections work better than pills? That's what the research process is like; it always leads to new questions. Even if researchers think they understand what was happening in one area of Guatemala, comparative research would be needed to find out if these beliefs are found throughout Guatemala or other areas of Central and South America. Do they apply to other medicines as well?

Although we don't yet have answers to these more extensive questions, anthropologists have developed efficient methods for assessing variation in beliefs within and between cultures. We now know that if we ask one or two informants, we cannot assume that the answer is cultural. But that doesn't mean that we need to ask hundreds of people. If a belief is cultural and therefore commonly held, asking 10 to 20 individuals the same question is sufficient to provide the researcher with a high probability that an answer is correct. (The agreement among respondents is called *cultural consensus*.) So, for example, Guatemalan respondents mostly agreed about which illnesses were contagious, but they disagreed a lot about whether a particular disease should be treated with a "hot" or a "cold" remedy. Using cultural-consensus methods, researchers can compare rural and urban residents, and they can also compare informants in different cultures. When we have more of these systematic comparisons, medical anthropologists and health practitioners may have a better understanding of how to implement medical care.

Sources: Kimball Romney A, Weller SC, Batchelder WH. 1986. Culture as Consensus: A Theory of Culture and Informant Accuracy. American Anthropologist. 88:313–338.

Weller SC. 1998. The Research Process. In: Ember CR, Ember M, Peregrine PN, editors. Research Frontiers in Anthropology. Upper Saddle River, NJ: Prentice Hall.

the strangers wished to perform. Afraid of the epidemic, the villagers appealed for help to their local priest, whose opinions on such matters they trusted. The priest went into a trance, explaining that the illness was the result of the goddess Thalerani's anger with the people. She could be appeased, he continued, only by massive feasts, offerings, and other demonstrations of the villagers' worship of her. Realizing that the priest was the village's major opinion leader, at least in medical matters, the frustrated health workers tried to get the priest to convince his people to undergo vaccination. At first, the priest refused to co-operate with the strange men, but when his favourite nephew fell ill, he decided to try any means available to cure the boy. He thereupon went into another trance, telling the villagers that the goddess wished all her worshippers to be vaccinated. Fortunately, the people agreed, and the epidemic was largely controlled (Niehoff 1966).

If channels of influence are not stable, using influential persons in a campaign can sometimes backfire. In the educational campaign in Haiti to promote the use of oral rehydration therapy, Mme. Duvalier, the first lady of Haiti at the time, lent her name to the project. Because there were no serious social or cultural barriers to the treatment and mothers reported that children took to the solutions well, success was expected. However, in the middle of the campaign, Haiti became embroiled in political turmoil and the first lady's husband was overthrown. Some of the public thought that the oral rehydration project was a plot by the Duvaliers to sterilize children, and this suspicion fuelled resistance (Coreil 1989:155). Even after the Duvalier regime had ended, people in Haiti were suspicious of any government-sponsored program.

Applied anthropologists often advocate integrating Indigenous healers into medical change programs. This idea may encounter considerable resistance by the medical profession and by government officials who view such healers negatively, but this strategy may be quite effective in more isolated areas where Indigenous healers are the only sources of health care. If they are involved in medical change programs, Indigenous healers are likely to refer patients to hospitals when they feel unable to cope with an illness, and the hospitals choose sometimes to refer patients to the healers (Warren 1989).

Other social groups and their attitudes can play important roles in shaping the outcome of the change program. Most often the people who are being helped have few privileges, little political and economic power, and low prestige (Goodenough 1963:416). Change or development is often regarded as a threat to those with more privilege. If those who do have power object to the new program, they may effectively sabotage it. The development agent, then, not only has to reckon with the local community but may also have to persuade more powerful groups in the society that the new program should be introduced.

Toward Collaborative Applied Anthropology

Most large-scale programs of planned change originate with governments, international aid organizations, or other agencies. Even if the programs are well intentioned and even if the appropriate evaluations are made to ensure that the population will not be harmed, the population targeted for the change is usually not involved in the decision making. Some anthropologists, like Wayne Warry, think that applied anthropology should be more collaborative. Warry explained that a First Nations elder asked him whether he (Warry) would tolerate his own methods and interpretations if he were the First Nations individual (Warry 1990). This question prompted Warry to become involved in a project with First Nations collaborators, directed by the Mamaweswen, the North Shore Tribal Council. The project assessed health-care needs and developed plans to improve local community health care. Funding was provided by the Canadian government as part of a program to transfer health care to the First Nations. First Nations researchers conducted the surveys and workshops to keep the community informed about the project. The tribal council also reviewed any publications and shares in any profits resulting from those publications.

Students in Mozambique wait to participate in a parade for International AIDS Day.

Applied anthropologists may be increasingly asked to work on behalf of local grassroots organizations. In some cases these small groups and networks of such groups are starting to hire their own technical assistance (Fisher 1996:57). When such organizations do the hiring, they control the decision making. There is increasing evidence that grassroots organizations are the key to effective development.

For example, Kenyan farmers who belong to grassroots organizations produce higher farm yields than those farmers who do not belong, even though the latter group is exposed to more agricultural extension agents (Oxby 1983; Fisher 1996). Grassroots organizations can succeed where government or outside projects fail. We have plenty of instances of people effectively resisting projects, but their willingness to change and their participation in the crucial decision making may be mostly responsible for the success of a change project.

Medical Anthropology

Illness and death are significant events for people everywhere. No one is spared. So it should not be surprising that how people understand the causes of illness and death, how they behave, and what resources they marshal to cope with these events are extremely important parts of culture. Some argue that we will never completely understand how to treat illness effectively until we understand cultural behaviours, attitudes, and values, and the larger social political milieu in which people live.

Anthropologists, particularly medical anthropologists, actively engaged in studying health and illness increasingly recognize the need to consider both social and biological factors—the biocultural model (see Chapter 1)—for understanding disease processes in populations. For instance, some populations have an appalling incidence of infant deaths due to diarrhea. The origin of this situation is mostly biological, in the sense that the deaths are caused by bacterial infection, but the question is, Why are so many infants exposed to those bacteria? Usually, the main reason is social. The affected infants are likely to be poor, and as a result are likely to live with infected drinking water. Similarly, malnutrition may be the biological result of a diet poor in protein, but such a diet is usually also a cultural phenomenon, reflecting a society with classes of people with very unequal access to the necessities of life.

People with more social, economic, and political power in a society are generally healthier (Hahn 1995). Inequality in health in socially stratified societies is not surprising. The poor usually have more exposure to disease because they live in more crowded conditions. The poor are also more likely to lack the resources to get quality care. For many diseases, health problems, and death rates, incidence or frequency varies directly with social class. In the United Kingdom, for example, people in the higher social classes are less likely to have headaches, bronchitis, pneumonia, heart disease, arthritis, injuries, and mental disorders, to name just a few of the differences (Mascie-Taylor 1990).

Inequities because of class and ethnicity are not limited to within-society differences. Power and economic differentials between societies also have profound health consequences. Over the course of European exploration and expansion, Indigenous peoples died in enormous numbers from introduced diseases, wars, and conquests; they had their lands expropriated and diminished in size and quality. When incorporated into colonial territories or into countries, Indigenous peoples usually become minorities and they are almost always very poor. These conditions of life not only affect the incidence of disease, but they also tend to lead to greater substance abuse, violence, depression, and other mental pathologies (Cohen 1999).

The medical profession's ways of treating illness may be able to treat some conditions well, but the medical profession cannot tell us why some groups are more affected than others, or why the effectiveness of treatment varies from group to group. Recognizing the interaction of culture and biology, medical anthropology and anthropology in general utilize the biocultural model for better understanding how illness is manifest and spread within a population.

Cultural Understandings of Health and Illness

Medical researchers and medical practitioners in Canada, the United States, and other Western societies do not exist in a social vacuum. Many of their ideas and practices are influenced by the culture in which they live. We may think of medicine as purely based on "fact." But on reflection, it is clear that many ideas stem from the culture in which the researchers reside. Discovering the health-related beliefs, knowledge, and practices of a cultural group—its **ethnomedicine**—is one of the goals of medical anthropology. How do cultures view health and illness? What are their theories about the causes of illness? Do those theories affect how illnesses are treated? What is the therapeutic process? Are there specialized medical practitioners, and how do they heal? Are there special medicines, and how are they administered? These are some of the questions asked by the anthropological study of ethnomedicine.

In their extensive research on Mayan ethnomedicine, Elois Ann Berlin and Brent Berlin made a strong case that although studies of the Maya have emphasized beliefs about illness that are based on supernatural causes, a good deal of Mayan ethnomedicine is about natural conditions, their signs and symptoms, and the remedies used to deal with those conditions. In regard to gastrointestinal diseases, the Berlins found that the Maya have a wide-ranging and accurate understanding of anatomy, physiology, and symptoms. Furthermore, the remedies they use, including recommendations for food, drink, and herbal medicines, have properties that are not that different from those of the Western medical profession (Berlin 1996).

Western medicine has increasingly become aware of the value of studying the "traditional" medicinal remedies discovered or invented by people around the world. In studying the indigenous medicines of the Hausa of Nigeria, Nina Etkin and Paul Ross asked individuals to describe the physical attributes of more than 600 plants and their possible medicinal uses, more than 800 diseases and symptoms, and more than 5000 prepared medicines. While many medicines were used for treating sorcery, spirit aggression, or witchcraft, most medicines were used for treating illnesses regarded by the Hausa as having natural causes. Malaria is a serious endemic medical problem in the Hausa region, as in many areas of Africa. The Hausa use approximately 72 plant remedies for conditions connected with malaria—among them anemia, intermittent fever, and jaundice. Experimental treatment of malaria in laboratory animals supports the efficacy of many of the Hausa remedies. Perhaps the most important part of the Etkin and Ross findings is the role of diet. While most medical research does not consider the possible medical efficacy of foods that people eat in combating illness, food is, of course, consumed in much larger quantities and more often than medicine. It is noteworthy therefore, that the Hausa eat many plants with antimalarial properties; in fact, dietary consumption of these plants appears to be the greatest during the time of year when the risk of malarial infection is at its highest (Etkin and Ross 1997).

Anthropology contributes to the understanding of health and illness through the development of culturally appropriate interventions. Among North American Indigenous peoples, there are strong cultural aspects of traditional medicine that can often be a vital part of both the individual and community response to illness. Further, some Indigenous people, particularly those in remote or small communities, may feel disenfranchised from the Western medical system and the biomedical

> **Ethnomedicine:** the health-related beliefs, knowledge, and practices of a cultural group.

Morning Tai Chi exercises in Shanghai, China.

paradigm. As a result, it is important that public health responses, at both the individual and population levels, recognize and respect the cultural perceptions of health within different groups.

The Biomedical Paradigm. In most societies, people simply think that their ideas about health and illness are true. Often it is not until they confront another medical system that people develop any awareness that there may be another way of viewing things. Western medical practice has spread widely. People with other medical systems have had to recognize that their ideas about health and illness may be considered deficient by Western practitioners, so it is often necessary to decide which course (Western or non-Western) to follow in dealing with illness. Change, however, is not entirely one-way. For example, for a long time the Chinese practice of acupuncture was disparaged by the Western medical profession, but now more medical practitioners are recognizing that acupuncture may provide effective treatment of certain conditions.

Most medical anthropologists use the term **biomedicine** to refer to the dominant medical paradigm in Western cultures today, with the *bio* part of the word indicating the biological emphasis of this medical system. As Robert Hahn pointed out, biomedicine appears to focus on specific diseases and cures for those diseases. Health is not the focus, as it is thought to be the *absence* of disease. Diseases are considered to be purely natural, and there is relatively little interest in the person or the larger social and cultural systems. Doctors generally do not treat the whole body but tend to specialize, with the human body partitioned into zones that belong to different specialties. Death is seen as a failure, and biomedical practitioners do everything they can to prolong life, regardless of the circumstances under which the patient would live his or her life (Hahn 1995).

Biomedicine: the dominant medical paradigm in Western societies today.

One of the most important discoveries that profoundly changed the course of Western medicine was Louis Pasteur's isolation of the organisms responsible for some major infectious diseases. Pasteur's discoveries stimulated the search for other disease-causing germs using scientific methods. But the *germ theory* of disease, although powerful, may have led researchers to pay less attention to the patient and the patient's social and cultural milieux (Loustaunau and Sobo 1997).

Many diseases, including infectious diseases like AIDS or chronic diseases like diabetes, may be viewed as "Western" diseases. Without acknowledging the perceived risks or responses of community members, it is difficult to develop meaningful and effective tools for educating people or combating a specific illness. To this end, research on AIDS in Indigenous groups has promoted understanding community response to HIV/AIDS through traditional mechanisms that recognize the traditional relationships between individuals, families, entire communities, and finally Mother Earth (Lambert 1993). For example, in Alberta, the Feather of Hope Aboriginal AIDS Prevention Society provides culturally sensitive HIV prevention programs to First Nations communities (Mill and DesJardins 1996). In particular, the society focuses on self-empowerment with respect to health and illness, which reflects broader socio-political aspects of self-determinism within First Nations peoples. Similarly, the Manitoba First Nations Centre for Aboriginal Health Research, a joint project of the University of Manitoba and the Assembly of Manitoba Chiefs, develops and supports research that assists in the promotion of healing, wellness, and improved health services in Indigenous communities. Medical anthropologists like John O'Neil and colleagues are engaged in research sponsored by the Canadian Institutes of Health Research (CIHR) to identify factors that enhance or constrain the development of a First Nations–controlled health-care system (O'Neil 1995; O'Neil and Commanda 1998; O'Neil et al. 1998, 2001; see also Lavoie et al. 2009 and O'Neil 2015). Of particular interest is the assessment of cultural perceptions of health risk, and how to develop a strategy that allows the resources and the appropriate political environment to realize community healing. In northern Saskatchewan, medical anthropologist Sylvia Abonyi and her colleagues at the Saskatchewan Population Health and Evaluation Research Unit (SPHERU) are also working together with Indigenous groups to deal with health issues. Working with the Prince Albert Grand Council (PAGC) and the Athabasca Health Authority (AHA), SPHERU researchers are developing tools for use in Indigenous health organizations. The goal of this research is to develop culturally appropriate indicators to gauge changes in health within the community, and to assess the impact of health-related services, because the ability to understand cross-cultural perceptions of health and illness is critical for any health system to effectively treat and prevent illnesses.

Health Conditions and Diseases

Epidemics of disease have killed millions of people within short periods of time throughout recorded history. The Black Death, a bubonic plague, killed between 25 and 50 percent of the population of Europe, perhaps 75 million people, during the 14th century; an epidemic in the 6th century killed an estimated 100 million people in the Middle East, Asia, and Europe. Less noted in our history books, but also devastating, was the enormous depopulation that accompanied the expansion of Europeans into the New World and the Pacific from the 1500s on. Not only were people killed directly by European conquerors; millions also died from introduced diseases to which the Indigenous people had little or no resistance, diseases such as smallpox and measles that the Europeans brought with them but were no longer dying from.

The current state of medical science and technology may lull us into thinking that epidemics are a thing of the past. Despite this, the establishment of diseases like **AIDS (acquired immune deficiency syndrome)** over the past few decades or the recent and sudden emergence of diseases like West Nile and SARS (severe acute respiratory

> **AIDS (Acquired Immune Deficiency Syndrome):** a disease that emerged in the 20th century, almost always lethal, presumably caused by the HIV virus or viruses.

syndrome) remind us that new diseases, or new varieties of old diseases, can appear at any time. SARS is a newly emerged disease caused by a coronavirus that spread globally through 30 countries in 2003. Its origins have been traced to Hong Kong, but genetic evidence suggests that several strains of the virus had occurred, but only one was associated with the subsequent outbreak in Hong Kong, which later spread to other areas of the world (Ruan et al. 2003; Guan et al. 2004). A sample of the virus from one of the first victims of SARS in Toronto was taken by the National Microbiology Laboratory in Winnipeg. From that, the genome of the SARS virus was cracked by scientists at the Michael Smith Genome Sciences Centre in Vancouver. Its origins remain debated, though it is possible that the human form is a mutation of an animal coronavirus. Currently, health authorities in China and Canada are working to develop several potential vaccines against the virus, in preparation for future outbreaks. Like all other organisms, disease-causing organisms also evolve—and as discussed in Chapter 6, human behaviour is a major factor in the evolution of diseases.

AIDS. The human immunodeficiency viruses (HIV) that presumably cause AIDS emerged only recently. Viruses and bacteria are always mutating, and new strains emerge that are initially a plague on our genetic resistance and on medical efforts to contain them.

Millions of people around the world already have the symptoms of AIDS and millions more are infected with HIV but do not know they are infected. According to World Health Organization estimates, some 40 million people, including 2.5 million children, have been infected with HIV. In 2014, approximately 1.2 million people died from AIDS, down from the more than 3 million people who died a decade earlier. AIDS is a frightening epidemic not only because of its likely toll but also because it takes a long time (on average, four years) after exposure for symptoms to appear.

Millions of children in sub-Saharan Africa are orphaned because of AIDS. These orphaned children in Uganda look on during a visit by Queen Elizabeth II to their centre.

This means that many people who have been infected by HIV but do not know they are infected may continue unknowingly to transmit the viruses to others (Bolton 1989).

Transmission occurs mostly via sexual encounters, through semen and blood. Drug users may also transmit HIV by way of contaminated needles. Mothers may transmit the virus to their babies in the womb. Transmission by blood transfusion has been virtually eliminated in this and other societies by medical screening of blood supplies, but in many countries there is still no routine screening of blood prior to transfusions.

Many people think of AIDS as only a medical problem that requires only a medical solution, without realizing that there are behavioural and cultural issues that need to be addressed as well. It is true that developing a vaccine or a drug to prevent people from getting AIDS and finding a permanent cure for those who have it will finally solve the problem of AIDS. However, for a variety of reasons, we can expect that the medical solution alone will not be sufficient, at least not for a while. First, to be effective worldwide, or even within a country, a vaccine has to be inexpensive and relatively easy to produce in large quantities; the same is true of any medical treatment for victims. Second, governments around the world have to be willing and able to spend the money and hire the personnel necessary to manage an effective program (Bolton 1989). Third, future vaccination and treatment will require the people at risk to be willing to get vaccinated and treated, which is not always easy to arrange. Witness the fact that the incidence of measles is on the rise in the United States because many people are not having their children vaccinated.

There are now expensive drug treatments that significantly reduce the HIV load, but we do not know if an effective and inexpensive vaccine or treatment will be developed soon. In the meantime, the risk of HIV infection can be reduced only by changes in social, particularly sexual, behaviour. But to persuade people to change their sexual behaviour, it is necessary to find out exactly what they do sexually, and why they prefer what they do. The reasons for preferring some activity may make it difficult to change behaviour.

Research so far suggests that different sexual patterns are responsible for HIV transmission in different parts of the world. In the United States, England, northern Europe, Australia, and Latin America, the recipients of anal intercourse, particularly men, are the most likely individuals to acquire HIV infection; vaginal intercourse can also transmit the infection, usually from the man to the woman. In Africa, the most common mode of transmission is vaginal intercourse, and so women get infected more commonly in Africa than elsewhere (Schoepf 1988; Carrier and Bolton 1991). Is it reasonable to expect that people can generally be persuaded to stop doing what they prefer to do?

As of now, there are only two known ways to reduce the likelihood of sexual HIV transmission. One way is to abstain from sexual intercourse; the other is to use condoms. Educational programs that teach how AIDS spreads and what the individual can do about it may reduce the spread somewhat. Such programs may fail, though, where people have incompatible beliefs and attitudes about sexuality. For example, people in some central African societies believe that deposits of semen after conception are necessary for a successful pregnancy and generally enhance a woman's health and ability to reproduce. It might be expected then that people who have these beliefs about semen would choose not to use condoms; after all, condoms in their view are a threat to public health (Schoepf 1988). Educational programs may also emphasize the wrong message. Promiscuity may increase the risk of HIV transmission, so hardly anyone would question the wisdom of advertising to reduce the number of sexual partners. What was not anticipated, however, was that individuals in monogamous relationships, who may feel safe, are less likely to use condoms or to avoid the riskiest sexual practices. Needless to say, sex with a regular partner who is infected is not safe (Bolton 1992).

The stigma associated with AIDS also hinders efforts to reduce its spread. Possible victims may be unwilling to find out if they have been infected. The stigma, in this and some other societies, is the widespread belief that homosexual men are particularly likely to get infected (Feldman and Johnson 1986). Of course, not everyone who gets infected has engaged in homosexual behaviour. Indeed, the majority of people now infected with AIDS in the world are heterosexual (Barnett and Blaikie 1992). Nevertheless, the disease's association with homosexuality, and a general prejudice against homosexuals, may contribute to the spread of AIDS. Some of those infected will continue to transmit the infection because they are afraid to find out that they might be infected. Much of the stigma associated with AIDS derives also from people's misinformation about exactly how AIDS is transmitted; indeed, many people fear contact with AIDS victims, as if any kind of contact could result in infection. Fear that they will be shunned if they are known to have AIDS may also contribute to some persons' unwillingness to be tested.

To solve the problem of AIDS, we may hope that medical science will develop an effective and inexpensive vaccination or treatment that can be afforded by all. In the meantime, we can try to understand why people engage in certain risky sexual practices. Such understanding may allow us to design educational and other programs that would more successfully inhibit the spread of AIDS.

Mental and Emotional Disorders

When Western anthropologists started describing mental illness in non-Western societies, there seemed to be unique illnesses in different cultures. These are referred to as **culture-bound syndromes**. For example, a medical disorder called *pibloktoq* occurred among some Inuit adults of Greenland, usually women, who became oblivious to their surroundings and acted in agitated, eccentric ways. They might strip themselves naked and wander across the ice and over hills until they collapsed of exhaustion. Another disorder, *amok*, occurred in Malaya, Indonesia, and New Guinea, usually among males. It was characterized by John Honigmann as a "destructive maddened excitement . . . beginning with depression and followed by a period of brooding and withdrawal [culminating in] the final mobilization of tremendous energy during which the 'wild man' runs destructively berserk" (Honigmann 1967). *Anorexia nervosa*, a disorder involving aversion to food, may be unique to the relatively few societies that idealize slimness (Kleinman 1988) (see Applied Anthropology, "Eating Disorders, Biology, and the Cultural Construction of Beauty").

Some scholars think that each society's views of the personality and concepts of mental illness have to be understood in its own terms. Western understandings and concepts cannot be applied to other cultures. For example, Catherine Lutz suggested that the Western concept of depression cannot be applied to the Pacific island of Ifaluk. The people there have many words for thinking or feeling about "loss and helplessness," but all their words are related to a specific need for someone, such as when someone dies or leaves the island. Such thoughts and feelings of loss are considered perfectly normal, and there is no word in their language for general hopelessness or "depression" (Lutz 1985). Therefore, Lutz questioned the applicability of the Western concept of depression as well as other Western psychiatric disorders.

Other researchers are not so quick to dismiss the possible universality of psychiatric categories. Some think they have found a considerable degree of cross-cultural uniformity in conceptions of mental illness. Jane Murphy studied descriptions by Inuit and the Yoruba, in Nigeria, of severely disturbed persons. She found that their descriptions not only were similar to each other, but also corresponded to North American descriptions of schizophrenia. The Inuktitut word for "crazy" is *nuthkavihak*. Inuit use this word when something inside a person seems to be out of order. *Nuthkavihak* people are described talking to themselves, believing themselves to be animals, making strange faces, becoming

> **Culture-Bound Syndromes:** illnesses unique to a specific culture.

PERSPECTIVES ON GENDER

Eating Disorders, Biology, and the Cultural Construction of Beauty

Cultures differ in terms of what they consider beautiful. In many cultures, fat people are considered more beautiful than thin people. Melvin Ember did fieldwork years ago on the islands of American Samoa. When he returned to the main island after three months on a distant island, a prominent chief said, "You look good. You gained weight." In reality, he had lost 30 pounds! The chief clearly thought that fat was better than thin and was trying to say something nice. Among the Azawagh Arabs of Niger, fatness was not merely valued and considered beautiful; great care was taken to ensure that young girls became fat by insisting and sometimes forcing them to drink large quantities of milk-based porridge.

Around the world, fatness is generally considered more desirable than thinness not only because it is considered more beautiful but also because it is thought to be a marker of health and fertility. This view is in strong contrast to the ideal in North America and many other Western societies, where fatness is thought to be unattractive and to reflect poor health. Thinness, particularly in the upper classes, is considered beautiful. How can we explain these differences in what is considered beautiful?

A common assumption is that fatness will be valued in societies subject to food scarcity. However, cross-cultural research suggests that the picture is more complicated. It appears that many societies with unpredictable resources actually value thinness, particularly in societies that have little or no technological means of storing food. At first glance, this seems puzzling. Shouldn't an individual who stores calories on the body be better off than an individual who is thin when facing starvation? Perhaps. But 10 thin individuals will generally consume less than 10 heavier people, so perhaps there is a group advantage to being thin. Indeed, many societies with frequent episodes of famine encourage fasting or eating very light meals, as among the Gurage of Ethiopia.

The strongest cross-cultural predictor of valuing fatness in women is what is often referred to as "machismo." Societies with a strong emphasis on male aggression and sexuality are the most likely to value fatness in women; those with little machismo value thinness. Why? One theory is that machismo actually reflects male insecurity and fear of women. Such men may not be looking for closeness or intimacy with their wives, but they may want to show how potent they are by having lots of children. If fatness suggests fertility, men may look for wives who are fatter. Consistent with this idea, the ideal of thinness in women became more common in North America with the rise of women's movements in the 1920s and late 1960s. Consider that Marilyn Monroe epitomized beauty in the 1950s; she was well rounded, not thin. Thin became more popular only when women began to question early marriage and having many children. Behaviours associated with machismo became less acceptable at those times.

Cultural beliefs about what is considered a beautiful body impose enormous pressures on females to achieve the ideal body type—whether it be fat or thin. In Canada and other Western countries, the effort to be thin can be carried to an extreme, resulting in the eating disorders anorexia and bulimia. The irony of "thinness" being idealized in many Western countries is that obesity is becoming more common in those societies. As of 2010, the incidence of obesity in adults increased in the United States to 36 percent, and medical researchers are worried about the increase in heart disease and diabetes resulting from obesity. Between 2001 and 2011, obesity rates in Canada rose from 9.9 percent to 11.3 percent for women, and 12.6 percent to 15.0 percent for men. By 2019, it is estimated that 55.4 percent of Canadian adults will be either overweight (34.2 percent) or obese (21.2 percent). Whether or not obesity is a result of an eating disorder (in the psychological sense) is debatable. Researchers are finding biological causes of obesity, such as resistance to the hormone leptin, which regulates appetite, suggesting that much of the obesity "epidemic" has biological causes. Still, fast food, increasing sedentariness, and extremely large portion sizes are probably contributing factors also.

Sources: Anderson-Fye EP. 2012. Anthropological Perspectives on Physical Appearance and Body Image. Encyclopedia of Body Image and Human Appearance. 1: 15–22.

Brown PJ, Sweeney J. 2009. The Anthropology of Overweight, Obesity, and the Body. AnthroNotes. 30(1):6–12.

Ember M, Ember CR, Skoggard I, editors. 2005. Encyclopedia of Diasporas: Immigrant and Refugee Cultures around the World, 2 vols. New York: Kluwer Academic/Plenum.

Friedman JM. 2003. A War on Obesity, Not the Obese. Science. 299:856–858.

Loustaunau MO, Sobo EJ. 1997. The Cultural Context of Health, Illness, and Medicine. Westport, CT: Bergin & Garvey. p. 85.

Ogden C, Carroll MD, Kit BK, Flegal KM. 2012. Prevalence of Obesity in the United States 2009–2010. NCHS Data Brief, no. 82 (January). Hyattsville, MD: National Center for Health Statistics.

Popenoe R. 2004. Feeding Desire: Fatness, Beauty, and Sexuality among a Saharan People. London: Routledge.

Twells LK, Gregory DM, Reddigan J, Midodzi WK. 2014. Current and Predicted Prevalence of Obesity in Canada: A Trend Analysis. Canadian Medical Association Journal. 2(1):E18–26.

Wolf N. 1991. The Beauty Myth: How Images of Beauty Are Used against Women. New York: Morrow.

violent, and so on. The Yoruba have a word, *were*, for people who are "insane." People described as *were* sometimes hear voices, laugh when there is nothing to laugh at, and take up weapons and suddenly hit people (Murphy 1981).

Robert Edgerton found similarities in conceptions of mental illness in four East African societies. He noted not only that the four groups essentially agreed on the symptoms of psychosis but also that the symptoms they described were the same ones that are considered psychotic here (Edgerton 1966). Edgerton believed that the lack of exact translation in different cultures, such as the one pointed out by Lutz regarding Ifaluk, does not make comparison impossible. If researchers can come to understand another culture's views of personality and if the researchers can manage to communicate these views to people of other cultures, we can compare the described cases and try to discover what may be universal and what may be found only in some cultures (Edgerton 1992).

Some mental illnesses, such as schizophrenia and depression, seem so widespread that many researchers think they are probably universal. Consistent with this idea is the fact that schizophrenic individuals in different cultures seem to share the same patterns of distinctive eye movements (Allen et al. 1996). Still, cultural factors may influence the risk of developing such diseases, the specific symptoms that are expressed, and the effectiveness of different kinds of treatment (Kleinman 1988; Berry et al. 1992). There may be some truly culture-bound (nearly unique) syndromes, but others thought at one time to be unique may be culturally varying expressions of conditions that occur widely. *Pibloktoq*, for example, may be a kind of hysteria (Honigmann 1967).

Biological but not necessarily genetic factors may be very important in the etiology of some widespread disorders such as schizophrenia (Kleinman 1988). With regard to hysteria, Anthony Wallace theorized that nutritional factors such as calcium deficiency may cause hysteria and that dietary improvement may account for the decline of this illness in the Western world since the 19th century (Wallace 1972). By the early 20th century, the discovery of the value of good nutrition, coupled with changes in social conditions, had led many people to drink milk, eat vitamin-rich foods, and spend time in the sun (although spending a lot of time in the sun is no longer recommended because of the risk of skin cancers). These changes in diet and activity increased the intake of vitamin D and helped people to maintain a proper calcium level. Consequently, the number of cases of hysteria declined.

Regarding *pibloktoq*, Wallace suggested that a complex set of related variables may cause the disease. Inuit live in an environment that supplies only a minimum amount of calcium. A diet low in calcium could result in two different conditions. One condition, rickets, would produce physical deformities potentially fatal in the Inuit hunting economy. Persons whose genetic makeup made them prone to rickets would be eliminated from the population through natural selection. A low level of calcium in the blood could also cause muscular spasms known as tetany. Tetany, in turn, may cause emotional and mental disorientation similar to the symptoms of *pibloktoq*. Such attacks last for only a relatively short time and are not fatal, so people who developed *pibloktoq* would have a far greater chance of surviving in the Arctic environment with a calcium-deficient diet than would people who had rickets.

Although researchers disagree about the comparability of mental illnesses among cultures, most agree that effective treatment requires understanding a culture's ideas about mental illness. Why people think it occurs, what treatments are believed to be effective, and how families and others respond to those afflicted must all be considered (Kleinman 1988; Kirmayer et al. 2000).

Environmental Anthropology

Environmental Contaminants

A variety of substances that can be found in the environment can have serious effects on health. As a result, considerable attention is now being paid to those substances, particularly contaminants that humans are introducing into the environment.

A *contaminant* is a substance foreign to the environment in which it is found. Industrial contaminants—the result of large-scale manufacturing processes—may or may not be harmful, depending on the kind of substance and the quantity present. The earliest evidence for the effects of industrial contaminants on the environment occurred in the 1950s when the effects of DDT—a pesticide—were observed in the reproductive failure of birds of prey (Berg et al. 2004). Polychlorinated biphenyls (PCBs) were commonly used in electrical transformers for many years. While they are no longer produced in North America, PCBs in the northern regions of Canada and Alaska are still carried by winds and ocean currents from other areas of the world (Van Oostdam et al. 1999). Very low levels of PCBs are found in water and soil, while higher levels can be found in animals. These are passed up the food chain when a larger predator eats a small animal. Exposure to PCBs can cause cancer as well as reduced immunity, low birth weights, and learning problems. Exposures are higher in the eastern than in the western region of the North and exposure among Dene–Métis populations is generally below a level of concern, although estimated intake has been found to be elevated for certain groups and is a cause for concern if exposures are elevated on a regular basis (Van Oostdam et al. 1999).

Mercury and cadmium are naturally occurring heavy metals that can be found in rocks, soil, and water. In high doses, mercury is toxic to living things, causing damage to the brain and nerves. Industrial activity has increased the quantity of mercury in the environment. Samples of human hair from Dene, Cree, and Inuit in the Canadian North have indicated that a significant proportion have mean mercury levels within the 5 percent risk range proposed by the World Health Organization for neonatal neurological damage (Van Oostdam et al. 1999). Most kinds of food contain some cadmium, but organs like the liver and kidneys contain the highest levels. Smoke from cigarettes contains cadmium, and smokers have more cadmium in their blood than non-smokers. Long-term exposure to high levels of cadmium can cause permanent kidney damage.

Many contaminants in food cannot be detected through the senses and are therefore a serious potential health concern, especially when they are not known. For example, environmental contaminants are a real concern among northern Indigenous peoples who eat caribou, fish, moose, seal, and whale, many of which are known to have trace levels of contaminants like PCBs, mercury, and cadmium (Kuhnlein and Chan 2000). Consumers of caribou meat in particular are exposed to radiation doses as much as seven times greater than non-consumers of traditional foods. This is due mostly to the cumulative presence of natural *radionuclides* in the food chain (Van Oostdam et al. 1999). However, because these traditional foods are a source of nutrition not easily replaced by store-bought foods, the implications of contaminants for health are important. Traditional foods are also an economic necessity in many communities (Van Oostdam et al. 1999). As a result, there has been considerable effort to monitor the level of contaminants in fish and wildlife collected from different regions in northern Canada over the last few decades (Chan 1998).

In response to requests from Indigenous peoples, the Centre for Indigenous Peoples' Nutrition and Environment (CINE) was created in 1993 at McGill University. The purpose of the centre was to engage in participatory research and education regarding issues about the safety of consumption of traditional Indigenous foods. Anthropologists and other researchers at CINE have been involved in the analysis of environmental contaminants for a variety of northern communities.

For example, at the request of the Deninu K'ue First Nation, in the Northwest Territories, researchers at CINE examined levels of cadmium in traditional foods and Dene–Métis food consumption data. They determined that dietary intake of cadmium from traditional foods posed no health risk to the inhabitants of Fort Resolution, a community on the shores of Great Slave Lake (Kim and Chan 1998). Similarly, Peter Berti and colleagues at CINE examined dietary data collected from over 1000 Indigenous adults from 16 communities in the Northwest Territories. Combining these data with data concerning the level of contaminants in a variety of traditional foods that were part of the peoples' diets, they calculated a relatively low dietary exposure to 11 chemical contaminants (Berti et al. 1998a, 1998b).

Natural Disasters and Famine

Natural events such as floods, droughts, earthquakes, and insect infestations are usually but not always beyond human control, but their effects are not (Aptekar 1994). We call such events accidents or emergencies when only a few people are affected, but we call them disasters when large numbers of people or large areas are affected. The harm caused is not just a function of the magnitude of the natural event. Between 1960 and 1980, 43 natural disasters in Japan killed an average of 63 people per disaster. During the same period, 17 natural disasters in Nicaragua killed an average of 6235 people per disaster. In the United States, between 1960 and 1976, the average flood or other environmental disturbance killed just one person, injured a dozen, and destroyed fewer than five buildings. These comparative figures demonstrate that climatic and other events in the physical environment become *disasters* because of events or conditions in the social environment.

If people live in houses that are designed to withstand earthquakes—if governing bodies require such construction and the economy is developed enough so that people can afford such construction—the effects of an earthquake will be minimized. If poor people are forced to live in deforested flood plains in order to be able to find land to farm (as in coastal Bangladesh), if the poor are forced to live in shanties built on precarious hillsides (like those of Rio de Janeiro), the floods and landslides that follow severe hurricanes and rainstorms can kill thousands and even hundreds of thousands.

Thus, natural disasters can have greater or lesser effects on human life, depending on social conditions. Therefore, disasters are also social problems, problems that have social causes and possible social solutions. Legislating safe construction of a house is a social solution. The 1976 earthquake in Tangshan, China, killed 250 000 people, mostly because they lived in top-heavy adobe houses that could not withstand severe shaking, whereas the 1989 earthquake in Loma Prieta, California, which was of comparable intensity, killed 65 people.

One might think that floods, of all disasters, are the least influenced by social factors. After all, without a huge runoff from heavy rains or snowmelt, there cannot be a flood. However, consider why so many people have died from Huang (Yellow) River floods in China. (One such flood, in 1931, killed nearly 4 million people, making it the deadliest single disaster in history.) The floods in the Huang River basin have occurred mostly because enormous quantities of silt wash into the river, raising the riverbed and increasing the risk of floods that burst the dams that normally would contain them. The risk of disastrous flooding would be greatly reduced if different social conditions prevailed—if people did not have to farm close to the river, or if the dams were higher and more numerous.

Famines, episodes of severe starvation and death, often appear to be triggered by physical events such as a severe drought or a hurricane that kills or knocks down food trees and plants. However, famines do not inevitably follow such an event. Social conditions can prevent a famine or increase the likelihood of one. Consider what is likely to happen in Samoa after a hurricane. Whole villages that have lost their coconut and breadfruit trees, as well as their taro patches, pick up and move for some time to other villages where there are relatives and friends. The visitors stay and are fed until some of their cultivated trees and plants start to bear food again, at which point they return home. This kind of inter-village reciprocity probably could occur only in a society that has relatively little inequality in wealth. Now, the central government or international agencies may also help out by providing food and other supplies.

Researchers point out that famine rarely results from just one low-yield food production season. During such a season, people can usually cope by getting help from relatives, friends, and neighbours, or by switching to less desirable foods. The famine in the African Sahel—the belt of marginal grassland that stretches across the African continent south of the Sahara Desert—in 1974 occurred after eight years of below-average precipitation. A combination of drought, floods, and a civil war in 1983–84 contributed to the subsequent severe famine in Ethiopia and Sudan (Mellor and Gavian 1987). Famine almost always has some social causes. Who has rights to the available food, and do those who have more food distribute it to those who have less? Cross-cultural research suggests that societies with individual property rights rather than shared rights are more likely to suffer famine (Dirks 1993). Nonetheless, government assistance can lessen the risk of famine in societies with individual property.

Relief provided by government may not always get to those who need it the most. In India, for example, the central government provides help in time of drought to minimize the risk of famine. However, food and other supplies provided to a village may end up being unequally distributed, following the rules of social and gender stratification. Members of the local elite arrange to function as distributors and find ways to manipulate the relief efforts to their advantage. Lower-class and lower-caste families still suffer the most. Within the family, biases against females, particularly young girls and elderly women, translate into their getting less food. It is no wonder, then, that in times of food shortage and famine, the poor and other socially disadvantaged persons are especially likely to die (Torry 1986).

Thus, the people of a society may not all be equally at risk in case of disaster. In socially stratified societies, the poor particularly suffer. It is they who are likely to be forced to overcultivate, overgraze, and deforest their land, making it more susceptible to degradation. A society most helps those it values the most.

To reduce the impact of disasters, then, we need to reduce the social conditions that magnify the effects of disasters. If humans are responsible for those social conditions, humans can change them. If earthquakes destroy houses that are too flimsy, we can build stronger houses. If floods caused by overcultivation and overgrazing kill defenceless people directly (or indirectly by stripping their soils), we can grow new forest cover and provide new job opportunities to floodplain farmers. If prolonged natural disasters or wars threaten famine, social distribution systems can lessen the risk. In short, we may not be able to do much about the weather or other physical causes of disasters, but we can do a lot—if we want to—about the social factors that make disasters disastrous.

Conservation

Another area of applied interest for physical anthropology is in primate conservation. As we have already discussed in Chapter 7 (see Applied Anthropology, "Endangered Primates," page 162), many groups of non-human primates face certain extinction, often the result of human behaviour. At the University of Calgary, Linda Fedigan, Canada Research Chair in Primatology and Bioanthropology, is involved in monitoring primate populations in the World Heritage Site Area de Conservación Guanacaste in Costa Rica, where she has studied capuchins, howlers, and spider monkeys for the past three decades. Fedigan's research aims to advance knowledge regarding primates and facilitate their conservation in the wild.

Kerry Bowman and his colleagues have established the Canadian Ape Alliance fund in order to coordinate efforts in raising awareness of the threats to the great apes and develop conservation strategies. The mission statement of this group is to promote conservation strategies that reflect local cultures, as well as economic and political realities. Similarly, the Jane Goodall Institute of Canada, established in 1997, implements a variety of educational programs to promote a better understanding of the relationship of all species on earth.

At the University of Toronto, Michael Schillaci is involved in research that is exploring the health of local primates and humans who coexist in a variety of environments in Asia. He is interested in trying to understand the risks of disease transmission to humans from interactions with monkeys, as well as to non-human primates from humans. For example, while many of the monkeys he studied in Jakarta, Indonesia, were infected with simian viruses known to be transmissible to humans, many of the Jakarta monkeys were infected with human diseases like measles (Schillaci et al. 2005, 2006; Karlsson et al. 2012).

Forensic Anthropology

Perhaps one of the most obvious applications of physical anthropology is the field of forensic anthropology. *Forensic anthropologists* are physical anthropologists trained in human skeletal biology. They use their expertise in the analysis of the human skeleton to help solve questions for medical and law enforcement personnel in cases where skeletal remains are discovered. Further, their expertise in archaeological excavation of human skeletons often provides them with an advantage when excavating an identified or suspected crime scene. Another role of the forensic anthropologist has been to assist in investigations of human rights violations around the world, particularly in the exhumation and analysis of mass graves.

Forensic anthropology has become extremely popular in last two decades, partly as a result of increased media attention, such as the popularity of the fictional works of forensic anthropologist Kathleen Reichs. However, in Canada the demand for the expertise of forensic anthropologists is relatively low, and most physical anthropologists provide consultation for police, medical examiners, and coroners on a part-time or ad hoc basis. The role of forensic anthropologists is to help reconstruct personal identity in cases where the victim is not known and is represented by skeletal remains. Their training in skeletal biology from archaeological contexts has provided them with the tools for quickly estimating age at death and determining sex, stature, and perhaps population affinity from the skeleton. Often human remains are discovered accidentally, and a forensic anthropologist is called in to help establish the antiquity or identity of the remains. Sometimes the nature of a scene, like the result of a mass disaster, requires a forensic anthropologist to assist in the identification of victims and the circumstances surrounding their deaths. For example, forensic anthropologists assisted in the recovery and identification of 256 victims of a military aircraft that crashed in Gander, Newfoundland, in 1985 (Hinkes 1989; Silversides 2001).

Other times, remains might be discovered under more clearly suspicious circumstances, and the data provided by a forensic anthropologist may assist in resolving a crime. For example, forensic anthropologists played a major role in the recovery and analysis of the Branch Davidian Compound victims near Waco, Texas, in early 1993 (Owsley et al. 1995; Ubelaker et al. 1995).

Now infamous, Canada's largest crime scene was also the largest forensic anthropological investigation in the country. In 2002, the largest serial-killer investigation in Canada began at the farm of Robert Pickton in Port Coquitlam, British Columbia. In January 2007, the case went to court and Robert Pickton was charged with 26 counts of first-degree murder. The Joint Missing Women Task Force of the Royal Canadian Mounted Police (RCMP) and the Vancouver Police Department worked with forensic anthropologists Tracy Rogers from the University of Toronto and Richard Lazenby from the University of Northern British Columbia. The 21-month-long search of a 7-hectare farm owned by Pickton involved dozens of senior undergraduate and graduate anthropology students with training in human skeletal biology, sifting through hundreds of thousands of cubic metres of soil, watching for and collecting thousands of specimens for evidence. The goal was to screen all the surface dirt piles and to excavate and screen the subsurface material until undisturbed, sterile ground was encountered. The combined process of excavation and sorting materials involved a team of over 100 forensic anthropology, biological anthropology, and archaeology technicians, working in combination with the RCMP, the Vancouver Police Department, and civilian heavy machinery operators—the first time in Canada that civilians have been used to such a degree in the processing of a crime scene.

Building on initiatives including Amnesty International's report on discrimination and

Aerial view of the forensic investigation site and surrounding area of Port Coquitlam, British Columbia.

Courtesy of Dr. Tracy Rogers, University of Toronto

violence against Indigenous women in Canada (Amnesty International 2004) and the Native Women's Association of Canada (NWAC) 2010 report that identified 582 missing and murdered Indigenous women and girls, the RCMP identified 1181 missing and murdered Indigenous women in its 2014 report (RCMP 2014). Following considerable public pressure, in 2015, the federal government announced a national inquiry into missing and murdered Indigenous women and girls. Consultations with key stakeholder organizations and communities took place in December 2015 and January 2016 as a basis for developing an implementation plan for the inquiry. The community-based, grassroots initiative Drag the Red, organized by Bernadette Smith in Winnipeg, has brought together families of victims, volunteers, and forensic experts to assist in locating and identifying any skeletal remains that may be in the Red River in Winnipeg. Emily Holland, a forensic anthropologist at Brandon University, got involved in the effort and provided basic training in recognizing bone and in search techniques to aid volunteers in their efforts, which are ongoing.

Forensic anthropology has also had a heightened role in investigations of international violations of human rights over the past decade. Forensic anthropologists from Canada and the United States have participated in assessments of war crimes and human rights violations in the former Yugoslavia, Serbia, and Albania and, more recently, following the conflicts in Afghanistan and Iraq (Skinner 1987; Primorac et al. 1996; Huffine et al. 2001; Komar 2003; Skinner et al. 2003; Williams and Crews 2003; Steadman and Haglund 2005; Baraybar 2014; Kimmerle 2014). In the wake of the September 11, 2001, terrorist attacks on the World Trade Center, forensic anthropologists and archaeologists assisted in the complex task of recovery and analysis of human remains in an effort to help bring closure to the families of the victims (Budimlija et al. 2003). At the same time forensic anthropologists aided in the recovery and identification of human remains from the associated plane crash in Somerset County, Pennsylvania.

A number of international organizations including Human Rights Watch, Physicians for Human Rights, and the United Nations coordinate or participate in forensic investigations of human rights violations around the world. These organizations often rely on the expertise of forensic anthropologists on a case-by-case basis, although some individuals are full-time consultants. The late Clyde Snow was perhaps the most famous practising forensic anthropologist to date. He worked on such prominent cases as identifying the remains of Dr. Josef Mengele, the Nazi war criminal who fled to Brazil; victims of serial killer John Wayne Gacy; Tutankhamen; and the victims of the Oklahoma City bombing (Anonymous 1997a). In Argentina in the 1980s he exhumed bodies from the mass graves of civilians killed by government death squads during the war, and he later worked in Guatemala, Ethiopia, Philippines, Croatia, and other areas.

In some areas of the world, full-time investigative teams have developed in response to local needs for justice and criminal investigations. Two examples are the Argentine Forensic Anthropology Team and the Guatemalan Forensic Anthropology Team.

Since it was founded in 1984, the Argentine Forensic Anthropology Team (EAAF) has investigated cases of persons who disappeared during the last military dictatorship (1976–83). In 1995 activities relating to the recovery of "disappeared"

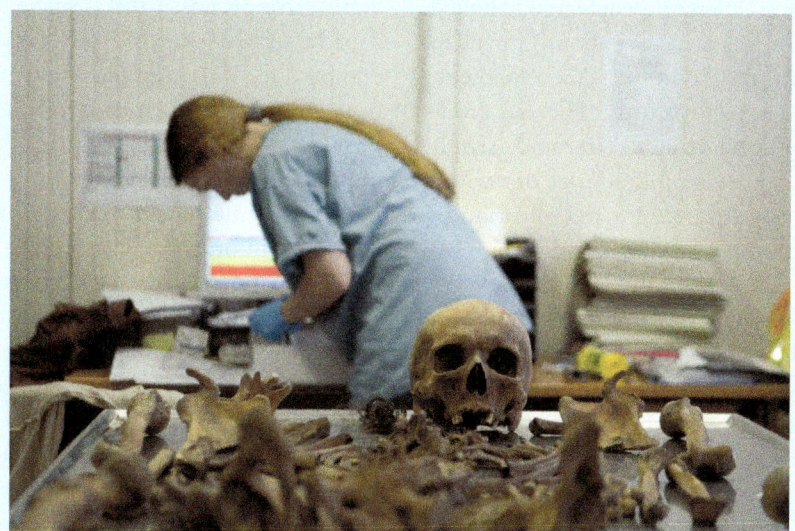
Anthropologist examining a human skull at the mortuary facility of ICMP commission of missing persons in town of Lukavac, Bosnia.

persons in Argentina increased significantly, and the EAAF continues to be active in Argentina and abroad. In 1997 the EAAF developed a data bank of blood samples from relatives of disappeared citizens. When a skeleton suspected to belong to a "disappeared" person is discovered, the DNA extracted from the remains and from blood samples in the data bank can be compared to help determine the identity of the individual (Anonymous 1997b). In 1997 members of the EAAF assisted in planning a forensic investigation in Colombia of the remains of victims killed in a battle between guerrilla troops and the Colombian army. In 1998, four EAAF members took part in the International Criminal Tribunal for the former Yugoslavia's ongoing forensic investigations in Bosnia.

In 1991 the Guatemalan Forensic Anthropology Team (Equipo de Antropología Forense de Guatemala, or EAFG) was formed through the initiative of Clyde Snow with the aid of the American Association for the Advancement of Science, which provided formal training by forensic anthropologists and pathologists from the United States. In the summer of 1992, EAFG began the first forensic investigation in Guatemala of several mass graves. It has continued to excavate and analyze remains from the graves of victims of massacres associated with the Guatemalan military during the early 1980s. Currently, EAFG consults on an international level with members of international organizations like the United Nations International Criminal Tribunals for Rwanda and for the former Yugoslavia, the Honduran government, the Haitian Truth Commission, and human rights organizations like Physicians for Human Rights.

Nutritional Anthropology

Anthropology has a long tradition of studying variation in human form. Since human variation is partly a result of growth differences among different people, many anthropologists become interested in the study of growth and development as indicators of general health within a population.

For applied anthropologists, **nutritional anthropology** may employ *longitudinal studies*, following the same children at repeated age intervals, or *cross-sectional studies*, looking at many

Nutritional Anthropology: seeks to understand the impact of various biocultural factors in the health and nutrition of a population. Nutritional anthropology can help to establish evidence on which public health policy changes or recommendations can be made.

different children at different age intervals. Applied anthropologists may collect data about growth in height and weight, skeletal or dental development, or physiological (sexual) maturity. The end product of such analyses is usually a better understanding of the impact or potential impact of various biocultural factors on the health and nutrition of the population. In this way, nutritional anthropology can help to establish evidence on which public health policy changes or recommendations can be made. In addition, monitoring people's growth in developing nations provides a basis for developing strategies for improving the health and quality of life for all people.

Growth

We can learn about the health of a population by taking body measurements, as these show levels of nutrition (Martorell and Ho 1984; Haas and Habicht 1990; Rona 1991). Studies of infant and childhood health often look at several of these **anthropometric measures** as indicators of health status. This is because body measurements are sensitive over the full range of malnutrition.

Anthropometric studies employ a variety of measurements, including height-for-age, weight-for-height, weight-for-age, arm circumference, and arm-circumference-for-height. Deficits in either of the first two are classified as *stunting* and *wasting* respectively. The most common expression of these deficits is comparison to a healthy population reference standard. The level of reduced growth for a given age is assessed against a reference mean or median. Values between 95 and 90 reflect mild growth deficit, between 90 and 85 moderate growth deficit, and less than 85 severe stunting or growth reduction (WHO [World Health Organization] 1986).

Reference standards—growth-for-age standards—for assessing growth are not universal and are often based on growth rates for well-nourished children from Western or developed nations.

> **Anthropometric Measures:** measurements of the human body for the purpose of understanding growth and variation.

Some have proposed that a single, universal standard be utilized so that all studies of growth are comparable. This argument rests on the assumption that all populations have the same genetic growth potential. Interpreting differences in growth from standards and saying what that means in terms of the health of the population require additional information about variation and differential nutrition within the populations (Johnston and Ouyang 1991:338).

Growth retardation is widely recognized as a response to the lack of an adequate diet. During periods of nutritional deficiency, bone continues to grow but at a reduced rate; the "undernourished child slows down and waits for better times" (Tanner 1990:130). The amount of "slowing" is related to the severity and duration of the malnutrition. Reduced growth is also associated with prolonged periods of infection. More frequent infections will lead to weight loss (wasting) and may prevent or impair normal growth.

Perhaps more than any other factor, socio-economic status promotes or reduces overall health within a community. Contemporary comparisons of subgroups or populations can provide information about the association between growth and social conditions.

Reduced survival of newborns in any environment is a result of biological, environmental, social, and economic factors; the last two determinants operate "through more basic proximate determinants that in turn influence the risk of disease and the outcome of disease processes" (Mosley and Chen 1984:27). At the individual level, factors related to parental education and cultural behaviours, like gender roles, are stressed. At the household level, simple considerations such as the availability of food, safe water, appropriate clothing and housing, and the interaction with preventive care are important. The community level includes such variables as political economy and public health systems that control availability and distribution of resources and directly shape the components at the household and individual levels (Mosley and Chen 1984).

In communities where population growth is extremely rapid, economic stress often results, and the resources available cannot always accommodate the constant demand. Such restraints in turn threaten or reduce the quality of health-care services, which in turn can adversely affect the mortality risks of all age groups, particularly infants. Within-family social structure associated with cultural traditions and beliefs can also serve to promote or prevent adequate infant growth. While women in traditional societies are usually responsible for care of the children, they may not have direct control over the resources on which health is dependent (Mosley and Chen 1984).

Undernutrition

What people eat is intrinsically connected to their survival and the ability of a population to reproduce itself, so we would expect that the ways people obtain, distribute, and consume food have been generally adaptive (Quandt 1996). For example, the human body cannot synthesize eight amino acids. Meat can provide all of these amino acids, and combinations of particular plants can also provide them for a complete complement of protein. The combination of maize and beans in many traditional Native American diets, or *tortillas* and *frijoles* in Mexico, can provide all the needed amino acids. In places where wheat (often made into bread) is the staple, dairy products combined with wheat also provide complete protein (McElroy and Townsend 2002). Even the ways that people have prepared for scarcity, such as breaking up into mobile bands, cultivating crops that can better withstand drought, and preserving food in case of famine, are probably adaptive practices in unpredictable environments. As we saw in the box on obesity, hypertension, and diabetes in Chapter 6, geneticists have proposed that populations in famine-prone areas may have had genetic selection for "thrifty genes"—genes that allow individuals to need a minimum of food and store the extra in fatty tissue to get them past serious scarcity. Customary diets and genetic changes may have been selected over a long stretch of time, but many serious nutritional problems observed today are due to rapid culture change.

Often the switch to commercial or cash crops has harmful effects on nutrition. For example, when the farmer-herders of the arid region in northeastern Brazil started growing sisal, a drought-resistant plant used for making twine and rope, many of them abandoned subsistence agriculture. The small landholders used most of their land for sisal growing, and when the price of sisal fell they had to work as labourers for others to try to make ends meet. Food then had to be mostly bought, but if a labourer or sisal grower didn't earn enough, there was not enough food for the whole family.

Analysis of allocation of food in some households by Daniel Gross and Barbara Underwood suggested that the labourer and his wife received adequate nutrition but the children often received much less than required. Lack of adequate nutrition usually results in retarded weight and height in children. As is commonly the case when there is substantial social inequality, the children from lower-income groups weigh substantially less than those from higher-income groups. But even though there were some economic differences before sisal production, the effects on nutrition appeared negligible before, judging from the fact that there was little or no difference in weight among adults from higher and lower socio-economic positions who grew up prior to sisal production. But more recently, 45 percent of the children from lower economic groups were undernourished as compared with 23 percent of those children from the higher economic groups (Gross and Underwood 1971).

This is not to say that commercialization is always deleterious to adequate nutrition. For example, in the Highlands of New Guinea there is evidence that the nutrition of children improved when families started growing coffee for sale. However, in this case the families still had land to grow some crops for consumption. The extra money earned from coffee enabled them to buy canned fish and rice, which provided children with higher amounts of protein than the usual staple of sweet potatoes (McElroy and Townsend 2002:187).

Nutritional imbalances for females have a far-reaching impact on reproduction and the health of the infants they bear. In some cultures, the lower status of women has a direct bearing on their access to food. While the custom of feeding males first is well known, it is less often realized that females end up with less nutrient-dense food such as meat. Deprivation of food sometimes starts in infancy where girl babies, as in India, are weaned earlier than boy babies (Quandt 1996). Parents may be unaware that their differential weaning practice has the effect of reducing the amount of high-quality protein that girl infants receive. Indeed, in Ecuador, Lauris McKee found that parents thought that earlier weaning of girls was helpful to them. They believed that mothers' milk transmitted sexuality and aggression, both ideal male traits, to their infants and so it was important that girl babies be weaned early. Mothers weaned their girls at about 11 months and their boys at about 20 months, a 9-month difference. McKee found that girl infants had a significantly higher mortality than boy infants in their second year of life, suggesting that the earlier weaning time for girls and their probable undernutrition may have been responsible (McKee 1984).

Body Composition

Body composition, in particular the distribution of fat, has increasingly been used to answer broader questions of human evolutionary development. Factors affecting how body fat is distributed include age, sex, maturation, ethnicity, and socio-economic status. The question of whether specific patterns of fat distribution in various populations represent an adaptive response to environmental stress continues to be evaluated. The implications of changes in environment associated with migration and modernization for such populations have been examined. Recent studies of body fat patterning in childhood as an indicator of health and risk of certain diseases in adulthood have produced some very interesting results from both academic and applied perspectives.

Body fat composition and distribution can be measured in a variety of ways, including traditional anthropometric assessment, dual-energy X-ray absorptiometry (DXA) and, most recently, 3D body scans (Garlie et al. 2010). Estrogen seems to promote the accumulation of body fat, and thus females with earlier **menarche**—the beginning of reproductive maturity—have more fat during pre-adolescence, adolescence, and later life (Marshall and Tanner 1986). A variety of studies observed a correlation between the patterns of fat distribution and rates of sexual maturity (Frisancho and Flegal 1982). The observed correlation between fat patterning and age at menarche is particularly interesting considering the well-known secular trend toward earlier age at menarche in many populations over the last century or so. Most noticeably, the age of onset of menarche has become two to four years earlier over the past century in Europe, North America, and other parts of the world (Marshall 1978; Marshall and Tanner 1986; Eveleth and Tanner 1990). Coincidentally, biological studies of modernization have consistently observed increased mean adult weight and the prevalence of obesity (Reed et al. 1970; Bindon and Baker 1985; McGarvey et al. 1989). While this has been associated with excess caloric intake and reduced physical activity, the correspondence with decreased age of sexual maturity should also be considered.

Despite the intrinsic factors that are associated with changes in growth, such as diet, many studies have observed that differences related to the environment in which an individual lives are also associated with total body fat (Johnston et al. 1974, 1984; Bogin and Sullivan 1986; Shepard 1991). Most environmental factors that affect growth can be linked either directly or indirectly to nutrition (Eveleth 1986). When under nutritional stress, individual fat distribution changes, with a reduction in the extremities and a relative increase around the torso (Bogin and MacVean 1981; Johnston et al. 1984; Cameron et al. 1992). Inadequate nutrition can slow or halt the production of fat cells but will have little permanent effect on fat distribution if it occurs while cells are increasing in size only (Tanner 1990). The fact that infants in developing countries often deviate from the expected pattern of fat deposition has been

---

Menarche: the onset of first menstruation in young women.

attributed to poor nutrition associated with breast-feeding and weaning (Eveleth 1986).

At the University of Toronto, Tracey Galloway is engaged in research that aims to assess chronic disease risks and health inequities in northern Indigenous populations. More specifically, her research looks at obesity and chronic diseases such as diabetes and hypertension. In their review of recent trends among Arctic populations, Galloway et al. (2012) observed continued trends toward increased obesity in Inuit adults and children, and they found that this condition was prevalent at younger ages in children.

A question of major interest to researchers in this field is whether obesity in childhood predisposes obesity in adulthood. Overnutrition in childhood can lead to increased risks of chronic diseases in adulthood such as diabetes (NIDDM), cardiovascular disease, and site-specific cancers. In many Westernized populations, obesity is the primary factor associated with high risks of hypertension and diabetes (Bruce 2000). Presently, childhood obesity is a major problem in childhood health in North America (Andersen 2000). Most studies suggest that while some obese infants and children do become obese adults, most return to near-normal weight for height in early or late childhood (Shapiro et al. 1984; Johnston 1985).

A major focus of anthropometry and especially 3D whole-body scan data is in the field of ergonomics—the science of design for how people relate to the products they use. For example, 3D body scanning has been explored for everything from motion capture in the entertainment industry to custom on-demand garment design and tailoring (e.g., Gill 2015) to safety systems, including automobiles, helmets, and so on. In addition to consumer ergonomics, both the Canadian and the U.S. military are interested in studying the body composition of soldiers in order to improve safety and equipment use in the field. With changes in the typical size and shape of soldiers over time and an increased diversity of body shapes within the military over the last few decades, including more female soldiers, there is a need for better designs (e.g., Mitchell et al. 2014). The Canadian Forces Anthropometric Survey (CFAS) (Keefe et al. 2012) was the first major 3D anthropometric survey of Canadian Forces personnel, combining data from 2200 full-body scans (Shu et al. 2015). Anthropometric studies of military personnel have focused on a variety of issues from changing body composition over time (e.g. Choi and Garlie 2015) to the impact on range of motion when soldiers are fully outfitted (Garlie 2011; Mitchell et al. 2014).

Archaeology as Culture History

Archaeology and the study of past societies provide an important historical framework for current issues in modern society. Bringing this information to the general public is important for establishing an awareness of cultural variability that is a part of the multicultural society in which Canadians live today, as well as the wider global community. In Canada, anthropological research into past societies offers an opportunity to explore the history and prehistory of Indigenous peoples. A primary concern with skeletal remains from North America in general is that these remains are often discovered accidentally and require reburial. Excavation is often undertaken relatively quickly and analysis (when desired by the community) is also limited by time. However, when proper analysis is undertaken, information that can be inferred from human skeletal remains and material culture becomes an important resource for understanding the past. Archaeology can help reconstruct cultural history, including that of Indigenous peoples in Canada.

Cultural Resource Management

Cultural resource management (CRM) is about the long-term stewardship of a region's cultural heritage sites—locations of historical, cultural, or spiritual significance to the populations. Because so many of these sites are of interest to the general public, CRM is designed not only to safeguard cultural heritage sites from potential damage, but also to provide access to the rich

> **Cultural Resource Management (CRM):** the long-term stewardship of a region's cultural heritage sites.

Students from a First Nations community in Manitoba work with a local archaeological consulting company to survey for sites in the community's traditional land use area.

historical and cultural information that can be gained from such sites to the general public. A variety of national and international agencies have the responsibility for large-scale CRM activities. These include UNESCO's World Heritage Convention, English Heritage in the United Kingdom, and the Quebec Archaeological Association (AAQ) and Parks Canada in Canada.

As one of the principal cultural resource management organizations in Canada, Parks Canada has a CRM policy guide. Managing cultural resources for public benefit can be difficult. Some of Canada's most significant cultural resources are, by their very nature, those for which protection and public presentation are most needed. In its commitment to responsible stewardship, Parks Canada balances public awareness and access to cultural resources, while preserving the irreplaceable resources being visited.

These challenges require a holistic framework for policy that deals with cultural resources as symbolic as well as physical entities. Canadian efforts to protect and present cultural resources for public benefit are part of a worldwide endeavour to protect, understand, and appreciate our human heritage. In the past few decades, Parks Canada has been involved with Indigenous communities on a variety of initiatives related to establishing and planning historic sites and new parks and to land claims settlements (Fox 1999). At the same time, other communities have begun to develop Indigenous tourism from a resource-based industry in the form of big-game hunting to ecotourism and cultural or ethnic tourism, balancing this development with elements of Indigenous land-based economy (Notzke 1999).

As a result of the increasing awareness of cultural heritage issues in Canada, courses in CRM are now offered at various institutions in Canada. The University of Victoria offers a CRM program aimed at people involved with museums, galleries, heritage agencies, and other cultural organizations throughout Canada. The University of Manitoba is developing an innovative new program in Aboriginal Cultural Resource Management that will provide a critical venue for dealing with the often conflicting economic and heritage conservation needs, including the discovery of burials.

With respect to human remains, there has been an increasing involvement of Indigenous populations in the repatriation and reburial of human remains from museums and institutions throughout the world. Many communities feel that human remains are not at rest until reburied. Perhaps the most famous example of this is the discovery of the Kennewick skull and the subsequent legal battle between American anthropologists and Indigenous groups for its reburial discussed earlier in this chapter (Chatters 2002; Holden 2004a, 2004b; Watkins 2004).

Canada has seen a variety of repatriations, few as sensational as the Kennewick case. In British Columbia, the Skidegate Repatriation and Cultural Committee has reburied over 390 human remains from various institutions. In 1998, the Canadian Museum of Civilization (now the Canadian Museum of History) repatriated a large skeletal sample from a 15th-century St. Lawrence Iroquois village to the Mohawk First Nation Council of Chiefs at Akwesasne for reburial.

Others are keen to see how anthropology can help reveal the life histories of their ancestors. While these may seem like two extremes, in fact there have been many successful partnerships between Indigenous communities and anthropologists recently in Canada. There have also been some internationally notable cases of co-operative, multidisciplinary research by Canadian physical anthropologists and archaeologists with great sensitivity to concerns of Indigenous communities—including repatriation—while still accomplishing significant research. These include the discovery and study of Kwaday Dän Sinchi, whose remains were found frozen in a B.C. glacier; the archaeological discovery of an extensive Indigenous settlement, including human remains, on the Canadian side of the river during the "twinning" of the Blue Water Bridge between Sarnia, Ontario, and Port Huron, Michigan; and the discovery of an Iroquois ossuary in suburban Toronto that resulted in a brief, but intensive, study of the human remains that were recovered, before their repatriation to the Six Nations reserve near Brantford in early 1998 (Williamson and Pfeiffer 2003). These cases all stand in sharp contrast to the often contentious nature of similar cases in the United States, like the Kennewick Man. The key to these successes has been mutual respect by all parties involved and an increasing role of Indigenous communities in controlling and directing research on their cultural heritage. As these partnerships continue to build, we will no doubt see tremendous benefits gained through the ongoing research in cultural heritage.

Museum Archaeology

Museums have been an important part of anthropology since the very beginnings of the field. As early anthropologists returned from archaeological excavations and ethnographic explorations, they brought with them artifacts from the peoples and cultures they encountered. These materials were collected in museums—often natural history museums since, at the time (the mid to late 19th

Commuters look at 4th-century ruins uncovered as part of a large-scale CRM project associated with the construction of the Athens metro system.

century), non-Western artifacts were not considered art, nor were the cultures of non-Western peoples considered part of history. Thus the objects non-Western peoples produced and the information about their cultures were deposited with similar items from other forms of animal life. Today we recognize this as an ethnocentric, perhaps even racist, view of non-Western people, but many anthropological and archaeological collections are still deposited and maintained in natural history museums. Many other museums exist today as well, from cultural museums to historic site museums to museums showcasing traditional works of art, and anthropologists work in all of these.

Anthropologists typically hold one of three positions in museums: curators, collections managers, or educators. Curators are responsible for the overall content and use of collections. They oversee the museum collections with an eye to their value for research and their importance to the history of their field. In some cases curators acquire (or accession) materials in order to fill areas that are inadequately represented in their collections; in other cases they have to make difficult decisions about discarding (or deaccessioning) materials that are no longer of use. Curators also lead teams that evaluate and develop the museum's exhibits. Collections managers work to ensure that the museum's collections are preserved. They make sure that storage facilities and records are properly maintained, and they regularly check the collections to make sure they are not deteriorating. When deterioration is found, collections managers work with conservators to repair damage and determine ways to keep further damage from occurring. Finally, museum educators work with the public to teach them about the peoples and cultures represented in the museum's collections.

Regardless of their position, public education is a central role for all museum anthropologists. A good example can be seen in recent work involving a traditional New Zealand Maori meeting

A Maori meeting house in New Zealand.

APPLIED ANTHROPOLOGY

Raised Field Agriculture

Most agricultural systems in the Americas today rely upon either animal power or large machines to cultivate the soil and harvest food. But in the past, people had no traction animals or machines to help with agricultural production. How did the ancient farmers in the Americas till the soil and harvest crops? The answer is that they used human labour. In most cases, animal or mechanical power is much more efficient than human power and allows more food to be grown on the same piece of land. Archaeologists, however, have found that some ancient, human-powered agricultural systems are actually better suited to specific local environments and produce more food than modern, mechanized systems. These archaeologists have started to use their knowledge of ancient food production to help modern communities improve their lives.

Archaeologist Clark Erickson calls this work "applied archaeology," and he has been conducting applied archaeological work in South America for decades. One of his most significant projects involved the reconstruction of raised fields in the community of Huatta near Lake Titicaca in highland Peru. The environment there is relatively harsh. Early agricultural development projects tried and failed to make the land surrounding Huatta productive. But Erickson recognized that most of the area surrounding the community had once been highly productive raised fields, and he wondered if rebuilding these ancient agricultural structures might help the community.

Raised fields are created by piling soil into a long mound, which becomes surrounded by a ditch as soil is taken from it and piled on the mound. Over time, the ditch fills with water and aquatic plants. The aquatic plants are harvested annually and placed on top of the mound as fertilizer. The water in the ditch both keeps the mound soil moist and helps control the soil temperature. As a system, raised fields form a self-sustaining agricultural microenvironment. The major drawback is that mechanized equipment cannot be used easily on these mounds and ditches, so significant amounts of human labour are often required.

Erickson began working with members of the Huatta community to rebuild several of the ancient raised fields. About five years later it was clear that raised field agriculture was well suited to the area. Raised fields were not as labour-intensive as initially thought and were as productive as nearby agricultural fields built upon better soils. More significantly, the "manure" from aquatic plants maintained the soils in the raised fields and actually improved them over time. So, although more labour-intensive, raised fields were able to bring otherwise marginal land into full agricultural production. Although many problems have arisen, including some failures, parts of the Lake Titicaca basin have been returned to raised field agriculture.

Raised field agriculture in practice.

Sources: Bandy M. 2005. Energetic Efficiency and Political Expediency in Titicaca Basin Raised Field Agriculture. Journal of Anthropological Archaeology. 24(3):271–296.

Erickson C. 1988. Raised Field Agriculture in the Lake Titicaca Basin. Expedition. 30(1):8–16.

Erickson C. 1989. Raised Fields and Sustainable Agriculture in the Lake Titicaca Basin of Peru. In: Browder J, editor. Fragile Lands of Latin America. Boulder, CO: Westview.

Erickson C. 1998. Applied Archaeology and Rural Development. In: Whiteford M, Whiteford S, editors. Crossing Currents: Continuity and Change in Latin America. Upper Saddle River, NJ: Prentice Hall.

Guttman-Bond E. 2010. Sustainability Out of the Past: How Archaeology Can Save the Planet. World Archaeology. 42:355–366.

Morris A. 2004. Raised Field Technology: The Raised Field Projects around Lake Titicaca. Burlington, VT: Ashgate.

house, or *marae*, on display at the Field Museum in Chicago. A *marae* is used in Maori culture as a place where individuals are allowed to air grievances and settle disputes in an atmosphere of respect and openmindedness. Field Museum curator of Pacific anthropology John Terrell wished that Chicago had such a space and then realized that the *marae* itself might be used as one; in other words, that the Maori *marae* might become a Chicago *marae*. Terrell worked with a group of Maori and a group of teachers from Chicago public schools to explore this idea, and today the *marae* is used by groups seeking to discuss difficult issues in a context of mutual respect. In this way Terrell was able to not only display an important cultural object but also, with the assistance of the collections manager and museum education staff, develop a way for the object to be used by the Chicago community in a manner similar to its use within Maori culture.

Landscape Archaeology

Archaeology and historical ecology can also contribute to our understanding of present-day environments. For example, archaeologists from the United States and Bolivia have presented new archaeological evidence on landscape transformation by prehistoric populations in Amazonia that has implications for applied studies of sustainable development, conservation of biodiversity, and Indigenous knowledge systems (Erickson 2000). Archaeological research at the Lake Titicaca region of Peru and Bolivia has documented large agricultural earthworks, long thought to be unproductive agriculturally and referred to as simply "raised fields." Based on an archaeological investigation of land use in prehistoric Bolivia, Clark Erickson and colleagues argued that Indigenous people in late prehistory transformed a marginal environment into a productive landscape capable of supporting large and dense populations. The raised fields were first used around 3000 years ago and subsequently abandoned sometime before the arrival of the Spaniards (Erickson 2000).

In the early 1980s, Erickson, along with Peruvian agronomist Ignacio Garaycochea, anthropologist Kay Candler, and agricultural journalist Dan Brinkmeier, persuaded some local farmers in the Huatta, a Quechua-speaking community near Lake Titicaca, to rebuild a few of the raised fields, plant indigenous crops, and farm them using traditional methods. Attempts to impose inappropriate Western crops and techniques in the Andes had failed miserably, but the archaeological evidence suggested that raised fields might be appropriate for the region. This small-scale experiment was considered successful and today some farmers in the region are using the technology of their ancestors once again to produce food (Erickson 2000) (see Applied Anthropology, "Raised Field Agriculture").

Making the World Better

Many social problems afflict our world, not just the ones discussed in this chapter. We don't have the space to discuss the international trade in drugs and how it plays out in violence, death, and corruption. We haven't discussed the negative effects of environmental degradation—water and air pollution, global warming, ozone depletion, destruction of forests and wetlands. We haven't said anything about overpopulation, the energy crisis, and a host of other problems we should care and do something about, if we hope to make this a better world.

Anthropology is now an applied as well as a basic science. What anthropology has discovered, and what it can discover, about humans can help solve problems in the real world. No longer is what we do purely academic. Most of the problems anthropology can help solve are of human making; therefore, they are susceptible to human unmaking.

SUMMARY AND REVIEW

APPLIED AND PRACTISING ANTHROPOLOGY

14.1 Explain what applied anthropology is.

- Many anthropologists find employment outside of academia—in medical schools, health centres, development agencies, urban-planning agencies, and other public and private organizations.
- Applied anthropologists can be involved in one or more phases of a program designed to change people's lives: assembling relevant knowledge, constructing alternative plans for a program, assessing social and environmental impacts of plans, implementing programs, and monitoring the program and its effects.
- The code of ethics specifies that applied anthropologists should not be involved in programs that have negative effects for target populations and that communities should be included as much as possible in planning the program of change.
- Above all, the code of ethics pledges a responsibility to ensure the welfare and dignity of those who are being studied and a responsibility to report openly and truthfully to those who will read or be affected by their research.
- Applied anthropologists play an important role in identifying long-term consequences and are regularly sought by governments and other agencies in planning projects.
- A growing trend is for anthropologists to become advocates for affected communities—such as Indigenous grassroots organizations—by involving the people in all stages of the project, from design, through execution, to publishing. Grassroots organizations can succeed where government or outside organizations fail.

What is the most important ethical question anthropologists should ask themselves before embarking on research?

MEDICAL ANTHROPOLOGY

14.2 Explain the perspective that medical anthropology brings to understanding health.

- Medical anthropologists investigate the cultural aspects of biomedical problems.
- Anthropologists, particularly those in medical anthropology, who are actively engaged in studying health and illness and associated beliefs and practices are increasingly realizing that biological and social factors need to be considered to reduce human suffering.
- Western medical researchers and medical practitioners may think of medicine as being purely based on "fact," but it is clear on reflection that many ideas stem from the culture in which the researchers reside.
- Biomedicine is the dominant Western medical paradigm today, focusing on diseases and cures. Health is seen as the absence of disease; death, as a failure. Medical interest tends not to consider psychological factors, social or cultural influences, or links within the human body.

In what way has the stigma associated with AIDS hindered efforts to reduce its spread?

ENVIRONMENTAL ANTHROPOLOGY

14.3 Describe the field of environmental anthropology.

- Environmental anthropology focuses on issues relating to the interaction of humans with local, regional, and global environments, particularly how to understand and alleviate degradation of the environment. There is increasing recognition that imposing environmental policies from the top down does not work well and efforts will more likely succeed if affected communities participate in the planning of programs. Biological anthropologists identify health concerns from environmental contaminants and make recommendations to communities and government for how to deal with these issues.

 *What are the social causes typically associated with famine?*

FORENSIC ANTHROPOLOGY

14.4 Describe the role of forensic anthropology in medical-legal cases.

- Forensic anthropology helps solve crimes by identifying human remains, usually by applying knowledge of physical anthropology.
- Many forensic anthropologists work to confirm abuses of human rights around the world, especially where there has been systematic killing of citizens.

 *What was the largest forensic anthropological investigation in Canada? Describe how it was conducted.*

NUTRITIONAL ANTHROPOLOGY

14.5 Describe the field of nutritional anthropology.

- Nutritional anthropologists study biocultural factors that influence nutrition and growth.
- Nutritional anthropology can help to establish evidence on which public health policy changes or recommendations can be made.
- Monitoring people's growth in developing nations provides a basis for creating strategies for improving the health and quality of life for all people.
- Anthropometric studies of changing body composition can inform design decisions and ergonomic applications in clothing, wearable technologies, and safety equipment.

 *What is the standard method for assessing growth deficits?*

ARCHAEOLOGY AS CULTURE HISTORY

14.6 Explain how archaeology can be used for understanding culture history.

- Cultural resource management involves recovering and preserving the archaeological record before programs of planned change disturb or destroy it.
- Cultural resource management educates the public about the past in an attempt to balance education about, access to, and preservation of heritage resources around the world.
- A companion to public archaeology is museum anthropology where materials are increasingly being presented in a less biased way from the perspective of non-Western cultures.

 *What positions do anthropologists typically hold in museums? What are their responsibilities in these positions?*

LANDSCAPE ARCHAEOLOGY

14.7 Describe how landscape archaeology can have an impact on society.

- Landscape archaeology can contribute to our understanding of modern-day environmental conditions.
- It can make a contribution to studies of sustainable development, conservation, biodiversity, and Indigenous knowledge.

 *What is raised field agriculture?*

THINK ON IT

1. What advantages do anthropologists have in trying to solve practical problems?

2. Is it ethical to try to influence people's lives when they have not asked for help?

3. Do global problems require solutions by global agencies? If so, which problems do?

4. What kinds of questions do environmental anthropologists ask? What are some of the methods they use to address these questions?

5. How have practices in museum anthropology changed over time?

6. What kinds of challenges do forensic anthropologists face in their research? Give examples.

Glossary

Absolute Dating a method of dating fossils in which the actual age of a deposit or specimen is measured. Also known as *chronometric dating*.
Acclimatization impermanent physiological changes that people make when they encounter a new environment.
Acculturation the process of extensive borrowing of aspects of culture.
Acheulian a stone toolmaking tradition dating from 1.5 million years ago. Compared with the Oldowan tradition, Acheulian assemblages have more large tools created according to standardized designs or shapes. One of the most characteristic and prevalent tools in the Acheulian tool kit is the so-called hand axe, which is a teardrop-shaped, bifacially flaked tool with a thinned, sharp tip. Other large tools may have been cleavers and picks.
Acquired Inheritance a theory proposed in the late 18th century that acquired characteristics could be inherited and therefore species could evolve. Individuals who in their lifetime developed characteristics helpful to survival would pass those characteristics on to future generations, thereby changing the physical makeup of the species.
Adapid a type of prosimian with many lemur-like features; appeared in the early Eocene.
Adaptation changes to biology or behaviour that increase the chances of surviving and leaving viable offspring in a new environment.
Adaptive the concept that a trait or behaviour increases chances of survival under certain environmental conditions. See also *Adaptive Trait*.
Adaptive Trait a trait that enhances survival and reproductive success in a particular environment. Usually applied to biological evolution, the term is also often used by cultural anthropologists to refer to cultural traits that enhance reproductive success.
AIDS (Acquired Immune Deficiency Syndrome) a disease that emerged in the 20th century, almost always lethal, presumably caused by the HIV virus or viruses.
Allele one member of a pair of genes.
Allen's Rule the rule that protruding body parts (particularly arms and legs) are relatively shorter in the cooler areas of a species' range than in the warmer areas.
Altruism the concept of caring for and sustaining members of the group who may no longer contribute to the group's survival.
Amino Acid Racemization a non-radiometric technique for dating materials that can be applied to organic material such as bone, mollusc shells, and eggshells.

Ancient DNA (aDNA) DNA extracted from archaeologically recovered materials.
Anthropoids one of the two suborders of primates; includes monkeys, apes, and humans.
Anthropological Linguistics the anthropological study of languages.
Anthropology the study of differences and similarities, both biological and cultural, in human populations. Anthropology is concerned with typical biological and cultural characteristics of human populations in all periods and in all parts of the world.
Anthropometric Measures measurements of the human body for the purpose of understanding growth and variation.
Applied Anthropology the branch of anthropology that concerns itself with applying anthropological knowledge to achieve practical goals, usually in the service of an agency outside the traditional academic setting. Also called *practising anthropology*.
^{40}Ar-^{39}Ar Dating Method used in conjunction with potassium-argon dating, this method gets around the problem of needing different rock samples to estimate potassium and argon. A nuclear reactor is used to convert the ^{39}Ar to ^{39}K, on the basis of which the amount of ^{40}K can be estimated. In this way, both argon and potassium can be estimated from the same rock sample.
Arboreal adapted to living in trees.
Archaeological Site areas of past human habitation or where fossil remains are found.
Archaeology the branch of anthropology that seeks to reconstruct the daily life and customs of peoples who lived in the past and to trace and explain cultural changes. Often lacking written records for study, archaeologists must try to reconstruct history from the material remains of human cultures. See also *Historical Archaeology*.
Archaic *Homo sapiens* specimens of early *Homo sapiens* that are not exactly like anatomically modern humans are distinguished as Archaic *Homo sapiens*. Neandertals are a specific group of Archaic *Homo sapiens*.
Arctic Small Tool Tradition culture that follows the Palaeo-Arctic tradition, representing the first humans to move into the eastern Canadian Arctic and Greenland. In Alaska the Arctic Small Tool tradition evolved into the Norton tradition, while in the eastern Arctic it became the Dorset culture.
Ardipithecus ramidus an intermittently bipedal species dated to 4 million years ago. It is a possible candidate for the hominin common ancestor.
Artifacts items manufactured by people and found in archaeological contexts.

Assimilation Theory a variation on the replacement theory that suggests modern human populations that evolved in Africa interbred and replaced populations they encountered in North Africa, Europe, and Asia.

Association the relationship between artifacts and features within archaeological sites.

Atlatl Aztec word for "spear-thrower."

Aurignacian Tools a stone tool technology associated with modern humans that began in Europe around 35 000 years ago. It includes the production of long, narrow blade tools.

Australopithecines a bipedal genus of hominin distinguished from the later genus *Paranthropus* by their lighter dentition and smaller faces.

Australopithecus genus of Pliocene and Pleistocene hominins.

Australopithecus afarensis a species of *Australopithecus* that lived 4 million to 3 million years ago in East Africa and was definitely bipedal.

Australopithecus africanus a species of *Australopithecus* that lived between about 3 million and 2 million years ago.

Australopithecus anamensis a species of *Australopithecus* that lived perhaps 4.2 million years ago.

Australopithecus bahrelghazali a species of *Australopithecus* discovered by French researchers in Chad in north-central Africa and reported in 1995. *A. bahrelghazali* is dated between 3.5 million and 3 million years ago and is thought to be a second hominin species contemporary with *A. afarensis*.

Australopithecus garhi a species discovered in 1999 in the Afar region of Ethiopia, dating to about 2.5 million years ago. *A. garhi* had a projecting ape-like face and small braincase, similar to *A. afarensis* but with much larger teeth.

Balancing Selection a type of selection that occurs when a heterozygous combination of alleles is positively favoured even though a homozygous combination is disfavoured.

Basicranium the base of the skull.

Behavioural Ecology the study of how all kinds of behaviour may be related to the environment. The theoretical orientation involves the application of biological evolutionary principles to the behaviour (including social behaviour) of animals, including humans. Also called *sociobiology*, particularly when applied to social organization and social behaviour.

Bergmann's Rule the rule that smaller-sized subpopulations of a species inhabit the warmer parts of its geographical range and larger-sized subpopulations the cooler areas.

Beringia the land mass that is now under water (the Bering Strait) between Siberia and Alaska.

Bifacial Tool a tool worked or flaked on two sides.

Bilophodont having four cusps on the molars that form two parallel ridges. This is the common molar pattern of Old World monkeys.

Biocultural Model a holistic approach that recognizes the interaction between biology and culture in human populations.

Biological (Physical) Anthropology the study of humans as biological organisms, dealing with the emergence and evolution of humans and with contemporary biological variations among human populations. Also called *physical anthropology*.

Biomedicine the dominant medical paradigm in Western societies today.

Bipedalism locomotion in which an animal walks on its two hind legs.

Blade a thin flake whose length is usually more than twice its width. In the blade technique of toolmaking, a core is prepared by shaping a piece of flint with hammer stones into a pyramidal or cylindrical form. Blades are then struck off until the core is used up.

Brachiators animals that move through the trees by swinging hand over hand from branch to branch. They usually have long arms and fingers.

Broca's Area the area of the brain related to language acquisition. It is important for understanding the origins of language in early hominins.

Burin a chisel-like stone tool used for carving and for making such artifacts as bone and antler needles, awls, and projectile points.

Canines the cone-shaped teeth immediately behind the incisors; used by most primates to seize food and in fighting and display.

Carpolestes a mouse-sized arboreal creature living about 56 million years ago; a strong candidate for the common primate ancestor.

Carrying Capacity the estimated population number and density that a given area of land can support, given the technology used by the people at the time.

Catarrhines the group of anthropoids with narrow noses and nostrils that face downward. Catarrhines include monkeys of the Old World (Africa, Asia, and Europe), as well as apes and humans.

Catastrophism the theory that the earth was shaped by a serious of catastrophic events including volcanic eruptions, floods, hurricanes, etc. It preceded later theories to explain evolutionary changes.

Ceramics objects shaped from clay and baked at high temperature (fired) to make them hard. Containers such as pots and jars are typical ceramics, though they can take on many forms and uses.

Cercopithecoids Old World monkeys.

Cerebral Cortex the "grey matter" of the brain; the centre of speech and other higher mental activities.

Chiefdom a political unit, with a chief at its head, integrating more than one community but not necessarily the whole society or language group.

Chromosomes paired rod-shaped structures within a cell nucleus containing the genes that transmit traits from one generation to the next.

Chronometric Dating See *Absolute Dating*.

Civilization urban society, from the Latin word for "city-state."

Cline the gradually increasing (or decreasing) frequency of a gene from one end of a region to another.

Conservation techniques used on archaeological materials to stop or reverse the process of decay.

Continental Drift the movement of the continents over the past 135 million years. In the early Cretaceous (about 135 million years ago) there were two "supercontinents": *Laurasia*, which included North America and Eurasia, and *Gondwanaland*, which included Africa, South America, India, Australia, and Antarctica. By the beginning of the Paleocene (about 65 million years ago), Gondwanaland had broken apart, with South America drifting west away from Africa, India drifting east, and Australia and Antarctica drifting south.

Coprolites the fossilized remains of feces.

Cretaceous geological epoch 135 million to 65 million years ago, during which dinosaurs and other reptiles ceased to be the dominant land vertebrates and mammals and birds began to become important.

Cross-cultural Researcher an ethnologist who uses ethnographic data about many societies to test possible explanations of cultural variation.

Crossing-Over exchanges of sections of chromosomes from one chromosome to another.

Cultural Anthropology the study of cultural variation and universals.

Cultural Ecologist a person concerned with the relationship between culture and the physical and social environments.

Cultural Relativism the attitude that a society's customs and ideas should be viewed within the context of that society's problems and opportunities.

Cultural Resource Management (CRM) the long-term stewardship of a region's cultural heritage sites.

Culture the set of learned behaviours, beliefs, attitudes, values, and ideals that are characteristic of a particular society or population.

Culture-Bound Syndrome illnesses unique to a specific culture.

Cuneiform wedge-shaped writing invented by the Sumerians around 3000 B.C.

Darwin, Charles (1809–82) a British naturalist who proposed the theory of evolution by natural selection. Most people equate the theory of evolution with Darwin because of the historical controversy his theory created at the time.

Datum a fixed, permanent reference point within or near an archaeological site used to define the location of all information and specimens collected from the site. As the datum is a permanent fixture, future investigations can be spatially related to all previous work at the site.

Dendrochronology an absolute dating technique based on counting annual tree rings in wood.

Denisovans a group of Siberian hominins contemporary with Neandertals and modern humans who all share a common ancestor based on DNA analysis.

Dentition the type, number, and arrangement of teeth.

Diagenesis chemical changes that occur in materials after deposition in the ground.

Diastema a gap between the canine and first premolar found in apes.

Differential Diagnosis the assessment of potential diseases that are consistent with the observable traits/criteria on bones within an individual.

Differential Reproductive Success differences in the chances of an organism surviving and leaving offspring that will also survive.

Diffusion the borrowing by one society of a cultural trait belonging to another society as the result of contact between the two societies.

Directional Selection a type of natural selection that increases the frequency of a trait (the trait is said to be positively favoured, or *adaptive*).

Diurnal active during the day.

DNA (Deoxyribonucleic Acid) a long, two-stranded molecule in the genes; directs the making of an organism according to the instructions in its genetic code.

Domestication modification or adaptation of plants and animals for use by humans. When people plant crops, we refer to the process as *cultivation*. It is only when the crops cultivated and the animals raised have been modified—are different from wild varieties—that we speak of plant and animal domestication.

Dominant the allele of a gene pair that is always phenotypically expressed in the heterozygous form.

Dryopithecus genus of ape from the later Miocene found primarily in Europe. It had thin tooth enamel and pointed molar cusps quite similar to those of the fruit-eating chimpanzees of today.

Ecofacts natural objects that have been used or affected by humans.

Egalitarian Society a society in which all persons of a given age-sex category have equal access to economic resources, power, and prestige.

Electron Spin Resonance Dating like thermoluminescence dating, this technique measures trapped electrons from surrounding radioactive material. The material to be dated is exposed to varying magnetic fields in order to obtain a spectrum of the microwaves absorbed by the tested material. Because no heating is required for this technique, electron spin resonance is especially useful for dating organic materials, such as bone and shell, that decompose if heated.

Endocast a preserved, fossilized relief of a hominin brain, created by the skull filling with minerals and taking on the morphology and structure of the brain. Endocasts are an important source of evidence for understanding the evolution of the brain and questions related to the origins of language, etc.

Environmental Archaeology a field of study that is interested specifically in ecological and climatic conditions of the past as a means for better understanding how various peoples lived—what conditions they lived in and how those conditions affected their lives.

Eocene a geological epoch 55 million to 34 million years ago during which the first definite primates appeared.

Epigenetics changes in gene expression (without changes in the DNA itself) that are inheritable.

Ethnocentric refers to judgment of other cultures solely in terms of one's own culture.

Ethnographer a person who spends some time living with, interviewing, and observing a group of people so that he or she can describe their customs.

Ethnographic Analogy method of comparative cultural study that extrapolates to the past from recent or current societies.

Ethnography a detailed description of aspects of cultural behaviours and customs based on observation.

Ethnohistorian an ethnologist who uses historical documents to study how a particular culture has changed over time.

Ethnology the study of how and why recent cultures differ and are similar.

Ethnomedicine the health-related beliefs, knowledge, and practices of a cultural group.

Experimental Archaeology a specialty within archaeology used to explore a variety of historical questions, especially those related to diet and subsistence, by reproducing or replicating technological traits and patterns observed in the archaeological record.

Explanation an answer to a question. In science, there are two kinds of explanation that researchers try to achieve: associations and theories.

Features the non-portable portions of an archaeological site, some of which can include artifacts.

Fission-Track Dating a chronometric dating method used to date crystal, glass, and many uranium-rich materials contemporaneous with fossils or deposits that are from 20 to 5 billion years old. This dating method entails counting the tracks or paths of decaying uranium-isotope atoms in the sample and then comparing the number of tracks with the uranium content of the sample.

Food Collection all forms of subsistence technology in which food-getting is dependent on naturally occurring resources—wild plants and animals.

Food Production the form of subsistence technology in which food-getting is dependent on the cultivation and domestication of plants and animals.

Foragers people who subsist on the collection of naturally occurring plants and animals. Also referred to as *hunter-gatherers*.

Foramen Magnum the hole in the base of the skull through which the spinal cord passes en route to the brain.

Fossilization the process of becoming a fossil by the replacement of organic materials with an inorganic mineral matrix.

Fossil Locales places where fossilized remains of once-living organisms are found.

Fossils the hardened remains or impressions of plants and animals that lived in the past.

F-U-N Trio fluorine (F), uranium (U), and nitrogen (N) tests for relative dating. All three minerals are present in groundwater. The older a fossil is, the higher its fluorine or uranium content will be, and the lower its nitrogen content.

Funerary Archaeology the study of burial customs from archaeological evidence.

Gas Chromatography an analytical technique for determining the relative proportions of different substances within a sample.

Gene chemical unit of heredity.

Gene Flow the process by which genes pass from the gene pool of one population to that of another through mating and reproduction.

Genetic Drift the various random processes that affect gene frequencies in small, relatively isolated populations.

Genetic Recombination a random shuffling of the parents' genes.

Genome the complete genetic makeup of an organism.

Genotype the total complement of inherited traits or genes of an organism.

Genus a group of related species; pl., *genera*.

Geographic Information System (GIS) an integrated software package for the input, analysis, and display of spatial information.

Gloger's Rule the rule that populations of birds and mammals living in warm, humid climates have more melanin (and therefore darker skin, fur, or feathers) than populations of the same species living in cooler, drier areas.

Group Selection natural selection of group characteristics.
Half-Life the time it takes for half of the atoms of a radioactive substance to decay into atoms of a different substance.
Haplorhines tarsiers and anthropoids.
Heritability the concept that traits are inherited from parent to offspring.
Heterozygous possessing differing genes or alleles in corresponding locations on a pair of chromosomes.
Hieroglyphics "picture writing," as in ancient Egypt and in Mayan sites in Mesoamerica (Mexico and Central America).
Historical Archaeology a specialty within archaeology that studies the material remains of recent peoples who left written records.
Historical Linguistics the study of how languages change over time.
Holistic refers to an approach that studies many aspects of a multifaceted system.
Hominins the group of hominoids consisting of humans and their direct ancestors. It contains at least two genera: *Homo* and *Australopithecus*.
Hominoids the group of catarrhines that includes both apes and humans.
Homo genus to which modern humans and their ancestors belong.
Homo antecessor a proposed last common ancestor between Neandertals and modern humans.
Homo erectus the first hominin species to be widely distributed in the Old World. The earliest finds are possibly 1.8 million years old. The brain (averaging 895–1040 cc) was larger than that found in any of the australopithecines or *H. habilis* but smaller than the average brain of a modern human.
Homo ergaster classification given by some for *Homo erectus* remains from Africa.
Homo floresiensis a distinct species closely related to *Homo erectus* and found only on the Indonesian island of Flores. They are tiny, with cranial capacities of about 380 cc.
Homo habilis early species belonging to our genus, *Homo*, with cranial capacities averaging about 630–640 cc, about 50 percent of the brain capacity of modern humans. Dating from about 2 million years ago.
Homo heidelbergensis classification given by some for *Homo erectus* remains from Europe.
Homo rudolfensis early species belonging to our genus, *Homo*. Similar enough to *Homo habilis* that some palaeoanthropologists make no distinction between the two.
Homo sapiens all living people belong to one biological species, *Homo sapiens*, which means that all human populations on earth can successfully interbreed. The first *Homo sapiens* may have emerged by 200 000 years ago.
Homo sapiens neandertalensis a variety of early *Homo sapiens*.
Homo sapiens sapiens modern-looking humans, undisputed examples of which appeared about 50 000 years ago; may have appeared earlier.
Homozygous possessing two identical genes or alleles in corresponding locations on a pair of chromosomes.
Horticulture plant cultivation carried out with relatively simple tools and methods; nature replaces nutrients in the soil, in the absence of permanently cultivated fields.
Human Palaeontology the study of the emergence of humans and their later physical evolution. Also called *palaeoanthropology*.
Human Variation the study of how and why contemporary human populations vary biologically.
Hybridization the creation of a viable offspring from the mating of two different species.
Hylobates the family of hominoids that includes gibbons and siamangs; often referred to as the *lesser apes* (as compared with the *great apes*, such as gorillas and chimpanzees).
Hypothesis a proposition intended to explain facts or phenomena.
Hypoxia a condition of oxygen deficiency that often occurs at high altitudes. The percentage of oxygen in the air is the same as at lower altitudes, but because the barometric pressure is lower, less oxygen is taken in with each breath. Often, breathing becomes more rapid, the heart beats faster, and activity is more difficult.
Incisors the front teeth; used for holding or seizing food and preparing it for chewing by the other teeth.
Indirect Percussion a toolmaking technique common in the Upper Palaeolithic. After shaping a core into a pyramidal or cylindrical form, the toolmaker could put a punch of antler or wood or another hard material into position and strike it with a hammer. Using a hammer-struck punch enabled the toolmaker to strike off consistently shaped blades.
Individual Selection natural selection of individual characteristics.
Insectivore the order or major grouping of mammals, including modern shrews and moles, that is adapted to feeding on insects.
Intensive Agriculture food production characterized by the permanent cultivation of fields and made possible by the use of the plow, draft animals or machines, fertilizers, irrigation, water-storage techniques, and other complex agricultural techniques.
^{40}**K (Potassium-40)** a radioactive form of potassium that decays at an established rate and forms argon-40 used in K-Ar dating.
Kenyanthropus platyops a nearly complete 3.5 million-year-old skull found in western Kenya. It is thought by

some scholars to be a species of australopithecine (and hence should not be regarded as a separate genus).

Kenyapithecus an ape-like primate from the middle Miocene found in East Africa. It had very thickly enamelled teeth and robust jaws, suggesting a diet of hard, tough foods. Probably somewhat terrestrial.

Knuckle Walking a locomotor pattern of primates such as the chimpanzee and gorilla in which the weight of the upper part of the body is supported on the thickly padded knuckles of the hands.

Lamarck, Jean-Baptiste (1744–1829) a French naturalist who proposed a theory of evolution through the inheritance of acquired characteristics.

Law associations or relationships that almost all scientists accept.

Law of Superposition a law that states that older layers at an archaeological site are generally deeper or lower than more recent layers. The law of superposition provides a framework with which to make inferences regarding the relationship and relative date of cumulative layers of different strata.

Levalloisian Method a method that allowed flake tools of a predetermined size to be produced from a shaped core. The toolmaker first shaped the core and prepared a "striking platform" at one end. Flakes of predetermined and standard sizes could then be knocked off. Although some Levallois flakes date from as far back as 400 000 years ago, they are found more frequently in Mousterian tool kits.

Linguistics the study of language.

Linnaeus, Carolus (1707–78) a Swedish naturalist who looked at the similarities and differences among organisms and created a system for naming, ranking, and classifying organisms that is still in use today. This system defined the fundamentals of biology in terms of nomenclature and classification.

Lithics the technical name for the tools made from stone.

Lumbar Curve found only in hominins; the bottom part of the vertebral column forms a curve, causing the spinal column to be S-shaped (as seen from the side).

Material Culture objects that people have and make.

Measure to describe how something compares with other things on some scale of variation.

Meiosis the process by which reproductive cells are formed. In this process of division, the number of chromosomes in the newly formed cells is reduced by half, so that when fertilization occurs the resulting organism has the normal number of chromosomes appropriate to its species, rather than double that number.

Menarche the onset of first menstruation in young women.

Mesolithic the archaeological period in the Old World beginning about 12 000 B.C. Humans were starting to settle down in semipermanent camps and villages as people began to depend less on big game (which they used to have to follow over long distances) and more on relatively stationary food resources such as fish, shellfish, small game, and wild plants rich in carbohydrates, proteins, and oils.

Messenger RNA (mRNA) a type of ribonucleic acid that is used in the cell to copy the DNA code for use in protein synthesis.

Microlith a small, razor-like blade fragment that was probably attached in a series to a wooden or bone handle to form a cutting edge.

Midden a pile of refuse, often shells, in an archaeological site.

Middle Palaeolithic the time period of the Mousterian stone tool tradition.

Miocene the geological epoch from 24 million to 5.2 million years ago.

Mitosis cellular reproduction or growth involving the duplication of chromosome pairs.

Molars the large teeth behind the premolars at the back of the jaw; used for chewing and grinding food.

Molecular Anthropology the study of anthropological questions using genetic evidence.

Mousterian Tool Assemblage named after the tool assemblage found in a rock shelter at Le Moustier in the Dordogne region of southwestern France. Compared with an Acheulian assemblage, the Middle Palaeolithic (40 000–300 000 years ago) Mousterian has a smaller proportion of large core tools such as hand axes and cleavers and a bigger proportion of small flake tools such as scrapers. Flakes were often altered or "retouched" by striking small flakes or chips from one or more edges.

Multiregional Hypothesis the theory that anatomically modern humans evolved *in situ* in a variety of different regions around the world.

Mutation a change in the DNA sequence, producing an altered gene.

Natural Selection the outcome of processes that affect the frequencies of traits in a particular environment. Traits that enhance survival and reproductive success increase in frequency over time.

Neandertal the common name for the species *Homo neandertalensis*.

Neolithic originally meaning "the new Stone Age," now meaning the presence of domesticated plants and animals. The earliest evidence of domestication comes from the Near East about 8000 B.C.

Nocturnal active during the night.

Normalizing Selection the type of natural selection that removes harmful genes that arose by mutation.

Nutritional Anthropology seeks to understand the impact of various biocultural factors on the health and nutrition of a population. Nutritional anthropology can help to establish evidence on which public health policy changes or recommendations can be made.

Obsidian Hydration the absorption of water by a piece of obsidian when it is newly exposed to the atmosphere through natural forces or human activity. The layer that is being weathered is invisible, but its thickness can be measured and will depend on the time it has been exposed.

Occipital Torus a ridge of bone running horizontally across the back of the skull in apes and some hominins.

Oldowan the earliest stone toolmaking tradition, named after the tools found in Bed I at Olduvai Gorge, Tanzania, from about 2.5 million years ago. The stone artifacts include core tools and sharp-edged flakes made by striking one stone against another. Flake tools predominate. Among the core tools, so-called choppers are common.

Oligocene the geological epoch 34 million to 24 million years ago during which definite anthropoids emerged.

Omnivorous eating both meat and vegetation.

Omomyid a type of prosimian with many tarsier-like features that appeared in the early Eocene.

Opposable Thumb a thumb that can touch the tips of all the other fingers.

Orrorin tugenensis an apparently bipedal primate dating to between 5.8 million and 6 million years ago, making it possibly the earliest known hominin.

Osteology the study of the form and function of the skeleton.

Palaeoanthropology the study of the emergence of humans and their later physical evolution. Also called *human palaeontology*.

Palaeo-Arctic Tradition the first undisputed cultural development in the Arctic, after the more tentative early occupation sites associated with the peopling of the New World. The earliest well-documented Palaeo-Arctic sites occur from 8000 B.C. to 5000 B.C.

Palaeodemography the study of demographic structure and processes in past populations from archaeological evidence.

Palaeoethnobotany the study of plant remains from archaeological contexts.

Palaeomagnetic Dating a method used to identify the geomagnetic patterns in rocks, and to date the fossils within those rocks.

Palaeopathology the study of health and disease in the past from skeletal evidence.

Paleocene the geological epoch 65 million to 55 million years ago.

Palynology the study of pollen from archaeological contexts.

Paranthropoids a later group of hominin usually differentiated from the australopithecines by their heavier dentition and larger faces.

Paranthropus aethiopicus the earliest paranthropoid.

Paranthropus boisei an East African robust australopithecine species dating from 2.3 million to 1 million years ago with somewhat larger cranial capacity than *A. africanus*. No longer thought to be larger than other australopithecines, it is robust primarily in the skull and jaw, most strikingly in the teeth. Compared with *P. robustus*, *P. boisei* has even more features that reflect a huge chewing apparatus.

Paranthropus robustus a South African species found in South African caves dating from about 2.3 million to 1 million years ago.

Parapithecids small monkey-like Oligocene primates found in the Fayum area of Egypt.

Percussion Flaking a toolmaking technique in which one stone is struck with another to remove a flake.

Phenotype the observable physical appearance of an organism, which may or may not reflect its genotype or total genetic constitution.

Physical Anthropology See *Biological Anthropology*.

Phytolith microscopic granules of silicon dioxide that enter a plant's cells and take their shape.

Pierolapithecus a middle Miocene ape that had wrists and vertebrae that would have made it capable of brachiation, but also relatively short fingers like modern monkeys.

Platyrrhines the group of anthropoids that have broad, flat-bridged noses, with nostrils facing outward; these monkeys are currently found only in the New World (Central and South America).

Plesiadapis The most well known of the plesiadapiforms, possibly an archaic primate.

Pliocene the geological epoch 5.2 million to 1.6 million years ago during which the earliest definite hominins appeared.

Polymerase Chain Reaction (PCR) technique for accurate recovery of ancient DNA. PCR requires only a few molecules for the amplification of DNA sequences from trace amounts of the original genetic material.

Pongids hominoids whose members include both the living and extinct apes.

Potassium-Argon (K-Ar) Dating a chronometric dating method that uses the rate of decay of a radioactive form of potassium (^{40}K) into argon (^{40}Ar) to date samples from 5000 to 3 billion years old. The K-Ar method dates the minerals and rocks in a deposit, not the fossils themselves.

Practising Anthropology See *Applied Anthropology*.

Prehensile adapted for grasping objects.

Prehistoric in the time before written records.

Premolars the teeth immediately behind the canines; used in chewing, grinding, and shearing food.

Pressure Flaking toolmaking technique whereby small flakes are struck off by pressing against the core with a bone, antler, or wood tool.

Primate a member of the mammalian order Primates divided into the two suborders of prosimians and anthropoids.
Primatologists people who study primates.
Probability Value (p-Value) the likelihood that the observed result could have occurred by chance.
Proconsul the best-known genus of proto-apes from the Early Miocene; found mostly in Africa.
Prognathic a physical feature that is sticking out or pushed forward, such as the faces in apes and some hominin species.
Propliopithecids ape-like anthropoids dating from the early Oligocene, found in the Fayum area of Egypt.
Prosimians literally "premonkeys," one of the two suborders of primates; includes lemurs, lorises, and tarsiers.
Provenience the location of an artifact or feature within a site. Also called *provenance*.
Quadrupeds animals that walk on all fours.
Rachis the seed-bearing part of a plant. In the wild variety the rachis shatters easily, releasing the seeds. Domesticated grains have a tough rachis, which does not shatter easily.
Radiocarbon Dating a dating method that uses the decay of carbon-14 to date organic remains. It is reliable for dating once-living matter up to 50 000 years old.
Random Sample a sample in which all cases selected have had an equal chance to be included.
Recessive an allele phenotypically suppressed in the heterozygous form and expressed only in the homozygous form.
Relative Dating a method of dating fossils that determines the age of a specimen or deposit relative to a known specimen or deposit.
Remodelling occurs after growth has ceased and replaces old tissue with new formed bone to maintain bone strength from microscopic fractures from normal biomechanical stress.
Ribosome a structure in the cell used in making proteins.
Sagittal Crest a ridge of bone along the midline of the top of the skull for muscle attachment.
Sagittal Keel an inverted V-shaped ridge running along the top of the skull in *Homo erectus*.
Sahelanthropus tchadensis a hominoid found in Chad dating to about 7 million years ago.
Sampling Universe the list of cases to be sampled from.
Scientific Method a process that involves the formulation of a problem, the collection of data through observation and experiment, and the formulation and testing of hypotheses.
Secular Trend a change in growth and developmental measures over time.
Sedentism settling in a single, permanent location.
Sediment the dust, debris, and decay that accumulates over time.

Segregation the random sorting of chromosomes in meiosis.
Settlement Archaeology the study of settlement patterns within the archaeological record.
Sexually Dimorphic refers to a species in which males differ markedly from females in size and appearance.
Shifting Cultivation a type of horticulture in which the land is worked for short periods and then left to regenerate for some years before being used again.
Sickle-Cell Anemia (Sicklemia) a condition in which red blood cells assume a crescent (sickle) shape when deprived of oxygen, instead of the normal (disk) shape. The sickle-shaped red blood cells do not move through the body as readily as normal cells, and thus cause damage to the heart, lungs, brain, and other vital organs.
Single-Origin (or Replacement) Hypothesis the theory that anatomically modern humans evolved in a single region, Africa, and then replaced all existing Archaic populations in other regions of the world.
Site Catchment Analysis an analysis based on the assumption that the more dispersed resources are from habitation sites, the less likely they are to be exploited by a population.
Site Formation Process environmental and cultural factors that affect how and where materials are deposited at an archaeological site or fossil locale.
Sivapithecus a genus of ape from the later Miocene known for its thickly enamelled teeth, suggesting a diet of hard, tough, or gritty items. Found primarily in western and southern Asia and now thought to be ancestral to orangutans.
Skeletal Age-Indicator Techniques osteological techniques that are used to estimate the age at death of an individual from skeletal remains.
Slash-and-Burn Techniques a form of shifting cultivation in which the natural vegetation is cut down and burned off. The cleared ground is used for a short time and then left to regenerate.
Socialization a term used by anthropologists and psychologists to describe the development, through the direct and indirect influence of parents and others, of children's patterns of behaviour (and attitudes and values) that conform to cultural expectations.
Sociobiology See *Behavioural Ecology*.
Socio-cultural Anthropology See *Cultural Anthropology*.
Sociolinguistics the study of cultural and sub-cultural patterns of speaking in different social contexts.
Speciation the development of a new species.
Species a population that consists of organisms able to interbreed and produce fertile and viable offspring.
Stable Isotopes isotopes of the same elements with different atomic masses.

State a political unit with centralized decision making affecting a large population. Most states have cities with public buildings; full-time craft and religious specialists; an "official" art style; a hierarchical social structure topped by an elite class; and a governmental monopoly on the legitimate use of force to implement policies.

Stationary in demography, a population is considered to be stationary when there is no in-migration or out-migration and the number of deaths equals the number of births per year.

Statistical Association a relationship or correlation between two or more variables that is unlikely to be due to chance alone.

Statistically Significant refers to a result that would occur very rarely by chance. The result would occur fewer than 5 times out of 100.

Stratigraphy the study of how different rock formations and fossils are laid down in successive layers or strata. Older layers are generally deeper or lower than more recent layers. See also *Law of Superposition*.

Strepsirhines lemurs and lorises.

Structural Linguistics the study of how languages are constructed. Also called *descriptive linguistics*.

Subsistence Technology the methods humans use to procure food.

Subsurface Techniques archaeological survey techniques that map features beneath the surface.

Surface Techniques archaeological survey techniques for finding and assessing archaeological sites from surface finds.

Taphonomy the study of changes that occur to organisms or objects after being buried or deposited.

Taurodontism having teeth with an enlarged pulp cavity.

Technology constructions such as traps, skills required to use these constructions, and the organizations needed to extract, process, and redistribute resources.

Terrestrial adapted to living on the ground.

Theory a set of statements or principles intended to explain a group of facts or phenomena.

Thermoluminescence Dating a dating technique that is well suited to samples of ancient pottery, brick, tile, or terracotta, which (when they were made) were heated to a high temperature that released trapped electrons from radioactive elements around it; the electrons trapped after manufacture emit light when heated, so the age of the object can be estimated by measuring how much light is emitted when the object is heated.

Trace Elements elements found in extremely small amounts within the body.

Type II Diabetes non-insulin-dependent diabetes mellitus (NIDDM), unlike insulin-dependent diabetes, that tends to manifest itself in adult patients as a result of a sedentary lifestyle, chronic obesity, and excess sugar intake.

Typology a way of organizing artifacts in categories based on their particular characteristics.

Unifacial Tool a tool worked or flaked on one side only.

Uniformitarianism the concept that processes in the past must have behaved in the same manner as they are observed to behave today, and will do so in the future. This is an assumption that is often applied to geological processes (e.g., erosion) or biological processes (e.g., interaction of mortality and fertility).

Upper Palaeolithic the period associated with the emergence of modern humans and their spread around the world.

Uranium-Series Dating a technique for dating *Homo sapiens* sites that uses the decay of two kinds of uranium (^{235}U and ^{238}U) into other isotopes (such as ^{230}Th—thorium). Particularly useful in cave sites. Different types of uranium-series dating use different isotope ratios.

Variable a thing or quantity that varies.

Variation differences in the genotype and phenotype of individual members of a species.

Vertical Clinging and Leaping a locomotor pattern characteristic of several primates, including tarsiers and galagos. The animal normally rests by clinging to a branch in a vertical position and uses its hind limbs alone to push off from one vertical position to another.

Virgin Soil Epidemic occurs when a disease enters a population that has not been previously exposed to it, or has not had exposure for a considerably long time. Because there is no previous immunity within a portion of the population, the disease tends to affect all members of the group equally.

"Y-5" Pattern refers to the pattern of cusps on human molars. When looked at from the top, the cusps of the molars form a Y opening toward the cheek.

Zooarchaeology the study of animals' remains from archaeological contexts.

Literature Cited

Abi-Rached L, Jobin MJ, Kulkarni S, McWhinnie A, Dalva K, Gragert L, Babrzadeh F, Gharizadeh B, Luo M, Plummer FA, Kimani J. 2011. The shaping of modern human immune systems by multiregional admixture with archaic humans. Science. 334(6052):89–94.

Adams R. 1981. Heartland of cities: surveys of ancient settlement and land use on the central floodplain of the Euphrates. Chicago: University of Chicago Press.

Adams RM. September 1960. The origin of cities. Scientific American. 153.

Aiello LC. 1992. Body size and energy requirements. In: Jones S, Martin R, Pilbeam D, editors. The Cambridge Encyclopedia of Human Evolution. Cambridge: Cambridge University Press. pp. 41–44.

Aiello LC. 1993. The origin of the New World Monkeys. In: Lavocat GW, Lavocat R, editors. The Africa–South America Connection. Oxford: Clarendon Press. pp. 100–118.

Aiello LC, Collard M. 29 November 2001. Palaeoanthropology—our newest oldest ancestor? Nature. 410:526–527.

Aiello LC, Dean C. 1990. An introduction to human evolutionary anatomy. London: Academic Press.

Aitken MJ. 1985. Thermoluminescence dating. London: Academic Press.

Alberts B, Bray D, Lewis J, Raff M, Roberts K, Watson JD. 1983. Molecular biology of the cell. New York: Garland.

Alemseged Z, Spoor F, Kimbel WH, Bobe R, Geraads D, Reed D, Wynn JG. 2006. A juvenile early hominin skeleton from Dikika, Ethiopia. Nature. 443:296–301.

Alexander JP. August 1992. Alas, poor *Notharctus*. Natural History. 55–59.

Allen JS, Lambert AJ, Attah Johnson FY, Schmidt K, Nero KL. 1996. Antisaccadic eye movements and attentional asymmetry in schizophrenia in three Pacific populations. Acta Psychiatrica Scandinavia. 94:258–265.

Allen KMS, Green SW, Zubrow EBW. 1990. Interpreting space: GIS and archaeology. London: Taylor & Francis.

Almécija S, Tallman M, Alba DM, Pina M, Moyà-Solà S, Jungers WL. 2013. The femur of *Orrorin tugenensis* exhibits morphometric affinities with both Miocene apes and later hominins. Nature Communications. 4:1–12.

Alperson-Afil N, Sharon G, Kislev M, Melamed Y, Zohar I, Ashkenazi S, Rabinovich R, Biton R, Werker E, Hartman G, Feibel C. 2009. Spatial organization of hominin activities at Gesher Benot Ya'aqov, Israel. Science. 326(5960):1677–1680.

Alroy J. 2001. A multispecies overkill simulation of the End-Pleistocene megafaunal mass extinction. Science. 292:1893–1896.

Ames KM, Richards MP, Speller CF, Yang DY, Lyman RL, Butler VL. 2015. Stable isotope and ancient DNA analysis of dog remains from Cathlapotle (45CL1), a contact-era site on the Lower Columbia River. Journal of Archaeological Science. 57:268–282.

Amnesty International. 2004. Stolen sisters: A human rights response to discrimination and violence against Indigenous women in Canada. London: Amnesty International.

Andersen RE. 2000. The spread of the childhood obesity epidemic. Canadian Medical Association Journal. 163:1461–1432.

Andrews P. 2000. Propliopithecidae. In: Tattersall I, Delson E, van Couvering J, editors. Encyclopedia of human evolution and prehistory. New York: Garland. pp. 485–487.

Ankel-Simons F. 2007. Primate anatomy. 3rd ed. San Diego: Academic Press.

Anonymous. 1967. Textor RB, comp. A cross-cultural summary. New Haven, CT: HRAF Press.

Anonymous. 5 March 1973. The first dentist. Newsweek. 73.

Anonymous. 1980. Paper. In: Academic American encyclopedia. Princeton, NJ: Areté.

Anonymous. 1988. Webster's new world dictionary. Third College ed. New York: Webster's New World.

Anonymous. 1990a. Appendix A: report of the Committee on Ethics, Society for Applied Anthropology, and Appendix F: Professional and ethical responsibilities, SFAA. In: Fluehr-Lobban C, editor. Ethics and the profession of anthropology: dialogue for a new era. Philadelphia: University of Pennsylvania Press.

Anonymous. 1990b. Appendix C: Statements on ethics: principles of professional responsibility, adopted by the Council of the American Anthropological Association, May 1971 (as amended through May 1976) and Appendix I: Revised principles of professional responsibility. In: Fluehr-Lobban C, editor. Ethics and the profession of anthropology: dialogue for a new era. Philadelphia: University of Pennsylvania Press.

Anonymous. 19 April 1996. The last of the Cahokians. Science. 351.

Anonymous. 1997a. Clyde Snow. Current Biography. 58:52–54.

Anonymous. 1997b. EAAF (Argentine Forensic Anthropological Team), annual report.

Anonymous. 1997c. The first tool kit. Science [31 January]. 623.

Anonymous. February 1998. Printing, typography, and photoengraving: history of prints: origins in China: transmission of paper to Europe (12th century). Britannica Online.

Anton SC. 1997. Developmental age and taxonomic affinity of the Mojokerto Child, Java, Indonesia. American Journal of Physical Anthropology. 102:497–514.

Aptekar L. 1994. Environmental disasters in global perspective. New York: G.K. Hall/Macmillan.

Arensburg B, Schepartz LA, Tillier AM, Vandemeersch B, Rak Y. 1990. A reappraisal of the anatomical basis for speech in Middle Palaeolithic hominids. American Journal of Physical Anthropology. 83(2):137–146.

Armelagos GJ, Harper KH. 2005. Genomics at the origins of agriculture, part two. Evolutionary Anthropology. 14:109–121.

Arsuaga JL, Martinez I, Gracia A, Lorenzo C. 1993. The Sima de los Huesos crania (Sierra de Atapuerca, Spain): a comparative study. Journal of Human Evolution. 33(2/3):219–282.

Arsuaga JL, Martinez I, Lorenzo C, Gracia A, Munoz A, Alonso O, Gallego J. 1999. The human cranial remains from Gran Dolina Lower Pleistocene site (Sierra de Atapuerca, Spain). Journal of Human Evolution. 37:431–457.

Asch NB, Asch DL. 1978. The economic potential of *Iva annua* and its prehistoric importance in the lower Illinois Valley. In: Ford RI, editor. The nature and status of ethnobotany. Anthropological Papers. Museum of Anthropology No. 67. Ann Arbor: University of Michigan. pp. 301–342.

Asfaw B, White T, Lovejoy CO, Latimer B, Simpson S, Suwa G. 1999. *Australopithecus garhi*: a new species of early hominid from Ethiopia. Science. 284(5414):629–635.

Ayala FJ. 22 December 1995. The myth of Eve: molecular biology and human origins. Science. 270(5244):1930–1936.

Badcock C. 2000. Evolutionary psychology: a critical introduction. Cambridge: Blackwell.

Bahn PG. 1998. Neanderthals emancipated. Nature. 394:719–720.

Bahn PG. 1999. The Cambridge illustrated history of archaeology. Cambridge: Cambridge University Press.

Bailey GN, editor. 1981. Hunter-gatherer economy in prehistory. Cambridge: Cambridge University Press.

Bailey RC, Head G, Jenike M, Owen B, Rechtman R, Zechenter E. 1989. Hunting and gathering in tropical rain forest: is it possible? American Anthropologist. 91:59–82.

Balter M. 2007. Seeking agriculture's ancient roots. Science. 316:1830–1835.

Balter M. 2009. Better homes and hearths, Neandertal-style. Science. 326:1056–1057.

Balzeau A, Grimaud HD, Jacob T. 2005. Internal cranial features of the Mojokerto Child fossil (East Java, Indonesia). Journal of Human Evolution. 48:535–553.

Barash DP. 1977. Sociobiology and behavior. New York: Elsevier.

Baraybar JP. 2014. Forensic anthropology: investigating human rights violations. In: Smith C, editor. Encyclopedia of global archaeology. New York: Springer. pp. 2835–2839.

Bard KA. 2008. An introduction to the archaeology of ancient Egypt. Malden, MA: Blackwell.

Barnett T, Blaikie P. 1992. AIDS in Africa: its present and future impact. London: Belhaven.

Barnosky A, Koch P, Feranec R, Wing S, Shabel A. 2004. Assessing the causes of Late Pleistocene extinctions on the continents. Science. 306:70–75.

Barrett DE. 1984. Malnutrition and child behavior: conceptualization, assessment and an empirical study of social-emotional functioning. In: Brozek J, Schürch B, editors. Malnutrition and behavior: critical assessment of key issues. Lausanne, Switzerland: Nestlé Foundation. pp. 280–306.

Bathurst RR. 2005. Archaeological evidence of intestinal parasites from coastal shell middens. Journal of Archaeological Science. 31(1):115–123.

Bathurst RR, Barta JL. 31 July 2004. Molecular evidence of tuberculosis induced hypertrophic osteopathy in a 16th-century Iroquoian dog. Journal of Archaeological Science. 31(7):917–925.

Beadle G, Beadle M. 1966. The language of life. Garden City, NY: Doubleday.

Bearder SK. 1987. Lorises, bushbabies, and tarsiers: diverse societies in solitary foragers. In: Smuts BB, Cheney DL, Seyfarth RM, Wrangham RW, Struhsaker TT, editors. Primate societies. Chicago: University of Chicago Press. pp. 11–24.

Beattie O, Apland B, Blake EW, Cosgrove JA, Gaunt S, Greer S, Mackie AP, Mackie KE, Straathof D, Thorp V, Troffe PM. 2000. The Kwäday Dän Ts'ínchi discovery from a glacier in British Columbia. Canadian Journal of Archaeology. 24(1):129–147.

Beaumont PB. 2011. The edge: more on fire-making by about 1.7 million years ago at Wonderwerk Cave in South Africa. Current Anthropology. 52:585–595.

Begun DR, 1998. Miocene apes. In: Ember CR, Ember M, Peregrine PN, editors. Research frontiers in anthropology. Upper Saddle River, NJ: Prentice Hall/Simon & Schuster Custom Publishing.

Begun DR. 2010. Miocene hominids and the origins of the African apes and humans. Annual Review of Anthropology. 39:67-84.

Begun DR, Ward CV. 2005. Comment on *Pierolapithecus catalaunicus*, a new Middle Miocene great ape from Spain. Science. 308:203c.

Bellwood P. 2005. First farmers. Malden, MA: Blackwell.

Benyshek DC, Martin JF, Johnston CS. 2001. A reconsideration of the origins of the Type 2 diabetes epidemic among Native Americans and the implications for intervention policy. Medical Anthropology. 20:25–64.

Berg C, Blomqvist A, Holm L, Brandt I, Brunström B, Ridderstråle Y. 2004. Embryonic exposure to oestrogen causes eggshell thinning and altered shell gland carbonic anhydrase expression in the domestic hen. Reproduction. 128:455–461.

Berg P, Singer M. 1992. Dealing with genes: the language of heredity. Mill Valley, CA: University Science Books. pp. 53, 221–244.

Berge C, Penin X, Pelle E. 2006. New interpretation of Laetoli footprints using an experimental approach and procrustes analysis: preliminary results. Comptes Rendus Palevol. 5:561–569.

Berger LR, de Ruiter DJ, Churchill SE, Schmid P, Carlson KJ, Dirks PH, Kibii JM. 2010. *Australopithecus sediba*: a new species of *Homo*-like australopith from South Africa. Science. 328 (April 9):195–204.

Berger LR, Hawks J, de Ruiter DJ, Churchill SE, Schmid P, Delezene LK, Kivell TL, Garvin HM, Williams SA, DeSilva JM, et al. 2015. *Homo naledi*, a new species of the genus *Homo* from the Dinaledi Chamber, South Africa. Elife. 4:e09560.

Berlin EA. 1996. General overview of Maya ethnomedicine: the gastrointestinal diseases. In: Berlin AE, Berlin B, editors. Medical ethnobiology of the Highland Maya of Chiapas, Mexico. Princeton, NJ: Princeton University Press. pp. 52–53.

Bermúdez de Castro JM, Arsuaga JL, Carbonell E, Rosas A, Martínez I, Mosquera M. 1997. A hominid from the Lower Pleistocene of Atapuerca, Spain: possible ancestor to Neandertals and modern humans. Science. 276:1392–1395.

Bermúdez de Castro JM, Nicolás ME. 1997. Palaeodemography of the Atapuerca-SH Middle Pleistocene hominid sample. Journal of Human Evolution. 33:333–355.

Berry JW, Poortinga YH, Segall MH, Dasen PR. 1992. Cross-cultural psychology: research and applications. New York: Cambridge University Press.

Berti PR, Chan HM, Receveur O, MacDonald CR, Kuhnlein HV. 1998a. Population exposure to radioactivity from consumption of caribou among the Dene/Métis of Denendeh (western Northwest Territories, Canada). Journal of Exposure Analysis and Environmental Epidemiology. 8:145–158.

Berti PR, Receveur O, Chan HM, Kuhnlein HV. 1998b. Dietary exposure to chemical contaminants from traditional food among adult Dene/Métis in the western Northwest Territories, Canada. Environmental Research. 76:131–142.

Bilsborough A. 1992. Human evolution. New York: Blackie Academic & Professional.

Bindon JR, Baker PT. 1985. Modernization, migration and obesity among Samoan adults. Annals of Human Biology. 12:67–76.

Binford LR. 1971. Post-Pleistocene adaptations. In: Struever S, editor. Prehistoric agriculture. Garden City, NY: Natural History Press. pp. 27–33.

Binford LR. 1972. Mortuary practices: their study and potential. In: An anthropological perspective. New York: Seminar Press. pp. 208–243.

Binford LR. 1973. Interassemblage variability: the Mousterian and the "functional" argument. In: Renfew C, editor. The explanation of culture change: models in prehistory. Pittsburgh: University of Pittsburgh Press. pp. 227–254.

Binford LR. 1984. Faunal remains from Klasies River mouth. Orlando, FL: Academic Press.

Binford LR. 1987. Were there elephant hunters at Torralba? In: Nitecki M, Nitecki DV, editors. The evolution of human hunting. New York: Plenum. pp. 47–105.

Binford LR. 1990. Mobility, housing, and environment: a comparative study. Journal of Anthropological Research. 46:119–152.

Binford LR, Ho CK. 1985. Taphonomy at a distance: Zhoukoudian, "the cave home of Beijing Man"? Current Anthropology. 26:413–442.

Binford SR, Binford LR. April 1969. Stone tools and human behavior. Scientific American. 220:70–84.

Bird A. 2007. Perceptions of epigenetics. Nature. 447(7143):396–398.

Bischoff I, Schröder S, Misof B. 2009. Differentiation and range expansion of North American squash bee, *Peponapis pruinosa* (Apidae: Apiformes) populations assessed by geometric wing morphometry. Annals of the Entomological Society of America. 102(1):60–69.

Black FL. 11 December 1992. Why did they die? Science. 258:1739–1740.

Blaffer Hrdy S. 1977. The langurs of Abu: female and male strategies of reproduction. Cambridge, MA: Harvard University Press.

Blanchard JF, Ludwig S, Wajda A, Dean H, Anderson K, Kendall O, Depew N. 1996. Incidence and prevalence of diabetes mellitus in Manitoba, 1986–1991. Diabetes Care. 19:807–811.

Blanton RE. 1976. The origins of Monte Albán. In: Cleland CE, editor. Cultural continuity and change. New York: Academic Press. pp. 223–232.

Blanton RE. 1978. Monte Albán: settlement patterns at the ancient Zapotec capital. New York: Academic Press.

Blanton RE. 1981. The rise of cities. In: Sabloff JA, editor. Supplement to the Handbook of Middle American Indians. Volume 1. Austin: University of Texas Press. p. 397.

Blanton RE, Kowalewski SA, Feinman G, Appel J. 1981. Ancient Mesoamerica: a comparison of change in three regions. New York: Cambridge University Press.

Blendon RJ, Benson JM, DesRoches CM, Raleigh E, Taylor-Clark K. 2004. The public's response to severe acute respiratory syndrome in Toronto and the United States. Clinical Infectious Diseases. 38:925–931.

Block JI, Boyer DM. 22 November 2002. Grasping primate origins. Science. 298:1606–1610.

Blumler MA, Byrne R. 1991. The ecological genetics of domestication and the origins of agriculture. Current Anthropology. 32:23–35.

Bocquet-Appel JP. 2008. Recent advances in paleodemography. Dordrecht: Springer.

Bodley JH. 1990. Victims of progress. 3rd ed. Mountain View, CA: Mayfield.

Boesch C, Boesch H. 1990. Tool use and tool making in wild chimpanzees. Folia Primatology (Basel). 54:86–99.

Bogin B. 1988. Patterns of human growth. Cambridge: Cambridge University Press.

Bogin B. 1997. Evolutionary hypotheses for human childhood. Yearbook of Physical Anthropology. 40:63–89.

Bogin B, MacVean RB. 1981. Nutritional and biological determinants of body fat patterning in urban Guatemalan children. Human Biology. 53:259–268.

Bogin B, Sullivan T. 1986. Socioeconomic status, sex, age, and ethnicity as determinants of body fat distribution for Guatemalan children. American Journal of Physical Anthropology. 69:527–535.

Bohannan P, Glazer M, editors. 1988. High points in anthropology. New York: Alfred A. Knopf.

Boldsen J. 2001. Epidemiological approach to the paleopathological diagnosis of leprosy. American Journal of Physical Anthropology. 115:380–387.

Bolton R. 1973. Aggression and hypoglycemia among the Qolla: a study in psychobiological anthropology. Ethnology. 12:227–257.

Bolton R. 1989. Introduction: the AIDS pandemic, a global emergency. Medical Anthropology. 10:93–104.

Bolton R. 1992. AIDS and promiscuity: muddled in the models of HIV prevention. Medical Anthropology. 14:145–223.

Bordaz J. 1970. Tools of the Old and New Stone Age. Garden City, NY: Natural History Press.

Bordes F. 22 September 1961. Mousterian cultures in France. Science. 803–810.

Bordes F. 1968. The Old Stone Age. New York: McGraw-Hill. pp. 51–97.

Borgerhoff Mulder M. 1992. Demography of pastoralists: preliminary data on the Datoga of Tanzania. Human Ecology. 20:383–405.

Bos KI, Herbig A, Sahl J, Waglechner N, Fourment M, Forrest SA, Klunk J, Schuenemann VJ, Poinar D, Kuch M, Golding GB. 2016. Eighteenth century *Yersinia pestis* genomes reveal the long-term persistence of an historical plague focus. eLife. Jan 21:e12994.

Bos KI, Stevens P, Nieselt K, Poinar HN, DeWitte SN, Krause J. 2012. *Yersinia pestis*: new evidence for an old infection. PLoS One. 7(11):e49803.

Boutton TW, Lynott MJ, Bumstead MP. 1991. Stable carbon isotopes and the study of prehistoric human diet. Critical Reviews in Food Science and Nutrition. 30:373–385.

Bowler PJ. 1989. Evolution: the history of an idea. Berkeley: University of California Press.

Boyd M, Surette C. 2010. Northernmost precontact maize in North America. American Antiquity. 75(1):117–133.

Boyd R, Richerson PJ. 1985. Culture and the evolutionary process. Chicago: University of Chicago Press.

Boyd R, Richerson PJ. 2005. The origin and evolution of cultures. New York: Oxford University Press.

Boyd R, Silk J. 2000. How humans evolved. 2nd ed. New York: Norton.

Brace CL. 1996. A four-letter word called race. In: Reynolds LT, Leiberman L, editors. Race and other misadventures: essays in honor of Ashley Montague in his ninetieth year. New York: General Hall.

Brace CL, Tracer DF, Yaroch LA, Robb J, Brandt K, Nelson AR. 1993. Clines and clusters versus "race": a test in ancient Egypt and the case of a death on the Nile. Yearbook of Physical Anthropology. 36:1–31.

Braidwood RJ. September 1960. The agricultural revolution. Scientific American. 203:130.

Braidwood RJ, Willey GR. 1962. Conclusions and afterthoughts. In: Braidwood RJ, Willey GR, editors. Courses toward urban life: archeological considerations of some cultural alternatives. Viking Fund Publications in Anthropology No. 32. Chicago: Aldine. p. 342.

Brain CK, Sillen A. 1 December 1988. Evidence from the Swartkrans Cave for the earliest use of fire. Nature. 540:464–466.

Branda RF, Eaton JW. 18 August 1978. Skin color and nutrient photolysis: an evolutionary hypothesis. Science. 536:625–626.

Brandon RN. 1990. Adaptation and environment. Princeton, NJ: Princeton University Press.

Bräuer G. 1984. A craniological approach to the origin of anatomically modern *Homo sapiens* in Africa and implications for the appearance of modern Europeans. In: Smith FH, Spencer F, editors. The origins of modern humans. Chicago: University of Chicago Press.

Britten RJ. 2002. Divergence between samples of chimpanzee and human DNA sequences is 5%, counting indels. Proceedings of the National Academy of Sciences USA. 99:13633–13635.

Brodey JE. 15 October 1971. Effect of milk on Blacks noted. New York Times. p. 15.

Bromage TG, Dean MC. 10 October 1985. Re-evaluation of the age at death of immature fossil hominids. Nature. 538:525–527.

Brooks AF, Jackson F, Grinker RR. 1993. Race and ethnicity in America. Anthro Notes 15(3):1–15. National Museum of Natural History Bulletin for Teachers.

Broom R. 1950. Finding the missing link. London: Watts.

Browman D, Fritz G, Watson PJ. 2009. Origins of food-producing economies in the Americas. In: Scarre C, editor. The human past. New York: Thames and Hudson.

Brown F, Harris J, Leakley R, Walker A. 29 August–4 September 1985. Early *Homo erectus* skeleton from west Lake Turkana, Kenya. Nature. 316:788–792.

Brown FH. 1988. Geochronometry. In: Tattersall I, Delson E, Van Couvering J, editors. Encyclopedia of human evolution and prehistory. New York: Garland. p. 225.

Brown FH. 1992. Methods of dating. In: Jones S, Martin R, Pilbeam D, editors. The Cambridge encyclopedia of human evolution. New York: Cambridge University Press. pp. 179–186.

Brown JA. 1983. Summary. In: Philips JL, Brown JA, editors. Archaic hunters and gatherers in the American Midwest. New York: Academic Press. pp. 5–10.

Brown JA. 1985. Long-term trends to sedentism and the emergence of complexity in the American Midwest. In: Price TD, Brown JA, editors. Prehistoric hunter-gatherers: the emergence of cultural complexity. Orlando, FL: Academic Press. pp. 201–231.

Brown JA, Price TD. 1985. Complex hunter-gatherers: retrospect and prospect. In: Price TD, Brown JA, editors. Prehistoric hunter-gatherers: the emergence of cultural complexity. Orlando, FL: Academic Press. pp. 435–441.

Brown P, Sutikna T, Morwood MJ, Soejono RP, Jatmiko, Saptomo EW, Due RA. 2004. A new small-bodied hominin from the Late Pleistocene of Flores, Indonesia. Nature. 431:1055–1061.

Bruce SG. 2000. The impact of diabetes mellitus among the Métis of Western Canada. Ethnicity & Health. 5(1):47–57.

Brumfiel E. 1976. Regional growth in the Eastern Valley of Mexico: a test of the "population pressure" hypothesis. In: Flannery KV, editor. The early Mesoamerican village. New York: Academic Press. pp. 234–250.

Brumfiel EM. 1983. Aztec state making: ecology, structure, and the origin of the state. American Anthropologist. 85:261–284.

Brunet M, Beauvilain A, Coppens Y, Heitz E, Moutaye AH, Pilbeam D. 16 November 1995. The first australopithecine 2,500 kilometers west of the Rift Valley. Nature. 378:273–275.

Brunet M, Guy F, Pilbeam D, Mackaye HT, Likius A, Ahounta D, Beauvilain A, Blondel C, Bocherens H, Boisserie JR, et al. 11 July 2002. A new hominid from the Upper Miocene of Chad, Central Africa. Nature. 418:145–151.

Brutsaert T. 2010. Human adaptation to high altitude. In: Muehlenbein M, editor. Human evolutionary biology. Cambridge: Cambridge University Press. pp. 170–191.

Bryan P. 2015. Experience and practical insights: 3D laser scanning for heritage. GeoInformatics. 18(8):10–13.

Bryant CA, Bailey DFC. 1990. The use of focus group research in program development. In: van Willigen J, Finan T, editors. Soundings: rapid and reliable research methods for practicing anthropologists. NAPA Bulletin No. 10. Washington, DC: American Anthropological Association. pp. 24–39.

Buckland PC, Amorosi T, Barlow LK, Dugmore AJ, Mayewski PA, McGovern TH, Sadler AEJ, Skidmore P. 1996. Bioarchaeological and climatological evidence for the fate of Norse farmers in Medieval Greenland. Antiquity. 70:86–88.

Budimlija ZM, Prinz MK, Zelson-Mundorff A, Wiersema J, Bartelink E, MacKinnon G, Nazzaruolo BL, Estacio SM, Hennessey MJ, Shaler RC. 2003. World Trade Center human identification project: experiences with individual body identification cases. Croatian Medical Journal. 44:259–263.

Burbano HA, Hodges E, Green RE, Briggs AW, Krause J, Meyer M, Good JM, Maricic T, Johnson PL, Xuan Z, Rooks M. 2010. Targeted investigation of the Neandertal genome by array-based sequence capture. Science. 328(5979): 723–725.

Burke A, Cinq-Mars J. 1998. Paleoethological reconstruction and taphonomy of *Equus lambei* from the Bluefish Caves, Yukon Territory, Canada. Arctic. 51(2):105–115.

Burke AM, editor. 2000. Special issue: hunting in the Middle Palaeolithic. International Journal of Osteoarcharchaeology. 10(5):281–285.

Butzer KW. 1982a. Archaeology as human ecology. Cambridge: Cambridge University Press.

Butzer KW. 1982b. Geomorphology and sediment stratigraphy. In: Singer R, Wymer J, editors. The Middle Stone Age at Klasies River mouth in South Africa. Chicago: University of Chicago Press. p. 42.

Byrne R. 1987. Climatic changes and the origins of agriculture. In: Manzanilla L, editor. Studies of agriculture. Oxford: British Archaeological Reports International Series 349. pp. 21–34.

Cameron N, Johnston FE, Kgamphe JS, Lunz R. 1992. Body fat patterning in rural South African Black children. American Journal of Human Biology. 4:353–364.

Campbell AM. 1991. Microbes: the laboratory and the field. In: Davis BD, editor. The genetic revolution: scientific prospects and public perceptions. Baltimore: Johns Hopkins University Press. pp. 28–44.

Campbell BG. 2001. Humankind emerging: the concise edition. Boston: Little, Brown. p. 202.

Campbell DT. 1965. Variation and selective retention in socio-cultural evolution. In: Barringer H, Blankstein G, Mack R, editors. Social change in developing areas: a re-interpretation of evolutionary theory. Cambridge, MA: Schenkman. pp. 19–49.

Cann R. 1988. DNA and human origins. Annual Review of Anthropology. 17:127–143.

Cann RL, Stoneking M, Wilson AC. 1987. Mitochondrial DNA and human evolution. Nature. 325(6099):31–36.

Cannon A. 1998. Contingency and agency in the growth of Northwest Coast maritime economies. Arctic Anthropology. 35:57–67.

Cannon A. 2000a. Assessing variability in Northwest Coast salmon and herring fisheries: bucket-auger sampling of shell midden sites on the central coast in British Columbia. Journal of Archaeological Science. 27:725–737.

Cannon A. January 2000b. Settlement and sea level on the central coast of British Columbia: evidence from shell midden cores. American Antiquity. 65(1):67–77.

Cannon A. 2002. Sacred power and seasonal settlement on the central Northwest Coast. In: Fitzhugh B, Habu J., editors. Beyond foraging and collecting: evolutionary change in hunter-gatherer settlement systems. New York: Springer. pp. 311–338.

Cannon A, Yang DY. 2006. Early storage and sedentism on the Pacific Northwest Coast: ancient DNA analysis of salmon remains from Namu, British Columbia. American Antiquity. 71: 123–140.

Carlson KJ, Stout D, Jashashvili T, De Ruiter DJ, Tafforeau P, Carlson K, Berger LR. 2011. The endocast of MH1, *Australopithecus sediba*. Science. 333(September 9):1402–1407.

Carneiro RL. 1968. Slash-and-burn cultivation among the Kuikuru and its implications for settlement patterns. In: Cohen Y, editor. Man in adaptation: the cultural present. Chicago: Aldine.

Carneiro RL. 21 August 1970. A theory of the origin of the state. Science. 733–738.

Carneiro RL. 1988. The circumscription theory: challenge and response. American Behavioral Scientist. 31:506–508.

Carpenter CR. 1940. A field study in Siam of the behavior and social relations of the gibbon (*Hylobates lar*). Comparative Psychology Monographs. 16:1–212.

Carretero JM, Lorenzo C, Arsuaga JL. 1999. Axial and appendicular skeleton of *Homo* antecessor. Journal of Human Evolution. 37:459–499.

Carrier J, Bolton R. 1991. Anthropological perspectives on sexuality and HIV prevention. Annual Review of Sex Research. 2:49–75.

Cartmill M. 1974. Rethinking primate origins. Science. 184:436–443.

Cartmill M. 1992a. New views on primate origins. Evolutionary Anthropology. 1:105–111.

Cartmill M. 1992b. Non-human primates. In: Jones S, Martin R, Pilbeam D, editors. The Cambridge encyclopedia of human evolution. Cambridge: Cambridge University Press.

Cartmill M. 1998. Explaining primate origins. In: Ember CR, Ember ME, Peregrine P, editors. Research frontiers in anthropology. Upper Saddle River, NJ: Prentice Hall/Simon & Schuster Custom Publishing.

Cartmill M. 2010. Primate classification and diversity. In: Platt M, Ghazanfar, A, editors. Primate neuroethology. Oxford: Oxford University Press.

Caussinus H, Courgeau D, Mandelbaum J. 2010. Estimating age without measuring it: a new method in paleodemography. Population. 65(1):117–145.

Cavalli-Sforza LL, Feldman MW. 2003. The application of molecular genetic approaches to the study of human evolution. Nature Genetics Supplement. 33:266–275.

Caws P. 1969. The structure of discovery. Science. 166:1375–1380.

Chambers E. 1989. Applied anthropology: a practical guide. Prospect Heights, IL: Waveland.

Chan HM. 1998. A database for environmental contaminants in traditional foods in northern and Arctic Canada: development and applications. Food Additives and Contaminants. 15(2):127–134.

Chang K-C. September 1970. The beginnings of agriculture in the Far East. Antiquity. 44(175):176.

Chang K-C. 1981. In search of China's beginnings: new light on an old civilization. American Scientist. 69:148–160.

Chang K-C. 1986. The archaeology of ancient China. New Haven, CT: Yale University Press.

Chaplin G, Jablonski NG, Cable NT. 1994. Physiology, thermoregulation and bipedalism. Journal of Human Evolution. 27:497–510.

Chard CS. 1969. Man in prehistory. New York: McGraw-Hill.

Charles-Dominique P. 1977. Ecology and behaviour of nocturnal primates. Martin RD, translator. New York: Columbia University Press.

Chase LA. 1937. The trend of diabetes in Saskatchewan 1905–1934. Canadian Medical Association Journal. 36:366–369.

Chase P, Dibble H. 1987. Middle Paleolithic symbolism: a review of current evidence and interpretations. Journal of Anthropological Archaeology. 6:263–269.

Chatters J. 2002. Last word on Kennewick Man? Archaeology. 55:17.

Cheney DL, Wrangham RW. 1987. Predation. In: Smuts BB, Cheney DL, Seyfarth RM, Wrangham RW, Struhsaker TT, editors. Primate societies. Chicago: University of Chicago Press. p. 236.

Chessa B, Pereira F, Arnaud F, Amorim A, Goyache F, Mainland I, Kao RR, Pemberton JM, Beraldi D, Stear MJ, Alberti A, et al. 2009. Revealing the history of sheep domestication using retrovirus integrations. Science. 324(5926):532–536.

Chia S, Neri LA, De La Torre A. 2014. Obsidian sourcing at Ulilang Bundok site and its implications for mobility, exchange, and social contexts in the Philippine Metal Age. Asian Perspectives. 53(1):97–115.

Childe VG. 1950. The urban revolution. Town Planning Review. 21:3–17.

Chivers DJ. 1974. The Siamang in Malaya. Basel, Switzerland: Karger.

Chivers DJ, editor. 1980. Malayan forest primates: ten years' study in tropical rain forest. New York: Plenum.

Choi HJ, Garlie TN. 2015. Comparison of body size among male and female African American military personnel between 1988 and 2012. Poster presented at: Annual Meeting of the Canadian Association for Physical Anthropology; Winnipeg, MB.

Chomsky N. 1975. Reflections on language. New York: Pantheon.

Ciochon R, Olsen J, James J. 1990. Other origins: the search for the giant ape in human prehistory. New York: Bantam.

Ciochon RL, Etler DA. 1994. Reinterpreting past primate diversity. In: Corruccini S, Ciochon RL, editors. Integrative paths to the past: paleoanthropological advances in honor of F. Clark Howell. Englewood Cliffs, NJ: Prentice Hall. pp. 37–68.

Clark AG, Glanowski S, Nielsen R, Thomas PD, Kejariwal A, Todd MA, Tanenbaum DM, Civello D, Lu F, Murphy B, et al. 12 December 2003. Inferring nonneutral evolution from human-chimp-mouse orthologous gene trios. Science. 302:1960–1963.

Clark G. 1975. The earlier Stone Age settlement of Scandinavia. Cambridge: Cambridge University Press.

Clark G, Piggott S. 1965. Prehistoric societies. New York: Knopf.

Clark JD. 1970. The prehistory of Africa. New York: Praeger.

Clark JD. 1977. Interpretations of prehistoric technology from ancient Egyptian and other sources. Part II: prehistoric arrow forms in Africa as shown by surviving examples of the traditional arrows of the San Bushmen. Paleorientology. 3:136.

Clarke RJ, Tobias PV. 1995. Sterkfontein Member 2 foot bones of the oldest South African hominid. Science. 269:521–524.

Clayman CB, editor. 1989. American Medical Association encyclopedia of medicine. New York: Random House. pp. 857–858.

Clutton-Brock J. 1988. Domestication of animals. In: Jones S, Martin R, Pilbeam D, editors. The Cambridge encyclopedia of human evolution. Cambridge: Cambridge University Press. pp. 380–385.

Clutton-Brock TH, Harvey P. 1977. Primate ecology and social organization. Journal of Zoology. 183:8–9.

Clutton-Brock TH, Harvey P. 1980. Primates, brains and ecology. Journal of Zoology. 190:309–323.

Coe MD. 2011. The Maya. 8th ed. New York: Thames and Hudson.

Cohen A. 1999. The mental health of Indigenous peoples: an international overview. Geneva: Department of Mental Health, World Health Organization.

Cohen JD. 2011. The beginnings of agriculture in China. Current Anthropology. 52(4 Suppl): S273–293.

Cohen MN. 1977a. The food crisis in prehistory: overpopulation and the origin of agriculture. New Haven, CT: Yale University Press.

Cohen MN. 1977b. Population pressure and the origins of agriculture. In: Reed CA, editor. Origins of agriculture. The Hague: Mouton. pp. 138–141.

Cohen MN. 1987. The significance of long-term changes in human diet and food economy. In: Harris M, Ross EB, editors. Food and evolution: toward a theory of human food habits. Philadelphia: Temple University Press. pp. 269–273.

Cohen MN. 1989. Health and the rise of civilization. New Haven, CT: Yale University Press.

Cohen MN. 1998. Were early agriculturalists less healthy than food collectors? In: Ember CR, Ember M, Peregrine PN, editors. Research frontiers in anthropology. Upper Saddle River, NJ: Prentice Hall/Simon & Schuster Custom Publishing.

Cohen MN, Armelagos GJ. 1984a. Paleopathology at the origins of agriculture. Orlando, FL: Academic Press.

Cohen MN, Armelagos GJ. 1984b. Paleopathology at the origins of agriculture: editor's summation. In: Cohen MN, Armelagos GJ, editors. Paleopathology at the origins of agriculture. Orlando, FL: Academic Press. pp. 585–602.

Cohen RN, Service ER, editors. 1978. Origins of the state: the anthropology of political evolution. Philadelphia: Institute for the Study of Human Issues.

Cole TJ. 2003. The secular trend in human physical growth: a biological view. Economics & Human Biology. 1(2):161–168.

Collier S, White JP. 1976. Get them young? age and sex inferences on animal domestication in archaeology. American Antiquity. 41:96–102.

Collins D. 1976. Later hunters in Europe. In: Collins D, editor. The origins of Europe. New York: Thomas Y. Crowell. pp. 88–125.

Connah G. 1987. African civilizations: precolonial cities and states in tropical Africa, an archaeological perspective. Cambridge: Cambridge University Press.

Connah G. 2009. Holocene Africa. In: Scarre C, editor. The human past. New York: Thames and Hudson.

Conroy GC. 1990. Primate evolution. New York: Norton. pp. 8–15.

Cook DC. 1981. Mortality, age structure and status in the interpretation of stress indicators in prehistoric skeletons: a dental example from the Lower Illinois Valley. In: Chapman R, Kinnes I, Randsborg K, editors. The archaeology of death. Cambridge: Cambridge University Press. pp. 133–144.

Cook DC, Buikstra JE. 1979. Health and differential survival in prehistoric populations: prenatal dental defects. American Journal of Physical Anthropology. 51:649–664.

Cooper A, Drummond AJ, Willerslev E. 2004. Ancient DNA: would the real Neandertal please stand up? Current Biology. 14:R431–R433.

Coqueugniot H, Hublin JJ, Veillon F, Houet F, Jacob T. 2004. Early brain growth in *Homo erectus* and implications for cognitive ability. Nature. 431:299–302.

Corballis MC. March/April 1999. The gestural origins of language. American Scientist. 87(2):138–145.

Coreil J. 1989. Lessons from a community study of oral rehydration therapy in Haiti. In: van Willigen J, Rylko-Bauer B, McElroy A, editors. Making our research useful: case studies in the utilization of anthropological knowledge. Boulder, CO: Westview Press. pp. 143–157.

Corruccini RS. 1992. Metrical reconsideration of the Skhul IV and IX and Border Cave 1 crania in the context of modern human origins. American Journal of Physical Anthropology. 87:433–445.

Cortopassi-Laurino M, Imperatriz-Fonseca VL, Roubik DW, Dollin A, Heard T, Aguilar I, Venturieri GC, Eardley C, Nogueira-Neto P. 2006. Global meliponiculture: challenges and opportunities. Apidologie. 37(2):275–292.

Crawford GW. 1992. Prehistoric plant domestication in East Asia. In: Cowan C, Watson PJ, editors. The origins of agriculture. Washington, DC: Smithsonian Institution Press. pp. 29–30.

Crawford GW, Smith DG. 1996. Migration in prehistory: Princess Point and the Northern Iroquoian case. American Antiquity. 61(4):782–790.

Crawford GW, Smith DG, Bowyer V. 1997. Dating the entry of corn (*Zea mays*) to the Lower Great Lakes region. American Antiquity. 62(1):112–119.

Crawford RD. 1984. Turkey. In: Mason IL, editor. Evolution of domesticated animals. New York: Longman. pp. 329–331.

Crockett C, Eisenberg JF. 1987. Howlers: variations in group size and demography. In: Smuts BB, Cheney DL, Seyfarth RM, Wrangham RW, Struhsaker TT, editors. Primate societies. Chicago: University of Chicago Press. pp. 54–68.

Crosby AW. 2004. Ecological imperialism: the biological expansion of Europe, 900–1900. Cambridge: Cambridge University Press.

Culotta E. 18 August 1995. New hominid crowds the field. Science. 269:918.

Cybulski JS, Katzenberg MA. 2014. Bioarchaeology in Canada: origins and contemporary issues. In: Odonnabhain B, Lozada Cerna MC, editors. Archaeological human remains. New York: Springer. pp. 85–103.

Czekala N, Sicotte P. 2000. Reproductive monitoring of free-ranging female mountain gorillas by urinary hormone analysis. American Journal of Primatology. 51:209–215.

Daiger S. 15 April 2005. Was the Human Genome Project worth the effort? Science. 308:362–364.

Dalton R. 7 July 2005. Scientists finally get their hands on Kennewick Man. Nature. 436:10.

Daniel IR. 2001. Early Eastern Archaic. In: Peregrine PN, Ember M, editors. Encyclopedia of prehistory. Volume 6: North America. Kluwer Academic: Plenum.

Daniel M, Green LW, Marion SA, Gamble D, Herbert CP, Hertzman C, Sheps SB. 1999. Effectiveness of community-directed diabetes prevention and control in a rural Aboriginal population in British Columbia, Canada. Social Science and Medicine. 48(6):815–832.

Dart R. 1925. *Australopithecus africanus*: the man-ape of South Africa. Nature. 115:195.

Darwin C. 1859. The origin of species. Reprinted in: Young LB, editor. 1970. Evolution of man. New York: Oxford University Press.

Darwin C. 1871. The descent of man. Reprinted in: Hutchins RM, editor. 1971. Great books of the Western world. Vol. 49. Chicago: Encyclopedia Britannica.

Dasen PR, Berry JW, Sartorius N, editors. 1988. Health and cross-cultural psychology: toward applications. Newbury Park, CA: Sage.

Dawson A. 1992. Ice Age Earth. London: Routledge.

Dawson PC, Bertulli MM, Levy R, Tucker C, Dick L, Cousins PL. 2013. Application of 3D laser scanning to the preservation of Fort Conger, a historic polar research base on northern Ellesmere Island, Arctic Canada. Arctic. 1:147–158.

Dean H, Mundy R, Moffatt M. 1992. Non-insulin-dependent diabetes mellitus in Indian children in Manitoba. Canadian Medical Association Journal. 147(1):1422–1425.

Defleur A, White T, Valensi P, Slimak L, Cregut-Bonnoure E. 1999. Neanderthal cannibalism at Moula-Guercy, Ardeche, France. Science. 286(5437):128–131.

de Lumley H. 1969. A Paleolithic camp at Nice. Scientific American. 220(5):42–50.

deMenocal PB. 2001. Cultural responses to climate change during the late Holocene. Science. 292:667–673.

deMenocal PB. 2011. Climate and human evolution. Science. 331:540–542.

Denham TP, Haberle SG, Lentfer C, Fullagar R, Field J, Therin M, Porch N, Winsborough B. 11 July 2003. Origins of agriculture at Kuk Swamp in the highlands of New Guinea. Science. 301:189–193.

d'Errico F, Henshilwood C, Nilssen P. 2001. An engraved bone fragment from c. 70,000-year-old Middle Stone Age levels at Blombos Cave, South Africa: implications for the origin of symbolism and language. Antiquity. 75:309–318.

d'Errico F, Henshilwood C, Vanhaeren M, van Niekerk K. 2005. *Nassarius kraussianus* shell beads from Blombos Cave: evidence for symbolic behaviour in the Middle Stone Age. Journal of Human Evolution. 48(1):3–24.

de Souza SM, de Carvalho DM, Lessa A. 2003. Paleoepidemiology: is there a case to answer? Memórias do Instituto Oswaldo Cruz. 1(98 Suppl):21–27.

Devillers C, Chaline J. 1993. Evolution: an evolving theory. New York: Springer-Verlag.

Devlin B, Fienberg SE, Resnick DP, Roeder K, editors. 1997. Intelligence, genes, and success: scientists respond to The Bell Curve. New York: Springer Verlag.

de Waal F, Lanting F. 1997. Bonobo: the forgotten ape. Berkeley: University of California Press.

DeWitte SN, Stojanowski CM. 2015. The osteological paradox 20 years later: past perspectives, future directions. Journal of Archaeological Research. 23(4):397–450.

Diamond J. December 1989. The accidental conqueror. Discover. 71–76.

Diamond J. November 1993. Who are the Jews? Natural History. 16.

Diamond J. 14 November 1997. Location, location, location: the first farmers. Science. 278:1243–1244.

Diamond JM. 2003. Guns, germs, and steel. New York: Norton.

Dickson DB. 1990. The dawn of belief: religion in the Upper Paleolithic of southwestern Europe. Tucson: University of Arizona Press.

Dickson JH, Oeggl K, Handley LL. 2003. The Iceman reconsidered. Scientific American. 288:70–79.

Dillehay T. 2000. The settlement of the Americas. New York: Basic Books.

Dincauze DF. 2000. Environmental archaeology: principles and practice. Cambridge: Cambridge University Press.

Dirks PH, Berger LR, Roberts EM, Kramers JD, Hawks J, Randolph-Quinney PS, Elliott M, Musiba CM, Churchill SE, de Ruiter DJ, Schmid P, et al. 2015. Geological and taphonomic context for the new hominin species *Homo naledi* from the Dinaledi Chamber, South Africa. eLife. 4:e09561.

Dirks R. 1993. Starvation and famine. Cross-cultural Research. 27:28–69.

Dobzhansky T. 1962. Mankind evolving: the evolution of the human species. New Haven, CT: Yale University Press.

Dobzhansky T. 1973. Genetic diversity and human equality. New York: Basic Books.

Dohlinow PJ, Bishop N. 1972. The development of motor skills and social relationships among primates through play. In: Dohlinow PJ, editor. Primate patterns. New York: Holt, Rinehart & Winston. pp. 321–325.

Donoghue HD, Marcsik A, Matheson C, Vernon K, Nuorala E, Molto JE, Greenblatt CL, Spigelman M. 2005. Co-infection of *Mycobacterium tuberculosis* and *Mycobacterium leprae* in human archaeological samples: a possible explanation for the historical decline of leprosy. Proceedings of the Royal Society of London B: Biological Sciences. 272(1561):389–394.

Donoghue HD, Spigelman M, Greenblatt CL, Lev-Maor G, Bar-Gal GK, Matheson C, Vernon K, Nerlich AG, Zink AR. 2004. Tuberculosis: from prehistory to Robert Koch, as revealed by ancient DNA. The Lancet Infectious Diseases. 4(9):584–592.

Dorit RL, Akashi H, Gilbert W. 1995. Absence of polymorphism at the ZFY locus on the human Y chromosome. Science. 268(5214):1183–1185.

Douglass AE. 1929. The secret of the Southwest solved by talkative tree rings. National Geographic Magazine. 56(6):736–770.

Douglass AE, University of Arizona, Laboratory of Tree-Ring Research. 1947. Precision of ring dating in tree-ring chronologies. Tucson: University of Arizona.

Doyle GA, Martin RD, editors. 1979. The study of prosimian behavior. New York: Academic Press.

Duarte C, Mauricio J, Pettit PB, Souto P, Trinkaus E, van der Plicht H, Zilhão J. 1999. The Early Upper Paleolithic human skeleton from the Abrigo do Lagar Velho (Portugal) and modern human emergence in Iberia. Proceedings of the National Academy of Sciences. 96(13):7604–7609.

Dudar JC, Waye JS, Saunders SR. 2003. Determination of a kinship system using ancient DNA, mortuary practice, and historic records in an upper Canadian pioneer cemetery. International Journal of Osteoarchaeology. 13(4):232–246.

Duhard J-P. 1993. Upper Paleolithic figures as a reflection of human morphology and social organization. Antiquity. 67:83–91.

Dunbar R, Shultz S. 2007. Evolution if the social brain. Science. 317:1344–1347.

Dunbar RIM. 1989. Ecological modelling in an evolutionary context. Folia Primatologica. 53:235–246.

Dunn FL, Janes CR. 1986. Introduction: medical anthropology and epidemiology. In: Janes CR, Stall R, Gifford SM, editors. Anthropology and epidemiology. Boston: D. Reidel. p. 334.

Dupras TL, Schwarcz HP. 2001. Strangers in a strange land: stable isotope evidence for human migration in the Dakhleh Oasis, Egypt. Journal of Archaeological Science. 28:1199–1208.

Dupré J. 2008. What genes are and why there are no genes for race. In: Koening BA, Lee SSJ, Richardson SS, editors. Revisiting race in a genomic age. New Brunswick, NJ: Rutgers University Press.

Durham WH. 1991. Co-evolution: genes, culture, and human diversity. Stanford, CA: Stanford University Press.

Early JD, Peters JF. 1992. The population dynamics of the Mucajai Yanomama. San Diego: Academic Press.

Ebrey PB. 2010. The Cambridge illustrated history of China. Cambridge: Cambridge University Press.

Edgerton RB. 1966. Conceptions of psychosis in four East African societies. American Anthropologist. 68:408–425.

Edgerton RB. 1992. Sick societies: challenging the myth of primitive harmony. New York: Free Press.

Eiseley LC. 1970. The dawn of evolutionary theory. In: Young LB, editor. Evolution of man. New York: Oxford University Press. pp. 13–15.

Eisenberg JF. 1977. Comparative ecology and reproduction of New World monkeys. In: Kleinman D, editor. The biology and conservation of the Callitrichidae. Washington, DC: Smithsonian Institution. pp. 13–22.

Eldredge N, Tattersall I. 1982. The myths of human evolution. New York: Columbia University Press.

Ember CR. 1978. Myths about hunter-gatherers. Ethnology. 17:439–448.

Ember CR. 1983. The relative decline in women's contribution to agriculture with intensification. American Anthropologist. 85:285–304.

Ember CR, Ember M. 1984. The evolution of human female sexuality: a cross-species perspective. Journal of Anthropological Research. 40:202–210.

Ember CR, Levinson D. 1991. The substantive contributions of worldwide cross-cultural studies using secondary data. Behavior Science Research, special issue. Cross-cultural and Comparative Research: Theory and Model. 25:79–140.

Ember M, Ember CR. 1979. Male–female bonding: a cross-species study of mammals and birds. Behavior Science Research. 14:37–56.

Emery KF, Wright EL, Schwarcz H. 2000. Isotopic analysis of ancient deer bone: biotic stability in collapse period Maya land use. Journal of Archaeological Science. 27(6):537–550.

Erickson C. 2000. An artificial landscape-scale fishery in the Bolivian Amazon. Nature. 408:190–193.

Ervin AM. 2000. Applied anthropology. Boston: Allyn and Bacon.

Eswaran V. 2002. A diffusion wave out of Africa. Current Anthropology. 43:749–774.

Etkin NL, Ross PJ. 1997. Malaria, medicine and meals: a biobehavioral perspective. In: Romanucci-Ross L, Moermann DE, Tancredi LR, editors. The anthropology of medicine: from culture to method. 3rd ed. Westport CT: Bergin and Garvey. pp. 169–209.

Evans J, O'Connor T. 1999. Environmental archaeology: principles and methods. Stroud: Sutton.

Eveleth PB. 1986. Population differences in growth: environmental and genetic factors. In: Falkner F, Tanner JM, editors. Human growth: a comprehensive treatise. Volume 3, Methodology and ecological, genetic, and nutritional effects on growth. 2nd ed. New York: Plenum Press. pp. 221–239.

Eveleth PB, Tanner JM. 1990. Worldwide variation in human growth. 2nd ed. Cambridge: Cambridge University Press.

Excoffier L, Langaney A. 1989. Origin and differentiation of human mitochondrial DNA. American Journal of Human Genetics. 44(1):73–85.

Fagan BM. 1989. People of the Earth: An introduction to world prehistory. 6th ed. Glenview, IL: Scott, Foresman.

Fagan BM. 1991. Ancient North America: the archaeology of a continent. London: Thames and Hudson.

Fagan BM. 2000. In the beginning: an introduction to archaeology. Upper Saddle River, NJ: Prentice Hall.

Falk D. 1988. Enlarged occipital/marginal sinuses and emissary foramina: their significance in hominid evolution. In: Grine FE, editor. Evolutionary history of the "robust" australopithecines. New York: Aldine. pp. 85–96.

Falk D, Hildebolt C, Smith K, Morwood MJ, Sutikna T, Brown P, Jatmiko, Saptomo EW, Brunsden B, Prior F. 2005. The brain of LB1, *Homo floresiensis*. Science. 308:242–245.

Farnsworth P, Brady JE, DeNiro MJ, MacNeish RS. 1985. A re-evaluation of the isotopic and archaeological reconstructions of diet in the Tehuacan Valley. American Antiquity. 1:102–116.

Feder KL, Park MA. 1997. Human antiquity: an introduction to physical anthropology and archaeology. 3rd ed. London: Mayfield.

Fedigan LM. 1982. Primate paradigms: sex roles and social bonds. Montreal: Eden Press.

Fedoroff N. 14 November 2003. Prehistoric GM corn. Science. 302:1158–1159.

Feibel CS, Brown FH. 1993. Microstratigraphy and paleoenvironments. In: Walker A, Leakey R, editors. The Nariokotome *Homo erectus* skeleton. Cambridge, MA: Harvard University Press. pp. 21–39.

Feinberg AP, Fallin MD. 2015. Epigenetics at the crossroads of genes and the environment. JAMA. 314(11):1129–1130.

Feinman GM, Kowalewski SA, Finsten L, Blanton RE, Nicholas L. 1985. Long-term demographic change: a perspective from the Valley of Oaxaca. Journal of Field Archaeology. 12:333–362.

Feldman DA, Johnson TM. 1986. Introduction. In: Feldman DA, Johnson TM, editors. The social dimension of AIDS: methods and theory. New York: Praeger.

Ferguson RB, Whitehead NL. 1992. The violent edge of empire. In: Ferguson RB, Whitehead N, editors. War in the tribal zone. Santa Fe: School of American Research Press. pp. 1–30.

Fischman J. 1994. Putting our oldest ancestors in their proper place. Science. 265:2011–2012.

Fish PR. 1981. Beyond tools: Middle Paleolithic debitage analysis and cultural inference. Journal of Anthropological Research. 37(4):374–386.

Fisher J. 1996. Grassroots organizations and grassroots support organizations: patterns of interaction. In: Moran EF, editor. Transforming societies, transforming anthropology. Ann Arbor: University of Michigan Press. pp. 57–101.

Fisher JW Jr. 1995. Bone surface modifications in zooarchaeology. Journal of Archaeological Method and Theory. 2(1):7–68.

Fisher WH. 1994. Megadevelopment, environmentalism, and resistance: the institutional context of Kayapó Indigenous politics in central Brazil. Human Organization. 53:220–232.

Fix AG. 1977. The demography of the Semai Senoi. Anthropological Papers No. 62. Ann Arbor: Museum of Anthropology, University of Michigan.

Fladmark KR, Nelson DE, Brown TA, Vogel JS, Southon JR. 1987. AMS dating of two wooden artifacts from the Northwest Coast. Canadian Journal of Archaeology. 11:1–12.

Flannery KV. 12 March 1965. The ecology of early food production in Mesopotamia. Science. 147:1247–1256.

Flannery KV. 1971. The origins and ecological effects of early domestication in Iran and the Near East. In: Struever S, editor. Prehistoric agriculture. Garden City, NY: Natural History Press. pp. 50–79.

Flannery KV. 1972. The cultural evolution of civilizations. Annual Review of Ecology and Systematics. 3:399–426.

Flannery KV. 1973a. The origins of agriculture. Annual Review of Anthropology. 2:274.

Flannery KV. 1973b. The origins of the village as a settlement type in Mesoamerica and the Near East: a comparative study. In: Tringham R, editor. Territoriality and proxemics R1. Andover, MA: Warner Modular. pp. 1–31.

Flannery KV. 1986. The research problem. In: Flannery KV, editor. Guilá Naquitz: Archaic foraging and early agriculture in Oaxaca, Mexico. Orlando, FL: Academic Press. pp. 3–18.

Fleagle JG. 1994. Anthropoid origins. In: Corruccini R, Ciochon RL, editors. Integrative paths to the past. Englewood Hills, NJ: Prentice Hall. pp. 17–35.

Fleagle JG. 1999. Primate adaptation and evolution. 2nd ed. San Diego: Academic Press.

Fleagle JG, Kay RF. 1983. New interpretations of the phyletic position of Oligocene hominoids. In: Ciochon RL, Corruccini RS. New interpretations of ape and human ancestry. New York: Plenum. pp. 181–210.

Fleagle JG, Kay RF. 1985. The paleobiology of catarrhines. In: Delson E, editor. Ancestors: the hard evidence. New York: Alan R. Liss. pp. 23–36.

Fleagle JG, Kay RF. 1987. The phyletic position of the Parapithecidae. Journal Human Evolution. 16:483–531.

Fleischer RL, Hart JW Jr. 1972. Fission-track dating: techniques and problems. In: Bishop WA, Miller JA, editors. Calibration of hominid evolution. Toronto: University of Toronto Press. pp. 135–170.

Fleischer RL, Price PB, Walker RM, Leakey LSB. 2 April 1965. Fission-track dating of Bed I, Olduvai Gorge. Science. 148:72–74.

Fogel M, Tuross N, Owsley DW. 1989. Nitrogen isotope traces of human lactation in modern and archaeological populations. Carnegie Institution, Annual Report of the Director. Geophysical Laboratory.

Fortey R. 1999. Life: a natural history of the first four billion years of life on Earth. New York: Vintage Books.

Fossey D. 1983. Gorillas in the mist. Boston: Houghton Mifflin.

Foster GM. 1962. Traditional cultures and the impact of technological change. New York: Harper & Row.

Fowler ML. August 1975. A pre-Columbian urban center on the Mississippi. Scientific American. 233:92–101.

Fox C, Harris S, Whalen-Brough E. 1994. Diabetes among Native Canadians in northwestern Ontario: 10 years later. Chronic Diseases in Canada. 15(3):92–96.

Fox WA. 1999. Aboriginal peoples, archaeology and Parks Canada. Plains Anthropologist. 44:35–42.

Franciscus RG, Trinkaus E. 1988. Nasal morphology and the emergence of *Homo erectus*. American Journal of Physical Anthropology. 75:517–527.

Frankel B, Trend MG. 1991. Principles, pressures and paychecks: the anthropologist as employee. In: Fluehr-Lobban C, editor. Ethics and the profession of anthropology: dialogue for a new era. Philadelphia: University of Pennsylvania Press. pp. 175–197.

Frayer DW. 1981. Body size, weapon use, and natural selection in the European Upper Paleolithic and Mesolithic. American Anthropologist. 83:57–73.

Frayer DW, Wolpoff MH. 1985. Sexual dimorphism. Annual Review of Anthropology. 14:431–432.

Frayer DW, Wolpoff MH, Thorne A, Smith F, Pope G. 1993. Theories of modern human origins: the paleontological test. American Anthropologist. 95:24–27.

Freeman LG. 1994. Torralba and Ambrona: a review of discoveries. In: Corruccini R, Ciochon RL, editors. Integrative paths to the past: paleoanthropological advances in honor of F. Clark Howell. Englewood Cliffs, NJ: Prentice Hall. pp. 597–637.

Fricke HC, O'Neil JR, Lynnerup N. 1995. Oxygen isotope composition of human tooth enamel from medieval Greenland: linking climate and society. Geology. 23:869–872.

Friedman SS. 1980. Holocaust. In: Academic American [now Grolier] Encyclopedia. Volume 10. Princeton, NJ: Arete. p. 206.

Frisancho AR, Flegal PN. 1982. Advanced maturation associated with centripetal fat pattern. Human Biology. 54:717–728.

Frisancho AR, Greksa LP. 1989. Development responses in the acquisition of functional adaptation to high altitude. In: Little MA, Haas JD, editors. Human population biology: a transdisciplinary science. New York: Oxford University Press. pp. 203–221.

Frisch RE. October 1980. Fatness, puberty, and fertility. Natural History. 89(10):16–27.

Fry I. 2000. The emergence of life on Earth: a historical and scientific overview. New Brunswick, NJ: Rutgers University Press.

Fuentes A, Wyczalkowski MA, MacKinnon K. 2010. Niche construction through cooperation: A nonlinear dynamics contribution to modeling facets of the evolutionary history of the genus *Homo*. Current Anthropology. 51:435–444.

Gabunia L, Vekua A, Lordkipanidze D, Swisher III CC, Ferring R, Justus A, Nioradze M, Tvalchrelidze T, Antón SC, Bosinski G, et al. 12 May 2000. Earliest Pleistocene hominid cranial remains from Dmanisi, Republic of Georgia: taxonomy, geological setting, and age. Science. 288(5468):1019–1025.

Gadjev I. 2015. Nature and nurture: Lamarck's legacy. Biological Journal of the Linnean Society. 114(1):242–247.

Galdikas BMF. 1979. Orangutan adaptation at Tanjung Puting Reserve: mating and ecology. In: Hamburg DA, McCown ER, editors. The great apes. Menlo Park, CA: Benjamin/Cummings. pp. 194–233.

Galik K, Senut B, Pickford M, Gommery D, Treil J, Kuperavage AJ, Eckhardt RB. 2004. External and internal morphology of the BAR 1002'00 *Orrorin tugenensis* femur. Science. 305(5689):1450–1453.

Galloway T, Blackett H, Chatwood S, Jeppesen C, Kandola K, Linton J, Bjerregaard P. 2012. Obesity studies in the circumpolar Inuit: a scoping review. International Journal of Circumpolar Health. 71. doi:http://dx.doi.org/10.3402/ijch.v71i0.18698.

Garlie TN. 2011. Encumbered anthropometry: a human systems integration approach for characterizing the encumbered soldier. Poster presented at: Annual Meetings of the Canadian Association for Physical Anthropology, Montreal.

Garlie TN, Obusek JP, Corner BD, Zambraski EJ. 2010. Comparison of body fat estimates using 3D digital laser scans, direct manual anthropometry, and DXA in men. American Journal of Human Biology. 22(5):695–701.

Gentner W, Lippolt HJ. 1969. The potassium-argon dating of Upper Tertiary and Pleistocene deposits. In: Brothwell D, Higgs E, editors. Science in archaeology. New York: Basic Books. pp. 72–84.

Gibbons A. 19 April 1995. First Americans: not mammoth hunters, but forest dwellers? Science. 272:346–347.

Gibbons A. 2001. The riddle of co-existence. Science. 291:1725–1729.

Gibbons A. 29 November 2002. One scientist's quest for the origin of our species. Science. 298:1708–1711.

Gibbons A. 2011. A new view of the birth of *Homo sapiens*. Science. 311:392–394.

Gibbons A. 2012. A crystal-clear view of an extinct girl's genome. Science. 337:1028–1029.

Gilbert MT, Jenkins DL, Götherstrom A, Naveran N, Sanchez JJ, Hofreiter M, Thomsen PF, Binladen J, Higham TF, Yohe RM, Parr R. 2008. DNA from pre-Clovis human coprolites in Oregon, North America. Science. 320(5877):786–789.

Gill JL, Williams JW, Jackson ST, Lininger KB, Swanson GS. 2009. Pleistocene megafaunal collapse, novel plant communities, and enhanced fire regimes in North America. Science. 326:1100–1103.

Gill S. 2015. Body scanning and its influence on garment development. In: Hays SG, Venkatraman P, editors. Materials and technology for sportswear and performance apparel. Boca Raton, FL: Taylor & Francis Group. pp. 311–326.

Gingerich PD. 1986. *Pleisiadipis* and the delineation of the order Primates. In: Wood B, Martin L Andrews P, editors. Major topics in primate evolution. Cambridge: Cambridge University Press. pp. 32–46.

Goebel T, Waters M, O'Rourke D. 2008. The late Pleistocene dispersal of modern humans in the Americas. Science. 319:1479–1502.

Goldizen AW. 1987. Tamarins and marmosets: communal care of offspring. In: Smuts BB, Cheney DL, Seyfarth RM, Wrangham RW, Struhsaker TT, editors. Primate societies. Chicago: University of Chicago Press. pp. 34–43.

Goodall J. August 1963. My life among wild chimpanzees. National Geographic. 124:272–308.

Goodenough WH. 1963. Cooperation in change. New York: Russell Sage Foundation.

Goodman AH, Armelagos GJ. September 1985. Disease and death at Dr. Dickson's Mounds. Natural History. 94:12–18.

Goodman AH, Lallo J, Armelagos GJ, Rose JC. 1984a. Health changes at Dickson Mounds, Illinois (A.D. 905–1300). In: Cohen MN, Armelagos GJ, editors. Paleopathology at the origins of agriculture. Orlando, FL: Academic Press. pp. 271–305.

Goodman AH, Martin DL, Armelagos GJ, Clark G. 1984b. Indications of stress from the bone and teeth. In: Cohen MN, Armelagos GJ, editors. Palaeopathology at the origins of agriculture. Orlando, FL: Academic Press. pp. 13–49.

Goodman M. 1992. Reconstructing human evolution from proteins. In: Jones S, Martin R, Pilbeam D, editors. The Cambridge encyclopedia of human evolution. Cambridge: Cambridge University Press. pp. 307–312.

Goren-Inbar N, Alperson N, Kislev ME, Simchoni O, Melamed Y, Ben-Nun A, Werker E. 2004. Evidence of hominin control of fire at Gesher Benot Ya'aqov, Israel. Science. 304:725–727.

Gorman C. 1970. The Hoabinhian and after: subsistence patterns in Southeast Asia during the Late Pleistocene and Early Recent Periods. World Archaeology. 2:315–316.

Gowland R, Knüsel C. 2006. The social archaeology of funerary remains. Oxford: Oxbow Books.

Gowland RL. 2015. Entangled lives: implications of the developmental origins of health and disease hypothesis for bioarchaeology and the life course. American Journal of Physical Anthropology. 158(4):530–540.

Gowlett JAJ. 2008. Deep roots of kin: Developing the evolutionary perspective from prehistory. In: Allen N, Callan H, Dunbar R, James W, editors. Early human kinship: from sex to social reproduction. Oxford: Blackwell. pp. 41–57.

Grant PR, Grant R. 26 April 2002. Unpredictable evolution in a 30-year study of Darwin's finches. Science. 296:707–711.

Graver AM, Molto JE, Parr RL, Walters S, Praymak RC, Maki JM. 2001. Mitochondrial DNA research in the Dakhleh Oasis, Egypt: a preliminary report. Ancient Biomolecules. 3:239–253.

Gray JP. 1985. Primate sociobiology. New Haven, CT: HRAF Press.

Grayson DK. 18 February 1977. Pleistocene avifaunas and the overkill hypothesis. Science. 195:691–692.

Grayson DK. 1989. Explaining Pleistocene extinctions: thoughts on the structure of a debate. In: Martin PS, Klein RG, editors. Quaternary extinctions: a prehistoric revolution. Tucson: University of Arizona Press. pp. 807–823.

Greenberg JH, Ruhlen M. November 1992. Linguistic origins of Native Americans. Scientific American. 267:94–99.

Greenfield HJ. 1999. The origins of metallurgy: distinguishing stone from metal cut-marks on bones from archaeological sites. Journal of Archaeological Science. 26(7):797–808.

Greenfield HJ. 2000. Integrating surface and subsurface reconnaissance data in the study of stratigraphically complex sites: Blagotin, Serbia. Geoarchaeology. 15:167–201.

Greenfield HJ. 2006. Slicing cut marks on animal bones: diagnostics for identifying stone tool type and raw material. Journal of Field Archaeology. 31(2):147–163.

Greksa LP, Beall CM. 1989. Development of chest size and lung function at high altitude. In: Little MA, Haas JD, editors. Human population biology: a transdisciplinary science. New York: Oxford University Press. pp. 222–238.

Grine FE. 1993. Australopithecine taxonomy and phylogeny: historical background and recent interpretation. In: Ciochon R, Fleagle J, editors. The human evolution source book. Upper Saddle River, NJ: Prentice-Hall. pp. 198–210.

Grine FE. 1998. Evolutionary history of the "robust" australopithecines: a summary and historical perspective. In: Grine FE, editor. Evolutionary history of the "robust" australopithecines. New York: Aldine. pp. 515–516.

Gross DR, Underwood BA. 1971. Technological change and caloric costs: sisal agriculture in northeastern Brazil. American Anthropologist. 73:725–740.

Grossman D. December 2002. Parched turf battle. Scientific American. 287:32–33.

Grün R, Beaumont PB, Stringer CB. 1990. ESR dating evidence for early modern humans at Border Cave in South Africa. Nature. 344:537–539.

Guan Y, Peiris JS, Zheng B, Poon LL, Chan KH, Zeng FY, Chan CW, Chan MN, Chen JD, Chow KY, et al. 2004. Molecular epidemiology of the novel coronavirus that causes severe acute respiratory syndrome. Lancet. 363:99–104.

Guthrie RD. 1984. Mosaics, allelochemics and nutrients: an ecological theory of Late Pleistocene megafaunal extinctions. In: Martin PS, Klein RG, editors. Quaternary extinctions: a prehistoric revolution. Tucson: University of Arizona Press. pp. 259–298.

Gutiérrez G, Sánchez D, Marín A. 2002. A reanalysis of the ancient mitochondrial DNA sequences recovered from Neandertal bones. Molecular Biology and Evolution. 19:1359–1366.

Haas J, Creamer W, Ruiz A. 2004. Dating the Late Archaic occupation of the Norte Chico region in Peru. Nature. 432:1020–1023.

Haas JD, Habicht JP. 1990. Growth and growth charts in the assessment of pre-school nutritional status. In: Harrison GA, Waterlow JC, editors. Diet and disease in traditional and developing societies. Cambridge: Cambridge University Press. pp. 160–183.

Habicht JKA. 1979. Paleoclimate, paleomagnetism, and continental drift. Tulsa, OK: American Association fo Petroleum Geologists.

Hackenberg RA. 1988. Scientists or survivors? the future of applied anthropology under maximum uncertainty. In: Trotter II RT, editor. Anthropology for tomorrow: creating practitioner-oriented applied anthropology programs. Washington, DC: American Anthropological Association. pp. 170–185.

Hahn RA. 1995. Sickness and healing: an anthropological perspective. New Haven CT: Yale University Press.

Haile-Selassie Y. 12 July 2001. Late Miocene hominids from the Middle Awash, Ethiopia. Nature. 412:178–181.

Haldane JBS. 1963. Human evolution: past and future. In: Jepsen GL, Mayr E, Simpson GG, editors. Genetics, paleontology, and evolution. New York: Atheneum. pp. 405–418.

Hall ET. 1966. The hidden dimension. Garden City, NY: Doubleday. pp. 144–153.

Hammer MF, Zegura SL. 1996. The role of the Y chromosome in human evolutionary studies. Evolutionary Anthropology. 5:116–134.

Hammer MF, Zegura SL. 2002. The human Y chromosome haplogroup tree. Annual Review of Anthropology. 31:303–321.

Hanna JM, Little MA, Austin DM. 1989. Climatic physiology. In: Little MA, Haas JD, editors. Human population biology: a transdisciplinary science. New York: Oxford University Press. pp. 133–136.

Hannah AC, McGrew WC. 1987. Chimpanzees using stones to crack open oil palm nuts in Liberia. Primates. 28:31–46.

Harcourt AH. 1979. The social relations and group structure of wild mountain gorillas. In: Hamburg DA, McCown ER, editors. The great apes. Menlo Park, CA: Benjamin/Cummings. pp. 187–192.

Harcourt-Smith WEH, Aiello LC. 2004. Fossils, feet and the evolution of human bipedal locomotion. Journal of Anatomy. 204:403–416.

Harington CR, Cinq-Mars J. 1995. Radiocarbon dates on saiga antelope (*Saiga-tatarica*) fossils from Yukon and the Northern Territories. Arctic. 48(1):105–115.

Harlan JR. June 1967. A wild wheat harvest in Turkey. Archaeology. 20(3):197–201.

Harpending HC, Batzer MA, Gurven M, Jorde LB, Rogers AR, Sherry ST. 1998. Genetic traces of ancient demography. Proceedings of the National Academy of Sciences. 95(4):1961–1967.

Harpending HC, Pennington R. 1991. Age structure and sex-biased mortality among Herero pastoralists. Human Biology. 63(3):329–353.

Harris DR. 1977. Settling down: an evolutionary model for the transformation of mobile bands into sedentary communities. In: Friedman J, Rowlands MJ, editors. The evolution of social systems. London: Duckworth. pp. 401–417.

Harris M. 1979. Cultural materialism: the struggle for a science of culture. New York: Random House.

Harris S, Caulfield LE, Sugamori ME, Whalen EA, Henning B. 1997. The epidemiology of diabetes in pregnant Native Canadians. Diabetes Care. 20(9):1422–1425.

Harris S, Perkins B, Whalen-Brough E. 1996. Non-insulin-dependent diabetes mellitus among First Nations children. Canadian Family Physician. 42:869–876.

Harrison GA, Tanner J, Pilbeam DR, Baker PT. 1988. Human biology: an introduction to human evolution, variation, growth, and adaptability. 3rd ed. Oxford: Oxford University Press.

Harrison GG. 1975. Primary adult lactase deficiency: a problem in anthropological genetics. American Anthropologist. 77:812–835.

Harrison PD, Turner II BL, editors. 1978. Pre-Hispanic Maya agriculture. Albuquerque: University of New Mexico Press.

Harrison T. 2002. Late Oligocene to Middle Miocene catarrhines from Afro-Arabia. In: Hartwig WC, editor. The primate fossil record. Cambridge: Cambridge University Press. pp. 311–338.

Hartwig WC. 1994. Pattern, puzzles and perspectives on platyrrhine origins. In: Corruccini RS, Ciochon R, editors. Integrative paths to the past: paleoanthropological advances in honor of F. Clark Howell. Englewood Cliffs, NJ: Prentice Hall. pp. 69–93.

Hassan FA. 1981. Demographic archaeology. New York: Academic Press.

Haug G, Günther D, Peterson LC, Sigman DM, Hughen KA, Aeschlimann B. 2003. Climate and the collapse of Maya civilization. Science. 299:1731–1735.

Hausfater G, Altmann J, Altmann S. 20 August 1982. Long-term consistency of dominance relations among female baboons. Science. 217:752–754.

Hauspie RC, Vercauteren M, Susanne C. 1996. Secular changes in growth. Hormone Research. 45(2 Suppl):817.

Hawkins A, Kleindienst M. 2001. Aterian. In Peregrine PN, Ember M, editors. Encyclopedia of prehistory. Vol. 1, Africa. New York: Kluwer Academic/Plenum. pp. 23–45.

Hayden B. 1997. The pithouses of Keatley Creek. New York: Harcourt Brace.

Health Canada. Medical Services Branch. 1997. Diabetes among First Nations people: information from the 1991 Aboriginal Peoples Survey carried out by Statistics Canada. Ottawa: Health Canada.

Hedican EJ. 1995. Applied anthropology in Canada: understanding Aboriginal issues. Toronto: University of Toronto Press.

Hegele RA. 2001. Genes and environment in Type 2 diabetes and atherosclerosis in Aboriginal Canadians. Current Atheroclerosis Reports. 3:216–221.

Helms MW. 1975. Middle America. Englewood Cliffs, NJ: Prentice Hall.

Henry DO. 1989. From foraging to agriculture: the Levant at the end of the Ice Age. Philadelphia: University of Pennsylvania Press.

Henry DO. 1991. Foraging, sedentism, and adaptive vigor in the Natufian: rethinking the linkages. In: Clark GA, editor. Perspectives on the past: theoretical biases in Mediterranean hunter-gatherer research. Philadelphia: University of Pennsylvania Press. pp. 365–368.

Henshilwood CS, d'Errico F, Marean CW, Milo RG, Yates R. 2001. An early bone tool industry from the Middle Stone Age at Blombos Cave, South Africa: implications for the origins of modern human behaviour, symbolism and language. Journal of Human Evolution. 41(6):631–678.

Henshilwood CS, d'Errico F, Van Niekerk KL, Coquinot Y, Jacobs Z, Lauritzen SE, Menu M, García-Moreno R. 2011. A 100,000-year-old ochre-processing workshop at Blombos Cave, South Africa. Science. 334(6053):219–222.

Henshilwood CS, d'Errico F, Watts I. 2009. Engraved ochres from the Middle Stone Age levels at

Blombos Cave, South Africa. Journal of Human Evolution. 57(1):27–47.

Herring DA, Hoppa RD. 1999. Endemic tuberculosis among nineteenth century Cree in the central Canadian subarctic. Perspectives in Human Biology. 4(1):189–199.

Herring DA, Saunders SR, Katzenberg MA. 1998. Investigating the weaning process in past populations. American Journal of Physical Anthropology. 105:425–439.

Herrmann E, Call J, Hernàndez-Lloreda MV, Hare B, Tomasello M. 2007. Humans have evolved specialized skills in social cognition: the cultural intelligence hypothesis. Science. 317:1360–1365.

Herrnstein RJ, Murray C. 1994. The bell curve: intelligence and class structure in American life. New York: Free Press.

Hewes GW. 1961. Food transport and the origin of hominid bipedalism. American Anthropologist. 63:687–710.

Higham C. 2009. East Asian agriculture and its impact. In: Scarre C, editor. The human past. New York: Thames and Hudson. pp. 234–263.

Higham C, Lu T. 1998. The origins and dispersal of rice cultivation. Antiquity. 72:867–877.

Higham T, Ramsey CB, Karavanić I, Smith FH, Trinkaus E. 2006. Revised direct radiocarbon dating of the Vindija G1 Upper Paleolithic Neandertals. Proceedings of the National Academy of Sciences of the United States of America. 103:553–557.

Hill JH. 1978. Apes and language. Annual Review of Anthropology. 7:89–112.

Hill JH. 1998. Do apes have language? In: Ember CR, Ember M, Peregrine PN, editors. Research frontiers in anthropology. Upper Saddle River, NJ: Prentice Hall, Prentice Hall/Simon & Schuster Custom Publishing.

Hinkes MJ. 1989. The role of forensic anthropology in mass disaster resolution. Environmental Medicine. 60:A60–A63.

Hockett CF, Ascher R. 1964. The human revolution. Current Anthropology. 5:135–168.

Hodgson J, Driscoll T. 2008. No evidence of a Neandertal contribution to modern human diversity. Genome Biology. 9:206.1–206.7.

Hoffecker JF, Powers WR, Goebel T. 1 January 1993. The colonization of Beringia and the peopling of the New World. Science. 46–53.

Holdaway RN, Jacomb C. 2000. Rapid extinction of the Moas (Aves: Dinornithiformes): model, test, and implications. Science. 287:2250–2257.

Holden C. 2004a. Kennewick Man—court battle ends, bones still off-limits. Science. 305:591.

Holden C. 2004b. Kennewick Man—scientists hope ruling will lead them to bones. Science. 303:943.

Hole F. 1992. Origins of agriculture. In: Jones S, Martin R, Pilbeam D, editors. The Cambridge encyclopedia of human evolution. New York: Cambridge University Press. pp. 373–379.

Hole F. 1994. Environmental shock and urban origins. In: Stein G, Rothman MS, editors. Chiefdoms and early states in the Near East: the organizational dynamics of complexity. Madison, WI: Prehistoric Press.

Hole F, Flannery KV, Neely JA. 1969. Prehistory and human ecology of the Deh Luran Plain. Memoirs of the Museum of Anthropology No. 1. Ann Arbor: University of Michigan.

Hole F, Heizer RH. 1973. An introduction to prehistoric archeology. New York: Holt, Rinehart & Winston.

Holliday R. 2006. Epigenetics: a historical overview. Epigenetics. 1(2):76–80.

Holloway RL. 1980. Indonesian "Solo" (Ngangdong) endocranial reconstructions: preliminary observations and comparisons with Neandertal and *Homo erectus* groups. American Journal of Physical Anthropology. 53:285–295.

Holloway RL. 1981. The Indonesian *Homo erectus* brain endocasts revisited. American Journal of Physical Anthropology. 55:502–521.

Holloway RT. July 1974. The casts of fossil hominid brains. Scientific American. 231:106–115.

Honigmann JJ. 1967. Personality in culture. New York: Harper & Row.

Hoppa RD. 1998. Mortality in a northern Ontario fur-trade community: Moose Factory, 1851–1964. Canadian Studies in Population. 25(2):175–198.

Hoppa RD, Garlie TN. 1998. Secular changes in the growth of Toronto children during the last century. Annals of Human Biology. 25(6):553–561.

Hoppa RD, Vaupel JW, editors. 2002. Palaeodemography: age distributions from skeletal samples. Cambridge: Cambridge University Press.

Houston SD. 1988. The phonetic decipherment of Maya glyphs. Antiquity. 62:126–135.

Howell FC. April 1966. Observations on the earlier phases of the European Lower Paleolithic. In: Recent Studies in Paleoanthropology. American Anthropologist (special publication). 68:88–201.

Howell N. 1979. Demography of the Dobe !Kung. New York: Academic Press.

Howell N. 1986. Anthropological demography. Annual Review of Anthropology. 15:219–246.

Huang HT. 2002. Hypolactasia and the Chinese diet. Current Anthropology. 43:809–819.

Hudson J, editor. 1993. From bones to behavior: ethnoarchaeological and experimental contributions to the interpretation of faunal remains. Occasional Paper No. 21. Carbondale: Center for Archaeological Investigations. Southern Illinois University at Carbondale.

Huffine E, Crews J, Kennedy B, Bomberger K, Zinbo A. 2001. Mass identification of persons missing from the break-up of the former Yugoslavia: structure, function, and role of the International Commission on Missing Persons. Croatian Medical Journal. 42:271–275.

Hull S, Fayek M. 2012. Cracking the code of pre-Columbian turquoise trade networks and procurement strategies. In: King JCH, Carocci M, Cartwright C, McEwan C, editors. Turquoise in Mexico and North America: science, conservation, culture and collections. London: Archetype. pp. 29–40.

Hull S, Fayek M, Mathien FJ, Roberts H. 2014. Turquoise trade of the Ancestral Puebloan: Chaco and beyond. Journal of Archaeological Science. 45: 187–195.

Huss-Ashmore R, Johnston FE. 1985. Bioanthropological research in developing countries. Annual Review of Anthropology. 14:475–528.

Huypens P, Sass S, Wu M, Dyckhoff D, Tschöp M, Theis F, Marschall S, Hrabě de Angelis M, Beckers J. 2016. Epigenetic germline inheritance of diet-induced obesity and insulin resistance. Nature Genetics. doi:10.1038/ng.3527.

Inhorn MC, Brown PJ. 1990. The anthropology of infectious disease. Annual Review of Anthropology. 19:89–117.

Irons W. 1979. Natural selection, adaptation, and human social behavior. In: Chagnon NA, Irons W, editors. Evolutionary biology and human social behavior: an anthropological perspective. North Scituate, MA: Duxbury. pp. 10–12.

Isaac G. 1971. The diet of early man: aspects of archaeological evidence from Lower and Middle Pleistocene sites in Africa. World Archaeology. 2:289.

Isaac G. 1977. Ologesailie: archaeological studies of a Middle Pleistocene lake basin in Kenya. Chicago: University of Chicago Press.

Isaac G. 1984. The archaeology of human origins: studies of the Pleistocene in East Africa, 1971–1981. In: Wendorf F, Close AE, editors. Advances in world archaeology. Vol. 3. Orlando, FL: Academic Press. pp. 1–87.

Jablonski NG. 2010. Skin coloration. In: Muehlenbein M, editor. Human evolutionary biology. Cambridge: Cambridge University Press. pp. 192–213.

Jablonski NG, Chaplin G. 2000. The evolution of human skin coloration. Journal of Human Evolution. 39:57–106.

Jackes M, Lubell D, Meiklejohn C. 1997a. Healthy but mortal: human biology and the first farmers in western Europe. Antiquity. 71:639–658.

Jackes M, Lubell D, Meiklejohn C. 1997b. On physical anthropological aspects of the Mesolithic-Neolithic transition in the Iberian Peninsula. Current Anthropology. 38(5):839–846.

Jacobs P, Blanchard JF, James RC, Depew N. 2000. Excess costs of diabetes in the Aboriginal population of Manitoba, Canada. Canadian Journal of Public Health. 91(4):298–301.

Janzen DH. 12 December 1973. Tropical agroecosystems. Science. 182:1212–1218.

Jayaswal V. 2002. South Asian Upper Paleolithic. In: Peregrine PN, Ember M, editors. Encyclopedia of prehistory. Vol. 8, South and Southwest Asia. New York: Kluwer Academic/Plenum. pp. 326–343.

Jelliffe DB, Jelliffe EFP. 9 May 1975. Human milk, nutrition and the world resource crisis. Science. 557–561.

Jenkins DL, Davis LG, Stafford TW, Campos PF, Hockett B, Jones GT, Cummings LS, Yost C, Connolly TJ, Yohe RM, Gibbons SC. 2012. Clovis age western stemmed projectile points and human coprolites at the Paisley Caves. Science. 337(6091):223–228.

Jennings JD. 1968. Prehistory of North America. New York: McGraw-Hill.

Johanson DC, Edey M. 1981. Lucy: the beginnings of humankind. New York: Simon & Schuster.

Johanson DC, White TD. 26 January 1979. A systematic assessment of early African hominids. Science. 321–330.

Johansson SR, Horowitz S. 1986. Estimating mortality in skeletal populations: influence of the growth rate on the interpretations of levels and trends during the transition to agriculture. American Journal of Physical Anthropology. 71:233–250.

Johnson AW, Earle TK. 2000. The evolution of human societies: from foraging group to agrarian state. Stanford, CA: Stanford University Press.

Johnson GA. 1977. Aspects of regional analysis in archaeology. Annual Review of Anthropology. 6:479–508.

Johnson GA. 1987. The changing organization of Uruk administration on the Susiana Plain. In: Hole F, editor. Archaeology of western Iran. Washington, DC: Smithsonian Institution Press. pp. 107–139.

Johnston FE. 1985. Health implications of childhood obesity. Annals of Internal Medicine. 103:1068–1072.

Johnston FE, Bogin B, MacVean RB, Newman BC. 1984. A comparison of international standards versus local reference data for the triceps and subscapular skinfolds of Guatemalan children and youth. Human Biology. 56:157–171.

Johnston FE, Hamill PV, Lemeshow S. 1974. Skinfold thicknesses in a national probability sample of US males and females 6 through 17 years. American Journal of Physical Anthropology. 40:321–324.

Johnston FE, Ouyang Z. 1991. Choosing appropriate reference data for the anthropometric assessment of nutritional status. In: Himes JH, editor. Anthropometric assessment of nutritional status. New York: Wiley-Liss. pp. 337–346.

Jolly A. 1985. The evolution of primate behavior. 2nd ed. New York: Macmillan.

Jolly C. 1970. The seed-eaters: a new model of hominid differentiation based on a baboon analogy. Man. 5:5–28.

Jones M, Liu X. 2009. Origins of agriculture in East Asia. Science. 324:730–731.

Jones S, Martin R, Pilbeam D, editors. 1992. The Cambridge encyclopedia of human evolution. New York: Cambridge University Press.

Jordanova LJ. 1984. Lamarck. Oxford: Oxford University Press.

Judge WJ, Dawson J. 16 June 1972. Paleo-Indian settlement technology in New Mexico. Science. 176:1210–1216.

Jungers WL. 1988. Relative joint size and hominoid locomotor adaptations with implications for the evolution of hominid bipedalism. Journal of Human Evolution. 17:247–265.

Jungers WL. 1998. New estimates of body size in australopithecines. In: Grine FE, editor. Evolutionary history of the "robust" australopithecines. New York: Aldine. pp. 115–125.

Jungers WL, Harcourt-Smith WE, Wunderlich RE, Tocheri MW, Larson SG, Sutikna T, Awe Due R, Morwood MJ. 2009a. The foot of *Homo floresiensis*. Nature. 459(7243):81–84.

Jungers WL, Larson SG, Harcourt-Smith W, Morwood MJ, Sutikna T, Awe Due R, Djubiantono T. 2009b. Descriptions of the lower limb skeleton of *Homo floresiensis*. Journal of Human Evolution. 57(5):538–554.

Kakekagumick KE, Hayward MN, Harris SB, Saksvig B, Gittelsohn J, Manokeesic G, Goodman S, Hanley AJ. 2013. Sandy Lake Health and Diabetes Project: a community-based intervention targeting Type 2 diabetes and its risk factors in a First Nations community. Frontiers in Endocrinology. 4:170.

Kaler SN, Ralph-Campbell K, Pohar S, King M, Laboucan CR, Toth EL. 2006. High rates of the metabolic syndrome in a First Nations community in western Canada: prevalence and determinants in adults and children. International Journal of Circumpolar Health. 65:389–402.

Kappelman J. 1993. The attraction of paleomagnetism. Evolutionary Anthropology. 2:89–99.

Karlsson EA, Engel GA, Feeroz MM, San S, Rompis A, Lee BP, Shaw E, Oh G, Schillaci MA, Grant R, Heidrich J, et al. 2012. Influenza virus infection in nonhuman primates. Emerging Infectious Diseases. 18(10):1672–1675.

Kasarda JD. August 1971. Economic structure and fertility: a comparative analysis. Demography. 8(3):307–318.

Katzenberg MA. 1984. Chemical analysis of prehistoric human bone from five temporally distinct populations in southern Ontario. Ottawa: National Museums of Canada.

Katzenberg MA. 1991. Stable isotope analysis of remains from the Harvie family. In: Saunders SR, Lazenby R, editors. The links that bind: the Harvie family nineteenth century burying ground. Occasional Papers in Northeastern Archaeology, No. 5. Dundas, ON: Copetown Press. pp. 65–69.

Katzenberg MA. 1992. Advances in stable isotope analysis of prehistoric bones. In: Saunders SR, Katzenberg MA, editors. Skeletal biology of past peoples: research methods. New York: Wiley-Liss. pp. 105–119.

Katzenberg MA. 1993. Applications of elemental and isotopic analysis to populations in Ontario prehistory. In: Sandford MK, editor. Investigations of ancient human tissues: chemical analyses in anthropology. Langhorne, PA: Gordon and Breach Science Publishers. pp. 335–360.

Katzenberg MA. 2000. Stable isotope analysis: a tool for studying past diet, demography and life history. In: Katzenberg MA, Saunders SR. Biological anthropology of the skeleton. New York: Wiley-Liss. pp. 305–328.

Katzenberg MA, Herring DA, Saunders SR. 1996. Weaning and infant mortality: evaluating the skeletal evidence. Yearbook of Physical Anthropology. 39:177–199.

Katzenberg MA, Oetelaar G, Oetelaar J, Fitzgerald C, Yang D, Saunders SR. 2005. Identification of historical human skeletal remains: a case study using skeletal and dental age, history and DNA. International Journal of Osteoarchaeology. 15(1):61–72.

Katzenberg MA, Pfeiffer S. 1995. Nitrogen isotope evidence for weaning age in a nineteenth century Canadian skeletal sample. In: Grauer AL, editor. Bodies of evidence: reconstructing history through skeletal analysis. New York: John Wiley & Sons. pp. 139–160.

Katzenberg MA, Saunders SR, Fitzgerald W. 1993. Age differences in stable carbon and nitrogen isotope ratios in a population of prehistoric maize horticulturists. American Journal of Physical Anthropology. 90:267–281.

Katzenberg MA, Schwarcz HP, Knyf M, Melbye FJ. 1995. Stable isotope analysis for maize horticulture and paleodiet in southern Ontario, Canada. American Antiquity. 60:335–350.

Kawai M. 1965. Newly-acquired pre-cultural behavior of the natural troop of Japanese monkeys on Koshima Islet. Primates. 6(1):1–30.

Kay RF. 1988a. Parapithecidae. In: Tattersall I, Delson E, Van Couvering J, editors. Encyclopedia of human evolution and prehistory. New York: Garland. pp. 441–442.

Kay RF. 1988b. Teeth. In: Tattersall I, Delson E, Van Couvering J, editors. Encyclopedia of human evolution and prehistory. New York: Garland. pp. 571–578.

Keefe AA, Angel H, Mangan B. 2012. Canadian Forces Anthropometric Survey (CFAS): final report. Report No. DRDC-RDDC-2015-R186. Toronto: Defence Research and Development Canada, Toronto Research Centre; Guelph, ON: HumanSystems Inc.

Kelley J. 1992. The evolution of apes. In: Jones S, Martin R, Pilbeam D, editors. The Cambridge encyclopedia of human evolution. New York: Cambridge University Press. pp. 223–230.

Kent S. 1996. Cultural diversity among twentieth-century foragers: an African perspective. Cambridge: Cambridge University Press.

Kerr RA. 16 January 1998. Sea-floor dust shows drought felled Akkadian Empire. Science. 279:325–326.

Keuhn S. 1998. New evidence for Late Paleoindian–Early Archaic subsistence behavior in the western Great Lakes. American Antiquity. 63:457–476.

Kim C, Chan HM. 1998. Risk assessment of cadmium exposure in Fort Resolution, Northwest Territories, Canada. Food Additives and Contaminants. 15:307–317.

Kimbel WH, Lockwood CA, Ward CV, Leakey MG, Rak Y, Johanson DC. 2006. Was *Australopithecus Anamensis* ancestral to *A. afarensis*? a case of anagenesis in the hominin fossil record. Journal of Human Evolution. 51:134–152.

Kimmerle EH. 2014. Practicing forensic anthropology: a human rights approach to the global problem of missing and unidentified persons. Annals of Anthropological Practice. 38(1):1–6.

King M-C, Motulsky A. 20 December 2002. Mapping human history. Science. 298:2342–2343.

Kingston JD, Marino BD, Hill A. 13 May 1994. Isotopic evidence for Neogene hominid paleoenvironments in the Kenya Rift Valley. Science. 264:955–959.

Kirmayer LJ, Brass GM, Tait CL. 2000. The mental health of Aboriginal peoples: transformations of identity and community. Canadian Journal of Psychiatry. 45:607–616.

Kivell TL, Deane AS, Tocheri MW, Orr CM, Schmid P, Hawks J, Berger LR, Churchill SE. 2015. The hand of *Homo naledi*. Nature Communications. 6:8431 doi:10.1038/ncomms9431.

Klaus HD. 2014. Frontiers in the bioarchaeology of stress and disease: cross-disciplinary perspectives from pathophysiology, human biology, and epidemiology. American Journal of Physical Anthropology.155(2):294–308.

Klein RG. June 1974. Ice-Age hunters of the Ukraine. Scientific American. 230:96–105.

Klein RG. 8 July 1977. The ecology of early man in southern Africa. Science. 197:111–126.

Klein RG. 1983. The Stone Age prehistory of southern Africa. Annual Review of Anthropology. 12:25–48.

Klein RG. 1987. Reconstructing how early people exploited animals: problems and prospects. In: Nitecki M, Nitecki DV, editors. The evolution of human hunting. New York: Plenum. pp. 11–45.

Klein RG. 1989. The human career: human biological and cultural origins. Chicago: University of Chicago Press.

Klein RG. 1994. Southern Africa before the Ice Age. In: Corruccini R, Ciochon RL, editors. Integrative paths to the past: paleoanthropological advances in Honor of F. Clark Howell. Englewood Cliffs, NJ: Prentice Hall.

Klein RG. 2003. Paleoanthropology. Whither the Neanderthals? Science. 299:1525–1527.

Klein RG. 2009. The human career: human biological and cultural origins. 3rd ed. Chicago: University of Chicago Press.

Klein RG, Edgar B. 2002. The dawn of human culture. New York: John Wiley and Sons.

Kleinman A. 1988. Rethinking psychiatry: from cultural category to personal experience. New York: Macmillan.

Klepinger LL. 1984. Nutritional assessment from bone. Annual Review of Anthropology. 13:75–96.

Klima B. 1962. The first ground-plan of an Upper Paleolithic Loess settlement in Middle Europe and its meaning. In: Braidwood RJ, Willey GR, editors. Courses toward urban life: archaeological consideration of some cultural alternatives. Viking Fund Publications in Anthropology No. 32. Chicago: Aldine. pp. 193–210.

Komar D. 2003. Lessons from Srebrenica: the contributions and limitations of physical anthropology in identifying victims of war crimes. Journal of Forensic Sciences. 48:713–716.

Konigsberg LW, Frankenberg SR. 1994. Palaeodemography: not quite dead. Evolutionary Anthropology. 3(3):92–105.

Konner M, Wortman C. 15 February 1980. Nursing frequency, gonadal function, and birth spacing among !Kung hunter-gatherers. Science. 207:788–791.

Kottak CP. 1996. The media, development, and social change. In: Moran EF, editor. Transforming societies, transforming anthropology. Ann Arbor: University of Michigan Press.

Kramer A. 1993. Human taxonomic diversity in the Pleistocene: does *Homo erectus* represent multiple

Kramer SN. 1963. The Sumerians: their history, culture, and character. Chicago: University of Chicago Press.

Krause J, Lalueza-Fox C, Orlando L, Enard W, Green RE, Burbano HA, Hublin JJ, Hänni C, Fortea J, de la Rasilla M, Bertranpetit J, et al. 2007. The derived FOXP2 variant of modern humans was shared with Neandertals. Current Biology. 17(21):1908–1912.

Krause J, Fu Q, Good JM, Viola B, Shunkov MV, Derevianko AP, Pääbo S. 2010. The complete mitochondrial DNA genome of an unknown hominin from southern Siberia. Nature. 464(7290):894–897.

Krause J, Pääbo S. 2016. Genetic time travel. Genetics. 203:9–12

Krebs JR, Davies NB, editors. 1984. Behavioural ecology: an evolutionary approach. 2nd ed. Sunderland, MA: Sinauer.

Krebs JR, Davies NB. 1987. An introduction to behavioural ecology. 2nd ed. Sunderland, MA: Sinauer.

Krings M, Geisert H, Schmitz RW, Krainitzki H, Paabo S. 1999. DNA sequence of the mitochondrial hypervariable Region II from the Neandertal type specimen. Proceedings of the National Academy of Sciences of the United States of America. 96:5581–5585.

Krings M, Stone A, Schmitz RW, Krainitzki H, Stoneking M, Paabo S. 1997. Neandertal DNA sequences and the origin of modern humans. Cell. 90:19–30.

Kuehn S. 1998. New evidence for Late Paleoindian–Early Archaic subsistence behavior in the western Great Lakes. American Antiquity. 63:475–476.

Kuhnlein HV, Chan HM. 2000. Environment and contaminants in traditional food systems of northern Indigenous peoples. Annual Review of Nutrition. 20:595–626.

Kushner G. 1991. Applied anthropology. In: Emener WG, Darrow M, editors. Career explorations in human services. Springfield, IL: Charles C. Thomas. pp. 46–61.

Laitman J, Heimbuch R. 1982. The basicranium of Plio-Pleistocene hominids as an indicator of their upper respiratory systems. American Journal of Physical Anthropology. 59:323–343.

Laitman J, Heimbuch RC. 1984. The basicranium and upper respiratory system of African *Homo erectus* and early *Homo sapiens*. American Journal of Physical Anthropology. 63:180.

Laitman JT, Heimbuch RC, Crelin ES. 1978. Developmental change in a basicranial line and its relationship to the upper respiratory system in living primates. American Journal of Anatomy. 152:467–482.

Laland KN, Odling-Smee J, Myles S. 2010. How culture shaped the human genome: bringing genetics and the human sciences together. Nature Reviews Genetics. 11(2):137–148.

Lalueza-Fox C, Römpler H, Caramelli D, Stäubert C, Catalano G, Hughes D, Rohland N, Pilli E, Longo L, Condemi S, de la Rasilla M, et al. 2007. A melanocortin 1 receptor allele suggests varying pigmentation among Neanderthals. Science. 318(5855):1453–1455.

Lambert DT. 1993. AIDS and the Aboriginal community. Canadian Journal of Public Health. 84(1 Suppl):S46–S47.

Langdon J. 2005. The human strategy. New York: Oxford University Press.

Larcombe L, Mookherjee N, Slater J, Slivinski C, Dantouze J, Singer M, Whaley C, Denechezhe L, Matyas S, Decter K, Turner-Brannen E, et al. 2015. Vitamin D, serum 25 (OH) D, LL-37 and polymorphisms in a Canadian First Nation population with endemic tuberculosis. International Journal of Circumpolar Health. 2015(74):28952.

Larcombe L, Orr PH, Lodge AM, Brown JS, Dembinski IJ, Milligan LC, Larcombe EA, Martin BD, Nickerson PW. 2008. Functional gene polymorphisms in Canadian Aboriginal populations with high rates of tuberculosis. Journal of Infectious Diseases. 198(8):1175–1179.

Larcombe L, Orr P, Turner-Brannen E, Slivinski CR, Nickerson PW, Mookherjee N. 2012. Effect of vitamin D supplementation on Mycobacterium tuberculosis-induced innate immune responses in a Canadian Dené First Nations cohort. PLoS One. 7(7):e40692.

Larcombe LA, Nickerson P, Hoppa RD, Matheson C. 2005. Detection of a single nucleotide polymorphism in the IL-6 promoter region of ancient nuclear DNA. Infection, Genetics and Evolution. 5(2):117–122.

Larcombe L, Rempel JD, Dembinski I, Tinckam K, Rigatto C, Nickerson P. 2005. Differential cytokine genotype frequencies among Canadian Aboriginal and Caucasian populations. Genes and immunity. 6(2):140–144.

Larsen CS. 1995. Biological changes in human populations with agriculture. Annual Review of Anthropology. 24:185–213.

Larsen CS. 1998. Bare bones anthropology: the bioarchaeology of human remains. In: Ember CR, Ember M, Peregrine PN, editors. Research frontiers in anthropology. Upper Saddle River, NJ: Prentice Hall/Simon & Schuster Custom Publishing.

Lavoie JG, O'Neil JD, Reading J, Allard Y. 2009. Community healing and Aboriginal self-government. In: Aboriginal self-government in Canada: current trends and issues. 3rd ed. Saskatoon: Purich. 2009:175–205.

Leakey LSB. September 1960. Finding the world's earliest man. National Geographic. 118:420–435.

Leakey M. 1971. Olduvai Gorge: excavations in Beds I and II. Cambridge: Cambridge University Press.

Leakey M. 1979. Olduvai Gorge: my search for early man. London: Collins.

Leakey M, Spoor F, Brown FH, Gathogo PN, Kiarie C, Leakey LN, McDougall I. 22 March 2001. New hominin genus from eastern Africa shows diverse Middle Pliocene lineages. Nature. 410:433–451.

Leakey MG, Feibel CS, McDougall I, Walker A. 17 August 1995. New four-million-year-old hominid species from Kanapoi and Allia Bay, Kenya. Nature. 376:565–571.

Leakey MG, Feibel CS, McDougall I, Ward C, Walker A. 1998. New specimens and confirmation of an early age for *Australopithecus anamensis*. Nature. 393:62–66.

Lee PC. 1983. Home range, territory and intergroup encounters. In: Hinde RA, editor. Primate social relationships: an integrated approach. Sunderland, MA: Sinauer. pp. 231–253.

Lee RB. 1972. Population growth and the beginnings of sedentary life among the !Kung Bushmen. In: Spooner B, editor. Population growth: anthropological implications. Cambridge, MA: MIT Press. pp. 329–342.

Lee RB. 1979. The !Kung San: men, women, and work in a foraging society. Cambridge: Cambridge University Press.

Le Gros Clark WE. 1964. The fossil evidence for human evolution. Chicago: University of Chicago Press.

Leonard WR. December 2002. Food for thought: dietary change was a driving force in human evolution. Scientific American. 287:108–115.

Leonard WR, Katzmarzyk PT. 2010. Body size and shape: Climatic and nutritional influences on human body morphology. In: Muehlenbein M, editor. Human evolutionary biology. Cambridge: Cambridge University Press. pp. 157–169.

Lev-Yadun S, Gopher A, Abbo S. 2000. The cradle of agriculture. Science. 288(5471):1602.

Lewin R. 7 January 1983. Fossil Lucy grows younger, again. Science. 219:43–44.

Lewis KP. 2000. A comparative study of primate play behaviour: implications for the study of cognition. Folia Primatologica. 71:417–421.

Liebenberg L. 2006. Persistence hunting by modern hunter-gatherers. Current Anthropology. 47:1017–1025.

Lieberman DE. 1995. Testing hypotheses about recent human evolution from skulls: integrating morphology, function, development, and phylogeny. Current Anthropology 36: 159–197.

Lieberman P. 2002. On the nature and evolution of the neural bases of human language. Yearbook of Physical Anthropoology. 45:36–62.

Lieberman L. 1999. Scientific insignificance. Anthropology Newsletter. 40:11–12.

Lieberman P. 1992. Human speech and language. In: Jones S, Martin R, Pilbeam D, editors. Cambridge encyclopedia of human evolution. Cambridge: Cambridge University Press. pp. 134–137.

Lieberman P, Laitman J, Reidenberg J, Gannon P. 1982. The anatomy, physiology, acoustics and perception of speech: essential elements in analysis of the evolution of human speech. Journal of Human Evolution. 22:447–467.

Lightfoot E, O'Connell TC. 2016. On the use of biomineral oxygen isotope data to identify human migrants in the archaeological record: intra-sample variation, statistical methods and geographical considerations. Plos One. 11(4):e0153850.

Lin DS, Connor WE. 2001. Fecal steroids of the coprolite of a Greenland Eskimo mummy, AD 1475: a clue to dietary sterol intake. American Journal of Clinical Nutrition. 74(1):44–49.

Linton R. 1936. The study of man. New York: Appleton-Century-Crofts.

Lombard M. 2014. *In situ* presumptive test for blood residues applied to 62 000-year-old stone tools. The South African Archaeological Bulletin. 69(199):80–86.

Loomis WF. 4 August 1967. Skin-pigment regulation of vitamin-D biosynthesis in man. Science. 157:501–506.

Lopinot NH, Woods W. 1993. Wood overexploitation and the collapse of Cahokia. In: Scarry CM, editor. Foraging and farming in the Eastern Woodlands. Gainesville: University Press of Florida. pp. 206–231.

Lopuchin AS. January/April 1975. Structures of biogenic origin from early Precambrian rocks of Euro-Asia. Origins of Life. 6(12):45–57.

Loustaunau MO, Sobo EJ. 1997. The cultural context of health, illness, and medicine. Westport, CT: Bergin & Garvey.

Lovejoy AO. 1964. The great chain of being: a study of the history of an idea. Cambridge, MA: Harvard University Press.

Lovejoy CO. 23 January 1981. The origin of man. Science. 211:341–350.

Lovejoy CO. 1988. Evolution of human walking. Scientific American. 259(5):118–125.

Lovejoy CO, Heiple K, Bernstein A. 1973. The gait of *Australopithecus*. American Journal of Physical Anthropology. 38:757–779.

Low B. 1990. Human responses to environmental extremeness and uncertainty. In: Cashdan E, editor. Risk and uncertainty in tribal and peasant economies. Boulder, CO: Westview Press. pp. 242–243.

Low BS. 1998. Behavioral ecology, "sociobiology" and human social behavior. In: Ember CR, Ember M, Peregrine PN, editors. Research frontiers in anthropology. Upper Saddle River, NJ: Prentice Hall/Simon & Schuster Custom Publishing.

Lowie RH. 1917, 1988. The determinants of culture. In: Bohannan P, Glazer M, editors. High points in anthropology. New York: Alfred A. Knopf.

Loy TH. 1998. Blood on the axe. New Scientist. 159(2151):40.

Loy TH, Dixon EJ. 1998. Blood residues on fluted points from eastern Beringia. American Antiquity. 63(1):21–46.

Loy TH, Hardy BL. 1992. Blood residue analysis of 90,000-year-old stone tools from Tabun Cave, Israel. Antiquity. 66(250):24–35.

Loy TH, Rhys Jones DE, Nelson BM, Meehan B. 1990. Accelerator radiocarbon dating of human blood proteins in pigments from Late Pleistocene art sites in Australia. Antiquity. 64(242):110–116.

Loy TH, Spriggs MJT, Wickler S. 1992. Direct evidence for human use of plants 28,000 years ago: starch residues on stone artefacts from the northern Solomon Islands. Antiquity. 66(253):898–912.

Lubell D, Jackes M, Schwarcz HP, Knyf M, Meiklejohn C. 1994. The Mesolithic–Neolithic transition in Portugal: isotopic and dental evidence of diet. Journal of Archaeological Science. 21:201–215.

Lumbreras L. 1974. The peoples and cultures of ancient Peru. Washington, DC: Smithsonian Institution Press.

Lutz C. 1985. Depression and the translations of emotional worlds. In: Kleinman A, Good B, editors. Culture and depression: studies in the anthropology and cross-cultural psychiatry of affect and disorder. Berkeley: University of California Press. pp. 63–100.

Lyell C. 1863. The geological evidences of the antiquity of man. London: Murray.

Mackie Q. 1995. Prehistory in a multicultural state: a commentary on the development of Canadian archaeology. In: Ucko PJ, editor. Theory in archaeology: a world perspective. London/New York: Routledge. pp. 175–193.

MacKinnon J, MacKinnon K. 1980. The behavior of wild spectral tarsiers. International Journal of Primatology. 1:361–379.

MacLarnon A, Hewitt G. 2004. Increased breathing control: another factor in the evolution of human language. Evolutionary Anthropology: Issues, News, and Reviews. 13(5):181–197.

MacMillan H, MacMillan AB, Offord DR, Dingle JL. 1996. Aboriginal health. Canadian Medical Association Journal. 155(11):1569–1578.

MacNeish RS. 1991. The origins of agriculture and settled life. Norman: University of Oklahoma Press.

Madigral L. 1989. Hemoglobin genotype, fertility, and the malaria hypothesis. Human Biology. 61:311–325.

Maestripieri D, Ross SK, Megna NL. 2002. Mother-infant interactions in western lowland gorillas (*Gorilla gorilla gorilla*): spatial relationships, communication, and opportunities for social learning. Journal of Comparative Psychology. 116(3):219–227.

Makristathis A, Schwarzmeier J, Mader RM, Varmuza K, Simonitsch I, Chavez JC, Platzer W, Unterdorfer H, Scheithauer R, Derevianko A, Seidler H. 2002. Fatty acid composition and preservation of the Tyrolean Iceman and other mummies. Journal of Lipid Research. 43:2056–2061.

Malainey ME. 2011. Lipid residue analysis. In: Malainey ME, editor. A consumer's guide to archaeological science. New York: Springer. pp. 201–218.

Malainey ME, Przybylski R, Sherriff BL. 1999. Identifying the former contents of late precontact period pottery vessels from western Canada using gas chromatography. Journal of Archaeological Science. 26(4):425–438.

Manchester K. 1987. Skeletal evidence for health and disease. In: Boddington A, Garland AN, Janaway RC, editors. Death, decay and reconstruction: approaches to archaeology and forensic science. Manchester: Manchester University Press. pp. 163–179.

Manzi G, Mallegni F, Ascenzi A. 2001. A cranium for the earliest Europeans: phylogenetic position of the hominid from Ceprano, Italy. Proceedings of the National Academy of Sciences of the United States of America. 98:10011–10016.

Marciniak S, Klunk J, Devault A, Enk J, Poinar HN. 2015. Ancient human genomics: the methodology behind reconstructing evolutionary pathways. Journal of Human Evolution. 79:21–34.

Marcus J. 1983. On the nature of the Mesoamerican City. In: Vogt EZ, Leventhal RM, editors. Prehistoric settlement patterns: essays in honor of Gordon R. Willey. Albuquerque: University of New Mexico Press. pp. 195–242.

Marcus J, Flannery KV. 1996. Zapotec civilization: how urban society evolved in Mexico's Oaxaca Valley. New York, NY: Thames and Hudson.

Marks J. December 1994. Black, white, other: racial categories are cultural constructs masquerading as biology. Natural History. 32–35.

Marshack A. 1972. The roots of civilization. New York: McGraw-Hill.

Marshall LG. 1984. Who killed Cock Robin? An investigation of the extinction controversy. In: Martin PS, Klein RG, editors. Quaternary extinctions: a prehistoric revolution. Tucson: University of Arizona Press. pp. 785–806.

Marshall WA. 1978. The relationship of puberty to other maturity indicators and body composition in man. Journal of Reproductive Fertility. 52:437–443.

Marshall WA, Tanner JM. 1986. Puberty. In: Falkner F, Tanner JM, editors. Human Growth 2: Postnatal growth. 2nd ed. London: Plenum Press. pp. 171–210.

Martin PS. 9 March 1973. The discovery of America. Science. 179:969–974.

Martin PS, Wright HE, editors, National Research Council (U.S.). 1967. Pleistocene extinctions: the search for a cause. New Haven, CT: Yale University Press.

Martin R. 1992. Classification and evolutionary relationships. In: Jones S, Martin R, Pilbeam D, editors. The Cambridge encyclopedia of human evolution. Cambridge: Cambridge University Press. pp. 17–19.

Martin RD. November 1975. Strategies of reproduction. Natural History. 84:48–57.

Martin RD, Bearder SK. 1979. Radio bush baby. Natural History. 88:77–81.

Martin RD, MacLarnon AM, Phillips JL, Dobyns WB. 2006. Flores hominid: new species or microcephalic dwarf? The Anatomical Record Part A: Discoveries in Molecular, Cellular, and Evolutionary Biology. 288:1123–1145.

Martin RD, Martin AE. 1990. Primate origins and evolution: a phylogenetic reconstruction. Princeton, NJ: Princeton University Press.

Martorell R. 1980. Interrelationships between diet, infectious disease and nutritional status. In: Greene L, Johnston FE, editors. Social and biological predictors of nutritional status, physical growth and neurological development. New York: Academic Press. pp. 81–106.

Martorell R, Ho TJ. 1984. Malnutrition, morbidity and mortality. In: Mosley WH, Chen LC, editors. Child survival: strategies for research. Population development review, supplement to Volume 10. New York: Population Council. pp. 49–68.

Martorell R, Rivera J, Kaplowitz H, Pollit E. 15 September 1991. Long-term consequences of growth retardation during early childhood. Paper presented at: The Sixth International Congress of Auxology; Madrid, Spain.

Mascie-Taylor CGN. 1990. The biology of social class. In: Mascie-Taylor CGN, editor. Biosocial aspects of social class. Oxford: Oxford University Press. pp. 118–121.

Matthews R. 2009. Peoples and complex societies of southwest Asia. In: Scarre C, editor. The human past. New York: Thames and Hudson.

Maxwell MS. 1985. Prehistory of the eastern Arctic. Orlando, FL: Academic Press.

Mayr E. 2 June 1972. The nature of the Darwinian revolution. Science. 981–989.

Mayr E. 1982. The growth of biological thought: diversity, evolution, and inheritance. Cambridge, MA: Belknap Press of Harvard University Press.

McCain G, Segal EM. 1988. The game of science. 5th ed. Monterey, CA: Brooks/Cole.

McCorriston J, Hole F. 1991. The ecology of seasonal stress and the origins of agriculture in the Near East. American Anthropologist. 93:46–69.

McCracken RD. 1971. Lactase deficiency: an example of dietary evolution. Current Anthropology. 37:227–275.

McDonald KA. 13 March 1998. New evidence challenges traditional model of how the New World was settled. Chronicle of Higher Education. A22.

McElroy A, Townsend PR. 2002. Medical anthropology in ecological perspective. 3rd ed. Boulder, CO: Westview.

McGarvey ST, Bindon JR, Crews DE, Schendel DE. 1989. Modernization and adiposity: causes and consequences. In: Little MA, Haas JD, editors. Human population biology. a transdisciplinary science. Oxford: Oxford University Press. pp. 263–279.

McGhee R. 1996. Ancient people of the Arctic. Vancouver: University of British Columbia Press.

McGovern PE, Hall GR. 2015. Charting a future course for organic residue analysis in archaeology. Journal of Archaeological Method and Theory. 23(2):1–31.

McHenry HM. 1982. The pattern of human evolution: studies on bipedalism, mastication, and encephalization. Annual Review of Anthropology. 11:151–173.

McHenry HM. 1998a. New estimates of body weight in early hominids and their significance to encephalization and megadontia in "robust" australopithecines. In: Grine FE, editor. Evolutionary history of the "robust" australopithecines. New York: Aldine. pp. 133–148.

McHenry HM. 1998b. "Robust" australopithecines, our family tree, and homoplasy. In: Ember CR, Ember M, Peregrine PN, editors. Research frontiers in anthropology. Upper Saddle River, NJ: Prentice Hall/Simon & Schuster Custom Publishing.

McHenry HM. 2002. "Robust" australopithecines: our family tree, and homoplasy. In: Peregrine PN, Ember CR, Ember M, editors. Physical anthropology: original readings in method and practice. Upper Saddle River, NJ: Prentice Hall.

McKee L. 1984. Sex differentials in survivorship and the customary treatment of infants and children. Medical Anthropology. 8:91–108.

McNeill WH. 1967. A world history. New York: Oxford University Press.

McNeill WH. 1998. Plagues and peoples. New York: Anchor Books/Doubleday.

Mellaart J. 1961. Roots in the soil. In: Piggott S, editor. The dawn of civilization. London: Thames & Hudson. pp. 41–64.

Mellaart J. April 1964. A Neolithic city in Turkey. Scientific American. 210:94–104.

Mellars P. 1994. The Upper Paleolithic revolution. In: Cunliffe B, editor. The Oxford illustrated prehistory of Europe. Oxford: Oxford University Press. pp. 42–78.

Mellars P. 1996. The Neanderthal legacy: an archaeological perspective from western Europe. Princeton, NJ: Princeton University Press.

Mellars P. 1998. The fate of the Neanderthals. Nature. 395:539–540.

Mellor JW, Gavian S. 30 January 1987. Famine: causes, prevention, and relief. Science. 235:539–544.

Meltzer DJ. 2009. First peoples in a new world: colonizing Ice Age America. Berkeley: University of California Press.

Mercader J, Panger M, Boesch C. 2002. Excavation of a chimpanzee stone tool site in the African rainforest. Science. 296:1452–1455.

Meyer M, Arsuaga J-L, de Filippo C, Nagel S, Aximu-Petri A, Nickel B, Martínez I, Gracia A, Bermúdez de Castro JM, Carbonell E, et al. 2016. Nuclear DNA sequences from the Middle Pleistocene Sima de los Huesos hominins. Nature. 531:504–507.

Mill JE, DesJardins DA. 1996. The Feather of Hope Aboriginal AIDS Prevention Society: a community approach to HIV/AIDS prevention. Canadian Journal of Public Health. 87:268–271.

Miller NF. 1992. The origins of plant cultivation in the Near East. In: Cowan CW, Watson PJ, editors. The origins of agriculture. Washington, DC: Smithsonian Institution Press. pp. 41–42.

Millon R. 1967. Teotihuacán. Scientific American. 216:38–48.

Millon R. 1976. Social relations in ancient Teotihuacán. In: Wolf ER, editor. The Valley of Mexico: studies in pre-Hispanic ecology and society. Albuquerque: University of New Mexico Press. pp. 215–220.

Milner GR, Boldsen JL. 2012. Transition analysis: a validation study with known-age modern American skeletons. American Journal of Physical Anthropology. 148:98–110.

Milner GR, Humpf DA, Harpending HC. 1989. Pattern matching of age-at-death distributions in palaeodemographic analysis. American Journal of Physical Anthropology. 80:49–58.

Milner GR, Wood JW, Boldsen JL. 2008. Advances in paleodemography. In: Katzenberg MA, Saunders SR, editors. Biological anthropology of the human skeleton. New York: Wiley. pp. 561–600.

Milton K. 1981. Distribution patterns of tropical plant foods as an evolutionary stimulus to primate mental development. American Anthropologist. 83:534–548.

Milton K. 1988. Foraging behaviour and the evolution of primate intelligence. In: Bryne RW, Whiten A, editors. Machiavellian intelligence: social expertise and the evolution of intellect in monkeys, apes, and humans. Oxford: Clarendon Press. pp. 285–305.

Miracle AW. 1998. A shaman to organizations. In: Ember CR, Ember M, Peregrine PN, editors. Research frontiers in anthropology. Upper Saddle River, NJ: Prentice Hall/Simon & Schuster Custom Publishing.

Mitchell KB, Garlie TN, Choi HJ. 2014. Anthropometry and range of motion (ROM) of the encumbered soldier. Poster presented at: Personal Armour Systems Symposium (PASS) 2014; Cambridge, UK.

Mojzsis SJ, Arrhenius G, McKeegan KD, Harrison TM, Nutman AP, Friend CR. 7 November 1996. Evidence for life on Earth before 3,800 million years ago. Nature. 384(6604):55–59.

Molnar S. 1998. Human variation: races, types and ethnic groups. 4th ed. Upper Saddle River, NJ: Prentice Hall.

Moore JA, Swedlund AC, Armelagos GJ. 1975. The use of life tables in paleodemography. In: Swedlunch AC, editor. Population studies in archaeology and biological anthropology. Memoirs of the Society for American Archaeology no. 30. pp. 57–70.

Morell V. 31 March 1995. The earliest art becomes older—and more common. Science. 267:1908–1909.

Morgan, LH. 1877. Ancient society. Reprinted in 1964. Cambridge, MA: Harvard University Press.

Morlan RE, Nelson DE, Brown TA, Vogel JS, Southon JR. 1990. Accelerator mass spectrometry dates on bones from Old Crow Basin, northern Yukon Territory. Canadian Journal of Archaeology. 14:75.

Morwood MJ, Brown P, Sutikna T, Saptomo EW, Westaway KE, Awe Due R, Roberts RG, Maeda T, Wasisto S, Djubiantono T. 2005. Further evidence for small-bodied hominins from the Late Pleistocene of Flores, Indonesia. Nature. 437(7061):1012–1017.

Morwood MJ, Soejono R, Roberts R, Sutikna T, Turney C, Westaway K, Rink W, Zhao J, van den Bergh G, Awe Due R, et al. 2004. Archaeology and age of a new hominin from Flores in eastern Indonesia. Nature. 431:1087–1091.

Mosley WH, Chen LC. 1984. An analytical framework for the study of child survival in developing countries. In: Mosley WH, Chen LC, editors. Child survival: strategies for research. Population development supplement to Volume 10. New York: Population Council. pp. 25–45.

Moss ML, Rodrigues AT, Speller CF, Yang DY. 9 October 2015.The historical ecology of Pacific herring: tracing Alaska Native use of a forage fish. Journal of Archaeological Science: Reports. doi:10.1016/j.jasrep.2015.10.005.

Moss ML, Yang DY, Newsome SD, Speller CF, McKechnie I, McMillan AD, Losey RJ, Koch PL. 2006. Historical ecology and biogeography of North Pacific pinnipeds: isotopes and ancient DNA from three archaeological assemblages. Journal of Island & Coastal Archaeology. 1:165–190.

Motesharrei S, Rivas J, Kalnay E. 2014. Human and nature dynamics (HANDY): modeling inequality and use of resources in the collapse or sustainability of societies. Ecological Economics. 101:90–102.

Motulsky A. 1971. Metabolic polymorphisms and the role of infectious diseases in human evolution. In: Morris LN, editor. Human populations, genetic variation, and evolution. San Francisco: Chandler.

Mourre V, Villa P, Henshilwood CS. 2010. Early use of pressure flaking on lithic artifacts at Blombos Cave, South Africa. Science. 330(6004):659–662.

Moyà-Solà S, Köhler M, Alba DM, Casanovas-Vilar I, Galindo J. November 19, 2004. *Pierolapithecus catalaunicus*: a new Middle Miocene great ape from Spain. Science. 306:1339–1344.

Müller H-G, Love B, Hoppa RD. 2002. A semiparametric method for estimating demographic profiles from age indicator data. American Journal of Physical Anthropology. 117(1):1–14.

Müller-Haye B. 1984. Guinea pig or cuy. In: Mason IL, editor. Evolution of domesticated animals. New York: Longman. pp. 329–331.

Murphy J. 1981. Abnormal behavior in traditional societies: labels, explanations, and social reactions. In: Munroe RH, Munroe RL, Whiting BB, editors. Handbook of cross-cultural human development. New York: Garland. pp. 809–826.

Murphy WA Jr, Nedden DD, Gostner P, Knapp R, Recheis W, Seidler H. 2003. The Iceman: discovery and imaging. Radiology. 226:614–629.

Myers FR. 1988. Critical trends in the study of hunter-gatherers. Annual Review of Anthropology. 17:261–282.

Nagel E. 1961. The structure of science: problems in the logic of scientific explanation. New York: Harcourt, Brace & World.

Napier JR. 1970. Paleoecology and catarrhine evolution. In: Napier JR, Napier PH, editors. Old World monkeys: evolution, systematics, and behavior. New York: Academic Press. pp. 53–95.

Napier JR, Napier PH. 1967. A handbook of living primates. New York: Academic Press.

Nash JM. 2001. The Iceman. Time. 158:42–43.

Naylor CD, Chantler C, Griffiths S. 2004. Learning from SARS in Hong Kong and Toronto. Journal of the American Medical Association. 291:2483–2487.

Neel JV. 1962. Diabetes mellitus: a "thrifty" genotype rendered detrimental by "progress"? American Journal of Human Genetics. 14:353–362.

Nelson AJ, Thompson JL. 1999. Growth and development in Neandertals and other fossil hominids: implications for the evolution of hominid ontogeny. In: Hoppa RD, FitzGerald CM, editors. Human growth in the past: studies from bones and teeth. Cambridge: Cambridge University Press. pp. 88–110.

Neumann K. 11 July 2003. New Guinea: a cradle of agriculture. Science. 301:180–181.

Nicolson NA. 1966. Infants, mothers, and other females. In: Smuts BB, Cheney DL, Seyfarth RM, Wrangham RW, Struhsaker TT, editors. Primate societies. Chicago: University of Chicago Press. pp. 330–342.

Niehoff AH. 1966. A casebook of social change. Chicago: Aldine.

Nielsen R, Bustamante C, Clark AG, Glanowski S, Sackton TB, Hubisz MJ, Fledel-Alon A, Tanenbaum DM, Civello D, White TJ, Sninsky JJ, et al. 3 May 2005. A scan for positively selected genes in the genomes of humans and chimpanzees. PLoS Biology. 3(6):e170.

Nissen HW. 1958. Axes of behavioral comparison. In: Roe A, Simpson GG, editors. Behavior and evolution. New Haven, CT: Yale University Press. pp. 183–205.

Noback ML, Harvati K, Spoor F. 2011. Climate-related variation of the human nasal cavity. American Journal of Physical Anthropology. 145(4):599–614.

Noble WC. 1968. Iroquois archaeology and the development of Iroquois social organization (1000–1650 A.D.): a study in culture change based on archaeology, ethnohistory and ethnology [Ph.D. dissertation]. [Calgary, AB]: Department of Archaeology, University of Calgary.

Normile D. 6 March 1998. Habitat seen playing larger role in shaping behavior. Science. 279:1454–1455.

Notzke C. 1999. Indigenous tourism development in the Arctic. Annals of Tourism Research. 26:55–76.

[NWAC] National Women's Association of Canada. 2010. Fact sheet: missing and murdered Aboriginal women and girls. [accessed June 2015]. http://www.nwac.ca/wp-content/uploads/2015/05/Fact_Sheet_Missing_and_Murdered_Aboriginal_Women_and_Girls.pdf.

Oakley KP. 1963. Analytical methods of dating bones. In: Brothwell D, Higgs E, editors. Science in archaeology. New York: Basic Books. pp. 24–34.

Oakley KP. 1964. On man's use of fire, with comments on tool-making and hunting. In: Washburn SL, editor. Social life of early man. Chicago: Aldine.

O'Connell CA, DeSilva JM. 2013. Mojokerto revisited: evidence for an intermediate pattern of brain growth in *Homo erectus*. Journal of Human Evolution. 65(2):156–161.

Ogden C, Carroll MD, Kit BK, Flegal KM. January 2012. Prevalence of obesity in the United States 2009–2010. NCHS Data Brief No. 82. Hyattsville, MD: National Center for Health Statistics.

Olsen S. 2002. Seeking the signs of selection. Science. 298:1324–1325.

Olszewski DI. 1991. Social complexity in the Natufian? Assessing the relationship of ideas and data. In: Clark GA, editor. Perspectives on the past: theoretical biases in Mediterranean hunter-gatherer research. Philadelphia: University of Pennsylvania Press. pp. 322–340.

Omoto K, Tobias PV, editors. 1998. The origins and past of modern humans—towards reconciliation. Singapore: World Scientific.

O'Neil J. 2015. Democratizing health services in the Northwest Territories: is devolution having an impact? Northern Review. 5:60–81.

O'Neil J, Assembly of Manitoba Chiefs, University of Manitoba, Centre for Aboriginal Health Research. 2001. Building capacity in applied Aboriginal population health research. Winnipeg, MB: Centre for Aboriginal Health Research.

O'Neil J, Commanda L. 1998. Determining the feasibility of the Canadian First Nations and Inuit Regional (Longitudinal) Health Surveys. International Journal of Circumpolar Health. 57(1 Suppl):611–616.

O'Neil J, Yassi A, Elias B. 1998. Cultural environmental health risk perception in the Canadian North. International Journal of Circumpolar Health. 57(1 Suppl):543–549.

O'Neil JD. 1995. Issues in health policy for Indigenous peoples in Canada. Australian Journal of Public Health. 19:559–566.

Orr CM, Tocheri MW, Burnett SE, Due Awe R, Saptomo EW, Sutikna T, Jatmiko, Wasisto S, Morwood MJ, Jungers WL. 2013. New wrist bones of *Homo floresiensis* from Liang Bua (Flores, Indonesia). Journal of Human Evolution. 64(2):109–129.

Ortner DJ. 1991. Theoretical and methodological issues in palaeopathology. In: Ortner DJ, Aufderheide AC, editors. Human palaeopathology: current synthesis and future options. Washington, DC: Smithsonian Institution Press. pp. 5–11.

Ortner DJ. 2012. Differential diagnosis and issues in disease classification. In Grauer AL, editor. A companion to paleopathology. New York: John Wiley & Sons. pp. 250–267.

Ousley S, Jantz R, Freid D. 2009. Understanding race and human variation: why forensic anthropologists are good at identifying race. American Journal of Physical Anthropology. 139(1):68–76.

Ovchinnikov IV, Gotherstorm A, Romanova GP, Kharitonov VM, Liden K, Goodwin W. 2000. Molecular analysis of Neanderthal DNA from the northern Caucasus. Nature. 404:490–793.

Owsley DW, Ubelaker DH, Houck MM, Sandness KL, Grant WE, Craig EA, Woltanski TJ, Peerwani N. 1995. The role of forensic anthropology in the recovery and analysis of Branch Davidian Compound victims: techniques of analysis. Journal of Forensic Science. 40:341–348.

Oxby C. 1983. Farmer groups in rural areas of the Third World. Community Development Journal. 18:50–59.

Pääbo S, Poinar H, Serre D, Jaenicke-Després V, Hebler J, Rohland N, Kuch M, Krause J, Vigilant L, Hofreiter M. 2004. Genetic analyses from ancient DNA. Annual Review of Genetics. 38:645–679.

Palkopoulou E, Mallick S, Skoglund P, Enk J, Rohland N, Li H, Omrak A, Vartanyan S, Poinar H, Götherström A, Reich D, et al. 2015. Complete genomes reveal signatures of demographic and genetic declines in the woolly mammoth. Current Biology. 25(10):1395–1400.

Park RW. 1993. The Dorset-Thule succession in Arctic North America: assessing claims for culture contact. American Antiquity. 58(2):203–234.

Park RW. 1997. Thule winter site demography in the High Arctic. American Antiquity. 62:2:273–284.

Park RW. 1998a. Current research and the history of Thule archaeology in Arctic Canada. In: Smith PJ, Mitchell D, editors. Bringing back the past: historical perspectives on Canadian archaeology. Mercury Series Paper 158. Hull: Canadian Museum of Civilization, Archaeological Survey of Canada. pp. 191–201.

Park RW. 1998b. Size counts: the miniature archaeology of childhood in Inuit societies. Antiquity. 72:269–281.

Park RW. 2000. The Dorset-Thule succession revisited. In: Appelt M, Berglund J, Gulløv HC, editors. Identities and cultural contacts in the Arctic. The Danish Polar Center Publication No. 8. Copenhagen: The Danish National Museum & Danish Polar Center. pp. 192–205.

Parker ST. 1990. Why big brains are so rare. In: Parker ST, Gibson KR, editors. "Language" and intelligence in monkeys and apes: comparative developmental perspectives. Cambridge: Cambridge University Press. pp. 129–154.

Parker Pearson M. 1999. The archaeology of death and burial. Phoenix Mill, UK: Sutton.

Partridge WL, Eddy EM. 1987. The development of applied anthropology in America. In: Eddy EM, Partridge WL, editors. Applied anthropology in America. New York: Columbia University Press. pp. 31–40.

Patterson TC. 1971. Central Peru: its population and economy. Archaeology. 24:318–319.

Patterson TC. 1973. Amer°ica's past: a New World archaeology. Glenview, IL: Scott, Foresman.

Patterson TC. 1981. The evolution of ancient societies: a world archaeology. Englewood Cliffs, NJ: Prentice Hall.

Pearsall D. 1992. The origin of plant cultivation in South America. In: Cowan CW, Watson PJ, editors. The origins of agriculture. Washington, DC: Smithsonian Institution Press. pp. 173–205.

Pelto PJ, Miller-Wille L. 1987. Snowmobiles: technological revolution in the Arctic. In: Bernard HR, Pelto PJ, editors. Technology and social change. 2nd ed. Prospect Heights, IL: Waveland Press. pp. 207–243.

Pennington R, Harpending HC. 1991. Effect of infertility on the population structure of the Herero and Mbanderu of southern Africa. Social Biology. 38:127–139.

Pennisi E. 2001. Malaria's beginnings: On the heels of hoes? Science. 293:416–417.

Pennisi E. 13 April 2007. Genomicists tackle the primate tree. Science. 316:218–221.

Peregrine PN. 2001. Southern and eastern Africa Later Stone Age. In Peregrine PN, Ember M, editors. Encyclopedia of prehistory. Vol. 1, Africa. New York: Kluwer Academic/Plenum. pp. 272–273.

Peregrine PN, Bellwood P. 2001 Southeast Asia Upper Paleolithic. In: Peregrine PN, Ember M, editors. Encyclopedia of prehistory. Vol. 3, East Asia and Oceania. New York: Kluwer Academic/Plenum. pp. 207–209.

Peregrine PN, Ember CR, Ember M. 2000. Teaching critical evaluation of Rushton. Anthropology Newsletter. 41:29–30.

Perry S, Manson JH. 2003. Traditions in monkeys. Evolutionary Anthropology: Issues, News, and Reviews. 12(2):71–81.

Petersen EB. 1973. A survey of the Late Paleolithic and the Mesolithic of Denmark. In: Kozlowski SK, editor. The Mesolithic in Europe. Warsaw: Warsaw University Press. pp. 94–96.

Pfeiffer JE. 1978. The emergence of man. 3rd ed. New York: Harper & Row.

Phillipson DW. 1993. African archaeology. 2nd ed. New York: Cambridge University Press.

Phillipson DW. 2005. African archaeology. 3rd ed. Cambridge: Cambridge University Press.

Picchi D. 1991. The impact of an industrial agricultural project on the Bakairi Indians of central Brazil. Human Organization. 50:26–38.

Picchi D. 1998. Bakairi: the death of an Indian. In: Ember MC, Ember CR, Levinson D, editors. Portraits of culture: ethnographic originals. Upper Saddle River, NJ: Prentice Hall/Simon & Schuster Custom Publishing.

Pickering R, Dirks PH, Jinnah Z, de Ruiter DJ, Churchill SE, Herries AI, Woodhead JD, Hellstrom JC, Berger LR. 9 September 2011. *Australopithecus sediba* at 1.977 Ma and implications for the origins of the genus *Homo*. Science. 333:1421–1423.

Pickford M, Senut B, Gommery D, Treil J. 2002. Bipedalism in *Orrorin tugenensis* revealed by its femora. Comptes Rendus de l'Académie des Sciences de Paris, Série Palevol. 1:191–203.

Pilbeam D. 1972. The ascent of man. New York: Macmillan.

Pilbeam D, Gould SJ. 6 December 1974. Size and scaling in human evolution. Science. 186:892–901.

Pinhasi R, Mays S, editors. 2008. Advances in human palaeopathology. Chichester, UK: John Wiley & Sons.

Piperno D, Stothert K. 2003. Phytolith evidence for early holocene cucurbita domestication in southwest Ecuador. Science. 299:1054–1057.

Piperno DR, Ranere AJ, Holst I, Iriarte J, Dickau R. 2009. Starch grain and phytolith evidence for early ninth millennium BP maize from the Central Balsas River Valley, Mexico. Proceedings of the National Academy of Sciences. 106(13):5019–5024.

Poinar HN. 2002. The genetic secrets some fossils hold. Accounts of Chemical Research. 35(8):676–684.

Poinar HN, Kuch M, Sobolik KD, Barnes I, Stankiewicz AB, Kuder T, Spaulding WG, Bryant VM, Cooper A, Pääbo S. 2001. A molecular analysis of dietary diversity for three archaic Native Americans. Proceedings of the National Academy of Sciences. 98(8):4317–4322.

Poinar HN, Schwarz C, Qi J, Shapiro B, MacPhee RD, Buigues B, Tikhonov A, Huson DH, Tomsho LP, Auch A, Rampp M, et al. 2006. Metagenomics to paleogenomics: large-scale sequencing of mammoth DNA. Science. 311(5759):392–394.

Poinar HN, Stankiewicz BA. 1999. Protein preservation and DNA retrieval from ancient tissues. Proceedings of the National Academy of Sciences. 96(15):8426–8431.

Polanyi KC, Arensberg CM, Pearson HW. 1957. Trade and market in the early empires. New York: Free Press.

Polednak AP. 1974. Connective tissue responses in Negroes in relation to disease. American Journal of Physical Anthropology. 41:49–57.

Pope GG. October 1989. Bamboo and human evolution. Natural History. 48–56.

Post PW, Daniels F Jr, Binford, Jr. RT. 1975. Cold injury and the evolution of "white" skin. Human Biology. 47:65–80.

Potts R. 1988. Early hominid activities at Olduvai. New York: Aldine de Gruyter.

Preuschoft H. 2004. Mechanisms for the acquisition of habitual bipedality: are there biomechanical reasons for the acquisition of upright bipedal posture? Journal of Anatomy. 204:363–384.

Preuschoft H, Chivers DJ, Brockelman WY, Creel N, editors. 1984. The lesser apes: evolutionary and behavioural biology. Edinburgh: Edinburgh University Press.

Price TD. 1984. The chemistry of prehistoric bone. Cambridge: Cambridge University Press.

Primorac D, Andelinovic S, Definis-Gojanovic M, Drmic I, Rezic B, Baden MM, Kennedy MA, Schanfield MS, Skakel SB, Lee HC. 1996. Identification of war victims from mass graves in Croatia, Bosnia, and Herzegovina by use of standard forensic methods and DNA typing. Journal of Forensic Science. 41:891–894.

Pringle H. 20 November 1998. The slow birth of agriculture. Science. 282:1446–1450.

Pringle H. 2011. The first Americans. Scientific American. 305:36–42.

Prinsloo LC, Wadley L, Lombard M. 2014. Infrared reflectance spectroscopy as an analytical technique for the study of residues on stone tools: potential and challenges. Journal of Archaeological Science. 41:732–739.

Prowse TL. 2016. Isotopes and mobility in the ancient Roman world. In: de Ligt L, Tacoma LE, editors. Migration and mobility in the early Roman Empire. Leiden, Netherlands: Brill. pp. 205–233.

Prowse TL, Schwarcz HP, Garnsey P, Knyf M, Macchiarelli R, Bondioli L. 2007. Isotopic evidence for age-related immigration to Imperial Rome. American Journal of Physical Anthropology. 132(4):510–519.

Public Health Agency of Canada. 2011. Diabetes in Canada: facts and figures from a public health perspective. Ottawa: Public Health Agency of Canada.

Quandt SA. 1996. Nutrition in anthropology. In: Sargent CF, Johnson TM, editors. Handbook of medical anthropology. Rev. ed. Westport, CT: Greenwood Press. pp. 272–289.

Radinsky L. 1967. The oldest primate endocast. American Journal of Physical Anthropology. 27:358–388.

Rasmussen DT. 2002. Early catarrhines of the African Eocene and Oligocene. In: Hartwig WC, editor. The primate fossil record. Cambridge: Cambridge University Press.

Rathje WL. 1971. The origin and development of Lowland Classic Maya civilization. American Antiquity. 36:275–285.

Ray AK, Roth EA. 1984. Demography of the Juang tribal population of Orissa. American Journal of Physical Anthropology. 65:387–393.

[RCMP] Royal Canadian Mounted Police. 2014. Missing and murdered Aboriginal women: a national operational overview. [accessed May 2016]. http://www.rcmp-grc.gc.ca/pubs/mmaw-faapd-eng.pdf.

Redman CL. 1978. The rise of civilization: from early farmers to urban society in the ancient Near East. San Francisco: Freeman.

Reed D, Labarthe D, Stallones R. 1970. Health effects of Westernization and migration among Chamorros. American Journal of Epidemiology. 92:96–112.

Reed DM. 1994. Ancient Maya diet at Copan, Honduras, as determined through the analysis of stable carbon and nitrogen isotopes. In: Sobolik KD, editor. Paleonutrition: the diet and health of prehistoric Americas. Occasional Paper No. 22. Carbondale: Southern Illinois University Center for Archaeological Investigations. pp. 210–221.

Reich D, Patterson N, Campbell D, Tandon A, Mazieres S, Ray N, Parra MV, Rojas W, Duque C, Mesa N, García LF. 16 August 2012. Reconstructing Native American population history. Nature. 488(7411):370–374.

Reich D, Green RE, Kircher M, Krause J, Patterson N, Durand EY, Viola B, Briggs AW, Stenzel U, Johnson PL, Maricic T. 2010. Genetic history of an archaic hominin group from Denisova Cave in Siberia. Nature. 468(7327):1053–1060.

Reitz EJ, Newsom LF, Scudder SJ, editors. 1996. Case studies in environmental archaeology: interdisciplinary contributions to archaeology. New York: Plenum Press.

Remis M. 1995. Effects of body size and social context on the arboreal activities of lowland gorillas in the Central African Republic. American Journal of Physical Anthropology. 97:413–433.

Renfrew C. 1969. Trade and culture process in European prehistory. Current Anthropology. 10:151–169.

Rice PC. 1981. Prehistoric Venuses: symbols of motherhood or womanhood? Journal of Anthropological Research. 37:402–414.

Rice PC, Paterson AL. 1985. Cave art and bones: exploring the interrelationships. American Anthropologist. 87:94–100.

Rice PC, Paterson AL. 1986. Validating the cave art–archeofaunal relationship in Cantabrian Spain. American Anthropologist. 88:658–667.

Richard AF. 1985. Primates in nature. New York: Freeman.

Richard AF. 1987. Malagasy prosimians: female dominance. In: Smuts BB, Cheney DL, Seyfarth RM, Wrangham RW, Struhsaker TT, editors. Primate societies. Chicago: University of Chicago Press. pp. 25–33.

Richards MP, Pettitt PB, Stiner MC, Trinkaus E. 2001. Stable isotope evidence for increasing dietary breadth in the European Mid-Upper Paleolithic. Proceedings of the National Academy of Sciences of the United States of America. 98:6528–6532.

Richmond BG, Jungers WL. 2008. *Orrorin tugenensis* femoral morphology and the evolution of hominin bipedalism. Science. 319(5870):1662–1665.

Riesenfeld A. 1973. The effect of extreme temperatures and starvation on the body proportions of the rat. American Journal of Physical Anthropology. 39:427–459.

Rightmire GP. 1984. *Homo sapiens* in sub-Saharan Africa. In: Smith FH, Spencer F, editors. The origins of modern humans: a world survey of the fossil evidence. New York: Alan R. Liss.

Rightmire GP. 1985. The tempo of change in the evolution of mid-Pleistocene *Homo*. In: Delson E, editor. Ancestors: the hard evidence. New York: Alan R. Liss. pp. 255–264.

Rightmire GP. 1988. *Homo erectus*. In: Tattersall I, Delson E, Van Couvering J, editors. Encyclopedia of human evolution and prehistory. New York: Garland. pp. 259–265.

Rightmire GP. 1990. The evolution of *Homo erectus*: comparative anatomical studies of an extinct human species. Cambridge: Cambridge University Press.

Rightmire GP. 1998. Human evolution in the Middle Pleistocene: the role of *Homo heidelbergensis*. Evolutionary Anthropology. 6:218–227.

Rightmire GP. 2000. *Homo erectus*. In: Tattersall I, Delson E, Van Couvering J, editors. Encyclopedia of human evolution and prehistory. New York: Garland. pp. 322–326.

Rijksen HD. 1978. A field study on Sumatran orang utans (*Pongo pygmaeus abelii* Lesson 1827): ecology, behaviour and conservation. Wageningen, Netherlands: H. Veenman and Zonen, B.V.

Ritenbaugh C, Goodby C. 1989. Beyond the thrifty gene: metabolic implications of prehistoric migration into the New World. Medical Anthropology. 11:227–236.

Roberts D. 2015. Can research on the genetics of intelligence be "socially neutral"? Hastings Center Report. 45(S1):S50–S53.

Roberts DF. 1953. Body weight, race, and climate. American Journal of Physical Anthropology. 2:553–558.

Roberts DF. 1978. Climate and human variability. 2nd ed. Menlo Park, CA: Cummings.

Robinson JG, Janson CH. 1987. Capuchins, squirrel monkeys, and atelines: sociological convergence with Old World primates. In: Smuts BB, Cheney DL, Seyfarth RM, Wrangham RW, Struhsaker TT, editors. Primate societies. Chicago: University of Chicago Press. pp. 69–82.

Robinson JG, Wright PC, Kinzey WG. 1987. Monogamous cebids and their relatives: intergroup calls and spacing. In: Smuts BB, Cheney DL, Seyfarth RM, Wrangham RW, Struhsaker TT, editors. Primate societies. Chicago: University of Chicago Press. pp. 44–53.

Rodrigues S, Robinson E, Gray-Donald K. 1999. Prevalence of gestational diabetes mellitus among James Bay Cree women in northern Quebec. Canadian Medical Association Journal. 160(9):1293–1297.

Rogers A, Iltis D, Wooding S. 2004. Genetic variation at the MC1R locus and the time since loss of human body hair. Current Anthropology. 45:105–108.

Rogers EM. 1983. Diffusion of innovations. 3rd ed. New York: Free Press.

Rona RJ. 1991. Nutritional surveillance in developed countries using anthropometry. In: Himes JH, editor. Anthropometric assessment of nutritional status. New York: Wiley-Liss. pp. 301–318.

Roosevelt AC. 1984. Population, health, and the evolution of subsistence: conclusions from the conference. In: Cohen MN, Armelagos GJ, editors. Paleopathology at the origins of agriculture. Orlando, FL: Academic Press. pp. 559–584.

Roosevelt AC, Lima da Costa M, Lopes Machado C, Michab M, Mercier N, Valladas H, Feathers J, Barnett W, Imazio da Silveira M, Henderson A, et al. 19 April 1996. Paleoindian cave dwellers in the Amazon: the peopling of America. Science. 272:373–384.

Rose MD. 1984. Food acquisition and the evolution of positional behaviour: the case of bipedalism. In: Chivers DJ, Wood BA, Bilsborough A, editors. Food acquisition and processing in primates. New York: Plenum. pp. 509–524.

Rosenberger AL. 1979. Cranial anatomy and implications of *Dolichocebus*, a late Oligocene ceboid primate. Nature. 279:416–418.

Ross MH. 1998. Ethnocentrism and ethnic conflict. In: Ember CR, Ember M, Peregrine PN, editors. Research frontiers in anthropology. Upper Saddle River, NJ: Prentice Hall/Simon & Schuster Custom Publishing.

Ruan YJ, Wei CL, Ee AL, Vega VB, Thoreau H, Su ST, Chia JM, Ng P, Chiu KP, Lim L, et al. 2003. Comparative full-length genome sequence analysis of 14 SARS coronavirus isolates and common mutations associated with putative origins of infection. Lancet. 361:1779–1785.

Rubicz R, Schurr TG, Babb PL, Crawford MH. 2003. Mitochondrial DNA variation and the origins of the Aleuts. Human Biology. 75:809–835.

Ruff CB, Walker A. 1993. Body size and body shape. In: Walker A, Leakey R, editors. The Nariokotome *Homo erectus* skeleton. Cambridge, MA: Harvard University Press. pp. 234–265.

Rumbaugh DM. 1970. Learning skills of anthropoids. In: Rosenblum LA, editor. Primate behavior. Vol. 1. New York: Academic Press. pp. 52–58.

Rushton JP. 1995. Race and crime: international data for 1989–1990. Psychological Reports. 76(1):307–312.

Rushton JP. 1996. Genetics and race. Science. 271(5249):579–580.

Russell DA, Séguin R. 1982. Reconstruction of the small cretaceous theropod *Stenonychosaurus inequalis* and a hypothetical dinosauroid. Syllogeus. 37:143.

Russon AE. 1990. The development of peer social interaction in infant chimpanzees: comparative social, Piagetian, and brain perspectives. In: Taylor Parker S, Gibson KR, editors. "Language" and intelligence in monkeys and apes: comparative development perspectives. New York: Cambridge University Press. pp. 379–419.

Sade DS. 1965. Some aspects of parent–offspring and sibling relationships in a group of rhesus monkeys, with a discussion of grooming. American Journal of Physical Anthropology. 23:1–17.

Sagan C. December 1975. A cosmic calendar. Natural History. 70–73.

Sala N, Arsuaga JL. 9 April 2016. Regarding beasts and humans: A review of taphonomic works with living carnivores. Quaternary International. doi:10.1016/j.quaint.2016.03.011.

Salzman PC. 2001. Understanding culture: An introduction to anthropological theory. Long Grove, IL: Waveland.

Sanders WT. 1968. Hydraulic agriculture, economic symbiosis, and the evolution of states in central Mexico. In: Meggers BJ, editor. Anthropological archaeology in the Americas. Washington, DC: Anthropological Society of Washington. pp. 88–107.

Sanders WT, Parsons JR, Santley RS. 1979. The basin of Mexico: ecological processes in the evolution of a civilization. New York: Academic Press.

Sanders WT, Price BJ. 1968. Mesoamerica. New York: Random House.

Sandford MK. 1992. A reconstruction of trace element analysis in prehistoric bone. In: Saunders SR, Katzenberg MA, editors. Skeletal biology of past peoples: research methods. New York: Wiley-Liss. pp. 79–103.

Sandford MK. 1993. Investigations of ancient human tissues: chemical analysis in anthropology. Langhorne, PA: Gordon and Breach Science Publishers.

Sandford MK, Weaver DS. 2000. Trace element research in anthropology: new perspectives and challenges. In: Katzenberg MA, Saunders SR, editors. Biological anthropology of the human skeleton. New York: Wiley-Liss. pp. 329–350.

Santayana G. 1905. The life of reason: Reason in common sense. London: Archibald Constable and Co.

Sarich VM. 1968. The origin of hominids: an immunological approach. In: Washburn SL, Phyllis CJ, editors. Perspectives on human evolution. Vol. 1. New York: Holt, Rinehart, & Winston. pp. 99–121.

Sarich VM, Wilson AC. 23 December 1966. Quantitative immunochemistry and the evolution of the primate albumins: micro-component fixations. Science. 154:1563–1566.

Sassaman K. 1996. Early Archaic settlement in the South Carolina coastal plain. In: Anderson DG, Sassaman K, editors. The Paleoindian and Early Archaic Southeast. Tuscaloosa: University of Alabama Press. pp. 58–83.

Sattenspiel L. 1990. Modeling the spread of infectious disease in human populations. Yearbook of Physical Anthropology. 33:245–276.

Sattenspiel L, Herring DA. 1998. Structured epidemic models and the spread of the 1918–1919 influenza epidemic in the central subarctic. Human Biology. 70:91–115.

Sauer NJ. 1992. Forensic anthropology and the concept of race: if races don't exist, why are forensic anthropologists so good at identifying them? Social Science & Medicine. 34(2):107–111.

Saunders SR. 1992. Subadult skeletons and growth related studies. In: Saunders SR, Katzenberg MA, editors. Skeletal biology of past peoples. New York: Wiley-Liss. pp. 1–20.

Saunders SR, Hoppa RD. 1993. Growth deficit in survivors and non-survivors: biological bias in subadult skeletal samples. Yearbook of Physical Anthropology. 36:127–151.

Savage-Rumbaugh ES. 1992. Language training of apes. In: Jones S, Martin R, Pilbeam D, editors. The Cambridge encyclopedia of human evolution. Cambridge: Cambridge University Press. pp. 138–141.

Savage-Rumbaugh ES. 1994. Hominid evolution: looking to modern apes for clues. In: Quiatt D, Itani J, editors. Hominid culture in primate perspective. Niwot: University Press of Colorado. pp. 7–49.

Savelle JM. 1997. The role of architectural utility in the formation of zooarchaeological whale bone assemblages. Journal of Archaeological Science. 24(10):869–885.

Savolainen P, Luo J, Lunderberg J, Leitner T. 2002. Genetic evidence for an East Asian origin of domestic dogs. Science. 296:1610–1614.

Scally A, Durbin R. 2012. Revising the human mutation rate: implications for understanding human evolution. Nature Reviews Genetics. 13(10):745–753.

Scarr S, McCartney K. 1983. How people make their own environments: a theory of genotype–environment effects. Child Development. 54:424–435.

Scarre C. 2012. Social stratification and the state in prehistoric Europe: the wider perspective. In: Cruz Berrocal M, García Sanjuán L, Gilman A, editors. The prehistory of Iberia: debating early social stratification and the state. New York: Routledge. pp. 381–406.

Schaller G. 1963. The mountain gorilla: ecology and behavior. Chicago: University of Chicago Press.

Schaller G. 1964. The year of the gorilla. Chicago: University of Chicago Press.

Schaller GB. 1972. The Serengeti lion: a study of predator–prey relations. Chicago: University of Chicago Press.

Schick KD, Toth N. 1994. Making silent stones speak: human evolution and the dawn of technology. New York: Simon & Schuster.

Schillaci MA, Jones-Engel L, Engel GA, Kyes RC. 2006. Exposure to human respiratory viruses among urban performing monkeys in Indonesia. American Journal of Tropical Medicine and Hygeine. 75(4):716–719.

Schillaci MA, Jones-Engel L, Engel GA, Paramastri Y, Iskandar E, Wilson B, Allan JS, Kyes RC, Watanabe R, Grant R. 2005. Prevalence of enzootic simian viruses among urban performance monkeys in Indonesia. Tropical Medicine & International Health. 10(12):1305–1314.

Schoeninger MJ. 1995. Stable isotopes studies in human evolution. Evolutionary Anthropology. 4:83–98.

Schoepf B. 1988. Women, AIDS, and economic crisis in central Africa. Canadian Journal of African Studies. 22:625–644.

Scholz M, Bachmann L, Nicholson GJ, Bachman J, Giddings I, Ruschoff-Thale B, Czarnetzki A, Pusch CM. 2000. Genomic differentiation of Neanderthals and anatomically modern man allows a fossil-DNA-based classification of morphologically indistinguishable hominid bones. American Journal of Human Genetics. 66:1927–1932.

Schopf JW. 20 June 2000. Solution to Darwin's dilemma: discovery of the missing Precambrian record of life. Proceedings of the National Academy of Sciences. 97(13):694–753.

Schrire C. 1984. Past and present in hunter-gatherer studies. Orlando, FL: Academic Press.

Schurr MR. 1997. Stable nitrogen isotopes as evidence for the age of weaning at the Angel site: a comparison of isotopic and demographic measures of weaning age. Journal of Archaeological Science. 24:919–927.

Schurr TG, Sherry ST. 2004. Mitochondrial DNA and Y chromosome diversity and the peopling of the Americas: evolutionary and demographic evidence. American Journal of Human Biology. 16(4):420–439.

Schwarcz HP. 1993. Uranium-series dating and the origin of modern man. In: Schwarcz HP, editor. The origin of modern humans and the impact of chronometric dating. Princeton, NJ: Princeton University Press. pp. 12–26.

Schwarcz HP, Grün R. 1992. Electron spin resonance (ESR) dating of the origin of modern man. Philosophical Transactions of the Royal Society of London Biological Sciences. 337:145–148.

Schwarcz HP, Melbye FJ, Katzenber MA, Knyf M. 1985. Stable isotopes in human skeletons of southern Ontario: reconstructing paleodiet. Journal of Archaeological Science. 12:187–206.

Schwarz C, Debruyne R, Kuch M, McNally E, Schwarcz H, Aubrey AD, Bada J, Poinar H. 24 March 2009. New insights from old bones: DNA preservation and degradation in permafrost preserved mammoth remains. Nucleic Acids Research. doi:10.1093/nar/gkp159.

Scott GR, Halffman CM, Pedersen PO. 1991. Dental conditions of Medieval Norsemen in the North Atlantic. Acta Archaeologica. 62:183–207.

Scudder T. 1987. Opportunities, issues, and achievements in development anthropology since the mid-1960s: a personal view. In: Eddy EM, Partridge WL, editors. Applied anthropology in America. New York: Columbia University Press. pp. 184–210.

Seidensticker J. 1985. Primates as prey of Panthera cats in South Asian habitats. American Journal of Primatology. 8:365–366.

Seielstad M, Bekele E, Ibrahim M, Touré A, Traoré M. 1999. A view of modern human origins from Y chromosome microsatellite variation. Genome Research. 9(6):558–567.

Sellers WI, Cain GM, Wang WJ, Crompton RH. 2005. Stride lengths, speed and energy costs in walking of *Australopithecus afarensis*: using evolutionary robotics to predict locomotion of early human ancestors. Journal of the Royal Society Interface. 2:431–441.

Semenov SA. 1970. Prehistoric technology. Thompson MW, translator. Bath, England: Adams & Dart.

Senner WM. 1989. Theories and myths on the origins of writing: a historical overview. In: Senner WM, editor. The origins of writing. Lincoln: University of Nebraska Press. pp. 1–26.

Senut B. 2006. Bipedalism and climate. Comptes Rendus Palevol. 5:89–98.

Serre D, Langaney A, Chech M, Teschler-Nicola M, Paunovic M, Mennecier P, Hofreiter M, Possnert G, Pääbo S. 2004. No evidence of Neandertal mtDNA contribution to early modern humans. PLoS Biology. 2:E57.

Service ER. 1975. Origins of the state and civilization: the process of cultural evolution. New York: Norton.

Service ER. 1979. The hunters. 2nd ed. Englewood Cliffs, NJ: Prentice Hall.

Seyfarth RM, Cheney DL. 1982. How monkeys see the world: a review of recent research on East African vervet monkeys. In: Snowdon CT, Brown CH, Petersen MR, editors. Primate communication. New York: Cambridge University Press. pp. 239–252.

Shanklin E. 1994. Anthropology and race. Belmont, CA: Wadsworth.

Shannon LM, Boyko RH, Castelhano M, Corey E, Hayward JJ, McLean C, White ME, Abi Said M, Anita BA, Bondjengo NI, et al. 2015. Genetic structure in village dogs reveals a Central Asian domestication origin. Proceedings of the National Academy of Sciences. 112(44):13639–13644.

Shapiro LR, Crowford PB, Clark MJ, Pearson DL, Raz J, Huenemann RL. 1984. Obesity prognosis: a longitudinal study of children from the age of 6 months to 9 years. American Journal of Public Health. 74:968–972.

Shaw B, Leclerc M, Dickinson W, Spriggs M, Summerhayes GR. 2016. Identifying prehistoric trade networks in the Massim region, Papua New Guinea: evidence from petrographic and chemical compositional pottery analyses from Rossel and Nimowa islands in the Louisiade Archipelago. Journal of Archaeological Science: Reports. 6:518–535.

Shepard RJ. 1991. Body composition in biological anthropology. Cambridge Studies in Biological Anthropology 6. Cambridge: Cambridge University Press.

Shipman P. 1984. Early hominid lifestyle: the scavenging hypothesis. Anthroquest. 28:910.

Shipman P. 1986. Scavenging or hunting in early hominids: theoretical framework and tests. American Anthropologist. 88:27–43.

Shipman P, Rose J. 1983. Early hominid hunting, butchering, and carcass-processing behaviors: approaches to the fossil record. Journal of Anthropological Archaeology. 2(1):57–98.

Shu C, Xi P, Keefe A. 2015. Data processing and analysis for the 2012 Canadian Forces 3D Anthropometric Survey. Procedia Manufacturing. 3:3745–3752.

Sicotte P. 1993. Inter-group encounters and female transfer in mountain gorillas: influence of group composition on male behavior. American Journal of Primatology. 30:21–36.

Sicotte P. 1995. Interpositions in conflicts between males in bimale groups of mountain gorillas. Folia Primatology (Basel). 65:14–24.

Sicotte P. 2002. The function of male aggressive displays towards females in mountain gorillas. Primates. 43:277–289.

Silk J. 2007. Social components of fitness in primate groups. Science. 317:1347–1351.

Silversides A. 2001. Lessons Canada learned in Swissair crash being applied in New York. Canadian Medical Association Journal. 165:1243.

Simmons AH, Köhler-Rollefson I, Rollefson GO, Mandel R, Kafafi Z. 1 April 1988. 'Ain Ghazal: a major Neolithic settlement in central Jordan. Science. 240:35–39.

Simons E. 1992. The primate fossil record. In: Jones S, Martin R, Pilbeam D, editors. The Cambridge encyclopedia of human evolution. New York: Cambridge University Press. pp. 199–208.

Simons E. 30 June 1995. Skulls and anterior teeth of *Catopithecus* (Primates: Anthropoidea) from the Eocene shed light on anthropoidean origins. Science. 268:1885–1888.

Simpson GG. 1971. The meaning of evolution. New York: Bantam.

Simpson SW. 1998. *Australopithecus afarensis* and human evolution. In: Ember CR, Ember M, Peregrine PN, editors. Research frontiers in anthropology. Upper Saddle River, NJ: Prentice Hall/Simon & Schuster Custom Publishing.

Simpson SW, Quade J, Levin NE, Butler R, Dupont-Nivet G, Everett M, Semaw S. 2008. A female *Homo erectus* pelvis from Gona, Ethiopia. Science. 322(5904):1089–1092.

Sinclair AR, Leakey MD, Norton-Griffiths M. 1986. Migration and hominid bipedalism. Nature. 324(6095):307–308.

Singer R, Wymer J. 1982. The Middle Stone Age at Klasies River mouth in South Africa. Chicago: University of Chicago Press.

Skinner M. 1987. Planning the archaeological recovery of evidence from recent mass graves. Forensic Science International. 34:267–287.

Skinner M, Alempijevic D, Djuric-Srejic M. 2003. Guidelines for international forensic bio-archaeology monitors of mass grave exhumations. Forensic Science International. 134:81–92.

Smith BD. 1992a. Prehistoric plant husbandry in eastern North America. In: Cowan CW, Watson PJ, editors. The origins of agriculture. Washington, DC: Smithsonian Institution Press. pp. 101–119.

Smith BD. 1992b. Rivers of change. Washington, DC: Smithsonian Institution Press.

Smith BH. 25 September 1986. Dental development in *Australopithecus* and early *Homo*. Nature. 323:327–330.

Smith FH. 1984. Fossil hominids from the Upper Pleistocene of central Europe and the origin of modern humans. In: Smith FH, Spencer F, editors. The origins of modern humans: a world survey of the fossil evidence. New York: Alan R. Liss. pp. 137–209.

Smith FH, Falsetti AB, Donnelley SM. 1989. Modern human origins. Yearbook of Physical Anthropology. 32:35–68.

Smith FH, Spencer F. 1984. The origins of modern humans: a world survey of the fossil evidence. New York: A.R. Liss.

Smith FH, Trinkaus E, Pettitt PB, Karavanic I, Paunovic M. 1999. Direct radiocarbon dates for Vindija G(1) and Velika Pecina Late Pleistocene hominid remains. Proceedings of the National Academy of Sciences. 96(22):12281–12286.

Smith JM. 1989. Evolutionary genetics. New York: Oxford University Press.

Smith MW. 1974. Alfred Binet's remarkable questions: a cross-national and cross-temporal analysis of the cultural biases built into the Stanford-Binet Intelligence Scale and other Binet tests. Genetic Psychological Monographs. 89:307–334.

Smuts BB, Cheney DL, Seyfarth RM, Wrangham RW, Struhsaker TT, editors. 1987. Primate society. Chicago: University of Chicago Press.

Soffer O. 1993. Upper Paleolithic adaptations in central and eastern Europe and man–mammoth interactions. In: Soffer O, Praslov ND, editors. From Kostenski to Clovis: Upper Paleolithic–Paleo-Indian adaptations. New York: Plenum. pp. 38–40.

Soffer O, Adovasio JM, Hyland DC. 2000. The "Venus" figurines: textiles, basketry, gender, and status in the Upper Paleolithic. Current Anthropology. 41:511–537.

Sohn S, Wolpoff MH. 1993. Zuttiyeh face: a view from the East. American Journal of Physical Anthropology. 91:325–347.

Solis RS, Haas J, Creamer W. 2001. Dating Caral, a preceramic site in the Supe Valley of the central coast of Peru. Science. 292:723–726.

Spence MW. 1992. Tlailotlacan: a Zapotec enclave in Teotihuacán. In: Berlo J, editor. Art, ideology, and the city of Teotihuacán. Washington, DC: Dumbarton Oaks Research Library and Collection. pp. 59–88.

Spence MW. 1996. Commodity or gift: Teotihuacán obsidian in the Maya region. Latin American Antiquity. 7(1):21–39.

Spencer F. 1984. The Neandertals and their evolutionary significance: a brief historical survey. In: Smith FH, Spencer F, editors. The origins of modern humans: a world survey of the fossil evidence. New York: Alan R. Liss. pp. 1–50.

Speth JD. 1998. Were our ancestors hunters or scavengers? In: Ember CR, Ember M, Peregrine PN, editors. Research frontiers in anthropology. Upper Saddle River, NJ: Prentice Hall/Simon & Schuster Custom Publishing.

Speth JD, Davis DD. 1976. Seasonal variability in early hominid predation. Science. 441–445.

Speth JD, Spielmann KA. 1983. Energy source, protein metabolism, and hunter-gatherer subsistence strategy. Anthropological Archaeology. 2:1–31.

Spigelman M, Matheson C, Lev G, Greenblatt C, Donoghue HD. 2002. Confirmation of the presence of Mycobacterium tuberculosis complex–specific DNA in three archaeological specimens. International Journal of Osteoarchaeology. 12(6):393–401.

Spurles PK, Babineau J. 2011. A qualitative study of attitudes toward public breastfeeding among young Canadian men and women. Journal of Human Lactation. 27(2):131–137.

Staller J, Tykot R, Benz B. 2006. Histories of maize: multidisciplinary approaches to the prehistory, linguistics, biogeography, domestication, and evolution of maize. Walnut Creek, CA: Left Coast Press.

Stanford C. 1998. Chimpanzee hunting behavior and human evolution. In: Ember CR, Ember M, Peregrine PN, editors. Research frontiers in anthropology. Upper Saddle River, NJ: Prentice Hall. Prentice Hall/Simon & Schuster Custom Publishing. pp. 35–41.

Stanford CB. 2006. Arboreal bipedalism in wild chimpanzees: implications for the evolution of hominid posture and locomotion. American Journal of Physical Anthropology. 129:225–231.

Stark B. 1986. The origins of food production in the New World. In: Meltzer D, Dowler D, Sabloff J, editors. American archeology: past and present. Washington, DC: Smithsonian Press. pp. 277–321.

Steadman DW, Haglund WD. 2005. The scope of anthropological contributions to human rights investigations. Journal of Forensic Science. 50(1):214–218.

Stedman HH, Kozyak BW, Nelson A, Thesier DM, Su LT, Low DW, Bridges CR, Shrager JB, Minugh-Purvis N, Mitchell MA. 2004. Myosin gene mutation correlates with anatomical changes in the human lineage. Nature. 428(6981):415–418.

Steegman AT Jr. 1975. Human adaptation to cold. In: Damon A, editor. Physiological anthropology. New York: Oxford University Press. pp. 130–166.

Steinbock RT. 1976. Palaeopathological diagnosis and interpretation. Springfield: Charles C. Thomas.

Stewart A, Friesen TM, Keith D, Henderson L. 2000. Archaeology and oral history of Inuit land use on the Kazan River, Nunavut: a feature-based approach. Arctic. 53(3):260–278.

Stewart TD. 1950. Deformity, trephanating, and mutilation in South American Indian skeletal remains. In Steward JA, editor. Handbook of South American Indians. Vol. 6, Physical anthropology, linguistics, and cultural geography. Bureau of American Ethnology Bulletin 143. Washington, DC: Smithsonian Institution.

Stini WA. 1971. Evolutionary implications of changing nutritional patterns in human populations. American Anthropologist. 73:1019–1030.

Stinson S. 1992. Nutritional adaptation. Annual Review of Anthropology. 21:143–170.

Stone L, Lurquin PE. 2007. Genes, culture, and human evolution. Malden, MA: Blackwell.

Stoneking M. 1994. Mitochondrial DNA and human evolution. Journal of Bioenergetics and Biomembranes. 26(3):251–259.

Strauss LG. 1982. Comment on White. Current Anthropology. 23:185–186.

Strauss LG. 1989. On early hominid use of fire. Current Anthropology. 30:488–491.

Stringer C. 1985. Evolution of a species. Geographical Magazine. 57:601–607.

Stringer CB. 1988a. The dates of Eden. Nature. 331:565–566.

Stringer CB. 1988b. Neandertals. In: Tattersall I, Delson E, Van Couvering J, editors. Encyclopedia of human evolution and prehistory. New York: Garland.

Stringer CB. 2003. Out of Ethiopia. Nature. 423:692–695.

Stringer CB, Hublin JJ, Vandermeersch B. 1984. The origin of anatomically modern humans in western Europe. In: Smith FH, Spencer F, editors. The origins of modern humans: a world survey of the fossil evidence. New York: A.R. Liss. pp. 51–135.

Stuart-Williams HL, Schwarcz HP. 30 June 1997. Oxygen isotopic determination of climatic variation using phosphate from beaver bone, tooth enamel, and dentine. Geochimica et Cosmochimica Acta. 61(12):2539–2550.

Stulp G, Barrett L. 2014. Evolutionary perspectives on human height variation. Biological Reviews. 91(1):206–234.

Susman RL, editor. 1984. The pygmy chimpanzee: evolutionary biology and behavior. New York: Plenum.

Susman RL. 9 September 1994. Fossil evidence for early hominid tool use. Science. 265:1570–1573.

Susman RL, Stern JK Jr, Jungers WL. 1985. Locomotor adaptations in the Hadar hominids. In: Delson E, editor. Ancestors: the hard evidence. New York: Alan R. Liss. pp. 184–192.

Sussman RW. 1972. Child transport, family size, and the increase in human population size during the Neolithic. Current Anthropology. 13:258–267.

Sussman RW. 1991. Primate origins and the evolution of angiosperms. American Journal of Primatology. 23:209–223.

Sussman RW, Kinzey WG. 1984. The ecological role of the Callitrichidae: a review. Journal of Physical Anthropology. 64:419–449.

Sussman RW, Raven PH. 19 May 1978. Pollination by lemurs and marsupials: an Archaic coevolutionary system. Science. 200:734–735.

Sutikna T, Tocheri MW, Morwood MJ, Saptomo EW, Due Awe R, Wasisto S, Westaway KE, Aubert M, Li B, Zhao JX, Storey M, et al. 2016. Revised stratigraphy and chronology for *Homo floresiensis* at Liang Bua in Indonesia. Nature. 532:366–369.

Svoboda T, Henry B, Shulman L, Kennedy E, Rea E, Ng W, Wallington T, Yaffe B, Gournis E, Vicencio E, et al. 2004. Public health measures to control the spread of the severe acute respiratory syndrome during the outbreak in Toronto. New England Journal of Medicine. 350:2352–2361.

Swisher CC, Curtis GH, Jacob T, Getty AG, Suprijo A, Widasmoro N. 25 February 1994. Age of the earliest known hominids in Java, Indonesia. Science. 263:1118–1121.

Swisher CC, Rink WJ, Antón SC, Schwarcz HP, Curtis GH, Suprijo A, Widasmoro N. 13 December 1996. Latest *Homo erectus* of Java: potential contemporaneity with *Homo sapiens* in Southeast Asia. Science. 274:1870–1874.

Sylvester AD. 2006. Locomotor decoupling and the origin of hominin bipedalism. Journal of Theoretical Biology. 242:581–590.

Szalay FS. 1968. The beginnings of primates. Evolution. 22:32–33.

Szalay FS. 1972. Paleobiology and the earliest primates. In: Tuttle R, editor. The functional and evolutionary biology of the primates. Chicago: University of Chicago Press. pp. 3–35.

Szalay FS. 1975. Hunting-scavenging protohominids: a model for hominid origins. Man. 10:420–429.

Szalay FS, Delson E. 1979. Evolutionary history of the primates. New York: Academic Press.

Szalay FS, Tattersall I, Decker R. 1975. Phylogenetic relationships of *Plesiadipis*—postcranial evidence. Contributions to Primatology. 5:136–166.

Szathmáry EJE. 1990. Diabetes in Amerindian populations: the Dogrib studies. In: Armelagos G, Swedlund A, editors. Health and disease of populations in transition. New York: Bergin and Garvey. pp. 75–103.

Szathmáry EJE. 1993. Genetics of Aboriginal North Americans. Evolutionary Anthropology. 1:202–220.

Szathmáry EJE. 1994. Non-insulin-dependent diabetes mellitus among Aboriginal North Americans. Annual Review of Anthropology. 23:457–482.

Tainter J. 1988. The collapse of complex societies. Cambridge: Cambridge University Press.

Tait H. 2008. Aboriginal Peoples Survey, 2006: Inuit health and social conditions. Ottawa, ON: Statistics Canada.

Tanner JM. 1966. The secular trend toward earlier physical maturation. Tijdschrift voor Sociale Geneeskunde. 44:524–538.

Tanner JM. 1990. Foetus into man: physical growth from conception to mortality. Cambridge: Harvard University Press.

Tanner JM. 1992. Growth as a measure of the nutritional and hygienic status of population. Hormone Research. 38(1 Suppl):106–115.

Tattersall I. 1982. The primates of Madagascar. New York: Columbia University Press.

Tattersall I. 1999. The last Neanderthal: the rise, success, and mysterious extinction of our closest human relatives. Boulder, CO: Westview Press.

Tattersall I, DeSalle R. 2011. Race? debunking a scientific myth. College Station, TX: Texas A&M University Press.

Tattersall I, Schwartz JH. 1999. Hominids and hybrids: the place of Neanderthals in human evolution. Proceedings of the National Academy of Science. 96:7117–7119.

Tattersall I, Schwartz JH. 2000. Extinct humans. Boulder, CO: Westview Press.

Teleki G. January 1973. The omnivorous chimpanzee. Scientific American. 228:32–42.

ten Bruggencate RE, Fayek M, Milne SB, Brownlee K. 2014. Characterizing quartz artefacts: a case study from Manitoba's northern boreal forest. Archaeometry. 56(6):913–926.

ten Bruggencate RE, Milne SB, Fayek M, Park RW, Stenton DR. 2015. Characterization of chert artifacts and two newly identified chert quarries on southern Baffin Island. Lithic Technology. 40(3):189–198.

Terborgh J. 1983. Five New World primates: a study in comparative ecology. Princeton, NJ: Princeton University Press.

Terhune CE, Kimbel WH, Lockwood CA. 2007. Variation and diversity in *Homo erectus*: a 3D geometric morphometric analysis of the temporal bone. Journal of Human Evolution. 53:41–60.

Thompson-Handler N, Malenky RK, Badrian N. 1984. Sexual behavior of *Pan paniscus* under natural conditions in the Lomako Forest, Equateur, Zaire. In: Susman RL, editor. The pygmy chimpanzee: evolutionary biology and behavior. New York: Plenum. pp. 347–366.

Thorne AG, Wolpoff MH. 1992. The multiregional evolution of humans. Scientific American. 266:76–83.

Thorpe SKS, Holder RL, Compton RH. 2007. Origin of human bipedalism as an adaptation for locomotion on flexible branches. Science. 316:1328–1331.

Tobias PV. 1987. The brain of *Homo habilis*: a new level of organization in cerebral evolution. Journal of Human Evolution. 16:741–761.

Tobias PV. 1994. The craniocerebral interface in early hominids: cerebral impressions, cranial thickening, paleoneurobiology, and a new hypothesis on encephalization. In: Corruccini R, Ciochon RL, editors. Integrative paths to the past: paleoanthropological advances in Honor of F. Clark Howell. Englewood Cliffs, NJ: Prentice Hall. pp. 185–203.

Tocheri MW, Jungers WL, Larson SG, Orr CM, Sutikna T, Jatmiko, Saptomo EW, Awe Due R, Djubiantono T, Morwood MJ. 2007. Morphological affinities of the wrist of *Homo floresiensis*. Paper presented at: Annual Meeting of the Paleoanthropology Society; Philadelphia, PA.

Toder R, Grutzner F, Haaf T, Bausch E. 2001. Species-specific evolution of repeated DNA sequences in great apes. Chromosome Research. 9:431–435.

Tomasello M. 1990. Cultural transmission in the tool use and communicatory signaling of chimpanzees? In: Taylor Parker ST, Gibson KR, editors. "Language" and intelligence in monkeys and apes: comparative developmental perspectives. New York: Cambridge University Press. pp. 274–311.

Torry WI. 1986. Mortality and harm: Hindu peasant adjustment to famines. Social Science Information. 25:125–160.

Toyne JM, White CD, Verano JW, Castillo SU, Millaire JF, Longstaffe FJ. 2014. Residential histories of elites and sacrificial victims at Huacas de Moche, Peru, as reconstructed from oxygen isotopes. Journal of Archaeological Science. 42:15–28.

Trinkaus E. 1983. The Shanidar Neanderthals. New York: Academic Press.

Trinkaus E. 1984. Western Asia. In: Smith FH, Spencer F, editors. The origin of modern humans: a world survey of the fossil evidence. New York: Alan R. Liss. pp. 251–253.

Trinkaus E. 1985. Pathology and the posture of the La Chapelle-aux-Saints Neandertal. American Journal of Physical Anthropology. 67:19–41.

Trinkaus E. 1986. The Neandertals and modern human origins. Annual Review of Anthropology. 15:193–218.

Trinkaus E. 1987. Bodies, brawn, brains and noses: human ancestors and human predation. In: Nitecki M, Nitecki DV, editors. The evolution of human hunting. New York: Plenum. pp. 107–145.

Trinkaus E. 2007. European early modern humans and the fate of the Neandertals. Proceedings of the National Academy of Sciences of the United States of America. 104:7367–7372.

Trinkaus E, Shipman P. 1993. Neandertals: images of ourselves. Evolutionary Anthropology. 1:194–201.

Turner BL. 1970. Population density in the Classic Maya lowlands: new evidence for old approaches. Geographical Review. 66:72–82.

Turner CG. 2005. A synoptic history of physical anthropological studies on the peopling of Alaska and the Americas. Alaska Journal of Anthropology. 3:157–170.

Turner II CG. February 1989. Teeth and prehistory in Asia. Scientific American. 88–96.

Tuross N, Dillehay TD. 1995. The mechanism of organic preservation at Monte Verde, Chile and the use of biomolecules in archaeological interpretation. Journal of Field Archaeology. 97–110.

Tuross N, Fogel ML. 1994. Stable isotope analysis and subsistence patterns at the Sully site. In: Owsley DW, Jantz RL, editors. Skeletal biology in the Great Plains: migration, warfare, health and subsistence. Washington, DC: Smithsonian Institution Press. pp. 283–289.

Tuttle RH. 1986. Apes of the world: their social behavior, communication, mentality, and ecology. Park Ridge, NJ: Noyes.

Tylor EB. 1871. Primitive culture. Reprinted in 1958. New York: Harper Torchbooks.

Ubelaker DH, Owsley DW, Houck MM, Craig E, Grant W, Woltanski T, Fram R, Sandness K, Peerwani N. 1995. The role of forensic anthropology in the recovery and analysis of Branch Davidian Compound victims: recovery procedures and characteristics of the victims. Journal of Forensic Science. 40:335–340.

Ucko PJ, Rosenfield A. 1967. Paleolithic cave art. New York: McGraw-Hill.

Ungar PS, Sponheimer M. 2011. The diets of early hominins. Science. 334:190–193.

Valladas H, Joron JL, Valladas G, Bar-Yosef O, Vandermeersch B. 18 February 1988. Thermoluminescence dating of Mousterian "Proto-Cro-Magnon" remains from Israel and the origin of modern man. Nature. 614–616.

van der Merwe NJ, Thackeray JF, Lee-Thorp JA, Luyt J. 2003. The carbon isotope ecology and diet of *Australopithecus africanus* at Sterkfontein, South Africa. Journal of Human Evolution. 44:581–597.

van Lawick-Goodall J. 1971. In the shadow of man. Boston: Houghton Mifflin.

Van Oostdam J Gilman A, Dewailly E, Usher P, Wheatley B, Kuhnlein H, Neve S, Walker J, Tracy B, Feeley M, et al. 1999. Human health implications of environmental contaminants in Arctic Canada: a review. Science of the Total Environment. 230:1–82.

Videan EN, McBrew WC. 2002. Bipedality in chimpanzee (*Pan troglodytes*) and bonobo (*Pan paniscus*): testing hypotheses on the evolution of bipedalism. American Journal of Physical Anthropology. 118:184–190.

Vigilant L, Stoneking M, Harpending H, Hawkes K, Wilson AC. 1991. African populations and the evolution of human mitochondrial-DNA. Science. 253:1503–1507.

Visaberghi E, Munkenbeck Fragaszy D. 1990. Do monkeys ape? In: Taylor Parker ST, Gibson KR, editors. "Language" and intelligence in monkeys and apes: comparative developmental perspectives. New York: Cambridge University Press. pp. 247–273.

Vogel JO. 2002. De-mystifying the past: Great Zimbabwe, King Solomon's Mines, and other tales of old Africa. In: Peregrine PN, Ember CR, Ember M, editors. Archaeology: original readings in method and practice. Upper Saddle River, NJ: Prentice Hall.

Vrba ES. 1995. On the connection between paleoclimate and evolution. In: Vrba ES, Denton GH, Partridge TC, Burckle LH, editors. Paleoclimate and evolution. New Haven, CT: Yale University Press. pp. 24–45.

Vrba ES. 1996. Climate, heterochrony, and human evolution. Journal of Anthropological Research. 52(1):1–28.

Wagner DM, Klunk J, Harbeck M, Devault A, Waglechner N, Sahl JW, Enk J, Birdsell DN, Kuch M, Lumibao C, Poinar D, et al. 2014. *Yersinia pestis* and the Plague of Justinian 541–543 AD: a genomic analysis. The Lancet Infectious Diseases. 14(4):319–326.

Waldram JB, Herring DA, Young TK. 1995. Aboriginal health in Canada: historical, cultural and epidemiological perspectives. Toronto: University of Toronto Press.

Walker A, Leakey R. 1988. The evolution of *Australopithecus boisei*. In: Grine F, editor. Evolutionary history of the "robust" australopithecines. New York: Aldine. pp. 247–258.

Wallace AFC. 1972. Mental illness, biology and culture. In: Hsu FLK, editor. Psychological anthropology. 2nd ed. Cambridge, MA: Schenkman. pp. 363–402.

Wallace AR. August 1858. On the tendency of varieties to depart indefinitely from the original type. Journal of the Proceedings of the Linnaean Society. Reprinted in Young LB, editor. 1970. Evolution of man. New York: Oxford University Press.

Walter RC. 1994. Age of Lucy and the first family: single-crystal 40Ar/39Ar dating of the Dena Dora and Lower Kada Hadar members of the Hadar Formation, Ethiopia. Geology. 22:6–10.

Ward S, Brown B, Hill A, Kelley J, Downs W. 27 August 1999. Equatorius: a new hominoid genus from the Middle Miocene of Kenya. Science. 285:1382–1386.

Warren DM. 1989. Utilizing Indigenous healers in national health delivery systems: the Ghanaian experiment. In: van Willigen J, Rylko-Bauer B, McElroy A, editors. Making our research useful: case studies in the utilization of anthropological knowledge. Boulder, CO: Westview Press. pp. 159–178.

Warry W. 1990. Doing unto others: applied anthropology, collaborative research and Native self-determination. Culture. 10:61–62.

Washburn S. 1960. Tools and human evolution. Scientific American. 203(3):62–75.

Watkins J. 2004. Becoming American or becoming Indian? NAGPRA, Kennewick and cultural affiliation. Journal of Social Archaeology. 4:60–80.

Watkins T. 2009. From foragers to complex societies in Southwest Asia. In: Scarre C, editor. The human past. New York: Thames and Hudson. pp. 200–233.

Weaver MP. 1993. The Aztecs, Maya, and their predecessors. 3rd ed. San Diego: Academic Press.

Webb EC, White CD, Longstaffe FJ. 2013. Exploring geographic origins at Cahuachi using stable isotopic analysis of archaeological human tissues and modern environmental waters. International Journal of Osteoarchaeology. 23(6):698–715.

Weiner JS. 1954. Nose shape and climate. Journal of Physical Anthropology. 4:615–618.

Weiss E. 2001. Kennewick Man's funeral: the burying of scientific evidence. Politics and the Life Sciences. 1:13–18.

Weiss H, Courty M-A, Wetterstrom W, Guichard F, Senior L, Meadow R, Curnow A. 1993. The genesis and collapse of third millennium north Mesopotamian civilization. Science. 261:995–1004.

Wenke RJ. 1990. Patterns in prehistory: humankind's first three million years. 3rd ed. New York: Oxford University Press.

Wenke RJ, Olszewski D. 2007. Patterns in prehistory. 5th ed. New York: Oxford University Press.

Werner D. November 1978. Trekking in the Amazon forest. Natural History. 87:42–54.

Weston E, Lister A. 2009. Insular dwarfism in hippos and a model for brain size reduction in *Homo floresiensis*. Nature. 459:85–88.

Wheat JB. January 1967. A Paleo-Indian bison kill. Scientific American. 44–47.

Wheatley D, Gillings M. 2002. Spatial technology and archaeology: the archaeological applications of GIS. New York: Taylor & Francis.

Wheatley P. 1971. The pivot of the four quarters. Chicago: Aldine.

Wheeler PE. 1991. The thermoregulator advantages of hominid bipedalism in open equatorial environments: the contribution of increased convective heat loss and cutaneous evaporative cooling. Journal of Human Evolution. 21:107–115.

White B. March 1973. Demand for labor and population growth in colonial Java. Human Ecology. 1(3):217–236.

White CD, Healy PF, Schwarcz HP. 1993. Intensive agriculture, social status, and Maya diet at Pacbitun, Belize. Journal of Anthropological Research. 49:347–375.

White CD, Price TD, Longstaffe FJ. 2007. Residential histories of the human sacrifices at the Moon Pyramid, Teotihuacan. Ancient Mesoamerica. 18(01):159–172.

White CD, Schwarcz HP. 1989. Ancient Maya diet at Lamanai, Belize: as inferred from isotopic and chemical analysis of human bone. Journal of Archaeological Science. 16:451–474.

White CD, Schwarcz HP. 1994. Temporal trends in stable isotopes for Nubian mummy tissues. American Journal of Physical Anthropology. 93:165–187.

White CD, Spence MW, Longstaffe FJ, Rattray E, Storey R. 2009. The Teotihuacan dream: an isotopic study of economic organization and immigration. Ontario Archaeology. 85–88:279–297.

White FJ. 1996. *Pan paniscus* 1973 to 1996: twenty-three years of field research. Evolutionary Anthropology. 5:11–17.

White LA. 1968. The expansion of the scope of science. In: Fried MH, editor. Readings in anthropology. 2nd ed., Vol. 1. New York: Thomas Y. Crowell. pp. 15–24.

White R. 1982. Rethinking the Middle/Upper Paleolithic transition. Current Anthropology. 23:169–175.

White TD. 28 March 2003. Early hominids—diversity or distortion? Science. 299:1994–1997.

White TD, Asfaw B, Beyene Y, Haile-Selassie Y, Lovejoy CO, Suwa G, WoldeGabriel G. 2009. *Ardipithecus ramidus* and the paleobiology of early hominids. Science. 326(5949):64–86.

White TD, Johanson DC, Kimbel WH. 1981. *Australopithecus africanus*: its phyletic position reconsidered. South African Journal of Science. 77:445–471.

White TD, Suwa G, Asfaw B. 1994. *Australopithecus ramidus*, a new species of early hominid from Aramis, Ethiopia. Nature. 371:306–312.

White TD, Suwa G, Asfaw B. 1995. *Australopithecus ramidus*, a new species of early hominid from Aramis, Ethiopia. Nature. 375:88.

Whiten A, Goodall J, McGrew WC, Nishida T, Reynolds V, Sugiyama Y, Tutin CE, Wrangham RW, Boesch C. 1999. Cultures in chimpanzees. Nature. 399:682–685.

Whiten A, Horner V, Litchfield CA, Marshall-Pescini S. 2004. How do apes ape? Learning & Behavior. 32(1):36–52.

Whiting JWM. 1964. Effects of climate on certain cultural practices. In: Goodenough W. Explorations in cultural anthropology. New York: McGraw-Hill.

Whittaker JC. 1994. Flintknapping: making and understanding stone tools. Austin: University of Texas Press.

[WHO] World Health Organization. 1986. Use and interpretation of anthropometric indicators of nutritional status. Bulletin of the World Health Organization. 64:929–941.

Wilford JN. 4 March 1997. Ancient German spears tell of mighty hunters of Stone Age. New York Times. C:6.

Wilford N. 5 September 1995. The transforming leap, from 4 legs to 2. New York Times. C:1 ff.

Wilkinson RL. 1995. Yellow fever: ecology, epidemiology, and role in the collapse of the Classic Lowland Maya civilization. Medical Anthropology. 16:269–294.

Williams ED, Crews JD. 2003. From dust to dust: ethical and practical issues involved in the location, exhumation, and identification of bodies from mass graves. Croatian Medical Journal. 44:251–258.

Williams GC. 1992. Natural selection: domains, levels, and challenges. New York: Oxford University Press.

Williamson RF, Pfeiffer S. 2003. Bones of the ancestors: the archaeology and osteology of the Moatfield ossuary. Hull, Quebec: Canadian Museum of Civilization.

Wilson EO. 1975. Sociobiology: the new synthesis. Cambridge, MA: Belknap Press of Harvard University Press. Quoted in Low B. 1998. Behavioral ecology, "sociobiology" and human behavior. In: Ember CR, Ember M, Peregrine PN, editors. Research frontiers in anthropology. Upper Saddle River, NJ: Prentice Hall/Simon & Schuster Custom Publishing.

Winnipeg Regional Health Authority. 2004. Diabetes Education Resource for Children and Adolescents (DER-CA) 2004 annual report. Winnipeg: Winnipeg Regional Health Authority.

Wittfogel K. 1957. Oriental despotism: a comparative study of total power. New Haven, CT: Yale University Press.

Wolf E. 1984. Culture: panacea or problem. American Antiquity. 49:393–400.

Wolpoff MH. 1971. Competitive exclusion among Lower Pleistocene hominids: the single species hypothesis. Man. 6:601–614.

Wolpoff MH. 1983. *Ramapithecus* and human origins: an anthropologist's perspective of changing interpretations. In: Ciochon RL, Corruccini RS, editors. New interpretations of ape and human ancestry. New York: Plenum. pp. 651–676.

Wolpoff MH. 1999. Paleoanthropology. 2nd ed. Boston: McGraw-Hill.

Wolpoff MH, Nkini A. 2001. Early and Early Middle Pleistocene hominids from Asia and Africa. In Delson E, editor. Ancestors: the hard evidence. New York: Alan R. Liss.

Wolpoff MH, Thorne AG, Jelinek J, Yinyun Z. 1994. The case for sinking *Homo erectus*: 100 years of *Pithecanthropus* is enough! In: Franzen JL, editor. 100 years of *Pithecanthropus*: the *Homo erectus* problem. Frankfurt am Main: Senckenbergische Naturforschende Gesellschaft. pp. 341–361.

Wong K. January 2003. An ancestor to call our own. Scientific American. 288:54–63.

Wong K. February 2005. The littlest human. Scientific American. 292:56–65.

Wood B. 2006. A precious little bundle. Nature. 443:278–281.

Wood B. 1994. Hominid paleobiology: recent achievements and challenges. In: Corruccini R, Ciochon RL, editors. Integrative paths to the past. Englewood Cliffs, NJ: Prentice Hall. pp. 147–165.

Wood B, Collard M. 1999. The human genus. Science. 284:65–71.

Wood BA. 1992. Evolution of australopithecines. In: Jones S, Martin R, Pilbeam D, editors. The Cambridge encyclopedia of human evolution. New York: Cambridge University Press. p. 236.

Wood JW, Milner GR, Harpending HC, Weiss KM. 1992. The osteological paradox: problems of inferring prehistoric health from skeletal samples. Current Anthropology. 33:343–370.

Wrangham RW. 1980. An ecological model of female-bonded primate groups. Behaviour. 75:262–300.

Wrangham RW. 2009. Catching fire: how cooking made us human. New York: Basic Books.

Wright GA. 1971. Origins of food production in southwestern Asia: a survey of ideas. Current Anthropology. 12:470.

Wright HT. 1986. The evolution of civilizations. In: Meltzer DJ, Fowler DD, Sabloff JA, editors. American archaeology past and future. Washington, DC: Smithsonian Institution Press. pp. 323–365.

Wright HT, Johnson GA. 1975. Population, exchange, and early state formation in southwestern Iran. American Anthropologist. 77:267–289.

Wright J. 1985. The development of prehistory in Canada, 1935–1985. American Antiquity. 50(2): 421–433.

Wright L, White C. 1996. Human biology in the Classic Maya collapse: evidence from palaeopathology and paleodiet. Journal of World Prehistory. 10:147–198.

Xinzhi W, Maolin W. 1985. Early *Homo sapiens* in China. In: Rukang W, Olsen JW, editors. Paleoanthropology and paleolithic archaeology in the People's Republic of China. Orlando, FL: Academic Press. pp. 91–106.

Yamei H, Potts R, Baoyin Y, Zhengtang G, Deino A, Wei W, Clark J, Guangmao X, Weiwen H. 3 March 2000. Mid-Pleistocene Acheulian-like stone technology of the Bose basin, South China. Science. 287(5458):1622–1626.

Yang DY, Cannon A, Saunders SR. 2004. DNA species identification of archaeological salmon bone from the Pacific Northwest Coast of North America. Journal of Archaeological Science. 31:619–631.

Yang DY, Eng B, Saunders SR. 2003. Hypersensitive PCR, ancient human mtDNA and contamination. Human Biology. 75:355–364.

Yang DY, Eng B, Waye JS, Dudar JC, Saunders SR. 1998. Improved DNA extraction from ancient bones using silica-based spin columns. American Journal of Physical Anthropology. 105(4):539–543.

Yang DY, Speller CF. 2006. Co-amplification of cytochrome b and D-loop mtDNA fragments for the identification of degraded DNA samples. Molecular Ecology Notes. 6:605–608.

Yang DY, Watt K. 2005. Contamination controls when preparing archaeological remains for ancient DNA analysis. Journal of Archaeological Science. 32:331–336.

Yellen JE, Brooks AS, Cornelissen E, Mehlman M, Stewart K. 1995. A Middle Stone Age worked bone industry from Katanda, Upper Semliki Valley, Zaire. Science. 268:553–556.

Young TK, Dean HJ, Flett B, Wood-Steiman J. 2000a. Childhood obesity in a population at high risk for type 2 diabetes. Journal of Pediatrics. 136(3):365–369.

Young TC Jr. 1972. Population densities and early Mesopotamian urbanism. In: Ucko P, Tringham R, Dimbleby GW, editors. Man, settlement and urbanism. Cambridge, MA: Schenkman. pp. 827–842.

Young TK, McIntyre LL, Dooley J, Rodriguez J. 1985. Epidemiological features of diabetes mellitus among Indians in northwestern Ontario and northeastern Manitoba. Canadian Medical Association Journal. 132:793–797.

Young TK, Reading J, Elias B, O'Neil JD. 2000b. Type 2 diabetes mellitus in Canada's First Nations: status of an epidemic in progress. Canadian Medical Association Journal. 163(5):561–566.

Young TK, Szathmáry EJ, Evers S, Wheatley B. 1990. Geographical distribution of diabetes among the Native population of Canada: A National Survey. Social Science and Medicine. 31(2):129–139.

Zeder MA, 2011. The origins of agriculture in the near east. Current Anthropology. 52(1 Suppl): S221–235.

Zeller A. 1987. Communication by sight and smell. In: Smuts BB, Cheney DL, Seyfarth RM, Wrangham RW, Struhsaker TT, editors. Primate societies. Chicago: University of Chicago Press. pp. 433–439.

Zeller A. 1992. Communication in the social unit. In: Burton FD, editor. Social processes and mental abilities in non-human primates. Queenston: Edwin Mellen Press. pp. 61–89.

Zeller A. 1994. Evidence of structure in macaque communication. In: Gardner RA, Gardner BT, Chiarelli B, editors. The ethological roots of culture. Dordrecht, Netherlands: Kluwer Academic. pp. 15–39.

Zhu H, Bhagatwala J, Huang Y, Pollock NK, Parikh S, Raed A, Gutin B, Harshfield GA, Dong Y. 2016. Race/ethnicity-specific association of vitamin D and global DNA methylation: cross-sectional and interventional findings. PloS One. 11(4):e0152849.

Zihlman A. 1992. The emergence of human locomotion: the evolutionary background and environmental context. In: Nishida T, editor. Topics in primatology. Tokyo: University of Tokyo Press.

Zimmer C. 19 November 1999. Kenyan skeleton shakes ape family tree. Science. 285:1335–1337.

Zimmer C. 2004. Faster than a hyena? Running may make humans special. Science. 306:1283.

Zohary, D. 1969. The progenitors of wheat and barley in relation to domestic and agriulture dispersal in the Old World. In: Ucko PJ, Dimbleby GW, editors. The domestication and exploitation of plants and animals. Chicago: Aldine.

Name Index

A
Abel, T., 183
Adams, R.M., 336
Aiello, L.C., 165, 188, 205, 209
Aitchiso, J., 278
Aitken, M.J., 46
Alberts, B., 98, 101, 103
Alemseged, Z., 215–216
Alexander, J.P., 186
Ali, J.R., 152
Allen, J.S., 131, 365
Allen, K.M.S., 70
Allman, J., 184
Alloway, B.V., 234
Almécija, S., 209
Almquist, A.J., 103, 157
Alperson-Afil, N., 243
Alroy, J., 300
Alvarez, L., 109
Ames, K.M., 58
Andersen, R.E., 375
Anderson-Fye, E.P., 364
Andersson, J.G., 240
Andrews, P., 188, 190
Ankel-Simons, F., 145, 154, 155, 156, 157, 158, 159, 160
Anonymous, 74, 170, 222, 295, 316, 317, 321, 343, 350, 370, 371
Anton, S.C., 237
Aptekar, L., 367
Arbib, M.A., 278
Arensburg, B., 260
Armelagos, G.J., 59, 64, 128, 134, 319, 320
Arsuaga, J.L., 62, 246
Asch, D.L., 310
Asch, N.B., 310
Ascher, R., 149
Asfaw, B., 211
Ayala, F.J., 267
Aziz, F., 234

B
Babineau, J., 354
Badcock, C., 107
Bahn, P.G., 86, 269
Bailey, D.F.C., 354
Bailey, G.N., 72
Bailey, R.C., 300
Baker, P.T., 374
Ball, T., 64
Balter, M., 256, 299
Balzeau, A., 245
Bandy, M., 379
Bar-Yosef, O., 240
Barash, D.P., 107
Baraybar, J.P., 370
Barbeau, C.M., 2
Bard, K.A., 333
Barnett, T., 363
Barnosky, A., 300
Barrett, D.E., 111
Barrett, L., 126
Barroso, I., 195
Barta, J.L., 58
Batchelder, W.H., 355
Bathurst, R.R., 58, 68
Beadle, G., 103
Beadle, M., 103
Beall, C.M., 123, 125
Bearder, S.K., 145, 152, 153
Beattie, O., 51
Beaumont, P.B., 242
Begun, D.R., 190, 191, 192, 193, 194
Bellwood, P., 280, 292, 297
Benyshek, D.C., 132
Berg, C., 366
Berg, P., 101
Berge, C., 215
Berger, L.R., 212, 246, 247
Berlin, B., 358
Berlin, E.A., 358
Bermúdez de Castro, J.M., 246
Berry, J.W., 365
Berti, P.R., 366–367
Beta Analytic Inc., 44
Bickmore, W.A., 195
Bilsborough, A., 31, 38, 45, 194, 200
Bin, G., 240
Bindon, J.R., 132, 374
Binford, L.R., 72, 242, 243, 256, 258, 296, 314, 317
Binford, S.R., 256
Bird, A., 107
Bischoff, J., 310
Bishop, N., 147
Black, D., 235
Black, F.L., 127
Blaffer Hrdy, S., 155–156
Blaikie, P., 363
Blanchard, J.F., 132
Blanton, R.E., 332, 337
Blendon, R.J., 127
Block, J.I., 181
Blumler, M.A., 314
Boas, F., 2, 3, 6, 87
Boaz, N.T., 103, 157
Bocquet-Appel, J.P., 61
Bodley, J.H., 75
Boesch, C., 169, 170
Boesch, H., 169, 170
Bogin, B., 125, 202, 237, 374
Bohannan, P., 87, 88
Bohlin, B., 235
Boldsen, J.L., 60, 61
Bolt, P., 64
Bolton, R., 111, 362
Bond, M., 152
Borchert, C.M., 171
Bordaz, J., 273, 274
Bordes, F., 241, 257
Borgerhoff Mulder, M., 294
Bos, K.I., 58
Boserup, E., 13
Boucher de Perthes, J., 86
Boule, M., 249–250
Boutton, T.W., 65
Bowler, P.J., 83
Bowman, K., 368
Boyd, M., 311
Boyd, R., 108, 112, 138, 139, 163, 167, 227
Boyer, D.M., 181
Brace, C.L., 106, 133, 135
Braidwood, R.J., 313
Brain, C.K., 242
Branda, R.F., 121
Brandon, R.N., 88
Bräuer, G., 264, 268
Brierley, J.A., 318
Brinkmeier, D., 380
Britten, R.J., 6
Brodey, J.E., 122
Bromage, T.G., 208, 216
Brooks, A.F., 135
Broom, R., 216, 217, 218, 219
Browman, D., 311
Brown, D.E., 132
Brown, F., 236
Brown, F.H., 42, 43, 45, 46, 236
Brown, J.A., 286, 297
Brown, P., 237, 238
Brown, P.J., 58, 128, 364
Bruce, S.G., 133, 375
Brues, A., 134
Brumfiel, E.M., 337, 341
Brumm, A., 234
Brunet, M., 209, 211, 212
Brush, S., 183
Brutsaert, T., 123
Bryan, P., 34
Bryant, C.A., 354
Buckland, P.C., 69
Budimlija, Z.M., 370
Buffon, G., 85
Buikstra, J.E., 59
Burbano, H.A., 252
Burke, A.M., 258, 269, 280
Burnet, T., 85
Butzer, K.W., 242, 256
Byrne, R., 314

C
Cameron, N., 374
Campbell, B.G., 215
Campbell, D.T., 112, 139
Campbell, K., 152
Candler, K., 380
Cann, R., 250, 251, 265, 267
Cannon, A., 35, 58, 61
Carlson, K.J., 212
Carneiro, R.L., 317, 336–337
Carpenter, C.R., 158
Carretero, J.M., 246
Carrier, J., 362
Carroll, M.D., 364
Cartmill, M., 146, 154, 155, 179, 184, 185
Caussinus, H., 61
Cavalli-Sforza, L.L., 266
Caws, P., 16
Chaline, J., 91, 109
Chalmers, T., 85
Chambers, E., 12
Chan, H.M., 366
Chang, K.-C., 299, 312, 334, 337
Chaplin, G., 122, 200
Chard, C.S., 297
Charles-Dominique, P., 153
Chase, L.A., 132
Chase, P., 259
Chatters, J., 376
Cheer, S.M., 131
Chen, F., 240
Chen, L.C., 372–373
Cheney, D.L., 149, 158
Chessa, B., 305
Chia, S., 73

Chikhi, L., 163
Childe, V.G., 313, 338
Chiozza, F., 163
Chivers, D.J., 158
Choi, H.J., 375
Chomsky, N., 170, 278
Chornogubsky, L., 152
Chouinard-Thuly, L., 278
Cinq-Mars, J., 280
Ciochon, R.L., 176, 179, 190, 192, 210, 232, 242, 251
Claassen, C., 54
Clark, A.G., 194
Clark, G., 298, 321
Clark, J.D., 223, 243, 244, 299
Clarke, R.J., 211
Clayman, C.B., 239
Clayton, D., 233
Clutton-Brock, J., 305, 311, 313
Clutton-Brock, T.H., 164, 165
Coe, M.D., 136, 333
Cohen, A., 358
Cohen, J.D., 312
Cohen, M.N., 59, 300, 301, 314, 319, 320
Cohen, R.N., 335
Cole, T.J., 126
Collard, M., 209, 234
Collier, J., 349
Collier, S., 305
Collins, D., 297
Collins, T., 184
Colquhoun, I.C., 162, 163
Commanda, L., 360
Conkey, M.W., 341
Connah, G., 299, 313, 326, 333, 334
Connor, W.E., 65
Conroy, G.C., 150, 179, 182, 185, 186, 188, 189, 190, 192, 211, 215, 217, 221
Cook, D.C., 59
Cooper, A., 252
Coqueugniot, H., 245
Corballis, M.C., 227
Coreil, J., 354, 356
Corruccini, R.S., 190, 269
Cortopassi-Laurino, M., 311
Costin, C.L., 341
Cotton, A., 163
Crawford, G.W., 63, 292
Crawford, R.D., 311
Crayle, J., 109
Crews, D.E., 132
Crews, J.D., 370
Crick, F., 98
Crockett, C., 155
Crosby, A.W., 136, 137
Cross, C.R., 278

Culotta, E., 211, 213
Cuvier, G., 84
Cybulski, J.S., 3
Czekala, N., 159

D

Daiger, S., 101
Dalton, R., 350
Daniel, I.R., 286
Daniel, M., 132, 133
Dart, R., 216, 219
Darwin, C., 81–82, 83, 85, 86, 87, 88, 89, 91, 96, 105, 106, 108, 109, 247
Dasen, P.R., 111
Davies. N.B., 107
Davis, D.D., 225
Dawson, A., 270
Dawson, G.M., 2
Dawson, J., 285
Dawson, J.W., 2
Dawson, P.C., 34
de la Torre, I., 278
de Lumley, H., 244
De Oliveira, F.B., 152
de Souza, S.M., 60
de Waal, F., 169
Dean, H., 132, 205
Dean, M.C., 208, 216
Defleur, A., 260
DeGreef, S., 248
Delson, E., 206, 216, 217
deMenocal, P.B., 213, 340
Denham, T.P., 312
d'Errico, F., 279
DeSalle, R., 140
DeSilva, J.M., 245
DesJardins, D.A., 360
Devillers, C., 91, 109
Devlin, B., 137
DeWitte, S.N., 60
Diamond, J., 129, 313, 330
Diamond, J.M., 338
Dibble, H., 259
Dickson, D.B., 245
Dickson, J.H., 51
Dillehay, T., 281, 282
Dillehay, T.D., 63
Dincauze, D.F., 68
Dirks, P.H., 246
Dirks, R., 318, 338, 368
Dixon, E.J., 63
Dobzhansky, T., 104, 108, 138, 208
Dohlinow, P.J., 147
Dolch, R., 163
Donald, M., 227
Donati, G., 163
Donoghue, H.D., 58
Dorit, R.L., 267

Douglass, A.E., 40
Doyle, G.A., 152
Dressler, W.W., 132
Driscoll, T., 252
Duarte, C., 268, 269
Dubois, E., 234–235
Dudar, J.C., 58
Duhard, J.-P., 277
Dunbar, R., 206
Dunbar, R.I.M., 167
Dunn, F.L., 58, 128
Dupras, T.L., 69
Dupré, J., 135
Durbin, R., 194
Durham, W.H., 4, 112, 116, 118, 122, 123, 129, 139

E

Earle, T.K., 338
Early, J.D., 294
Eaton, J.W., 121
Ebrey, P.B., 136
Ecker, J.R., 195
Eddy, E.M., 349
Edey, M., 214
Edgar, B., 279
Edgerton, R.B., 365
Eilers, R.G., 318
Eiseley, L.C., 82
Eisenberg, J.F., 155
Eldredge, N., 108, 109, 216
Ember, C.R., 117, 130, 138, 139, 169, 238, 294, 319, 364
Ember, M., 117, 130, 138, 169, 238, 364
Emery, K.F., 72
Erickson, C., 379, 380
Ervin, A.M., 349
Eswaran, V., 267
Etkin, N.L., 358
Etler, D.A., 176, 179
Evans, C., 278
Evans, J., 68
Eveleth, P.B., 125, 374, 375
Everett, M., 100
Excoffier, L., 267

F

Fagan, B.M., 46, 70, 71, 273, 284, 285, 286, 334
Falk, D., 204, 237
Fallin, M.D., 107
Farnsworth, P., 308
Favory, F., 316
Fayek, M., 73
Feder, K.L., 235, 268, 305, 309
Fedigan, L.M., 147, 156, 368
Fedoroff, N., 308
Feibel, C.S., 236

Feinberg, A.P., 107
Feinman, G.M., 337
Feldman, D.A., 363
Feldman, M.W., 266
Ferguson, R.B., 338
Fischman, J., 209
Fish, P.R., 256
Fisher, J., 357
Fisher, J.W., Jr., 61
Fisher, W.H., 353
Fix, A.G., 294
Fladmark, K.R., 43
Flannery, K.V., 293, 296, 299, 301, 304, 305, 308, 309, 310, 314, 327, 329
Fleagle, J.G., 154, 156, 158, 179, 180, 186, 187, 188, 189, 192, 193, 210, 213, 218, 219, 220, 232, 238, 246, 247, 251
Flegal, K.M., 364
Flegal, P.N., 374
Fleischer, R.L., 45
Fogel, M., 66, 67
Fortey, R., 81
Fossey, D., 159, 162
Foster, G.M., 75, 353, 354
Fowler, K., 117, 130
Fowler, M.L., 334
Fox, W.A., 376
Franciscus, R.G., 236
Frankel, B., 349
Frankenberg, S.R., 61
Frayer, D.W., 167, 266, 267, 301
Freedman, D., 110, 111
Freeman, L.G., 242
Fricke, H.C., 69
Friedman, J.M., 364
Friedman, S.S., 135
Frisancho, A.R., 125, 374
Frisch, R.E., 303
Fry, I., 81
Fuentes, A., 206
Fulford, A.J., 132

G

Gabunia, L., 232, 233
Gadjev, I., 83
Galdikas, B.M.F., 7, 158, 162
Galik, K., 209
Galloway, T., 375
Gamble, C., 253, 277
Gao, X., 240
Garber, P., 184
Garlie, T.N., 125, 374, 375
Gavian, S., 368
Gentner, W., 43
Gérin, L., 3
Gero, J.M., 341

Gibbons, A., 209, 254, 260, 265, 280
Gibson, K.R., 167
Gilad, Y., 195
Gilbert, M.T., 281
Gill, J.L., 300
Gill, S., 375
Gillings, M., 70
Gingerich, P.D., 179
Girardot, J.J., 316
Glazer, M., 87, 88
Goebel, T., 281
Goin, F., 152
Goldberg, P., 240
Goldizen, A.W., 155
Goodall, J., 148, 160, 162
Goodby, C., 132
Goodenough, W.H., 356
Goodman, A.H., 59, 320
Goodman, M., 161
Goren-Inbar, N., 243
Gorman, C., 299
Gould, S.J., 108, 109, 207
Gowland, R.L., 60, 72
Gowlett, J.A.J., 227
Granger, D.E., 240
Grant, P.R., 107, 109
Grant, R., 107
Graver, A.M., 58
Gray, J.P., 147
Grayson, D.K., 300
Greenberg, J.H., 281, 283
Greenfield, H.J., 62, 70
Gregory, D.M., 364
Gregory, T.R., 195
Greksa, L.P., 123, 125
Grine, F.E., 219
Gross, D.R., 373
Grossman, D., 339
Grün, R., 234, 264, 268
Guan, Y., 361
Guthrie, R.D., 300
Gutiérrez, G., 252
Guttman-Bond, E., 379

H

Haas, J., 334
Haas, J.D., 372
Habicht, J.K.A., 182
Habicht, J.P., 372
Hackenberg, R.A., 349
Haglund, W.D., 370
Hahn, R.A., 357, 359
Haile-Selassie, Y., 209
Haldane, J.B.S., 140
Hall, E.T., 21
Hall, G.R., 63
Hammer, M.F., 266
Hammond, S., 233
Hanna, J.M., 118

Hannah, A.C., 170
Harcourt, A.H., 159
Hardy, B.L., 63
Harington, C.R., 280
Harlan, J.R., 296
Harpending, H.C., 60, 268, 294
Harper, K.H., 128
Harris, D.R., 301, 302
Harris, M., 336
Harris, S., 132
Harrison, G.A., 105, 116, 118, 120, 125, 129
Harrison, G.G., 4
Harrison, P.D., 333
Harrison, T., 190
Hart, H.R., Jr., 45
Hartwig, W.C., 188
Harvey, P., 164, 165
Hassan, F.A., 300, 301
Hastorf, C., 341
Haug, G., 339, 340
Hauser, M.D., 278
Hausfater, G., 147
Hauspie, R.C., 126
Hawkins, A., 280
Hawthorne, H., 349
Hayden, B., 70
Hays, T.E., 183
Health Agency of Canada, 92
Health Canada, 92, 132
Heath, D.C., 146
Hedican, E.J., 349
Hegele, R.A., 132
Heimbuch, R.C., 171, 245, 260
Heizer, R.H., 43
Helms, M.W., 330, 332
Hennig, B.J., 132
Henry, D.O., 297, 314
Henshilwood, C.S., 279
Herring, D.A., 67, 68, 128
Herrmann, E., 206
Herrnstein, R., 137
Hewes, G.W., 202
Hewitt, G., 245
Higham, C., 299, 312
Higham, T., 268
Hill, J.H., 150
Hinkes, M., 134
Hinkes, M.J., 369
Ho, C.K., 243
Ho, T.J., 372
Hockett, C.F., 149
Hodgson, J., 252
Hoffecker, J.F., 281, 284
Holdaway, R.N., 300
Holden, C., 376
Hole, F., 43, 293, 305, 307, 310, 312, 314, 337

Holliday, R., 107
Holloway, R.L., 245
Holloway, R.T., 216
Honigmann, J.J., 363, 365
Hooke, R., 85
Hoppa, R.D., 59, 61, 117, 125, 128, 130
Horowitz, S., 61, 319
Houston, S.D., 333
Howell, F.C., 242
Howell, N., 294, 303, 319
Huang, H.T., 123
Huber, M., 152
Hudson, J., 61
Huffine, E., 370
Hull, S., 73
Hunt, T., 195
Hunter, J., 55
Huss-Ashmore, R., 125
Hutton, J., 85
Huxley, J., 108
Huxley, T., 86, 249
Huypens, P., 107

I

Illerhaus, B., 176, 253
Inhorn, M.C., 58, 128
Irons, W., 163
Irwin, M., 163
Isaac, G., 224, 225, 242

J

Jablonski, N.G., 121, 122
Jackes, M., 319, 320
Jacobs, P., 133
Jacomb, C., 300
James, G.D., 132
Jane Goodall Institute, The, 163
Janes, C.R., 58, 128
Janson, C.H., 155
Janzen, D.H., 317
Jayaswal, V., 280
Jelliffe, D.B., 353
Jelliffe, E.F.P., 353
Jenkins, D.L., 65, 281
Jenness, D., 2, 3
Jennings, J.D., 285
Jespersen, O., 278
Johanson, D.C., 214, 215
Johansson, S.R., 61, 319
Johnson, A.W., 338
Johnson, G.A., 301, 327, 328, 337
Johnson, S., 163
Johnson, T.M., 363
Johnston, F.E., 125, 372, 374, 375
Jolly, A., 165, 166, 170
Jolly, C., 203

Jones, F.W., 184
Jones, J., 292
Jones, M., 299
Jones, S., 194, 195, 201
Jordanova, L.J., 83
Judge, W.J., 285
Jungers, W.L., 209, 214, 217, 238

K

Kakekagumick, K.E., 133
Kaler, S.N., 132
Kalnay, E., 341
Kappelman, J., 46
Karlsson, E.A., 369
Kasarda, J.D., 318
Katzenberg, M.A., 3, 58, 65, 67, 68
Katzmarzyk, P.T., 118, 120
Kawai, M., 166
Kay, R.F., 178, 186, 188, 189
Kearney, R., 278
Keefe, A.A., 375
Keeley, L., 224, 241
Kelley, J., 191
Kent, S., 295
Kerr, R.A., 339
Kettlewell, H.B.D., 91
Kim, C., 366
Kimball Romney, A., 355
Kimbel, W.H., 211
Kimmerle, E.H., 370
King, M.-C., 135
Kingston, J.D., 200
Kinzey, W.G., 155
Kirk, R., 134
Kirmayer, L.J., 365
Kit, B.K., 364
Kivell, T.L., 247
Klaus, H.D., 60
Klein, R.G., 32, 39, 44, 207, 217, 218, 219, 220, 222, 223, 241, 242, 245, 255, 256, 257, 258, 259, 269, 274, 279
Kleindienst, M., 280
Kleinman, A., 363, 365
Klepinger, L.L., 65
Klima, B., 272
Knight, A., 132
Knight, C., 171
Knüsel, C., 72
Komar, D., 370
Konigsberg, L.W., 61
Konner, M., 319
Kono, R.T., 234
Kordos, L., 193
Kottak, C.P., 139
Krainitzki, H., 252
Kramer, A., 234

Kramer, S.N., 329
Krause, J., 57, 252, 260
Krebs, J.R., 107
Krings, M., 250, 251, 252
Kuhnlein, H.V., 366
Kurniawan, I., 234
Kushner, G., 13, 348, 349

L

LaFleur, M., 163
Laitman, J.T., 171, 245, 260
Laland, K.N., 118, 278
Lalueza-Fox, C., 252
Lamarck, J.-B., 83, 86, 87, 107
Lambert, D.T., 360
Landecker, H., 100
Langaney, A., 267
Langdon, J., 200, 204, 206, 238
Lanting, F., 169
Larcombe, L.A., 58, 107, 128
Larsen, C.S., 66, 120, 319
Lavoie, J.G., 360
Le Gros Clark, W., 157, 216
Leakey, L.S.B., 39, 162, 219, 220, 223
Leakey, M., 212, 214, 219, 220, 223, 225, 226
Leakey, M.G., 209, 211, 213
Leakey, R., 219, 221
Lee, P.C., 156
Lee, R.B., 302
Leonard, W.R., 118, 120, 207, 243
Leroi-Gourhan, A., 274
Lev-Yadun, S., 296
Levinson, D., 139
Lewin, R., 194
Lewis, C.A., 109
Lewis, H.M., 278
Lewis, K.P., 147
Li, Y., 64
Liebal, K., 278
Lieberman, D.E., 267
Lieberman, L., 134, 138
Lieberman, P., 171, 227, 278
Lightfoot, E., 69
Lin, D.S., 65
Linnaeus, C., 82, 86, 87
Linton, R., 73
Lippolt, H.J., 43
Lister, A., 237
Littlefield, A., 134
Liu, J., 240
Liu, L., 64
Liu, X., 299
Lombard, M., 63
Loomis, W.F., 122
Lopinot, N.H., 340

Lopuchin, A.S., 80
Louis, E.E., 163
Loustaunau, M.O., 360, 364
Lovejoy, A.O., 82
Lovejoy, C.O., 202–203, 204, 214, 217, 239
Low, B., 317
Low, B.S., 110, 111, 163
Lowie, R.H., 73, 87–88
Loy, T.H., 63
Lu, T., 312
Lubell, D., 66, 319
Lumbreras, L., 334
Lurquin, P.E., 122, 129
Lutz, C., 363, 365
Lyell, C., 85

M

MacDowell, L.S., 282
MacKinnon, J., 154
MacKinnon, K., 154
MacLarnon, A., 245
MacMillan, H., 132
MacNeish, R.S., 292, 305, 310, 312, 313
MacVean, R.B., 374
Madigral, L., 129
Maestripieri, D., 148
Makristathis, A., 51
Malainey, M.E., 65
Manchester, K., 58
Manson, J.H., 166
Manzi, G., 246
Maolin, W., 250
Marciniak, S., 58
Marcus, J., 299, 308, 309, 332
Marks, J., 133, 136
Marroig, G., 152
Marshack, A., 276, 277
Marshall, L.G., 300
Marshall, W.A., 374
Martin, A., 55
Martin, A.E., 178, 186, 189, 194
Martin, P.S., 271, 298, 300
Martin, R., 31, 150, 151, 201, 292
Martin, R.D., 146, 152, 153, 166, 178, 181, 186, 189, 194, 238
Martorell, R., 125, 372
Mascie-Taylor, C.G.N., 357
Matthews, R., 329
Maxwell, M.S., 287, 288
Mayr, E., 82, 83, 84, 86, 108
Mays, S., 58
McCain, G., 15–16, 17
McCarthy, R., 278

McCartney, K., 111
McCorriston, J., 314
McCracken, R.D., 122–123
McDermott, L., 277
McDonald, K.A., 280, 283
McElroy, A., 373
McGarvey, S.T., 132, 374
McGhee, R., 286, 287, 288
McGovern, P.E., 63
McGrew, W.C., 170, 203
McHenry, H.M., 206, 215, 217, 219, 220, 221
McIlwraith, T., 3
McKee, L., 374
McNeill, W.H., 136, 139
Meiklejohn, C., 319
Mellaart, J., 297, 308
Mellars, P., 254, 272
Mellor, J.W., 368
Meltzer, D.J., 281
Meltzer, D.K., 281
Mendel, G., 91, 96–97
Mercader, J., 170
Meyer, M., 260
Midodzi, W.K., 364
Mill, J.E., 360
Miller, N.F., 292
Miller-Wille, L., 75
Millon, R., 330, 331, 332
Milne, S.B., 34
Milner, G.R., 61, 335
Milton, K., 165, 167
Minugh-Purvis, N., 253
Miracle, A.W., 13
Mitchell, K.B., 375
Mittermeier, R.A., 163
Mojzsis, S.J., 80
Molina, E.C., 152
Molnar, S., 130, 133
Moore, J.A., 61
Moore, M.W., 234
Morell, V., 275
Morgan, L.H., 87
Morgan, T.J.H., 278
Morlan, R.E., 280
Morris, A., 379
Morrison, K.D., 341
Morwood, M.J., 234, 237, 238
Moser, S., 248
Mosley, W.H., 372–373
Moss, M.L., 58
Motesharrei, S., 341
Motulsky, A., 126, 129, 135, 137
Mourre, V., 279
Moyà-Solà, S., 191
Müller, H.-G., 61
Müller-Haye, B., 311
Munkenbeck Fragaszy, D., 148

Murphy, J., 363, 365
Murphy, M.S., 341
Murphy, W.A., Jr., 51
Murray, C., 137
Myers, F.R., 295

N

Nagel, E., 14, 15
Napier, J.R., 144, 154, 156
Napier, P.H., 144, 154
Nargolwalla, M.C., 193
Nash, J.M., 51
Nash, S., 163
Naylor, C.D., 127
Neave, R., 248
Neel, J.V., 130, 131
Nelson, A.J., 237, 253
Neumann, K., 312
Nickerson, P., 58, 128
Nicolson, N.A., 147
Niehoff, A.H., 352, 356
Nielsen, R., 58
Nishida, T., 163
Nissen, H.W., 112
Nkini, A., 234
Noback, M.L., 120
Noble, W.C., 72
Normile, D., 158, 161
Norton, C.J., 240
Notzke, C., 376
Novo, N., 152

O

Oakley, K.P., 40, 200
O'Brien, P., 335
O'Connell, C.A., 245
O'Connell, T.C., 69
O'Connor, T., 68
Ogden, C., 364
Olduvai, G., 39
Olsen, J.W., 240
Olsen, S., 101
Olszewski, D.I., 297, 311, 326, 327, 330, 332, 334, 335
Omoto, K., 268
O'Neil, J., 360
Orlove, B., 183
Ortner, D.J., 59
Ousley, S., 133
Ouyang, Z., 372
Ovchinnikov, I.V., 252
Owsley, D.W., 369
Oxby, C., 357

P

Pääbo, S., 57, 58, 252
Palkopoulou, E., 58
Park, M.A., 235, 268
Park, R.W., 287, 288

NAME INDEX

Parker, S.T., 165, 167
Parker Pearson, M., 72
Partridge, W.L., 349
Pasteur, L., 360
Patel, E., 163
Paterson, A.L., 276
Patterson, T.C., 257, 272, 300, 301
Pauketat, T., 335
Peacock, H., 163
Peacock, N., 9
Pearsall, D., 293
Pearson, J.D., 132
Pelto, P.J., 75
Pennington, R., 294
Pennisi, E., 129, 157
Peregrine, P.N., 117, 130, 138, 280
Perry, S., 166
Peter, N., 117
Peters, J.F., 294
Petersen, E.B., 298
Pfeiffer, J.E., 259
Pfeiffer, S., 67, 377
Phillipson, D.W., 136, 241, 256, 257, 274, 292, 300, 303, 313
Picchi, D., 352
Pickering, R., 212
Pickford, M., 209
Piggott, S., 321
Pika, S., 278
Pilbeam, D., 201, 203, 207, 216, 292
Pilbeam, D.R., 166
Pinhasi, R., 58
Piperno, D., 308, 310
Plundering Earth Is Nothing New, 318
Poinar, H.N., 58
Polanyi, K.C., 337
Polednak, A.P., 121
Pope, G.G., 242
Popenoe, R., 364
Post, P.W., 122
Potts, R., 226
Powell, J., 282
Power, C., 171
Prag, J., 248
Prentice, A.M., 132
Preuschoft, H., 158, 204
Price, B.J., 336, 337
Price, T.D., 65, 297
Primorac, D., 370
Pringle, H., 281, 308
Prinsloo, L.C., 63
Pritchard, J.K., 195
Prowse, T.L., 69
Public Health Agency Canada, 92
Puspaningrum, M.R., 234

Q

Quandt, S.A., 373, 374

R

Radinsky, L., 186
Randrianambinina, B., 163
Rasmussen, D.T., 188, 189
Rasolofoharivelo, T., 163
Rathje, W.L., 337
Ratsimbazafy, J., 163
Raven, P.H., 185
Ray, A.K., 294
Razafindramanana, J., 163
RCMP, 370
Reading, J., 132, 133
Reddigan, J., 364
Redman, C.L., 316, 327
Reed, D., 233, 374
Reed, D.M., 72
Reich, D., 260, 283
Reichs, K., 369
Reisner, M., 318
Reitz, E.J., 68
Relethford, J., 122
Remis, M., 159
Rempel, J.D., 128
Rendell, L.E., 278
Renfrew, C., 321
Rhine, S., 134
Rice, P.C., 276, 277
Richard, A.F., 145, 152, 154, 163, 184
Richards, M.P., 258
Richerson, P.J., 108, 112, 138, 139
Richmond, B.G., 209
Riesenfeld, A., 120
Rightmire, G.P., 232, 234, 235, 236, 246, 247, 264, 268
Rijksen, H.D., 158, 159
Ritenbaugh, C., 132
Rivas, J., 341
Roberts, C., 55
Roberts, D., 138
Roberts, D.F., 118, 119, 120
Robins, A.H., 121
Robinson, J.G., 155
Robinson, J.T., 219
Rodrigues, S., 133
Rogers, A., 233, 239
Rogers, T., 369
Rona, R.J., 372
Roosevelt, A.C., 280, 319, 320
Rose, J., 242
Rose, M.D., 200, 211
Rosenberger, A.L., 188
Rosenfeld, A., 275
Ross, M.H., 136
Ross, P.J., 358

Roth, E.A., 294
Ruan, Y.J., 361
Rubicz, R., 283
Ruff, C.B., 236
Ruhlen, M., 281, 283
Rumbaugh, D.M., 169
Rushton, J.P., 137, 138
Russell, D.A., 88
Russon, A.E., 147
Rylands, A.B., 163

S

Sade, D.S., 147
Sagan, C., 80, 81
Sahlins, M.D., 88
Sala, N., 62
Salzman, P.C., 16
Samuel, D., 64
Sanders, W.T., 330, 336, 337
Sandford, M.K., 65, 68
Santayana, G., 316
Sapir, E., 2, 3
Sarich, V.M., 194, 195
Sassaman, K., 286
Sattenspiel, L., 58, 128
Sauer, N.J., 133
Saunders, S.R., 59
Savage-Rumbaugh, E.S., 150, 191, 203
Savelle, J.M., 61
Savolainen, P., 305, 311
Scally, A., 194
Scarr, S., 111
Scarre, C., 292, 296, 303
Schaller, G., 109–110, 159
Schick, K.D., 61–62, 223, 224, 241, 255, 272
Schillaci, M.A., 368–369
Schmitz, R.W., 252
Schoeninger, M.J., 65
Schoepf, B., 362
Scholz, M., 252
Schopf, J.W., 80
Schrire, C., 295
Schultz, S., 206
Schurr, M.R., 68
Schurr, T.G., 283
Schwarcz, H.P., 46, 65, 67, 69, 72, 264
Schwartz, J.H., 213, 245, 268
Schwarz, C., 58
Schwitzer, C., 162, 163
Scott, G.R., 69
Segal, E., 195
Segal, E.M., 15–16, 17
Séguin, S., 88
Seidensticker, J., 158
Seielstad, M., 267
Sellers, W.I., 214–215
Semenov, S.A., 303

Senner, W.M., 170
Senut, B., 209
Serre, D., 252
Service, E.R., 321, 328, 329, 333, 335, 336, 338
Setiawan, R., 234
Setiyabudi, E., 234
Seyfarth, R.M., 149
Shanklin, E., 133
Shannon, L.M., 305
Shapiro, L.R., 375
Shaw, B., 73
Shen, G., 240
Shepard, R.J., 374
Sherry, S.T., 283
Shi, C., 240
Shipman, P., 202, 204, 225, 242, 250
Shu, C., 375
Shultz, S., 167
Sicotte, P., 159
Silk, J.B., 167, 206, 227
Sillen, A., 242
Silversides, A., 369
Simmons, A.H., 307
Simons, E., 187, 194
Simoons, F.J., 122–123
Simpson, G., 108
Simpson, G.G., 140
Simpson, S.W., 207, 213, 215, 221
Sinclair, A.R., 204
Singer, M., 101
Singer, R., 264, 268
Skinner, M., 370
Skoggard, I., 364
Smay, D., 134
Smith, B.D., 293, 310, 311
Smith, B.H., 208, 216
Smith, D.G., 63
Smith, F.H., 250, 268
Smith, G.E., 184
Smith, H., 3
Smith, J.M., 91
Smith, M.W., 138
Smith, V., 233
Smuts, B.B., 144
Sobo, E.J., 360, 364
Soffer, O., 274, 277
Sohn, S., 269
Solis, R.S., 334
Speller, C.F., 58
Spence, M.W., 331, 332
Spencer, F., 249, 250
Spencer, H., 87
Speth, J.D., 224, 225, 315
Spielmann, K.A., 315
Spigelman, M., 58
Sponheimer, M., 219
Spring, A., 13
Spurles, P.K., 354

Staller, J., 308
Stanford, C., 160, 161, 164
Stanford, C.B., 203
Stankiewicz, B.A., 58
Stark, B., 313
Steadman, D.W., 370
Stedman, H.H., 208
Steegman, A.T., Jr., 120
Steinbock, R.T., 59
Stenton, D.R., 34
Stepp, J.R., 183
Sterling, E.J., 163
Stewart, A., 70
Stewart, T.D., 118
Stini, W.A., 167
Stinson, S., 118
Stock, J.T., 202
Stojanowski, C.M., 60
Stokstad, E., 92
Stone, A., 252
Stone, L., 122, 129
Stoneking, M., 252, 267
Storey, M., 234
Stothert, K., 310
Strauss, L.G., 254, 270
Street, S.E., 278
Stringer, C., 219, 246, 253, 264, 266, 269
Stuart-Williams, H.L., 69
Stulp, G., 126
Sullivan, T., 374
Surette, C., 311
Susman, R.L., 160, 211, 220, 221, 222
Sussman, R.W., 155, 182, 184–185, 302
Sutikna, T., 237
Svoboda, J., 127
Swanstrom, R., 109
Sweeney, J., 364
Swisher, C., 233, 235
Sylvester, A.D., 204
Szalay, F.S., 179, 184, 185, 216, 217, 225
Szathmáry, E.J.E., 132, 283

T

Tainter, J., 343
Tait, H., 132
Tanner, J.M., 125, 126, 372, 374
Tattersall, I., 109, 140, 152, 206, 213, 216, 220, 233, 245, 254, 268
Tecumseh Fitch, W., 278
Tejedor, M., 152
Teleki, G., 161
ten Bruggencate, R.E., 73
Terborgh, J., 165
Terhune, C.E., 234

Terrell, J., 380
Thomas, D.H., 282
Thompson, J.L., 176, 237, 253
Thompson-Handler, N., 168
Thomsen, C.J., 86
Thorne, A.G., 270
Thorpe, S.K.S., 200
Tinsman, J., 163
Tobias, P.V., 172, 206, 211, 221, 227, 235, 236, 268
Tocheri, M.W., 238
Toder, R., 6
Tomasello, M., 147
Torry, W.I., 368
Toth, N., 61–62, 223, 224, 241, 255, 272
Townsend, P.R., 373
Toyne, J.M., 69
Trend, M.G., 349
Trinkaus, E., 202, 236, 250, 252, 253, 259, 266, 269
Turner, B.L., 333
Turner, B.L., II, 333
Turner, C.G., II, 283
Turner, T., 183
Tuross, N., 63, 67
Tuttle, R.H., 159, 161
Twells, L.K., 364
Tylor, E.B., 87

U

Ubelaker, D.H., 56, 369
Ucko, P.J., 275
Underwood, B.A., 373
Ungar, P.S., 219
Uomini, N.T., 278
Ussher, J., 84

V

Valladas, H., 264
Van Couvering, J., 206
van den Bergh, G.D., 234
Van der Leeuw, S., 316
van der Merwe, N.J., 66, 219
van Lawick-Goodall, J., 148, 160
Van Oostdam, J., 366
Vaupel, J.W., 61
Videan, E.N., 203
Vigilant, L., 251, 265
Visabergi, E., 147–148
Vogel, J.O., 334
von Koenigswald, G.H.R., 235
Vrba, E.S., 182, 202

W

Waddington, C., 107
Wagner, D.M., 58
Waldram, J.B., 132

Walker, A., 219, 236
Wallace, A.F.C., 365
Wallace, A.R., 85–86, 96, 105
Wallis, J., 163
Walter, R.C., 215
Wang, J., 64
Ward, C.V., 192
Ward, S., 191
Warren, D.M., 356
Warry, W., 356
Washburn, S., 203
Watkins, J., 376
Watkins, T., 297
Watson, J., 98
Watt, K., 58
Weaver, D.S., 68
Weaver, M.P., 332
Webb, E.C., 69
Weidenreich, F., 235
Weiner, J.S., 120
Weiner, S., 240
Weiss, E., 350
Weiss, H., 339
Weller, S.C., 355
Wells, J.C.K., 202
Wenke, R.J., 311, 326, 327, 330, 332, 334, 335, 336
Wenzhong, P., 240
Werner, D., 295
Weston, E., 237
Wheat, J.B., 284, 285
Wheatley, D., 70
Wheatley, P., 336
Wheeler, P.E., 200
White, B., 318
White, C.D., 67, 69, 72
White, F.J., 160, 168
White, J.P., 305
White, L.A., 20
White, R., 270
White, T.D., 209, 213, 215, 259–260
Whitehead, N.L., 338
Whiten, A., 148, 169, 278
Whiting, J.W.M., 14, 15, 16, 17, 18–19
Whittaker, J.C., 224, 241, 255, 272, 273, 303
Wiebe, B.H., 318
Wilford, J.N., 258
Wilford, N., 211
Wilkinson, R.L., 343
Willems, G., 248
Willey, G.R., 313
Williams, E.D., 370
Williams, G.C., 89
Williams, J.S., 341
Williamson, E.A., 163
Williamson, R.F., 377
Wilson, A.C., 194, 195
Wilson, D., 2

Wilson, E.O., 110
Wintemberg, W., 3
Wittfogel, K., 336
Wolf, E., 226
Wolf, N., 364
Wolfenden, R., 109
Wolff, 146
Wolpoff, M.H., 167, 203, 204, 234, 237, 266, 267, 269, 270
Wong, K., 209, 237
Wood, B., 178, 216, 220, 234
Wood, B.A., 217
Wood, J.W., 59, 60, 319
Woods, W., 340
World Bank, 132
World Health Organization (WHO), 92, 372
Worsaae, J.J.A., 86–87
Wortman, C., 319
Wrangham, R.W., 158, 166, 207, 243
Wright, G.A., 314
Wright, H.E., 271, 298
Wright, H.T., 327, 328, 336, 337
Wright, L., 72
Wright, P.C., 163
Wu, X., 240
Wymer, J., 264, 268

X

Xing, F., 64
Xing, G., 240
Xinzhi, W., 250
Xu, Q., 240

Y

Yamei, H., 242
Yang, D.Y., 58
Yellen, J.E., 270
Yi, S.V., 195
Young, T.C., Jr., 337
Young, T.K., 132, 133
Yousuke, K., 234
Yu, L., 64
Yurnaldi, D., 234

Z

Zeder, M.A., 305
Zegura, S.L., 266
Zeller, A., 148
Zhang, S., 240
Zhang, X., 240
Zhong, M., 240
Zhou, S., 109
Zhu, H., 107
Zihlman, A.L., 171, 204
Zimmer, C., 204
Zohary, D., 304

Subject Index

Note: Entries for figures are followed by "*f*"

A

abiotic evidence, 68
Aboriginal peoples.
    See Indigenous peoples
Aborigines, 164, 321
absolute dating, 38
absolute dating methods, 40–47
    amino acid racemization,
        46–47
    argon-argon dating, 43–45
    dendrochronology, 40–42,
        41f
    electron spin resonance
        dating, 46
    fission-track dating, 45
    obsidian hydration, 47
    palaeomagnetic dating,
        45–46
    potassium-argon (K-Ar)
        dating, 43–45
    radiocarbon dating, 42–43
    thermoluminescence
        dating, 46
    uranium-series dating, 46
accelerated mass spectrometry
    (AMS) radiocarbon
    dating, 43
accidental juxtaposition, 73
acclimatization, 117
accomplishment, 22
acculturation, 75
Acheulian tool tradition, 240,
    241–242
acquired inheritance, 83
acupuncture, 359
adapids, 180, 186
adaptation, 15, 81, 118, 138–139
    see also primate adaptations
adaptive, 163, 226
adaptive radiation, 213
adaptive traits, 88, 108
advanced spectroscopic
    techniques, 63
Aegyptopithecus, 188, 189f
aerial photography, 34
Afar region, Ethiopia, 211
Afghanistan, 370
Africa, 136, 152, 189
    domestication, 312–313
    early bipedal hominins,
        194, 195, 200
    early *Homo sapiens,* 257
    East Africa. *See* East Africa

Homo erectus, 232, 233, 239
Middle Stone Age, 254, 256
origins of modern humans,
    264–266
pre-agricultural period, 299
primates, movement of, 188
states, 333
Upper Palaeolithic cultures,
    279–280
African great apes, 156
African Sahel, 367–368
age estimation, 53–55, 55f
age of the apes, 183
agents of change, 354
agriculture
    agricultural activities, 54
    intensive agriculture, 296,
        317, 321
    raised field agriculture, 379
    women's contributions to, 13
AIDS (acquired immune
    deficiency syndrome),
    131, 348, 360, 361–363
Aishihik First Nation, 51
Akkadian empire, 339
Alabama, 300
Alaska, 134, 281
Albania, 370
alcoholic beverages, 139
Aleut, 283
Ali Kosh, Iran, 305–307
allele, 97
Allen's rule, 120, 120f
alphabet, 74
altruism, 259
Alvarez, Louis, 109
Amazonia, 380
Ambrona, 242
American Association of
    Physical Anthropologists,
    351
American Geophysical Union,
    339
American Samoa, 11
American Sign Language
    (ASL), 149
Amerind family of languages,
    282
amino acid racemization,
    46–47
amino acids, 373
Amnesty International, 369–370
amok, 363

analysis
    animal remains, 61–62
    artifacts, 51–53
    chemical analysis, 32, 66
    coprolites, 61, 65
    experimental archaeology,
        62–63
    human remains, 53–61
    palaeoethnobotany, 61,
        63–65
    past diets, 61
    and reconstruction, 62
    stable isotopes, 65–68
    trace elements, 65–68
    zooarchaeology, 61–62
anaphase stage, 98f
ancient beer, 64
ancient DNA (aDNA), 56–58,
    58f
Ancient Society (Morgan), 87
Andaman Islanders, 321
Andean high-altitude dwellers,
    123
Andes, the, 123
angiosperms, 185
animal domestication. *See*
    domestication
animal pests, 33
animal remains, 61–62
Anopheles gambiae mosquito, 129
anorexia nervosa, 363
anthropoids, 150, 154–161
    cercopithecines monkeys,
        156
    colobine monkeys, 155–156
    emergence of, 186–189
    Fayum Oligocene
        anthropoids, 187–189
    gibbons, 157–158, 158f, 168
    hominins, 12, 161
    hominoids, 156–157,
        189–194
    New World monkeys,
        154–155, 188
    Old World monkeys,
        155–156, 189, 200
    orangutans, 144, 158–159
    siamangs, 157–158
anthropological curiosity, 4–5
anthropological fields. *See*
    fields of anthropology
anthropological linguistics, 5,
    10–11

anthropology, 2
    see also specific fields of
        anthropology
    anthropological curiosity,
        4–5
    biocultural model, 12
    explanations. *See*
        explanations
    fields of anthropology, 5–13
    history of, in Canada, 2–3
    holistic approach, 4
    making the world better,
        380
    relevance of, 20–22
    scope of, 3–4
anthropometric measures, 372
anthropometry, 375
antibiotic-resistant disease
    strains, 91, 92
antibiotics, 92
antimalarial drugs, 355
antler tools, 272
Apache, 282–283
apartheid, 135
ape pelvis, 205
apes, 156–157
Apidium, 188
applied anthropologists, 12–13
applied anthropology, 12–13,
    342, 348–349
    biodiversity, study of, 183
    collaborative applied
        anthropology, 356–357
    endangered primates,
        162–163
    environmental collapse, 316
    ethics, 350–351
    facial reconstruction, 248
    first North Americans, 282
    food production, and the
        environment, 318
    history of, 349–350
    modernization, health
        consequences of, 131
    planned change, evaluation
        of. *See* planned change
    predicting societal collapse,
        348
    "race" in forensic
        anthropology, 134
    raised field agriculture, 379
    understanding failure of
        applied projects, 355

SUBJECT INDEX

applied archaeology, 379
Ar-39, 40
Ar dating method, 45
Arabs, 21
arboreal, 144
arboreal quadrupeds, 178
arboreal theory, 184
archaeobotany, 63–65
archaeological record, 32
archaeological sites, 27, 30
    excavation, 36–38
    finding archaeological sites, 34–36
    fossil locales, 30
    site prospection, 34–36
    types of sites, 30
archaeology, 5, 8
    cave archaeology, 37
    as cultural history, 375–380
    cultural resource management (CRM), 375–377
    landscape archaeology, 380
    museum archaeology, 377–380
ARCHAEOMEDES project, 316
archaeozoology, 61–62
Archaic *Homo sapiens*, 245–247, 260
Archaic peoples of Highland Mesoamerica, 299
Archaic peoples of North America, 286
archaic primates, 179
Arctic Small Tool tradition, 286, 287–288
Ardipithecus (genus), 210
Ardipithecus ramidus, 209
Argentina, 370
Argentine Forensic Anthropology Team (EAAF), 370–371, 371f
argon-argon dating, 43–45
Aristotle, 82
art, 275–277
artifacts, 30, 32, 34, 51–53
Aryan race, 135
Asia, 136, 232, 242, 279–280, 282
Asmat, New Guinea, 21f
assimilation theory, 267
association, 30–31
associations, 14
Atapuerca, Spain, 246
Athapaskan languages, 283
Atlantic coast, 286
atlatls, 43, 274
Aurignacian tools, 270
Austin, 149–150
Australia, 280

Australian Aborigines, 164, 321
australopithecine sites, 210f
australopithecines, 199f, 205, 206, 208, 211, 213–217
Australopithecus, 199, 210, 211, 249
Australopithecus afarensis, 211, 213–216, 215f, 220
Australopithecus africanus, 207f, 215, 216–217, 217f, 218f, 220, 239
Australopithecus anamensis, 209, 211, 213
Australopithecus bahrelghazali, 212
Australopithecus fricanus, 211
Australopithecus garhi, 211, 213f
Australopithecus robustus, 218f
Axum, 333
Azawagh Arabs, 364
Aztecs, 137, 137f

B

baboons, 156, 200, 242
backdirt, 37
bacteria, 81, 296
Baghdad, 74
Bakairi Indians, 352
balancing selection, 116, 129
Balkans, 135
bamboo, 241–242
bananas, 312
Bangladesh, 367
Barbeau, Charles Marius, 2
basic research, 12
basicranium, 171
Beagle, 85
beans, 309
beauty, 364
beer, 64
behavioural abilities of humans, 169–172
behavioural ecology, 107, 161
behavioural traits, 107–113
Belize, 72
The Bell Curve (Murray and Herrnstein), 137
Bergmann's rule, 118, 125
Bering land bridge, 105
Bering Strait, 281
Beringia, 281, 281f, 282
Bermudan land snails, 108
bias-free test, 138
Bible, 84
bifacial tools, 223, 241
Big Bang, 80
big game, 300
big-game eating, and *Homo erectus*, 242
bilophodont, 157
Binford-Flannery model, 314

bioarchaeology, 6f
biocultural model, 12
biodiversity, 183
biological anthropology, 5–8
biological diversity in human populations, 118–133
    body build, 118–120
    facial construction, 118–120
    height, 125–126
    high altitude, adaptation to, 123–125
    infectious diseases, susceptibility to, 126–128
    lactase deficiency, 122–123
    sickle-cell anemia, 116
    skin colour, 120–122, 121f
    Type II diabetes, 130–133
biological fallacy of race, 133–135
biological variation, 133
    see also biological diversity in human populations
biological warfare, 137
biology, 81–83
biomedical paradigm, 359–360
biomedicine, 359
biotic evidence, 68
bipedalism, 168, 200–205, 201f, 209, 227
bird extinctions, 300
birth spacing, 318
bison, 284, 285
BK II, Tanzania, 242
Black, Davidson, 235
black moths, 90
Black Skull, 218f
blades, 256, 272, 303
blood traces, 63
blood types, 137
Bluefish Caves site, Yukon Territory, 280
Boas, Franz, 2, 3, 6f, 87
body build, 118–120
body composition, 374–375
body language, 227
body mass, 119f
body size, 164–165
Bohlin, Birger, 235
Bolivia, 380
bone artifacts, 32
bone tools, 272
bones, 33, 52, 66
bonobo, or pygmy, chimpanzee *(Pan paniscus)*, 160, 169
Border Cave, South Africa, 268
boring, 35
Borneo, 158
bottle-feeding, 139, 354

bottle gourds, 308
Bouchard, Lucien, 91
Boucher, Jacques, 86
Boule, Marcellin, 249–250
brachiators, 157–158, 179
brain
    basicranium, 171
    brain size, 145
    early hominins, 205–207, 206f
    endocast, 172
    expansion of, 205–207
    human brain, 168
    relative brain size, and primates, 164
Branch Davidian Compound, 369
Branisella, 186
Brazil, 280, 373
breast-feeding, 66–68, 353, 353f, 354
broad-spectrum collecting, 292, 300–301
Broca's area, 172
Broken Hill mine, Zambia, 246
Bronze Age, 86
bubonic plague, 137
Buffon, Georges, 85
buildings, 33
bullae, 328
Burgess Shale, 108
burials, 28, 29, 72, 258–259
burins, 256
Burnet, Thomas, 85
bushbabies, 152
butchering marks, 61, 62f
butchering site, 244

C

C3 plants, 65
C4 plants, 65
cactus finches *(Geospiza scandens)*, 106–107
Cactus Hill site, Virginia, 281, 284f
cadmium, 366
Cahokia, 320, 334, 335, 340, 343
calibration curve, 43, 44f
Cambrian explosion of life, 108
Cambrian period, 31f
campsites, and *Homo erectus*, 243–244
Canadian Ape Alliance fund, 368
Canadian Archaeological Association, 351
Canadian Association for Physical Anthropology, 351

Canadian Institutes of Health Research (CIHR), 360
Canadian Museum of Civilization, 376
Canadian Museum of History, 376
canines, 145
cannibalism, 259–260
carbon-14, 43, 44f, 65–66
carbon isotopic analyses, 65–66
caring, 348
carnivore gnawing, 61
Carpolestes, 181
Carpolestes simpsoni, 181
carrying capacity, 71
Çatal Hüyük, Turkey, 307–308
catarrhines, 154, 188
catastrophism, 84
Catopithecus, 187
cave archaeology, 37
cave paintings, 276
cebids, 155
Cenozoic era, 182
Central America, 343
Centre for Indigenous Peoples' Nutrition and Environment (CINE), 366
Ceprano, Italy, 246
ceramics, 29, 32, 52
cercopithecines monkeys, 156
cercopithecoids, 155
cereals, 66
cerebral cortex, 168
cerrado, 352
Chad, 194, 209
Chalmers, Thomas, 85
Champagne First Nation, 51
change, 226–227
Chavín, 334
chemical analysis, 32, 66
Chenopodium, 54
Cherokee syllabic writing system, 74
chewing teeth, 145
Chicago, 380
chiefdoms, 329, 335
child burials, 327
child dependency, 208
child-rearing customs, 110, 111f
childhood obesity, 375
children
 age estimation, 53
 child burials, 327
 dental development, 56f
 infant mortality, 67–68
Chile, 280
chimpanzee hunting, 161

chimpanzees, 159–161, 168
 communication, 149–150
 and human upper limbs, 83f
 and language, 171
 quadrupedal locomotion, 204
 tool use and toolmaking, 148, 168, 169–170, 226
China, 33f, 64, 66, 74, 85, 136, 139, 232, 235, 266, 336, 337
choking, 89
choppers, 223, 224f
chromosome pairs, 97–98
chromosomes, 97, 99f, 102
chronic diseases, 131, 360
chronometric dating, 38
circumscription, 336–337
cities
 Mesoamerica, 330–333
 Monte Albán, 332
 other areas, 333–334
 Sumer, 328–330
 Teotihuacán, 330–332
civilization, 136, 326
 see also cities; states
 archaeological inferences, 326–328
 emergence of, 327f
class, 82
class stratification, 338
classification, 17, 150–151
clavicle, 145
clearing of forests, 34
climate, 117
cline, 105
cloning, 139
closed systems, 149
clothing, 243
clouded leopard, 158
Clovis complex, 284
co-evolution, 112
co-operative hunting, 242
code of ethics, 350
coffins, 28
cognitive mapping, 167
cold climates, 317
cold light, 46
collaborative applied anthropology, 356–357
collagen, 43
collapse of states, 338–343
collarbone, 145
Collier, John, 349
Collins, Treacher, 184
colobine monkeys, 155–156
colonization, 75
colonizing apes, 202
Columbia, 353–354

commodity sealings, 328
common chimpanzee (*Pan troglodytes*), 160
communication
 language. *See* language
 mother–infant communication, 171
 primate communication, 148–150
comparative anatomy, 32
computer-assisted biomechanical modelling, 32
conceptual perspectives, 164
Congo River basin, 334
conquest, 75, 136–137
conservation, 51, 368–369
construction, 34
contact period, 28
contaminant, 366
contemporary culture change, 139
continental drift, 181f, 182, 189
continuity, 266
controlled excavation, 37
Copán, 72
coprolites, 61, 65
core samples, 35
corn, 66, 112, 311
Cree, 128, 366
Cretaceous period, 181, 182
Crick, Francis, 98
Cro-Magnon humans, 264, 268
Croatia, 370
cross-cultural researcher, 10
cross-sectional studies, 371
crossing-over, 102–103
CT scans, 32
cultivation, 34, 304, 312
cultural antecedent, 73
cultural anthropology, 10
cultural barriers, 353
cultural borrowing, 75
cultural change, 73
 acculturation, 75
 cultural diffusion, 73–75
 discovery, 73
 invention, 73
cultural diffusion, 73–75
cultural diversity, 138–139
cultural ecologists, 11
cultural environment, 117–118
cultural evolution, 112
cultural innovations, 239
cultural relativism, 87
cultural resource management (CRM), 375–377
cultural transmission, 112

culture, 8, 117, 164
 adaptive nature of, 226
 archaeology as cultural history, 375–380
 beauty, 364
 and change, 226–227
 early hominins, 221–227
 emergence of modern humans, 269–270
 learned and shared, 226
 Lower Palaeolithic culture, 240–247
 Middle Palaeolithic cultures, 254–260
 and stone tools, 226–227
 Upper Palaeolithic cultures, 270–280
culture-bound, 20
culture-bound syndromes, 363
culture-test, 138
cuneiform, 329f, 330
curators, 378
cut marks, 242
Cuvier, Georges, 84

D

D-isomers, 47
dairying, 123
Dakhleh Oasis, Egypt, 69, 299
darker-skinned humans, 121
Darwin, Charles, 81, 83, 85–86, 87f, 89, 91, 105, 108, 247
dating techniques, 38–47, 47f
 absolute dating methods, 40–47
 amino acid racemization, 46–47
 argon-argon dating, 43–45
 dendrochronology, 40–42, 41f
 electron spin resonance dating, 46
 fission-track dating, 45
 obsidian hydration, 47
 palaeomagnetic dating, 45–46
 potassium-argon (K-Ar) dating, 43–45
 radiocarbon dating, 42–43
 relative dating methods, 38–40
 thermoluminescence dating, 46
 uranium-series dating, 46
datum, 37
Dawson, George Mercer, 2, 3
Dawson, John William, 2
DDT, 91, 366

decay rate, 41–42
decline of states, 338–343
declining health, 319–320
deer, 72
definite apes, 189
demographic collapse, 71, 267–268
demography, 60
dendrochronology, 40–42, 41f
Dene, 366
Deninu K'ue First Nation, 366
Denisovans, 260
dental development, 56f
dentition, 156, 157f, 177–178
deodorants, 21
deoxyribonucleic acid. *See* DNA (deoxyribonucleic acid)
Department of Energy, 101
dependency, 147, 147f
depositional context, 31
depression, 363, 365
The Descent of Man and Selection in Relation to Sex (Darwin), 86
descriptive linguist, 11
descriptive linguistics, 10
detailed excavation, 37
developing nations, 136
developing world, 131
development, 147
development plans, 30
development programs, 13
diabetes, 130–133, 375
diagenesis, 68
diastema, 157
Dickson Mounds, 320
differential diagnosis, 59
differential reproductive success, 88, 112
diffusion, 73–75
direct contact, 74
directional selection, 116, 117f
discovery, 73
diseases, 360–363
    see also health and illness; specific diseases
    drug-resistant disease strains, 91, 92
    infectious diseases, 59, 126–128, 136–137
    new strains of common diseases, 91
    Western diseases, 360
disproportionate limbs, 178–179
diurnal, 146
diversity, 5, 88
division of labour, 172, 208–209

Dmanisi, 233
DNA (deoxyribonucleic acid), 56, 98–101, 99f
    ancient DNA (aDNA), 56–58, 58f
    extraction of, 57
    functional DNA, 195
    junk DNA, 195
    messenger RNA (mRNA), 101
    mitochondrial DNA (mtDNA), 250–252, 252f, 265–266, 267
    non-coding DNA, 195
    ownership of DNA, 100
Dobzhansky, Theodosius, 104, 108
Dolichocebus, 186, 188
Dolní Vĕstonice, 272, 274
domestication, 61, 304
    Africa, 312–313
    East Asia, 311–312
    Mesoamerica, 308–310
    Near East, 305–308, 306f
    New World *vs.* Old World, 311
    North America, 310–311
    South America, 310–311
dominant, 96
Dordogne River, France, 256
Dorset, 287–288
Drachenloch cave, Swiss Alps, 259
Drag the Red, 370
Dragon Bone Hill, Zhoukoudian, 235
droughts, 367
drug-resistant disease strains, 91, 92
Dryopithecines, 192, 193
Dryopithecus, 191, 192, 193
dual-inheritance theory, 107–108
Dubois, Eugène, 234–235
dwellings, 71, 71f

E

early Arctic populations, 286–287
early Eocene primates, 186
early hominins
    see also specific hominins
    Archaic *Homo sapiens*, 245–247, 260
    australopithecines. *See* australopithecines
    bipedalism, 200–205, 201f
    brain, expansion of, 205–207, 206f
    "costs" of bipedalism, 204–205

cultures, 221–227
early species of *Homo*, 220–221
environmental change, evolutionary consequences of, 202
face, 207–208
first definite hominins, 210–213
Homo erectus. See Homo erectus
jaws, 207–208
language, 227
lifestyles, 223–226
Neandertals. *See* Neandertals
one model of human evolution, 220
other evolved traits, 208–209
paranthropoids, 199f, 212, 217–220
teeth, 207–208
tool traditions, 221–223
transition to hominins, 209–220
trends in hominin evolution, 200–209
early *Homo sapiens. See* Neandertals
early Miocene proto-apes, 189–191
early primates, 185
early species of *Homo*, 220–221
early toolmaking, 8
Early Uruk period, 328
earthquakes, 367, 368
East Africa, 45, 200, 202, 205, 210, 211, 235, 236
East African hominins, 199
East Asia, 311–312
Eastern societies, 139
eating disorders, 364
eco-tourism, 162
ecofacts, 30, 33
ecological modelling, 164
economic anthropologists, 11
economic inequality, 342
economic specialization, 329
economic unsustainability, 342
Ecuador, 374
egalitarian societies, 326
Egypt, 64, 67f, 74, 85, 135
Egypt Exploration Society, 64
Eldredge, Niles, 108
electrical resistance, 36
electrical resistivity meters, 36
electron microscopy, 32
electron spin resonance dating, 46
electronic techniques, 35

elites, 342
Ellesmere Island, 34
emotional disorders, 363–365
endangered primates, 162–163
endocast, 172
England, 74
environment
    environmental change, 202
    environmental collapse, 316
    environmental degradation, 339
    and food production, 318
environmental anthropology, 365–369
environmental archaeology, 68–69
environmental collapse, 316
environmental contaminants, 365–367
environmental restraints, 316–317
Eocene epoch, 180, 185
Ephesus, 339f
epidemiology, 8, 60
epigenetics, 83, 107
erosion, 29, 85
estimation of age, 55f
ethics, 350–351
Ethiopia, 205, 209, 210, 351f, 370
ethnic cleansing, 135
ethnocentric, 20
ethnographer, 9
ethnographic analogy, 60, 164
ethnography, 9
ethnohistorian, 9–10
ethnology, 9
ethnomedicine, 358
Europe, 243, 297–298
European Union (EU), 316
evidence, 16–20, 30–31
    artifacts, 30, 32, 34
    ecofacts, 30, 33
    features, 30, 33
    fossils, 6, 30, 31–32
evolution, 107
    see also modern evolutionary theory
    and biology, 81–83
    and drug-resistant disease strains, 92
    environmental change, consequences of, 202
    evolution of evolution, 81–88
    and geology, 84–88
    Homo erectus, 238–240
    model of human evolution, 220
    natural selection. *See* natural selection

Neandertals, 260
observed examples of, 90–91
origin of species, 89–91
predating material culture, 32
primate evolution. *See* primate evolution
speed of, 108
trends in hominin evolution, 200–209
evolutionary psychology, 107
evolutionary theory, 82
excavation, 36–38
experimental archaeology, 62–63
experimental observations, 164
explanations, 13
associations, 14
evidence, 16–20
hypothesis, 16, 17–18
measurement, 17–18
relations, 14
sampling, 18
scientific method, 16
statistical evaluation, 18–20
testing explanations, 16–20
theories, 14–16
external pressure for cultural change, 75
extinctions, 162, 300
extractive foraging, 167
Eynan site, Israel, 297

F

F-U-N trio, 40
face, early hominins, 207–208
facial construction, 118–120
facial expressions, 148
facial reconstruction, 248
famine, 320, 367–368
Faroe Islands, 126
fatness, 364
fauna, 38
Fayum area, Egypt, 186–187
Fayum Oligocene anthropoids, 187–189
parapithecids, 187–188
propliopithecids, 187, 188–189
Feather of Hope Aboriginal AIDS Prevention Society, 360
features, 30, 33
female sexuality, 168–169
fertility, 277
field surveying, 34
field walking, 34
fields of anthropology, 5–13
anthropological linguistics, 5, 10–11

applied anthropology, 12–13
archaeology, 5, 8
physical anthropology, 5–8
socio-cultural anthropology, 5, 8–10
specialization, 11
Fiji Islands, 126
finches of Galápagos Islands, 106, 109
finding archaeological sites, 34–36
fire, 239, 242–243
first definite hominins, 210–213
first migrants, 233
First Nations and Inuit Health Branch (FNIHB), 133
First Nations health care, 360
first North Americans, 282
fishing, 244, 317
fission-track dating, 45
flake tools, 223, 241
flesh-eating disease, 91
flint tools, 306
floods, 367
flora, 38
fluorine tests, 40
Folsom point, 284
food, 72, 257–258
analysis of past diets, 61
broad-spectrum collecting, 292, 300–301
Europe, 297–298
food collection, 293–296
food production. *See* food production
Mesoamerica, 298–299
microlithic technology, 303
Near East, 296–297
original locations of main food crops, 293f
other areas, 299–300
pre-agricultural developments, 296–303
food-carrying, 202
food collection, 293–296
food production, 54, 61, 295
agriculture. *See* agriculture
consequences, 315–322
development of, 313–315
domestication of plants and animals, 304–313
and elaboration of material possessions, 320–322
and the environment, 318
environmental restraints, 316–317
and health, 319–320
horticulture, 295–296, 317
population growth, 317–319

pull models, 313
push models, 313
foraging societies, 164, 294
foramen magnum, 205
foraminifera, 69
forelimbs, 144
forensic anthropologists, 369
forensic anthropology, 134, 369–371
form, 52
formal analysis, 52
formative era, 328–329, 330
former Yugoslavia, 370
formula-feeding, 352–353
Fort Resolution, 366
fossil locales, 30
fossil record and evidence, 80, 84, 144
emergence of modern humans, 268–269
fossil remains, 27
incompleteness of, 31
and primate evolution, 176–179
fossilization, 31
fossilized feces. *See* coprolites
fossils, 6, 30, 31–32
fossilization, 31
learning from fossils, 31–32
founder effect, 105
FOXP2, 278
France, 74
front teeth, 145
fruit-eating primates, 164
functional DNA, 195
funeral rituals, 258–259
funerary archaeology, 72
furs, 239

G

Gacy, John Wayne, 370
galactosemia, 104
Galápagos Islands, 106
galaxies, 80
Galdikas, Biruté, 7f
garbage heap, 27–28
gas chromatography, 64
Gault site, Texas, 281
gelada baboon, 155
gender. *See* women
gender-role specialization, 172
gender roles, 54
gene flow, 89, 105–106
gene frequencies, 89
genera, 82
genes, 97–101
genetic bottlenecks, 267, 268
genetic drift, 89, 105, 107
genetic engineering, 139
genetic homogeneity, 127

genetic recombination, 101–103
genocide, 269
genome, 101
genotype, 97
genus, 82
geographic barriers, 90
geographic information system (GIS), 70
geographic positioning system (GPS), 70
Geological Survey, 2
geology, 84–88
Gérin, Léon, 3
germ theory, 137, 360
Germany, 74, 125, 135
Gesher Benot Ya'aqov, Israel, 243
Ghana, 136, 334
gibbons, 157–158, 158f, 168
Gigantopithecus, 192
giraffes, 83, 89, 89f
glaciation, 271f, 282
Gloger's rule, 121
Godin Tepe, Zagros Mountains, Iran, 64
Gold Coast, 334
Gombe National Park, Tanzania, 160
Gona, Ethiopia, 222
Gondwanaland, 182
Gönnersdorf cave, Rhine River, 277
goosefoot, 311
gorillas, 159, 168
Gould, Stephen Jay, 108
gradualist view of evolution, 108
grassroots organizations, 357
gravers, 256
Gravettian period, 277
grazing animals, 314
Great Zimbabwe, 334
Greater Mesopotamia, 327
Greece, 74
Greenland, 318
grey langur monkeys, 147
grey-speckled moths, 90
grid system, 36f, 37
ground finches (*Geospiza fortis*), 107
ground-penetrating radar, 36
ground stone woodworking tools, 286
group selection, 163
group size, and primates, 165–166
growth, 60, 372–373
growth-for-age standards, 372
growth retardation, 372

H

Guatemala, 111, 125, 355, 370
Guatemalan Forensic Anthropology Team, 371
Guilá Naquitz, 310
Guinea, West Africa, 170

H

Hadar, Ethiopia, 213
Haida, 282
hairless, 239
Haiti, 354, 356
half-life, 42
hand axes, 241
hands, 145, 202
haplorhines, 154, 180
Harappa, 334, 334f
Hausa, 358
Hawthorne, Harry, 349
Hayonim, 297f
head binding, 118
Head-Smashed-In Buffalo Jump, Alberta, 37
health and illness, 59
  cultural understandings of, 358–360
  culture-bound syndromes, 363
  emotional disorders, 363–365
  and food production, 319–320
  health conditions, 360–363
  Indigenous populations, 357–358
  mental disorders, 363–365
  and modernization, 131
Health Canada, 132
hearths, 33
heavy metals, 366
Hebrew, 135
height, 125–126
HeLa cells, 100
Henson, Jim, 91
heredity, 96–101
heritability, 88, 112
heritable, 163
Herrnstein, Richard, 137
heterozygotes, 129
heterozygous, 97, 129
hieroglyphics, 329f, 330
high altitude, 123–125
High Plains, 286
high-status burials, 72
highland Andean societies, 118
Highlands of New Guinea, 373
Himalayas, 123, 125
hind limbs, 144
historical archaeology, 8
historical linguistics, 10
history of anthropology, 2–3
The History of the Earth (Hutton), 85
Hitler, Adolf, 135
HIV/AIDS. *See* AIDS (acquired immune deficiency syndrome)
HMS *Erebus*, 37
HMS *Terror*, 37
H5N1 strain of bird flu, 127f
Hobbits, 234
holistic, 4
holistic approach, 4
Holland, Emily, 370
Holocaust, 135
homesites, 256–257
hominins, 12, 161
  see also specific hominins
  divergence of hominins from other hominoids, 194–195
  early hominins. *See* early hominins
  evolution. *See* early hominins
  first migrants, 233
  Homo erectus. *See Homo erectus*
  models for hominin behaviour, 161–164
  transition to hominins, 209–220
hominoids, 156–157
  divergence of hominins from other hominoids, 194–195
  early Miocene proto-apes, 189–191
  emergence of, 189–194
  late Miocene apes, 191–194
  Middle Miocene apes, 191
Homo, 199
Homo antecessor, 246
Homo erectus, 206, 221, 232–240, 260, 266, 267, 278
  Acheulian tool tradition, 240, 241–242
  big-game eating, 242
  campsites, 243–244
  evolution of, 238–240
  fire, 239, 242–243
  Homo floresiensis, 237–238
  Java discovery, 234–235
  language, 245
  later finds, 234–235
  Lower Palaeolithic culture, 240–247
  oldest known specimen, 235
  physical characteristics, 236–237
  religion, 244–245
  ritual, 244–245
  tools, 240–242
Homo ergaster, 233–234, 237
Homo floresiensis, 234, 237–238
Homo habilis, 172, 205–206, 207f, 221, 236, 239
Homo heidelbergensis, 234, 246–247, 247f
Homo naledi, 246
Homo neandertalensis, 247f
Homo rudolfensis, 221, 239
Homo sapiens, 7, 82, 247f, 266
  Archaic *Homo sapiens*, 245–247, 260
  evolutionary timeline, 254f
  Middle Palaeolithic cultures, 254–260
  mitochondrial DNA (mtDNA), 250–252
  modern *Homo sapiens*. *See* modern humans
  Neandertals. *See* Neandertals
  sites, 251f
Homo sapiens daliensis, 250
Homo sapiens neandertalensis, 250
  see also Neandertals
Homo sapiens sapiens, 116, 246, 264
  see also modern humans
homogeneity, 246
homozygous, 97, 129
Homunculus, 186
Honduras, 72
Hooke, Robert, 85
horizontal control, 37
horticulture, 295–296, 317
hot zones, 92
howler monkey, 154f
Huang (Yellow) River floods, 367
Huatta, Peru, 379
Human and Nature DYnamics (HANDY), 342
human evolution. *See* evolution
human genetics, 7
Human Genome Project (HGP), 101
Human Organization (Partridge and Eddy), 349
human palaeontology, 5
human remains
  age estimation, 53–55, 55f
  analysis of, 53–61
  ancient DNA (aDNA), 56–58, 58f
  infectious lesions, 59
  osteology, 53
  palaeodemography, 60–61
  sex determination, 55–56, 57f
Human Rights Watch, 370
human sacrifice, 331
human traits
  behavioural abilities, 169–172
  bipedalism, 168
  brain, 168
  division of labour, 172, 208–209
  female sexuality, 168–169
  hunting very large animals, 172
  language, 170–172
  physical traits, 168–169
  terrestrial, 172
  toolmaking, 169–170
human variation, 7, 116–118
  adaptation, 138–139
  biological diversity. *See* biological diversity in human populations
  cultural diversity, 138–139
  cultural environment, 117–118
  future of, 139–140
  natural selection, 116–117
  physical environment, 117
  "race" and racism, 133–138
humans, 156–157, 161
  see also Homo sapiens; modern humans
humility, 22
hunter-gatherers, 294
hunting, 257–258
Hutterites, 105, 135
Hutton, James, 85
Huxley, Thomas, 86, 108, 249
hybridization, 106–107, 106f
hylobates, 156
hypertension, 131, 375
hypoglycemia, 111–112
hypothesis, 16, 17–18
hypoxia, 123

I

Ice Man, 51
ice sheets, 281, 281f
Iceland, 318
Ifaluk, 363, 365
illness. *See* health and illness
imitation, 148
immunity, 126
imperialism, 340–341
Inca, 118, 340–341
incisors, 145
India, 368, 374

SUBJECT INDEX

Indigenous peoples
   acculturation of, 75
   applied anthropology, 349
   environmental contaminants, 366–367
   First Nations health care, 360
   health, 357–358, 375
   Indigenous healers, 356
   in North America, origins of, 281
   traditional medicine, 358–359
   Type II diabetes, 130, 132–133
   violence against Indigenous women, 370
indirect percussion, 272
individual selection, 163
Indo-European languages, 135
Indonesia, 127f
Indus Valley of northwestern India, 334
industrialized societies, 321
infant dependency, 208
infant mortality, 67–68
infanticide, 155
infectious diseases, 59, 126–128, 136–137
infectious lesions, 59
influence, 354
influenza, 126, 128
influenza pandemic, 128
inherited traits, 97–101
innovation, 73
inoculation, 351
insect infestations, 367
insectivores, 182, 183
insects, 33
Institute for the Study of Ancient and Forensic DNA, 58
intelligence
   living primates, 167
   and "race," 137–138
intensive agriculture, 296, 317, 321
interaction sphere, 337
interbreeding, 90, 269
intermediate contact, 74
international human rights violations, 370
Inuit, 75, 164, 283, 288, 321, 363, 366
Inuit-Aleut, 283
invention, 73
Iran, 328
Iraq, 336, 337, 370
Iron Age, 86
iron deficiency, 118
Iroquois ossuary, 377

irrigation, 335–336
ischial callosities, 156
Islamic societies, 139
Israel, 269
Italy, 74
ivory tools, 272

J

Jane Goodall Institute of Canada, 368
Japan, 139, 367
Japanese Canadians, 135
Java, 233, 234–235, 245
jaws, early hominins, 207–208
Jenness, Diamond, 2, 3
jewellery, 72
Jews, 135
Joint Missing Women Task Force, 369
Jones, Frederic Wood, 184
junk DNA, 195

K

Kalahandi, Orissa, India, 354
Kalahari Desert, 20
Kanzi, 149–150
Karisoke, 162
the Kayapo, 183, 295, 353
Kazan River, Nunavut, 70
Keatley Creek, British Columbia, 70
Kennewick case, 376
Kennewick Man, 350, 377
Kentucky, 300
Kenya, 124f, 194, 205, 210, 221
Kenyanthropus platyops, 212
Kenyapithecus, 191, 192
Kettlewell, H.B.D., 91
Khirokitia, 321
kill floor, 285
kingdom, 82
Klasies River, South Africa, 257, 268
Knights of St. John, 74
Knights Templar, 74
KNM-ER 3733, 235
KNM-ER 3883, 235
KNM-WT 15000, 236
knock-kneed posture, 205
knuckle walking, 159
Koko, 149
!Kung, 20, 164, 302–303, 302f
Kwäday Dän Ts'ìnchi, 51, 377
kwashiorkor, 15

L

L-isomers, 47
La Chapelle-aux-Saints, France, 250, 259

La Quinta, France, 253
La Venta, Mexico, 327
Lacks, Henrietta, 100
lactase, 123
lactase deficiency, 122–123
Lactobacillus, 123
lactose intolerance, 4, 122–123
Laetoli, Tanzania, 211, 213, 214f
Lake Titicaca, 380
Lake Turkana, Kenya, 211, 235
Lamanai, 72
Lamarck, Jean-Baptiste, 83, 107
Lana, 149
landfill sites, 28, 28f
landscape archaeology, 380
language
   early hominins, 227
   Homo erectus, 245
   humans and, 170–172
   modern humans, 277–279
   Neandertals, 260
   origin of, 171
   spoken, 170, 278
language-acquisition device, 170
languages, 10–11, 149
larynx, 171
laser-scanning technology, 34
last ice age, 270–271, 282
late Miocene apes, 191–194
Laurasia, 182
Laurier, Wilfrid, 2
law of superposition, 38
laws, 14
Leakey, Louis, 162
leapers, 179
learning from others, 147–148
lemur-like forms, 151–152
lemurs, 151–152, 162, 168
Les Archives de Folklore, Université Laval, 2
lesions, 59
Levalloisian method, 256
Liang Bua site, 234
lice, 233
The Life of Reason (Santayana), 316
lifestyles, early hominins, 223–226
light-coloured skin, 121–122
Lima, Peru, 334
linguistics, 10
Linnaean Society of London, 86
Linnaeus, Carolus, 82

lions, 109–110
lithics, 32
   see also stone tools
Little Foot, 211
living floors, 33
living primates
   anthropoids, 150, 154–161, 186–189
   body size, 164–165
   classification of primates, 150–151
   common primate traits, 144–151, 146f
   distinctive human traits, 168–172
   endangered primates, 162–163
   group size, 165–166
   intelligence, 167
   models for hominin behaviour, 161–164
   physical features, 144–146
   primate adaptations, 164–167
   primate communication, 148–150
   primate evolution. *See* primate evolution
   prosimians, 150, 151–154, 153f
   relative brain size, 165, 166f
   sexual dimorphism, 166–167
   social features, 146–150
   suborders, 150–151
local channels of influence, 354–356
local trade, 337
"Long Ago Person Found," 51
long-distance trade, 73, 322, 337
longitudinal studies, 371
loris-like forms, 152–153
lorises, 152
Lower Palaeolithic culture, 240–247
   Acheulian tool tradition, 240, 241–242
   Archaic *Homo sapiens*, 245–247
   big-game eating, 242
   campsites, 243–244
   fire, 239, 242–243
   language, 245
   religion, 244–245
   ritual, 244–245
Lower Palaeolithic sites, 245
Lowie, Robert H., 87–88
Lucy, 214–215
lumbar curve, 217

SUBJECT INDEX

Luo, 296
Lyell, Charles, 85

M

macaques, 155, 156
machismo, 364
macrobands, 299
Macrobius, 82
macroscopic observation, 53
Madagascar, 152, 162
Maglemosian culture of Northern Europe, 298
magnetic resistance, 36
magnetometer, 36
maize, 72, 308, 309, 309f, 311
Malapa Cave, South Africa, 212
malaria, 129, 355, 358
malnutrition, 111, 357
Mamaweswen, 356
mammal extinctions, 300
Mammalia, 144
mammalian radiations, 182
mammals, 81, 144
mammoth shelters, 275f
mammoths, 274, 284
Manitoba First Nations Centre for Aboriginal Health Research, 360
Maori, 378–380
marginal areas, 294
marmosets, 155
marriage, 238
Mars, 80, 80f
Martin, Robert, 31
master chronology, 40
Mata Menge, 234
material culture, 27–29, 32
material possessions, 320–322
Mauer, Heidelberg, Germany, 246
Mayan lowlands, 337
the Mayans, 72, 136, 339–340
  cities, 343
  ethnomedicine, 358
  Mayan civilization, 72, 342
Mayr, Ernst, 108
Mbuti Pygmies, 321
McIlwraith, Thomas, 3
McMaster Ancient DNA Centre, 58
MC1R, 239
measles, 126, 127, 128
measure, 17
measurement, 17–18
meat, 373
mechanical techniques, 35
medical anthropologists, 11
medical anthropology, 6f, 357–365
  biomedical paradigm, 359–360

cultural understandings of health and illness, 358–359
megafauna, 286
meiosis, 97–98, 98f, 99f, 103
Melanesia, 280
melanin, 103, 121
meme, 112
menarche, 374
Mendel, Gregor, 91, 96–97, 96f, 105
Mendel's experiments, 96–97
Mengele, Josef, 370
mental disorders, 363–365
mercury, 366
Mesoamerica, 72, 136, 315
  Archaic peoples of Highland Mesoamerica, 299
  cities, 330–333
  domestication, 308–310
  food, 298–299
  states, 330–333
Mesolithic, 270, 292
Mesopotamia, 64
Mesozoic, 182
message sealings, 328
messenger RNA (mRNA), 101
metaphase stage, 98f
microbands, 299
microenvironments, 118
microlithic technology, 303
microliths, 272, 273–274, 303
microscopic changes, 53
midden, 27–28, 33
Middle Kingdom, 67f
Middle Miocene apes, 191
Middle Palaeolithic, 232, 245, 254
Middle Palaeolithic cultures, 254–260
  altruism, 259
  cannibalism, 259–260
  food, 257–258
  funeral rituals, 258–259
  homesites, 256–257
  language, 260
  Mousterian tool assemblage, 254–256
  tool assemblages, 254–256
Middle Pleistocene, 235
Middle Stone Age, 254, 256
Middle Uruk, 328
migrants, 331
migration, 60–61
milk, 4
Milky Way, 80
Milne, Brooke, 34
Miocene, 183, 189, 194, 195, 200

mitochondria, 250
mitochondrial DNA (mtDNA), 250–252, 252f, 265–266, 267
mitosis, 97–98
models for hominin behaviour, 161–164
modern evolutionary theory
  see also evolution
  behavioural traits, natural selection of, 107–113
  heredity, 96–101
  variability, 101–107
modern humans
  art, 275–277
  coexistence with Neandertals, 268–269
  early Arctic populations, 286–287
  emergence of, 264–270
  language, 277–279
  last ice age, 270–271
  Neandertals, evolutionary relationship with, 260
  New World, earliest humans in, 280–288
  origins of modern humans, 264–268
  Palaeo-Indians, 283–286
  tools, 272–274
  Upper Palaeolithic cultures, 270–280
  Upper Palaeolithic Europe, 271–272
modern synthesis, 108
modernization, and health, 131
Mohawk First Nation Council of Chiefs, 376
molars, 145
molecular anthropology, 63, 260
molecular clock, 194–195
monkeys, 168
Monk's Mound, 334
Monroe, Marilyn, 364
Monte Albán, 332
Monte Verde, Chile, 280
Monte Verde site, Chile, 284f
Moors, 74
Moose Factory, 128
Morgan, Lewis Henry, 87
Morocco, 74
morphology, 29
mother–infant communication, 171
Mount Carmel, Israel, 254
Mousterian tool assemblage, 254–256, 255f, 274
Mrs. Ples, 217f
multifaceted approach, 4

multiregional hypothesis, 266–267
Murray, Charles, 137
museum archaeology, 377–380
museums, 351
mutations, 103–105, 108, 116
mycobacterium tuberculosis, 92
MYH16, 208
myths of racism, 136–138

N

Na-Dené, 282, 283
Nariokotome, Lake Turkana, 236
National Aboriginal Diabetes Association (NADA), 133
National Human Genome Research Institute, 195
National Indian Foundation (FUNAI), 352
National Institutes of Health, 101
Native American graves, 350
Native American Protection and Repatriation Act, 350
Native Americans, 122, 349
Native Women's Association of Canada (NWAC), 370
Natufians, 297
natural disasters, 367–368
A Natural History (Buffon), 85
natural observations, 164
natural physical processes, 29
natural selection, 85, 86, 116–117
  and adaptive traits, 91
  balancing selection, 116, 129
  behavioural traits, 107–113
  bipedalism, 203
  directional selection, 116, 117f
  and drug-resistant disease strains, 92
  group selection, 163
  individual selection, 163
  normalizing selection, 116, 129
  principles of, 88–89
naturalistic paintings, 275
nature, 110–113
Navaho, 282
Nazca state, 334
the Ndumba, 183
Neander Valley, 247
Neandertals, 137, 234, 247–254, 249f
  altruism, 259

cannibalism, 259–260
coexistence with modern humans, 268–269
evolutionary relations, 260
evolutionary timeline, 254f
food, 257–258
funeral rituals, 258–259
growth and development, 253
homesites, 256–257
language, 260
Middle Palaeolithic cultures, 254–260
Mousterian tool assemblage, 254–256
resource strategies, 258
tool assemblages, 254–256
Near East
domestication, 305–308, 306f
food, 296–297
Natufians, 297
Neolithic, 304
Neolithic Cyprus, 321
Neolithic revolution, 292
neutral mutations, 103–104
New Guinea, 280
New World, 126, 137, 280
animal domestication, 311
Arctic Small Tool tradition, 286
demographic collapse, 71
Dorset, 287–288
earliest humans, 280–288
early Arctic populations, 286–287
Palaeo-Indians, 283–286
primates in, 152
Thule, 62, 287
New World monkeys, 154–155, 188
New Zealand Maori, 378–380
Nicaragua, 367
Nightingale, Florence, 91
Nile Valley, Egypt, 333
Nim, 149
nitrogen, 66
nitrogen-14, 42
nitrogen tests, 40
nocturnal, 152, 164
non-coding DNA, 195
non-genetic factors, 128
non-insulin-dependent diabetes mellitus (NIDDM), 130
non-invasive site inspection techniques, 36
nonrandom sample, 18
normalizing selection, 116, 129
North America, 282, 310–311, 334

North Shore Tribal Council, 356
Norton tradition, 286–287
Notharctus, 186
nurture, 110–113
nuthkavihak, 363
nutritional anthropology, 371–375
nutritional supplements, 111

O

Oaxaca, 337
obesity, 131, 364, 375
obsidian, 47
obsidian hydration, 47
occipital torus, 236
Office of Women in the U.S. Agency for International Development, 13
Ogallala aquifer, 318
Oklahoma City bombing, 370
Old Crow site, Yukon Territory, 280
Old Kingdom, 333
Old World, 264, 266, 272, 300, 311, 326
Old World monkeys, 155–156, 189, 200
Oldowan, 223
Olduvai Gorge, Tanzania, 39f, 45, 223, 223f, 224, 235
Oligocene, 187
Olorgesailie, Kenya, 242
Olsen-Chubbuck site, Colorado, 285
omnivorous, 145
Omo, Ethiopia, 268
omomyids, 180, 186
open-air sites, 257
open systems, 149
operational definition, 17
opposable thumbs, 145
orangutans, 144, 158–159
order, 82
Oreopithecus, 191, 192
organic residues, 63
origin of language, 171
origin of species, 89–91
Origin of Species by Means of Natural Selection, The (Darwin), 86, 247
origins of modern humans, 264–268
assimilation theory, 267
cultural evidence, 269–270
fossil evidence, 267–268
genetic evidence, 267–268
multiregional hypothesis, 266–267

single-origin hypothesis, 264–266, 267
Orrorin tugenensis, 194, 209
osteology, 53
Ouranopithecus, 191
"out of Africa" hypothesis. *See* single-origin hypothesis
overextension, 343
overgrazing, 318
overkill hypothesis, 300
overnutrition, 375
oxygen, 123
oxygen isotopes, 69

P

p-value, 19
Pacbitun, 72
Pachakuti, 340
Pacific Coast, 286
Pacific Islands, 74
pair bonding, 238–239
Paisley Caves, Oregon, 281
Palaeo-Arctic tradition, 286
Palaeo-Indians, 283–286
palaeoanthropology, 5–6
palaeodemography, 60–61
palaeoecology, 68
palaeoethnobotany, 61, 63–65
palaeomagnetic dating, 45–46
palaeopathology, 58–60
Palaeopathology at the Origins of Agriculture (Cohen and Armelagos), 319
Paleocene, 179, 181, 182
palynology, 68–69
pandemic, 126
paper, 74
Papua New Guinea, 73
paranthropoid sites, 210f
paranthropoids, 199f, 212, 217–220
Paranthropus, 210
Paranthropus aethiopicus, 212, 217–219
Paranthropus boisei, 212, 218f, 219–220, 221, 239
Paranthropus robustus, 212, 219, 220
parapithecids, 187–188
parasites, 233
Park, Robert, 34
Parks Canada, 376
particular environment, 88
past diets, 61
past environments, 68–69
Pasteur, Louis, 360
patterned variation, 38
PCBs. *See* polychlorinated biphenyls (PCBs)
Peacock, Nadine, 9f

peat bogs, 298
Peking Man, 235
peptide bonds, 102f
percussion flaking, 222–223, 273f
perfect human, 139–140
personality differences, 111–112
Peru, 334, 336–337
Peunayong Market, Indonesia, 127f
phenotype, 97
Philippines, 370
phylogenetic timelines, 220f
physical anthropology, 5–8
physical differences, 20–21
physical environment, 117, 316
physical features
Homo erectus, 236–237
human variation in, 118–122
living primates, 144–146
physical sciences, 14
physical traits of humans, 168–169
Physicians for Human Rights, 370
physiological differences, 111–112
phytoliths, 38, 63
pibloktoq, 363, 365
Pickton, Robert, 369
Pierolapithecus, 191
Pithecanthropus erectus, 234
pits, 33
Plains peoples, 285
planned change
evaluation of effects of, 351–352
implementation difficulties, 352–356
local channels of influence, 354–356
resistance, 352–354
plant domestication. *See* domestication
Plato, 82
platyrrhines, 154, 154f, 188
play, 144, 147
Pleistocene, 208
Pleistocene megafauna, 271
plesiadapiforms, 179
Plesiadapis, 179
Pliocene, 194, 200, 202, 213
Plotinus, 82
Poinar, Hendrik, 58
polishes, 63
political anthropologists, 11
pollens, 33, 69
polychlorinated biphenyls (PCBs), 366

polymerase chain reaction (PCR), 57
Polynesia, 131
polypeptide chain, 102f
pongids, 156
population biology, 7
population collapse, 71
population fission, 105
population growth, 301–303
   and food production, 317–319
   and origin of the state, 336–337
population size and composition, 70–71
post-Acheulian, 254
post-partum sex taboo, 14, 15, 16, 17, 19f
potassium-40 (40K), 43
potassium-argon (K-Ar) dating, 43–45
pottery, 29
practising anthropology, 348
   see also applied anthropology
pre-agricultural developments, 296–303
pre-Clovis occupation, 281
prehensile, 145
prehistoric, 9
premolars, 145
pressure flaking, 272, 273
prides, 109–110
primate adaptations, 164–167
   body size, 164–165
   group size, 165–166
   relative brain size, 165, 166f
   sexual dimorphism, 166–167
primate communication, 148–150
primate conservation, 368
primate evolution, 177f
   anthropoids, 186–189
   arboreal theory, 184
   biodiversity, 183
   dentition, 177–178
   divergence of hominins from other hominoids, 194–195
   early Eocene primates, 186
   early primates, 185
   emergence of primates, 179–186
   the environment, 181–184
   evolutionary relationships, 178f
   fossil record, 176–179
   hominoids, 189–194
   locomotion, 178–179, 180f
   posture, 178–179
   reconstruction of, 176
   visual predation theory, 185
primate palaeontologists, 31
primate traits, 144–151, 146f
   physical features, 144–146
   social features, 146–150
primates, 6, 81
   see also living primates; primate evolution
primatologists, 6
primatology, 144
Primitive Culture (Tylor), 87
Principles of Geology (Lyell), 85
probabilistically, 14
probability value, 19
Proconsul, 190, 191f
Proconsul africanus, 190f
prognathic, 236
progress, 88
propliopithecids, 187, 188–189
prosimians, 150, 151–154, 153f
   lemur-like forms, 151–152
   loris-like forms, 152–153
   tarsiers, 153–154, 153f
protein, 102f
protein residues, 63
protein synthesis, 101, 102f
proto-apes, 189
proto-hominins, 200
provenience, 27
psychological anthropologists, 11
psychological factors, 354
Public Health Agency of Canada, 132
pull models, 313
punctuated equilibrium, 107, 108
push models, 313

Q

Qolla, 111–112
quadrupeds, 151
Québec, 3

R

"race," 133–138
   biological fallacy of race, 133–135
   and civilization, 136
   conquest, and infectious disease, 136–137
   in forensic anthropology, 134
   and intelligence, 137–138
   myths of racism, 136–138
   as social construct, 135–136
racemization, 47
rachis, 304
racial classification, 135
racism, 136–138
   see also "race"
radiocarbon dating, 42–43
radionuclides, 366
rain shadow, 182
raised field agriculture, 379
random assortment, 102
random sample, 18
rate of decay, 41–42
raw materials, 73
recessive, 96
reconstruction, 51
   and analysis, 62
   facial reconstruction, 248
   of the past, 27
   past diets, 61
   past environments, 68–69
   of primate evolution, 176
   settlement patterns, 69–72
   social systems, 72–73
red colobus monkey, 161
referential communication, 149
referential perspectives, 164
Reichs, Kathleen, 369
relations, 14
relative dating, 38
relative dating methods, 38–40
religion, and *Homo erectus*, 244–245
remains of human cultures, 8
remodelling, 53
replacement hypothesis. *See* single-origin hypothesis
replication, 17
reptiles, 81
research, 12
   see also explanations
residential schools, 75
residue analysis, 63
resistance to planned change, 352–354
resource availability, 72
Rhône Valley, France, 316
ribonucleic acid (RNA), 101
ribosome, 101
rice, 312
rickets, 365
Rift Valley, 212
Rio de Janeiro, Brazil, 367
ritual
   funeral rituals, 258–259
   Homo erectus, 244–245
   Lower Palaeolithic culture, 244–245
Roman Catholicism, 75
Roman Empire, 343
Rudabánya, Hungary, 193
Rushton, Philippe, 137–138

S

sagittal crest, 212
sagittal keel, 235, 236
Sahara Desert, 299
Sahelanthropus tchadensis, 194, 209
Sahlins, Marshall D., 87–88
salinization, 318
Samarkand, 74
Sami, 75
Samoans, 131
sampling, 18
sampling universe, 18
San Joaquin Valley, California, 318
Sandy Lake Health and Diabetes Project (SLHDP), 133
Sapir, Edward, 2, 3
Sarah, 149
SARS (severe acute respiratory syndrome), 126–127, 360–361
satellite imaging, 34
Scandinavia, 297f
scanning electron microscope (SEM), 64
schizophrenia, 363, 365
scientific method, 16
scrapers, 223, 256
sea water, 69
seafood, 244
secular trend, 125
sedentism, 61, 293
   and broad-spectrum collecting, 301
   increased sedentism, 299–300
   and population growth, 301–303, 314, 317
sediment, 35, 256
sediment magnetism, 36
seeds, 63
segregation, 102
selective mortality, 59
Semang of Malaya, 321
September 11, 2001, terrorist attacks, 370
Sequoya, 74
Serbia, 370
settlement archaeology, 69–72
settlement data, 70
settlement patterns, 69–72
sex determination, 55–56, 57f
sex-linked traits, 103
sexual dimorphism, 156, 158, 160, 166–167, 238

sexual reproduction strategies, 81
sexually dimorphic, 56
Shang dynasty, 136, 334
Shanidar I, 259
Shell Mound Archaic, 54
shellfish, 298
shellfishing, 54
Sherman, 149–150
shifting cultivation, 295
short hair, 75
shovel-shaped incisors, 283, 283f
shovel shining, 35
Shriver site, Missouri, 281
siamangs, 157–158
Siberia, 281
sickle-cell anemia, 116, 128–130
sicklemia, 128
Sicotte, Pascale, 159f
significant statistical associations, 19
silverback, 159
Simpson, George, 108
Sinanthropus pekinensis, 235
single-origin hypothesis, 264–266, 267
Sioux Lookout Zone, 132
site catchment analysis, 71–72
site evaluation, 36
site formation processes, 27–29
site integrity, 36
site prospection, 34–36
  subsurface techniques, 34–36
  surface techniques, 34
sites. *See* archaeological sites
Sivapithecines, 192–193
Sivapithecus, 191, 192
skeletal age-indicator techniques, 53, 55f
skeletal biology, 53
skeletons. *See* human remains
Skidegate Repatriation and Cultural Committee, 376
skin colour, 103, 120–122, 121f, 135
skin reflectance, 122
skulls, 29
slash-and-burn techniques, 295
Slavs, 135
smallpox, 137, 354
smilodectes, 179f
Smith, Bernadette, 370
Smith, G. Elliot, 184
Smith, Harlan, 3
Snow, Clyde, 370, 371
social classes, 125

social factors, 354
social features of primates, 146–150
  dependency, 147, 147f
  development, 147
  learning from others, 147–148
  play, 147
  primate communication, 148–150
social groups, 356
social learning, 147
social sciences, 12, 14
social systems, 72–73
socialization, 110
societal collapse, 342
Society for Applied Anthropology, 350
socio-cultural anthropology, 5, 8–10, 11
socio-economic status, 372
sociobiological approach, 112
sociobiology, 107, 161
sociolinguist, 11
sociolinguistics, 10
Socrates, 82
soil samples, 38
Soriacebus, 186
South Africa, 135, 199
South America, 136, 152, 188, 310–311, 334
South Asia, 280
Southeast Asia, 266, 299, 312
Spain, 74
Spanish conquest of Mexico, 75
spears, 258
specialization, 11
speciation, 90
species, 82, 89–90, 106
Spencer, Herbert, 87
spoken language, 170, 278
squashes, 309, 310
St. Acheul, France, 241
stable isotopes, 65–68
Standard Cross-Cultural Sample, 138
states, 326, 327
  Cahokia, 335
  circumscription, 336–337
  consequences of state formation, 337–338
  decline and collapse of, 338–343
  irrigation, 335–336
  Mesoamerica, 330–333
  Monte Albán, 332
  origin of the state, theories about, 335–337
  other areas, 333–334
  population growth, 336–337

Sumer, 328–330
Teotihuacán, 330–332
trade, 337
war, 336–337
stationary, 60
statistical association, 14
statistical evaluation, 18–20
statistically significant, 19
Stenton, Doug, 34
stereoscopic vision, 145
stimulus diffusion, 74
Stone Age, 86
stone flake tools, 223
stone tools, 52, 52f
  see also specific tools
  Acheulian tool tradition, 240, 241–242
  bifacial tools, 223, 241
  chipped stone tools, 62
  and culture, 226–227
  early hominins, 221–223
  Homo erectus, 240–242
  lithics, 32
  Oldowan, 223
  percussion flaking, 222–223, 273f
  unifacial tool, 223
strata, 38
strategic modelling, 164
stratigraphy, 38–40, 39f
strepsirhines, 154, 180
Streptococcus A, 91
streptomycin, 92
structural linguist, 11
structural linguistics, 10
stunting, 372
sub-fields of anthropology, 6f
sub-Saharan Africa, 135, 256, 333–334
subsistence technology, 293–294
subsurface techniques, 34–36
Sumer, 328–330
Sumerian civilization, 329–330
sumpweed, 310
supercontinents, 182
surface techniques, 34
symbolic communication, 149
syphilis, 137
systema naturae, 82
Szalay, Frederick, 184

T

Tai Chi, 359f
Taï chimpanzees, 169–170
Taiwanese women, 352
tanning, 117
Tanzania, 205, 210, 221
taphonomy, 29, 224
taro, 312
tarsiers, 153–154, 153f

taurodontism, 236
taxa, 82
technology, 320
teeth
  chemical analysis, 66
  early hominins, 207–208
Telles-Sawwan, Iraq, 327
temperament, 110
temperate climate plants, 65
Temple of Quetzalcoatl, 331
teosinte, 308, 309f
Teotihuacán, 330–332, 331f, 337, 342
termite "fishing," 148
Terra Amata, 244, 244f
Terrell, John, 380
terrestrial, 155
terrestrial quadrupeds, 178
test pits, 35, 35f
test pitting, 35
tetany, 365
Tetonius, 186
theories, 14–16
theory of evolution, 81–82, 83
thermoluminescence, 46
thermoluminescence dating, 46
Theropithecus oswaldi, 242
thinness, 364
Thomsen, C. J., 86
3D laser scanning, 34
thrifty gene, 130, 131
Thule, 62, 287, 288
tools
  see also stone tools; specific tools
  Arctic Small Tool tradition, 286, 287–288
  Aurignacian tools, 270
  and the brain, 206
  early hominins, 221–223
  evolution of techniques, 274
  Homo erectus, 240–242
  indirect percussion, 272
  microliths, 272, 273–274, 303
  Middle Palaeolithic cultures, 254–256
  Middle Stone Age, 256
  Mousterian, 254–256, 255f, 274
  Palaeo-Indians, 284–285
  pressure flaking, 272, 273
  toolmaking, 169–170, 204
  Upper Palaeolithic tools, 272–274
  use of tools, 274
  as weapons, 203
Torralba, 242

tourism, 21f, 34
toxic-shock syndrome (TSS), 91
trace elements, 65–68
trade, 73, 337
trading patterns, 73
transfer RNA (tRNA), 102f
translation, 102f
trapùan arroyo, 285
tree-dwelling monkeys, 169
Tremacebus, 186
trenching, 35, 35f
trial-and-error methods, 355
trilobites, 31f, 108
troops, 156
tropical forests, 317
tropical grasses, 65
Ts'ai Lun, 74
tuberculosis, 92
Tupari, 126
Tutankhamen, 370
Tylor, Edward Burnett, 87
Type II diabetes, 130–133
types, 17
typology, 52

U

Ukraine, 124f
ultraviolet radiation, 122
Umatilla, 350
unconscious invention, 73
undernutrition, 373–374
underwater archaeology, 37
unifacial tool, 223
uniformitarianism, 85
unique offspring, 102
United Kingdom, 357
United Nations, 13, 370
United States, 367, 380
Upper Palaeolithic, 270, 271f
Upper Palaeolithic cultures, 270–280

art, 275–277
language, 277–279
last ice age, 270–271
tools, 272–274, 273f
Upper Palaeolithic Europe, 271–272
Upper Palaeolithic Europe, 271–272
uracil, 101
uranium-series dating, 46
uranium tests, 40
U.S. Agency for International Development, 13
U.S. Army Corps of Engineers, 350
use-wear analysis, 53
Ussher, James, 84

V

variability
  epigenetics, 83, 107
  gene flow, 89, 105–106
  genetic drift, 89, 105, 107
  genetic recombination, 101–103
  hybridization, 106–107, 106f
  mutations, 103–105, 108, 116
  sources of, 101–107
variables, 14
variation, 5, 88, 112
  see also human variation
varieties, 133
Velika Pećina, Croatia, 268
Venezuela, 352
Venus figurines, 277
Venus of Willendorf, 276f
vertebrates, 81
vertical clingers, 178–179
vertical clinging and leaping, 151
vertical control, 37
vervet monkeys, 149

Viking Greenland settlement, 69
Vindija, Croatia, 268
virgin soil epidemic, 126
vision, 145
visual predation theory, 185
vitamin D, 122, 123
vocalizations, 170
volcanic events, 45
von Koenigswald, G.H.R., 235

W

Waddington, Conrad, 107
Wallace, Alfred Russel, 85–86, 105
Wanka, 340
war, 336–337
warm-blooded, 144
Washoe, 149
wasting, 372
Watson, James, 98
weapons, 169, 203
wear patterns, 63
were, 365
West Nile, 360
West Nile virus, 126
Western clothing, 74
Western diseases, 360
Western medical practice, 359
Western medicine, 358
Western societies, 139
whalebone, 62
whooping cough, 128
Wilberforce, Samuel, 86
wild wheat, 296
Wilson, Daniel, 2
windward side, 182
Wintemberg, William, 3
Woman's Role in Economic Development (Boserup), 13
women

agriculture, contributions to, 13
mother–infant communication, 171
nutritional imbalances, 373–374
Shell Mound Archaic, 54
violence against Indigenous women, 370
women's status, 340–341
Women in Agricultural Development Project, 13
Wonderwerk cave, South Africa, 242
wood artifacts, 32
workshops, 244
World Health Organization (WHO), 92, 361, 366
Worsaae, Jens Jacob Asmussen, 86–87
written records, 8

X

X chromosome, 103, 265–266

Y

"Y-5" pattern, 156–157
Y chromosome, 103, 265–266
Yanamarca Valley, Peru, 340
Yoruba, 363, 365
Yucatán Peninsula, 340

Z

Zambia, 13
Zawi Chemi Shanidar, Iraq, 304
Zhoukoudian, 235
Zhoukoudian cave, 240, 242, 245
ziggurat, 329f
Zinjanthropus, 219
zooarchaeology, 61–62